Agricultural Price Formation in Theory and Reality

Agricultural Price Formation in Theory and Reality

Edited by

Ulrich Koester and

Stephan von Cramon-Taubadel

Cambridge
Scholars
Publishing

Agricultural Price Formation in Theory and Reality

Edited by Ulrich Koester and Stephan von Cramon-Taubadel

This book first published 2023

Cambridge Scholars Publishing

Lady Stephenson Library, Newcastle upon Tyne, NE6 2PA, UK

British Library Cataloguing in Publication Data
A catalogue record for this book is available from the British Library

ISBN (10): 1-5275-2829-4
ISBN (13): 978-1-5275-2829-1

TABLE OF CONTENTS

FOREWORD

This textbook is based on a translation of the German textbook "Agrarpreisbildung: Theorie und Anwendung" that we published with Springer in 2021. Besides translating and updating parts of the original German text, we have added two chapters: Chapter 7 by David Zilberman on "Innovation in Agriculture", and Chapter 11 by Jens-Peter Loy on "Price Formation in Food Retailing".

Most degree programs in economics do not include courses devoted solely to the fundamentals of pricing in a particular sector. Why, therefore, have we written a textbook for a course on pricing in agriculture? Our motivation is as follows:

Textbooks on price theory at the Bachelor level usually explain price formation based on neoclassical economic theory and the construct of the 'homo oeconomicus'. The homo oeconomicus is not a real human being, but an imaginary economic agent, such as an individual, a firm or a household, that aims to maximise its utility. Its utility function is constant, stable and socially independent. Homo oeconomicus knows everything about its economic and social environment and thus also about all of its alternatives. It does not need to consider the reactions of others to its own decisions. Hence, in the world of homo oeconomicus, uncertainty about the behaviour of others or about changes in the economic environment plays no role. Based on this construct, neoclassical price theory explains the determination of market equilibrium and how it reacts to changes in exogenous factors. Neoclassical price analysis is predominately comparative static, and dynamic paths between equilibria are usually not considered.

In reality, uncertainty about the behaviour of other participants plays an important role on markets. Individuals, firms and households interact, and market outcomes depend on these interactions. The nature of market equilibria and how they react to changes in exogenous factors therefore depend on institutions which govern interactions between market participants by defining how participants are expected, permitted or obliged to behave. For example, how farm land prices react to changes in agricultural product prices depends on the design of land lease contracts as well as the laws that regulate what may and may not be stipulated in these contracts. Moreover, the distribution of the economic gains that result from market interactions also depends on institutions. Under such conditions, price determination is not merely a technical question of maximising a known utility function under conditions of perfect information. Instead, price theory needs to account for institutions. Furthermore, if markets are to contribute to solving societal problems, then economists also need to consider how to design institutions that support this contribution.

Based on these considerations, some authors conclude that the neoclassical approach in economics is irrelevant (Boettke, 1997). We disagree. We present the neoclassical approach, but supplement it with insights from institutional economics where necessary, to cast light on aspects of price formation on real-world agricultural markets. Neoclassical price theory uses mathematics (marginal analysis) to show how individual economic agents react to incentives, and how their decisions are coordinated by the price mechanism. While this approach is subject to limitations, it is powerful and flexible. Neoclassical instruments can be used in many areas of economics, and economic research in recent decades has shown that the neoclassical approach can also generate useful insights in fields such as the New Institutional Economics (NIE).

In this textbook we therefore attempt to extend the instruments of neoclassical price theory by including insights from the NIE. In the NIE, institutions are understood to be norms that restrict or otherwise influence the social behaviour of individuals and thus make it more predictable. Institutions thus understood include informal restrictions such as customs and traditions, formal regulations such as laws, property rights or contracts, as well as the instruments that are used to enforce these regulations. Rules of particular importance for price formation on agricultural markets include inheritance laws, land transfer laws, laws on the taxation of income from agricultural activity and from the sale of agricultural land, regulations on the use of agricultural pesticides and animal feed, foreign trade regulations, and quantitative restrictions such as production quotas. Informal institutions, such as family farming traditions that extend over generations, or a long-standing membership in a local cooperative or farmers' union, can also affect behaviour and price formation in agriculture.

In the NIE, an organisation is defined as a group of persons with a common goal. North (1990) refers to institutions as 'the rules of the game', and to organisations as the 'players of the game'. Organisations that are important for agricultural price formation include various legal forms of agricultural enterprise, private and public consultancies, public administrations at supranational, national, regional and local levels, private and public companies, auctions, and commodity futures markets.

Since many institutions and organisations in agriculture differ from those in other industries and sectors, agricultural price formation can also differ and deviate from what is predicted by the neoclassical theory commonly presented in bachelor's programs. We have therefore written and compiled this textbook to go beyond the standard neoclassical presentation found in the leading general microeconomic textbooks, and to extend the presentation found in textbooks on agricultural price formation, such as Tomek and Kaiser (2014), to reflect the importance of institutions and organisations.

Acknowledgement

Completing this textbook has taken longer than anticipated, and we thank the contributing authors for their patience and forbearance as we first completed the German version and then embarked on the task of translating, editing, and incorporating new chapters into this English version.

The individual chapters (with the exception of David Zilberman' chapter on "Innovations in Agriculture") were first translated from German with the help of DeepL by Fenja Bahr and Kirsten Kriegel in Kiel, to whom we are very grateful. Stephan von Cramon then thoroughly edited each chapter and interacted with the corresponding authors to produce the final versions. Manuel Droste, Jan Simon Erchinger and Anna von Kameke in Göttingen provided excellent assistance with the formatting and proofreading of the individual chapters – they caught many errors and inconsistencies, and greatly improved the final product. Finally, we thank Adam Rummens at Cambridge Scholars Publishing for his professional advice and his patience as several deadlines were extended on the way to completion. It goes without saying that we remain responsible for any remaining errors and shortcomings.

Ulrich Koester (Kiel) Stephan von Cramon-Taubadel (Göttingen)

References

Boettke PJ (1997) Where did economics go wrong? Modern economics as a flight from reality. Critical Review, 11(1): 11-64.

North D (1990) Institutions, Institutional Change and Economic Performance. Cambridge University Press, Cambridge.

Tomek WA and Kaiser HM (2014) Agricultural Product Prices, 4th Edition. Cornell University Press, Ithaca.

CHAPTER ONE

THE IMPORTANCE OF INSTITUTIONS FOR AGRICULTURAL PRICE FORMATION

ULRICH KOESTER AND
STEPHAN VON CRAMON–TAUBADEL

1.1. Introduction and learning objectives

Neoclassical economics aims to present the necessary conditions for an optimal allocation of factors. The allocation is optimal if the production of goods valued at market prices cannot be expanded profitably by reallocating factors. In this equilibrium state, certain marginal conditions must apply which, among other things, also determine the remuneration for factors such as capital and labour as well as the market prices of the individual produced products.

As with any theory, neoclassical theory is based on underlying assumptions and definitions. How exactly it can explain a specific economic situation, such as current reality, depends on the closeness to reality of these assumptions and definitions.

Neoclassical theory is characterised in particular by the use of mathematical analysis and has proven to be a good starting point for explaining economic reality in many situations. However, it is often only a starting point and cannot provide exhaustive explanations. This is especially the case when it comes to explaining the level and change of agricultural prices.

The aim of this chapter is twofold:

- First, we will show how price formation for products and factors in agriculture can be explained by means of the premises of neoclassical economics combined with concepts and findings from the so-called New Institutional Economics (NIE).

– Second, we will demonstrate that the explanation and understanding of specific economic situations and changes can be improved by extending the basic premises of neoclassical theory.

Hence, we do not consider the NIE to be a substitute for neoclassical analysis, but rather a complement which can help to reduce or overcome important limitations of neoclassic analysis.

1.2. On the concept of institutions and the significance of institutional economics

The literature distinguishes between **Old and New Institutional Economics** (OIE and NIE). The differences between the OIE and the NIE are based less on the different terms they employ for institutions than on differences in their methodologies. Ostrom [1] (1990, p. 51) defines **institutions** as follows:

> "'Institutions can be defined as the sets of working rules that are used to determine who is eligible to make decisions in some arena, what actions are allowed or constrained, what aggregation rules will be used, what procedures must be followed, what information must or must not be provided, and what payoffs will be assigned to individuals dependent on their actions … All rules contain prescriptions that forbid, permit, or require some action or outcome. Working rules are those actually used, monitored, and enforced when individuals make choices about the actions they will take."

North (1990, p. 7) defines institutions more briefly:

> "Institutions are the rules of the game in a society or, more formally, are the humanly devised constraints that shape human interactions".

These definitions are widely followed in literature. Some authors subsume rules and organisations under the term institutions. Thus, the World Bank (2002, p. 7) writes: "*Institutions are rules, enforcement mechanisms, and organisations*". In most cases, however, the literature differentiates between institutions and **organisation**: the former are interpreted as the **rules of a**

---

[1] Elinor Ostrom was awarded the Nobel Prize in economics in 2009, together with Oliver Williamson, to whom we refer later in this chapter.

Figure 1.5: The expected and actual development of production in a typical transition country from a neoclassical perspective

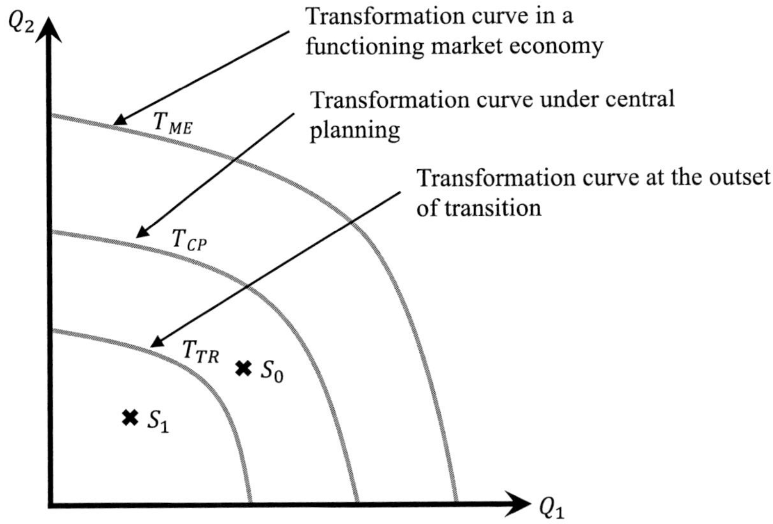

Source: Own depiction.

In order to explain what actually transpired in transition economies, it helps to recognised that the amount of production in an economy depends not only on the available resources and technology, but also on the existing rules and organisations (the institutions). A change in laws, for example labour market regulations, can lead to a shift in the transformation curve. It can also impose restrictions (e.g. shortened working hours) that make it impossible to fully exploit the technically possible production capacity. In the latter case, a production point is realised that lies not on but rather below the transformation curve. Alternatively, one might also define the transformation curve as the set of all maximum possible product combinations that can be produced with given resources, technology <u>and</u> institutions.

The initial situation in a typical transition economy can be represented as follows using neoclassical instruments. Transformation curve T_{ME} shows the production possibilities in a market economy with adequate institutions. T_{ME} lies above transformation curve T_{CP}, which shows the production possibilities for the same economy under central planning. Planned economy production was less efficient than market economy production because, for example, planners did not have sufficient information to optimally coordinate individual decisions. The difference between the two curves is also due to the fact that in a market economy system, other specific institutions, e.g. a regulatory framework, make it possible to achieve more efficient production than is possible in a planned economy system. In fact, however, neither planned nor market economies produce on the technically possible transformation curve, since not all existing institutions are fully enforced. In Figure 5 we assume that point S_0, which lies below the maximum attainable transformation curve T_{CP}, was reached under central planning before transformation began, and that production point S_1 was attained thereafter, i.e. that both production possibilities and production fell following the onset of transformation.

The transition from a planned to a market economy could only have led to an increase in production if the institutions in the planned economy had been fundamentally changed at the same time and adapted to those in efficient market economies. However, such institutional change takes time. Old planned-economy networks often linger. Institutions in the form of laws can be enacted relatively quickly, but the implementation of these laws often causes at least temporary problems. For example, it takes time to establish a functioning legal system for private-sector litigation, a tax authority with qualified tax experts, and a court of auditors to control state expenditures. It especially takes time to establish and safeguard private property.

In addition, the behaviour of individuals in planned economies is different from that in market economies. It is therefore understandable that the transformation curve T_{CP} in the formally central-planned economies did not shift outwards to T_{ME} initially, but rather inward to T_{TR}. The constitutive and regulative principles of a market-economy system formulated by Eucken[4] require a strong state in which both the government and the population are convinced of the advantages of a market-economy order and are in a position to implement these principles. It was naive to expect that the governments of individual transition countries would be able to institutionalise and enforce an efficient market-economy system immediately following the onset of transformation. Reflecting this, Figure

---

[4] Eucken (1950) defined seven constitutive (C) and four regulative (R) principles of a market economy (see van Suntum et al., 2011): C1 – functioning price system; C2 – monetary stability; C3 – open markets; C4 – private property; C5 – freedom to engage in contracts; C6 – liability; C7 – predictable and reliable economic policy; R1 – anti-monopoly policy; R2 – progressive income taxation; R3 – correction of externalities; R4 – regulation to protect workers' rights (e.g. against child labour).

game, and the latter as the players. The difference in definition is unimportant for the substance of the NIE, which considers both institutions in the narrow sense (rules) and organisation as subjects of research.

The OIE emerged at the beginning of the last century. It aimed at a critique of the market economy system and, unlike the NIE, was largely descriptive. Thorstein Veblen (1899), John Rogers Commons (1893, 1934) and Wesley Clair Mitchell (1903, 1914) are often cited as its founders. The NIE, like the OIE, focuses on the concept of institutions. In contrast to the OIE, however, it does not reject the research methods and results of neoclassical economics. Instead it aims to extend neoclassical economics by adding more realistic premises.

The work of Ronald Coase (1937) is regarded as the starting point of the NIE. Coase showed that transaction costs, which were neglected by the neoclassical analysis of the time, are of great importance for explaining economic problems and thus also for the functioning of both market and planned economies.[2] Even though this seminal work appeared in 1937 and revealed fundamental weaknesses of neoclassical analysis, it did not initially lead to an expansion of neoclassical economics. It was only later that the term New Institutional Economics was established in the literature, especially by Nobel Prize winner Oliver Williamson (1975). In the 1980s and 1990s, a comprehensive NIE literature emerged, which is summarised in a survey article by Williamson (2000).

In agricultural economics, the importance of the NIE was underscored by the experiences of the former planned economies in Central and Eastern Europe after they began the transition to more market-based economies in 1989. Figure 1 shows that it took 20 years for gross domestic product (GDP) in Russia to return to its 1989 level; in Ukraine GDP had not returned to 1989 levels after 23 years. Over the same period, income disparities in these countries increased considerably. Consequently, many individuals must have become much poorer in the course of the transformation.

[2] We discuss transaction costs in greater detail in Section 3 of this chapter, and in Chapter Two.

Figure 1.1: The development of real GDP in Ukraine and 33 transition countries (index 1989 = 100)

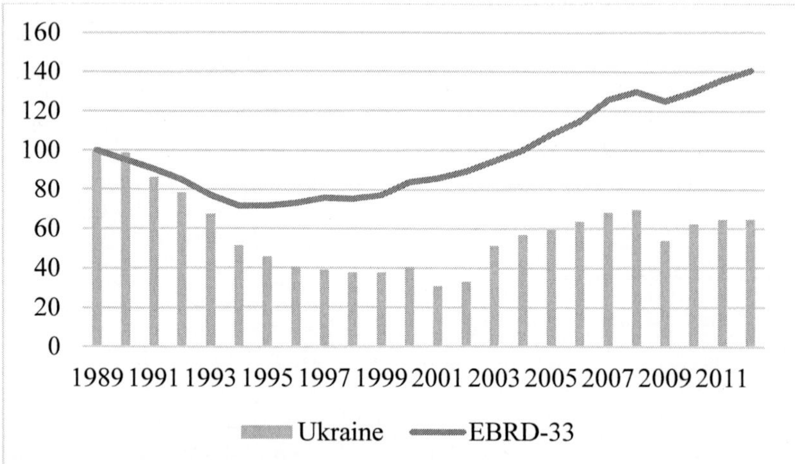

Source: EBRD (2012, p. 157).

Figure 1.2: The development of real GDP in Russia and 33 transition countries (index 1989 = 100)

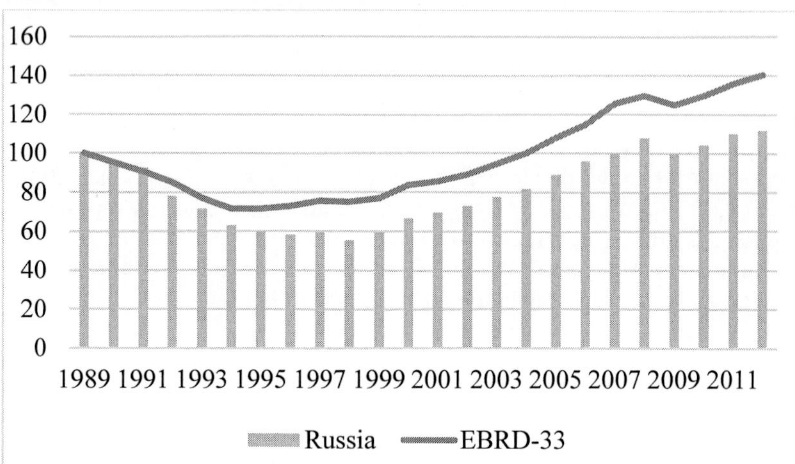

Source: EBRD (2012, p. 141).

The importance of institutions can also be illustrated by comparing the development of agricultural production in Germany's new federal states following Reunification with the development in Ukraine (Figures 3 and 4). In the new Länder (former German Democratic Republic - GDR), agricultural production initially remained roughly constant into the mid-1990s, while agricultural employment immediately fell rapidly. In Ukraine – as in many other former Soviet Union countries - employment remained roughly constant, but production fell rapidly. This decline in agricultural production in Ukraine occurred although Western agricultural economists suspected that there was considerable inefficiency in the use of factors, especially labour, in Ukrainian agriculture before transformation began. It was also known that yields per hectare or animal unit were significantly lower than in Western countries due to inefficient use of technologies. Many experts therefore expected that agricultural production would increase rapidly with transformation, not decrease. What actually occurred after transformation began cannot be explained using standard neoclassical theory, but it can be explained by drawing on NIE.

Figure 1.3: The evolution of agricultural production and employment in the federal states of the former GDR (1989-1994, index 1988 = 100)

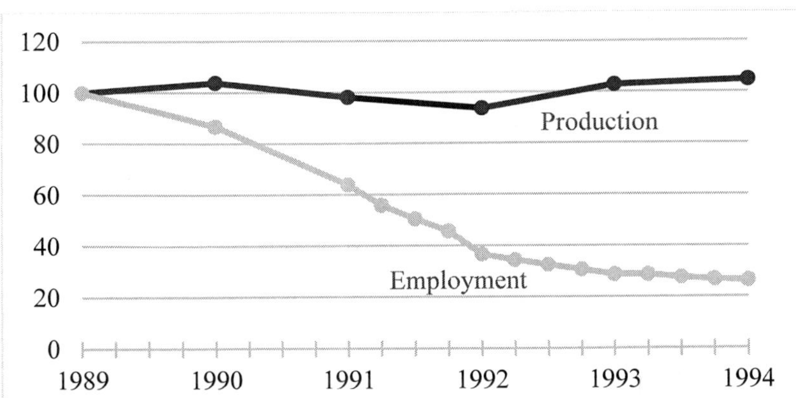

Source: Statistisches Bundesamt (1994, various pages; 1995, p. 680); Sachverständigenrat (1996, p. 376), own calculations.

Figure 1.4: The evolution of agricultural production and employment in Ukraine (1990-1997, index 1990 = 100)

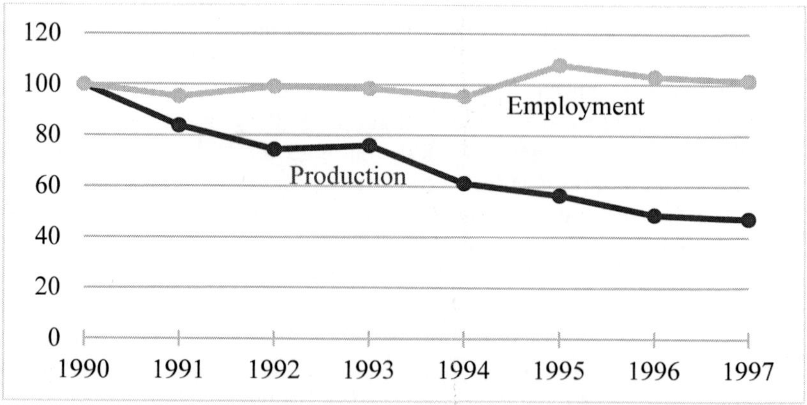

Source: State Committee of Statistics (no date), own calculations.

Which amounts of which goods are produced in an economy is explained in neoclassical economics with the help of a **transformation curve** (also referred to as a **production possibility curve**).[3] Assume that only two goods (q_1 and q_2) are produced. The transformation curve is the set of all maximum possible combinations of q_1 and q_2 that can be produced with the given resource endowment and technology, i.e. for any quantity of q_1 (q_2) the maximum quantity of q_2 (q_1) that can also be produced. Figure 5 shows a set of typical transformation curves.

[3] We formally derive the transformation curve in Chapter Two.

Figure 1.5: The expected and actual development of production in a typical transition country from a neoclassical perspective

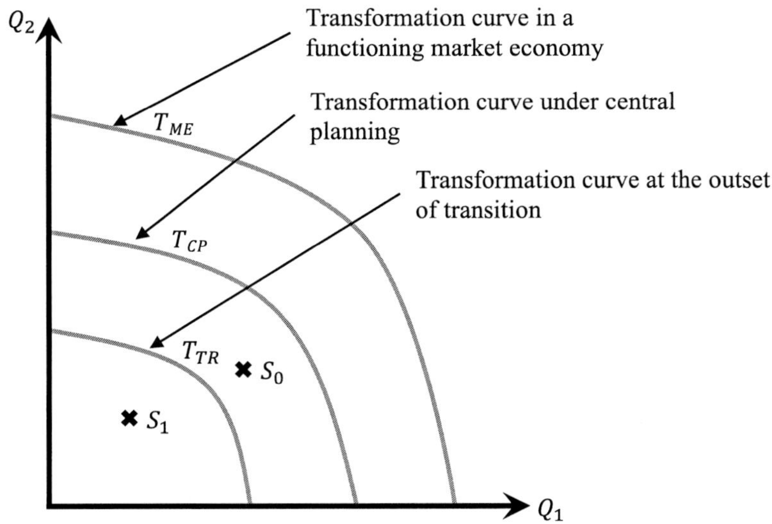

Source: Own depiction.

In order to explain what actually transpired in transition economies, it helps to recognised that the amount of production in an economy depends not only on the available resources and technology, but also on the existing rules and organisations (the institutions). A change in laws, for example labour market regulations, can lead to a shift in the transformation curve. It can also impose restrictions (e.g. shortened working hours) that make it impossible to fully exploit the technically possible production capacity. In the latter case, a production point is realised that lies not on but rather below the transformation curve. Alternatively, one might also define the transformation curve as the set of all maximum possible product combinations that can be produced with given resources, technology and institutions.

The initial situation in a typical transition economy can be represented as follows using neoclassical instruments. Transformation curve T_{ME} shows the production possibilities in a market economy with adequate institutions. T_{ME} lies above transformation curve T_{CP}, which shows the production possibilities for the same economy under central planning. Planned economy production was less efficient than market economy production because, for example, planners did not have sufficient information to optimally coordinate individual decisions. The difference between the two curves is also due to the fact that in a market economy system, other specific institutions, e.g. a regulatory framework, make it possible to achieve more efficient production than is possible in a planned economy system. In fact, however, neither planned nor market economies produce on the technically possible transformation curve, since not all existing institutions are fully enforced. In Figure 5 we assume that point S_0, which lies below the maximum attainable transformation curve T_{CP}, was reached under central planning before transformation began, and that production point S_1 was attained thereafter, i.e. that both production possibilities and production fell following the onset of transformation.

The transition from a planned to a market economy could only have led to an increase in production if the institutions in the planned economy had been fundamentally changed at the same time and adapted to those in efficient market economies. However, such institutional change takes time. Old planned-economy networks often linger. Institutions in the form of laws can be enacted relatively quickly, but the implementation of these laws often causes at least temporary problems. For example, it takes time to establish a functioning legal system for private-sector litigation, a tax authority with qualified tax experts, and a court of auditors to control state expenditures. It especially takes time to establish and safeguard private property.

In addition, the behaviour of individuals in planned economies is different from that in market economies. It is therefore understandable that the transformation curve T_{CP} in the formally central-planned economies did not shift outwards to T_{ME} initially, but rather inward to T_{TR}. The constitutive and regulative principles of a market-economy system formulated by Eucken[4] require a strong state in which both the government and the population are convinced of the advantages of a market-economy order and are in a position to implement these principles. It was naive to expect that the governments of individual transition countries would be able to institutionalise and enforce an efficient market-economy system immediately following the onset of transformation. Reflecting this, Figure

---

[4] Eucken (1950) defined seven constitutive (C) and four regulative (R) principles of a market economy (see van Suntum et al., 2011): C1 – functioning price system; C2 – monetary stability; C3 – open markets; C4 – private property; C5 – freedom to engage in contracts; C6 – liability; C7 – predictable and reliable economic policy; R1 – anti-monopoly policy; R2 – progressive income taxation; R3 – correction of externalities; R4 – regulation to protect workers' rights (e.g. against child labour).

5 assumes that the transformation curve shifted inward to T_{TR}, and that the realised production point S_1 was below T_{TR} due to a lack of enforcement of the nascent legal regulations.

Not only the economic downturn in numerous transition countries but also the different amounts of time that it took for individual countries to recover from this downturn, and the economic rise of countries such as China and Vietnam that only partially liberalised, have led to a stronger emphasis on the NIE, also in agricultural economics. This is due in part to the fact that many agricultural economists expected that the agricultural sector would benefit especially strongly from transformation. Many agricultural economists assumed that agricultural production in the transition countries would increase and that the agricultural structure would change from large farms to more efficient smaller family farms. However, these expectations were not borne out.

In the following general discussion of institutions that are important for agricultural price determination we will draw on the above-mentioned survey article by Williamson (2000). In later chapters, specific institutions that play an important role on individual agricultural product and factor markets are discussed in greater detail. Williamson distinguishes between four hierarchically arranged **levels of institutions** (Figure 6). The institutions on the first level refer to behaviour by producers, consumers and political actors that is not based on rational considerations but is rather embedded in the prevailing social order. These are behaviours that occur spontaneously in accordance with habit and tradition, because everyone else in society follows them and finds them appropriate, and/or because one assumes without further reflection that they are good for oneself and/or the society of which one is part. These behaviours depend, among other things, on the prevailing culture of a society and tend to be long-lived. Since they are deeply rooted in the thinking of individuals and the mental models that they employ, they are referred to as '**embedded institutions**' in the literature.

What role do embedded institutions play in pricing in agricultural markets? First of all, it is useful to differentiate between embedded institutions on the supply side of agricultural markets and those on the demand side.

Figure 1.6: Williamson's hierarchy of institutions

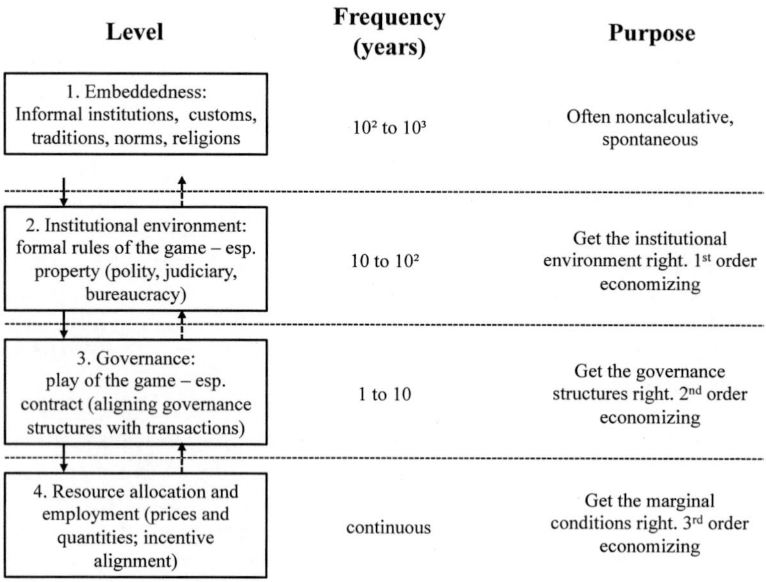

Source: Williamson (2000, p.597).

1.2.1. The importance of embedded institutions on the supply side

On the supply side, the simplest neoclassical model is based on the assumption that producers pursue the goal of profit maximisation and have complete information at their disposal. They view the market price as given, and the marginal cost curve is rising and known.

However, these assumptions do not account for a number of relevant embedded institutions. First, the objective of many agricultural producers is not exclusively to maximise profits. Farmers in Western Europe usually manage farms that have been inherited over many generations. Maintaining family tradition therefore often plays an important role in the decision to take over or continue what might be an unprofitable farm. In addition, the decision to become a farmer is also a decision for a certain way of life, e.g. entrepreneurship, country living. Furthermore, a past decision to become a farmer is often difficult to revise, because it involves making investments in human (training) and physical capital that generate low returns outside of agriculture.

Finally, some farmers fear a loss of reputation with their colleagues and in their social setting if they exit farming. They prefer to cover financial losses from year to year by drawing down on the (often considerable) equity value of their farms, and thus postpone the decision to exit farming to the next generation. For example, according to the agricultural reports of the German Government between 1990 and 2015/16, in all but two years the equity capital losses of the full-time and main-occupation farms in Germany exceeded 40% of their accounting values. Hence, many farms, generally the same ones from year to year, lost money but nevertheless continued to operate.

These factors together contribute to a deviation from the profit maximisation objective. As a result, the aggregated individual supply curves are not identical to the sectoral marginal cost curve, and the neoclassical decision rule 'price equals marginal costs' does not apply, as at least some enterprises are prepared to supply at prices that do not fully cover their marginal costs. This leads to a sub-optimal allocation of production factors and slows structural change in agriculture; the rate at which individual farms exit and other farms grow by taking over their land is reduced. The market mechanism therefore does not always lead to an economically optimal allocation of production factors in agriculture due to the special objective function (embedded institutions) of individual farmers.

Second, embedded institutions in the form of cultural and religious norms can influence supply behaviour in agriculture. These include, for example, regulations governing working on certain days, the use of certain technologies, or the employment of women, children or members of certain social groups. Embedded institutions in the form of traditions and cultural norms also influence the willingness of farmers to cooperate and thus the use or utilisation of technologies characterised by economies of scale, or, for example, the willingness to take measures to increase productivity, such as land consolidation. Farmers who attach particular importance to independence and are therefore not willing to cooperate, or are only willing to cooperate to a limited extent, can thus contribute to a suboptimal use of production factors from a macroeconomic point of view. The willingness to introduce innovations and to experiment with new methods can strongly depend on how traditional and hierarchically structured a society is. In some societies, younger, more experimentally-inclined individuals enjoy greater freedoms than in others (e.g. the Amish in North America). In some societies, chiefs or 'elders' decide on the allocation of scarce resources such as communal land and water, in other societies these decisions are reached by government agencies or on markets. Cultural norms about the inheritance of agricultural holdings or areas also play an important role in this context: a traditional inheritance system that distributes land evenly among heirs can, for example, lead to increased fragmentation of holdings compared with a system that passes the consolidated holding on to a single heir.

Economic systems also belong to the embedded institutions that have considerable and long-lasting effects on individual behaviour and thus also on the intensity of innovations in a society. Alesina and Fuchs-Schündeln (2007) demonstrate that former communist systems have had long-lasting effects on the behaviour of individuals in a society. For example, market systems emphasise private incentives and thus also the search for innovations more strongly than centrally-planned systems. It is therefore not surprising that in the former planned economies relatively few individuals displayed a willingness to re-launch or establish family farms. Koester (2005) and Koester and Petrick (2010) conclude that embedded institutions have also contributed to the emergence and survival of extremely large agro-holdings in Russia.

1.2.2. The importance of embedded institutions on the demand side

Agricultural goods are not homogeneous. Farmers produce, for example, private and public goods. The demand for public goods is determined by political decisions but is also strongly influenced by public awareness and perceptions of the environment, biodiversity and landscapes. The extent to which public goods are demanded and financed by society thus also depends on embedded institutions. A case in point are debates over the perceived advantages of smallholder agriculture and regional production, and whether they should be subsidised.

The demand for food is also determined by embedded institutions. Eating habits vary from country to country and even from family to family due to tradition, religion and differences in the willingness to try new foods. An obvious example of this is religious regulations such as kosher rules; but the reluctance of many German consumers to eat horsemeat is also an example of an embedded institution. Even the cultural question of whether to eat with knife and fork or, for example, with chopsticks can influence what is eaten.

1.2.3. The importance of embedded institutions for policy decisions

Embedded institutions influence not only supply and demand in agricultural markets, but also political decisions on the regulation of these markets. Which rules (laws) are introduced, even in democratic systems, is influenced by citizens' preferences, but also by their representatives, the members of parliament as the legislative branch and the government as the executive branch. The resulting decisions and their implementation are shaped, sometimes considerably, by the embedded institutions of the decision-makers. Throughout history, for example, embedded institutions have often led farmers to be regarded as particularly honest, hard-working and thus worthy of support. Even Cato the Elder was convinced of the special qualities of farmers:

> "But it is from the tillers of the soil that spring the best citizens, the staunchest soldiers; ... Such as devote themselves to that pursuit are least of all men given to evil counsels" (Cato the Elder, about 160 BCE).

One of the founding fathers of the USA, Thomas Jefferson, expressed a similar sentiment, sometimes referred to as the **'Jeffersonian Ideal'**:

> "Those who labour in the earth are the chosen people of God, if ever he had a chosen people, whose breasts he has made his peculiar deposit for substantial and genuine virtue. .... Corruption of morals in the mass of cultivators is a phenomenon of which no age nor nation has furnished an example" (Jefferson 1787).

The German Agriculture Act, which was adopted in 1955 and is still in force today, was shaped by a similar attitude towards agriculture and farmers. The then Chancellor of Germany Adenauer expressed the following views on the importance of agriculture and the objectives of agricultural policy:

> "I have always been a friend of agriculture, for one reason alone, because I am deeply convinced that the maintenance of a healthy farming community is one of the most fundamental tasks of an intelligent and sensible government even in our time. ... The agricultural price level, which can largely be influenced by domestic and trade policy measures, must, in my opinion, be kept in parity with the other prices of the German economy, in particular also with regard to wages and here again primarily with regard to agricultural wages. The Federal Government will take all appropriate measures to ensure that prices develop in line with actual production costs. ... We will become much more independent and stable through an increase in domestic production, which is associated with restrictions on imports.

> This would make an extraordinary contribution to strengthening our entire state" (Adenauer 1951).

The deeply rooted conviction reflected in Adenauer's words was decisive not only for the German Agriculture Act of 1955, but also later in the 1960s for the design of the first European Union market intervention systems (see Koester 2000).

In conclusion, embedded institutions are of great importance for the development of the current situation on many national agricultural markets and thus for the situation and development of world agricultural markets.

1.2.4. The importance of the institutional environment for agricultural price formation

Williamson (2000) refers to the institutions on the second level of his hierarchy (see Figure 6) as the '**institutional environment**', which comprises the fundamental rules of the game such as the legal system, property rights and the regulation of markets.

Agriculture produces not only search goods, but also experience goods and trust goods. As a result, the markets for these products in individual countries are more or less strongly influenced by laws and their enforcement. These laws serve to protect the producers of agricultural products when purchasing agricultural inputs, but also to protect traders and consumers. Of particular importance are laws that regulate the approval and use of certain inputs (e.g. herbicides and pesticides), certain products (e.g. genetically modified organisms) and land use (e.g. the designation of protected areas, and building laws that regulate the location of livestock facilities). Legal regulations concerning the land market are of particular importance for agricultural price formation; we describe this in detail in Chapter 3.

Since laws differ from country to country, even within the EU, they also influence the international competitiveness of agriculture and the upstream and downstream industries. When this is the case, for example when a state imposes stricter standards on the spreading of manure to avoid or reduce environmental damage, should the state compensate farmers for the effects of these rules?

In principle, (agricultural) economic policy measures should only be considered if they increase social welfare. This is the case with policies that eliminate the effects of market failures or the undesirable side-effects of other agricultural policy measures. In the optimum, the marginal social costs of an economic activity should equal its marginal social benefits. The marginal social costs are identical to the opportunity costs of producing an additional unit. State intervention which aims, for example, at avoiding environmental damage, increases private production costs, but it increases social welfare if it aligns private and social marginal costs and thus forces producers to take the total opportunity costs of their decisions into account. Paying subsidies to the producer to compensate for the additional private costs would undermine this alignment and thus lead to a suboptimal situation.

Another way of looking at this is to refer once more to the transformation curve. As explained above, a country's transformation curve is determined not only by the available resources and the given technology, but also by the existing institutions. These include not only the embedded institutions discussed above, but also the institutional environment. This environment can include legal regulations that have a negative impact on producers, but are desired by society, at least in the opinion of policy makers. In addition to regulations that are introduced for environmental reasons, this includes numerous social laws and labour regulations. If, for example, these regulations contribute to improved quality of life and increasing political and economic stability in a country, they can strengthen its competitiveness; they will then contribute to an outward shift of the transformation curve.

Whether state regulations influence a country's agricultural prices depends on how trade is regulated, the relative size of the country and the level of transaction costs. For internationally non-tradable goods, price changes will depend on changes in the private costs as a result of government regulations, and the price elasticities of domestic supply and demand. In the case of tradable goods in a large country[5], government regulations influence price formation at home but also abroad. In the case of tradable goods in a small country, price effects depend on the type of government regulation – border measures such as customs duties or export taxes will change domestic prices, but measures that only affect domestic production or consumption will have no impact on the domestic price level, which depends on the world market.

---

[5] A country is considered to be 'large' in economic terms (independent of the size of its population or physical area) if changes that take place on its domestic markets influence world market prices.

1.2.5. The importance of governance for agricultural price formation

The laws that make up the institutional environment and provide rules of the game for economic actors will only be capable of contributing efficiently to the coordination of economic activity if they are well-designed and enforced. Who adopts laws and how they are enforced is referred to as '**governance**', which represents the third level of Williamson's (2000) hierarchy (Figure 6).

The importance of the legal and administrative enforcement of laws in the EU has been pointed out by the European Court of Auditors in a number of reports. In these reports the Court criticises that the effects of individual EU laws cannot be adequately verified and therefore no macroeconomic cost-benefit analysis of these laws can be carried out. This finding applies in particular to laws designed to protect the environment, including biodiversity; it also applies to measures that are supposed to achieve the agricultural policy objective of ensuring a fair standard of living for individuals working in agriculture (European Court of Auditors 2016).

A particular problem with the effectiveness of formal legislation occurs in countries where a large share of the GDP is produced illegally, i.e. on black markets. Depending on the extent of this production, it can influence price formation on official markets. This influence can be illustrated using the milk market as an example. In most countries it is prohibited by law to sell raw milk directly from farms to households or on farmers' markets. Despite this prohibition, however, in some Central Asian countries, much raw milk is sold directly to consumers, bypassing official marketing channels. Obviously, the sellers view the risk of being caught and having to pay a fine as lower in monetary terms than the additional profit they realise by bypassing official marketing channels. As a result, both supply and demand on the official markets are lower.

The EU has often struggled to enforce specific agricultural regulations in individual EU member states. For example, in the 1990s there were numerous reports of farmers in Italy claiming subsidies for olive trees that did not exist. Although the EU implemented a milk quota system in 1984, this system had not been fully implemented in Italy as late as 1995. In that year the expansion of the EU to include three new members (Austria, Finland and Sweden) was being negotiated. The accession of new member states requires unanimous approval by all current member states, and Italy was only prepared to vote in favour in return for a reduction in the fines that were due for its failure to implement the milk quota, and for an increase in its national quota allocation. More recently, in late 2016, the EU Commission took Germany to court for its failure to implement EU 'Water Framework Directive', a law that regulates groundwater quality and specifically nitrate levels in groundwater (EU Commission 2020).

1.3. The importance of transaction costs for agricultural price formation

Embedded institutions, the institutional environment, and governance are important determinants of the functioning of markets, especially in agriculture, as they determine the level of **transaction costs**. Transaction costs arise when goods and services are exchanged between economic actors. Transaction costs include (Richter and Furubotn 1996):

- search and information costs,
- negotiation and decision costs,
- monitoring and enforcement costs.

The simple neoclassical model does not consider transaction costs. Markets develop spontaneously under these conditions, since buyers and sellers can meet at any time and without cost. In reality, however, transaction costs affect the performance of markets and can even prevent their emergence.

Exchange takes place on markets, but also within enterprises, whenever a client (in the literature on transaction costs often called the 'principal') demands a certain service from one or more contractors ('agents'), and the agents expect a fee for this service. In the following we first consider the importance of transaction costs for price determination on agricultural markets.

1.3.1. The importance of transaction costs for the prices of private agricultural goods

Search and information costs play an important role on agricultural product and input markets. Agricultural products can be divided into search, experience and trust goods, each with its special types and levels of transaction costs. Search and information costs are affected by the heterogeneity of the product in question and the numbers of suppliers and consumers in space and time. These costs include not only the costs incurred in searching for a prospective buyer or seller, but also the costs of obtaining reliable information about the quality of the product in question and about the contractual loyalty of potential exchange partners. Naturally, these costs are higher if qualities vary widely (as is the case for many agricultural products such as wheat and milk), and if the enforcement of contracts is uncertain and expensive due to unreliable legal channels or corruption. Search and information costs are therefore higher for contracts between contractual partners who are dealing with one another for the first time compared with long-term partners. It is therefore understandable that buyers of ecologically produced products, which are trust goods, often prefer to buy directly from a known producer. Familiarity with the seller and the inspection of the production site can strengthen trust.

The transaction costs associated with trade in agricultural products are influenced by the rules of international trade as well as by agricultural production technology. Changes in these factors can lead to the emergence of new institutions, as illustrated by the following examples.

- In the last decades of the 19th century, the net trade positions of France and Russia on world wheat markets changed fundamentally. France became a net importer of wheat and Russia a net exporter. French importers often found that the quality of the Russian wheat did not meet agreed standards. In order to avoid costly and risky legal disputes, the French importers engaged a company that had been founded in Switzerland in 1878, the Société Générale de Surveillance (SGS 2021VI). Today SGS offers inspection, testing, certification, and verification services in 120 countries worldwide. Inspection services include testing and verification of the quantity, weight and quality of goods traded. SGS thus reduces uncertainty for grain traders, who are willing to pay for the resulting reduction and stabilisation of their transaction costs.

- The first commodity futures market for grain was established in Chicago in 1848 on the initiative of private companies. The aim was to reduce transaction costs, which had risen significantly in previous years as a result of a new production technology, the combine harvester. This technology was patented in the USA in 1835 and spread rapidly. While combine harvesters reduced the costs of harvesting grain, they also increased transaction costs for grain traders. Before the advent of combine harvesters, farmers harvested grain on the stalk and stored it in their barns, threshing it with immobile threshing machines throughout the year. The supply of grain was therefore distributed over several months, and grain traders needed only limited storage capacity, as they usually passed on the grain that they had bought from farmers immediately to mills. The spread of combine harvesters made grain sales much more seasonal. As most farmers had only limited grain storage capacities on their farms, they tried to sell large parts of their grain immediately after the harvest. This created two problems for the traders: they needed larger storage capacities, and they had to manage the increased price risk associated with longer storage periods. Hence, the transaction costs faced by traders increased as a result of a new technology on the farm. In response, traders initiated the establishment of a futures market for grain in Chicago; in other words, they responded to the increased transaction costs by creating a new institution.[6]

- In recent decades, transaction costs in agricultural markets have changed significantly due to new information technologies. Jensen (2007) shows how the introduction of mobile telephones along the coast of Kerala in India radically changed pricing in local fish markets, to the great benefit of producers and consumers. Before the introduction of mobile telephones, there were often large surpluses on some markets depending on the size of the daily catch, which can vary considerably along the coast. When such surpluses occurred, the price fell to zero and fish had to be thrown away at the end of the market day due to a lack of refrigerated storage capacities. On the same day, however, there could be deficits and high prices at other, low-catch locations along the coast. Using mobile phones, fishermen could coordinate the distribution of their daily catches among the individual markets, which stabilised prices and almost eliminated instances of wastage. Since Jensen's ground-breaking work, many studies have demonstrated similar effects of modern information and communication technologies on agricultural markets.

These examples show that institutions can change over time without government activity. However, much institutional change is due to government activity such as changes in or the introduction of new legislation.

Transaction costs depend not only on the characteristics of the product in question but also on **uncertainty** that can arise from the unpredictable

[6] How futures markets function and influence agricultural prices is the topic of Chapter 13.

behaviour of trading partners. Sometimes trading partners cannot fulfil their contractual obligations due to circumstances beyond their control. For example, a farmer might not be able to deliver a contracted amount because of an extremely poor harvest. But sometimes contracts are not fulfilled due to **opportunistic behaviour**; a farmer might not fulfil contractual obligation because the current spot market price is higher than the contracted price.

Even for completely homogeneous goods, market transaction costs can vary among buyers and sellers depending on their perceived reliability and contract loyalty. Following the onset of transition in Central and Eastern European countries, for example, transaction costs for the sellers of agricultural products were relatively high because it was not possible to draw on the experience of past transactions with the individual potential partners. It is therefore understandable that at the beginning of transition, market transactions were primarily carried out in the form of **barter trade**. However, the transaction costs for barter transactions are as a rule much higher than on functioning markets. Barter trade requires a coincidence of interests – sellers need to find partners who demand the product that they wish to sell, and who are offering products that they wish to purchase – and the associated search costs can be very high.

However, barter trade has the advantage that the contracting parties *uno actu* fulfil their obligations, e.g. when a farmer barters grain from the last harvest for fertiliser for next year's crop. Under normal market conditions, the number of transactions that occur is much larger because the seller of a product receives money that can be used to purchase any good or service. If there is a time lag between the two transactions, e.g. between the sale of grain and the purchase of fertiliser, uncertainty arises. This uncertainty is particularly high when the value of money changes over time due to inflation. For example, the inflation rate in Ukraine in 1993 was over 4700 % (Statista 2021). Buyers and sellers were therefore afraid to exchange goods for money; they preferred barter trade.

When conditions such as lack of trust and monetary instability lead to barter trade, farms tend to specialise in the production of goods that can be used by workers and their families, and that can be easily bartered for other goods on regional markets. Farms pay wages with these goods rather than money. However, this specialisation weakens the division of labour between enterprises and regions, thereby reducing the efficiency of resource use in the economy. As a result, for example, animal production on large farms in Central and Eastern Europe fell strongly after transition began while the share of animal production on small-scale household farms increased – large farms paid their workers in grain and other feedstuffs, which were then fed to animals in household holdings.

1.3.2. Transaction costs and farm size and organisation

Transaction costs influence farm sizes, even under free market conditions and in the absence of embedded institutions. Figure 7 describes the interplay of factors that influence the choice of farm size. We assume that the chosen technology depends on the size of the farm and that average production costs fall with increasing farm size. In Figure 7, this curve, which describes how inputs are transformed into agricultural products on the farm, is referred to as 'transformation costs'. The curve labelled 'internal transaction costs' captures the costs incurred in monitoring labour on the farm. We assume that larger farms require larger numbers of employees and, hence, incur higher costs of monitoring labour. Internal transaction costs can also increase with farm size due to internal transport costs, for example if some fields are located far from the farm centre.

Figure 1.7: The relevance of transaction costs for the determination of the optimal farm size

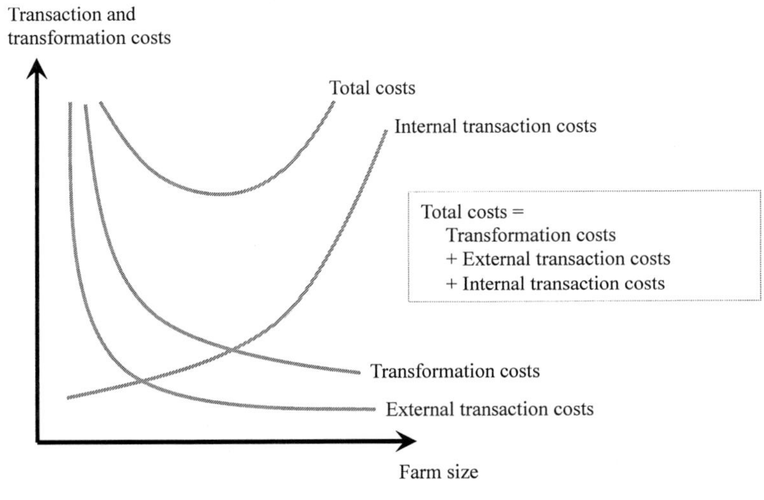

Source: Own design.

In addition to transformation costs and internal transaction costs, 'external transaction costs' also play an important role. External transaction costs include the market transaction costs discussed above. For example, large farms are more likely to have storage facilities that allow them to choose when to sell. They might be able to secure volume discounts on input purchases (and volume premia on their sales), and they will generally be in a better position to use marketing options such as futures markets, because they can distribute the fixed costs of participation over a larger production volume. Finally, operational transport costs are often lower for farms that sell higher sales volumes. For example, milk producers with large delivery volumes to a dairy often receive higher farm-gate prices for their milk than smaller farms located the same distance from the dairy.

The exact shapes of the various cost curves depicted in Figure 7 will vary depending on the type of farm (e.g. crop, livestock, horticulture), the technologies used and many other factors such as proximity to markets and management skills (e.g. the ability to motivate workers). But the basic forms of these curves will be the same across a wide variety of settings, leading to a U-shaped total cost curve and a more or less narrow range of optimal farm sizes.

In most market economies, agricultural holdings are organised as businesses or partnerships. The choice of organisational form is also determined by the transaction costs between principals and agents. On a family farm, principle-agent (manager-worker) relations blur and overlap with family relations (e.g. father-daughter, owner-inheritor). The result is often high motivation and low monitoring, but in some cases inter-generational conflict can inflate transaction costs. In the case of a corporation or company, the farm manager (agent) is selected and supervised by the owners (principals). Experience with large corporate farms in Eastern Europe and Central Asia shows that the principals (owners) often find it difficult to effectively monitor the agent (manager) because they are far from the many and complex day-to-day decisions that farm managers must take, and especially the large numbers of sales and purchases that they make. It is relatively easy for an agent to engage in opportunistic behaviour by arranging ‘deals’ whereby, for example, an input supplier charges an inflated price on paper, and splits the difference with the farm manager, all at the expense of the owners. If the farm manager is a part-owner or is paid a share of the farm profits, the incentives for such opportunistic behaviour can be reduced.

1.3.3. Transaction costs on agricultural input markets

Information costs on agricultural input markets are of particular importance for agricultural price formation. The most important agricultural input factors, apart from labour, are capital and land.

The use of capital and land, and the acquisition of agricultural skills are associated with investments that are often financed by loans that need to be repaid over the course of an uncertain future. Therefore, the risk for investors and lenders is relatively high. Creditors will have more confidence in borrowers with whom they have a history of trading relationships, or who can provide collateral. It is therefore not surprising that at the beginning of the transition process in Central and Eastern Europe, private traders often acted as creditors, and the next harvest often served as collateral. However, the resulting loans were initially only used to finance short-term investments, such as the purchase of agricultural inputs. Providing long-term loans requires greater trust on the part of lenders. This trust is strengthened if borrowers can provide collateral in the form of marketable, durable assets. Therefore, access to agricultural credit is facilitated by ownership of land. Agricultural development in many transition countries often was and sometimes still is severely hampered by missing or incomplete privatisation of agricultural land.

1.3.4. The importance of transaction costs for public goods produced in agriculture

Agriculture can produce **public goods** either as a by-product of private good production, or in return for payment. In a market economy, society will not be willing to pay for a public good if the social demand curve cuts the abscissa to the left of the quantity supplied (see Figure 8). However, this theoretical consideration is of little practical help as it is difficult to quantify the marginal social willingness to pay for public goods. It can be assumed that the willingness to pay will depend on the income of the potential consumers and on the nature of the public good in question (e.g. the maintenance of an open cultural landscape, or planting a strip of wildflowers). Where there is no market, the state can decide to influence the allocation of resources by promoting the production of public goods. Determining the optimal amounts of public goods and promoting them involves considerable transaction costs. These costs will vary depending on whether the desired public good is regional, supranational or international. For example, it will be easier to determine the willingness to pay for a local public good that is produced in a particular region and only consumed by inhabitants of that region. Matters become considerably more complicated if the public good in question is produced and consumed in many (or all) countries (e.g. the mitigation of climate change).

Figure 1.8: Hypothetical demand and supply curves for a public good

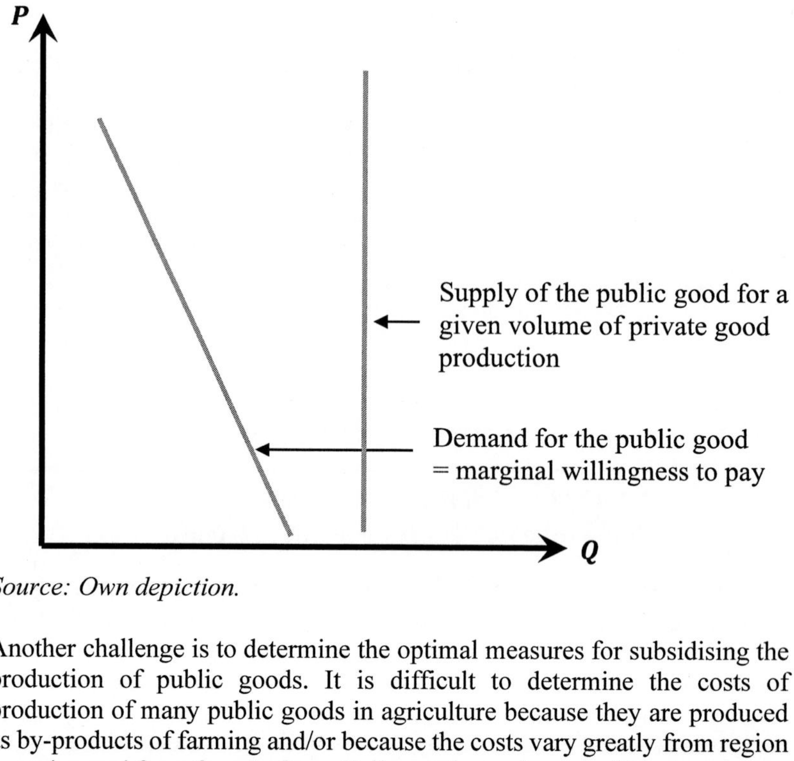

Source: Own depiction.

Another challenge is to determine the optimal measures for subsidising the production of public goods. It is difficult to determine the costs of production of many public goods in agriculture because they are produced as by-products of farming and/or because the costs vary greatly from region to region and from farm to farm. Policy-makers often use the average costs of the resources needed for producing a public good as a basis for calculating subsidy levels. However, this leads to overcompensation of all farmers who have lower than average production costs. This overcompensation will be higher if subsidies are made available and farmers are free to decide whether they wish to participate in the programme and claim them. In this case, it is to be expected that only those farmers with below-average costs will participate.

In the EU, many policy measures to encourage the production of public goods are jointly financed. The resulting so-called **common pool problem** leads member states to subsidize more public good production than they would under national financing (Osterloh et al., 2008). The EU's Common Agricultural Policy (CAP) provides many examples. In 1992, the so-called 'Second Pillar' of the CAP was introduced to support agri-environmental policy and to promote rural areas. Before that, rural development policy had only played an important role in the United Kingdom. The availability of joint financing in the Second Pillar has greatly increased member states' interest in promoting rural areas. The European Court of Auditors has published a series of critical assessments of the resulting programs, for example:

> "The 'accompanying measures' to the changes made by the 1992 reform … included: an agri-environment measure, which aimed at compensating farmers for using environmentally beneficial but costly farming techniques; and an afforestation measure, which aimed at compensating farmers for relevant expenses and loss of agricultural income resulting from planting trees on their farmland. … However, neither the Community nor the Member States targeted the use of Community funds according to pre-established environmental priorities … In consequence funds were not allocated to the zones with the greatest agri-environmental problems and/or potential. … The effectiveness of some programmes is hampered by inadequacies in programme design. In some cases, aid rates are too low to attract farmers to environmentally friendly farming techniques; in other cases, because aid rates are based on the average cost to farmers of compliance with programme requirements, farmers received rates of aid significantly in excess of their actual costs" (European Court of Auditors 2000, p. 2).

Even though the Court of Auditors' report does not explicitly refer to transaction costs in this statement, it nevertheless highlights the importance of transaction costs for efforts to support the provision of public goods in agriculture.

1.3.5. Transaction costs in the adoption and implementation of new laws and their importance for agricultural price formation

Agricultural prices result not only from the free play of market forces, but also from a multitude of state regulations (laws) and their enforcement. Transaction costs arise in the political process that leads to the adoption of laws, when governments and administrations decide on the selection and the dosage of instruments, in the enforcement of laws, and when the effectiveness of laws and their implementation are monitored and reviewed.

New legislative proposals may be justified for different reasons. For example, market failures may have been diagnosed; a lack of effectiveness and efficiency of existing laws may have been determined; policy makers may wish to place more emphasis on the pursuit of non-economic _ ; the earlier justification for an existing law may have lost validity as a result of changes in the economic and/or political environment.

The costs of decision-making would be low if problems could be diagnosed easily and there was broad agreement on the methods and results of diagnoses. Such unambiguity is not to be expected in democratic systems, or only rarely. As a rule, even if there is agreement on the facts, there will be differences in the evaluation of the facts and in the selection of instruments for improvement. Often policy makers take decisions without first compiling rigorous diagnoses, even in cases in which they are legally required to do so. For example, the German "Haushaltsgrundsatzgesetz" (Budget Principles Act) stipulates that:

> "Appropriate efficiency analyses shall be conducted for all measures having financial impact." (Federal Ministry of Finance 1969, article 6, paragraph 2).

An **economic efficiency analysis** is a comprehensive macroeconomic cost-benefit study. It is thus not limited to simply projecting financial costs; it must also examine whether implementation of the proposed measure can be expected to lead to an efficient achievement of clearly defined objectives.

Prior to 2013, the EU did not have an analogous law. Since the adoption of Regulation (EU) 1306/2013, the EU Commission is charged with monitoring and evaluating agricultural policy measures:

> "Every measure under the CAP should be subject to monitoring and evaluation in order to improve its quality and to demonstrate its achievements" (EU 2013, paragraph 68).

However, Regulation 1306/2013 simply calls on the EU Commission to determine "a list of indicators" for assessing the performance of the CAP and does not explicitly call for rigorous economic efficiency analysis. In the absence of such analysis, politicians lack a basis for economically rational decisions.

In addition, even where rigorous cost-benefit analysis is carried out, individual decision-makers may not agree on the implications for policy. It cannot be assumed that all decision-makers are interested in maximising overall economic welfare. In most cases, they are equally or more interested in the distributional effects of potential interventions; in many cases they are exposed to pressure from interest groups and their lobbyists. Sometimes their scope for decision-making is restricted by international treaties and obligations. Finally, decision-makers might use different discount rates to determine the current value of the future streams of costs and benefits that are triggered by a policy measure, and thus arrive at different assessments of this measure.

Since farmers are more directly and strongly affected by agricultural prices than most other groups in society, such as consumers, they have a powerful incentive to invest resources in lobbying to influence political decisions that affect agricultural prices. As a result, agricultural policy makers in democratic systems will tend to place a greater weight on farmers' interests than on the interests of other groups. In his seminal work on collective action, Olson (1965) explained that successful lobbying generates an outcome that has public-good characteristics: for example, price support that benefits all farmers, whether or not they have contributed to the lobbying effort. As a result, individual farmers will have an incentive to free ride (let others do the lobbying, but benefit from the fruits of this lobbying). This freeriding problem is typically better overcome by small, relatively homogeneous groups (e.g. farmers in industrialised countries) than by large, inhomogeneous groups (e.g. consumers).

Agricultural policy making in Brussels or elsewhere is based on a time-consuming and costly process of collecting and evaluating information, and harmonising interests. Economic expertise can contribute to this process, reduce costs and lead to improved decisions, but any assessment of the current situation and of the effects of alternative policy measures necessarily contains subjective value judgements and is not just a technical exercise.

1.3.6. Transaction costs in the implementation of alternative policies

Market intervention is always associated with administrative costs. The more the intervention depends on direct information from farms, the higher the administrative costs. Border measures such as customs duties and levies are generally associated with lower administrative costs than on-farm measures such as regulations on permissible production quantities (such as quotas) or on the use of factors (such as prescribed crop rotations, acreage set aside, or measures to improve biodiversity). However, the transaction costs associated with some border measures (such as complex rules of origin in a free trade area, tariff rate quotas or the former EU agri-monetary system) can also be significant. Furthermore, the transaction costs associated with on-farm measures will depend on farm structures. In Ukraine, where roughly 20,000 commercial enterprises of over 1,000 hectares each farm roughly 80% of the agricultural land (Vlasenko and Vlasovets 2016, p. 160), the costs of implementing on-farm measures will be much lower than, for example, in Germany with more than 200,000 farms.

The more detailed information from agricultural holdings or from downstream or upstream enterprises is required to implement certain measures or to assess the impact of these measures, the higher the administrative costs will be. For example, the shift in EU agricultural policy from price support to direct payments to farms that was initiated by the so-called MacSharry Reforms beginning in 1992 have led to an increase in so-called 'irregularities' (EU jargon) and fraud in the implementation of agricultural policy measures in individual EU countries. The European Court of Auditors has pointed out in several reports that the implementation of agricultural policy measures in member states that suffer from relatively high corruption is causing problems. Corruption in the enforcement of agricultural policy measures increases the overall economic costs of these measures, which should be accounted for in a comprehensive evaluation of the measures.

1.3.7. Transaction costs in the ex-post evaluation of policy measures that affect agricultural prices

It is relatively easy to determine the direct price effects of border measures such as tariffs on internationally traded products. However, even in this case, determining the spillover effects of these measures on the prices of agricultural products that are not traded internationally can be costly. Changes in the prices of traded goods caused by border measures will also influence the prices of non-traded goods via cross-price in supply and demand. Thus, the 2014 Russian embargo on agricultural imports from the EU affected not only prices for butter, cheese and other traded dairy products, but also the prices of raw milk and fresh milk that are not traded.

Quantifying these effects as a basis for assessing the effects of the Russian embargo entails considerable costs.

1.4. Keywords

- barter trade
- common pool problem
- economic efficiency analysis
- embedded institution
- governance
- institutional environment
- institutions
- Jeffersonian Ideal
- Old and New Institutional Economics
- opportunistic behaviour
- organisation
- public goods
- production possibility curve
- rules of a game
- transaction costs
- transformation curve
- uncertainty
- Williamsons levels of institutions

References

Adenauer A (1951) Deutsche Bauern-Korrespondenz 4. Vol. 4, February 26, 1951. Quoted by Puvogel C., (1957), Der Weg zum Landwirtschaftsgesetz. Bayerischer Landwirtschaftsverlag, Bonn, p. 30.

Alesina A and Fuchs-Schündeln N (2007) Good-Bye Lenin (or Not?): The Effect of Communism on People's Preferences. American Economic Review 97: 1507-1528.

Cato the Elder, about 160 BCE, De agricultura. https://penelope.uchicago.edu/Thayer/E/Roman/Texts/Cato/De_Agricultura/A*.html#0, accessed on September 24, 2021.

Coase R (1937) The Nature of the Firm. Economica 4: 386-305.

Commons JR (1893) The Distribution of Wealth. Macmillan and Co., New York.

Commons JR (1934) Institutional Economics: Its place in political economy. The Macmillan Company, New York.

Eucken W (1950) The Foundations of Economics. History and Theory of Economic Reality. London, Edinburgh, Glasgow.

European Court of Auditors (2000) Special Report No 14/2000 on "Greening the CAP" together with the Commission's replies. https://www.eca.europa.eu/Lists/ECADocuments/SR00_14/SR00_14_EN.PDF, accessed on September 24, 2021.

European Court of Auditors (2016) Supporting farmers' incomes: Is the Commission's performance measurement system well designed and based on sound data? https://www.eca.europa.eu/Lists/ECADocuments/SR16_01/SR_FARMERS_EN.pdf, accessed on September 24, 2021.

EU (2013) Regulation (EU) No 1306/2013 on the financing, management and monitoring of the common agricultural policy. Official Journal of the European Union, L 347/549, https://eur-lex.europa.eu/legal-content/EN/TXT/PDF/?uri=CELEX:32013R1306&from=EN, accessed on September 24, 2021.

EU Commission (2020) Vertragsverletzungsverfahren: Kommission leitet in 17 Fällen rechtliche Schritte gegen Deutschland ein. https://ec.europa.eu/germany/news/20190725-vertragsverletzungsverfahren_de, accessed on September 24, 2021.

EBRD (European Bank for Reconstruction and Development) (2012) Transition Report 2012: Integration Across Borders. EBRD, London.

Federal Ministry of Finance (1969) Budgetary Principles Act (Haushaltsgrundsatzgesetz), English translation, https://www.bundesfinanzministerium.de/Content/EN/Gesetze/Laws/1969-08-19-budgetary-principles-act.html, accessed on September 24, 2021.

Jefferson T (1787) Notes on the State of Virginia. Digitised by the University of Virginia American Studies Program 1998-99. http://www.xroads.virginia.edu/~Hyper/JEFFERSON/header.html accessed on September 24, 2021.

Jensen R (2007) The Digital Provide: Information (Technology), Market Performance, and Welfare in the South Indian Fisheries Sector. Quarterly Journal of Economics 122: 879-924.

Koester U (2000) The Role of Germany in the Common Agricultural Policy. In: Tangermann S (Ed.) Agriculture in Germany. DLG-Verlag, Frankfurt, pp. 209-230.

Koester U (2005) A revival of large farms in Eastern Europe—how important are institutions? Agricultural Economics 32: 103-113.

Koester U and Petrick M (2010) Embedded Institutions and the Persistence of Large Farms in Russia. IAMO Discussion Paper No. 131, https://www.iamo.de/fileadmin/documents/dp131.pdf, accessed on September 24, 2021.

Mitchell WC (1903) A History of the Greenbacks. University of Chicago Press, Chicago.

Mitchell WC (1914) Human Behavior and Economics. A Survey of Recent Literature. Quarterly Journal of Economics 29: 1-47.

North D (1990) Institutions, Institutional Change and Economic Performance. Cambridge University Press, Cambridge.

Olson M (1965) The logic of collective action. Vol. 124. Harvard University Press.

Osterloh S, Heinemann F and Mohl P (2008) EU Budget Reform Options and the Common Pool Problem. Unpublished manuscript, http://aei.pitt.edu/33114/1/osterloh._steffen.pdf, accessed on September 24, 2021.

Ostrom E (1990) Governing the Commons: The Evolution of Institutions for Collective Action. Cambridge University Press, Cambridge.

Richter R and Furubotn E (1996) Neue Institutionenökonomik. 2nd edition. Mohr Siebeck, Tübingen.

Sachverständigenrat (1996) Jahresgutachten des Sachverständigenrates zur Begutachtung der gesamtwirtschaftlichen Entwicklung 1995/96. Wiesbaden.

SGS (Société Générale de Surveillance) (2021) https://www.sgsgroup.de/en/our-company/about-sgs/sgs-in-brief accessed on September 24, 2021.

State Committee of Statistics /no date) Ukraine Economic Trends. Unpublished document, Kiev.

Statista (2021) Ukraine: Inflationsrate von 1993 bis 2020 und Prognosen bis 2026. https://de.statista.com/statistik/daten/studie/232421/umfrage/inflationsrate-in-der-ukraine/. accessed on September 24, 2021.

Statistisches Bundesamt (1994) Fachserie 18, Reihe 1.3. Wiesbaden.

Statistisches Bundesamt (1995) Statistisches Jahrbuch. Wiesbaden.

Veblen TR (1899) The Theory of the Leisure Class: An Economic Study of Institutions. Macmillan, New York.

Vlasenko T and Vlasovets V (2016) Status and trends of agricultural enterprises in Ukraine in terms of market agricultural machinery. ECONTECHMOD 5:159-170.

van Suntum U, Böhm T, Oelgemöller J and Ilgmann C (2011) Walter Eucken`s principles of economic policy today, CAWM Discussion

Paper, No.49, Westfälische Wilhelms-Universität Münster, Centrum für Angewandte Wirtschaftsforschung (CAWM), Münster.
Williamson OE (1975) Markets and Hierarchies: Some Elementary Considerations. American Economic Review 63: 316-325.
Williamson OE (2000) The New Institutional Economics: Taking Stock, Looking Ahead. Journal of Economic Literature 38: 595-613.
World Bank (2002) World Development Report. World Bank, Washington DC.

CHAPTER TWO

THE DERIVATION OF OPTIMAL PRICE RELATIONS IN CLOSED AND IN OPEN ECONOMIES: THE NEOCLASSICAL APPROACH

ULRICH KOESTER AND
STEPHAN VON CRAMON–TAUBADEL

2.1. Introduction and learning objectives

The aim of this chapter is to show how equilibrium prices are determined under neoclassical conditions, thereby maximising the efficiency of factor use and welfare in society. This chapter is primarily intended for students who are not familiar with neoclassical economics as presented in standard textbooks, or who are looking to refresh their knowledge. We therefore do not consider extensions based on institutional economics in this chapter.

This chapter has three sections. The first section explains the determination of prices for consumption goods in a closed economy. The second section then deals with the determination of prices for factors of production given equilibrium prices for goods. Finally, the third section describes the special features of price determination in an open economy. Most of the explanations in this chapter are based on a simplified model of a closed economy with two individuals (consumers), two goods[1] and two production factors. This (2 * 2 * 2)-model is developed in Appendix 2.1. It can be generalised to an (m * n * l)-model that allows for more than 2 individuals, goods and production factors, but the key results and insights remain the same.

---

[1] We use the term ‘goods’ to refer to goods as well as services, which are also produced and consumed.

In this first part of this chapter:

- we explain the derivation of optimal price relations for consumption goods in a closed barter economy,
- we show how exchange equilibria are achieved with money in a market economy system,
- we describe the importance of transaction costs and the role of money as an institution, and
- we outline how the market price mechanism can maximise economic welfare.

2.2. Achieving optimal price relations for consumer goods through barter

2.2.1. Barter and Pareto optimum in consumption

In Appendix 2.1 (equation 49) we show that economic welfare is maximised when, among other things, the following condition is met:

$$\frac{\frac{\partial U^1}{\partial Q_1^{D1}}}{\frac{\partial U^1}{\partial Q_2^{D1}}} = \frac{\frac{\partial U^2}{\partial Q_1^{D2}}}{\frac{\partial U^2}{\partial Q_2^{D2}}} \qquad (1)$$

The expressions on the left and right sides of equation (1) are called **marginal rates of substitution** between goods 1 and 2 for individuals 1 and 2, respectively. They indicate the slope of the indifference curves for each respective individual.[2] Equation (1) thus states that economic welfare is maximised when the marginal rates of substitution between goods are the same for all individuals or, alternatively, that all individuals should consume combinations of goods for which their indifference curves have the same slope,

---

[2] The slope of an indifference curve can be determined by taking the total differential of the utility function $U^i(Q_1^{Di}, Q_2^{Di})$ and equating it to zero. One obtains for individual i:

$$dU^i = \frac{\partial U^i}{\partial Q_1^{Di}} dQ_1^{Di} + \frac{\partial U^i}{\partial Q_2^{Di}} dQ_2^{Di} = 0 \text{ and thus } -\frac{dQ_2^{Di}}{dQ_1^{Di}} = \frac{\frac{\partial U^i}{\partial Q_1^{Di}}}{\frac{\partial U^i}{\partial Q_2^{Di}}}.$$

i.e. are tangent to one another. This condition is called **exchange efficiency** in economics.

The concept of exchange efficiency can be illustrated with the help of the so-called **Edgeworth box** (Figure 2.1). The total quantities of goods 1 and 2 available are Q_1^S and Q_2^S (S indicates supply), which defines the size of the box. In the initial situation, marked by the point p^I, individual 1 consumes Q_1^{D1} and Q_2^{D1}, and individual 2 consumes Q_1^{D2} and Q_2^{D2} (D indicates demand). This allocation of goods in the initial situation generates a certain level of utility (U) for each individual, indicated by the indifference curve I_0^1 for individual 1 and by the indifference curve I_0^2 for individual 2.

Figure 2.1: Exchange efficiency in the Edgeworth box

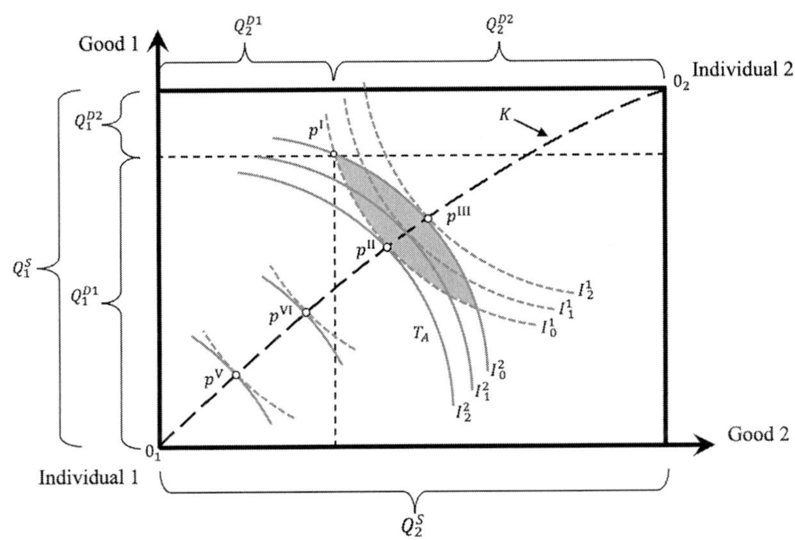

Source: Own depiction

Individual 1 would increase his utility if he could reach an indifference curve above the indifference curve I_0^1 (movement towards northeast). Individual 2 would increase her utility if she could reach an indifference curve above I_0^2 (movement towards southwest). By bartering (individual 1 exchanges good 1 in return for good 2, and vice versa) both outcomes are possible. All exchange outcomes that lead from p^I to a point within the shaded 'lens' in Figure 2.1 mean an increase in utility for at least one of the individuals compared with the situation in p^I.

From p^{I}, therefore, **Pareto improvements** are possible; p^{I} itself can therefore not be a **Pareto optimum**. However, certain points within the shaded area that could be reached by exchange represent Pareto optima. The condition for a Pareto optimum is that two indifference curves are tangent to one another. This applies, for example, for the point p^{II} in Figure 2.1. If a combination of consumption quantities such as p^{II} is realised, neither individual can increase his/her utility without reducing the utility of the other. Since the indifference curves I_0^1 and I_2^2 are at a tangent to one another at point p^{II}, they must have the same slope at this point. As shown above, the marginal rate of substitution equals the slope of an indifference curve. Thus, in a Pareto optimum such as p^{II}, the substitution marginal rates must be the same for both individuals, which confirms the algebraic result in equation (1).

In the Edgeworth box in Figure 2.1 we can see that point p^{III}, where the indifference curves I_2^1 and I_0^2 are tangent to one another, also represents a Pareto optimum. In fact, between p^{II} and p^{III} there is a multitude of Pareto-optimal points which can be reached by exchange starting from the initial situation in p^I. Which of these points is reached depends on the negotiation skills of the individuals or their relative the power (i.e. whether one is able to dictate terms to the other). For example, if the Pareto-optimal point p^{II} is ultimately reached, which is on the same indifference curve for individual 1 as point of departure p^{I}, then only individual 2 would have achieved an increase in utility through the exchange. In p^{III} the opposite would apply; only the first individual's utility would increase. Although the distribution of utility between individuals 1 and 2 in p^{II} is clearly different from the distribution of utility in p^{III}, both points are equally optimal according to the Pareto criterion. The Pareto criterion makes it possible to differentiate between optimal and suboptimal allocations (in Figure 2.1, optimal and suboptimal allocations of a given quantity of goods among individuals); however, it does not consider distributional issues, i.e. the fact that some Pareto optima might be considered more fair or equitable than others.

There are many possible Pareto optima, not only between p^{II} and p^{III} in Figure 2.1, but more generally between 0_1 und 0_2 (including, for example, p^{IV} and p^{V}). The complete set of all such Pareto optima is called an **exchange** or **contract curve**. A **utility possibility curve** can be derived from the contract curve by measuring the utility attained by each individual for each point on the contract curve. The corresponding coordinates (utility pairs) are then plotted on a graph in which the first individual's utility is plotted on one axis, and the second individual's utility on the other. The utility possibility curve is thus the set of all possible combinations of the maximum utility levels that two individuals can attain from a given quantity of goods.

2.2.2. Transaction costs and the realisation of exchange equilibria in a market economy system

In the discussion above we assumed that the exchange of goods between individuals does not incur any costs. However, a society would be ill-advised if it attempted to achieve an optimum through **barter trade**. As discussed in chapter 1, each exchange of goods in a barter economy requires a double coincidence: an individual supplying one good must find a trading partner who is interested in this good (both the quality and the quantity), and who is simultaneously offering another good (quality and quantity) that the individual is willing to accept in return. It is to be expected that potential exchange partners will usually need to search for a long time until such a coincidence is found. This search will be associated with costs that might be so high that exchange only rarely takes place and the members of a society are therefore obliged to be predominantly self-sufficient. In this case, the economy does not benefit from specialisation and the division of labour, and therefore produces a smaller volume of goods (which reduces the dimensions of the Edgeworth box in Figure 2.1).

North (1990, p. 30) divides a good's production costs into **transformation costs** and **transaction costs**[3]. Transformation costs arise in the physical transformation of goods; they represent the production costs that are usually considered in neoclassical theory. According to North, transaction costs are incurred in the exchange of goods. The costs of the above-mentioned search for barter partners are typical transaction costs. In an empirical study North shows that transaction costs for certain goods in the USA amount to more than 40% of the total production costs. The magnitude of the transaction costs is determined by the nature of the goods and, as discussed in chapter 1, by the existing **institutions**. If a society creates institutions that reduce search and information costs for potential market partners, transaction costs are reduced. This in turn fosters specialisation and the division of labour in the economy. By playing an active role in the creation and monitoring of

[3] Douglass C. North won the 1993 Prize in Economic Sciences in Memory of Alfred Nobel together with Robert W. Fogel "for having renewed research in economic history by applying economic theory and quantitative methods in order to explain economic and institutional change" (Nobelprize.org 2021).

institutions, the state can thus contribute to the efficiency of the economic system.

The transaction costs associated with the exchange of goods can be reduced in a market economy by the introduction of money. Instead of exchanging goods for goods, goods can be exchanged for money, and money for goods. The act of exchange is thus divided into two parts that are only indirectly connected to each other, namely by the restriction that each individual's total income and total expenditure must balance at least in the long term (and possibly in the short term if an individual's liquidity is constrained). In this process, money assumes the functions of a unit of account, a medium of exchange and a store of value. By accepting the institution of money, transaction costs can be considerably reduced. First, the need for a double coincidence that characterises barter trade is eliminated. Second, the number of possible exchange relationships – and thus the information needs of the economic actors – are considerably reduced.

This can be shown using the example in Table 2.1. Assume that there are four goods in an economy: cereals, leather, metal, and textbooks. The possible exchange relationships between these goods are shown in Table 2.1. Altogether there are n^2 such relationships (with $n = 4$ in the present example). For example, 5 kg of grain are exchanged for 1 kg of leather, or 0.2 kg of leather for 1 kg of grain.

Table 2.1: Hypothetical exchange ratios between four goods

Product	Cereals	Leather	Textbooks	Metal
Cereals	1	5	20	10
Leather	0.2	1	4	2
Textbooks	0.05	0.25	1	0.5
Metal	0.1	0.5	2	1

Of course, potential exchange partners do not require information about all of these relationships. First, the n exchange relationships between a good and itself (the 'ones' on the diagonal of Table 2.1) have no information value. Furthermore, the values above the diagonal are simply the inverse of the values below. Thus, for 4 goods there are only six relevant exchange relationships. In general, for n goods the number of relevant exchange relationships is therefore reduced to:

$$\frac{n^2-n}{2} = \frac{n(n-1)}{2} \qquad (2)$$

With the introduction of money as a reference unit (also called **numéraire**) the number of relevant exchange relations is reduced even further, to n, i.e. one price for each individual good. In the example in Table 2.1, only four exchange ratios are required instead of six. In a world with many thousands of heterogeneous goods, the difference between n and $\frac{n(n-1)}{2}$ is much greater.

The realisation of exchange equilibria (i.e. points on the contract curve in Figure 2.1) thus does not require that goods are actually exchanged for goods. By introducing money, the need for double coincidence is eliminated and the number of exchange relationships to be determined can be considerably reduced.

2.2.3. How the market and price mechanism leads to optimal price relations

In introductory lectures on economics students learn how an individual optimally allocates a fixed amount of income between the purchases of two goods. The individual's utility is maximised when the budget line is tangent to the indifference curve. This condition holds when:[4]

$$\frac{\frac{\partial U}{\partial Q_1}}{\frac{\partial U}{\partial Q_2}} = \frac{P_1}{P_2} \qquad (3)$$

In section 2.1.1 above, we established that economic welfare is maximised when the following condition is met:

$$\frac{\frac{\partial U^1}{\partial Q_1^{D1}}}{\frac{\partial U^1}{\partial Q_2^{D1}}} = \frac{\frac{\partial U^2}{\partial Q_1^{D2}}}{\frac{\partial U^2}{\partial Q_2^{D2}}} \qquad (1)$$

In equation (1) the notation has changed slightly to include indices that reflect the fact that two consumers are being considered. It can easily be shown that in a world with n consumers the following general condition must apply:

[4] See for example Chiang (1974, pp. 391-393).

$$\frac{\frac{\partial U^1}{\partial Q_1^{D1}}}{\frac{\partial U^1}{\partial Q_2^{D1}}} = \frac{\frac{\partial U^2}{\partial Q_1^{D2}}}{\frac{\partial U^2}{\partial Q_2^{D2}}} = \cdots = \frac{\frac{\partial U^n}{\partial Q_1^{Dn}}}{\frac{\partial U^n}{\partial Q_2^{Dn}}} \qquad (4)$$

Note that the marginal rate of substitution appears in equation (3) as well as in equations (1) and (4). The condition in equation (3) implies that the individual maximises his utility by choosing a consumption point for which the marginal rate of substitution is equal to the ratio of the prices for the two goods. The condition in equation (4) implies that economic welfare is maximised when the marginal rate of substitution is the same for all consumers.

In a market economy with perfect competition, all consumers are price takers. Accordingly, all individuals will base their consumption decisions on the same price relations and, if they satisfy the condition in equation (3), will choose optimal consumption points that are characterised by identical marginal rates of substitution. Consequently, by basing their consumption decisions on the same price relations, they automatically fulfil the condition in equation (4) for the maximisation of economic welfare.

2.3. Optimal factor price ratios in a closed economy

Introduction and learning objectives

In the previous section of this chapter we showed which price relations between consumption goods are consistent with a Pareto optimal economic outcome. In this section we present analogous results for the production side of the economy by explaining which factor price relations must apply under Pareto optimal conditions. The results that we present are analogous because just as consumers choose optimal combinations of goods to maximise utility, so do producers choose optimal combinations of production factors to maximise profit.

In addition, there is an important link between the consumption and the production sides of the economy. This is because households need income to buy the goods that they demand from producers. Households generate this income by making the production factors that they own available to producers in return for remuneration. For example, households supply labour, or retired farmers rent their land to active farmers. **General equilibrium** in an economy is achieved when all product and factor markets clear, i.e. the demand for goods that is generated by factor income coincides with the supply of goods that is produced using factor input. Supply and demand on factor markets and the generation of factor income are the subject of the so-called **marginal productivity theory**.

In this section we will continue to draw on the simple (2 * 2 * 2)-model of a **closed economy**. First, we will present important aspects of marginal productivity theory. After that we will examine in greater detail the connection between optimal conditions in consumption on the one hand, and optimal conditions in production on the other.

In this second section of the chapter we:

- explain the derivation of optimal factor price relations in a closed economy,
- show how the market and price mechanism can lead to an economic optimum in production,
- present the basics of marginal productivity theory, and
- explain the relationship between optimal good price ratios and optimal factor price ratios.

2.3.1. Achieving production equilibria

In Appendix 2.1 (equation 53) we show that in order to maximise economic welfare the following condition (referred to as **production efficiency**) must also be met:

$$\frac{\frac{\partial Q_1^S}{\partial C_1}}{\frac{\partial Q_1^S}{\partial L_1}} = \frac{\frac{\partial Q_2^S}{\partial C_2}}{\frac{\partial Q_2^S}{\partial L_2}} \tag{5}$$

The expressions on the left and right sides of equation (5) are called **marginal rates of substitution** between production factors, in this case capital (C) and labour (L), in the production of goods 1 and 2, respectively. In the first section of this chapter, other marginal rates of substitution were presented; these referred to the slopes of indifference curves and thus to the possibility of individuals substituting good 1 for good 2 without changing their levels of utility. The marginal rates of substitution in equation (5) refer instead to the slopes of isoquants. An **isoquant** is the set of all technically possible and efficient combinations of production factors that produce the same output. Consequently, the marginal rate of substitution between factors is a measure of a producer's ability to substitute factors without changing the level of production achieved[5]. The marginal rate of substitution between factors in production is also called the **marginal rate of factor substitution** to distinguish it from the marginal rate of substitution in consumption.

As was the case for consumption of goods in the previous section, an Edgeworth box can be used to explain the production efficiency condition in equation (5). In Figure 2.2 we assume that there are two producers who produce goods 1 and 2, respectively. The isoquants of producer 1 are convex to the southwest and the isoquants of producer 2 to the northeast. The width and height of the Edgeworth box are defined by the amounts of capital and labour available in the economy, respectively, and any point inside the box therefore describes an allocation of the available production factors between the two producers. The assumed shape of the isoquants reflects the assumption of limited substitutability between the factors – it takes progressively more units of one input to replace each consecutive unit of the other. We can see that at point p production efficiency is not achieved, because by reallocating capital and labour between the two producers it would be possible to increase the output of one or both goods. Production efficiency is achieved at points such as p^{I}, p^{II}, and p^{III}, where two isoquants are tangent to one another, i.e. where the marginal rate of factor substitution is the same for both producers.

---

[5] The slope of an isoquant can be determined by taking the total differential of the production function $Q_i^S(C_i, L_i)$ and equating it to zero. One obtains for good i: $dQ_i^S = \frac{\partial Q_i^S}{\partial C_i} dC_i + \frac{\partial Q_i^S}{\partial L_i} dL_i = 0$ and thus $-\frac{dL_i}{dC_i} = \frac{\frac{\partial Q_i^S}{\partial C_i}}{\frac{\partial Q_i^S}{\partial L_i}}$.

Figure 2.2: Production efficiency in the Edgeworth box

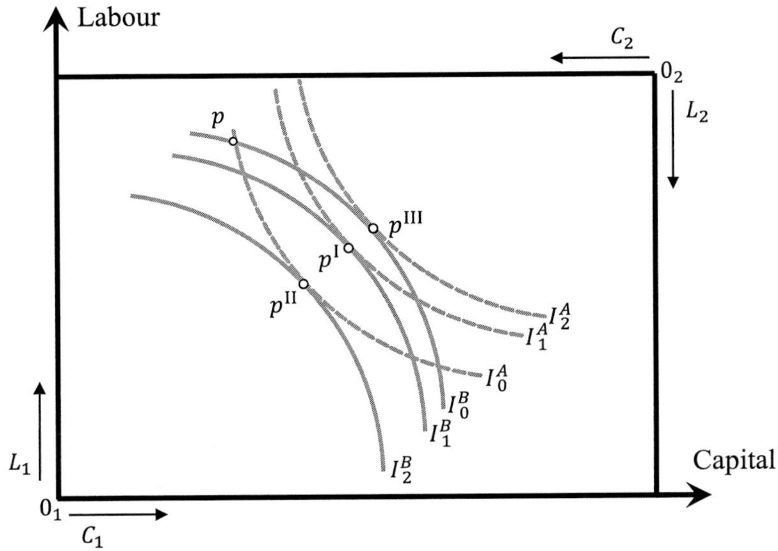

Source: Own depiction

As was the case for exchange efficiency, there are many Pareto optimal points where production efficiency is achieved. Each of these points is characterised by the fact that two isoquants are tangent to one another. And each of these points corresponds to a certain combination of produced quantities of goods 1 and 2 (Q_1^S and Q_2^S). Just as a utility possibility curve can be derived from the contract curve of the Edgeworth box for exchange efficiency, a so-called **transformation curve** or **production possibility curve** can be derived from the set of Pareto optimal production points (see Figure 2.3). The transformation curve is the set of all Pareto optimal combinations of Q_1^S und Q_2^S that can be produced with the available production factors and technology.[6] In Figure 2.3 the points p to p^{III} have been transferred from Figure 2.2. If a product quantity combination is produced which, like p, lies below the transformation curve, this means that allocation of production factors is inefficient. Movements towards the north-east in Figure 2.3 reflect increases in production efficiency.

[6] Recall that we discussed in Chapter 1 how the shape of the transformation curve is also affected by institutions.

Figure 2.3 – The transformation or production possibility curve

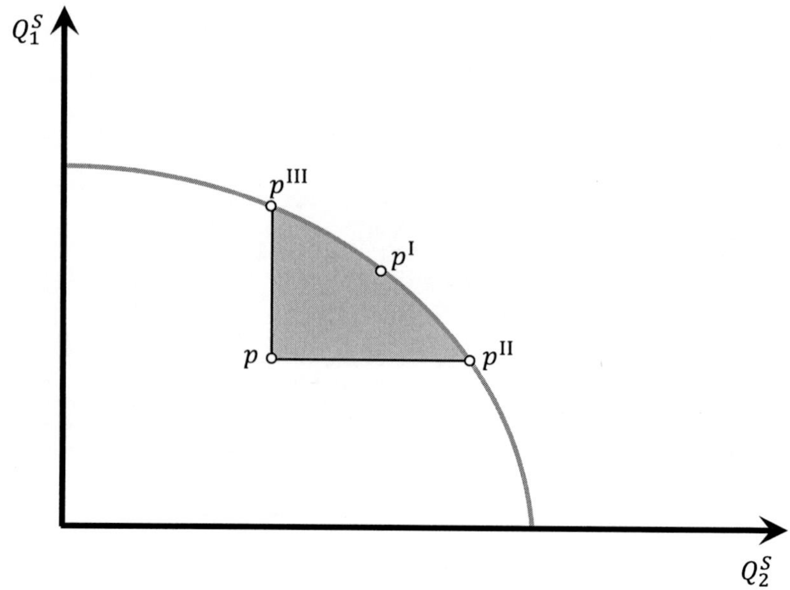

Source: Own depiction.

2.3.2. How the market and price mechanism leads to a Pareto optimal production outcome

Can it be assumed that the market and price mechanism will lead to the realisation of a Pareto optimal point on the transformation curve? In Appendix 2.2 the following condition is derived for a profit maximising producer:

$$\frac{\frac{\partial Q_j^S}{\partial C_j}}{\frac{\partial Q_j^S}{\partial L_j}} = \frac{P_C}{P_L} \tag{6}$$

According to this condition, every profit-maximising producer will, in producing a good j, choose a factor combination for which the marginal rate of factor substitution is equal to the factor price ratio. In a market economy with perfect competition, all producers are price takers, i.e. they consider all good and factor prices as given. Thus, all producers will face the same factor price ratio and, if they adhere to the condition in equation (6), will optimally choose factor combinations that are characterised by the same marginal rate of factor substitution. Consequently, the production efficiency condition in equation (5) for the maximisation of economic welfare is simultaneously fulfilled.

2.3.3. Fundamentals of marginal productivity theory

Since it can be assumed that the total factor supply in an economy is fixed in the short term, factor prices are determined by factor demand. The core concept for understanding factor demand is the so-called **marginal value product**, defined as physical marginal productivity of the factor in question multiplied by the price of the good being produced. In Appendix 2.2 (Equations 61 and 62) we derive the following conditions for a profit-maximising producer:

$$P_j \frac{\partial Q_j^S}{\partial C_j} = P_C \tag{7}$$

$$P_j \frac{\partial Q_j^S}{\partial L_j} = P_L \tag{8}$$

In equations (7) and (8), the expression on the left-hand side is the marginal value product of the respective factor. The expression on the right-hand side is the corresponding factor price. In profit-maximising optimum, the marginal value product is therefore equal to the factor price. Since producers face given prices in perfect markets, they can only adjust the factor input quantities and thus the marginal physical productivity of the individual factors in order to attain these conditions. Therefore, the part of price theory that deals with the demand for factors of production is called **marginal productivity theory**.

In order to present the basics of this theory, we assume a strictly quasi-concave production function. One of the two production factors (L and C) is assumed to be variable (L), while the other ($\bar{C}$) is fixed (as indicated by the bar above the symbol C). The quantity of the good i (Q_i^S) that is produced using variable L and fixed $\bar{C}$ is valued with the constant product price P_i. The monetary production function (the relationship between the factor input quantity L and the output quantity Q_i^S multiplied by the product price P_i, also called the **yield function**) is shown in the top panel of Figure 2.4. Marginal and average productivity curves can be derived from the production function, and the corresponding marginal value product and average value product curves ($P_i \frac{\partial Q_i^S}{\partial L_i}$ and $P_i \frac{Q_i^S}{L_i}$ in the bottom panel of Figure 2.4) can be derived from the yield function.

The maximum marginal value product is determined by the inflection point of the yield function (p^I). Point p in Figure 2.4, which is formed by a ray from the origin tangent to the yield curve, indicates the factor input quantity at which the maximum average value product is reached. At point p the following relationship holds:

$$\tan\alpha = P_i \frac{Q_i^S(L_i)}{L_i} = P_i \frac{\partial Q_i^S}{\partial L_i} \quad (9)$$

In other words, the ray from the origin and the yield function have the same slope at point p. Hence, for the factor input quantity L_i^p corresponding to p, the marginal value product curve and the average value product curve must intersect.

Figure 2.4: The relationship between the production function and factor demand

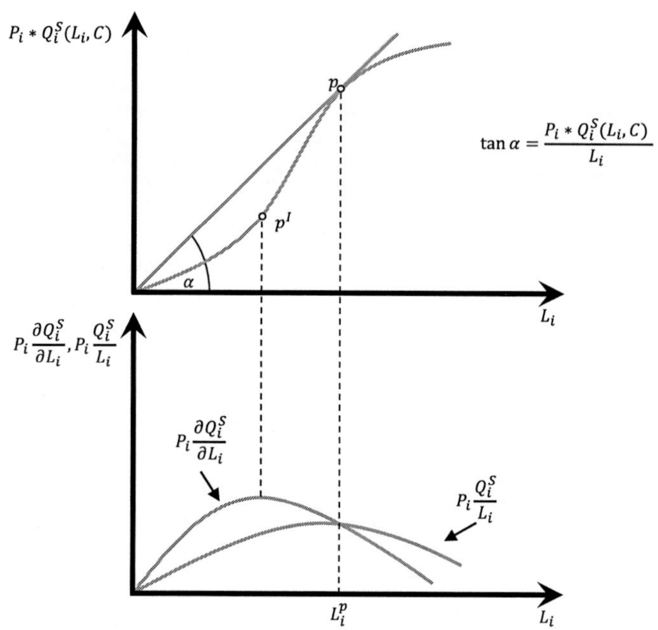

Source: Own depiction

A producer's **factor demand curve** under perfect competition on good and factor markets is identical with the falling part of the marginal value product curve to the right of its intersection with the average value product curve (i.e. to the right of L_i^p in Figure 2.4). In the following we demonstrate that factor inputs less than L_i^p are incompatible with profit-maximising behaviour. If, for example, a company were to use a factor input quantity to the left of L_i^p (e.g. L_i^* in Figure 2.5), the average value product of the factor would be smaller than its marginal value product. If we assume that production factors are remunerated according to their marginal value product (see equations 7 and 8 above), a factor price of P_L^* would have to be paid for L_i^*. The factor income would thus correspond to the area of the rectangle $0bce$ in Figure 2.5. However, a factor income of this amount would not be feasible, since the producer's total revenue from sale of the produced good ($0ade$) is lower.[7]

If the producer uses the quantity L_i^p, a factor price of P_L^p must be paid. At L_i^p, equation (9) holds (marginal value product = average value product). If factors are remunerated according to their marginal value products, the total factor income of L in the production of the good i is:

$$P_L^p L_i^p = P_i \frac{Q_i^S}{L_i^p} L_i^p \tag{10}$$

or

$$P_L^p L_i^p = P_i Q_i^S \tag{11}$$

Equation (11) states that the income of the variable factor L in the production of the good i is equal to the total value of the good i produced (the producer's revenue). In this case, there would be no revenue left for the remuneration of the fixed factor $\bar{C}$. The production of the good i would only be possible if C were a free good, in other words not scarce.

[7] The area of the rectangle $0ade$ measures total revenue because its height ($0a$) equals the average value product $P_i \frac{Q_i^S}{L_i^*}$, and its width ($0e$) equals the factor quantity L_i^*. The product of these two terms therefore equals revenue $P_i Q_i^S$.

Figure 2.5: Deriving the factor demand curve

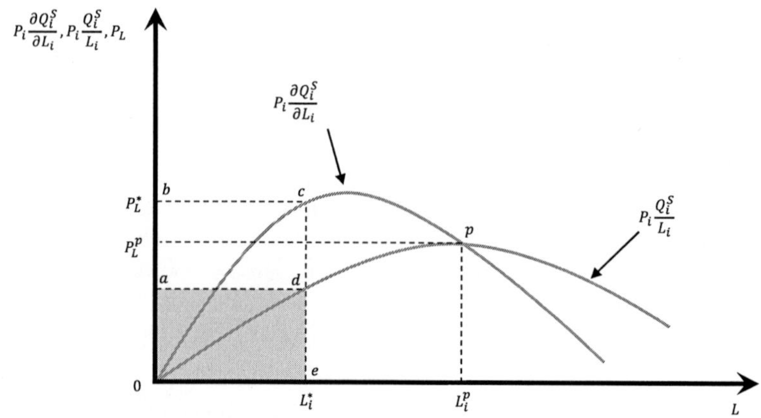

Source: Own depiction

It is therefore clear that no profit-maximising company would choose factor inputs smaller than L_i^p. The part of the marginal value product curve to the left of the intersection with the average value product curve (i.e. to the left of L_i^p) is therefore irrelevant for factor demand. We next prove that factor inputs greater than L_i^p (such as L_i^{**} in Figure 2.6) are consistent with profit-maximising behaviour. For the quantity L_i^{**}, the marginal value product is smaller than the average value product. The variable factor receives the factor price P_L^{**} according to its marginal value product. Hence, the total cost of using the quantity L_i^{**} equals the area *0ade* in Figure 2.6. This factor remuneration is smaller than the producer's revenue from the sale of the goods produced, which corresponds to the area *0bce*. Consequently, in this case it would be possible to remunerate the fixed factor $\bar{C}$. The highest possible remuneration of the factor $\bar{C}$ in the production of the good i is determined by deducting the remuneration of the variable factor L ($P_L^{**}L_i^{**}$) from the producer's revenue ($P_iQ_i^S$). Hence

$$P_C\bar{C}_i = P_iQ_i^S - P_L^{**}L_i^{**} \tag{12}$$

which corresponds to the area *abcd* in Figure 2.6.

Figure 2.6: Remuneration of variable and fixed factors according to marginal productivity theory

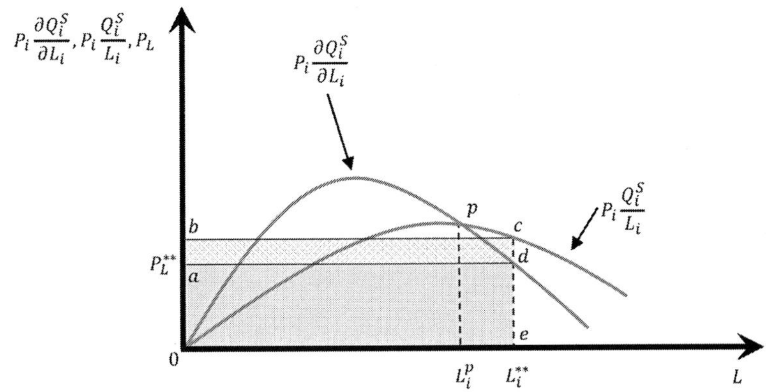

Source: Own depiction.

Based on these considerations we can determine the **functional distribution of income**. The functional distribution of income indicates how total income from the sale of goods is distributed among the factors (e.g. labour and capital) that were used to produce the goods. Indicators of the functional income distribution are, for example, the **wage share** and the **capital income share**, defined respectively as:

$$\frac{P_L L_i}{P_i Q_i^S}, \text{ and} \tag{13}$$

$$\frac{P_C C_i}{P_i Q_i^S} \tag{14}$$

In the discussion above and in Figure 2.6 we implicitly assumed that the sum of the wage share and the capital income share is 1, i.e. that the sum of the factor remunerations is equal to total revenue. However, this will only be the case if the production function is characterised by **constant returns to scale**. Constant returns to scale mean that when all factor input quantities are increased by a given percentage, the output of good i increases by the same percentage. So-called linear-homogeneous production functions are characterised by constant returns to scale and therefore play an important role in price theory. In Appendix 2.3 the characteristics of linear-homogeneous production functions are discussed in greater detail.

2.3.4. Simultaneous optimum in consumption and production sector

In the first section of this chapter we explained exchange efficiency (equal marginal rates of substitution between goods for all individuals). In this section we explained production efficiency (equal marginal rates of factor substitution in all production processes). At the beginning of this second section we stressed that there is an important link between exchange and production efficiency, because in equilibrium there must be sufficient demand at market prices to purchase all of the goods that are supplied. Demand for goods is determined by the incomes that households earn by supplying factors of production such as labour to producers; the supply of goods is determined by technology and the quantities of factors of production such as labour that producers demand. If the relationship between demand and supply for even one good or factor of production is not balanced, the economy is not in general equilibrium.

These relationships are illustrated schematically for one factor of production L and one good i in Figure 2.7. For a given factor input L_i^* a certain quantity of good i (Q_i^s) is produced according to the applicable production function. This is depicted in the northeast quadrant of Figure 2.7. If Q_i^s is supplied, and given the demand function for good i depicted in the northwest quadrant of Figure 2.7, product price P_i^* will result in equilibrium. However, the factor input L_i^*, and therefore Q_i^s, will only be optimal if the factor market is also in equilibrium. Such an equilibrium is depicted in the southeast quadrant of Figure 2.7, where the factor input L_i^* corresponds to the intersection of given factor supply and factor demand curves at factor price P_L^*.

Figure 2.7: Simultaneous balance on product and factor markets

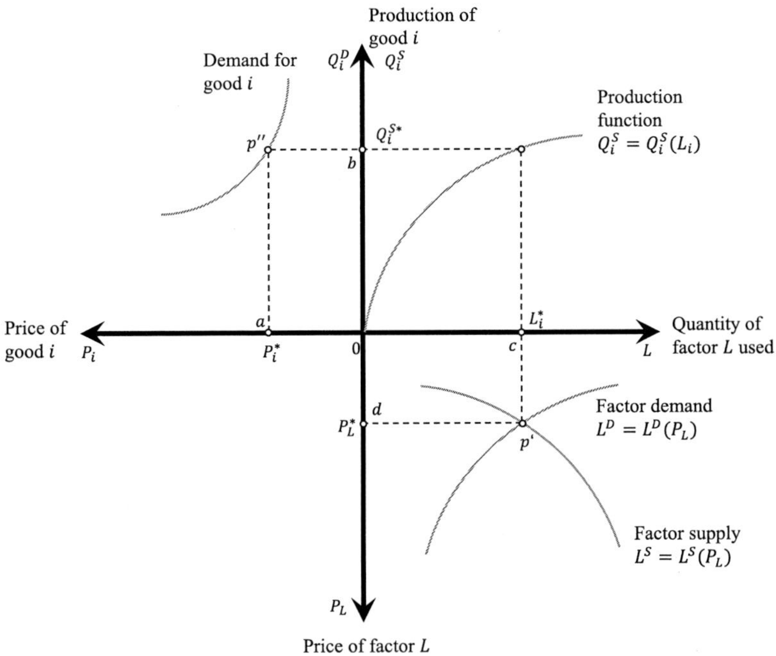

Source: Own depiction.

One more condition must be met for the situation in Figure 2.7 to be a general equilibrium. If the production of the good i is to continue in the long run, thus ensuring the employment of the factors of production, then the purchasing power generated by the sum of factor earnings must be sufficient to buy all of the Q_i^S that is produced. This will be the case when:

$$P_L^* L_i^* = P_i^* Q_i^{S*} \tag{15}$$

or, alternatively, when the area *0cp'd* equals the area *0ap''b* in Figure 2.7.

Of course, in a modern economy a wide range of goods and services are produced using multiple production factors. In our previous model with two goods and two factors, the following condition must be met, analogous to (15), for the economy to be in equilibrium:

$$\sum_{i=1}^{2} P_L^* L_i^* + \sum_{i=1}^{2} P_C^* C_i^* = \sum_{i=1}^{2} P_i^* Q_i^{S*} \tag{16}$$

More generally, for n goods and m factors of production, equation (16) is called Walras' Law.[8]

2.4. The derivation of optimal price relations in an open economy

Introduction and learning objectives

The previous two sections of this chapter assumed a closed economy, i.e. an economy that does not engage in foreign trade. In a closed economy in equilibrium, domestic supply must equal domestic demand for all goods. An **open economy**, in contrast, trades goods with other economies. Depending on whether an open economy is large or small in the economic sense, there are different optimal price ratios for **tradable** and **non-tradable goods**. These price ratios may differ from those in a closed economy. Since most economies engage in trade – often with agricultural goods – it is clear that the analysis of price determination in open economies is of great practical importance. In the following third section of this chapter, we therefore extend the results of the previous sections to consider the case of an open economy.

In this section we will:

- explain the difference between tradable and non-tradable goods,
- explain the importance of price relations on world markets for maximising the welfare of a small economy,
- derive optimal price ratios that apply in the case of a large economy, and
- derive selected implications for agricultural policy in an open economy.

2.4.1. Tradable and non-tradable goods

In an open economy with free trade, it is important to distinguish between internationally tradable and internationally non-tradable goods. Internationally non-tradable goods are non-tradable either because of their specific

---

[88] Léon Walras (1834-1910) was a French economist who made fundamental contributions to general equilibrium theory.

characteristics (e.g. immobility) or because domestic supply and demand conditions result in **autarchy** prices that are both higher than the country's export prices and lower than its import prices. The following equation therefore holds for internationally non-tradable goods:

$$P_{Ex} \leq P \leq P_{Im} \tag{17}$$

with:

P_{Ex} = the price for which the good can be sold on export markets,

P = the domestic autarchy price, and

P_{Im} = the price for which the good can be imported.

While the distinction between tradable and non-tradable is sometimes based on the physical properties of a good, it is more often a question of international competitiveness. Goods that are not tradable at a certain point in time may become tradable at a later date, if domestic market conditions, world market conditions or transport and transaction costs change in the meantime.

Further, it follows from equation (17) that whether a country is an exporter or importer of a given good depends not only on the production and demand conditions in the country, but also on the level of world market prices and the difference between P_{Im} and P_{Ex}. This difference depends on the proximity of the country to world markets, which depends both on physical distance (e.g. New Zealand is geographically far away from many potential trading partners), and on infrastructure (does the country have ports and good road/rail connections between these ports and domestic markets, or is it perhaps landlocked and reliant on neighbouring countries for access to world markets). The farther a country is from its potential trading partners, the greater the difference between P_{Im} and P_{Ex}.

For a non-tradable good, the domestic price is determined by the intersection of domestic supply and demand curves. Hence, for non-tradable goods, the market is only cleared if the domestic quantity supplied equals the domestic quantity demanded. In a two-person model this equilibrium condition can be depicted as follows:

$$P_j\left(Q_j^{D1} + Q_j^{D2}\right) = P_j Q_j^S \tag{18}$$

with:

Q_j^S = the quantity of the domestically produced good j

P_j = the price of the good j, and

Q_j^{Di} = the quantity of the good j demanded by individual i.

For internationally tradable goods, trade is balanced when the value of all imported goods equals the value of all exported goods. As a consequence, the total value of all tradable goods that are demanded domestically, regardless whether they import or export goods, will equal the corresponding total value of all tradable goods that are supplied:

$$\sum_{i=1}^{H} P_i(Q_i^D - Q_i^S) = 0 \qquad (19)$$

with: $i = 1,2,\ldots,H$ tradable goods.[9]

The model that we elaborate in Appendix 2 can be extended to include tradable goods by replacing the market equilibrium restriction in equation (37) by equation (19). The formal derivation of the resulting optimal price relations is analogous to Appendix 2. There is only one major difference in the welfare-maximising results: for tradable goods, domestic prices must equal world market prices. It follows that **world market prices** have a decisive influence on the structure of domestic production and consumption. We discuss the implication of this statement in the following.

2.4.2. The importance of price relations on world markets for maximising domestic welfare

Would a country be well advised to rely on world market prices as a basis for domestic production and consumption decisions? World market prices - not least for agricultural products - are influenced by a large number of government interventions on individual national markets. In many countries, domestic prices for agricultural products are higher than world market prices; in some countries they are lower. Farmers therefore often argue that world market prices for agricultural goods are distorted and should therefore not be used to determine domestic prices.

---

[9] Good i is imported if $Q_i^D \geq Q_i^S$, and exported if $Q_i^S \geq Q_i^D$.

It is true that world market prices for many agricultural products do not reflect the result of undistorted market forces. From the point of view of a single economy, however, this is irrelevant. What matters is whether the country can buy or sell the quantities it demands or supplies at the prevailing world market prices. If domestic production and consumption decisions, and therefore a country's exports and imports, have an effect on world market prices, then indeed the country would be ill-advised to base its production and consumption decisions on current world market prices. In this case, the country is referred to as a **large country** in the economic sense. For a large country the world market price is not given; the country has market power because the amounts that it demands or supplies influence this price. To maximise welfare, it should take this influence into account. We consider optimal price relations for large countries in more detail in section 2.4.3 below.

For **small countries**, however, domestic production and consumption decisions have no effect on the current or future level of world market prices. Such countries can maximise their welfare by allowing domestic prices to equal world market prices for all tradable goods. It follows, of course, that world market prices for tradable goods will also influence the prices of non-tradable goods, when tradable goods (such as fossil fuels) are used as inputs in the production of non-tradable goods (such as a ride in a taxi), or when tradable and non-tradable goods are substitutes in consumption or production.

The welfare gains that a country can realise by adjusting its domestic price relations to world market price relations are illustrated in Figure 2.8. In the initial situation it is assumed that no trade takes place. The country is therefore self-sufficient, which is indicated by the letter *A* for autarchy. According to the optimal conditions, the marginal rate of transformation must be equal to the marginal rate of substitution. Such a situation is realized at point p_A where the indifference curve I_A is tangent to the country's transformation (or production possibility) curve T. The resulting domestic price relationship equals the slope of the iso-revenue curve G_A. In this autarchic situation, the quantities produced domestically are Q_{1A} and Q_{2A}.

Figure 2.8: Welfare gains through adjustment of domestic price relations to world market price relations

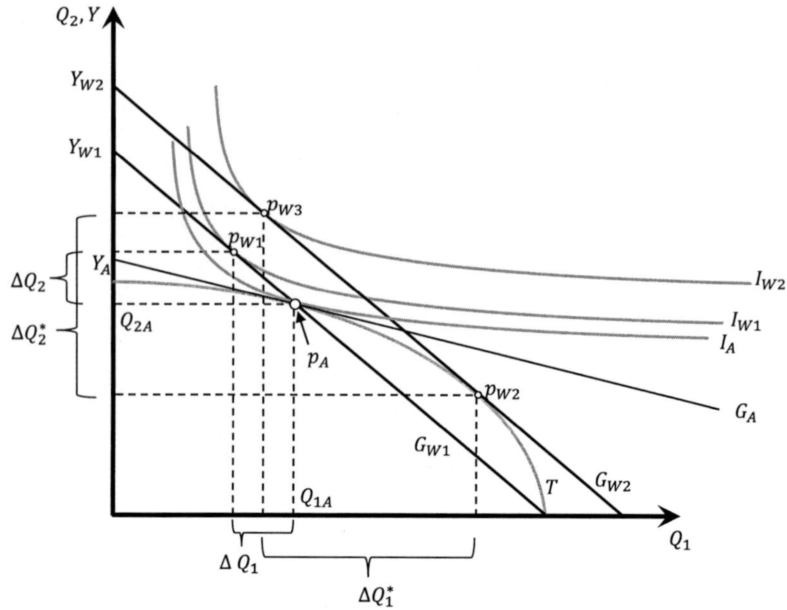

Source: Own depiction

We now demonstrate that the country can achieve welfare gains by adjusting both its consumption and production structures to world market price relations. Beginning with the consumption side, first assume that the country continues to produce quantities Q_{1A} and Q_{2A} domestically. Perhaps the country has a transformation curve that does permit any changes in the domestic production structure (i.e. the transformation curve consists only of the point p_A), or perhaps the country does not want to change its domestic production structure for political reasons (e.g. there is political resistance to the closure of certain production sites). Nevertheless, the country is willing to allow its domestic consumption structure to be influenced by the world market prices. The world market price relationship is represented by the slope of the straight line G_{W1}. The straight line G_{W1} runs through the point p_{W1} where it is tangent to the indifference curve I_{W1}. Hence, the country adjusts its consumption structure by exporting the quantity ΔQ_1 and importing the quantity ΔQ_2. Note that at the prevailing world market prices, the value of the Q_2 that is imported equals the value of the Q_1 that is exported.

By adjusting its domestic consumption to world market prices, the country realises an increase in welfare from utility level I_A to utility level I_{W1}.

If not only domestic consumption but also domestic production adjusts to world market prices, additional welfare gains can be realised. In this case, production shift from point p_A to point p_{W2}, while consumption shifts to point p_{W3}. At point p_{W2} the marginal rate of transformation equals the world market price relation. This means that the ratio of the domestic marginal costs of producing goods 1 and 2 equal the ratio of the world market prices for these goods. At point p_{W3} the marginal rate of substitution equals the world market price relation. This means that the ratio of the domestic marginal utilities of consuming goods 1 and 2 also equals the ratio of the world market prices for these goods. As a consequence of the adjustment of the domestic production structure the country's welfare increases further. At point p_{W3}, the iso-revenue curve G_{W2} is tangent to the indifference curve I_{W2}, which lies above the indifference curve I_{W1}. The transition from I_{W1} to I_{W2} therefore represents the additional welfare gain which arises from the adjustment of the domestic production structure. After adjusting both the consumption and the production structure, the country exports the quantity ΔQ_1^* and imports the quantity ΔQ_2^*.

Under which conditions will the adoption of world market price relations increase domestic welfare? The example in Figure 2.8 shows us that it is not a necessary condition that there are comparative cost differences between the countries, i.e. that their transformation curves differ. A necessary condition is merely (if transaction costs are neglected) that the price relations in autarchy differ from those which would result if international trade took place. Such differences in autarchic price relations could, for example, be the consequence of different consumer preferences in the two countries, even if their transformation curves are identical. Given differences in consumer preferences (and possibly also comparative costs), the magnitude of the welfare gains from trade depends on the curvature of the transformation and indifference curves.

Figure 2.8 can also be used to show how to quantify the gains from international trade. On the consumption side, the additional consumption of good 2 that is possible as a consequence of the adjustment to world market price relations can be used as a measure of the welfare gains. We use the price of good 2 as a measure of the value of goods in the country, and set this price equal to one (i.e. we define good 2 as the numéraire). The intersections of the iso-revenue lines G_A, G_{W1} and G_{W2} with the vertical axis (at points Y_A, Y_{W1} and Y_{W2}, respectively) measure the total real income of the economy. This measurement could also be done on the horizontal axis by defining good 1 as the numéraire. The transition from one indifference curve to another thus corresponds to a quantifiable change in the country's real income.

2.4.3. Optimal price ratios for a large country

Unlike a small country, a large country needs to take its ability to exercise market power on the world market into account when setting its internal prices. As an importer, a large country faces the exporting countries' upward sloping supply curve; if it demands more (less), the world market price will increase (decrease). As a consequence, not world market prices are decisive for price setting, but rather **marginal expenditure**. Marginal expenditure indicates by how many units a country's expenditure on an imported good changes if it increases the imported quantity by one unit. Analogous considerations apply to a large country that is a supplier on world markets. In this case, the country faces the importing countries' downward sloping demand curve. The more (less) a large country exports, the lower (higher) the export prices will be. Hence its **marginal revenue** is lower than the world market price.

The situation confronting a large importer is illustrated in Figure 2.9. This country acts as a buyer on the world market. If it does not consider its market power, this country will choose point b and import the quantity Q_0 at the price P_{W0}. The importer's marginal expenditure curve, however, lies above the world market supply curve, because by varying its import quantities the large importer can manipulate the world market price. Since each additional unit of imports leads to a higher price that affects not only the additional unit but all previously imported units as well, the marginal expenditure is higher than the price. The country can therefore act like a **partial monopsonist.**[10] It will demand the quantity at which its marginal expenditure curve intersects its import demand curve (point c), leading to the import quantity Q_1 and the world market price P_{W1}. The reduction in the world market price from P_{W0} to P_{W1} reduces the country's expenditure on the import quantity Q_1 by the amount $Q_1(P_{W0} - P_{W1})$. This horizontally shaded area in Figure 2.9 is referred to as the **Terms of Trade effect**. At the same time, the country incurs a welfare loss equal to the shaded triangle *bcd* in Figure 2.9 because the reduction in imports triggers a reallocation of domestic resources.

---

[10] A partial monopsonist is not the only customer, so he/she cannot set the price alone as a monopsonist could. But a partial monopsonist's demand does influence the price, while all other customers are price takers.

The maximum profit that the large importer realises is the sum of the positive terms of trade effect and the negative allocation effect.

Figure 2.9: A large importer's demand on the world market

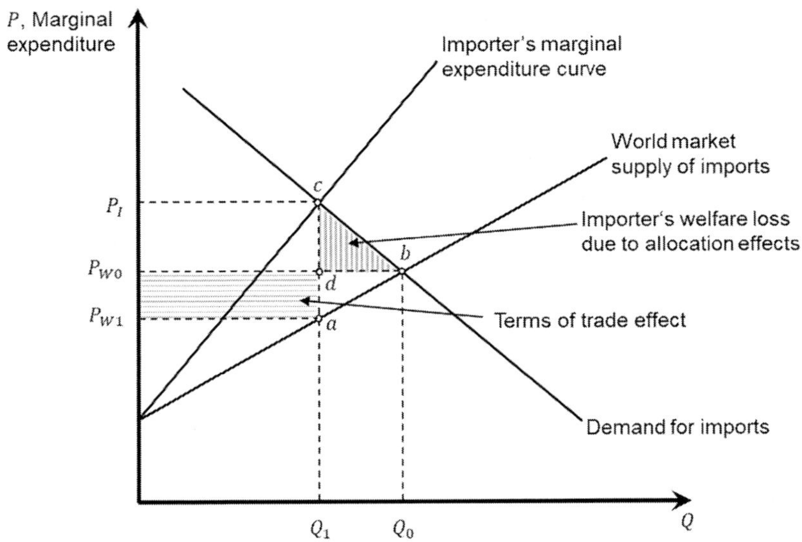

Source: Own depiction

The world as a whole loses the area *abc* in Figure 2.9, because for each unit of the good that is foregone between Q_1 and Q_0, the willingness to pay exceeds the marginal costs of production. However, from the point of view of the large importer an optimum is achieved in which marginal expenditure is equal to both marginal costs and the domestic marginal willingness to pay. The large importer can therefore maximise its welfare by imposing a levy equal to the segment ac or the difference between P_I and P_{W1}. The size of the **optimal levy** can be derived algebraically as follows. According to the definition:

$$P_I = P_W(1 + t) \tag{20}$$

where:

P_I = the domestic price,

t = the duty rate, and

P_W = the world market price.

The expenditure on imports is the product of the import quantity and the world market price. Hence:

$$E = P_W Q_{Im} \tag{21}$$

where:

E = the import expenditure, and

Q_{Im} = the import quantity.

Differentiating equation (21) with respect to Q_{Im} we obtain the following expression for marginal expenditure $\frac{\partial E}{\partial Q_{Im}}$:

$$\frac{\partial E}{\partial Q_{Im}} = P_W + Q_{Im} \frac{\partial P_W}{\partial Q_{Im}} \tag{22}$$

We multiply the last term in equation (22) by $\frac{P_W}{P_W}$, which leads to the following result:

$$\frac{\partial E}{\partial Q_{Im}} = P_W \left(1 + \frac{1}{\varepsilon_{Ex}}\right) \tag{23}$$

where:

ε_{Ex} = price elasticity of export supply on the world market.

The large importer maximises welfare by choosing an import quantity that equates its domestic price to its marginal expenditure on imports. Therefore:

$$P_I = \frac{\partial E}{\partial Q_{Im}} = P_W \left(1 + \frac{1}{\varepsilon_{Ex}}\right) \tag{24}$$

However, equation (20) also applies, and thus:

$$P_I = P_W(1+t) = P_W\left(1+\frac{1}{\varepsilon_{Ex}}\right).$$

Hence,

$$1+t = 1+\frac{1}{\varepsilon_{Ex}}$$

or

$$t = \frac{1}{\varepsilon_{Ex}} \qquad (25)$$

According to equation (25), the optimum duty is equal to the reciprocal of the price elasticity of supply on the world market.

The case of a large exporting country is similar and presented in Figure 2.10. If it does not consider its market power, this country will choose point *b* and export the quantity Q_0 at the price P_{W0}. However, the exporter's marginal revenue curve lies below the world market demand curve, because by varying its export quantities the large exporter can manipulate the world market price. The country can therefore act like a partial monopolist. To maximise its welfare, this country will choose point a where its marginal revenue curve intersects its export supply curve, leading to the import quantity Q_1 and the world market price P_{W1}. The country thus increases the revenue it receives for the export quantity Q_1 by the amount $Q_1(P_{W1} - P_{W0})$ (the horizontally shaded terms of trade effect in Figure 2.10). At the same time, the partial monopolist incurs welfare losses due to allocation effects in the amount of the triangle *abd*. The maximum profit that the large exporter realises is the sum of the positive terms of trade effect and the negative allocation effect. The world as a whole loses the area *abc*.

Figure 2.10: A large exporter's supply on the world market

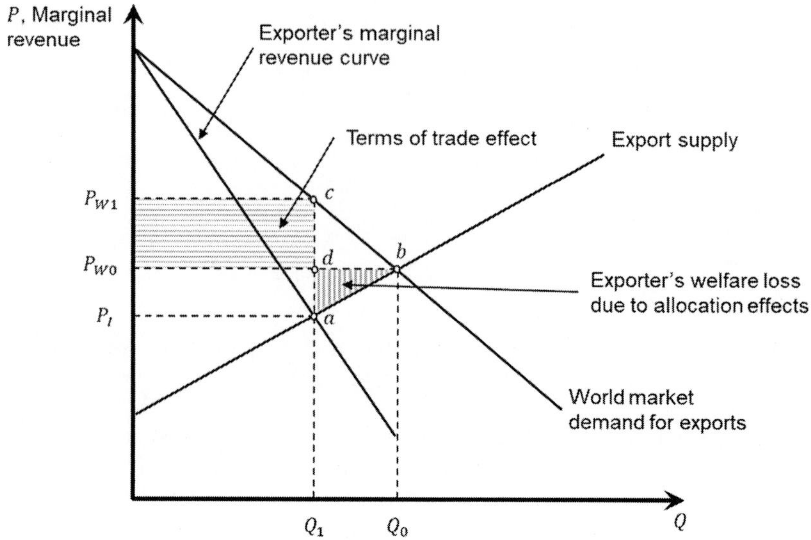

Source: Own depiction

Analogous to the derivation of the optimal import duty in the case of a large importing country, it can be shown that the **optimal export tax** of a large exporting country is given by the following condition:

$$s = \frac{1}{\varepsilon_{Im}} \tag{26}$$

where:

s = the export tax, and

ε_{Im} = the price elasticity of import demand on the world market.

According to equation (26), the optimal export tax rate equals the reciprocal of the price elasticity of world demand for imports.

2.4.4. Implications of selected agricultural market policy instruments

It can be seen from the above that from an economic welfare perspective, small countries should not implement protectionist policies. Instead, under the conditions listed above, free trade will maximise economic welfare. In reality, however, many countries, including small countries, interfere with foreign trade. On agricultural markets this intervention is usually due to political considerations, as farmers often lobby for protection against foreign competition. In the following, we will assume that the government has been persuaded to grant such protection by supporting agricultural prices. The question is how the state should support individual agricultural prices.

It follows from the optimal conditions for a small country that the welfare losses caused by price support are smaller the less the domestic price relations deviate from world market price relations (i.e. when the distortion in domestic price relations is small). If it were possible to support all domestic prices by the same percentage above world market prices, domestic price relations would be equal to world market price relations. In such a case, the nominal rate of protection would be the same for all products. The **nominal rate of protection** (NRP) is defined as:

$$NRP = \frac{p_D - p_W}{p_W} = \frac{p_D}{p_W} - 1 \tag{27}$$

where P is either the domestic (D) or the world market (W) price. The nominal protection rate thus indicates by what percentage a domestic price is higher than the corresponding world market price. If the NRP is the same for two goods, the following holds:

$$\frac{p_{D1}}{p_{W1}} - 1 = \frac{p_{D2}}{p_{W2}} - 1 \tag{28}$$

where the indices 1 and 2 represent goods 1 and 2, respectively. From equation (28) we obtain:

$$\frac{p_{D1}}{p_{W1}} = \frac{p_{D2}}{p_{W2}} \text{ or, equivalently } \frac{p_{D1}}{p_{D2}} = \frac{p_{W1}}{p_{W2}} \tag{29}$$

and domestic price relations are equal to world market price relations. Accordingly, the price support leads to no change in the price ratios faced by consumers and there will therefore be no substitution effects in demand. In this case the external protection leads neither to a distortion of the consumption structure nor to welfare losses on the demand side.

If welfare losses are to be avoided on the supply side (i.e. in production), price support must not change the relative value added of products. This means that the **effective rates of protection** must be the same for all goods. The effective rate of protection ERP is defined as:

$$ERP = \frac{VA_D - VA_W}{VA_W} = \frac{VA_D}{VA_W} - 1 \qquad (30)$$

where VA = value added at domestic (D) or world market prices (W).

The ERP thus indicates the percentage by which price support increases domestic value added over the value added that would result at world market prices. In the following, we show that if NRPs are identical for output and input prices, the ERP equals the NRP. We begin with the definition of domestic value added (VA_D) for an output (O) produced using one input (I):

$$VA_D = P_{OD}Q_O - P_{ID}Q_I \qquad (31)$$

where

P_{OD} and P_{ID} = the domestic prices of the output and the input, respectively, and

Q_O and Q_V= the quantities of output produced and input used, respectively.

Correspondingly, value added at world market prices (VA_W) is defined as:

$$VA_W = P_{OW}Q_O - P_{IW}Q_I \qquad (32)$$

For domestic prices applies:

$$P_{OD} = (1 + t)P_{OW} \qquad (33)$$

and

$$P_{ID} = (1 + t)P_{IW} \qquad (34)$$

By inserting equations (33) and (34) into equation (31) we obtain:

$$VA_D = (1 + t)VA_W \qquad (35)$$

and thus:

$$EPR = t = NPR. \qquad (36)$$

While the support for output prices increases the producers' value added (they receive a transfer of $P_{OD} - P_{OW}$ per unit produced), the support for input prices reduces their value added (they lose $P_{ID} - P_{IW}$ per unit of input used). If the NRP for output prices is higher (lower) than the NRP for input prices, the percentage increase in value added is higher (lower) than indicated by the NRP. If, the NRP is identical for output and input prices, value added is increased by the same percentage as the output and input prices, i.e. $ERP = NRP$.

In reality, of course, it will not be possible to increase all domestic inputs and outputs by the same percentage with respect to world market prices. Border measures such as import duties only directly affect the prices of tradable goods. The prices of non-tradable goods are indirectly affected by price support for internationally tradable goods, but usually less so in percentage terms. Furthermore, it would make little sense to attempt to increase the prices of all tradable goods by the same percentage. If policy makers wanted to do so, they could devalue the exchange rate instead of using border measures and protection.

Thus, the policy prescription derived above (apply equal NRPs for all products) can only roughly be translated into practical policy. In practice, policy makers could aim to implement equal *NRP*s for (tradable) products that are highly substitutable in production or consumption. Otherwise, policy-induced changes in domestic price relationships for highly substitutable products would lead to relatively large changes in production or consumption, and correspondingly large welfare losses.

The result that equal ERPs are less welfare-reducing than unequal ERPs has important implications for agricultural policy. Assume that the policy makers' objective is to increase the income of the factors of production that are specific to agriculture, i.e. factors of production that have no alternative use in the short and medium term. These include agricultural land, but also the agricultural labour force and a large proportion of the buildings and machinery used in farming. Assume further that policy makers can only pursue their objective by using price support instruments such as import duties. Under these assumptions, it does not make sense to increase factor incomes in agriculture solely by supporting output prices, i.e. by indirect subsidisation. From an economic welfare perspective, it is advisable to combine the price support for outputs with a tax on the use of inputs. The more mobile (i.e. the less agriculture-specific) inputs are, the more production-distorting effects will result from unequal protection rates for output and input prices. The more mobile inputs are, the more a policy of agricultural output price support will lead to an expansion of agricultural production. This will draw mobile inputs into farming, making them more expensive and scarcer and thus implicitly taxing other sectors of the economy that also rely on these inputs. Since the mobility of inputs generally increases with economic development (i.e. the degree of division of labour), it follows that the welfare losses associated with price support policies will increase as well.

2.5. Keywords

- autarchy
- barter trade
- capital income share
- closed economy
- constant returns to scale
- contract curve
- Edgeworth box
- effective rates of protection
- exchange
- exchange efficiency
- factor demand curve
- functional distribution of income
- general equilibrium
- institutions
- isoquant
- large country
- marginal expenditure
- marginal productivity theory
- marginal rate of factor substitution
- marginal rates of substitution
- marginal revenue
- marginal value product
- nominal rate of protection
- non-tradable goods
- numéraire
- open economy
- optimal export tax
- optimal levy
- Pareto improvements
- Pareto optimum

- partial monopsonist
- production efficiency
- production possibility curve
- small country
- Terms of Trade effect
- tradable
- transaction costs
- transformation costs
- transformation curve
- utility possibility curve
- world market prices
- yield function

References

Chiang AC (1974) Fundamental Methods of Mathematical Economics, 2nd Edition, McGraw-Hill, New York.

NobelPrize.org (2021) The Sveriges Riksbank Prize in Economic Sciences in Memory of Alfred Nobel 1993, https://www.nobelprize.org/prizes/economic-sciences/1993/summary/, accessed October 07, 2021.

North DC (1990) Institutions, Institutional Change and Economic Performance. Cambridge.

Exercises

a. A company produces 200 units of a good at a unit price of 5.00 € using factors of production x_1 and x_2. 40 units of x_1 are used at a price of 4.00 € each. The company uses 20 units of factor x_2. The production function is linear homogeneous and the company is a price taker on product and factor markets. Calculate:
   a) The marginal physical productivity of the factor x_1
   b) The marginal physical productivity of the factor x_2
   c) The factor income shares of x_1 and x_2.
b. The company in exercise 1 can only change the factor intensity by varying the factor x_1 (x_2 is a fixed amount of land, for example). Assume that the price of x_1 increases to 6.00 € per unit. The company therefore uses only 30 units of this factor and produces 180 units of the good at the unchanged price of 5.00 € per unit. Calculate:
   a) The marginal physical productivity of the factor x_1

b) The marginal physical productivity of the factor x_2
c) The factor income shares of x_1 and x_2
d) Explain verbally and graphically why the marginal productivity of factor x_2 has changed.

c. Explain with the help of marginal productivity theory how foreign investment can increase incomes in both the source and destination countries of the investment. What determined whether this is the case?

d. Assume a linear-homogeneous production function with a production elasticity of labour equal to 0.7. The labour input increases by 5%. How much do the following items change as a result?
a) The wage and capital income ratios
b) Total production
c) Labour productivity
d) The marginal productivity of labour.

e. In an autarchic region, per hectare cassava yields are twice as high as those for millet. Assume that both cassava and millet require the same amounts of other production factors, and that local consumers equally prefer both crops. If the production function is linear homogeneous, explain how a change in the production structure can lead to a Pareto improvement. Illustrate this result graphically.

f. The wage income share in Germany (and in many other countries) has changed over the decades. Which assumptions that we made in Figure 2.7 above (to explain simultaneous equilibrium on good and factor markets) do not apply in reality?

g. Rising world market prices for oil lead to the following discussion between two ministers in an oil importing country.

Minister A: "The costs of subsidising oil imports with the aim of keeping domestic price levels low are very high, and they have to be financed by collected taxes. But we have to be fair, we can't take the easy way out and let the domestic price rise to the world market price level, because that would impose an excessive burden on low-income families".

Minister B: "I think that we would all be better off if we allowed the domestic oil price to rise to the world market price level, and provided consumers with direct income transfer in the form of a negative income tax. We could thus provide low-income families with income transfers even if they do not pay income tax".

Minister A: "But by doing so, we would only be taking money out of one pocket via higher oil prices, and putting it back into the other pocket via direct income transfers. In reality nothing would change".

How would you analyse this problem from an economic perspective, and what advice would you give? Consider two representative families, a taxpaying family and a low-income family that pays no tax.

h. In 1977, a team of Chinese economists was commissioned to evaluate China's international cereal trade. The team was able to draw on the following information: the calorie content of wheat is approximately 90% of the calorie content of rice; Chinese rice yields are 2.58 times higher than Chinese wheat yields; from 1961 to 1976 China's cereal trade in cereals was characterised by rice exports and wheat imports (see Table). The experts concluded that China would have been better off producing less wheat and more rice in every year since 1971.

   a.
      i. How did the experts justify their conclusion?
      ii. From a macroeconomic perspective, under what general condition is it profitable to replace wheat production by rice production?
      iii. By what percentage could wheat consumption have been increased between 1970 and 1976 if all wheat production had been replaced by rice production?
   b. The experts also concluded that Chinese society would have been better off if less rice and more wheat had been consumed.
      i. Using 1976 as an example, calculate the increase in calorie consumption as a percentage of calorie exports.
      ii. Why is the degree of self-sufficiency misleading when it comes to assessing food security in China?
   c. The experts also concluded that Chinese society would have been better off if less rice and more wheat had been consumed.
      iii. Using 1976 as an example, calculate the increase in calorie consumption as a percentage of calorie exports.
      iv. Why is the degree of self-sufficiency misleading when it comes to assessing food security in China?

Table: China's rice and wheat trade

Year	net rice exports		net wheat imports	
	Quantity	Price	quantity	price
1970	1.819	115	4.973	71
1971	2.116	122	3.398	75
1972	1.997	120	4.696	81
1973	3.500	200	5.386	104
1974	2.883	326	5.346	214
1975	2.722	321	3.347	191
1976	2.186	299	1.998	170

d. The experts also concluded that Chinese society would have been better off if less rice and more wheat had been consumed.
   v. Using 1976 as an example, calculate the increase in calorie consumption as a percentage of calorie exports.
   vi. Why is the degree of self-sufficiency misleading when it comes to assessing food security in China?

Appendix 2.1

The following derivations are based on a simple model with two individuals (i) and two production factors, capital (C) and labour (L), that are used to produce two consumer goods (Q) according to neoclassical production technology. The goal is to maximise social welfare (W), which is a function of the two individuals' utility functions (U^i), by optimally allocating the two factors of production between the production of the two goods.

The Lagrange function to be maximised is:

$$\mathcal{L} = W[U^1(Q_1^{D1}, Q_2^{D1}), U^2(Q_1^{D2}, Q_2^{D2})] - \lambda_1[P_1 Q_1^S(C_1, L_1) - P_1(Q_1^{D1} + Q_2^{D2})] - \lambda_2[P_2 Q_2^S(C_2, L_2) - P_2(Q_2^{D1} + Q_2^{D2})] - \lambda_3[C - C_1 - C_2] - \lambda_4[L - L_1 - L_2] (37)$$

The eight first-order conditions that result are:

$$\frac{\partial \mathcal{L}}{\partial Q_1^{D1}} = \frac{\partial W}{\partial U^1}\frac{\partial U^1}{\partial Q_1^{D1}} + \lambda_1 P_1 = 0 \quad (38)$$

$$\frac{\partial \mathcal{L}}{\partial Q_2^{D1}} = \frac{\partial W}{\partial U^1}\frac{\partial U^1}{\partial Q_2^{D1}} + \lambda_2 P_2 = 0 \tag{39}$$

$$\frac{\partial \mathcal{L}}{\partial Q_1^{D2}} = \frac{\partial W}{\partial U^2}\frac{\partial U^2}{\partial Q_1^{D2}} + \lambda_1 P_1 = 0 \tag{40}$$

$$\frac{\partial \mathcal{L}}{\partial Q_2^{D2}} = \frac{\partial W}{\partial U^2}\frac{\partial U^2}{\partial Q_2^{D2}} + \lambda_2 P_2 = 0 \tag{41}$$

$$\frac{\partial \mathcal{L}}{\partial C_1} = -\lambda_1 P_1 \frac{\partial Q_1^S}{\partial C_1} + \lambda_3 = 0 \tag{42}$$

$$\frac{\partial \mathcal{L}}{\partial C_2} = -\lambda_2 P_2 \frac{\partial Q_2^S}{\partial C_2} + \lambda_3 = 0 \tag{43}$$

$$\frac{\partial \mathcal{L}}{\partial L_1} = -\lambda_1 P_1 \frac{\partial Q_1^S}{\partial L_1} + \lambda_4 = 0 \tag{44}$$

$$\frac{\partial \mathcal{L}}{\partial L_2} = -\lambda_2 P_2 \frac{\partial Q_2^S}{\partial L_2} + \lambda_4 = 0 \tag{45}$$

From equations (38) and (40) we obtain:

$$\frac{\partial W}{\partial U^1}\frac{\partial U^1}{\partial Q_1^{D1}} = \frac{\partial W}{\partial U^2}\frac{\partial U^2}{\partial Q_1^{D2}}. \tag{46}$$

Similarly, from equations (39) and (41) we obtain:

$$\frac{\partial W}{\partial U^1}\frac{\partial U^1}{\partial Q_2^{D1}} = \frac{\partial W}{\partial U^2}\frac{\partial U^2}{\partial Q_2^{D2}}. \tag{47}$$

Therefore:

$$\frac{\frac{\partial W}{\partial U^1}}{\frac{\partial W}{\partial U^2}} = \frac{\frac{\partial U^2}{\partial Q_1^{D2}}}{\frac{\partial U^1}{\partial Q_1^{D1}}} = \frac{\frac{\partial U^2}{\partial Q_2^{D2}}}{\frac{\partial U^1}{\partial Q_2^{D1}}}, \tag{48}$$

and as a result:

$$\frac{\frac{\partial U^1}{\partial Q_1^{D1}}}{\frac{\partial U^1}{\partial Q_2^{D1}}} = \frac{\frac{\partial U^2}{\partial Q_1^{D2}}}{\frac{\partial U^2}{\partial Q_2^{D2}}}. \tag{49}$$

This result implies that the marginal rate of substitution between good 1 and good 2 is the same for both individuals. This condition is explained in Section 2.1 above and illustrated using an Edgeworth box.

From equations (42) and (43) we obtain:

$$-\lambda_1 P_1 \frac{\partial Q_1^S}{\partial C_1} = -\lambda_2 P_2 \frac{\partial Q_2^S}{\partial C_2}. \tag{50}$$

Similarly, from equations (44) and (45) we obtain:

$$-\lambda_1 P_1 \frac{\partial Q_1^S}{\partial L_1} = -\lambda_2 P_2 \frac{\partial Q_2^S}{\partial L_2}. \tag{51}$$

Therefore:

$$\frac{\lambda_1 P_1}{\lambda_2 P_2} = \frac{\frac{\partial Q_2^S}{\partial C_2}}{\frac{\partial Q_1^S}{\partial C_1}} = \frac{\frac{\partial Q_2^S}{\partial L_2}}{\frac{\partial Q_1^S}{\partial L_1}}, \tag{52}$$

and as a result:

$$\frac{\frac{\partial Q_1^S}{\partial C_1}}{\frac{\partial Q_1^S}{\partial L_1}} = \frac{\frac{\partial Q_2^S}{\partial C_2}}{\frac{\partial Q_2^S}{\partial L_2}}. \tag{53}$$

This result implies that the marginal rate of factor substitution between capital and labour is the same in the production of both goods. This condition is explained in Section 2.2 above and also illustrated using an Edgeworth box.

Finally, from equations (38) and (39) we obtain:

$$\frac{\partial W}{\partial U^1} \frac{\partial U^1}{\partial Q_1^{D1}} = -\lambda_1 P_1 \tag{54}$$

and

$$\frac{\partial W}{\partial U^1} \frac{\partial U^1}{\partial Q_2^{D1}} = -\lambda_2 P_2. \tag{55}$$

Inserting equations (54) and (55) into equations (42) and (43) leads to:

$$\frac{\partial W}{\partial U^1}\frac{\partial U^1}{\partial Q_1^{D1}}\frac{\partial Q_1^S}{\partial C_1} = -\lambda_3 \tag{56}$$

$$\frac{\partial W}{\partial U^1}\frac{\partial U^1}{\partial Q_2^{D1}}\frac{\partial Q_2^S}{\partial C_2} = -\lambda_3. \tag{57}$$

Equations (56) and (57) are combined to produce:

$$\frac{\partial U^1}{\partial Q_1^{D1}}\frac{\partial Q_1^S}{\partial C_1} = \frac{\partial U^1}{\partial Q_2^{D1}}\frac{\partial Q_2^S}{\partial C_2} \tag{58}$$

and thus

$$\frac{\frac{\partial U^1}{\partial Q_2^{D1}}}{\frac{\partial U^1}{\partial Q_2^{D1}}} = \frac{\frac{\partial Q_2^S}{\partial C_2}}{\frac{\partial Q_1^S}{\partial C_1}}. \tag{59}$$

This result implies that the marginal rate of substitution between good 1 and good 2 (which according to equation (49) is the same for all consumers) is equal to the marginal rate of transformation between goods 1 and 2. This condition is also discussed in Section 2.2.

Appendix 2.2

The producer's decision problem is: which combination of the factors capital and labour should be used to produce which quantity (Q_j^S) of good j? If we assume profit-maximising behaviour, the producer' decision problem can be stated as:

$$Max: \pi = P_j Q_j^S(C_j, L_j) - P_C C_j - P_L L_j \tag{60}$$

where

π = profit, and

P_j, P_C and P_L are the prices of good j, capital and labour, respectively.

Taking the partial derivatives of the profit function (60) and setting them equal to zero we obtain the following first-order conditions:[11]

[11] The fulfilment of the second-order conditions for a maximum is ensured by the assumed strict quasi-concavity of the production function (see chapter 2.2).

$$\frac{d\pi}{dC_j} = P_j \frac{\partial Q_j^S}{\partial C_j} - P_C = 0 \tag{61}$$

$$\frac{d\pi}{dL_j} = P_j \frac{\partial Q_j^S}{\partial L_j} - P_L = 0 \tag{62}$$

From equations (61) and (62) we obtain:

$$P_j = \frac{P_C}{\frac{\partial Q_j^S}{\partial C_j}} \tag{63}$$

$$P_j = \frac{P_L}{\frac{\partial Q_j^S}{\partial L_j}} \tag{64}$$

so that:

$$\frac{P_C}{\frac{\partial Q_j^S}{\partial C_j}} = \frac{P_L}{\frac{\partial Q_j^S}{\partial L_j}} \text{ or } \frac{\frac{\partial Q_j^S}{\partial C_j}}{\frac{\partial Q_j^S}{\partial L_j}} = \frac{P_C}{P_L} \tag{65}$$

Hence, the profit-maximising producer chooses an optimal factor combination for which the marginal rate of factor substitution equals the factor price ratio.

Appendix 2.3: The linear-homogeneous production function

Homogeneity of a function of degree λ means that multiplying the independent variables by a constant k changes the value of the function by the factor k^λ. Hence, for a function f which is homogeneous of degree λ the following applies:

$$f(kx_1, kx_2, \dots, kx_n) = k^\lambda * f(x_1, x_2, \dots, x_n) \tag{66}$$

For example, the function

$$y = 3x^2 + 2z^2 \tag{67}$$

is homogeneous of degree 2, because a multiplication of the independent variables x and z by k results in a change of the value of the function by the factor k^2.

The terms 'homogeneous of degree 1' and 'linear homogeneous' are used synonymously. This can lead to confusion, because a linear homogeneous function - i.e. a function that is homogeneous of degree 1 - does not have to be linear: the adjective 'linear' describes the homogeneity of the function and not the function itself. The following function, for example, is non-linear in x and z, but homogeneous of degree 1 and therefore linearly homogeneous:

$$y = 3x^{0.25} * 2z^{0.75} \tag{68}$$

The function in equation (68) belongs to the family of so-called Cobb-Douglas functions, named after their inventors C.W. Cobb and P.H. Douglas. The Cobb-Douglas function is generally:

$$y = \beta_0 x^{\beta_1} z^{\beta_2}, \tag{69}$$

and it is only linear homogeneous if $\beta_1 + \beta_2 = 1$.

In economics, the Cobb-Douglas function is often used to map production processes. A typical Cobb-Douglas production function with 2 inputs, L and C, and output Q is:

$$Q = \beta_0 L^{\beta_1} C^{\beta_2} \tag{70}$$

In equation (70) β_1 and β_2 are referred to as **partial elasticities of production**. The partial elasticity of production is defined as the relative (percentage) change in the quantity produced when the input of a factor changes by one percent. For the factor labour, for example, the partial elasticity of production is defined as follows:

$$\frac{\frac{\partial Q}{Q}}{\frac{\partial L}{L}} = \frac{\partial Q}{\partial L}\frac{L}{Q} \tag{71}$$

The identity of the partial elasticity of production in equation (71) with the coefficient β_1 in equation (70) can be proved by taking logarithms of equation (70):

$$\ln Q = \ln \beta_0 + \beta_1 \ln L + \beta_2 \ln C \tag{72}$$

and totally differentiating the result:

$$d(\ln Q) = d(\ln \beta_0) + d(\beta_1 \ln L) + d(\beta_2 \ln C)$$

or

$$d(\ln Q) = \beta_1 d(\ln L) + \beta_2 d(\ln C). \tag{73}$$

Since the change in a logarithmic quantity is equal to the relative change of the original quantity (i.e. $d(\ln x) = \frac{dx}{x}$), equation (73) can be transformed into:

$$\frac{dQ}{Q} = \beta_1 \frac{dL}{L} + \beta_2 \frac{dC}{C}. \tag{74}$$

Holding the quantity of the factor C (L) constant, we obtain:

$$\frac{\frac{dQ}{Q}}{\frac{dL}{L}} = \beta_1 \text{ (or } \frac{\frac{dQ}{Q}}{\frac{dC}{C}} = \beta_2\text{)}. \tag{75}$$

Linear-homogeneous production functions have several properties that play important roles in price theory. These properties are presented in the following.

1. The scale elasticity of a linear-homogeneous production function equals one.

The scale elasticity indicates by how much production changes if all factor input quantities increase or decrease together by 1%. A scale elasticity of one means that if all factor input quantities increase by 1%, production also increases by 1%. Since the following applies to a linear-homogeneous function:

$$f(kx_1, kx_2, \dots, kx_n) = k * f(x_1, x_2, \dots, x_n) \tag{76}$$

it follows that the scale elasticity of such a function must equal one.

If the scale elasticity of a production technology equals one, larger producers to not do not have any competitive advantage vis-à-vis smaller producers. Since any increase in scale increases both costs and production by the same percentage, unit costs remain unchanged. Another term for scale elasticity is **returns to scale**. An elasticity of scale of one is also referred to as **constant returns to scale**; when the elasticity of scale is greater than one (i.e. a production function that is homogeneous of degree > 1), we refer to **increasing returns to scale**.

The assumption of constant returns to scale is crucial for the existence of a competitive equilibrium. With increasing returns to scale, for example, unit costs decrease with increasing company size. Hence, if production technology is characterised by increasing returns to scale, larger producers can squeeze smaller ones out of the market, which sooner or later will lead to a monopoly situation. As was shown in section 2.1.2, however, the market and price mechanism can only lead to a Pareto optimum if there is perfect competition on all goods markets.

2. The sum of the partial elasticities of production of a linear-homogeneous production function is equal to one.

This property follows directly from the first. Since the scale elasticity of a linear-homogeneous function is equal to one, we know that a change of all input amounts by a common percentage causes a change in production by the same percentage (i.e. for a given $\frac{dL}{L} = \frac{dC}{C}$ it follows that $\frac{dQ}{Q} = \frac{dA}{A} = \frac{dK}{K}$). Equation (74) can therefore be transformed into:

$$\frac{dQ}{Q} = (\beta_1 + \beta_2)\frac{dC}{C} \tag{77}$$

or

$$\frac{\frac{dQ}{Q}}{\frac{dC}{C}} = (\beta_1 + \beta_2) = 1 \tag{78}$$

The fact that the partial elasticities of production add up to one gives rise to an important theorem, **Euler's theorem**, which states that if all factors of production are remunerated according to their marginal value products, the sum of factor incomes is equal to the value of production. This can be shown as follows:

The starting point of the proof is equation (78):

$$\beta_1 + \beta_2 = \frac{dQ}{dL}\frac{L}{Q} + \frac{dQ}{dC}\frac{C}{Q} = 1 \tag{79}$$

If this equation is multiplied by $P_Q * Q$, the result is:

$$P_Q Q = \frac{dQ}{dL}\frac{L}{Q}P_Q Q + \frac{dQ}{dC}\frac{C}{Q}P_Q Q, \text{ or } P_Q Q = \frac{\partial Q}{\partial L}P_Q L + \frac{\partial Q}{\partial C}P_Q C. \tag{80}$$

If factors of production are remunerated according to their marginal value products (so that $\frac{\partial Q}{\partial L}P_Q = P_L$, and $\frac{\partial Q}{\partial C}P_Q = P_C$), then:

$$P_Q Q = P_L L + P_C C \tag{81}$$

If Euler's theorem applies, all factors can be fully remunerated according to their marginal value products, and there is no residual or excess profit. Obviously, this statement is of great importance for the functioning of a competitive market economy.

3. In a linear-homogeneous production function, factor productivity depends only on factor intensity.

The productivity of a factor is defined as the quotient of the production quantity to the input quantity of the factor. Hence the productivity of labour and capital are defined as:

$\frac{Q}{L}$ or $\frac{Q}{C}$, respectively.

The factor intensity is defined as the relation of the factor input quantities:

$\frac{L}{C}$ or $\frac{C}{L}$ = the factor intensity.

To show that factor productivity depends only on factor intensity, namely that:

$$\frac{Q}{L} = f\left(\frac{L}{C}\right), \tag{82}$$

we begin with the production function:

$$Q = f(L, C) \tag{83}$$

Dividing the equation by L we obtain:

$$\frac{Q}{L} = f\left(1, \frac{C}{L}\right) = f\left(\frac{C}{L}\right) \tag{84}$$

Thus, the more C that is used, the higher the productivity of L.

This relationship can also be derived specifically for the Cobb-Douglas production function $Q = \beta_0 L^{\beta_1} C^{\beta_2}$. Dividing by L, and since $\beta_1 + \beta_2 = 1$, we obtain:

$$\frac{Q}{L} = \frac{\beta_0 L^{\beta_1} C^{\beta_2}}{L} = \frac{\beta_0 C^{\beta_2}}{L^{1-\beta_1}} = \frac{\beta_0 C^{\beta_2}}{L^{\beta_2}} = \beta_0 \left(\frac{C}{L}\right)^{\beta_2}, \tag{85}$$

which proves that the factor productivity $\frac{Q}{L}$ depends solely on (and is an increasing function of) the factor intensity $\frac{C}{L}$.

CHAPTER THREE

PRICE FORMATION ON AGRICULTURAL LAND MARKETS

ULRICH KOESTER AND
STEPHAN VON CRAMON–TAUBADEL

3.1. Introduction and learning objectives

Factor mobility is a crucial determinant of structural change in all economic sectors. In agriculture, the immobile factor land plays a special role. Comparable situations exist only in a few other sectors, for example those which depend on rare ore deposits, oil fields, or fishing grounds. Since land extends over space, land markets cannot be treated as point markets. In the following chapter we must therefore begin by considering aspects of spatial pricing.

Agricultural holdings can lease and/or buy land. The decision to lease farm land is usually based on short- to medium-term considerations. In contrast, the purchase of farm land is usually based on long-term considerations. The purchase price of farm land depends on the long-term expectations of those working in the sector, and the relationship between purchase and lease prices at any given time thus reflects the expectations of land buyers and suppliers about future developments in agriculture.

In this chapter we will:

- explain the concept of the land rent and distinguish between the main components of land rent,
- explain the relationship between land rent and the lease price of land,

- discuss the relationship between lease and purchase prices for agricultural land,
- describe the importance of expectations for price formation on agricultural land markets, and
- highlight the importance of institutions and transaction costs for price formation on agricultural land markets.

3.2. Key Concepts

We begin by explaining a number of terms that we will use frequently in this chapter.

A **rent** in the economic sense is an income that exceeds opportunity costs. Rents are therefore **residual incomes**. The opportunity cost of a factor of production is the income it would earn if put to its best possible alternative use. Rents arise in the long run only in the case of limited supply and limited substitutability of a factor. Such limits can be physical (there is only so much agricultural land on the planet) but also institutional, for example when a government imposes production quotas or awards patent rights. If the supply of a factor is elastic or if the factor can be substituted, then competition will eventually eliminate any rents that arise in the short run.

If land is a scarce factor of production in agriculture, then it will receive an income that is higher than the income needed to channel it into agricultural production. The **land rent** is the difference between the total value added generated on a given area of land over a given period (which equals the sum of all factor incomes) and the incomes of the other factors employed on that land over the same period, each of which is paid its marginal value product. As a rule, land rents are measured per hectare (or other measure of area such as acre) and year. The annual per hectare land rent is thus a residual income based on the assumption that all other factors are perfectly mobile and remunerated according to their marginal value products. From an economic welfare perspective, we initially assume that the opportunity cost of agricultural land is zero, in other words that it has no alternative, non-agricultural uses. This assumption is certainly not realistic for much agricultural land in a densely populated country such as Germany, where alternative uses do exist (e.g. housing, or reforestation to act as a carbon sink). From a business perspective, if a hectare of land is agricultural by assumption, then its opportunity cost in one type of use (e.g. wheat production) is determined by its best possible alternative agricultural use (perhaps maize, barley, or grazing animals).

The **contribution margin** is the income available to remunerate all fixed factors of production. Since all factors are variable in the long term, the contribution margin per hectare can only be greater than the land rent if the adjustment of some other factors is constrained and/or some other factors are not paid their full marginal value products.

The **lease price** is the price which the land user has to pay the land owner for the temporary use of land, typically per hectare and year. It is useful to distinguish between the lease price for a specific piece of land, and the lease price for an entire farm. If all factors are fully adjusted to maximise profits, and if they are all paid according to their marginal value products, the lease price is usually higher than the land rent, and the per hectare lease price for a plot of land will be higher than the per hectare lease price for an entire farm.

The **purchase price** is the payment for the transfer of all rights of disposal and use of land. Later in this chapter we discuss in greater detail the relationship between the lease price and the purchase price, and between the land rent and the purchase price.

3.3. Explanation of land use prices using the land rent theory

The so-called **land rent theory** explains the determination of land rents as a function of the demand for land use. Assume that the supply of land is perfectly inelastic and that the production function is linear homogeneous.[1] The assumption of a perfectly inelastic supply of land is realistic for many countries and especially for most industrialised countries.

Land rent theory distinguishes between three different components of land rent; the **intensity rent**, the **quality rent,** and the **location rent**, which we explain in the following. We begin by assuming that land is homogeneous, i.e. that there are no quality differences between land in different locations, and no preferences for specific locations and thus no differences in the willingness to pay for different plots of otherwise identical land. Furthermore, it is assumed that all available land is exclusively for agricultural use. To simplify the graphs and equations that we use below,

[1] See Appendix 2.3 in Chapter 2.

we assume without loss of generality that only labour is used in addition to land in agricultural production.

3.3.1. Intensity rent

This component of land rent is a function of the intensity of land use, i.e. the per hectare use of other production factors such as labour. In the right panel of Figure 3.1 we assume that the demand for land (B) meets a completely inelastic land supply. Furthermore, we assume an initial equilibrium with demand curve D_0, in which the land rent P_0^B is zero. In this situation, with labour (L) input Q_0^L and wage rate P_0^L (in the left panel of Figure 3.1), it is not possible to remunerate the land because labour claims the entire value of production. This can only occur if a quantity of land of at least Q_0^B is available so that equilibrium with the demand D_0 occurs where the price of land is zero. This is the case in Figure 3.1 for the supply curve S (and any supply curve to the right of S).

Figure 3.1: Land rent as an intensity rent

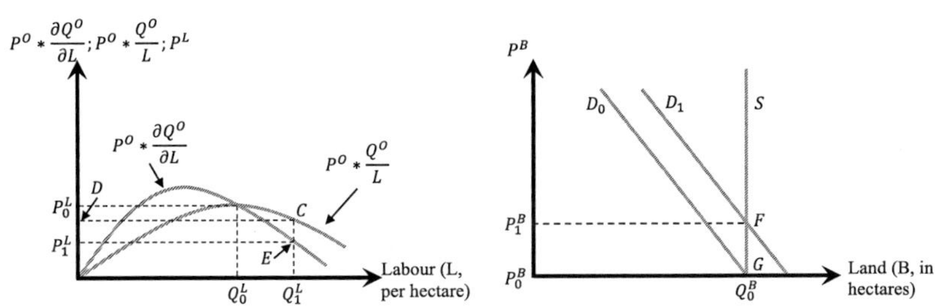

Source: Own depiction

An exogenous reduction in the wage rate from P_0^L to P_1^L leads to an increase in the intensity of land use (increase in per hectare labour use from Q_0^L to Q_1^L) and an increase in the demand for land. The demand curve shifts to the right (movement from D_0 to D_1), resulting in the factor price P_1^B. Given the output price and quantity P^O and Q^O, respectively, land now receives a per hectare income equal to its marginal value product $P^O * \partial Q^O / \partial B = P_1^B$ multiplied by the land input, which remains at Q_0^B because the supply of land is perfectly inelastic. For the given labour input Q_1^L therefore, the land rent corresponds to the area $CDP_1^L E$ in the left panel of Figure 3.1. Since the left panel of Figure 3.1 measures labour input per hectare, the area equals the remuneration of one hectare: $CDP_1^L E = P_1^B$

The size of the intensity rent thus depends on the amount of labour input. By assumption we are considering only labour in addition to land, and a linear-homogeneous production function. The more labour-intensive farming is, the higher the labour input per hectare, the lower the marginal productivity of the labour, and the higher the marginal productivity of the land.

3.3.2. Quality rent

The quality rent results from differences in the agronomic quality of land, i.e. if we relax the assumption that land is homogenous. The quality rent, which was already analysed two centuries ago by David Ricardo (1817), is one of the classic examples of a permanent rent.

For simplification, assume that there is only high-quality (good) and low-quality (bad) farm land (Figure 3.2). If the price of the labour is higher than P^{L^*}, then no land will be cultivated. As the price of labour falls below P^{L^*}, the good land will be cultivated first. Below P^{L^*} (where the marginal value product of good land equals its average value product), residual income for good land will remain after labour has been remunerated. Hence, as long as the price of the labour lies between P^{L^*} and P^L, per hectare labour quantities to the right of point E will be employed and the good land will receive a rent. Consequently, only the good land will be cultivated. If the price of labour falls below P^L, then the bad land will also receive a rent, and both the good and the bad land will be cultivated. Since the marginal value product of labour must be the same everywhere (otherwise it would be reallocated between good and bad land), the marginal value products of good and bad land will differ. The quality rent is therefore an increasing function of the quality of land.

Figure 3.2: The land rent as quality rent

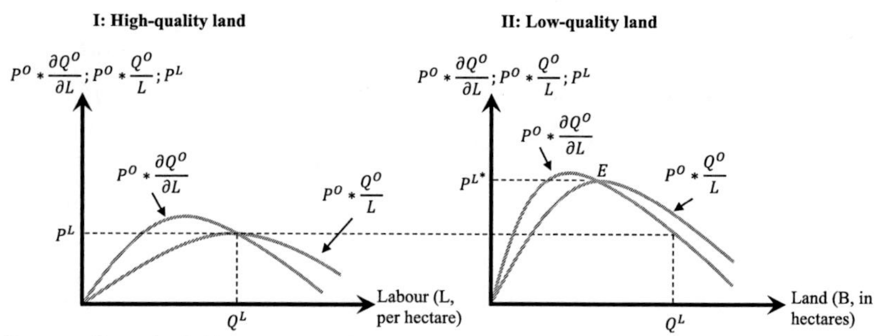

Source: Own depiction

3.3.3. Location rent

The location rent is the result of different farm-gate product (output) prices which arise because some farms are farther from consumption or sales markets than others. The location rent is another long-known classical example of a permanent rent in economics; it played an important role in Johann Heinrich von Thünen's (1910) location theory. Since the production value and thus the marginal value product change when output prices change, the remuneration of the production factors and thus the factor intensities must also change depending on the location. In Figure 3.3, we assume that some land is near to markets while other land is far. Net of transport costs from the farm to the market, the output produced near to markets, all other things being equal, fetches a higher farm-gate price than output produced on land that is farther from markets ($P^O_{Near} > P^O_{Far}$). As a result, the marginal and average value product curves are higher at locations close to the market than at locations further away. The points at which they equal zero (at the origin, and where the marginal or average productivity is zero) are identical for both locations, i.e. only the concavity of the curves increases. For a given labour input quantity Q^L, the land rent is thus higher near to markets (P^LBCD to P^LEFG in Figure 3.3). The closer to markets production takes place, the higher the farm-gate output price obtained, and thus the higher the location rent.

Figure 3.3: Land rent as location rent

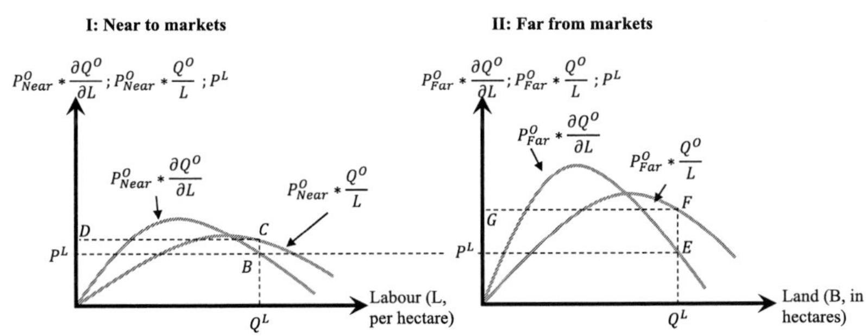

Source: Own depiction

3.3.4. Land rent, contribution margin and land use price

In reality, land is very heterogeneous in terms of quality, local climate and other factors such as water availability, and geographic location. This results in a complex spatial pattern of land rents and thus lease prices. Under conditions of perfect competition, when all other factors are remunerated according to their marginal value products, the lease price for a plot of land will equal its land rent. The land rent will be paid to the landowner, and in the long term, if all factors are remunerated according to their marginal value products and opportunity costs, pure tenant farms will receive no land rent.

In Figure 3.4, the total amount of land available is divided between two tenant farms X and Y. In equilibrium under perfect competition, the lease price is the same for both farms and equals the land rent on both farms. Equilibrium is therefore where the marginal value product curves of the two farms (MVP_0^X and MVP_0^Y) intersect. Thus, in the initial equilibrium the lease price will be $P_0^B = Rent_0^X = Rent_0^Y$, farm X will cultivate the quantity B_0^X of the available land and farm Y the remaining quantity B_0^Y. If farm Y adopts new technologies while farm X does not, the marginal value product of land on farm Y will shift from WGP_0^Y to WGP_1^Y. As a result, the land rent of the last hectare on farm Y will increase from $Rent_0^Y$ to $Rent_1^Y$. Farm Y will therefore be able to pay a higher lease price for land than farm X. If there is perfect competition, land will 'migrate' from farm X to farm Y until a new equilibrium is reached where the land rent is once more the same on both farms. The result is a lease price of P_1^B and a new distribution of land between the two farms (B_1^X and B_1^Y).

In practice, regional land markets are rarely polypolistic, but rather oligopolistic or monopolistic. Often, only a few local suppliers and/or demanders interact, and often the relationships between these entities are complex, characterised by kinship or rivalry. Furthermore, land lease contracts are often concluded for more than one year, and the lease price will not necessarily adapt immediately to changes in the land rent. Leases do sometimes contain clauses that create at least an indirect link between the lease price and the land rent; for example, a contract might link the lease price to a grain price index.

Figure 3.4: Mobility of the factor land between farms with perfect adjustment under neoclassical conditions

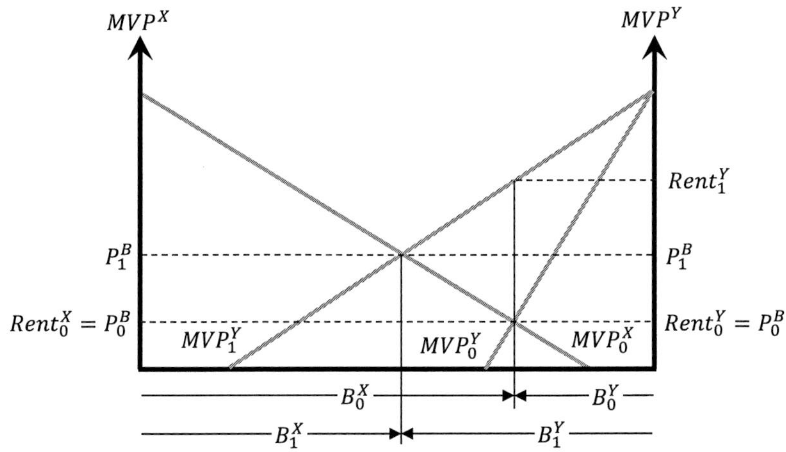

Source: Own depiction

3.4. The relationship between lease and purchase prices for land

So far, we have considered the formation of the lease price for land in agriculture, i.e. the price for one year's use of a plot of land. By purchasing a plot of land, the buyer can secure the right to the sum of all future lease income that can be generated on this land. Consequently, there is a relationship between land lease and purchase prices, which we will explain below. We will first assume that the economic entities have perfect information about the future. In reality, of course, economic entities only have limited information about the future conditions under which long-lived factors such as land can be used. Therefore, in a subsequent section we will discuss the importance of expectations about future developments for the formation of land prices.

3.4.1. The relationship between land lease and purchase prices with perfect information

As explained above, in equilibrium and under polypolistic conditions the annual lease price equals the annual land rent. Therefore, by purchasing a plot of land, the buyer can secure the sum of all future land rents that can be earned on that plot. Land rents that are earned in the future must be discounted to give a present value. A profit-maximising purchaser of land who is solely interested in agricultural use will not be willing to pay a purchase price that exceeds the sum of all discounted future land rents that can be earned on the land.[2] If we assume that the land rent and interest rate remain constant over time, the following relationship between the lease and purchase prices for land results:

$$P^{B,Purchase} = P_0^{B,Lease} + P_1^{B,Lease}(1-r) + P_2^{B,Lease}(1-r)^2 + \cdots + P_T^{B,Lease}(1-r)^T \quad (1)$$

where

$P^{B,Purchase}$= the purchase price for land,

$P_t^{B,Lease}$= the lease price for land at the time t,

r= the interest rate, and

T= the planning horizon in years.

If we assume constant lease prices over time and an infinite time horizon, equation (1) can be transformed as follows:

$$P^{B,Purchase} = P^{B,Lease}[1 + (1-r) + (1-r)^2 + \cdots + (1-r)^\infty] \quad (2)$$

Generally, if $|x| < 1$, then:

$$1 + x + x^2 + \cdots + x^\infty = \frac{1}{1-x}. \quad (3)$$

Inserting $x = (1-r)$ into equation (2), we obtain

$$P^{B,Purchase} = P^{B,Lease}\left[\frac{1}{1-(1-r)}\right] = P^{B,Lease}\left[\frac{1}{r}\right]. \quad (4)$$

Therefore:

$$r = \frac{P^{B,Lease}}{P^{B,Purchase}} \quad (5)$$

---

[2] We assume that there are no speculative motives for buying the land, for example no expectation that the land will be re-zoned for housing.

According to equation (5), the ratio of the lease to the purchase price of land under conditions of perfect information equals the discount rate (assumed to be constant) at which future lease income is discounted. If the purchase price is high in relation to the lease price, the discount rate is low, indicating that future lease income has a relatively high present value. If the purchase price is low in relation to the lease price, the discount rate is high, indicating that future lease income has a low present value.

In reality, the relationship between lease and purchase prices will be more complex than depicted in equation (5). No one knows with certainty at any given time how future land rents and interest rates will develop. Furthermore, different individuals will use different subjective **discount rates** to determine the prices that they are willing to pay to purchase land, not the economy-wide interest rate. We return to this issue later in the chapter.

3.4.2. The effect of a persistent change in agricultural prices

In the following we explore the implications for land prices of an isolated, permanent change in agricultural output prices. Such price changes can occur, for example, as a result of sudden changes on world agricultural markets, or changes in agricultural policy such as the removal of barriers to trade. Of course, agricultural prices are constantly changing, so the assumption of a one-off and persistent change is not realistic. Nevertheless, this thought experiment serves to demonstrate the fundamental relationship between product price changes and lease prices.

We begin with the following equation:

$$PQ = P^iQ^i = P^LQ^L + P^KQ^K + P^VQ^V + P^BQ^B \qquad (6)$$

where

Q= the quantity of agricultural output produced;

P= the price of the agricultural product;

Q^i= the quantity of the i-th production factor used, where i = labour (L), capital (K), intermediate inputs (V), and land (B); and

P^i= the price of the corresponding i-th production factor.

For simplification, we assume in equation (6) that all agricultural products can be aggregated to a single output Q; P is therefore an output price index. Analogous assumptions hold for the variables on the right side of equation (6) (e.g., V is an aggregate of different intermediate inputs such as seed, fertiliser, etc.).

In order to determine the relationship between the product price P and the lease price of land P^B, we make the following additional assumptions. First, we assume a linear-homogeneous production function for agricultural output: [3]

$$Q = f(Q^A, Q^K, Q^V, Q^B) \quad (7)$$

In addition, we assume that all factor prices except the lease price of land are fixed (which is indicated by a bar '¯'):

$$P^L = \bar{P}^L \quad (8)$$

$$P^K = \bar{P}^K \quad (9)$$

$$P^V = \bar{P}^V \quad (10)$$

Equations (8) to (10) indicate that labour, capital and intermediate inputs are variable, and that the supply of these factors is perfectly elastic. Hence, agriculture is a price-taker for these factors. This is a realistic assumption if agriculture is a relatively small sector of the economy, in which case all of the factors used in agriculture other than land are fully variable, and their prices depend on the remuneration they receive in other sectors. Finally, we assume that the available quantity of land is also fixed:

$$Q^B = \bar{Q}^B \quad (11)$$

The assumptions in equations (7) to (11) allow us to re-write equation (6) as follows:

$$P\big(f(Q^L, Q^K, Q^V, Q^B)\big) = \bar{P}^L Q^L + \bar{P}^K Q^K + \bar{P}^V Q^V + P^B \bar{Q}^B \quad (12)$$

Next, we convert equation (12) into its so-called **equilibrium displacement form** by converting the levels of variables into rates of change. First, we take the total differential:

---

[3] See Appendix 2.3 in Chapter 2.

$$QdP + P\left(\frac{\partial Q}{\partial Q^L}dQ^L + \frac{\partial Q}{\partial Q^K}dQ^K + \frac{\partial Q}{\partial Q^V}dQ^V\right) = \bar{P}^L dQ^L + \bar{P}^K dQ^K + \bar{P}^V dQ^V + \bar{Q}^B dP^B \quad (13)$$

Dividing by PQ we obtain:

$$\frac{dP}{P} + \left(\frac{\partial Q}{Q}\frac{Q^L}{\partial Q^L}\frac{dQ^L}{Q^L} + \frac{\partial Q}{Q}\frac{Q^K}{\partial Q^K}\frac{dQ^K}{Q^K} + \frac{\partial Q}{Q}\frac{Q^V}{\partial Q^V}\frac{dQ^V}{Q^V}\right)$$
$$= \frac{Q^L\bar{P}^L}{PQ}\frac{dQ^L}{Q^L} + \frac{Q^K\bar{P}^K}{PQ}\frac{dQ^K}{Q^K} + \frac{Q^V\bar{P}^V}{PQ}\frac{dQ^V}{Q^V} + \frac{\bar{Q}^B P^B}{PQ}\frac{dP^B}{P^B} \quad (14)$$

Recall the definition of ε_{Q,Q_i}, the partial elasticity of production with respect to a factor i:[4]

$$\varepsilon_{Q,Q_i} = \frac{\partial Q}{Q}\frac{Q^i}{\partial Q^i} = \frac{\frac{\partial Q}{Q}}{\frac{\partial Q^i}{Q^i}} \quad (15)$$

Furthermore, if the factors of production are remunerated according to their marginal value products, then:

$$\frac{\partial Q}{\partial Q^i}P = P^i, \text{ or } \frac{\partial Q}{\partial Q^i} = \frac{P^i}{P}$$

and therefore

$$\varepsilon_{Q,Q_i} = \frac{\partial Q}{Q}\frac{Q^i}{\partial Q^i} = \frac{\partial Q}{\partial Q^i}\frac{Q^i}{Q} = \frac{P^i}{P}\frac{Q^i}{Q}$$

This enables us to restate equation (14) as follows:

$$\frac{dP}{P} + \left(\varepsilon_{Q,Q^L}\frac{dQ^L}{Q^L} + \varepsilon_{Q,Q^K}\frac{dQ^K}{Q^K} + \varepsilon_{Q,Q^V}\frac{dQ^V}{Q^V}\right)$$
$$= \left(\varepsilon_{Q,Q^L}\frac{dQ^L}{Q^L} + \varepsilon_{Q,Q^K}\frac{dQ^K}{Q^K} + \varepsilon_{Q,Q^V}\frac{dQ^V}{Q^V}\right) + \frac{\bar{Q}^B P^B}{PQ}\frac{dP^B}{P^B} \quad (16)$$

and thus

$$\frac{dP}{P} = \frac{\bar{Q}^B P^B}{PQ}\frac{dP^B}{P^B}, \quad (17)$$

---

4 See Appendix 2.3 in Chapter 2.

which can be rearranged as

$$\frac{dP^B}{P^B} = \frac{dP}{P}\frac{PQ}{\bar{Q}^B P^B}. \tag{18}$$

According to equation (18), the percentage change in the lease price of land ($\frac{dP^B}{P^B}$) is equal to the percentage change in the agricultural output price ($\frac{dP}{P}$) multiplied by the inverse of the cost share of land in total revenue ($\frac{PQ}{\bar{Q}^B P^B}$). Since this cost share is always less than 1, its inverse must always be greater than 1, and therefore the percentage change in the lease price of land is always greater than the percentage change in the agricultural output price that triggered it. For example, if the share of land in the value of production is 15%, a 1% increase in agricultural prices results in a 6.6% increase in the lease price of land.

These results show that in long-run equilibrium, changes in agricultural prices lead to changes in output quantities, but not to a higher remuneration of the factors other than land that are used in agriculture. In the long run, after all adjustments in input use and production have taken place, only landowners benefit from an increase in agricultural output prices. However, this conclusion only holds if all farmers are profit maximisers, an assumption that we will return to below. In addition, this conclusion only holds if agriculture is a relatively small sector for which the prices of production factors other than land (labour, capital and intermediate inputs) are fixed. In many low-income and emerging economies, however, agriculture is a relatively large sector employing 30% or more of the labour force. In such countries, an increase in agricultural prices can trigger an expansion in production, leading to an increase not only in land but also in labour prices (i.e. wages). As Ivanic and Martin (2014) demonstrate, taking these wage effects into account is crucial when assessing the implications of high agricultural prices (e.g. during the so-called food price crisis of 2007/08) for poverty and hunger.

3.4.3. The effect of a constant rate of change in land lease prices[5]

If we assume that land lease prices follow a constant rate of change (w) over time, then the relationship between purchase and lease prices of land derived

[5] This section is based on Niehans (1966).

above (equation 5) must be modified accordingly. The new relationship between lease and purchase prices is:

$$P^{B,Purchase} = P_0^{B,Lease} + P_1^{B,Lease}(1-r)(1+w) + P_2^{B,Lease}(1-r)^2(1+w)^2 + \cdots + P_2^{B,Lease}(1-r)^T(1+w)^T \quad (19)$$

If, as above, we assume an infinite time horizon, equation (19) can be transformed as follows:

$$P^{B,Purchase} = P^{B,Lease}\left[\begin{array}{c}1 + ((1-r)(1+w)) + ((1-r)(1+w))^2 + \cdots \\ +((1-r)(1+w))^\infty\end{array}\right] \quad (20)$$

The sum in square brackets in equation (20) is finite only if $((1-r)(1+w)) < 1$. If this condition is not met, the sum in square brackets and thus the purchase price of land is infinite. The condition $((1-r)(1+w)) < 1$ is always fulfilled if the interest rate r is positive and the rate of change in the lease price change w is negative. In this case, future income leasing out land is not only discounted, but it also decreases nominally over time. Otherwise, if the interest rate and the rate of change w are both positive, the above condition is met if $|r| < w$. In this case, equation (20) can be transformed as follows:

$$P^{B,Purchase} = P^{B,Lease}\frac{1}{1-((1-r)(1+w))} = P^{B,Lease}\frac{1}{r-w+rw} \quad (21)$$

and it follows that

$$\frac{P^{B,Lease}}{P^{B,Purchase}} = r - w + rw. \quad (22)$$

The significance of this relationship between the interest rate and the rate of change in the land lease price is illustrated in Figure 3.5 and Table 3.1. First, the results in Table 3.1 confirm that the purchase price of land becomes infinite if the rate of change in the land lease price exceeds the interest rate ($w > r$). Otherwise, we see that for a given rate of change in the land lease price, the purchase price of land is highly sensitive to changes in r. The higher the expected rate of change in land lease prices, the stronger the purchase price reacts to changes in the interest rate. If the expected rate of change in land lease prices is high, for instance because world market prices for agricultural products are rising strongly, purchase prices for land increase very rapidly as a result of reductions in the interest rate (see also Figure 3.5). This can explain why land prices in many parts of the world increased so strongly in the years after the so-called food price crisis of 2007/08, when food prices were high and interest rates low.

Figure 3.5: The purchase price of land price as a function of the rate of change in land lease prices and the interest rate

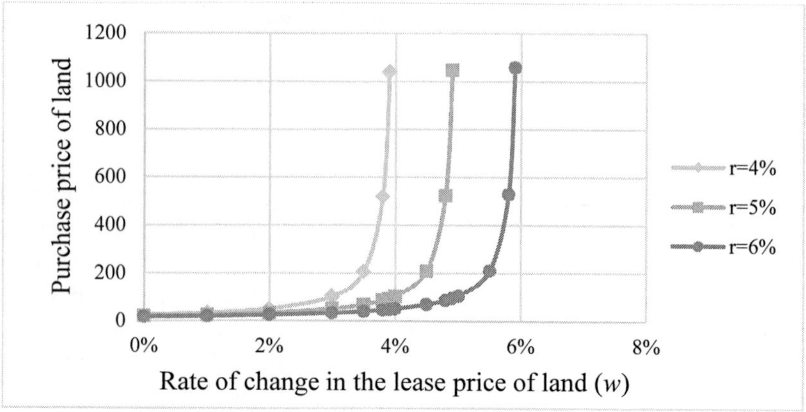

Source: Own calculations.

Table 3.1: The ratio of the purchase price to the land lease price as a function of the rate of change in the land lease price (*w*) and the interest rate (*r*)

w in %	interest rate in %		
	$r = 4\%$	$r = 5\%$	$r = 6\%$
0,0%	25	20	17
1,0%	34	25	20
2,0%	51	34	26
3,0%	103	52	34
3,5%	207	69	41
3,8%	519	87	47
3,9%	1039	94	49
4,0%	∞	104	52
4,5%	∞	209	70
4,8%	∞	524	87

4,9%	∞	1049	95
5,0%	∞	∞	105
5,5%	∞	∞	211
5,8%	∞	∞	529
5,9%	∞	∞	1059

3.4.4. Uncertain expectations regarding future lease prices and future interest rates

In reality, future streams of income, for example from land, are not discounted using a single interest rate. Instead, market participants use discount rates that can differ considerably. Each participant's discount rate r consists of two main components. The first component measures the opportunity costs of the capital used to buy land. The second component can be interpreted as a risk premium, since future land rents and lease income depend, among other things, on unforeseeable developments in agricultural policy, as well as on weather- and production-related risks.[6] This link between lease prices and agricultural policy, for example through support prices, was explained above (see equation 18). Changes in the ratio of the lease to the purchase price of land over time can thus be interpreted as an indicator of land market participants' average **expectations** regarding the future profitability of farming. If, for example, the implicit discount rate increases (e.g. if the purchase price falls while the lease price remains constant – see equations 5 and 22), this suggests that expectations about future income from land lease have worsened, perhaps due to pessimistic forecasts of world market price developments, or concerns that reform might reduce the protection of domestic agriculture.

Figure 3.6 shows the evolution of the number of trainees in agriculture per thousand full-time farms in Germany from 1968 to 1994. The evolution of this series can be interpreted as an indicator of expectations in agriculture – the more optimistic the expectations, the more young individuals will want to pursue careers in agriculture and, thus, become trainees.[7] For example, in Figure 3.6 we see that the number of trainees per thousand full-time farms increased during the phase of high agricultural prices in the early 1970s and

---

[6] Weersink et al. (1999) study these effects in greater detail.

[7] However, this series does not account for the age structure of the owners of full-time farms, which will also influence the number of trainees

decreased when the EU shifted to the so-called restrictive price policy in the mid-1980s.

Figure 3.6 also shows the development of the ratio of lease to purchase prices for agricultural land in Germany between 1975 and 1994. It is striking that this implicit discount rate is very low over the entire period. A possible explanation for this is that land purchase is subject to considerably higher transaction costs than land lease, which artificially depresses the ratio of lease to purchase price. Lence and Miller (1999) examine this influence of transaction costs on the relationship between lease and purchase prices in the US state of Iowa between 1900 and 1994. Furthermore, the assumption of an infinite time horizon used to derive equations (5) and (22) leads to an underestimation of the discount rate. In addition, the purchase prices for land are also influenced by the demand for land for non-agricultural use, as well as by tax laws (income, wealth and inheritance taxes).

Figure 3.6: The relationship between lease and purchase prices for land (implicit discount rate) and the number of trainees in agriculture per 1000 full-time farms in Germany

Source: Own calculations with BLE (various issues), BMEL (various issues) and Statistisches Bundesamt (various issues).

Regardless of its absolute level, note that the implicit discount rate in Figure 3.6 is negatively correlated with the number of trainees per 1000 full-time farms. When the number of trainees increases, suggesting optimism about the future profitability of agriculture, the purchase price of land increases relative to the lease price, which also suggests optimism. Hence, the implicit discount rate is indeed a good indicator of expectation in agriculture.

3.5. Extensions of the basic model

3.5.1. The implications of heterogeneous land

Under neoclassical conditions and perfect competition, there is only one price for a homogeneous good or factor of production. As discussed above (location rent and quality rent), land is not homogeneous. Land in different locations and of different qualities is valued differently by buyers and sellers. In industrialised countries, most demand for agricultural land is exercised by farmers. An individual farmer's willingness to pay for a certain plot of land will depend to a large extent on the location of that plot relative to the rest of his/her farm; whether the plot would reduce or increase the fragmentation of the farm's land. In addition, different potential buyers will have different expectations about the future (see above). It follows that different potential buyers will be willing to pay different amounts for the same plot of land.

Moreover, at any given place and time, there will only be a limited number of opportunities for potential buyers to purchase land. Generally speaking, the only suppliers of farm land are farmers who are ceasing agricultural production. Most of the time there will only be a few such suppliers - often only one - and only a few potential buyers in the vicinity, with varying degrees of willingness to pay. It is therefore not surprising that there are often considerable differences in regional land prices, and that land prices can vary greatly over time. There will therefore be more than the one price for agricultural land that is predicted by the simple neoclassical model.

3.5.2. Relaxing the assumption that farmers only maximise profit

The demand curve for a factor of production is given by its marginal value product, if the producer is a profit maximiser. However, farmers are often not profit maximisers. European agriculture is largely characterised by family farming. Farmers generally inherit farms that have been in the hands of the family for generations. As a result, they feel tied to their farms and strive to preserve or increase the inheritance, and view farming not only as a source of income but also as a vocation and livelihood. Since family farm owners often display pronounced preferences for agricultural activity and life in the countryside, their mobility is often very limited.

As a consequence, the rents that accrue to land can vary considerably between farms. Agricultural accounting data show that individual farmers sometimes incur considerable losses of wealth year after year. They would be better off economically if they sold or leased their land. Nevertheless, they continue to farm and postpone the decision to cease farming until the next generation, even though the income from renting or selling their land would be higher than the income from farming it themselves. This is especially true if farmers cannot find alternative, off-farm employment, which is often the case especially for older farmers. As a consequence of this behaviour and these conditions, a given demand for land meets less supply than would be expected under neoclassical conditions, resulting in a lower volume of land market transactions and higher land prices.

It can be observed that per hectare lease prices for individual plots of land are generally higher than per hectare lease prices for entire farms. This is not surprising. The lease price for an entire farm will reflect the expected average land rent over all of the different plots that make up the farm. The lease price for an individual plot of land will reflect the contribution margin that a farmer expects to generate by adding that plot to his/her farming operation. The contribution margin of an additional plot of land can be considerably higher than its land rent if, for example, adding that plot to the farm enables a farmer to use available machinery and labour to full capacity.

3.5.3. The influence of path dependency on land prices

We speak of **path dependency** when the past development of certain variables has an influence on their future development. In the neoclassical model, the past is only relevant for today's decisions if it influences profit maximisation. Thus, according to the neoclassical model, fixed costs incurred by past investments have no influence on today's decisions. Today's decisions are only based on the costs and benefits of adjusting variable input use.

Agricultural structures are path dependent, and they influence the development of land prices. In some countries or cultures, farms are inherited in equal shares by all eligible heirs. This can lead to a structure characterised by many small farms that do not employ the available labour and other inputs to full capacity. As a result, land prices in such a situation will likely be higher than in countries or cultures in which a single heir inherits the entire farm, especially if farmers, as discussed above, feel attached to the land or have no off-farm employment alternatives.

3.5.4. Assumption: significance of restricted rights of disposal

Rights of disposal can be classified into **ownership rights** and **use rights**. The right of ownership can be individualised - as is largely the case in market economies - or it can be centralised state ownership, with or without common land, for example ownership by a village community. Where ownership rights are individualised, the owner is largely free to use the land, and to transfer ownership or the right of use. Where ownership belongs to the state, individuals can have at most temporary use rights. In the real world, however, there is no such clear demarcation. Even in market economies with individualised ownership rights, these rights are restricted to a certain extent, for example by special agricultural and environmental laws. For example, ownership rights are restricted when the owner is not free to choose a buyer and negotiate the selling price. Rights of land use are often restricted by law (e.g. limits on fertiliser or agricultural chemical use) or even by tradition.

Restrictions on ownership and use rights vary considerably between countries. In some countries of the former Soviet Union, such as Belarus, Tajikistan and Uzbekistan, private ownership of agricultural land is not permitted. In Mongolia, private ownership of pastureland is not permitted. In many of the former centrally planned economies, even after land was formally privatised, owners were not allowed to sell their land for a number of years. In Ukraine, for example, land plots (shares) were distributed among 6.9 million active or former collective farm workers in the 1990s. However, a moratorium was imposed on the sale and purchase of land and only (partially) lifted in July 2021. In some countries, citizens are allowed to sell and purchase agricultural land, but foreigners are prohibited. In some countries, land transactions are reviewed and must be approved by authorities. Similarly, in some countries only farmers are allowed to purchase agricultural land, or local farmers are given a right of first refusal on land sales to non-farmers or absentee farmers.

It is obvious that these laws and restrictions will have an influence on the land market. Some of these laws even suppress the emergence of a land market. Furthermore, they can affect the land rents, both from a private and a social perspective. In the following sections we discuss the effects of selected restrictions on the functioning of land markets.

3.5.4.1. Unrestricted individual use of state-owned land

In an influential paper, Hardin (1968) described how unrestricted individual use of state- or publicly-owned land can lead to the so-called "**tragedy of the commons**". When deciding how to use grazing land, a utility-maximising individual with unrestricted use rights who does not cooperate with others will compare expected private benefits with expected private costs, and neglect the possible activities/responses of other users of the same land. Based on these considerations, he/she will tend to use the land more intensively than if it were his/her private property. As a consequence, the land will be overgrazed and its productive capacity will deteriorate.

Of course, this will only lead to an allocation problem if land becomes scarce, i.e. if the marginal private willingness to pay for the available land is greater than zero. The situation is illustrated in Figure 3.7. We initially assume that land is homogeneous. For the available quantity of land ($\bar{Q}$) the marginal willingness to pay is zero. Such a situation existed for world agriculture in past millennia. For hunters and gatherers as well as for the first farmers, land was not scarce; there was therefore no need to define private rights of disposal. If, however, the demand for land increases (i.e. the demand curve shifts to the right and the marginal willingness to pay increases), unrestricted individual use of land can lead to problems.

Figure 3.7: Unlimited rights of disposal for land when land is not in short supply

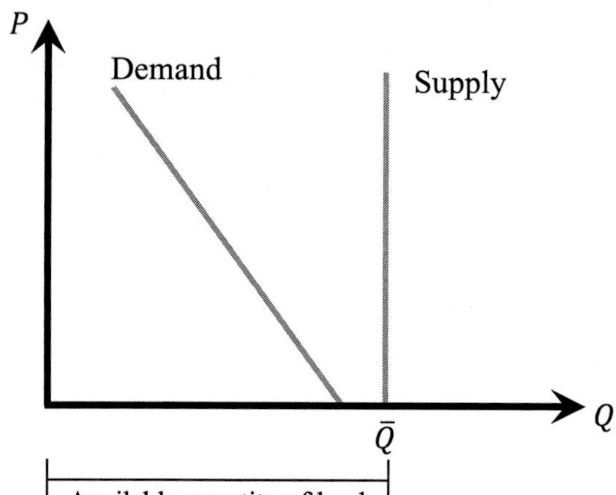

Source: Own depiction

What are further consequences of unrestricted individual use rights? In reality, land is not homogeneous. Therefore, even in countries with a relatively large supply of land - such as Mongolia - the marginal willingness to pay may be positive for high-quality land, but negative for low-quality or very remote land. Unrestricted use rights for land can therefore - compared with individualised rights - lead to overuse of high-quality land and reduced use of economically less valuable land. Since the quality of land is also determined by its proximity to water supply and market and population centres, the unrestricted individual use rights also lead to regional differences in the intensity of land use, with overgrazing in some regions, and little or no use in others.

If numerous individuals have unrestricted rights of use to a plot of land, there is, of course, no market price for that plot. Nevertheless, land rents are generated on that plot. Each individual land user can compare his/her expected benefit of using the land with his/her variable costs. If the benefits exceed the costs, the individual's marginal willingness to pay for use of the plot will be positive. However, the aggregated marginal willingness to pay over all individual users of the plot will be lower than if the use of the plot were restricted. This is because under unrestricted use the benefits expected by the individual user will be reduced by everyone else's use. As a consequence, the land will be used inefficiently, even if there is no overuse and/or no deterioration of the land over time.

Not only land use but also the use of other factors of production will be inefficient if individuals have unrestricted use rights to land. Livestock numbers will likely be higher than when private land use rights are enforced. In addition, in regions such as Central Asia harsh winters can result in insufficient fodder supplies and livestock losses. A market for fodder, especially hay, will not develop, as hay production for private use and sale is not possible if the land can be used without restriction. Investments and access to credit will also suffer. Individual farmers will not invest in improving the land itself because the returns from such investment will accrue to all users. Instead, individuals will invest in increasing herd sizes, improving winter quarters for animals and improving marketing possibilities, e.g. means of transport. Access to credit will be limited because land cannot be used as collateral. Farmers who require credits, for example to purchase fodder in a hard winter, will therefore have to resort to unofficial credit markets with high interest rates.

3.5.4.2. State ownership and private use by municipalities

Sometimes state-owned land, usually pasture, is managed by local municipalities which allow members to graze private animals on it. As a traditional form of economy, such "**commons**" are still widespread in the Alpine region, on the Swedish island of Gotland, occasionally in the northern and southern Black Forest (Hotzenwald) and in southern Bavaria, but above all in rural areas of low-income countries. The municipalities regulate the use of such commons, restricting the number of animals that individual producers are allowed to graze. Such regulation can avoid the overuse and underinvestment described above. However, a decisive factor is whether and how this regulation adapts to changes in the environment, such as changes in the carrying capacity of the land area, or improved animal performance as a result of breeding progress or improved feeding technology. In response to such changes, the community must revise and enforce both the total number of animals that may be grazed, and the allocation of this total number among the individual producers. Revision and enforcement of rules for the use of common resources is difficult, and as a result the management of common land is often suboptimal and the collectively generated land rent is often lower than in the case of private ownership. Elinor Ostrom was awarded the Nobel Prize in Economics in 2009 for her research on the management of common resources such as grazing land and the factors that determine why management systems are successful in some cases, and less so in others.

3.5.4.3. State ownership and private use by tenants

In principle, land can be used efficiently if the user is not also the owner. Management by both landowners and tenants is widespread in market economies. Here, we consider a special situation in which the state as owner is the sole lessor and only leased land is farmed. This situation exists for example in Israel.

If efficient use of land is to be achieved, the state must lease the land to the potential tenant who is expected to use the land most efficiently in the future. However, when the lease contract is being negotiated and concluded, the state has no information about how different potential tenants will manage land in the future. It can be assumed that the most efficient tenants will be willing to pay the highest lease prices under competitive conditions. Therefore, the state as lessor must try to determine potential tenants' willingness to pay. If the state wants to keep transaction costs low, it will offer whole farms or areas of land that are large enough to establish farms.

As a rule, however, only a few parties will be interested in such large parcels of land, and it is questionable that these few potential tenants will reveal their true willingness to pay. In such a situation the state can set a minimum lease price and enter into negotiations with potential tenants. This happens, for example, in Germany when state-owned farms are leased to tenants. In this case, the state uses statistics on past and current average lease prices or land values to establish the minimum lease or purchase price

However, the use of average past lease or purchase prices as a basis for future contract is unlikely to lead to efficient use of land. Current market prices for long-lived factors of production such as land are not based on prices paid in the past, but on expected future revenues and costs. In addition, average values are always a poor guide for determining prices. Market prices are formed by supply and demand at the margin, for a particular plot or parcel of land with specific characteristics (quality, location).

Using average past prices as a basis for future prices is especially problematic if there are large differences in the marginal willingness to pay for land and if future changes in basic current conditions such as technologies are expected. Since farm accounting data reveals great heterogeneity in the commercial success of farms, potential tenants' marginal willingness to pay for land is also heterogeneous. As a result, a past average price will not reflect the most efficient potential tenant's marginal willingness to pay. In addition, future changes in technologies as well as in input and output prices cannot be predicted with certainty. Land lease and purchase prices depend on expectations regarding such future changes, and different potential tenants will have different subjective expectations, and different personal preferences. These differences will also lead to a large variance in the marginal willingness to pay for land. It will therefore not be possible for the state, as the only supplier of land, to set lease or purchase prices that lead to efficient land use.

When the state leases land to tenants, defining the optimal duration of the lease contracts is also a difficult issue. The lease prices agreed at a certain point in time depend on the future evolution of factors such as input and output prices that determine future land rents. Since these factors and expectations for their continued evolution change over time, optimal lease prices change as well. Thus, even if an optimal long-term lease price can be determined now, it will no longer be optimal at some later date after important framework conditions and expectations have changed. The longer the duration of a lease contract, the more serious this problem becomes.

One might conclude that short-term lease contracts therefore lead to greater efficiency, because they can be adjusted to account for changes in framework conditions more frequently. As a rule, however, tenants prefer long-term contracts. Efficient land use requires the use of various forms of capital. Capital such as farm machinery is variable in the long run, but otherwise quasi-fixed; its resale value is lower - often significantly lower - than its book or market value. The limited mobility of capital means that leases for entire farms or large parcels of land are usually long-term contracts. However, this implies that the state as the lessor of farms and large parcels of land is not in a position to set a lease price that leads to the same allocative efficiency as would be achieved under private ownership of the land.

3.5.5. Importance of leasing and ownership of agricultural land in market economy systems

In market economies, the ownership of agricultural land is largely unrestricted. This does not mean, however, that agricultural enterprises cultivate only land that they own. The proportion of leased land varies considerably between countries, ranging from 15 to 90 percent in the EU (see Table 3.2). The differences between countries are not only limited to the share of lease overall, but also to differences in the shares of entire farm lease and individual plot lease in the total leased area. This coexistence of farm and plot leases can contribute to a higher allocative efficiency of land than lease or ownership alone.

Table 3.2: The share of leased land in agricultural area in EU countries (2007, in %)

Share of leased land (%)	**EU countries**
15-30	Ireland *(16.5%)*, Poland *(27.5%)*, Denmark *(28,3%)*
30-45	Austria *(31%)*, Slovenia *(31.8%)*, Portugal *(31.8%)*, Spain *(33.6%)*, Finland *(34.8%)*, Italy *(38.8%)*, Netherlands *(40,3%)*
45-60	Luxembourg *(50.7%)*, **EU** ***(52.5%)***, Sweden *(53.4%)*, Estonia *(59,8%)*
60-75	Lithuania *(60.1%)*, Cyprus *(64.0%)*, Hungary *(67.2%)*, Belgium *(74,1%)*

75-90	Malta *(81.2%)*, France *(84.5%)*, Czech Republic *(87.9%)*, Bulgaria *(89%)*
More than 90	Slovakia *(96,3%)*

Source: Střeleček et al. (2011).

3.5.5.1. Importance of uncertainty for the choice between lease and purchase

Purchasers of land face a greater uncertainty than those who lease land, because the decision to purchase has implications that reach farther into the uncertain future. Since more capital is tied up in the case of land purchase, the consequences of incorrect forecasts of future developments are also greater than in the case of land lease. As explained above, the relationship between purchase and lease prices is determined by the market participants' expectations, but also by the agricultural structure and changes in the macroeconomic environment. Uncertainty and the consequences of incorrect forecasts of future developments are smaller when a single plot of land rather than an entire farm is being purchased. Thus, it is to be expected that in regions with a relatively large proportion of owned land and primarily plot lease, the lease price will be relatively high in relation to the purchase price.

Interestingly, purchase prices for farm land in the Netherlands are much higher than in Denmark. According to Eurostat (2018), the average price for agricultural land in the Netherlands in 2016 was roughly 63,000 Euro/hectare; in Denmark the average price was only 22,000 Euro/hectare. Agriculture is very efficient in both countries, so that one would expect land prices to be roughly similar. The considerable price difference can be explained by different institutional arrangements. In Denmark a large proportion of land purchases involve entire farms. Farm successors - even if they are direct descendants of the owner – must acquire the farm from the predecessor by purchase. In the Netherlands, land purchases mainly involve individual plots of land by farmers looking to enlarge their holdings. As explained above, per hectare prices of individual plots will generally be higher than per hectare prices for entire farms. A further factor contributing to the relatively low purchase prices in Denmark is that the transactions take place mainly between family members and that personal preferences therefore influence the price.

3.5.5.2. The importance of structural change for the relative advantage of lease compared to purchase

Land transfer by lease as opposed to purchase can lead to an acceleration of structural change. Landowners will be more inclined - especially in uncertain times - to lease rather than sell land. It can therefore be expected that the more uncertain landowners and land users are, the more land transactions will involve lease rather than sale and purchase. In the 1990s, for example, roughly 7% of the farm land in the EU-15 was bought and sold each year, compared with only 1-2% in the countries of Central and Eastern Europe (Schulze 1999, p. 4). Furthermore, due to uncertainty, the ratio of lease to purchase prices is much higher in many countries of Central and Eastern Europe than in Germany.

3.5.5.3. The importance of transaction costs for the relative advantage of lease compared to purchase

Transaction costs arise on land markets for different reasons, including market imperfections and legal regulations. Transaction costs are caused by imperfect markets, for example, when the economic and political situation is very uncertain and it is therefore not possible to forecast the development of variables that determine the land price, such as output and factor prices. As a consequence, lease transactions will be preferred to purchase and sale.

The effects of transaction costs on lease and purchase markets are shown in Figure 3.8. In this figure we depict demand and supply curves both without (D and S) and with transaction costs ($D + T^D$ and $S + T^S$). In addition, we assume - in line with real observations - that transaction costs are higher on purchase markets for both suppliers and for those who demand than they are on lease markets (i.e. both T^D and T^S are higher in the right panel of Figure 3.8 than in the left panel). On both markets we see that with transaction costs, the volume of transactions is lower than it is without ($Q_1 < Q_0$). Moreover, we can also see that the reduction in transaction volumes caused by transaction costs is higher on the purchase than on the lease market. Indeed, it is conceivable that transaction costs lead to a situation in which the volume of transactions falls to zero, as is depicted in the right panel of Figure 3.8. This situation has been observed in several Central and Eastern European countries, especially in the early years of transition; agricultural land was left fallow even though farms were interested in expanding their areas.

Figure 3.8: The importance of transaction costs for the volume of land market transactions

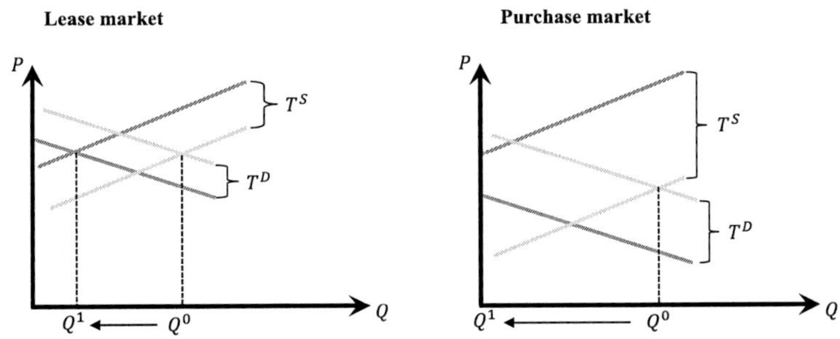

T^S= Transaction costs on the supply side
T^D= Transaction costs on the demand side

Source: Own depiction.

Such a situation can arise for two reasons. First, if property rights are not secure, lessors cannot be sure that lease payments will be made and that leased land will be returned in good condition at the end of the contract period. Similarly, if property rights are not secure or very expensive to enforce, buyers cannot be sure that they will become the recognised legal owners of the land that they pay for. Second, even if the ownership rights are clearly defined and enforceable, agricultural land might nevertheless remain unused if there is a high degree of uncertainty on markets. As explained above, farmers will generally prefer short-term over long-term leases. However, formerly fallow land is often not very productive in the first years and only attains its full productivity after a few years of cultivation. In this case, potential tenants will be interested in short-term leases as well.

3.5.5.4. The importance of capital requirements and access to credit markets for land lease and purchase

Agriculture is one of the most capital-intensive sectors in modern market economies. Farmers on efficient farms therefore often depend on credit. Access to credit markets is easier for farms with large shares of equity capital rather than debt financing. Leased farms therefore have less access to credit markets than farms that own most or all of their land. This disadvantage for leased farms is also detrimental for the economy as a whole if credit markets do not function well. In this case, lenders will tend to focus heavily on the security of loan repayment and therefore on the amount of collateral that farms have, rather than on the expected profitability of the investments that farms would like to finance. This means that lenders will tend to finance investments on farms with large shares of owned land that appear secure, rather than the investments that promise the highest return. As an example of this, after the reunification of Germany, many new cooperatives in Eastern Germany (the former German Democratic Republic - GDR) found it especially hard to obtain loans. These cooperatives did not own the land that they farmed; this land had either been returned to its pre-1945 owners, or it belonged to individuals who had obtained title under GDR law, or it belonged to the state. The cooperatives leased their land from these different types of owners, and hence had little or no equity that could serve as collateral for loans. In addition, these cooperatives had no credit histories under market conditions, so lenders could not use their past behaviour to assess their future creditworthiness.

3.6. State intervention on agricultural product and factor markets in Germany and the EU

State intervention on agricultural output and factor markets is widespread even in market economies. Government use of selected policy instruments in pursuit of agricultural policy goals. When choosing these instruments, however, governments often fail to consider that interventions on output markets also lead to changes on factor markets and, in particular, influence land price formation. Above we explained how changes in agricultural output prices lead to changes in land. In the following we will explain how output quotas, acreage set-aside programs, and direct income payments influence the formation of land prices.

3.6.1. The effects of production quotas on land prices

Implementing production quotas is only considered by policy makers if domestic prices are supported above the level of world market prices, and if domestic production at these prices exceeds domestic demand. In 1984, for example, the EU introduced a quota system for milk in order to reduce subsidised exports of dairy products. Of course, export volumes could also have been reduced by lowering the prices of dairy products (butter and skimmed milk powder); this alternative was recommended by many agricultural economists, but rejected by EU policy makers whose primary aim was to support agricultural incomes.

In the following we show that a major effect of such a production quota is to reduce land rents. On the output market in the left panel of Figure 3.9, domestic prices (P^{Dom}) are supported by policy measures (such as export subsidies and import duties) at a level above world market price (P^{W}). At P^{Dom}, supply (Q^{S}) exceeds demand (Q^{D}). The export surplus ($Q^{S} - Q^{D}$) is dumped on the world market by means of export subsidies of ($P^{Dom} - P^{W}$) per unit of output (e.g. per ton of butter). The government thus incurs expenditure of $(P^{Dom} - P^{W})(Q^{A} - Q^{N})$.

In order to reduce this expenditure, the government decides to implement a production quota. In Figure 3.9 we assume that the total volume of permitted production is fixed by the quota at $\bar{Q}$. Farmers are provided with licences that permit them to produce certain quantities that in aggregate add up to $\bar{Q}$. Hence, in addition to the traditional factors of production such as labour, land and capital, farmers now also need licences in order to produce.

Figure 3.9: The effect of a production quota on land prices

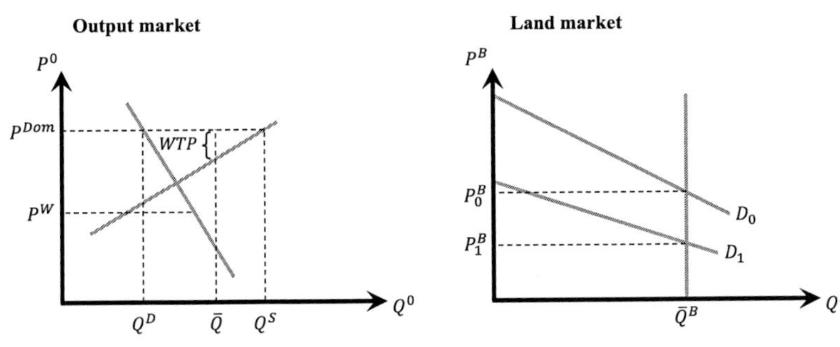

Source: Own depiction.

The quota system therefore effectively creates a new, artificial but essential factor of production – the licences. Before the quota was imposed, the farms' value added was identical to the sum of their payments to labour, capital and land; after implementation part of the value added accrues to the licences. If farmers are allowed to trade quota licences, then a market price for these licences will emerge. However, if we neglect transaction costs it is irrelevant whether the quota licences may be traded. With or without trade and explicit price formation, the decisive question is whether some farmers are willing to pay for additional licences to expand their production.

In Figure 3.9, the marginal willingness to pay for licences equals WTP, which equals the difference between the marginal revenue (P^{Dom}) and the marginal costs of the last unit of output produced at $\bar{Q}$. Since profit-maximising farmers can earn additional contribution margin if they expand production beyond $\bar{Q}$, they are willing to pay a price for the right to expand production. The right to produce that is conveyed by a quota licence can thus be considered an additional factor of production.

How does the addition of quota licences affect the distribution of value added among the (now) four factors of production? We saw above that land income is as residual income. If labour and capital are remunerated according to their opportunity costs, and if these costs do not change as a result of the quota system, only the use of labour and capital will decrease as a result of the quota. As can be seen in the right panel of Figure 3.9, the reduced use of labour and capital will reduce the marginal value product of land, and the demand for land will therefore shift to down from D_0 to D_1. As a result, land prices will fall, from P_0^B to P_1^B. Ultimately, the reduced value added and the income that accrues to quota licences will be at the expense of land income. If the remuneration of labour and capital is not fully in line with the opportunity costs, i.e. if the mobility of these factors is limited, then their remuneration will also decrease as a result of the quota.

3.6.2. The effect of acreage set-aside on land prices

Voluntary set-aside of agricultural land was first introduced in the EU in 1988 as an attempt by policy makers to reduce agricultural production and the associated use of export subsidies. Farmers were given incentives to take land out of production. In 1992 set-aside was made mandatory as part of the so-called MacSharry reform of the EU's Common Agricultural Policy. In 2008, set-aside was eliminated as part of the so-called Health Check reform.

First, we will examine how mandatory set-aside without incentives (i.e. without payments) affects land use prices.

Compulsory set-aside without payments

If land use is reduced by x percent by law, and labour and capital inputs remain unchanged in the short term, the income earned by land will increase, decrease or remain constant depending on the price elasticity of demand for land. Studies have shown that the price elasticity of demand for land is less than 1 in absolute terms. The lease price of land will increase and the total income earned by land will therefore increase as a result of compulsory set-aside.

In the long term, with full mobility of labour and capital, other effects will emerge. If labour and capital are remunerated according to their opportunity costs, set-aside leads to reduced use of labour and capital. Given a linear-homogeneous production function, labour and capital use will be reduced by the same percentage as land use. After these adjustments the lease price of land will be the same as before the set-aside. However, to the extent that labour mobility in particular is limited, mandatory set-aside can lead to higher lease prices in the long term.

Voluntary set-aside with incentive payments

The long-term increase in lease prices will be even more pronounced if set-aside is voluntary and farmers receive incentive payments that depend on the quality of the land. Germany, as a member of the EU, implemented such a system from 1988 to 1992. The incentive payment was determined using the econometric relationship between land quality (measured according to an agronomic point system used in Germany) and the contribution margin in individual regions. Based on the estimated linear relationship, farmers were offered incentive payments according to the quality of their land. While the estimated relationship between land quality and contribution margin is statistically significant, the scheme did not account for the fact that most observations do not lie directly on the estimated line, but instead are scattered around it. In other words, on land of a given quality, some farmers earn more than the expected contribution margin, others earn less. If policy makers offer a payment corresponding to the estimated average contribution margin to profit-maximising farmers, only those farmers who generate below-average contribution margins will accept; for all other farmers it is more profitable to farm the land rather than set it aside. As a result, the farmers who did set aside were overcompensated (i.e. they received incentive payments in excess of the foregone contribution margins), and lease prices increased in the long run.

3.6.3. The effect of decoupled income transfers compared with product price reductions

The MacSharry reform of 1992 initiated a fundamental shift in the EU's Common Agricultural Policy, gradually replacing support with direct income transfers. Farmers were compensated for the first cut in support prices for cereals (30 percent over three years) by means of direct payments per hectare of land planted to cereals. The intention was to fully compensate farmers for the loss of income caused by the price cuts. The effect of this change in agricultural policy on lease prices for land depends largely on the specific design of the direct payments and their level compared with the price support that they replaced.

Policy makers had to solve three basic problems in determining the level of compensation payments. First, they needed information on cereal yields in each region before the price cuts. This information was reliably available for regions in the old federal states (Länder) of Germany, where farms had been operating under old policies for many decades. However, reliable information was not available for the new Länder in the former German Democratic Republic, where farms had just begun to operate under market conditions following reunification in 1990. Older statistics did show that regions in the new Länder had produced higher yields than regions in the old Länder before the beginning of the Second World War. When calculating the level of compensation payments, policy makers therefore assumed that these pre-Second World War yield ratios would return after adjustment. Regions in the new Länder were therefore overcompensated, irrespective of their development potential.

Second, policy makers needed information on how the price cuts would affect yields. In the absence of this information, they assumed that the yields would remain unchanged. In the short term this is a realistic assumption. However, by failing to account for ongoing yield increases, it led to an overestimation of the income losses caused by the price cuts, and thus the required level of compensation payments.

Third, policy makers required information on the reduction in farm gate prices that was caused by cuts in support prices. They assumed a one-to-one relationship, i.e. that farm gate prices would fall by the same amount as the support prices. However, past experience suggested that farm gate prices would fall by less, and this was borne out following the MacSharry cuts in cereal support prices. This also led to overcompensation. All in all, the assumed yield and price changes that were used to calculate compensation payments resulted in overcompensation in both the old and the new Länder, but especially in the new.

This overcompensation increased average land lease prices, but it also changed the spatial pattern of land rents in Germany.[8] Farmers who produced above-average yields in a region (because they farmed above-

[8] Compensation payments were calculated differently in other EU member states, but similar issues with compensation arose in these countries as well.

average quality land, or were especially skilled at crop production) were undercompensated, and farmers with below-average yields were overcompensated, because they all received the same compensation based on regional average yields. As a result, own demand for land is likely to have increased, further increasing lease prices.

3.7. Keywords

- commons
- contribution margin
- discount rate
- equilibrium displacement form
- expectations
- land rent
- intensity rent
- land rent theory
- location rent
- lease price
- ownership rights
- path dependency
- purchase price
- quality rent
- rent
- residual income
- rights of disposal
- the tragedy of the commons
- use rights

References

Bachmann G (2014) Abgestimmte Strategie für die Böden fehlt. Ernährungsdienst Agrarzeitung, Vol. 8, August 2014.

BLE (Bundesanstalt für Landwirtschaft und Ernährung) (annual) Statistik über die praktische Berufsbildung in der Landwirtschaft der Bundesrepublik Deutschland. BLE, Bonn.

BMEL (Bundesministerium für Ernährung und Landwirtschaft) (annual) Statistik der Fachschulen in der Land- und Forstwirtschaft und in der ländlichen Hauswirtschaft. BMEL, Berlin.

Eurostat (2018) Land prices vary considerably between and within Member States. Eurostat Newsrelease 48/2018. Eurostat, Luxembourg.

https://ec.europa.eu/eurostat/documents/2995521/8756523/5-21032018-AP-EN.pdf/b1d0ffd3-f75b-40cc-b53f-f22f68d541df. Accessed on November 3, 2021.

Hardin G (1968) Tragedy of the Commons. Science 162: 1243-1248.

Ivanic M and Martin W (2014) Short- and Long-Run Impacts of Food Price Changes on Poverty. World Bank Policy Research Working Paper No. 7011, World Bank Development Research Group, Washington D.C.

Lence SH and Miller DJ (1999) Transaction Costs and the Present Value Model of Farmland: Iowa, 1990-1999. American Journal of Agricultural Economics 81: 257-272.

Niehans J (1966) Eine vernachlässigte Beziehung zwischen Bodenpreis, Wirtschaftswachstum und Kapitalzins. Schweizerische Zeitschrift für Volkswirtschaft und Statistik 102: 1-10.

Ricardo D (1817) Principles of Political Economy and Taxation. Introduction by Donald Winch. J.M.Dent. London.

Schulze E (1999) Zur Entwicklung von Boden- und Pachtmärkten in mittel- und osteuropäischen Ländern. Presentation at the 13th Mittel- und Osteuropäischem Seminar, IAMO, Halle. http://www.uni-kiel.de/agrarmarketing/Gewisola99/posterschulze.pdf. Accessed November 3, 2021.

Statistisches Bundesamt (annual) Statistisches Jahrbuch. Statistisches Bundesamt, Wiesbaden.

Střeleček F, Lososova J and Zdeněk R (2011) Farm land rent in the European Union. Acta Universitatis Agriculturae et Silviculturae Mendelianae Brunensis 59: 309-318.

von Thünen JH (1910) Der isolierte Staat in Beziehung auf Landwirtschaft und Nationalökonomie. Gustav Fischer Verlag, Jena. New edition based on the 1850 original.

Weersink A, Clark S, Turvey CG and Sarker R (1999) The Effect of Agricultural Policy on Farmland Values. Land Economics 75: 425-439.

Exercises

a. In the agricultural economic literature, it is frequently claimed that agricultural price support ultimately leads to increased prices for agricultural land, i.e. that landowners and not necessarily farmers are the main beneficiaries of support. Discuss this assertion. What assumptions about the nature of the supply of the individual factors of production underlie this assertion? How can institutional factors affect how much landowners benefit from price support?

b. Explain the effect on land prices of restrictions on the ownership of farm land by non-farmers and/or foreign citizens.

c. Assume neoclassical conditions (perfect information, perfect factor mobility, and homogeneous land) and explain why mandatory set-aside will have no influence on land prices. Why will it have an influence on land prices in reality?

d. Assume neoclassical conditions and explain why a direct payment that is coupled to production will be completely passed on to landowners in the form of increased land prices. Why will the transfer to landowners be less than complete in reality?

e. Discuss the following statement by Bachmann (2014, p. 3, own translation): "An asymmetric purchase of arable land occurs when prices are paid that are several times higher than the amount that could be refinanced using proceeds from agricultural production on the land".

f. Using marginal productivity theory, explain why smaller farms should be willing to pay higher lease and purchase prices for agricultural land than larger farms. Explain why smaller farms are not willing to pay higher lease and purchase prices in reality, despite this theoretical expectation.

g. In 1993, the so-called MacSharry reform of EU's Common Agricultural Policy was implemented. Among other things, this reform reduced price support for cereals and compensated farmers for the resulting loss of income through direct payments tied to land use. What effect do you think these changes had on the implicit discount rate discussed in section 3.4, and depicted in Figure 3.6?

h. Assume that the state provides farmers with incentive payments for unlimited set-aside. Assume further that the per hectare payments are higher than the lease prices that were paid for land before the policy was implemented. What effect will this measure have on land use?

CHAPTER FOUR

SPECIFIC CHARACTERISTICS OF AGRICULTURAL LABOUR MARKETS

ULRICH KOESTER AND
STEPHAN VON CRAMON–TAUBADEL

4.1. Introduction and learning objectives

Employment and the incomes earned on agricultural labour markets have a major influence on agricultural policy in most if not all countries. Under the **Agricultural Act of 1955**, which remains in force today, the German government is tasked with using general economic and agricultural policy instruments to ensure that the social situation of people working in agriculture is aligned with that of comparable occupational groups. The Agricultural Act refers to "economic disadvantages" vis-à-vis other sectors that need to be offset by means of policy measures.[1] Implicit in these provisions is the assumption that without state intervention, the market mechanism alone will not lead to sufficient remuneration of workers in agriculture.

EU agricultural policy is based on similar considerations. In the original **Treaty of Rome** signed in 1957, the first two paragraphs of Article 39 state:

> "1. The objectives of the common agricultural policy shall be:
>
> (a) to increase agricultural productivity by promoting technical progress and by ensuring the rational development of agricultural production and optimum utilisation of the factors of production, in particular labour;

---

[1] Federal Government of Germany (1955, para. 1).

(b) thus to ensure a fair standard of living for the agricultural community, in particular by increasing the individual earnings of persons engaged in agriculture" (EU Publications Office, 2021).

Except for a renumbering, Article 39 has survived all subsequent modifications of the EU treaties completely unchanged.

Since incomes in agriculture are obviously of great political importance, it is worth taking a closer look at the factors that determine them. Therefore, in this chapter we will:

- explain how prices (wages) on agricultural labour markets are formed under standard neoclassical conditions,
- discuss which special characteristics of agricultural markets influence price formation on agricultural labour markets,
- analyse how agricultural labour markets are influenced by selected institutions, including agricultural policy measures.

In the first part of this chapter, we will analyse what level of remuneration of agricultural labour can be expected in the absence of state intervention. We will begin with the simplest possible case of a closed economy with a relatively small agricultural sector and neoclassical assumptions, such as profit maximisation, perfect competition and no transaction costs. In subsequent sections we will then relax some of these assumptions to produce a more nuanced and realistic picture of agricultural labour markets.

In particular, we will focus on the importance of two types of institutions. First, labour is a factor of production in agriculture, but it is not an inanimate physical object like a hectare of land or a barn, it is composed of individuals. We will therefore consider how traditional types of behaviour by farmers (first-order institutions according to Williamson's (2000) scheme) affect price formation on agricultural labour markets. Second, we will discuss the influence of formal laws and policies (second-order institutions according to Williamson) on agricultural labour markets.[2]

[2] Williamson's (2000) classification of institutions is discussed in detail in Chapter 1.

4.2. Price formation on agricultural labour markets under neoclassical conditions: basic assumptions

We begin by making the following assumptions:

a) The prices of all agricultural products and production factors are determined on perfect markets. This means that all market participants:
   i. are profit or utility maximisers;
   ii. have independent utility functions;
   iii. have no personal, material or time preferences; and
   iv. have perfect information.

b) Production and utility functions are linearly homogeneous and twice differentiable. Accordingly, the marginal productivity of a factor of production falls with increasing input of that factor, all other things being equal. Similarly, the marginal utilities of consumption (and leisure time) decrease with increased consumption (and leisure time), all other things being equal.

c) Players can react immediately to any changes in the market data without having to consider transaction costs.

d) All outputs and factors of production are homogeneous; it follows that labour supply and demand are infinitely divisible, and that the unit of labour provided by one worker can be substituted by a unit from any other worker. Furthermore, the question who owns a specific factor of production, especially land, has no influence on its use or its price.

e) Workers are fully mobile.

f) There is no state intervention in prices or quantities on the labour market. It follows that the marginal value product of labour equals its net remuneration. Thus, under full employment the remuneration of labour equals its opportunity costs.

g) All prices are determined under perfect competition. Market participants have no market power on any markets.

4.3. Self-employment in agriculture under neoclassical conditions

Farmers in market economies work largely independently as owners or tenants of agricultural holdings. In the following, we illustrate the optimal use of labour under these conditions. We assume a one-period model in which the farmer chooses between **on-farm work** and leisure. On-farm self-employment is the only way in which the farmer can earn income. The additional options of off-farm work and part-time farming will be considered later in this chapter.

Assume that the farmer has the following utility function:

$$U = U(Y, F) \qquad (1)$$

where

U = utility,

Y = real income, and

F = leisure time.

Since we consider a one-period model, there are no savings; all income (Y) is thus spent on the purchase of goods and services for consumption. We assume that the farmer aims to maximise utility (U), and that consumption and leisure time are substitutes. This substitutive relationship is reflected in the shape of the indifference curve I_0 in Figure 4.1, which is convex to the origin.[3] In practical terms, this means that the farmer is prepared to forego a relatively large amount of income in order to enjoy the first hour of leisure time, but progressively less income for each additional hour of leisure.

[3] The convexity of the indifference curve is guaranteed by the assumed strict quasi-concavity of the utility function in equation (1) – see Chiang (1974, pp. 391-397).

Figure 4.1: The optimal choice of working/leisure time and real income for a self-employed farmer

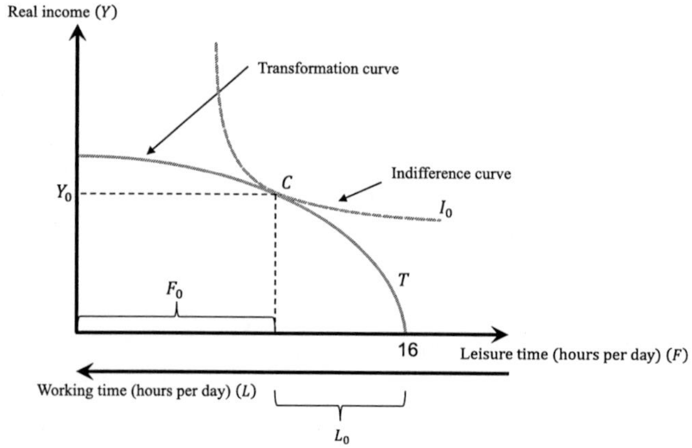

Source: Own depiction.

We next assume that income earned is the following function of the number of hours (L) worked:

$$Y = Y(L) \tag{2}$$

where

L = labour input, and

$\frac{\partial Y}{\partial L} > 0$ and $\frac{\partial^2 Y}{\partial L^2} < 0$.

The signs of these derivatives ensure that the marginal productivity of labour is positive but falls with the number of hours worked. In addition, the following daily time constraint applies for each farmer:

$$L + F + X = 24 \tag{3}$$

i.e., the number of hours worked (L), plus the hours of leisure time (F), plus an allowance for food and rest (X) must add up to the 24 hours in a day. Hence, labour input is given by:

$$L = 24 - F - X. \tag{4}$$

A function that reflects these characteristics and trade-offs is the transformation curve T in Figure 4.1. Starting at 16 hours of leisure time ($L = 0$) and thus no income, it increases but at a decreasing rate for each hour of leisure that is exchanged for labour and thus income.

The farmer's optimal combination of leisure (F_0), on-farm work (L_0) and income (Y_0) occurs where the indifference curve is tangent to the transformation curve. This is point C in Figure 4.1. In C, the slope of the transformation curve is equal to the slope of the indifference curve. The slope of the indifference curve can be determined by setting the total differential of equation (1) to zero:

$$dU = \frac{\partial U}{\partial Y} dY + \frac{\partial U}{\partial F} dF = 0 \qquad (5)$$

and

$$\frac{\frac{\partial U}{\partial F}}{\frac{\partial U}{\partial Y}} = -\frac{dY}{dF} \qquad (6)$$

The slope of the transformation curve is also $-dY/dF$.[4] In C, the farmer has chosen a combination of income and leisure from the objectively feasible set of combinations (given by the transformation curve) that maximises his/her subjective utility (represented by the indifference curve). For each point that deviates from C, the higher (lower) in income that would be possible through more (less) work and therefore less (more) leisure time is rated worse by the farmer than the income earned in point C.

Implicitly, the farmer is weighing the following variables when choosing the optimal amount of on-farm work:

- the marginal utility of income,
- the marginal utility of leisure, and
- the marginal monetary return on labour.

[4] The slope of the transformation curve in equation (2) is $\frac{dY}{dL}$. Since, from equation (4), $dL = -dF$, we can conclude that $\frac{dY}{dL} = -\frac{dY}{dF}$.

Hence, the farmer's chosen optimum will change if:

- the farmer's preference structure changes. Preferences for income and leisure time can change with age, for example, or when the farmer starts a family. As a result, individuals with different preferences will work different amounts of time;

- the transformation curve shifts. This can happen, for example, due to technological advances that increase productivity and thus the monetary yield of an hour of labour.

In this simple case, economic optimum for society as a whole is attained when all farmers choose their individual optima as outlined above. Other members of society are neither positively nor negatively affected by an individual farmer's variation in labour input, since a one-period model without savings has been assumed, i.e. the farmer generates income through production that is spent entirely on goods consumed by that farmer.

In the next section we will consider the possibility of off-farm employment. One important consequence of the presentation so far is that choice between on farm and off-farm employment depends on utility and not solely on income. On-farm employment will be chosen if off-farm employment leads to a lower level of utility. This can be the case even if off-farm employment generates a higher income, if it is not possible to achieve an optimal combination of real income and leisure time in off-farm employment.

4.4. Off-farm employment with free choice of working hours

At any given time, some farmers will be considering switching from on-farm to **off-farm employment**. We will first analyse this decision under the assumption that the individual (who is then no longer a farmer) is free to choose any combination of leisure and off-farm employment that he/she desires.

The decision is illustrated in Figure 4.2. The transformation curve is a straight line with a slope (the tangent of the angle α) that equals the hourly wage rate. Given the preferences reflected in the indifference curve I_0, the individual will supply L_0 hours of labour and enjoy F_0 hours of leisure.

However, it is not necessarily the case that exactly the L_0 hours of labour that the individual wishes to supply will also be demanded by employers at the given wage rate. Labour market regulations and the results of collective bargaining agreements between employers and unions can also constrain an individual's ability to achieve the optimum depicted in Figure 4.2, for example by imposing a fixed number of working hours per week. Thus, off-farm employment differs from self-employment on the farm in that individuals are no longer able to freely choose how many hours they work.

Figure 4.2: The optimal choice of working time and real income for off-farm employment

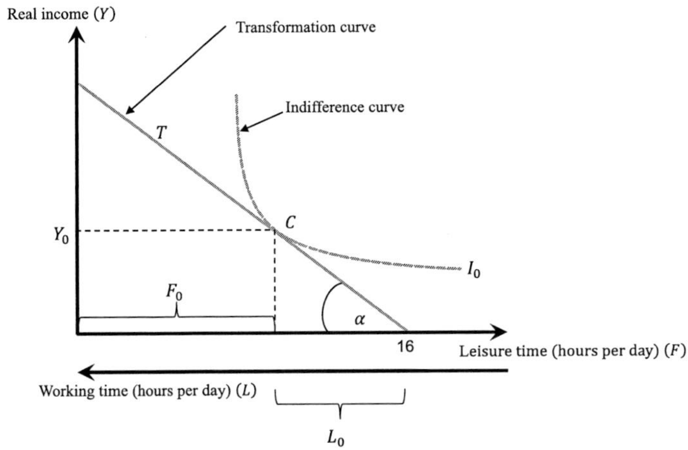

Source: Own depiction.

Indeed, since individuals have different preferences and skills, it can be assumed that the individual optimum in Figure 4.2 will only be achieved in exceptional cases. Most individuals in society will want to supply either too much (marginal value product < wage) or too little (marginal value product > wage) labour and thus find themselves in a constrained optimum.

4.5. Part-time farming with free choice of working hours

So far, we have considered on-farm and off-farm employment as mutually exclusive options. However, many farmers can also choose a combination of on-farm self-employment and off-farm wage labour. This situation is illustrated with the help of Figure 4.3, which combines element of Figures 4.1 and 4.2.

Figure 4.3: The optimal combination of on-farm and off-farm employment

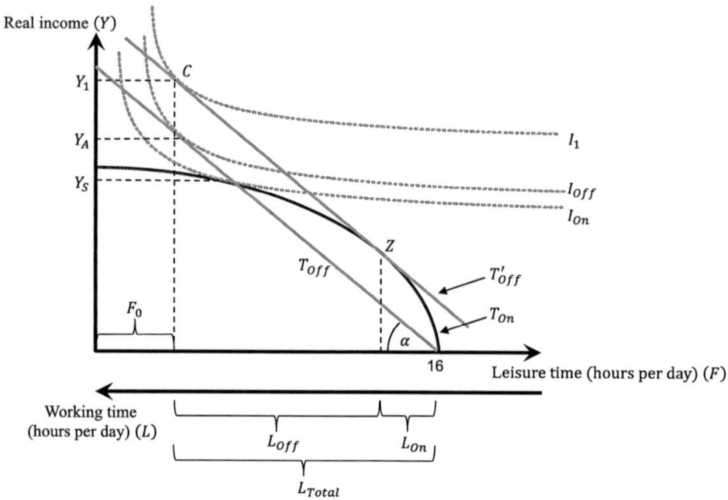

Source: Own depiction

For on-farm self-employment we assume the same production function as above (equation 2), which is characterised by $\partial Y/\partial L > 0$ and $\partial^2 Y/\partial L^2 < 0$, and which is labelled T_{On} in Figure 4.3. A constant wage rate, corresponding to the tangent of the angle α, applies to off-farm employment, and leads to the transformation curve labelled T_{Off}. The optimal division of working time between on-farm and off-farm employment is achieved if the marginal income earned from the last hour of work is the same in both occupations. Otherwise, the individual could increase his/her income by shifting working time between on-farm and off-farm employment without having to forego leisure time. We depict this geometrically in Figure 4.3 by shifting the transformation curve for off-farm employment parallel upwards until we obtain T'_{Off}, which is tangent to T'_{Off} at point Z. To the left of Z, the slope $\partial Y/\partial L$ of T'_{Off} (the wage rate) is greater than the slope of T_{On}, i.e. the individual could increase his/her income by working less on the farm, and more off of it. To the right of Z the opposite holds; the marginal income from an hour of on-farm work is greater than the wage rate.

In Figure 4.3 the individual reaches point C on the indifference curve I_1 by working L_{Total} hours altogether; L_{Off} as off-farm wage labour, and L_{On} as on-farm self-employment. In pure on-farm (off-farm) employment the individual could only attain the lower level of utility associated with indifference curve I_{On} (I_{Off}).

The analysis that we have presented here demonstrates that even under the assumptions of a simple neoclassical model, a wide variety of organisational forms for agricultural holdings are possible in a market economy. Holdings can be organised as **full-time or as part-time** family farms, with and without hired labour. This variety emerges because the shape of the transformation curve T_{On} will vary across different farms (size, location, past investments) and individuals (training, management skills). Similarly, the slope of the transformation curve T_{Off} will vary between individuals – some farmers may be able to earn higher wages off-farm than others. Finally, different individuals will have different preferences for income and leisure time, and for agricultural vs. non-agricultural work. As a result, a multitude of different constellations and optimal solutions are possible in Figure 4.3, and observed in reality.

Note that the economic welfare of society as a whole is maximised if individuals each chose their optimal combinations of on-farm and off-farm employment as outlined above. Under the assumptions that we have made, this individual optimising behaviour does not give rise to market failure, and there is therefore no need for government intervention on agricultural labour markets. Given these assumptions, the following conditions will hold on the labour market:

1. The individual remuneration per hour will equal the marginal value product of work, and it will be the same across all possible types of employment; and

2. Each individual will work a different number of hours.

However, some of the assumptions that we made above are unrealistic. In the following sections we therefore explore the consequences of relaxing them.

4.6. The importance of transaction costs for the agricultural labour market

Self-employed farmers cannot switch without friction to off-farm occupations. By friction we mean that the switch is associated with sometimes considerable **transaction costs**. In some cases, the farmer might be able to continue to reside at home but nevertheless have to bear the monetary and opportunity costs of commuting to work. Even if all other factors are complete mobile, the farmer has to take the costs of commuting into account when considering the option of off-farm employment. These costs will reduce the angle α in Figures 4.2 and 4.3 and, all other things being equal, shift the optimal solution towards more on-farm and less off-farm employment, and towards more full-time and less part-time farming. The reduction in α will vary from farm to farm depending on the distance to the off-farm employment opportunity, infrastructure quality and congestion.

Transaction costs in the labour market include the risk of unemployment. Self-employed farmers cannot be dismissed. Unlike employees outside of agriculture, they therefore do not need to take the risk of unemployment into account. Hence, even if less income is earned on-farm than could be earned with the same number of hours off-farm, it could be rational to continue to work on-farm. The risk of unemployment also reduces the angle α in Figures 4.2 and 4.3.

The neoclassical model that we have used here assumes that all factors are remunerated according to their marginal value products. We therefore did not consider the possibility that farmers will also take income from land and agricultural fixed capital into account when choosing their optimal amounts and allocations of labour. For example, farmers might earn higher returns on land and capital by managing their farms themselves rather than selling or leasing them, because of transaction costs on land markets (see Chapter 3) and on markets for fixed assets. Under these conditions, they must consider that the choice between on-farm and off-farm employment also affects a third source of income, from the ownership of land and fixed capital. If shifting to off-farm work leads to lower returns on land and capital, then, again, the angle α in Figures 4.2 and 4.3 will be reduced, with the effects discussed above.

The effects of limits on working hours

As discussed above, minimum or maximum working times established by law or in collective bargaining agreements lead to sub-optimal working times for individual employees. If L_{off} in Figure 4.3 cannot be freely chosen but is rather fixed, it is unlikely that the optimum point C will be attained. Of course, there may be compelling economic and social reasons for limiting daily or weekly working hours.

Farms that produce seasonal and especially perishable horticultural products are particularly affected by such limits. Food waste will generally be higher if working hours are limited rather than flexible during harvest periods, when the optimal timing of labour input depends on specific day-to-day weather conditions and is correspondingly difficult to plan in advance. Farms that hire wage labour will be more affected by such limits than farms which rely exclusively on family labour even during harvest periods. It follows that legal or negotiated limits on working hours will affect the competitiveness of farms with highly seasonal production and seasonal labour. For such farms, the limits will increase the economic incentives to replace labour by mechanisation.

The effect of farm size and organisation

Agricultural products are produced using very different technologies. Some farms are highly labour-intensive, others highly capital-intensive. If all farms operated with the same linear-homogeneous production function, we would expect that smaller holdings that are highly labour-intensive would generate the highest land rents and therefore be most competitive on land lease and purchase markets. These smaller holdings would therefore grow, which would increase the marginal productivity of labour and labour earnings.

However, it is generally observed that smaller farms are not more but rather less competitive on the land market than large farms. We can only conclude that production functions vary between farms and that they are often characterised by increasing rather than constant returns to scale.

In addition, agricultural enterprises in the western industrialised countries are mainly family farms, defined as farms on which all or most of the means of production are family property and the farm manager and her/his family members do most of the work. In Germany, a **full-time farm** is defined as farm from which the manager and family members earn more than 50 per cent of their total income from agricultural work. In contrast, **part-time farms** generate less than 50 per cent of their income from agricultural activity. The various factors that affect the optimal combination of on-farm and off-farm income, and thus whether a farm is full- or part-time were discussed above. If the land area available to a farm is small, it may be difficult to employ the available family labour in a manner that generates as much income as could be generated off-farm.

The heterogeneity of labour

Labour would be homogeneous if there were no professional, personal and geographical differences between the workers themselves or between the types of labour that are demanded by employers. In the simple model above, we assumed that labour is homogeneous and that individuals have no preferences or special aptitudes for specific occupations. We relax these assumptions in the following.

Agricultural workers, especially farm managers, have several specific qualifications. Farm managers must have economic and technical knowledge, be willing to take decisions, and be prepared to work in a manner that is often physically and mentally far more demanding than what is expected of employees who work under the conditions set out in collective bargaining agreements. It is therefore understandable that farm managers expect to earn higher incomes than typical employees.

However, under market conditions these expectations are not always fulfilled. Incomes in agriculture will be low especially if farmers do not switch to alterative, off-farm employment even though they feel that their incomes are too low. Switching to off-farm employment occurs only slowly; labour in agriculture is not perfectly mobile. As a rule, a farmer will not be able to find off-farm employment that fully remunerates all of his/her **sector-specific qualifications**, for example special skills in animal husbandry or crop production. When this is the case, farmers will stay in agriculture even though their incomes do not meet expectations and lag behind those in other sectors. As a result, an **income disparity** might arise, defined as a situation in which farmers' incomes are lower than the incomes of comparable occupational groups.

The importance of personal preferences

When young people make career decisions, they consider expected income, but other factors as well. Figure 4.4 shows that apprentices with the same level of schooling earn very different amounts in different occupations. Starting salaries and salary progressions for university graduates also vary greatly depending on occupation. These salary differences cannot be explained by differences in formal education alone. Since salaries and wages are prices for the factor labour, price differences across occupations are presumably due to differences in supply and demand. If employees had no personal preferences for specific occupations, they could move freely from one occupation to another. In this case, the labour supply curve, from the perspective of individual employers, would be perfectly elastic and there would be no differences in wages/salaries across occupations. Since we observe large and persistant differences, it must be the case that individuals prefer some occupations more than others, and are willing to accept less income than might otherwise be possible in a less-preferred occupation.

Personal preferences are likely to be of particular importance for those employed in agriculture, especially where family farms predominate. Owners and heirs often see it as their responsibility to preserve the family farm for future generations. Farmers in Germany and other countries are often embedded in local institutions such as voluntary fire brigades and other village associations that provide a sense of identity and influence how leisure time is spent. Most farmers, therefore, are not pure profit maximisers.

The importance of imperfect information and uncertainty for agricultural labour markets

If all farmers had full information about their lifetime income possibilities when they made career decisions, income differences would only be based on differences in individual talents and preferences. However, since no one can accurately predict the future, at least some individual decisions to pursue specific careers will likely turn out to be suboptimal *ex post*. The fact that there is a net movement of employees out of agriculture in most market economies supports this conjecture.

The decision-making problem of employees in agriculture can be illustrated using Figure 4.5. We assume that the career choice is made at time t_0. At t_0, an individual knows that on-farm incomes are lower than off-farm income; however, the individual is willing to accept the income disparity of $Y_O^{Off} - Y_O^{On}$ because he/she prefers to work in agriculture. Hence, $Y_O^{Off} - Y_O^{On}$ provides a monetary evaluation of the individual's preference for on-farm compared with off-farm work. At t_0, the income disparity is not expected to increase over time, so the individual expects that the same disparity will still exist at time t_n and chooses to become a farmer.

Figure 4.4: Monthly earnings by apprentices in selected occupations in West and East Germany (2020, in €)

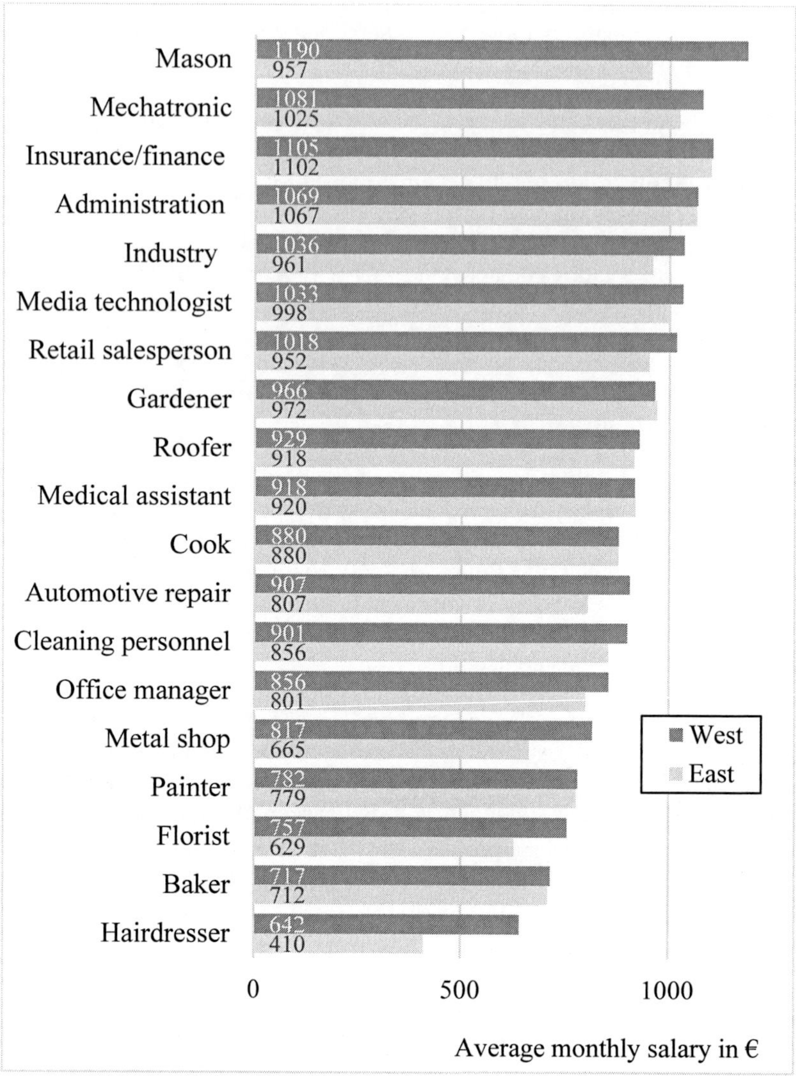

Source: Own presentation with data from Bundesinstitut für Berufsausbildung (2021).

However, at time t_n it turns out that the income disparity has grown. On-farm income has increased to Y_1^{On}, but off-farm income has increased more, to Y_1^{Off}. If the individual's preference for on-farm work has not increased as much as the income disparity, then he/she might consider leaving agriculture. However, when t_n arrives, Y_1^{Off} might not be an accurate measure of the individual's opportunity costs. During the years spent on the farm between t_0 and t_n, the individual has acquired specific skills which generate returns in agriculture, but little or no returns in other sectors. While the individual could choose between Y_0^{On} and Y_0^{Off} at t_0, at t_n he/she can only choose between Y_1^{On} and some income below Y_1^{Off} that is earned by less-qualified workers. Under these circumstances the individual might therefore decide to remain in agriculture even though the income disparity vis-à-vis similarly qualified workers in other sectors has grown.

Gisser and Davila's (1998) comparison of agricultural and non-agricultural wages in the USA is illustrative in this respect. The authors found that wages in agriculture were on average 27.1% lower than wages outside of agriculture in nominal terms. When differences in the cost of living between rural and urban areas were accounted for, this nominal difference reduced to a real (purchasing-power) difference of only 13.5%. However, when Gisser and Davila divided their sample into two groups according to age (under and over 35 years of age), the real wage disparity in the under-35 group was on average only 1.2% (and not statistically significant), whereas the wage disparity in the above-35 group was 21.4%. This suggests that younger people employed in agriculture can switch to off-farm employment more easily than older people, or they have recently chosen agriculture after carefully comparing the options. This higher mobility leads to an almost complete parity between agricultural and non-agricultural wages among younger people. For older people employed in agriculture, switching to off-farm employment is associated with higher transaction costs and they are therefore willing to accept increasing wage disparities over time.

Unexpected developments in sectoral wages influence the movement of labour between sectors. Workers can move from agriculture to other sectors due to pull or pressure effects. **Pull effects** occur when higher-paid opportunities arise in another sector. Even if incomes in agriculture have risen more than expected since employment began, if they have risen even more in other sectors, this might pull labour out of agriculture. Hence, movements of labour out of agriculture are not always the result of low incomes in agriculture.

Figure 4.5: The development of on-farm and off-farm incomes over time (schematic)

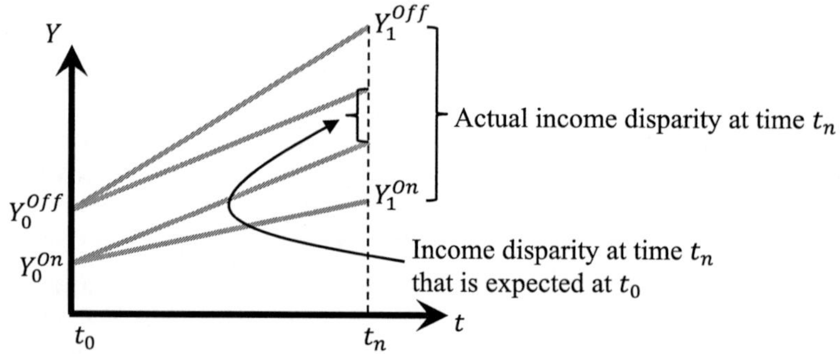

Y_0^{Off} Off-farm income at time t_0
Y_0^{O} On-farm income at time t_0

Source: Own depiction.

Push effects occur when individuals in agriculture earn incomes that are not sufficient for maintaining a standard of living that meets their subjective expectations. When self-employed farmers decide whether to continue farming or to leave agriculture, they do not only compare their agricultural labour income with potential off-farm income. Instead, they also have the option of drawing down on farm equity. For example, German farm accounting data show that in 2018/19 the farms in the bottom third of the profitability distribution realised average net reductions in farm equity of 204 €/hectare (BMEL 2020, table annex, p. 34).[5] Rather than reinvesting to maintain the value of their farms' assets such as machinery and buildings, these farmers allowed the value of their assets to decline. These farmers could have earned higher incomes by renting out their land, selling their farm assets, and switching to off-farm employment.[6] Instead, by continuing to manage loss-making farms, these farmers revealed their preferences for remaining farmers over maximising income. Essentially, the ability to withdraw from farm equity allowed them to resist the temptation of higher

---

[5] In the same year, the farms in the top one-third of the profitability distribution realised net equity gains of 335 €/hectare.

[6] This statement is only true if the farms had no other sources of income beside agriculture. Modern agricultural enterprise structures are often complex. It could be, for example, that some of these farms charged their private expenditures against farm operations, leading to net equity losses for the farm, while other branches of the family enterprise (for example a biogas fermenter or wind power generator) realised profits and equity gains.

incomes outside of agriculture. Obviously, if a substantial number of farmers behave in this manner, average labour incomes in agriculture will lag behind those in other sectors.

Following reunification in Germany, most of those employed in agriculture in the new Eastern provinces (Länder) did not have the same options as self-employed family farm operators in the Western Länder. These employees were hired labour on large collective farms who had no stakes in farm equity. Private cultivation of agricultural land in the former GDR was only possible on small household plots. The transition from state-planned agriculture with collective ownership led to a drastic reduction in the amount of labour input into agriculture (see Figure 1.3 in Chapter 1). Workers in agriculture were under strong pressure to leave their jobs, even though the alternative to agricultural employment was very often only unemployment.

These considerations lead to a simple conclusion: even if individuals are fully informed at the time they make career choices, income disparities between sector can nevertheless emerge over time. Information on current wages and incomes is available to individuals when they decide what training to acquire or what to study in preparation for a career, but future wages and incomes are a matter of expectations, which can prove to be false.

4.7. The significance of the business cycle for wages in agriculture

Business cycles are cyclical patterns of economic growth followed by contraction. Sectors are affected differently by these cycles, for example because the income elasticity of demand for goods and services differs across sectors. As a result, sectors are subjected to different pressures and adjustment needs in the course of a business cycle. In the following, we will analyse the effects on agriculture of a slowdown or contraction in the economy as a whole.

Initially, we might expect that agriculture will be less negatively affected by an economic slowdown than other sectors because the demand for food as a whole is income inelastic in industrialised countries. In a slowdown, therefore, the demand curve for agricultural goods will shift towards the origin, but it will shift less than the demand for other goods. However, the effect of an economic slowdown on prices and incomes is also influenced by the price elasticity of demand, the price elasticity of supply and the shifts in the supply curve.

In the following we use a simple market model to study the interaction between these various factors. To begin, we define four equations:

Demand function: $Q^D = Q^D(Y, P)$ (7)

Supply function: $Q^S = Q^s(P, T)$ (8)

Market equilibrium condition: $Q^D = Q^s$ (9)

Per capita income in agriculture: $Y^L = \frac{P * Q^S - K}{L}$. (10)

In equation (7) through (10):

Q^D = the quantity demanded,

Q^S = the quantity supplied,

Y = national income,

P = the market price,

T = the available technology,

Y^L = per capita income in agriculture,

L = the number of workers in agriculture, and

K = the cost of other inputs in agriculture.

First, we totally differentiate equations (7) and (8), which produces

$$dQ^D = \frac{\partial Q^D}{\partial Y} dY + \frac{\partial Q^D}{\partial P} dP \quad (11)$$

and

$$dQ^S = \frac{\partial Q^S}{\partial T} dT + \frac{\partial Q^S}{\partial P} dP. \quad (12)$$

Next, we divide equations (11) and (12) by Q^D and Q^S, respectively, and make several additions to obtain the equilibrium displacement forms of the demand and supply equations:[7]

$$\frac{dQ^D}{Q^D} = \frac{\partial Q^D}{\partial Y}\frac{Y}{Q^D}\frac{dY}{Y} + \frac{\partial Q^D}{\partial P}\frac{P}{Q^D}\frac{dP}{P} \rightarrow \frac{dQ^D}{Q^D} = \eta\frac{dY}{Y} + \varepsilon^D\frac{dP}{P} \quad (13)$$

and

$$\frac{dQ^S}{Q^S} = \frac{\partial Q^S}{\partial T}\frac{T}{Q^S}\frac{dT}{T} + \frac{\partial Q^S}{\partial P}\frac{P}{Q^S}\frac{dP}{P} \rightarrow \frac{dQ^S}{Q^S} = \frac{dT}{T} + \varepsilon^S\frac{dP}{P} \quad (14)$$

where

η = income elasticity of demand,

ε^D = price elasticity of demand, and

ε^S = price elasticity of supply.[8]

From equation (9) we know that $\frac{dQ^D}{Q^D} = \frac{dQ^S}{Q^S}$. We can therefore equate equations (13) and (14) to obtain:

$$\eta\frac{dY}{Y} + \varepsilon^D\frac{dP}{P} = \frac{dT}{T} + \varepsilon^S\frac{dP}{P}, \quad (15)$$

which can be rearranged to the following expression for the proportional change in the price level

$$\frac{dP}{P} = \frac{1}{\varepsilon^S - \varepsilon^D}\left(\eta\frac{dY}{Y} - \frac{dT}{T}\right). \quad (16)$$

According to equation (16), the effect of income changes on agricultural prices depends on the expression $\frac{\eta}{\varepsilon^S - \varepsilon^D}$. The denominator $(\varepsilon^S - \varepsilon^D)$ will be positive for normal supply and demand reactions, and the income elasticity of demand for food is also positive. Therefore, we can conclude that an

---

[7] See equations (12) to (16) in Chapter 3 for a more detailed explanation of the steps in this derivation.

[8] The technology elasticity of supply $\frac{\partial Q^S}{\partial T}\frac{T}{Q^S}$ equals 1 by definition, in other words 1% technological progress shifts the supply curve 1% to the right.

economic slowdown that reduces income will also reduce food prices. This reduction in prices will be small as

η becomes smaller,

ε^S becomes larger, and

the absolute value of ε^D becomes larger.

If supply is perfectly price elastic ($\varepsilon^S = \infty$), then agricultural prices will not respond at all to an economic slowdown, but agricultural supply is not perfectly price elastic, especially not in the short run. η is indeed small for agricultural products, which suggests that the price response $\frac{dP}{P}$ will also be small. However, ε^S and ε^D are also relatively small, which points to a larger influence of business cycles on agricultural prices.

In addition, technical change, which continues during an economic slowdown, also has the effect of reducing prices in equation (16). Enterprises in other sectors which are operating below capacity in an economic slowdown will not invest in expansion but rather seek to reduce production and adopt cost-saving technologies. Farms, however, will be comparatively eager to adopt new technologies that increase output. Enterprises in other sectors can lay off workers to reduce costs in an economic slowdown. However, this is not an option for a self-employed farmer unless he/she can find alternative employment, which is especially unlikely during an economic slowdown. This suggests that while the rate of technical change will fall and the supply curve might even shift to the left in other sectors during an economic slowdown, technical change will continue unabated and the supply curve will shift to the right in agriculture.

Further manipulations of the model introduced above, which are presented in Appendix 4.1 at the end of this chapter, lead to the following equation for the proportional change in per capita income:

$$\frac{dY^L}{Y^L} = \frac{R}{V}\left[\frac{dY}{Y}\left(\frac{\eta(1+\varepsilon^S)}{\varepsilon^S - \varepsilon^D}\right) - \frac{dT}{T}\left(\frac{(1+\varepsilon^D)}{\varepsilon^S - \varepsilon^D}\right)\right] - \frac{dK * K}{K * V} - \frac{dL}{L} \quad (17)$$

where

$R = (P * Q^S)$ is the revenue from sale of agricultural products, and

$V = Y^L * L = (P * Q^S) - K$ is the total value added in agriculture.

Equation (17) indicates that in an economic slowdown, per capita incomes will fall more strongly in percentage terms than agricultural price. The term in square brackets in equation (17) is similar to the proportional price change in equation (16), but it is enhanced by the multiplier, $\frac{R}{V}$. The change in per capital income in equation (17) also depends on the rate of decline in the agricultural labour force, $\frac{dL}{L}$. This rate will be lower in an economic slowdown that otherwise, which puts additional pressure on per-capita incomes in agriculture. This means that incomes in agriculture are flexible downwards in an economic slowdown – even if agricultural output prices are administered and remain unchanged. While other sectors can react by laying off employees, employment in agriculture sometimes even increases during an economic slowdown in some countries as agriculture serves as an employer of last resort. In a sense, other sectors at least partially externalize the effects of the economic slowdown be releasing labour which is then supported by social safety nets (e.g. unemployment insurance) or agriculture.

Agriculture's contribution to cushioning the employment effects of an economic slowdown is helpful in the short term, but problematic in the medium and long term. Every economic slowdown has structural effects on agriculture and thus changes the development of productivity in the sector and the costs of the agricultural policy interventions. If less efficient farms do not cease production, output and employment in agriculture might even increase in an economic downturn, and structural change might slow down. This can lead to increased economic costs in the future. Stepping up protectionist measures in an effort to support incomes in agriculture during an economic downturn may appear to be a sensible policy that has positive distribution effects and reduces unemployment. In the long run, however, such measures will result in pent-up structural change, greater income disparities, **hidden unemployment** and increasing future "**X inefficiency**" in agriculture (Leibenstein 1966).[9]

---

[9] In a controversial paper published in 1966, Liebenstein argued that in the absence of strong pressure from competition, most firms will not use the resources at their disposal efficiently, leading to what he termed X-inefficiency. Essentially, Liebenstein argued that firms do not minimise costs unless forced to do so by competition.

4.8. The effects of agricultural policy on labour earnings in agriculture

A variety of policy measures in the EU are aimed at increasing the labour earnings in agriculture. Policy makers in Germany and EU justify these measures by referring to laws such as the Agricultural Act of 1955 and the Treaty of Rome that we cited at the beginning of this chapter. In the following section, we will first consider whether policy makers have sufficient information to design targeted measures to support labour earnings in agriculture. We will then discuss what factors must be considered when designing such support measures. We end the chapter with a brief review of the effects of selected EU and national policies.

4.8.1. Information requirements for targeted measures to support labour earnings in agriculture

State intervention in agricultural labour markets can be justified for allocative reasons (i.e. because it improves resource use and boosts total economic output) or for distributional reasons (i.e. because it increases equity). Laws such as the Agricultural Act of 1955 and the Treaty of Rome refer to both of these justifications. However, framework laws are no guarantee for targeted and efficient policies. A policy can be considered targeted if it achieves its stated goal while minimising side effects. A policy is efficient if it achieves its stated goal at the lowest possible economic cost.

The EU Commission publishes statistics that show how the average agricultural incomes of full-time agricultural holdings have developed over time compared with incomes in other sectors and in the economy as a whole. These statistics do not provide sufficient information for the design and operation of a targeted and efficient income support policy. In particular, these statistics do not tell us how the total incomes of agricultural households, including both their on-farm and their off-farm incomes, have developed, and what contribution past agricultural policies have made to this development. The European Court of Auditors has repeatedly criticised in particular the lack of reliable statistics on the non-agricultural incomes of farm households in Germany and other EU member states. For example, in a special report published in 2016 the Court of Auditors concluded that:

> "The Commission has not clearly established the statistical data needed to effectively assess the performance of CAP measures in support of farmers' incomes. No representative data are available on the disposable income of farm households, which would facilitate assessing the achievement of the

> treaty objective of ensuring a fair standard of living for farmers. Furthermore, there is no reliable system to allow comparisons to be made between agricultural incomes and those in other sectors of the economy, which could justify EU income support for farmers." (European Court of Auditors 2016, p. 8).

It is known that many farm households earn substantial non-agricultural income in addition to their agricultural income. If their non-agricultural income is not considered, these households will appear to be needier than they actually are. Agricultural income support policies that fail to take the non-agricultural incomes of farm households into account cannot be targeted or efficient.

4.8.2. Externalities on agricultural labour market as a justification for government policies

Externalities result when there are differences between private and social marginal costs or between private and social marginal willingness to pay. If private incentives lead individuals to leave farming, even though it would be better from an economic welfare perspective if they remained in agriculture or, *vice versa*, if they remain in farming for private reasons although it would be better for the economy as a whole if they left, then there is an externality on the agricultural labour market. Externalities are often cited to justify government interventions.

If farmers were only interested in their labour incomes, they would leave agriculture if they could earn more in off-farm employment. That would be the case if the marginal value product of their off-farm labour, net of transaction costs and including possible income from farm assets (especially renting out land), were greater than the marginal value product of their on-farm labour. In this case, switching from on-farm to off-farm employment would increase the output of the economy as a whole and the farmers' private decisions would lead to a positive outcome from an economic welfare perspective.

However, as discussed above, farmers are likely to base their decisions not only on monetary income but also on non-monetary factors such as a preference for maintaining the family farm. As a result, the behaviour of individual farmers may not be optimal from an economic welfare perspective, i.e. with respect to the goal of maximising the monetary value of total economic output. Remaining in agriculture is nevertheless rational if it maximises the individual farmer's subjective utility. Since it is not possible to objectively measure an individual's utility, we have to assume that an individual's behaviour reveals his/her underlying preferences. Hence, if farmers do not switch to off-farm employment this reveals that they enjoy a higher level of utility in farming. The total value of economic output might not be maximised, but the sum of all individual utilities is.

This statement is only valid if the individual farmers are fully informed about the present and future developments, and if their decisions do not create any positive or negative effects for other individuals. We discussed above in detail the role of (possibly wrong) expectations regarding future developments and factors that can lead to growing income disparities between on-farm and off-farm incomes. As long as the individuals involved are maximising their individual utilities, these factors alone do not result in a sub-optimal allocation of resources between sectors and a reduction in economic welfare.

However, if other individuals are affected by a farmer's decision to remain in agriculture, then a sub-optimal allocation of resources can result. Since the switch to off-farm employment generally entails ceasing farming, when farmers decide to stay in agriculture, less land becomes available to other farms, which limits their ability to grow and take advantage of economies of scale. In this case, the total economic cost of a farmer' decision to remain in agriculture might exceed the economic costs from his/her private perspective. The result is an externality and, possibly, a justification for government intervention on agricultural labour markets.

Another type of externality related to agricultural labour markets can occur if the shift from on-farm to off-farm employment leads to a de-population of rural areas. Beyond some critical threshold, the population density might become so low that it becomes difficult or impossible to maintain basic **public and social infrastructure** such as school and medical services, public transportation and amenities such as sports facilities and theatres. As this infrastructure deteriorates, it can become increasingly difficult to attract new non-agricultural businesses and employers to a region, triggering a vicious circle of de-population and infrastructure decline. While the danger of such a vicious circle is perhaps less pronounced in most regions of a densely populated and comparatively decentralised country such as Germany, it is very present in the rural areas of countries such as Canada or Kazakhstan.

4.8.3. Policy measures to reduce labour market divergence

As a matter of principle, an efficient measure to correct an externality should address the precise cause of the externality as directly as possible. If the externality is caused by too few farmers deciding to leave agriculture for other sectors, then policy instruments that encourage more farmers to leave agriculture should be considered. Reductions in the number of people employed in agriculture result from illness and retirement, as well as from decisions to switch to off-farm employment. Policy instruments could, for example, aim at encouraging early retirement by improving pensions for retired farmers, making appropriate changes to tax and inheritance laws, and supporting retraining. Policies could also aim at influencing young individuals' decisions to begin farming. The decision whether or not to continue a farm in the next generation is of great importance in this respect. It is essential that prospective farmers base their decisions, which will have implications for themselves and for others over many decades, on a sober assessment of the best possible information. Support for rural development (both private enterprise but also the public and social infrastructure mentioned above) can also influence decisions to continue or begin farming if it creates jobs in the countryside.

4.8.4. Production-related measures

Policy measures that change the prices of agricultural goods, e.g. through price support or **direct payments** that are coupled to production, are not targeted and therefore cannot be an efficient means of supporting agricultural labour income. If the supply of all factors other than land is completely elastic, changes in agricultural output prices or coupled direct payments will only lead to changes in land prices (see Chapter 3). Hence, landowners are the main beneficiaries of such measures. Landowners are not necessarily farmers, and in many cases their land ownership means that they are comparatively wealthy, not poor. Price support and coupled direct payments therefore provide poorly targeted income support. Furthermore, to the extent that price support or coupled direct payments (despite the leakage to landowners), do provide some support to agricultural labour income, they will increase the use of labour in agriculture, or at least reduce the rate at which labour leaves agriculture for other sectors. As discussed above, this can lead to negative effects from an economic welfare perspective, by delaying structural change and fostering a sub-optimal allocation of resources.

4.8.5. Measures directly aimed at the labour input

Only a few measures in EU or German agricultural policy are specifically designed to change wages or incomes in agriculture. However, these measures include the EU's direct payments to farmers, which account for roughly 41,5 billion Euro (roughly 70% of the entire EU agricultural budget), of which roughly 4,8 billion Euro are spent in Germany (EU Commission 2019). EU policy makers frequently argue that these direct payments are essential to support the incomes of farmers in the member states. However, since these payments are made to farmers per hectare of land farmed, they largely accrue to landowners and not necessarily the low-income farmers who are most in need of support. The European Court of Auditors report cited in section 4.8.1 above provides more critical information on this point. Moreover, again, to the extent that these direct payments do provide income support, they will also tend to slow down structural change in agriculture, thus contributing to inefficient factor use.

A related EU measure targets the support of young farmers. This support takes the form of a five-year top-up of the direct payments mentioned above. This top-up can be claimed for up to 90 hectares of land by farmers under the age of 40. It is based on the consideration that young farmers often plan initial investments to improve the productivity and efficiency of the farms that they inherit or begin to operate. Special state support for these young farmers could therefore have the positive effect of encouraging these investments and thus increasing both private profitability and overall economic welfare. A negative effect could be, however, that not all recipients of the payments make investments that prove to be profitable from an economic welfare perspective. Some of the payments are therefore not targeted. An additional, perhaps larger negative effect, is that the payments provide incentives for young people to start farming and might, at the margin, lead to some farms being continued in the next generation that would otherwise have ceased production. This could lead to a larger number of individuals employed in agriculture that would have been the case without the special payments. Holst and von Cramon-Taubadel (2017) argue that there is a reliable flow of suitably trained young farm managers into agriculture in Germany and, thus, no need to provide additional incentives in the form of subsidies.

4.9. Keywords

- Agricultural Act of 1955
- Direct payments
- Externality
- Full-time and part-time farming
- Hidden unemployment
- Income disparity
- On-farm and off-farm employment
- Public and social infrastructure
- Push and pull effects
- Sector-specific qualifications
- Transaction costs
- Treaty of Rome
- X-inefficiency

References

Bundesinstitut für Berufsbildung (2021) Datenbank Ausbildungsvergütung: Tarifliche Ausbildungsvergütungen 2020 in Ost- und Westdeutschland. https://www.bibb.de/system/external_service_provider/2020_Dav_Gesamtuebersicht_Ausbildungsver-1.pdf. Accessed November 12, 2021.

BMEL (Bundesministerium für Ernährung und Landwirtschaft) (2020) Die wirtschaftliche Lage der landwirtschaftlichen Betriebe: Buchführungsergebnisse der Testbetriebe des Wirtschaftsjahres 2018/19. https://www.bmel-statistik.de/fileadmin/daten/BFB-0111001-2019.pdf. Accessed November 12, 2021.

Chiang AC (1974I Fundamental Methods of Mathematical Economics, 2nd ed., New York, McGraw-Hill.

EU Commission (2019) Indicative Figures on the Distribution of Aid, by Size-Class of Aid, Received in the Context of Direct Aid Paid to the Producers According to Council Regulation (EC) No 1307/2013 (Financial Year 2018). https://ec.europa.eu/info/sites/info/files/food-farming-fisheries/farming/documents/direct-aid-indicative-figures-2018_en.pdf. Accessed November 12, 2021.

EU Publications Office (2021) Consolidated version of the Treaty on the Functioning of the European Union. https://eur-lex.europa.eu/legal-content/EN/TXT/PDF/?uri=CELEX:12012E/TXT. Accessed November 12, 2021.

European Court of Auditors (2016) Is the Commission's system for performance measurement in relation to farmers' incomes well designed and based on sound data? Special Report No. 1/2016, https://www.eca.europa.eu/Lists/ECADocuments/SR16_01/SR_FARMERS_EN.pdf. Accessed November 12, 2021.

Federal Government of Germany (1955) Landwirtschaftsgesetz. https://www.gesetze-im-internet.de/lwg/LwG.pdf. Accessed November 12, 2021.

Gisser M and Dávila A (1998) Do Farm Workers Earn Less? An Analysis of the Farm Labor Problem. American Journal of Agricultural Economics 80: 669-682.

Holst C and von Cramon-Taubadel S (2017) Zukünftige Herausforderungen der deutschen Landwirtschaft vor dem Hintergrund der aktuellen Alters- und Ausbildungsstruktur landwirtschaftlicher Betriebsleiterinnen und Betriebsleiter. Schriftenreihe der Rentenbank 33: 43-74.

Leibenstein H (1966) Allocative Efficiency vs. "X Efficiency". The American Economic Review 56(3): 392-415.

Williamson OE (2000) The New Institutional Economics: Taking Stock, Looking Ahead. Journal of Economic Literature 38: 595–613.

Exercises

1. Discuss the following statement: If labour productivity increases less in one sector than in the rest of the economy, economic welfare will increase if labour shifts from the sector with the slower growth in labour productivity to other sectors with higher labour productivity growth.

2. If labour income is lower in one sector than in the rest of the economy, will individual welfare necessarily be lower in this sector? Might it even be higher? Discuss.

3. What determinants influence the coexistence of full-time and part-time farming in many countries?

4. Assume that a permanent increase in world market prices for agricultural products takes place. What effects will this price increase have on labour incomes in agriculture in an open economy if labour is completely mobile? What effects will it have if labour mobility is limited?

5. Suppose the government wants to increase labour incomes in agriculture and can only achieve this by means of border measures (protection). Why are measures that only target the prices for agricultural goods

(outputs) less efficient from an economic welfare perspective than measures that also lead to price increases for variable inputs?

Appendix 4.1: The derivation of equation (17) for the change in per capital income in agriculture

We begin with the definition of the per capita income in agriculture in equation (10):

$$Y^L = \frac{P * Q^S - K}{L} \tag{10}$$

which can be rearranged to

$$Y^L * L = (P * Q^S) - K. \tag{18}$$

Totally differentiating equation (18) leads to:

$$(dY^L * L) + (dL * Y^L) = (dP * Q^S) + (dQ^S * P) - dK \tag{19}$$

$$(dY^L * L) = (dP * Q^S) + (dQ^S * P) - dK - (dL * Y^L)\,. \tag{20}$$

We divide both sides of equation (20) by $(Y^L * L)$ to obtain

$$\frac{dY^L}{Y^L} = \frac{(dP*Q^S)}{Y^L*L} + \frac{(dQ^S*P)}{Y^L*L} - \frac{dK}{Y^L*L} - \frac{(dL*Y^L)}{Y^L*L} \tag{21}$$

or

$$\frac{dY^L}{Y^L} = \frac{1}{V}[(dP * Q^S) + (dQ^S * P)] - \frac{dK*K}{V*K} - \frac{dL}{L} \tag{22}$$

where

$V = Y^L * L = (P * Q^S) - K$ is the total value added of agricultural production.

Next, we multiply and divide term in square brackets on the right-hand-side of equation (22) by $R = (P * Q^S)$, the revenue from the sale of agricultural output:

$$\frac{dY^L}{Y^L} = \frac{R}{V}\left[\left(\frac{dP*Q^S}{P*Q^S}\right) + \left(\frac{dQ^S*P}{P*Q^S}\right)\right] - \frac{dK*K}{K*V} - \frac{dL}{L} \tag{23}$$

which simplifies to

$$\frac{dY^L}{Y^L} = \frac{R}{V}\left[\left(\frac{dP}{P}\right) + \left(\frac{dQ^S}{Q^S}\right)\right] - \frac{dK*K}{K*V} - \frac{dL}{L}. \tag{24}$$

We can now use equation (16) to replace $\frac{dP}{P}$, and equation (14) to replace $\frac{dQ^S}{Q^S}$. This leads to:

$$\frac{dY^L}{Y^L} = \frac{R}{V}\left[\frac{1}{\varepsilon^S-\varepsilon^D}\left(\eta\frac{dY}{Y} - \frac{dT}{T}\right) + \frac{dT}{T} + \frac{\varepsilon^S}{\varepsilon^S-\varepsilon^D}\left(\eta\frac{dY}{Y} - \frac{dT}{T}\right)\right] - \frac{dK*K}{K*V} - \frac{dL}{L}. \tag{25}$$

Collecting terms finally leads to:

$$\frac{dY^L}{Y^L} = \frac{E}{W}\left[\frac{dY}{Y}\left(\frac{\eta(1+\varepsilon^S)}{\varepsilon^S-\varepsilon^D}\right) - \frac{dT}{T}\left(\frac{(1+\varepsilon^D)}{\varepsilon^S-\varepsilon^D}\right)\right] - \frac{dK*K}{K*W} - \frac{dL}{L}. \tag{17}$$

CHAPTER FIVE

PRICE FORMATION ON AGRICULTURAL CREDIT MARKETS

ULRICH KOESTER AND
STEPHAN VON CRAMON–TAUBADEL

5.1. Introduction and learning objectives

Over time, capital has become increasingly important for the competitiveness of individual farms and the agricultural sector as a whole. Changes in factor price ratios and technological advances require increased capital input in farming. Since equity capital is often not available in sufficient quantities, farms must increasingly rely on debt financing. In addition to loans, capital can also be acquired in other ways, e.g. via participation in partnerships, or the sale of shares in corporations. In most market-economies, however, farms mainly access capital by taking out loans. This chapter will focus on the credit market in agriculture. We will show that it differs considerably from other sectoral credit markets, and that this can provide a justification for state intervention in the agricultural credit market.

In this chapter we will explain:

- how the capital intensity of production and, therefore, the interest rate influence agricultural price relations,

- that the functioning of agricultural credit markets cannot be explained without considering the effect of institutions,

- why the development of agricultural credit markets crucially depends on trust,

- how secure property rights contribute to the expansion of agricultural credit markets, and

- that government measures can have positive or negative effects on the development of agricultural credit markets.

5.2. The capital intensity of German agriculture

> "The capital stock of agriculture, forestry and fisheries, defined as gross fixed assets (excluding land) at replacement prices, has increased rapidly in recent years. The capital input per employee (capital intensity) has increased even more rapidly. Today, agriculture is one of the most capital-intensive sectors, with €536,100 per employee. In the manufacturing sector (industry), for example, the capital intensity is considerably lower at €313,800 per employee. In trade, the capital intensity is €128,200, and in construction only €41,400 per employee. … At the end of June 2018, the volume of borrowed capital in German agriculture and forestry reached €50.5 billion, which is only slightly lower than in the previous year. Long-term loans account for 84 percent of this borrowing and serve to finance long-term investments. Short-term (less than one year) and medium-term (less than 5 years) loans play a minor role with a share of 16 percent. German agriculture and forestry use borrowed capital primarily to improve economic performance. The currently low interest rates contribute to this." (DBV 2018, p. 71-72).

It may seem puzzling that agriculture, which as described above is comparatively capital-intensive, and which is characterised by enterprises (farms) that have above-average equity capital shares, nevertheless has more difficulty obtaining access to capital markets than other sectors. Explaining this puzzle is one of the objectives of this chapter. But first we will discuss the influence of interest rates on agricultural price relations.

5.3. The importance of interest rates for the interdependence of agricultural prices

Interest is a price that the borrower pays the lender in return for the transfer of purchasing power. The **interest rate** indicates the percentage share of a loan that the borrower pays the lender per unit of time, usually one year. Interest and interest rates are therefore prices that are paid for the right to make use of money, i.e. for a service. Capital markets and interest rates are extremely important for the development of agriculture; indeed, Nobel Prize winner Theodor Schulz[1] claimed that the interest rate is the most important price for the development of agriculture.

Neoclassical price theory begins by analysing price determination for homogeneous goods and services. Homogeneous goods and services are identical in all essential material and immaterial characteristics. This also implies that none of the exchange partners has a special preference for any other partner, and that the place and time at which exchange takes place are of no importance. This simple neoclassical analysis does not consider transaction costs. These assumptions are restrictive, but nevertheless useful for illustrating the principles of price determination in simple settings.

The interest rate a borrower has to pay depends on the willingness of the lender to provide purchasing power to individual borrowers. Differences between the interest rates for loans with different maturities, and for loans provided to different borrowers, are largely determined by differences in transaction costs. The borrower of a loan takes on payment obligations that extend into the future. Hence, the lender's confidence in the borrower's future willingness and ability to pay is an important determinant of the interest rate for that loan. It is therefore understandable that at any given point in time there will be a large number of different interest rates in the economy.

Despite this large number of different interest rates in reality, in the following we assume that there is only one representative interest rate. This (unrealistic) assumption makes it easier to analyse and explain the importance of the interest rate for the relationships between agricultural product and factor prices, and for the development of the agricultural sector. Figure 5.1 summarises the most important relationships.

[1] Theodore W. Schulz received the Nobel Prize in Economics together with Arthur Lewis in 1979, for his contributions to the "analysis of the role of investment in human capital for economic development, particularly in agriculture" (Nobelprize.org 2021a).

Figure 5.1: Importance of interest rates for the interdependence of agricultural prices

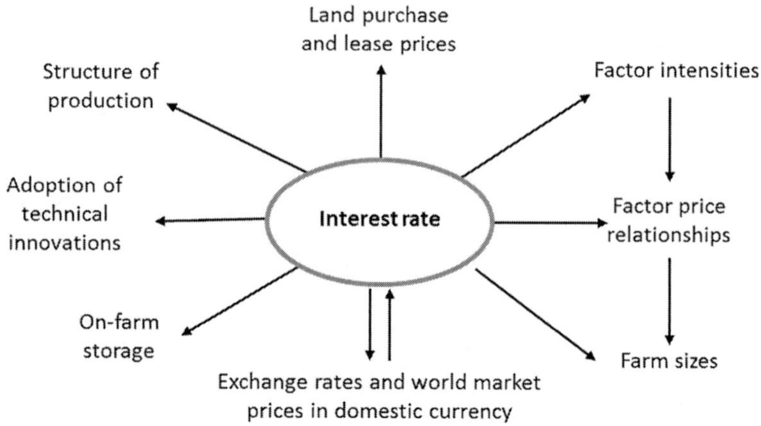

Source: Own depiction.

The importance of interest rates for the level of land prices

The importance of the interest rate for the purchase price of land was discussed in detail in chapter 3. Here we simply reiterate the importance of expectations for the determination of land price. In an economy with very low interest rates and expected land price increases, land prices will rise even if the profits generated by the most efficient agricultural holdings approach zero.

Investments in agricultural land by non-farmers and the expansion of corporate farms are reinforced by low interest rates and positive expectations of land price changes. Rising land prices, which are encouraged by low interest rates and expectations of continued price increases, also have a direct impact on lease prices. A potential tenant's willingness to pay for land lease will be based on the contribution margin or rent that he/she expects to earn on the land. However, he/she will often be competing with others who are interested in purchasing the land, and whose willingness to pay is not only determined by returns to land as a factor of production but also by expected future price increases.

The importance of interest rates for factor price relations and structural change in agriculture

The interest rate not only influences the land price and thus the demand for land as a specific factor of production in agriculture, it also influences **factor price relations** between credit and labour. Low interest rates reduce the production costs of capital-intensive agricultural products. They also tend to favour large farms, which are typically more capital-intensive than smaller farms. Low interest rates can thus accelerate **structural change** towards larger farms.

This effect will be felt in particular when decisions on inter-generational transfer of farms are taken. When interest rates are low, potential farm successors will be more likely to invest in physical capital and land, thus accelerating structural change and the decline in farm numbers. As explained above, low interest rates and expected price increases for agricultural land will reduce the competitiveness of family farms on the land lease market. Of course, if land is purchased by non-farmers rather than leased to family farms, the new owners might also consider leasing it to family farms. Evidence from Germany, however, suggests that this rarely takes place. Non-agricultural investors tend to buy larger parcels of contiguous land and then make these parcels available *en bloc* to existing agricultural holdings, either by leasing the land or as shareholders. Family farms, in contrast, are typically more interested in leasing smaller plots of land that are close to and thus complement their existing holdings in terms of management and logistics. As a result, family farms lose competitiveness vis-à-vis large farms when interest rates are low.

The importance of the interest rate for the operational storage of seasonal products

Storage ties up capital and is therefore a type of investment. The costs of storage are thus also determined by the level of interest rates. Low interest rates will therefore contribute to the increased storage of seasonal products, and thus also have an influence on seasonal price patterns.

Interdependencies between interest rates, exchange rates and agricultural price relations

Exchange rates are prices in domestic currency for foreign currencies. Exchange rates are particularly important for the pricing of products that are traded internationally. A country's exchange rate is determined, among other things, by the difference between domestic and foreign interest rates. Interest rate differentials with respect to the US are especially important, because much (agricultural) trade takes place in US-dollars. If interest rates in the EU are lower than in the US, *ceteris paribus*, capital will flow from the EU to the USA. The supply of Euros in the US will thus increase, and the price of Euros in US-dollars decrease; the result is a revaluation of the US-dollar and a devaluation of the Euro. The devaluation of the Euro means that the equivalent in Euro of a given price in US-dollars will increase. Since agriculture in the EU largely produces internationally tradeable goods, lower interest rates in the EU than in the US will cause agricultural prices in the EU to be higher than they would be if interest rates were the same in both countries. This will boost the EU's competitiveness on international markets. The opposite chain of effects will take place if interest rates are higher in the EU than in the US.

The mechanism described above is important, but exchange rates are not exclusively determined by interest rate differentials. The value of a reserve currency such as the US-dollar also depends on expectations regarding future economic growth, the investment climate and the future direction of economic policy. Furthermore, exchange rate fluctuations will also affect the prices of tradeable agricultural inputs (such as fossil fuels or fertiliser), so their net effects on international competitiveness vary from product to product depending on the costs shares of tradeable and non-tradeable (e.g. land) factors.

The importance of interest rates for the introduction of technical progress

Farmers adopt new technologies in response to incentives and competitive pressure. [2] Since the adoption of new technologies usually requires investments and is associated with uncertain expectations, interest rates also influence this adoption. Low interest rates lead to lower costs of investing in a new technology, and to a higher present value of future returns from the technology. Hence, low interest rates, even if seen as positive by many farmers individually, can accelerate structural change.

---

[2] The importance of technical change and innovations for agricultural price determination is discussed in Chapters 6 and 7.

5.4. The neoclassical analysis of agricultural credit markets

In the basic neoclassical model, all individual actors have all the information that they need to make optimal (profit- or utility-maximising) decisions. Under these conditions the credit market functions like any other market for factors of production. When loans are needed to purchase capital goods (e.g. machinery, buildings) or variable inputs (e.g. seeds, fertilisers, feed), the marginal value product of capital is compared with the interest rate. From an economic welfare perspective, the use of capital will be optimal if its marginal value product is the same in all uses, i.e. on all farms and in all other enterprises. In this simple conceptual framework, we assume that all potential borrowers and lenders have complete knowledge about the marginal value product of all short-term and long-term investments – in other words that there is no risk or uncertainty. In addition, we also ignore the fact that some investments (e.g. in a large piece of farm machinery) cannot be divided into small marginal increments – one either makes the entire investment, or not.

If these assumptions are met, then we can draw the smooth, falling marginal value product curve for capital that is depicted in Figure 5.2. If farmers are profit-maximisers, all loans with a marginal value product greater than or equal to the given interest rate will take place, leading to increased production capacities through increased capital input (including land purchases), or the substitution of labour by capital. If interest rates fall, the optimal loan volume will increase, thus increasing the rate of structural change in agriculture; if interest rates rise, the optimal loan volume and the rate of structural change will fall.

Figure 5.2: Demand curve for loans with perfect information and a smooth marginal value product curve

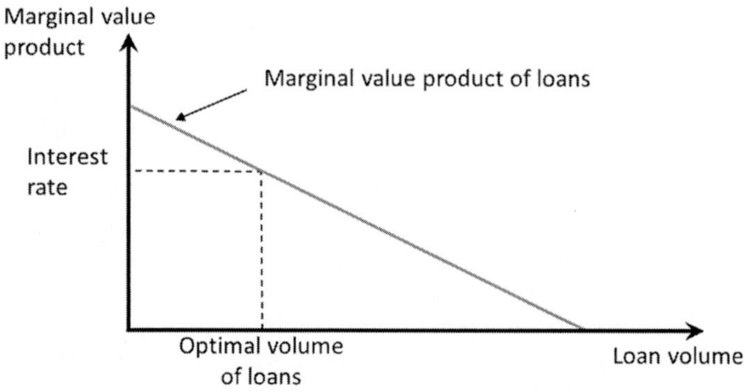

Source: Own depiction.

In reality, the marginal value product curve for capital will not be smooth for individual farms or for agriculture as a whole. Changes in the capital stock often occur in jumps, because many investments cannot be divided arbitrarily. Alternative investment projects that generate different returns can be ranked by their rates of return, leading to the stepped marginal value product curve depicted in Figure 5.3. All those investment projects that yield a return in excess of the interest rate are realised; all other projects are deferred.

Figure 5.3: Demand curve for loans with perfect information and a stepped marginal value product curve

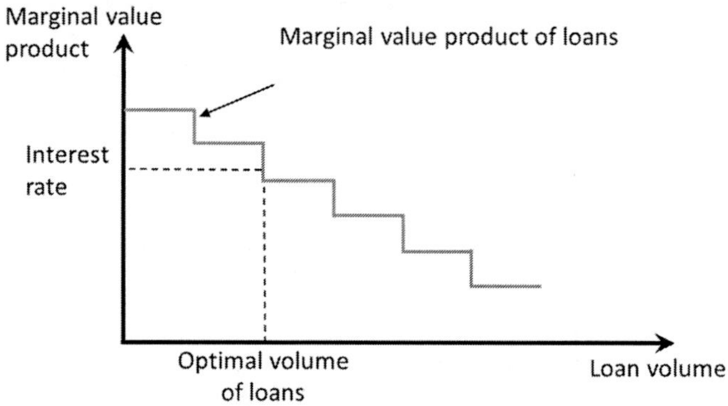

Source: Own depiction.

The assumption of complete information also applies to information about the decisions of other investors in the same sector. However, this is often an unrealistic assumption. For example, one farmer's decision to invest in a new biogas plant might lower the profitability of a nearby farmer's existing biogas plant, by increasing the local competition for the required biomass (e.g. maize silage).

The neglect of transaction costs in the simple neoclassical analysis of agricultural credit markets is also important. Lenders are usually only indirectly interested in the profitability of the investments or purchases of equipment that they fund via loans; they are primarily interested in the security of the loan repayment. Trust in the behaviour of the potential borrower is therefore crucial. Lenders will naturally place greater trust for example in family members, or in persons who have reliably repaid loans in the past, than in potential borrowers who are entering the credit market for the first time.

In the following sections we will expand on these brief remarks about the general limitations of neoclassical analysis of credit markets.

5.5. Specific features of the demand for agricultural credit

Imperfect information about future market developments affects agricultural credit depending on the terms of loans and the uses to which they are put. We begin by considering the demand for short-term loans.

5.5.1. The demand for short-term loans

Short-term credits can be used to finance consumption or variable inputs. Since incomes in agriculture can vary considerably from year to year, smallholder farmers in low-income countries are sometimes forced to borrow money to smooth consumption, for example to provide all members of the household with sufficient healthy food in a bad year. Potential borrowers in such a situation often have very limited or no access to formal credit markets because they can offer lenders no collateral and they have no credit histories as a basis for trust. Hence, they must often resort to informal lenders who charge much higher interest rates. To avoid becoming dependent on such lenders, smallholders often focus on producing food for own consumption (subsistence farming) rather than specialising on individual crops. In this way, the (mal)functioning of short-term credit markets will affect specialisation, the division of labour and productivity growth in agriculture and the economy as a whole.

If formal credit markets are underdeveloped, the demand for short-term credits to finance storage will also be low. The higher the interest rate, the less profitable it will be to store own production in anticipation of higher prices later in the year. In order to finance consumption, farmers might be forced to sell their products immediately after the harvest when supply is high and prices low, rather than spread their sales over time to obtain higher average prices.

A similar situation can arise when farmers demand short-term credits to finance variable inputs such as fertiliser, agricultural chemicals or medicine for sick animals. If formal credit markets are underdeveloped and farmers can only access informal loans at high interest rates, then the volume of loans demanded will be sub-optimal from an economic welfare perspective, as many short-term investments that could generate positive returns at formal market interest rates are not made.

5.5.2. The demand for long-term loans

The demand for long-term loans is determined by changes in factor price relations for labour, capital and land. These factor price relations change as a result of factor price changes in other sectors, and due to the adoption of new technologies in agriculture and other sectors. Of course, the access to long-term loans also depends on trust and whether potential borrowers can provide securities or have established positive credit records.

Economic growth is generally associated with increasing wages. As a result, the opportunity costs of labour increase relative to the price of capital. For profit maximising enterprises, including farms, these price changes change the optimal factor input combination. As a result, the demand for loans for investments in **capital deepening** increases. Capital deepening refers to the implementation of new technologies that reduce the need for other factors and increase the capital intensity of production. The goal is to increase the marginal value product of labour by increasing the capital input per unit of labour, and thus to ensure that returns to labour in agriculture keep pace with increasing wages in other sectors.

Capital deepening leads to a reduction in labour input, which is not an attractive option for all farms. Investment in a modern milking parlour that reduces the need for labour is an example of capital deepening that might be chosen by a farm that has employed and can release hired wage labourers, but that is less likely be chosen by a farm that uses exclusively family labour. Such farms will demand loans for investments in **capital widening**, which are investments that increase the capital stock while maintaining the input of other factors. Typical examples of capital widening are investments to purchase more land, extend the dairy barn, or build a new biogas plant. By increasing the total production capacity of a farm, such investments are supposed to increase the income generated by the given quantity of labour.

Opportunities for profitable capital widening are limited in agriculture compared with other sectors. This is because capital widening in agriculture often requires not only more physical capital in the form of farm machinery, buildings and livestock, but also more land. A farm can only increase its area if other farms in the vicinity are willing to make land available for lease or purchase. Expansion of one farm thus requires contraction or complete exit of another. As a result, the demand for long-term loans for investments in capital widening depends not only on the profitability of these investments, but also on the current and expected situation on land markets.

In addition, the profitability of a long-term investment in agriculture depends on many variables such as future price trends that are uncertain and based on subjective evaluations and expectations. Given this uncertainty, potential lenders who are not knowledgeable about agriculture will not be in a good position to accurately assess the likely profitability of a proposed investment. Hence, it is plausible that the less knowledgeable a lender is about agriculture, the more he/she will make loans conditional on collateral such as land and other assets. If a potential borrower is not in a position to provide sufficient collateral, the lender will either charge a higher interest rate, or refuse to provide a loan in the first place.

5.5.3. Sector-specific capital and the demand for loans in agriculture

Because information is not perfect when an investment is made it is sometimes necessary to revise an ongoing investment project. The cost of making such revisions is an increasing function of the difference between the book values of the investment goods and their market values. Such differences often arise in the case of long-term investments in agriculture. Most agricultural machinery, for example, can only be used in agriculture. If an investment in agricultural machinery turns out to be less profitable than expected, for example because agricultural output prices are lower than was expected at the time of investment, then the demand for this (now used) machinery will be low. As a result, the market price of the machinery can fall below its book value. Hence, even though the machinery is generating a low return on its book value, it might nevertheless make sense to continue to use it rather than to sell it at the lower market price. Decisions on the profit-maximising future use of an investment good should be based on comparison with its opportunity costs, not with its hypothetical book value. Of course, the continued use of the machinery, even if it is the profit-maximising decision, might not generate sufficient returns for repaying the original loan, leading to the risk of default.

Investments in agricultural land are associated with special risks because land is such a long-lasting asset. Small changes in interest rates or expectations of future lease prices can lead to large changes in the willingness of potential investors to pay for land, and they can make the revision of investment plans very expensive. Technological change, price volatility[3], and changes in domestic agricultural policies and policies in trading partners are also sources of uncertainty that can influence the profitability of investments in agriculture. In general, investments in sector-specific factors of production are associated with considerable risk, and the demand for long-term loans is therefore, in reality, lower than it would be under perfect information.

As a result, imperfect information can lead to market failure on agricultural credit markets. Uncertainty about future developments can lead lenders to demand higher interest rates and more collateral than would otherwise be the case. This, coupled with uncertainty on the part of borrowers, can lead to a total volume of loans in agriculture that is too low from an economic welfare perspective, because projects that could generate returns that exceed the opportunity costs of capital do not get financed.

This can especially be the case if agriculture is facing large changes, such as the transition from planned to market economies that took place in Central and Eastern Europe in the 1990s and 2000s. Farms in these countries needed to make large investments in order to close the technological gap to agriculture in other countries and improve their international competitiveness. However, there was much uncertainty about the future course of agricultural and economic policy in these countries, farms often had no collateral, lenders had no experience with lending to farms under market conditions, and at least initially there was no functioning legal

[3] Price volatility is the subject of Chapter 12.

framework for contract enforcement. Under these conditions, both the demand curve and the supply curve for agricultural credit were shifted to the left and many potentially profitable investments did not take place. Governments in these countries often tried to improve the situation for example by providing state credits to agriculture, establishing state-funded agricultural banks, or subsidising commercial loans to farms.

5.6. Special features of the supply of agricultural credit

5.6.1. Private lenders

Private lenders are obviously interested in reliable repayment of the loans that they provide. However, as a rule, individual lenders do not have reliable information on the profitability of the use of these loans. Furthermore, many lenders do not have the specific expertise that is required to evaluate the business plans and profitability calculations submitted by potential borrowers in agriculture. As a consequence, other factors, including in particular trust in the creditworthiness of potential borrowers, also play an important role in decisions to grant agricultural loans. Creditworthiness depends on both objective criteria and subjective assessment by the lender.

Information on a potential borrower's history of past loan repayment is an objective criterion. However, this criterion can only be used if easily accessible and reliable information on repayment histories is available. If such information is not available, as was for example the case in transition economies during the first years of adjustment from central planning to market institutions, the supply of loans will be reduced. Information on repayment histories is always missing when young farmers approach a lender for the first time, especially when someone from outside agriculture would like to enter farming. Such borrowers will generally require large loans for investments in sector-specific capital goods and land that are of limited liquidity. Lenders' willingness to grant loans will be particularly limited if there is no private ownership of land or if land markets are not very active. As a result of these features of agricultural credit supply, a variety of special institutions have evolved in agriculture.

Historically in many countries, agricultural lending first took place outside the banking sector. Small, short-term loans, which were needed primarily to bridge individual farmers' liquidity shortages before the harvest season, or to finance yield-increasing inputs such as fertilisers, were often provided by input suppliers or traders who already transacted with the potential borrowers. Trust in the borrower's willingness to repay was of fundamental importance for these loans. Such trust can accumulate over time as a result of repeated fulfilment of contracts.

Given the importance of trust, it is not surprising that the first credit arrangements were often between relatives and friends, and only later shifted to informal, unregulated arrangements for example with traders and input suppliers. The development of formal credit markets lagged behind that of product markets. Thus, the first German bank, the Fugger Bank, was not founded until 1486. It concentrated primarily on loans and deposits from large companies and royal houses. Even the founding of the first savings-and-loan institutions (Sparkassen) in Germany in 1738 was of little significance for agriculture, partly because these banks were located in cities and partly because loans were granted on the basis of previous deposits. For German agriculture, the transition from informal credit markets to official credit transactions between banks and borrowers only began with the founding of the first rural credit cooperatives (the Raiffeisen banks) in 1872.

5.6.2. Partners in the food chain as loan providers

We mentioned above that input suppliers and traders were among the first providers of credit to agriculture. Interest was often paid in the form of real goods, e.g. grain, and this is still the case in many low-income countries today. Since the borrower often has no alternative sources of credit, the lender has market power and can discriminate between borrowers, charging each an interest rate based on lender's perceived risk. From an economic welfare perspective, the result of this lack of competition on the market for agricultural credit is excessive interest rates and a sub-optimal total volume of loans to agriculture.

Contract farming is based on contracts between farms and processors that process agricultural raw products into food and other products. Since the processors are interested in specific qualities and quantities of certain products, contracts often prescribe certain production methods to be used by the farms. In other words, the processors are directly involved in some aspects of the on-farm production process. As a result of this involvement, the processors are often well-informed about the situation on the farms with which they contract and are therefore in a good position to assess the creditworthiness of these farms. Contract farming thus often involves the granting of loans to agricultural enterprises.

Whether farmers are well advised to take advantage of such loans from processors depends on the alternatives, for example the interest rates on loans from commercial lenders such as banks. Farms and processors have to agree on a number of important provisions in a contract, including the price that the processor will pay for the raw product, the quantity and quality of raw product that the farm must deliver, penalties and bonuses for deviations from the agreed quantity and quality, and the interest rate and other conditions of any loan that is part of the agreement. The interactions between all of these provisions can be complex, and it may be difficult for the farmer to determine whether a contract is advantageous compared with alternatives. If the processor has market power (i.e. is the only buyer of a particular agricultural product in the region) it might force farmers to accept contracts that are disadvantageous for them.

On the other hand, however, even if a processing firm has market power vis-à-vis farmers, it will not necessarily be in its best interests to use this market power to the disadvantage of those farmers. For example, if the processor has made specific investments in machines for processing a particular raw product, and if it is under pressure to fulfil delivery contracts with retailers, then it needs a reliable and sufficient supply of that particular raw product to survive. Under these conditions it will have an incentive to offer contracts that are attractive to farmers, to ensure that they are willing to produce the quantities and qualities on which the processor depends, now and in the future.[4]

5.6.3. Microfinance

Since the 1970s, **microfinance organisations** have gained in importance, particularly in developing countries and some transition economies. The Bengali entrepreneur, Mohamed Yunus, made a significant contribution to the spread of this form of enterprise and was awarded the Nobel Peace Prize in 2006 for his achievements.[5]

The basic idea is based on the following considerations. In some countries, especially in low-income countries and transition economies, there are many potential entrepreneurs who have low savings and no liquid assets. These people are therefore not considered creditworthy by commercial banks, even if they have plans for highly profitable investments. These

[4] See Sexton (2013) and Adjemian et al. (2016) for a discussion of when processors can and cannot be expected to take advantage of market power vis-à-vis farmers.
[5] See Nobelprize.org 2021b.

disadvantages are particularly important in rural areas, where there are only few or no commercial banks. If there are commercial banks, they often do not have employees with sufficient experience and expertise to assess the profitability of the investment proposals submitted by potential borrowers.

Microfinance organisations address both of these reasons for the underdevelopment of rural credit markets. They specialize in providing small loans to poor people. Bank employees are trained to assess potential loans in rural areas. They assess the expected return on proposed investments, but they also make personal visits to potential borrowers in their homes. The bank employee's personal assessment of the person applying for the loan, and his/her family, is important for determining creditworthiness.

To further reduce the risk of non-repayment, the microfinance organisations grant only short-term, low-volume loans to individual, first-time borrowers. If these first loan are repaid, the borrowers become eligible for larger loans with longer terms. In addition, so-called microcredits are often provided to groups of borrowers who are jointly responsible for repayment. This creates peer pressure to repay loans, which also increases creditworthiness. In this way, microfinance organisations have helped small farmers with little or no assets and savings to increase investments in rural areas, thus helping to raise the income of poor population groups.

5.7. Alternatives to borrowing money for farms

Over time, several alternative sources of credit besides commercial lenders have emerged in agriculture. Most of these alternatives developed as substitutes for the purchase of agricultural machinery. In the following we will discuss the examples of leasing, contracting, machinery rings and producer associations.

In the case of **leasing** farm machinery, a supplier who owns machines leases them to farms. Typically, the owner makes the machines available to the farmer when required during the season, and is paid after the harvest. Because the lease price can be paid out of current revenue, the farm does not need to borrow money to purchase the machines. However, the farm is generally only able to pay the lease price after the crop has been harvested and sold. Hence, leasing depends on trust by the owner that the farmer will produce a crop and honour the lease contract. In a sense, leasing replaces the long-term loan that the farm would require to purchase the machinery outright with a series of short-term credit arrangement between the farm and the owner of the machinery.

Leasing of farm machinery became common in transition economies where there was either limited private ownership of land and/or land markets were inactive (e.g. due to an embargo on the purchase and sale of agricultural land, as was in place for many years in Ukraine). Under these conditions, potential borrowers were unable to offer sufficient collateral and market interest rates were relatively high. Macroeconomic instability (e.g. high inflation rates, unstable exchange rates) also contributed to high interest rates and limited access to credit for many farms.

Agricultural contractors offer not only agricultural machinery to farmers, but also the labour and other inputs required to complete task such as soil preparation and seeding with that machinery. Agricultural contractors are often found in regions with small to medium-sized farms. The contractor can operate machines at a higher capacity than a single, smaller farmer could. This spreads the fixed costs of purchasing a machine over more operating hours and results in lower costs per hour of operation. In addition, the contractor generally has a higher level of expertise in operating (and maintaining and repairing) the machines than an individual farmer.

Sometimes a group of farmers will unite to form a **machinery ring** and buy machinery together. This typically takes place among member farms that are small and that would individually operate machinery far below capacity. To avoid conflicts, the members of a machinery ring have to establish rules about the order and extent of the use of the jointly-owned machinery, for example during the harvest times when the demand for machinery services peaks. Avoiding conflict will likely be easier if the member farms are all of similar size and have different crop rotations so that not all members demand large amounts of the same machinery service at the same time.

Similar to machinery rings, **producer associations** are groupings of agricultural holdings. However, they are not limited to the use of jointly financed machinery, and in some cases, machinery plays no role at all in the establishment and operation of a producer association. The aim of a producer association is to increase its members' profits, for example through coordination such as joint marketing of special crops, or joint purchase of inputs. A successful producer association can boost investments and the demand for loans by member farms both individually and jointly (for example, when an association of fruit producers invests in a joint packing station or storage facilities).

5.8. Market-based solutions to improve the functioning of agricultural credit markets

As outlined in the previous sections, a variety of market-based solutions have contributed to increasing trust and to overcoming problems of imperfect information on agricultural credit markets. These solutions include microfinance, leasing and contract farming. In the following we discuss the importance of collateral and information in greater detail.

Compared with most non-agricultural enterprises, farms own a large proportion of their business assets such as land and buildings. As a result, in Germany for example, farm bankruptcies are rare.[6] One might therefore expect that farms should have little difficulty in receiving loans. However, a farm's creditworthiness in the eyes of potential lenders depends on the marketability of its agricultural assets, especially land. While farm land is a marketable asset in Germany, in some low-income and transition countries, land laws have not been clarified, legal claims to land are not easily enforceable, or there is no active land market. Where this is the case, farms will not be in a position to use land as collateral to secure loans.

Following German reunification, for example, many farms in the new Eastern Länder were (re)established as cooperatives or other legal entities that rented most or all of the land that they farmed from owners (who had received this land as the result of a restitution process). These enterprises faced difficulties in securing loans because they could provide no collateral – they farmed the land, but they did not own it.

In most countries of the former Soviet Union, farm land was privatised through the distribution of ownership rights.[7] Individuals, often the employees of the former collective farms, received land shares, but initially without legally specified ownership rights. Typically, individuals were given certificates entitling to a certain amount of land, but these certificates did not specify the precise location of that land, and legally it was often only

[6] According to the Statistisches Bundesamt (2018, 2019), only 93 and 97 farms filed for bankruptcy in 2018 and 2019, respectively. That is less than 0.04% of the over 250,000 farms in Germany in those years. By German law a firm must file for bankruptcy if it is unable to meet its financial obligations within three weeks. Many of the (few) farms that did file for bankruptcy probably could have avoided this step, if they had sold farm land, which takes longer than three weeks.

[7] For a detailed description of the different approaches to and consequences of the restitution/distribution of farm land following the onset of transition in Central and Eastern Europe, see Swinnen et al. (1997).

possible to rent land, not to purchase or sell it. The new owners were therefore unable to use their land to secure loans. Often their only option was to rent their land back to the successor enterprises that arose out of the former collective farms. However, since these enterprises rented and did not own the land that they farmed, their access to private loans was also limited. It is therefore understandable that governments in these countries sought ways to improve farmers' access to loans and thus accelerate the agriculture modernisation. Measures such as state loans and subsidies were mentioned above, and we will return to these below.

Above we have stressed the importance of information and the effects of uncertainty on agricultural credit markets. Lenders are sometimes uncertain about the expected profitability of the investments that borrowers make with loans, and thus about the borrowers' solvency and ability to repay. Lenders might also worry that the sectoral or macroeconomic situation will change to the borrower's disadvantage. Uncertainty might also be related to personal circumstances, for example if the borrower's health deteriorates. The functioning of the credit market can be strengthened if measures are taken that reduce such sources of uncertainty, thus increasing lenders' and borrowers' willingness to provide and take out loans.

One such measure is the use of credit specialists and *ex ante* evaluation. Lenders can employ credit specialists who review the investment plans submitted by potential borrowers, and assess the creditworthiness of the borrowers themselves. If specialist have little experience and sector-specific know-how, reviews will focus primarily on collateral and the security of repayment. But experienced credit specialists with the appropriate know-how will be able to identify profitable investment opportunities, even if the potential borrowers cannot provide large amounts of collateral.

Of course, this assumes that the potential borrowers are able to draw up a realistic and credible investment plans. Most lenders require such plans, and for potential borrowers it is in any case advisable to only apply for a loan on the basis of a sound investment plan. However, not all farmers have the expertise required to prepare a convincing investment plan. A farm advisory service can be helpful in this regard, if the advisors are adequately trained. Government funding for the training of agricultural advisors and their activities can thus help to improve the functioning of agricultural credit markets.

Banks that want to be successful in agricultural lending also require qualified experts. They need credit specialists who understand farming and agricultural markets, and who can critically assess the investment plans submitted by farmers. This is true regardless of whether an investment plan has been prepared by a farmer alone, or with the help of a farm advisor. Farm advisors may tend to be too positive about the profitability of the investment that they help to plan, especially if they are being paid by the farms for this help. This can lead to conflict of interest. Conflict of interest can also arise if loans to agriculture are heavily subsidised, which increases the profitability of successful loan applications and, hence the incentives for drafting overly-optimistic investment plans.

Evidence of this is provided by the example of subsidised loans to farmers in Germany. Table 5.1 presents information from an evaluation of the profitability of subsidised farm loans in Schleswig-Holstein, the northern-most state (Land) in Germany. Farms applied for these loans by submitting investment plans that include a projection of farm income per employee and total farm profits in the target (fourth) year after the investment. At the time their applications for loans were submitted and approved, the farms that received subsidised loans projected similar profits and incomes per employee in the target year. However, when the target year arrived, large differences in performance had emerged. In Table 5.1 the farms are divided into four quartiles based on their performance in the target year. The first line of Table 5.1 shows that the farms all received similar loan volumes (255,962 – 273,156 DM). The third and fifth lines show that the farms projected similar profits (74,262 – 81,248 DM) and incomes per employee (37,606 – 41,563 DM) for the target year. The second and fourth lines of Table 5.1, however, reveal that actual profits and incomes in the target year varied far more than projected; from 23,389 to 122,514 DM per farm, and from 12,192 to 109,415 DM per employee, respectively.

On average, the farms in the first quartile had more equity capital than the farms in the second and fourth quartiles, and they had less debt capital than farms in all of the other three quartiles. Nevertheless, they generated average incomes of only 12,192 DM per employee in the target year, rather than the projected 37,606 DM. Although they had received heavily subsidised loans, these farms recorded average net equity capital losses of 26,552 DM. These results indicate that investment plans in agriculture can be highly unreliable and must be evaluated critically, especially when not only commercial investments but also government subsidies are at stake.

Table 5.1: The performance of farms that received subsidised loans in Schleswig-Holstein (in DM)

	1st quartile	2nd quartile	3rd quartile	4th quartile
Volume of the subsidised investment	262,757	273,156	255,962	264,278
Actual income per employee in year 4	12,192	39,571	61,064	109,415
Income per employee in year 4 according to investment plan	37,606	39,346	40,599	41,563
Actual profit in year 4	23,389	62,273	90,647	122,514
Profit in year 4 according to investment plan	74,262	76,422	77,402	81,248
Equity capital in year 4	80,1467	796,867	830,789	767,079
Debt capital in year 4	284,671	313,949	288,504	340,969
Change in equity capital	-26,552	2,994	27,127	36,305

Source: Striewe et al. (1996, p. 431). Calculations for 308 farms in Schleswig-Holstein that received subsidised loans between 1988 and 1990. The quartiles were constructed using information on the income per farm employee: the threshold between the 1st and 2nd quartiles is 30,029 DM; between the 2nd and 3rd quartiles 50,662 DM; between the 3rd and 4th quartiles 73,331 DM.

Besides investment plans, information on potential borrowers' past histories of loan repayment is an important indicator of creditworthiness for lenders. In many countries, organisations have been established to compile such information and make it available to lenders. In Germany, this organisation is called the *Schufa*.[8] This organisation was founded in the 1920s by private initiative and later transformed by a group of banks into a holding company. Its task is to collect information on the financial behaviour of individuals and enterprises, including loan repayment and, as the case may be, default histories, but also credit card use and payment of bills for electricity and other services. Lenders can obtain information about the creditworthiness of potential borrowers from the *Schufa* at low cost. The *Schufa* will not

[8] *Schufa* stands for '*Schutzgemeinschaft für allgemeine Kreditsicherung*', roughly 'protection association for general credit security'.

make information on potential borrowers available without their consent, but lenders will naturally have less confidence in the creditworthiness of a potential borrower who is unwilling to provide this consent. Furthermore, individuals and enterprises know that failure to repay a loan or to pay bills on time will affect their *Schufa* records, and thus increase the costs of future loans.

Organisations like the *Schufa* can greatly improve the functioning of credit markets. However, such institutions will not necessarily emerge in all countries as a result of private initiative as was the case in Germany. The start-up costs for such an institution are relatively high, and it can take some time before it accumulates a database that is extensive enough to provide information that lenders find useful and, hence, are willing to pay for. Government support for the establishment of such organisations can therefore be a sensible public investment.

5.9. Government intervention to correct market failure on agricultural credit markets

As we have outlined above, there are many reasons to expect that both the supply of and the demand for loans in agriculture will be too low from an economic welfare perspective. As a result, the use of debt capital in agriculture will be suboptimal and many potentially profitable investments will not take place. Government intervention can help to correct such market failures. Of course, not all government intervention is designed to correct market failure; sometimes it is motivated by political objectives such as redistribution in favour of certain groups in society.

In the following we will discuss several individual causes of market failure and how government intervention can most efficiently contribute to correcting them. Efficiency in this context means that the government intervention should achieve the greatest possible correction of the market failure at the lowest possible cost. When evaluating a specific intervention, attention must therefore also be paid to its possible side effects. For example, it is not enough that government subsidies for loans to farms increase the volume of investments in agriculture, if many of the subsidised investments turn out to be unprofitable from an economic welfare perspective. Asymmetric information between borrowers and lenders can make the design of efficient government intervention especially difficult.

5.9.1. Justifications for state intervention in the agricultural credit market

State intervention in agricultural credit markets can be justified if the profitability of investments in agriculture is higher from an economic welfare perspective than it appears to private investors. Farming is inherently risky, and farmers, like most individuals, are generally risk averse, especially where the survival of a family farm is at stake. Hence, farmers might fail to make investments that would on average generate benefits for the economy as a whole, because they appear too risky from their individual perspectives. Furthermore, individual farmers will not consider negative correlations between individual risks. For example, a downturn in world market prices for grains will have a negative effect on the profitability of investments in grain farming, but it will reduce feed costs and can therefore increase the profitability of investments made by livestock farmers. Similarly, local weather conditions that cause problems for farms that specialise in one crop can be beneficial for farms that specialise in another. Under these conditions, government provision of reduced-interest loans and other credit subsidies to farmers can generate net benefits for the economy as a whole.

However, the emphasis is on 'can' – the existence of market failure is no guarantee that government intervention will be beneficial. Consider the example of reduced-interest loans. Subsidising loans to agriculture does not reduce the uncertainty associated with investment, nor does it reduce the risk aversion of individual farmers in a targeted manner, it only addresses a symptom of the underlying market failure. Targeted policy measures would address the root cause of the market failure, which in this case is uncertainty about future market conditions. Targeted measures in this case would include promoting the establishment and functioning of futures markets, supporting improved market information systems, and subsidising insurance against risk. Another option might be to promote cooperation among farms with different production profiles so that they can jointly benefit from negative correlations between individual risks.

General loan subsidies are also inefficient because government officials will generally not have sufficient information and expertise to distinguish between investments that are likely to generate benefits for the economy as a whole, and investments that are not. It can be assumed that farms applying for subsidised credit will submit optimistic investment plans. The example of subsidised credit to farms in Schleswig-Holstein discussed in the previous section (see Table 5.1) suggests that some of these investment plans will be overly optimistic, and that the government officials who ultimately decide which applications succeed are not able to identify and sort out these applications. In addition, government officials might feel pressure to consider factors besides economic efficiency when evaluating applications, for example to favour farmers in regions that tend to support a particular political party, or in the Minister's electoral district.

It is perhaps telling that when politicians and farm representatives justify agricultural credit subsidies, they rarely appeal to market failure on credit markets and economic welfare considerations. Instead, they commonly appeal to justifications such as:

- the goal of increasing the productivity of agriculture;
- the need to provide special support to young farmers;
- the objective of supporting agricultural incomes;
- the need to support the production of positive environmental effects;
- the need to support farms in disadvantaged regions; or
- the objective of increasing self-sufficiency for specific agricultural products.

These can all be legitimate agricultural policy objectives. However, they do not arise primarily as a result of market failure in agricultural credit markets, so it is unlikely that intervention on credit markets is the most efficient way to pursue them.

5.9.2. The extent and problems of investment promotion in Germany

Table 5.1 presented evidence on the questionable effectiveness and efficiency of Germany's farm investment subsidy program. Several additional problematic side-effects of this program also bear mention. For example, many recipients of investment subsidies will attempt to expand their operations, thus increasing the demand for and prices of limited factors of production such as land and milk production quotas. This will have made it more difficult for other, possibly more efficient farms to grow and survive. Koester and Forstner (2015, p. 53) summarised the results of an evaluation report as follows:

"Investment subsidies have so far been an important instrument of agricultural policy. Every year, about 2,500 farms with an investment volume of roughly 750 million Euros receive subsidised credits. The investment subsidy program has been subject to evaluation since 2000, and the evaluation results so far are sobering. The subsidised investments were often not profitable for the participating farms, either because the investment plans had been 'sugar-coated' or non-economic investment objectives were pursued. Empirical analyses show no significant differences between the profitability of the farms that received investment subsidies and the profitability of those that did not; indeed, often the non-subsidised farms performed better. It is estimated that between 30 and 50 % of the subsidised investments would have taken place anyhow, which means that subsidies often generated windfall gains for farms, but no benefits for the economy as a whole. …

In the current funding period, investment aids are supposed to foster knowledge transfer and innovation – especially partnerships between science, consultancy and practice - to make a greater contribution to improving productivity and efficiency in agriculture. This approach represents a departure from the "mass funding" that has been practiced for years. In Germany, investment subsidies are increasingly targeted at the provision of public goods such as animal welfare, and environmental and climate protection. This increases the consistency of the investment aid program, by focussing support on fewer, targeted investments. However, it also makes it more difficult to measure and evaluate the efficiency of the investment subsidies. The new diversity of objectives that must be considered when evaluating and selecting eligible investments will pose major problems for the administration".

5.10. Keywords

- Agricultural producer association
- Agricultural contractor
- Capital deepening
- Capital widening
- Contract farming
- Factor price relations
- Interest
- Interest rate
- Leasing
- Machinery Ring
- Microfinance organisations
- Storage

References

Adjemian MK, Saitone TL and Sexton RJ (2016) A Framework to Analyse the Performance of Thinly Traded Agricultural Commodity Markets. American Journal of Agricultural Economics 98: 581-596.

DBV (Deutscher Bauernverband) (2018) Situationsbericht 2018/19. Deutscher Bauernverband e.V. Berlin

Koester U and Forstner B (2015) Agrarinvestitionsförderung – Wohl oder Übel? LandInForm 4: 53.

Nobelprize.org (2021a) Theodore W. Schultz: Facts. https://www.nobelprize.org/prizes/economic-sciences/1979/schultz/facts/. Accessed on November 23, 2021.

Nobelprize.org (2021b) Muhammad Yunus: Facts. https://www.nobelprize.org/prizes/peace/2006/yunus/facts/. Accessed on November 23, 2021.

Sexton RJ (2013) Market Power, Misconceptions, and Modern Agricultural Markets. American Journal of Agricultural Economics 95: 209-219.

Statistisches Bundesamt (various issues) Unternehmen und Arbeitsstätten: Insolvenzverfahren. Fachserie 2 Reihe 4.1 Statistisches Bundesamt, Wiesbaden. https://www.destatis.de/DE/Themen/Branchen-Unternehmen/Unternehmen/Gewerbemeldungen-Insolvenzen/Publikationen/_publikationen-innen-insolvenzen.html. Accessed on November 23, 2020,

Striewe L, Loy J-P and Koester U (1996) Analyse und Beurteilung der einzelbetrieblichen Investitionsförderung in Schleswig-Holstein. Agrarwirtschaft 45: 423-434.

Swinnen J, Buckwell A and Mathijs E (1997) Agricultural privatization, land reform and farm restructuring in Central and Eastern Europe, Aldershot: Ashgate.

Exercises

1. Why are commercial banks that are located in cities and towns often hesitant to provide loans to agricultural enterprises?

2. Why do farmers often have to pay higher interest rates for loans than entrepreneurs in other sectors?

3. Explain why subsidising loans to agricultural enterprises can be justified from an economic welfare perspective.

4. The government of a country establishes a special credit program to support farms that wish to invest in own storage facilities for grain. The official explanation provided by the government is that this will enable farmers to store grain so that they do not have to sell immediately following the harvest but rather can wait for better prices in later months. Discuss the merits of this explanation and possible effects of this special credit program.

5. Explain how the provision of subsidised loans for the construction of dairy barns led to increased prices for milk production quotas and agricultural land, and thus imposed costs on small family farms that wanted to increase their incomes by expanding their operations.

6. Discuss the effectiveness of subsidised credit programs for farms as a means of fostering rural development. Consider in particular the different effects of capital deepening and capital widening.

CHAPTER SIX

TECHNICAL CHANGE AND PRICE FORMATION IN AGRICULTURE

ULRICH KOESTER AND
STEPHAN VON CRAMON–TAUBADEL

6.1. Introduction and learning objectives

Most agricultural commodities - beef, wheat, eggs, or apples – have remained physically more or less unchanged in recent history. However, how these commodities are produced, i.e. by what methods and with which factors of production, has changed hugely. The production function, which was the basis for many of our considerations and derivations in the previous chapters, is therefore subject to constant shifts and changes. These shifts and changes are caused by technical change, which is a driving force behind agriculture's sectoral terms of trade and thus also of structural change in agriculture.

In this chapter we will explain:

- how technical change is defined and classified
- the importance of technical change for individual sectors and the economy as a whole in closed and open economies,
- how technical change influences the long-run development of agricultural prices, and
- the methods used by economists to measure the rate of technical change in agriculture.

6.2. Defining technical change

Technical change is defined as the introduction of new production processes that make it possible to:

a) produce more output with a given amount of input, or the same output with a smaller amount of input;

b) use a given amount of input to produce the same quantity but a higher quality of output;

c) increase the output quantity by using qualitatively improved inputs;

d) create previously unknown outputs, or to include previously unknown inputs in the production process.

Technical change according to a) shifts the production function upwards (from f_0 to f_1 in the left panel of Figure 6.1), or shifts the isoquants towards the origin (from I_0 to I_1 in the right panel of Figure 6.1). Technical progress according to d) leads to the creation of a completely new production function and set of isoquants. Cases b) and d) are distinct conceptually, but often difficult to distinguish in practice. A new wheat variety with increased protein content can be considered an improvement in quality (b), but also as a completely new product (d). If such a new wheat variety is used as an input in the milling industry, the result can be more output (flour) per ton on input (wheat), which would fall under a) above. However, this might equally be interpreted as an example of c) whereby output is increased by using improved inputs. Technical change in agriculture can also lead to an improved understanding of existing input-output relationships and thus new or more efficient input use.

Technical change also takes place when a farm's physical input and output quantities remain unchanged, but demands on the farm manager's time are reduced. This could be due to cooperation with other farms, or the use of new information technologies that lead to a reduction in transaction costs within the farm or between the farm and upstream or downstream enterprises that it deals with. In both of these examples input use is reduced. For example, transaction costs incurred in the marketing of agricultural products can be reduced by the use of new online market information systems or organisations such as commodity futures markets.

Figure 6.1: The effect of technical progress on production functions and the isoquants

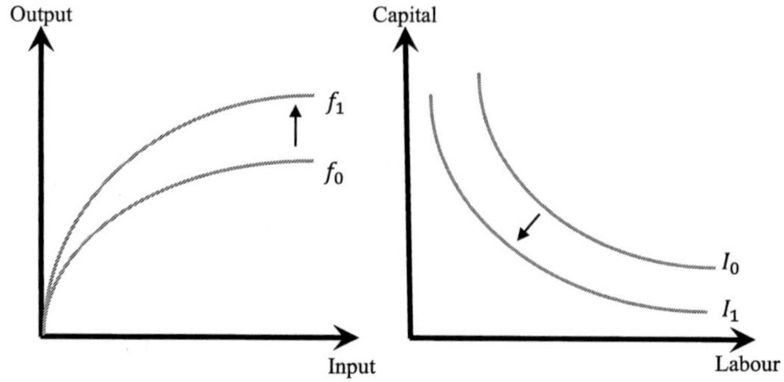

Source: Own depiction.

Finally, technical change also occurs when new processes make production more environmentally friendly, less harmful to the health of the workers, or less detrimental to animal welfare. These examples highlight that technical change that increases private profits does not necessarily increase overall economic welfare. A new process that reduces monetary production costs, but at the same time creates more negative externalities, for example, groundwater pollution or greenhouse gas emissions, might, when all costs and benefits are considered, be regarded as a negative technical change. Negative technical change might be implemented if private decision makers do not have to pay prices for inputs that equal their economic shadow prices, or if the costs of by-product 'bads' that they produce (such as pollution) are not accounted for.

In the right panel of Figure 6.1 we implicitly assumed that technical change works independently of the input combination, i.e. that the isoquant's shift towards the origin from f_0 to f_1 is proportionally equal for all combinations of labour and capital. In reality, however, most technical change does depend on input combinations. In the next section we discuss classifications of technical change that are based on its effects on input combinations and the shape of the isoquants.

6.3. Selected classifications of technical change

A variety of classifications of technical change have been proposed in economics. In the following we present some of the most common classifications.

6.3.1. The classification of technical change according to Brinkmann (1922)

Mechanical-technical change typically results in the replacement of human labour by capital. The first examples of mechanical-technical change (e.g. the introduction of the plough) expanded the area that a single farmer could farm; later examples (e.g. combine harvesters) also reduced the amount of hard physical work that is required of farmers. In today's industrialised countries, mechanical-technical change particularly benefits those farms that can either lay off workers or whose managers can use the hours of labour saved by mechanisation to take on part-time, off-farm work. In general, large farms benefit the most from mechanical-technical change (e.g. milking robots or 6-row sugar beet harvesters) because it is often characterised by increasing returns to scale. In other words, as depicted in Figure 6.2, the total average costs of these technologies fall over an initial range of output.

Figure 6.2: Total average costs (TAC) for different production processes

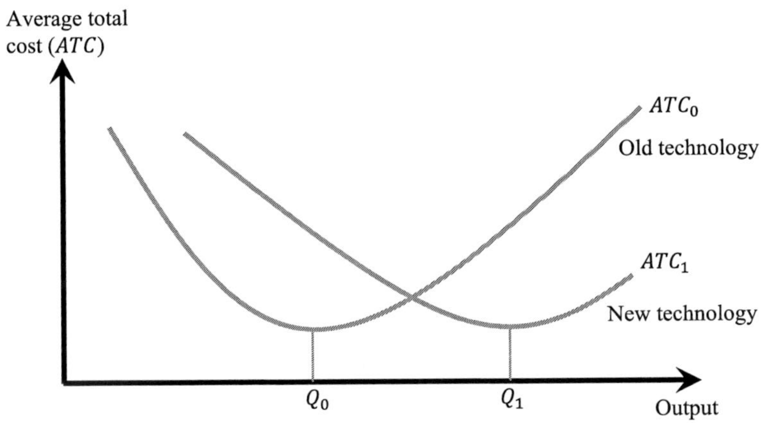

Source: Own depiction.

Biological-technical change is primarily the result of plant and animal breeding research, e.g. increasing the milk yield per cow, increasing the per hectare crop yields, or improving the product quality. Biological-technical change often increases factor productivity and thus the optimal intensity of factors use. However, some biological-technical change makes it possible to reduce the use of factors. For example, the development of monogerm sugar beet seed led to a large reduction in the demand for labour in sugar beet cultivation. Up to the 1950s, sugar beet cultivation was a labour-intensive activity and therefore also suitable for smaller farms. Nowadays sugar beet cultivation is capital-intensive, and most production takes place on large farms.

Organisational-technical change includes new management systems and organisational forms for farms, such as partnerships or corporations. This type of technical change leads to an improved utilisation of existing production capacities (especially farm machines and the family workforce). An example of organisational-technical change is crop management software that monitors and can help to optimise a farm's crop production. Other examples of organisational-technical change are machinery rings and contract farming, which were discussed in Chapter 5. Improved management can have major effects on farm profitability. Farm accounting data in industrialised countries show that there are considerable differences the input-output relationships observed on farms, and in their economic performance. In general, it can be observed that managers' professional training is positively correlated with efficiency and profitability.

Brinkmann's classification of technical change is useful, but not always well-suited for economic analysis. First, innovations do not fit neatly into one of Brinkmann's categories: so-called precision agriculture, for example, combines elements of mechanical-technical and organisational-technical change. Second, Brinkmann's scheme describes the nature of technical change and not its economic effects on input use and output. We present some alternative classification schemes that are more amenable to economic analysis in the following sections.

6.3.2. Output increasing versus cost saving technical change

As defined above, technical change can lead both to an increase in output for a given level of input use, and to a reduction in the input use required for a given level of output. In both cases, all other things being equal, technical change will lead to a reduction in costs per unit of output and, thus, an increase in output in the long run. This output growth will take place regardless of whether the technical change initially leads to a reduction in input use for a given level of output, or to an immediate increase in output.

From a farm management perspective, however, it is important which operational adjustments are made necessary by the introduction of technical change. Not all farms have the same ability and opportunities to adapt. Hence, in some settings implementing **cost-saving technical change** will be more advantageous than implementing **output-increasing technical change**. The labour situation on a farm is often decisive in this regard. Family farms, for example, may not be able to reduce their labour input in the short term. If so, they will be less interested in technical change that saves labour costs than farms that employ wage labour and who can vary their labour use more easily. Instead, they will prefer technical progress that increases output without reducing labour use.

Changes in the policy environment, such as the introduction of production quotas or acreage set-aside programmes, will also affect the relative advantageousness of different types of technical change for farm managers. If output is restricted by production quotas, output-increasing technical change is less attractive than it would otherwise be. For example, the use of the hormone BST (Bovine Somatotropin) increases the milk yields in dairy farming. Under the conditions of the EU's milk quota system, which was introduced in 1984, using BST would therefore have led to a reduction in the number of dairy cows needed to fill the quota. The result would have been a reduced utilisation of existing stable capacities on dairy farms in the EU – capacities for which there are often no alternative uses. Hence, the potential cost savings of using BST per litre of milk produced were less with the milk quota system than they would have been without. This might have contributed to the decision not to approve BST in the EU (although other arguments, such as animal welfare concerns and a general rejection of hormone use in livestock production in many EU member states, also played a role in this decision).

Note that the implementation of production quotas does not make every technical change less attractive to farmers. Milking robots and automatic feeding systems for dairy cows can reduce the costs of producing a litre of milk. In addition, the implementation of a quota system might increase both the level and the stability of farm profits. This in turn can increase the creditworthiness of farms, and their propensity to invest in cost-saving technical change.

Production quotas for milk and sugar were introduced in the EU and elsewhere to limit supply and thus increase market prices. Monopolists also limit their supply to achieve higher prices. Hence, they too will initially prefer cost-saving technical change, since output-increasing technical change would boost supply. This would lead to falling product prices, which (depending on the price elasticity of demand) would cancel out some or perhaps even all of the benefits of the increased production.

These examples show that depending on the environment in which a farm operates, cost-saving technical change can appear more or less advantageous than output-increasing technical change. As a result, the demand for individual types of technical change will differ from farm to farm, and across regions and countries. These differences in demand will affect product development and applied research on technical change; they might even effect basic research. In this context, economists refer to **induced technical change**, to which we will return in Section 6.3.4 below.

6.3.3. Neutral and non-neutral technical change

The most common classification into **neutral or non-neutral technical change** was proposed by Hicks (1932).[1] This classification hinges on how the relative marginal productivities of labour and capital change as a result of the technical change, under the assumption that their prices remain unchanged. If both marginal productivities increase proportionally, the technical change is Hicks-neutral.

If, however, the marginal productivity of one factor increases relative to that of the other, then the technical change is **non-neutral** according to Hicks. For example, if a technical change increases the marginal productivity of labour relative to that of capital, then, if relative input prices remain unchanged, the use of labour will become relatively more attractive. If it is possible to substitute inputs for one another, producers will respond by increasing their labour input relative to capital – production will become more labour intensive. In this case the technical change would be labelled capital-saving (or labour-increasing) according to Hicks. In the opposite case, if the marginal productivity of capital increases relative to that of labour, the technical change is labour-saving or capital-increasing.

[1] Other classifications of technical change into neutral and non-neutral were proposed by Harrod (1942) and Solow (1956).

Figure 6.1: Hicks-neutral technical change

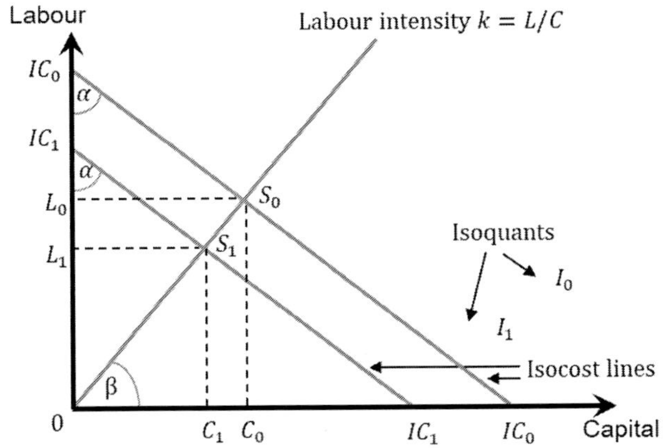

Source: Own depiction

Figure 6.3 illustrates the effect of Hicks-neutral technical change. We assume that there are only two inputs, capital and labour. In the initial situation, the input combination (C_0, L_0) is used to realise the production point S_0 on the isoquant I_0. The labour intensity (k = the ratio of labour to capital input) equals the slope of the ray from the origin to S_0, i.e. $k = \tan(\beta) = \frac{L_0}{C_0}$. The input price relation can be derived from the definition of the isocost line IC_0:

$$Cost = CP_C + LP_L \tag{1}$$

where

C = the capital input,

L = the labour input,

P_C = the price of capital, and

P_L = the price of labour.

If no capital is used ($C = 0$), the labour input $L = \frac{Cost}{P_L}$ (obtained by setting $C = 0$ in equation 1). Similarly, if $L = 0$, then $C = \frac{Cost}{P_K}$. It follows that

$$tan(\alpha) = \frac{\frac{Cost}{P_L}}{\frac{Cost}{P_C}} = \frac{P_C}{P_L} \qquad (2)$$

As a result of technical change, the isoquant shifts towards the origin from I_0 to I_1, i.e. the same output quantity can be produced with fewer inputs. The new isoquant I_1 is tangent to the isocost line IC_1 at the production point S_1. Since, if relative input prices are constant, the labour intensity remains unchanged (i.e. $\tan(\beta) = k = \frac{L_1}{C_1} = \frac{L_0}{C_0}$), the technical change is Hicks-neutral.

Figure 6.4: Non-neutral technical progress according to Hicks

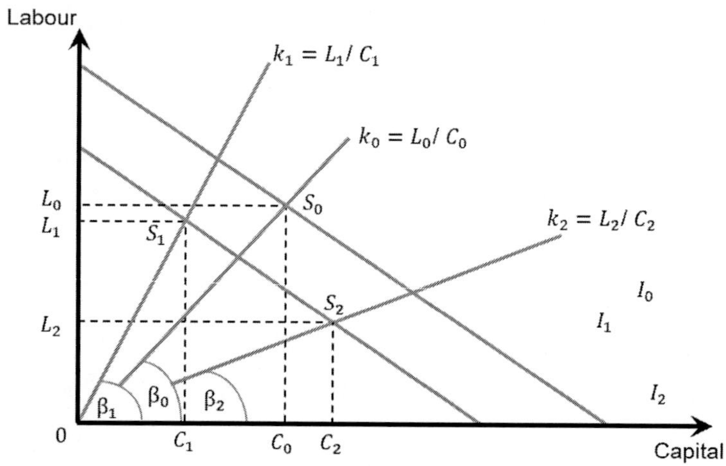

Source: Own depiction

Figure 6.4 illustrates non-neutral technical change according to Hicks. As in Figure 6.3, we begin with the input combination (K_0, L_0) and production point S_0 on the isoquant I_0. Capital-saving technical change results in a new isoquant such as I_1. Assuming constant relative input prices, the new optimal point S_1 is characterised by a higher input of labour relative to capital as $\tan(\beta_1) = k_1 = \frac{L_1}{C_1} > \tan(\beta_0) = k_0 = \frac{L_0}{C_0}$. In contrast, labour-saving technical change results in an isoquant such as I_2, with a production point S_2 that is characterised by an increased input of capital relative to labour corresponding to $\tan(\beta_2) = k_2 = \frac{L_2}{C_2}$.

6.3.4. Induced and autonomous technical change

The distinction between **autonomous and induced technical change** also goes back to Hicks and is closely linked to his distinction between neutral and non-neutral technical change. Technical change is called autonomous if it does not result from economic pressure and incentive mechanisms but rather occurs spontaneously. This could occur, for example, if opening a country's borders introduced an existing but previously unavailable technology. The discovery of the so-called gene-editing technology CRISPR-Cas9, which is expected to have far-reaching consequences for agriculture, goes back to basic research on bacteria in the 1980s and can therefore be regarded as an example of autonomous technical change.[2] **Induced technical change**, in contrast, is the consequence of relative input scarcities. Through targeted, applied research and/or product development, a company will look for technical change that reduces the costs of production by reducing and increasing the efficiency of the use of relatively scarce inputs. Grubb et al. (2002, p. 278) suggest that "Autonomous technical change may be most obviously associated with "supply push" of technologies developed in university and government research, whereas induced technical change tends to be more associated with ongoing innovation and development of applied technologies by the private sector." Vernon Ruttan and Yujiro Hayami made important contributions to our understanding of induced technical change ("induced innovations") in agriculture (Otsuka and Runge 2011).

Incentives for the development and adoption of technological change are influenced not only by relative scarcities on input markets, but also, as was explained above in the case of production quotas, by the policy environment. For instance, research activities might be attracted to products that benefit from high levels of price support compared with products that receive little or no such support. However, whether price support also leads to a greater adoption of technical change also depends on its effects on structural change. Higher prices allow some farms that would otherwise have to cease production, the marginal suppliers, to continue farming. This inhibits the growth of more efficient farms. Hence, the effects of price support on the supply of and demand for technical change are complex. The more efficient holdings will presumably want to expand even if access to agricultural land is limited. Under these conditions they will be especially interested in land-saving technical change. Their demand for this type of

---

[2] See Jakobs (2016).

change, strengthened by price support, will create incentives for the research, development and adoption of corresponding innovations.

In a similar vein, De Janvry and Dethier (1985) differentiate induced technical change into purely price-induced innovations and those that arise from institutional circumstances. Of course, the institutional environment can distort price relations. For instance, in low-income countries it is often the case that more research activity is focused on export products that earn foreign exchange than on products for the domestic market. Agricultural products that are mainly produced by smallholders for subsistence, such as millet, cassava, and sweet potato, are often called **orphan crops**; they tend to be neglected in private research because they only generate small profits for commercial breeders, seed companies and suppliers of other inputs. Where this is the case, national and international public agricultural research can play an important role.

The nature of technical change also influences the profitability of technology transfer between countries. A technical change that is profitable in one country, might be much less so in another. If research is induced by factor scarcities, the resulting technical change will tend to shift the isoquants towards the origin mainly in the vicinity of the current factor intensity. In a country where labour is scarce, for example, there will be incentives to generate labour-saving technical change (i.e. that shifts the isoquant from I_0 to I_2 in Figure 6.4). This type of technical change will, however, generate fewer benefits for a country that is rich in labour and produces using an input combination such as k_1. For example, so-called precision farming will generate few benefits in countries where grain fields are small and grain production is labour-intensive.

6.3.5. Technical progress through the inclusion of new products in the agricultural production process

Over time, the introduction of new products has diversified agricultural production in most countries. Some new products were introduced from other continents - such as the introduction of the so-called new world crops potato, corn, and sunflower into Europe. New products are also created through breeding research with previously known products. Agricultural research has contributed to large increases in the yields of cereals and other products as well as in animal production that sparked the so-called 'green revolution'. The genetic modification of crops has also expanded the geographic ranges of many products. It is now possible to grow potatoes and some vegetables even in Mongolia despite its only three-month growing season. As a consequence, diets in Mongolia have shifted from primarily animal- to more plant-based within a relatively short span of time.

The effects of technical change on agricultural production are not always targeted and direct; technical change can also affect agriculture indirectly through its effects on upstream and downstream industries and other sectors. An example of technical change in a downstream industry that has affected agriculture is the development of a large palette of processed potato products, which has led to changes in the types of potatoes that producers grow and the contractual arrangements that they enter into with processors. In the upstream industries, new types of feed and crop protection products have affected agricultural production. Innovations in communications technology, satellite control, artificial intelligence and robotics are examples of technical change in other sectors that are profoundly affecting agricultural production.

6.4. The effects of technical change on agricultural input markets

The effects of technical change in a sector such as agriculture depend on its relative importance in the economy as a whole. If agriculture is large enough relative to the rest of the economy, then its demand for factors of production such as labour and capital will affect wages and interest rates in the economy as a whole. Similarly, if agriculture is relatively large, technical change that increases agricultural export surpluses or agriculture's demand for an imported input such as fuel can affect a country's balance of payments and the exchange rate. Economists refer to such effects that spill over from one sector to the economy as a whole as **general equilibrium effects**.

In the following we will not consider such general equilibrium effects of technical change in agriculture. In other words, we will assume that the agricultural sector is small relative to the economy as a whole. This assumption is realistic for most industrialised economies, where agriculture only accounts for a small share of the gross national product and, therefore, has only negligible general equilibrium effects.[3] However, we will analyse

[3] 2001 was the last year in which agriculture's share of GNP exceeded 1% in Germany (1.07%). Since then it has fluctuated between 0.8 and 0.6% in most years (Statista 2021).

the effects of technical change in agriculture with and without trade, i.e. for an open and for a closed economy.

6.4.1. The effects of technical change in agriculture in an open economy

We assume that the country is too small to affect world market prices for agricultural products and therefore must take these prices as given. Hence, from the country's perspective, both the demand for its exports and the supply of its imports are perfectly price elastic. Increasing domestic production therefore does not lead to price reductions.

According to marginal productivity theory (see Chapter 2), the falling section of the marginal value product curve (MVP) to the right of the point where it intersects the average value product curve (AVP) is identical to the factor demand curve, when there is perfect competition on product and factor markets. Figure 6.5 illustrates the effects of technical change on agricultural labour. The marginal value product curve shifts outward due to technical change (from MVP_0 to MVP_1). As a result, the quantity of labour demanded at the given wage rate P_L (recall that we assume that there are no general equilibrium effects) increases from L_0 to L_1.

Figure 6.5: The effects of technical change in agriculture on labour use in a small, open economy

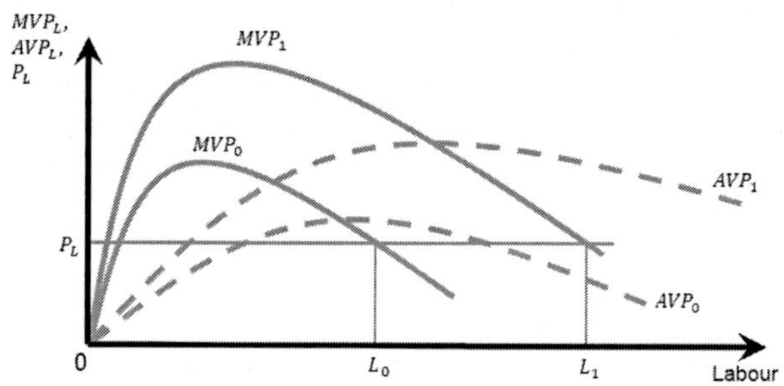

MVP = Marginal value product of labour = $\frac{\delta Q}{\delta L} * P_Q$

AVP = Average value product of labour = $\left(\frac{Q}{L}\right) * P_Q$

P_L = Price of labour (wage rate)

Q = Output quantity

P_Q= Output price

Source: Own depiction

With a few changes in labels, Figure 6.5 could also be used to illustrate the effects of technical change in agriculture on capital (and intermediate inputs such as fertiliser and fuel). The effects would be identical because changes in agriculture's demand for capital have no effects on interest rates (or fertiliser and fuel prices). However, Figure 6.5 cannot be used to illustrate the effects of technical change on land. Since land is a sector-specific and limited factor of production, changes in its marginal value product lead to price increases. Indeed, if the supply of land is completely price inelastic, as shown in Figure 6.6, the adjustments to technical change only affect the land P_B. These adjustments can be broken down into two distinct effects:

- **1st effect:** The marginal productivity of the land increases as a direct effect of technical change. As a result, the marginal value product of land increases from MVP_0 to MVP_1, and the land price increases from P_B^0 to P_B^1.

- **2nd effect:** The marginal productivity of land increases further as a result of increased per hectare factor intensity. Recall that as illustrated in Figure 6.5, technical change leads to an increase in the use of labour, capital and intermediate goods. The marginal value product and price of the land thus rise further, to MVP_2 and P_B^2, respectively.

Figure 6.6: The effects of technical change in agriculture on land use in a small, open economy

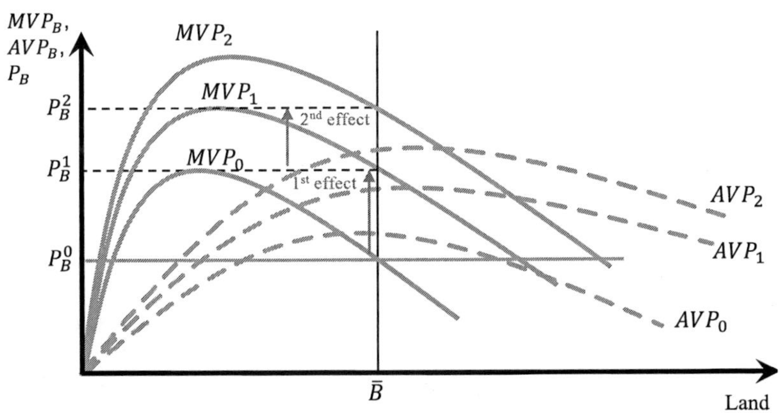

Source: Own depiction

In summary, in a small, open economy with a relatively small agricultural sector, technical change in agriculture leads to higher factor demand for variable production factors and higher factor prices for sector-specific production factors. Under these conditions, and all other things being equal, technical change leads to an increasing number of agricultural workers, increasing use of other production factors (except land), and to increasing land use prices.

6.4.2. The effects of technical change in agriculture in a closed economy

If no trade takes place, the price of the agricultural product is not given by the world market price but rather is determined as a result of the interplay of supply and demand on the domestic market. If production increases because of technical change, the supply curve shifts to the right and the price of the agricultural product decreases. In section 4.7 of chapter 4 we developed a simple algebraic model of changes in agricultural prices over time as a function of income changes and technical change. Using this model, we derived the following equation:

$$\frac{dP}{P} = \left(\frac{1}{\varepsilon^S - \varepsilon^D}\right)\left(\eta\frac{dY}{Y} - \frac{dT}{T}\right) \qquad \text{(chapter 4, equation 16)}$$

where

Y = income,

P = the agricultural output price,

η = the income elasticity of demand,

ε^S = the price elasticity of supply, and

ε^D = the price elasticity of demand.

This equation shows that technical change ($\frac{dT}{T} > 0$) has a negative effect on the agricultural output price, the magnitude of which depends on the price elasticities of supply and demand. This implies that the short-term positive effect (increased output) of technical change for innovative farms that are first to adopt the new technology will fade in the medium and long term. As other farms also adopt, the supply curve shifts and prices fall. We can distinguish between three effects on demand for inputs:

- **1st effect:** Technical change leads to an increase in the marginal value product and thus increased input demand.

- **2nd effect:** Production increases, which leads to lower product prices; this lowers the marginal value product of all inputs.

- **3rd effect:** Changes in the marginal productivities of different inputs can trigger changes in factor intensities, which will lead to further effects on marginal productivities.

The first two effects are shown in Figure 6.7 for labour. First, technical change increases the marginal productivity of labour and thus shifts the demand for labour (its marginal value product) to the right (from MVP_0 to MVP_1). If the labour input cannot be adjusted in the short term, the wage level will increase from P_L^0 to P_L^1. However, since the supply of labour is completely elastic at least in the long term, the increased demand for labour (after an initial adjustment phase) leads to a new equilibrium with increased labour input L_1 at the wage P_L^0. Second, however, due to the increase in production and the falling output price, the marginal value product falls. If the output price falls more than the marginal productivity increases (in percentage terms), the final marginal value product curve (MVP_2 in Figure 6.7) will lie to the left of MVP_0. After all adjustments, the labour input is L_2. The increase in marginal productivity, which led to the 1st effect in Figure 6.7, is referred to as the direct effect of technical change, and the price reduction, which leads to the 2nd effect, as the indirect effect.

While technical change does not change input prices, it does lead to falling prices for fixed factors such as land in a closed economy, as illustrated in Figure 6.8. In addition to the two effects that we just described for labour, the third effect mentioned above, which is based on changes in factor intensities, also plays a role. The reduced use of other inputs such as labour that we saw in Figure 6.7 leads to an additional decrease in the marginal value product of land (from MVP_2 to MVP_3). If the supply of land is completely inelastic, technical change in a closed economy will lead to falling land prices.

Figure 6.7: The effects of technical change in agriculture on labour use in a closed economy with price inelastic demand for agricultural outputs

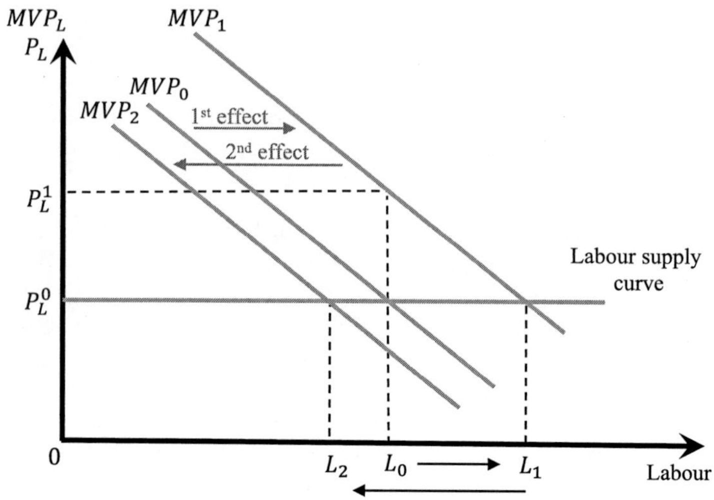

Source: Own depiction.

Figure 6.8: The effects of technical change in agriculture on land use in a closed economy with price inelastic demand for agricultural outputs

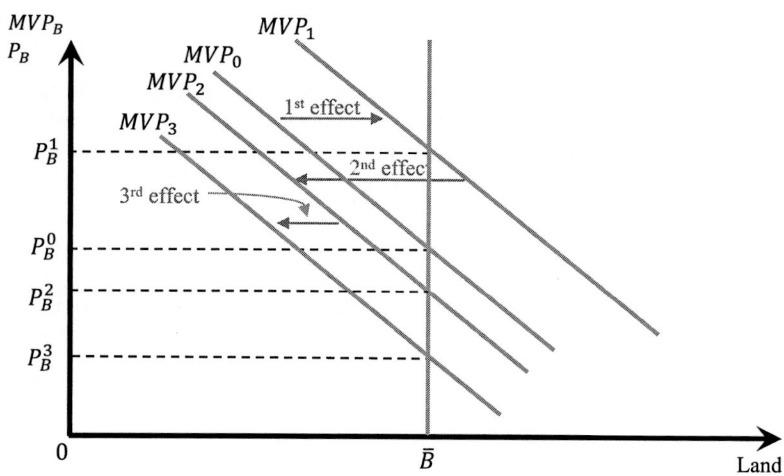

Source: Own depiction.

6.5. The effects of technical change on prices of agricultural outputs

In the previous section we discussed the fact that in a closed economy, the production increase caused by technical change leads to price reductions for agricultural outputs. Based on equation (16) from chapter 4 we can derive the *ceteris paribus* effect of technical change on agricultural product prices as follows:

$$\frac{dP}{P} = -\left(\frac{1}{\varepsilon^S - \varepsilon^D}\right) * \frac{dF}{F}. \qquad (3)$$

Equation (3) can be used to determine the change in the price of an individual product or of aggregated agricultural output as a whole. We see that the magnitude of the price change for a given rate of technical change depends on the price elasticities of supply and demand.

Cochrane (1958) described the fundamental relationship between technical change and agricultural prices in his so-called **treadmill theory**. Technical change leads to a reduction in production costs and thus increases profits. However, because some farmers are better managers and more willing to take risks, they will adopt new technologies earlier than others. These early innovators benefit the most from the technical change because their production increases are too small to have a noticeable effect on agricultural prices; they produce more and can sell it at an unchanged price, thus realising so-called **pioneer profits**. However, over time other farmers will also adopt the new technology, and as they do, production will increase to the point that it begins to depress prices. This forces **marginal producers**, whose marginal costs are no longer covered by the lower prices, to reduce their production or to stop producing altogether. The treadmill keeps turning as the price reductions increase the pressure on the remaining active farmers to seek out and adopt further new technologies. What is rational for the individual farmer leads to price reductions, pressure to adapt, and structural change at the sectoral level.

However, note that Cochrane's treadmill theory can only explain the pressure on farmers and structural change that results from technical change in a closed economy, or in a large, open economy that can affect world market prices. In a small, open economy, the effect on world markets of technical change at home is negligible; world market prices will not change because a small country produces a few percentage points more agricultural output. For such a county, both ε^S and ε^D in equation (3) are infinite and technical change will therefore have no effect on prices. Thus, technical change in a small open country will not lead to price changes or treadmill effects for tradable goods.

In the case of a closed economy outlined by Cochrane, the adoption of technical change has positive effects from an economic welfare perspective. Due to the technical change, fewer resources are required for the production of agricultural goods and food prices fall, which increases real incomes in other sectors. However, social hardship might arise in the form of falling agricultural incomes for farmers who do not introduce the new technologies. Even the farmers who do introduce the new technologies can experience income reductions, if factors of production (especially labour) are immobile (see the discussion of labour mobility and income disparities in chapter 4). Hence, the farm managers who generate welfare gains for the economy as a whole by taking risks, investing and adopting new technologies, sometimes experience social hardship in return. Agricultural policies in many industrialised countries aim to reduce these social hardships via a wide variety of measures, often at high costs and with differing success.

As outlined above, treadmill effects can unfold in a closed economy, but not in a small, open economy. Of course, the world as a whole is effectively a closed economy. At the global level, therefore, Cochrane's treadmill theory can help explain both the observed long-term decline in real prices for agricultural goods on world markets, as well as the observed structural change in agriculture in almost all countries worldwide. World market prices for agricultural products have tended to fall over the last roughly 100 years, as illustrated for the case of wheat in Figure 6.9.

This trend is even more remarkable if one considers that the world population has more than quadrupled over the same period (see Figure 6.10). Falling prices despite an increasing global population were only possible because the rate of technical change was strong, leading to production increases that outpaced population growth. As a result, technical change in agriculture has contributed to reducing (but unfortunately not completely eliminating) hunger in the world. According to the FAO (2020), between 1999/2001 and 2016/2018, the number of undernourished people fell from 916.3 million (14.9% of the world population) to 809.9 million (10.7% of the world population).

Figure 6.9: The long-run development of real wheat prices (1850-2018)

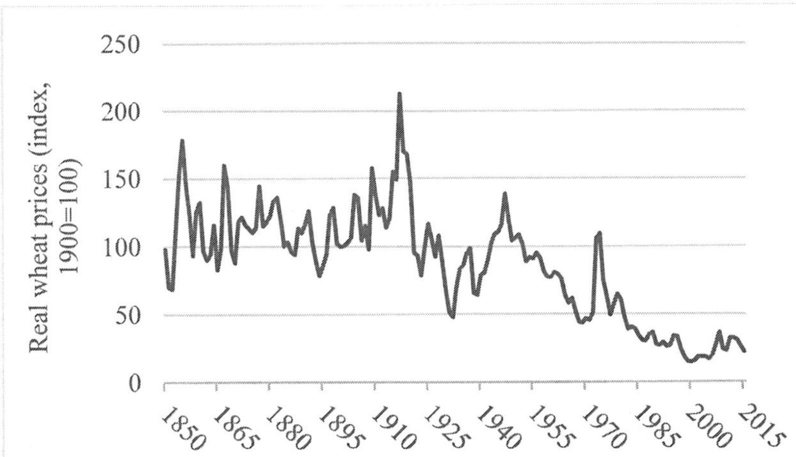

Source: Jacks (2019), own presentation.

Figure 6.10: The development of the world's population since 1850

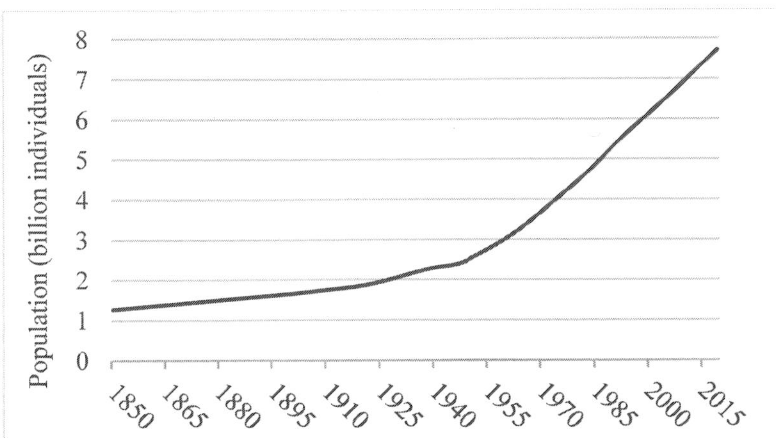

Source: Our World in Data (2020).

However, as can be seen in Figure 6.9, world market prices have not fallen continuously over time. There have also been episodes of sharply increasing prices, such as in the early 1970s and again in the mid-2000s.[4] These episodes have led some scientists to forecast that the era of falling world market prices for agricultural products is over. Such forecasts are often named "neo-Malthusian", after Thomas R. Malthus, who predicted long-term rising agricultural prices at the end of the 18th century and, as a result, famine, war and other calamities (Malthus 1798).

Looking back, Malthus could not foresee the rapid technical change, also in agriculture, that would unfold in the course of the industrial revolution. Hence, he could not foresee the growth of global agricultural production which ushered in an era of falling agricultural prices. As Fuglie et al. (2012, p. 1) write: "Improving agricultural productivity has been the world's primary defence against a Malthusian crisis". There have been episodes of price increases that deviate from the long-term trend, but they have always been of relatively short duration. Furthermore, a strong argument can be made that these episodes were caused or at least aggravated by political measures. For example, the agricultural price peak in the early 1970s was intensified and maybe even triggered by rapid increases in the price of oil following the establishment of the OPEC cartel of oil-exporting countries. The so-called L.I.F.T. (Lower Inventories for Tomorrow) program, which was introduced by the Canadian government in 1970 to reduce domestic grain production in response to low world market prices, also had a reinforcing effect.

The high prices in the mid-2000s were at least partially due to the subsidisation of biofuels in many countries, which had the effect of increasing demand for agricultural products. This is sometimes referred to as the food-fuel conflict. This high-price phase was also interpreted by some observers as the beginning of a new era of long-term increasing agricultural prices (see, for example, von Witzke 2008). However, in retrospect it appears to have been another temporary episode. Figure 6.11 shows how world market prices for selected agricultural products have evolved in real terms since 1990, as well as the corresponding OECD/FAO forecasts until 2030. We see first that the high prices, which began in the mid-2000s, had largely subsided by the mid-2010s. Furthermore, we see that the OECD and FAO are forecasting constant or slightly falling prices for the most important agricultural products in the coming decade. Of course, the fact

[4] In Figure 6.9 the price increase in the mid-2000s does not appear as striking as the price increase in the early 1970s. However, in both cases, prices roughly doubled.

that agricultural prices have tended to fall over the last 100 years does not prove that they will continue to fall, and separating short- and medium-term fluctuations from long-term trends is only possible well after the fact. Climate change, and a slowdown in the rate of technical change in agriculture, coupled with continued global population growth, are factors that some argue will lead to a persistently positive agricultural price trend in the future.

Figure 6.11: Actual and forecast real world market prices for selected agricultural products (1990-2030, 2019 = 100)

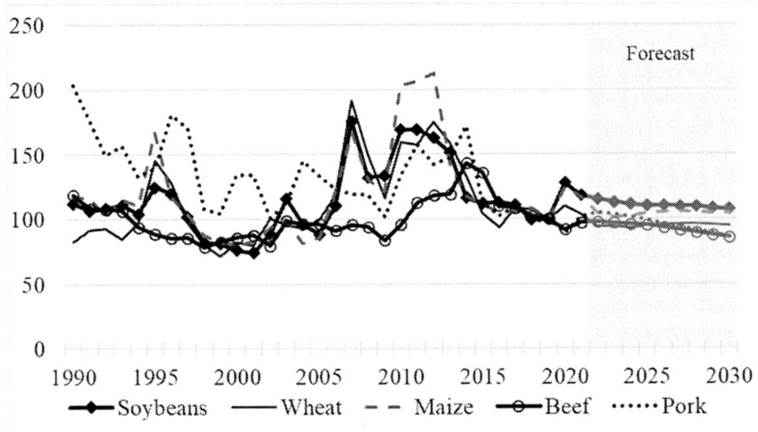

Source: OECD/FAO (2021).

6.6. Measuring technical change in agriculture: methods and selected results

So far in this chapter we have seen that the rate of technical change in agriculture plays a crucial role in the long-run evolution of agricultural prices and thus for structural change in agriculture as well as for combating hunger worldwide. For these reasons, public and private stakeholders in agriculture are very interested in information on past rates of technical change and the factors that have influenced them, as well as in forecasts of future rates of technical change in agriculture. For example, if it is true that the rate of technical progress in agriculture is declining, as some neo-Malthusians argue (see section 6.6.2 below), then feeding a growing world population will become even more challenging in the future than it has been in the past. Against this background, it is not surprising that the quantification and explanation of technical change have been key topics in agricultural economic research for many decades.

In the following, we provide a brief overview of the methods that have been developed to measure technical change in agriculture. We describe some methodological challenges that make it difficult to measure technical change, and we present the results of selected empirical studies on the rate of technical change in agriculture.

6.6.1. Quantifying technical change in agriculture: methods and challenges

In many practical discussions, the development of yields per hectare, milk yields per cow and similar indicators are used as an indication of technical progress in agriculture. Figure 6.12 shows for example the development of wheat yields (in bushels per acre) in the United States as a whole and in the State of Kansas since 1866.

Graph 6.12: The development of wheat yields in the US and in Kansas (1866-2019, in bushels/acre)

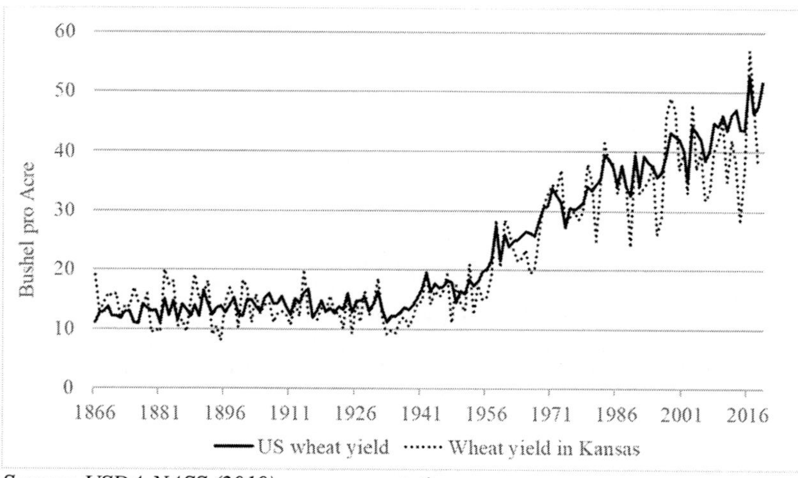

Source: USDA-NASS (2019), own presentation.

We see that wheat yields remained almost constant from 1866 to around 1950 and were also highly unstable. Yield instability was higher at the regional level (shown for the example of Kansas) than nationally. In a large country such as the USA, with many different agro-climatic zones, regional yield fluctuations tend to offset, which stabilises the national average. In the 1950s, a structural break in the development of yields took place in the USA (and in many other countries). Wheat yields increased steadily and became more stable.[5] Therefore, technical change not only led to increased yields but also to lower production risk.

Crop yields per hectare, milk yields per cow, and weight gains per kilogram of feed in animal production are so-called **partial factor productivities**. Partial factor productivities give the relation between the production quantity of a certain product and the amount of a specific input used, such as land or feed. Partial factor productivities are influenced by technical change, but by other factors as well. Increased wheat yields can result from successful breeding programs, but also from increased use of fertiliser or improved mechanisation in crop production. Improved seed varieties often only unfold their true potential in combination with increased use of other inputs such as fertilisation and irrigation. Wheat yields can also increase if farmers allocate scarce production factors (e.g. particularly fertile fields) away from other crops in favour of wheat. In this case wheat yields may increase, but at the cost of stagnating or even falling yields of other crops.

Since an increase in partial factor productivity is not necessarily due to technical change, the rate of technical change cannot be measured adequately using partial factor productivities alone. Instead, researchers try to estimate the rate of technological progress based on so-called **total factor productivity** (TFP). The TFP in period t is defined as the ratio of an index of total output in period t to an index of total input use in the same period t:

$$TFP_t = \frac{f(Y_{1t},Y_{2t},\ldots,Y_{mt})}{g(X_{1t},X_{2t},\ldots,X_{nt})}. \tag{4}$$

In equation (4), $f(.)$ is a function that aggregates the m different outputs of a production process into an index of total output; similarly, $g(.)$ is a function that aggregates the n inputs that were used to produce the output $f(.)$ into an index of total input use. The change in TFP from one period to the next is, therefore, a measure of those changes in total output which cannot be attributed to changes in total input use. By considering all inputs and outputs, the TFP avoids misinterpretations that can arise when partial productivity measures are used.

[5] The absolute annual yield fluctuations in Figure 6.12 increased after 1950, but the relative yield fluctuations decreased. Prior to 1950, the average absolute percentage change in yield over the previous year in the United States (Kansas) was 7.2% (15.5%). After 1950 it was only 4.7% (12.8%).

While the *TFP* concept is certainly appealing, it is difficult to operationalise in empirical analysis.[6] First, suitable aggregation functions $f(.)$ and $g(.)$ must be defined. A common solution is to aggregate using prices as weights. For example, the aggregated input index is calculated as the input price multiplied by the input quantity summed over all n inputs, in other words, the monetary value of the total input use. While this seems reasonable, the research still has to decide which year's prices to use as weights; prices change over time, but the indices $f(.)$ and $g(.)$ are supposed to only measure changes in output and input quantities. A variety of different weighting schemes and indices have been developed, which we will not discuss in detail here. However, the indices that have the best theoretical properties (e.g. Fisher or Tornqvist indices), generally place the highest demands on data availability and quality.

Even if the problem of aggregation can be adequately solved, further challenges remain that make measuring the rate of technical change difficult. In the following we use Figure 6.13 to explain some of these challenges.

Figure 6.13: Challenges in measuring technological change

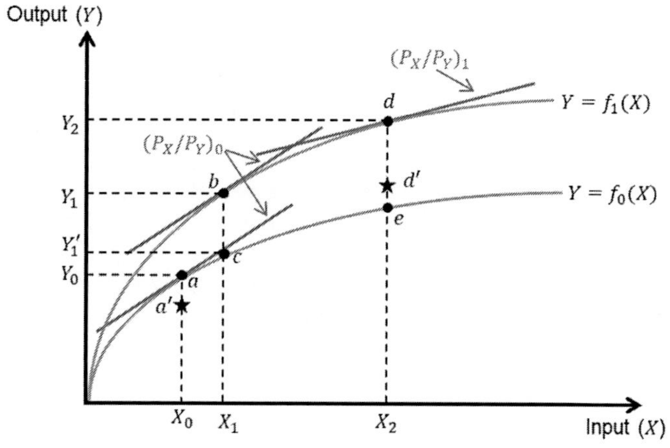

Source: Own depiction.

[6] The literature on measuring technical change and the evolution of productivity in agriculture is very extensive. An overview is provided by Fuglie et al. (2012), in particular Zhao et al. (Chapter 4) and Fuglie (Chapter 16). Ghosh and Kraay (2000) is another accessible source.

In Figure 6.13 we assume that the aggregation has been solved. X, therefore, is an index of total input use, and Y is an index of total output. In the initial situation, Y_0 is produced using X_0, so we observe point a on the production function $Y = f_0(X)$. The ratio of the input price to the output price $\left({P_x}/{P_Y}\right)_0$ is tangent to the production function at point a; the condition for profit maximisation is therefore met.[7]

If technical change shifts the production function upwards from $Y = f_0(X)$ to $Y = f_1(X)$, the new profit-maximising point is b. Output increases from Y_0 to Y_1. However, part of this increase (from Y_0 to Y_1') is due to the increase in factor input (from X_0 to X_1) and not due to technical change; only the increase from Y_1' to Y_1 is due to an increase in TFP.

The correct decomposition of these effects becomes more complicated if the ratio of input to output prices changes at the same time as technical change takes place. For example, if the price ratio falls to $\left({P_x}/{P_Y}\right)_1$ (i.e. production becomes more profitable overall because the input price decreases relative to the output price), a new profit maximum is reached at point d, with input X_2 and output Y_2. Part of the total increase in output from Y_0 to Y_2 is then due to increased input use (input from X_0 to X_2), and only the additional output between points e and d is a consequence of technical change. The point e, however, is never observed but must be estimated to answer the question: how much output would result if we combined today's input levels with yesterday's technology? To answer this question, assumptions e.g. about the mathematical form and properties of the production function must be made.

A further difficulty is that so far, we have ignored inefficiencies and the heterogeneity of farmers. In reality, farms rarely produce exactly on the production function. This is because not all farm managers are equally skilled, because prices and expectations can change within a production period, or because unexpected shocks (e.g. weather) can occur, to name just a few possible sources of inefficiency. Suppose we observe the point a' in the initial situation, which is below the production function $Y = f_0(X)$. The

---

7 Recall: Profit $\pi = P_Y * Y - P_X * X$. The first-order condition for profit-maximizing is $\frac{\partial \pi}{\partial X} = P_Y * \frac{\partial Y}{\partial X} - P_X = 0$. The solution $\frac{\partial Y}{\partial X} = \frac{P_X}{P_Y}$ implies that marginal productivity $\frac{\partial Y}{\partial X}$ (the slope of the production function) equals $\frac{P_X}{P_Y}$ (the ratio of input to output prices).

distance between a and a' represents inefficiency, an additional amount of production that could be generated with the correct implementation of the given technology, but that is not generated for the reasons mentioned above. After the introduction of technical progress, we might observe for example point d', which lies below the production function $Y = f_1(X)$. The relative distance between d and d' (the inefficiency after the introduction of the new technology) may be greater than the relative distance between a and a' because farmers must first learn how to use the new technology and adapt it to their specific conditions. To correctly determine the change in TFP, observations such as a' and d' must be used to infer the position of the production function before and after the introduction of technical change, respectively. This inference requires further assumptions (e.g. about the heterogeneity of producers and the distribution and causes of inefficiency).

Finally, we list four additional challenges to measuring technical change that are the subject of ongoing research efforts.

1. Measuring capital and labour inputs is difficult. The amount and price of a standardised variable input such as fertiliser can be determined relatively easily. However, the price of using a tractor for one hour, or a barn for one year depends on assumptions about the value of the tractor or barn, and the depreciation rate. To measure labour input correctly, the qualification of the employed workers must be considered, since different workers are equipped with different levels of knowledge and abilities.

2. In order to measure technical change, not only changes in the quantity of inputs and outputs must be accounted for, but also changes in their quality. The quality of labour has increased over time due to improved education and training. The quality of capital (e.g. the performance of farm machinery) has also improved, as has the quality of many agricultural outputs (for example in terms of shelf-life, homogeneity, and safety). Over time, the entirely new, previously unknown inputs (e.g. milking robots) and outputs (e.g. biogas) enter the production function. Quality improvements and the development of new inputs and outputs are often the result of technical change; if these improvements are adequately considered, the resulting measures of technical change and TFP will be distorted.

3. Some production processes take longer than a year. A newly planted fruit orchard, for example, may have to grow a few years before it yields

marketable output. The annual productivity of such an orchard will appear to be very low in the first years, and very high in later years.

4. To fully quantify the effects of technical change, all of the outputs that result from a production process must be considered, even those that are difficult to measure. These include, for example, the environmental effects of agricultural production, including both the positive effects (such as the preservation of open alpine pastures by dairy farming in mountain regions) and the negative effects (e.g. the nitrate pollution of the groundwater or the decline in biodiversity in intensively farmed arable regions). Without reliable information on the extent of these environmental effects and their costs, the productivity of a technology and the rate of technical change may be under- or overestimated. In this context, many researchers prefer to use the term multifactor productivity (MFP) rather than TFP to highlight that their calculations account for many inputs and outputs, but not all.

6.6.2. Selected empirical results

Given the many and often fundamental challenges outlined in the previous section, the results of quantitative studies on the rate of technical change in agriculture must be interpreted with caution. Alston et al. (2010, pp. 479-480) summarise the situation as follows:

> "Agricultural productivity is interesting and important but surprisingly difficult to measure meaningfully and discuss in simple and definitive terms. […] The implications of a change in TFP can depend on the source of the change. Also, measurement issues have implications for the interpretation of the measures. At best we can measure MFP indexes that may be only rough approximations in some cases for the TFP concepts that we have in mind. In practice, even the simplest productivity measures can be fraught with the difficulty of measurement and interpretation once we allow for the complexities of heterogeneous inputs and outputs and multiyear production processes."

Despite these caveats, researchers continue to focus on this important problem, and make progress. Comparing different studies can provide clues on the determinants of differences between countries and developments over time. One of the most important questions given the global importance of the rate of technical change in agriculture is whether it is increasing or decreasing. Alston et al. (2010, p. 481) conclude, for example, that "we cannot escape the conclusion that agricultural productivity growth has slowed, especially in the world's richest countries". Other authors, however, arrive at less pessimistic results. Table 6.1 summarises some results from recent analyses by these authors.

Table 6.1: Annual growth of agricultural TFP in the world, the United States, and Germany (in %).

Period	World (USDA)	USA (USDA)	USA (Alston et al.)	Germany (USDA)
1941-1950			1.58	
1951-1960			2.26	
1961-1970	0.12	0.33	1.66	2.09
1971-1980	0.34	0.81	2.32	0.85
1981-1990	0.76	0.67	1.66	3.30
1991-2000	1.61	2.38	1.26	1.97
2001-2007	1.78	2.10	0.83	1.10
2001-2010	1.72	2.10		1.64
2011-2015	1.15	1.81		1.43

Source: Own calculations with USDA-ERS (2020) and Alston et al. (2015).

The USDA's estimates in Table 6.1 are based on an analysis with comparatively aggregated FAO data on factor use and production in agriculture. The advantage of this approach is that it enables a comparison between countries based on uniform data and methodology. The estimates produced by Alston et al. (2015) are the result of detailed study with more disaggregated data for the United States (74 different agricultural products and 58 production factors in 48 US states).

First, we notice the clear differences between the different estimates for the US. The TFP growth rates estimated by Alston et al. (2015) are higher in the decades before the turn of the century than in the decades after; the USDA's estimates suggest the opposite. These differences underline the fact that the results of TFP estimates depend heavily on the methods and data used. It is also striking that regardless of the method and data, TFP does not develop continuously over time. The highly volatile estimates for Germany in Table 6.1 may be due to reunification, which led to a pronounced (and statistically difficult to grasp) structural break in input use and output in German agriculture.

The international comparison in Figure 6.14 reveals considerable differences in TFP growth rates among the 24 countries listed. Particularly striking are the persistently high growth rates in China, which are largely attributable to the radical economic and specifically agricultural reforms introduced in China in the late 1970s. The productivity of agriculture has also been growing steadily in Brazil for several decades. The results for Russia up to the late 1990s should be treated with special caution because the breakup of the Soviet Union and transition from a planned economy to a market economy led to major structural breaks, including in the reliability of official statistics. Since the turn of the century, the productivity of Russian agriculture has also seen strong growth rates. Figure 6.14 further suggests that the variation in TFP growth rates between countries fell after 2000. A possible explanation is that globalisation has contributed to a more widespread diffusion and adoption of technical change in agriculture.

Figure 6.14: International comparison of the development of total factor productivity

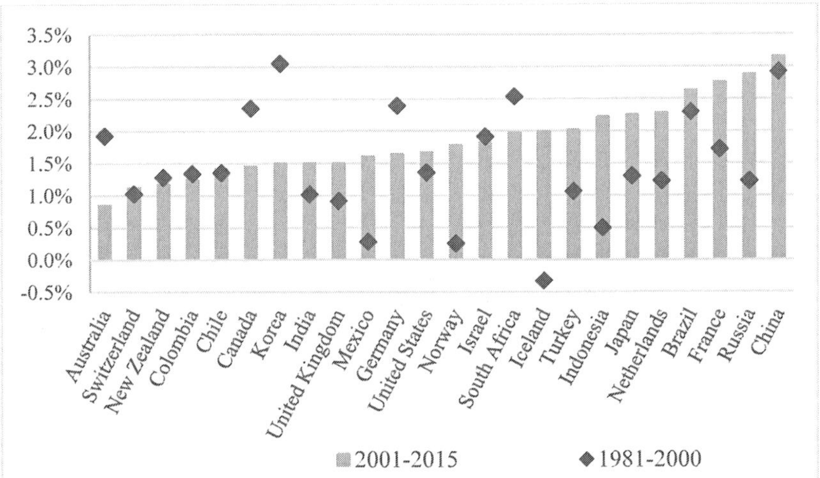

Source: Own calculations with USDA-ERS (2020).

6.7. Keywords

- Autonomous and induced technical change
- Biological-technical, mechanical-technical and organisational-technical progress
- General equilibrium effects
- Induced technical change

- Marginal producers
- Multifactor productivity
- Neutral and non-neutral technical change
- Orphan crops
- Output-increasing and cost-saving technical change
- Partial factor productivity
- Pioneer profits
- Technical change
- Total factor productivity
- Treadmill theory

References

Alston J, Babcock B and Pardey P (Eds.) (2010) The Shifting Patterns of Agricultural Production and Productivity Worldwide. Midwest Agribusiness Trade and Research Information Center, Iowa State University, Ames.

Alston J, Andersen MA and Pardey P (2015) The Rise and Fall of U.S. Farm Productivity Growth, 1910–2007. University of Minnesota Staff Paper.

Brinkmann T (1922) Die Ökonomik des landwirtschaftlichen Betriebs. In: Grundriß der Sozialökonomie, VII. Abteilung, Tübingen.

Cochrane WW (1958) Farm prices - myth and reality. Minneapolis.

De Janvry A and J-J Dethier (1985) Technological innovation in agriculture: The political economy of its rate and bias. The World Bank. Consultative Group on International Agricultural Research, Study Paper No.1. Washington, D.C.

FAO (Food and Agriculture Organisation) (2020) FAOSTAT Suite of Food Security Indicators. FAO, Rome. http://www.fao.org/faostat/en/#data/FS. Accessed on November 24, 2021.

Fuglie KO (2012) Productivity Growth and Technology Capital in the Global Agricultural Economy. In: Fuglie KO, Wang SL and Ball VE (Eds.) Productivity Growth in Agriculture: An International Perspective, CAB International, Wallingford UK.

Fuglie KO, Wang SL and Ball VE (2012) Productivity Growth in Agriculture: An International Perspective, England, UK: CAB International.

Ghosh SR and Kraay, A. (2000) Measuring growth in total factor productivity. PREM Notes; no. 42. Economic Policy. Washington, D.C.: World Bank Group.

http://documents.worldbank.org/curated/en/418451468336625510/Measuring-growth-in-total-factor-productivity. Accessed on November 24, 2021.

Grubb M, Köhler J and Anderson D (2002) Induced technical change in energy and environmental modelling: Analytic approaches and policy implications. Annual Review of Energy and the Environment 22: 271-308.

Harrod RF (1942) Towards a Dynamic Economics: Some Recent Developments of Economic Theory and their Application to Policy. Macmillan, London

Hicks JR (1932) The Theory of Wages. Macmillan, London.

Jacks DS (2019) From Boom to Bust: A Typology of Real Commodity Prices in the Long Run. Cliometrica 13: 202-220. Data series can be downloaded from:
http://www.sfu.ca/~djacks/data/boombust/index.html.
Accessed on November 24, 2021.

Jakobs A (2016) Die vergessenen Pioniere. Neue Zürcher Zeitung, October 23, 2016.

Malthus TR (1798) An Essay on the Principle of Population, as it Affects the Future Improvement of Society. Johnson, London.

OECD/FAO (2021) OECD-FAO Agricultural Outlook, OECD Agriculture statistics (database),
http://dx.doi.org/10.1787/agr-outl-data-en. Accessed on November 24, 2021.

Otsuka K. and Runge CF (Eds.) (2011) Can Economic Growth Be Sustained? The Collected Papers of Vernon W. Ruttan and Yujiro Hayami. Oxford University Press, Oxford.

Our World in Data (2020) World population by region. Global Change Data Lab. https://ourworldindata.org/search?q=world+population. Accessed on November 24, 2020.

Solow RF (1956) A contribution to the theory of economic growth. Quarterly Journal of Economics 70: 65–94.

Statista (2021) Anteil der Landwirtschaft an der gesamtwirtschaftlichen Bruttowertschöpfung in Deutschland in den Jahren 2000 bis 2018. https://de.statista.com/statistik/daten/studie/242847/umfrage/anteil-der-landwirtschaft-an-der-bruttowertschoepfung-in-deutschland/. Accessed on November 24, 2021.

USDA-ERS (United States Department of Agriculture Economic Research Service) (2020) International Agricultural Productivity Database 1961-2015. USDA, Washington DC.

https://www.ers.usda.gov/data-products/international-agricultural-productivity/. Accessed on November 24, 2021.
USDA-NASS (United States Department of Agriculture National Agricultural Statistics Service) (2019) Quick Stats. USDA, Washington DC. https://quickstats.nass.usda.gov/. Accessed on November 24, 2021.
von Witzke H (2008) Teure Lebensmittel: Strohfeuer oder neuer Megatrend auf den Weltagrarmärkten? Zukünftige Entwicklung von Nachfrage und Produktion. Humboldt-Universität zu Berlin. https://www.agrar.huberlin.de/de/institut/departments/daoe/ihe/Veroeff/IndV_Agrar_lang.pdf. Accessed on November 24, 2021.
Zhao S, Sheng Y and Gray EM (2012) Measuring Productivity of the Australian Broadacre and Dairy Industries: Concepts, Methods and Data. In: Fuglie KO, Wang SL and Ball VE (Eds.) (2012) Productivity Growth in Agriculture: An International Perspective, CAB International, Wallingford UK.

Exercises

1. Consider a closed economy with two sectors. One produces an output with the inputs land, labour, and capital; the other produces another product using only labour and capital. How does neutral technical change in the first sector affect input use and prices in the two sectors?

2. Can a country which trades internationally maintain its level of economic welfare over time if it does not make use of technical change while other countries do?

3. The development of factor intensities in agriculture over time is characterised by increasing use of capital and decreasing use of labour. Based on this observation, can we conclude that technical change in agriculture has been labour-saving?

4. How does the introduction of a milk quota affect the direction of technical change in milk production if the quota imposes limits on:
   a) The amount of milk produced?
   b) The amount of milk fat produced?

5. An empirical study has shown that especially innovative German companies did not reduce their employment but increased it, even though innovation is usually associated with labour-saving technologies. Suggest an explanation. (Hint: Think about the price effects of technical change.)

6. Explain why technical change in agriculture reduces or even reverses many of the relative advantages of family farming.

7. Explain why the rates of technical change in agriculture were generally considerably lower in the centrally planned economies than in the market economies, even though the centrally planned countries spent considerable sums on agricultural research.

8. Which technical changes in agriculture do you expect will play an especially important role in the next 10 (25) years, and what implications will these changes have for input use and structural change in farming?

CHAPTER SEVEN

INNOVATION IN AGRICULTURE

DAVID ZILBERMAN[1]

7.1. Introduction and learning objectives

The last two centuries have witnessed an immense increase in human population, from about 1 billion in 1800 to 7 billion in 2011. At the same time, per capita calorie production, which was around 2000 calories per day in Western Europe in 1800, is now over 2800 calories per day, and obesity has become a global health challenge (Federico 2004). While most of humanity was farming in 1800, employment in agriculture today is around 5% of total employment in developed countries, and is rapidly declining in developing countries. Agricultural production has transformed from being labour- and land-intensive to relying heavily on equipment, chemicals, new seeds, and irrigation (Sunding and Zilberman 2001). These transformations resulted from continuous technological change and innovation. Schultz (1964) suggest that a major feature of modern agriculture is a high rate of innovation, replacing physical labour with human capital (knowledge) and physical capital, and that agricultural systems are constantly adjusting to new knowledge and technologies, both produced in agriculture and imported from other sectors.

In this chapter we will provide:

- an introduction to basic concepts and tools to understand and analyse innovations in agriculture and in the food supply chain,

- information on detailed and richer surveys of agricultural innovation that are available elsewhere, including the recent handbook chapter

[1] I want to thank Jessica Blelloch, Hamza Husain, Jacob Lefler, and Jie Song for excellent research support.

by Alston and Pardey (forthcoming) and surveys by Sunding and Zilberman (2001) and Feder, Just and Zilberman (1985),

- an overview of different categories of innovation and the institutional setup of innovation in agriculture,
- a theory of innovation with tools to assess new technologies,
- a discussion of the political economy of innovation,
- a review of theories and measures of adoption and diffusion of innovations, and
- a presentation of several types of innovation that are especially important in agriculture today.

7.2. Background on innovation

An innovation is a new product or practice that allows for a new way of performing a task. Agricultural innovations are vast and diverse. Because modelling and analysis need to account for the novel features of the technology and the economy in which it is introduced, it is useful to classify innovations according to several criteria. First, innovations can be **categorised based on their outcome**, such as yield-increasing, cost-reducing, input-saving, risk-reducing, or quality-enhancing. [2] These categories are very useful in communications with practitioners and scientists. A major debate about genetically modified crop varieties is to what extent they increase yields per acre, save pesticide use, and affect profitability (Klümper and Qaim 2014). Another **categorisation is based on the manner in which the technology is implemented**, distinguishing between mechanical (e.g. tractors), biological (e.g. seed varieties), chemical (e.g. fertiliser and pesticide), institutional (e.g. cooperatives), and managerial (e.g. integrated pest management). [3] Recently, we have witnessed the emergence of digital and genomic innovations, each of which may affect agricultural productivity as well as the structure of agriculture and agribusiness. Furthermore, agriculture is part of the agri-food system, and farmers rarely sell directly to consumers. Instead, agricultural products move through a supply chain that includes processing and distribution. Innovations within the larger agri-food system affect farming and vice-

[2] See also chapter 6.

[3] This categorisation is discussed in detail in chapter 6.

versa. For example, the development of refrigeration and climate control led to the reallocation of production across regions, longer supply chains, the introduction of new varieties, and changes in the seasonal patterns of production (Barrett et al. forthcoming).

Nobel laureate Theodore Schultz (1975) argued that economic systems were mostly agrarian and behaving in a manner consistent with competitive equilibrium for millennia, but have been growing substantially in the developed world since the mid-19th century, with rapidly growing introduction of innovation, increasingly relying on scientific knowledge. He emphasised the importance of **human capital**—the knowledge, skills and capability that make humans more productive. Human capital is a stock that can be enhanced and improved. Schultz (1975) distinguished between worker ability—the capacity to conduct physical activities that can be enhanced by improved health and nutrition, and allocative ability—the capacity to make decisions and adapt to changes that can be enhanced by education and increased knowledge.

Schultz (1964) also emphasised that improved human capital combined with institutions like markets and **intellectual property protection** are crucial to technological changes and innovations in agriculture. Another Nobel laureate Paul Romer (1990, 1994) introduced the notion of **endogenous growth**, which suggests that economic growth is the outcome of economic activities and is not external to the system. In particular, Romer (1994) stressed that accumulated knowledge has features of a public good. It can be used by multiple agents (non-rivalry), and while access may be limited by the intellectual property constraint, it may be shared by multiple agents (partial non-excludability). Therefore, accumulated knowledge is a source of economy of scale, leading to further innovations and growth.

Romer (1994) suggested that the innovations are created, developed, and implemented by complementary inputs, including physical capital, human capital embodied by researchers, as well as experts in law and finance. Low transaction costs and a high level of interaction among researchers contribute to the success of innovation and growth. Therefore, many **innovative activities take place in clusters** which include research centres and other economic sectors that lead to research implementations. The so-called Silicon Valley is an obvious example of such an innovation centre. Agricultural innovation centres have emerged around the University of California, Davis in the United States, and Wageningen University in the Netherlands, among others.

The notion of endogenous growth highlights the importance of managing research as an economic activity and allocating resources among research projects considering the expected benefits and costs. Economists tend to model innovation by the manner in which they shift the production function. Consider a production function represented by $Y = F(aX_1, bX_2)$ where Y is output, X_1 and X_2 are inputs. Parameters a and b are technology parameters, and larger a and b reflect increased productivity. For example, an increase in a from 1 to 2 is equivalent to doubling the physical input of X_1. If a technology increases the productivity of all inputs proportionally, it reflects a neutral technology, but if it increases the productivity of a relative to that of b, it is biased and tends to save X_1 (assuming the function F is concave and the producer is a price taker). Standard economic models consider two inputs: capital and labour. Capital-intensive technologies are those that save labour. In agriculture, we consider multiple inputs, including land, labour, equipment, and climate (temperature, rainfall, etc).

Technologies themselves are outcomes of economic activities. Evenson and Kislev (1976) developed a model of research efforts in which a research organisation conducts N trials, each trial has an outcome, and the final result is the best outcome (e.g. highest yield). Their model fits biological research, but it can also be applied to many other research efforts in which the outcome is a random variable. Consider a situation in which the benefit of the research effort, $B(N)$, has mean $u(N)$ and variance $v(N)$, both of which depend on the number of trials (N). The cost of research is a convex function of the number of trials, denoted by $c(N)$. The optimal number of trials selected by a risk-averse research institute is determined solving

$$max\ N\ E[NB(N)] = u(N) - rv(N) - c(N) \tag{1}$$

where r is the cost of risk, measured by variance (for simplicity reflecting constant absolute risk aversion), and $E[NB(N)]$ is the expected net benefit (expected benefit minus cost of risk and cost of research). The optimal number of trials is where the marginal expected gain ($u'(N) = \frac{\partial u(N)}{\partial N}$) minus the cost of the marginal risk of the experiment ($rv'(N)$) equals the marginal cost of the experiment, $c'(N)$. This model can be expanded to select investments in multiple lines of research. Binswanger (1974) developed a model of induced innovation, showing that the direction of technological change reflects the rewards, the costs, and the risks of alternative research efforts. For example, labour-saving technologies are more likely to be developed when labour is relatively scarce, and the research effort is not very costly or risky. Large organisations or governments that are less risk-averse are more likely to invest in risky research. Governments are more likely to support research efforts that are profitable given their conditions. The US government supported labour-saving research and technologies while the West was being settled and labour was scarce. Israel supported research to develop drip irrigation to address water scarcity, and Brazil invested in research to improve the productivity of its soils.

The creation and implementation of innovations is a process that includes multiple steps. This process often requires research efforts that result in a discovery that leads to an idea for an innovation. The transformation of this idea into a product requires experimentation and development efforts that upscale the innovation. In some cases, this requires testing for efficacy and safety, development of manufacturing practices, and supply chain and marketing efforts that lead final users, whether consumers or farmers, to adopt the innovation. Different stages in the innovation process may be performed by different entities. The **basic research** that precedes discoveries tends to be conducted by publicly supported research institutes and universities. The **applied research** and development efforts are supported both by public and private funding. The commercialisation in most cases is done privately.

Intellectual property arrangements are crucially important in providing incentives for research and especially commercialisation. Researchers who generate innovations which are deemed novel by patent agencies are given a monopoly over the use of the patent (and other arrangements like plant protection rights) for a significant period of time, and the right to use a patent can be transferred or sold (Graff 2007). Many universities and other public research institutes have established offices of technology transfer that provide the right to develop a technology further. These rights are transferred to start-ups or major companies that have the incentives to invest in the patent because of the intellectual property rights. Frequently, researchers participate in or even start companies that utilise the patents, and these start-ups have played a very important role in the emergence of biotechnology in the United States and globally (Graff et al. 2002).

Of course, the design of the patent system, as well as addressing its limitations, is a subject of continuous research. For example, developers of products that benefit the poor or specialty crops are significantly constrained if they do not have access to intellectual property protection, for example due to high transaction costs in the patent system. While in developed countries both private and public sectors invest significantly in agricultural research, in developing countries most investment is funded by the public sector. Generally, the public sector has a relative advantage in basic research, and the private sector in development and commercialisation. Public and private research therefore tend to be complementary, especially in developed countries, and increasing public research leads to an expansion of private research (Alston and Pardey forthcoming). Furthermore, there is a growing collaboration between public and private research efforts, where the private sector supports research in universities and gains access to the technology and knowledge, which serves to enhance productivity and innovation (Rausser et al. 2016). In developing countries, because of the weak private sector, the public sector conducts both basic and applied research. The paucity of a private sector actively engaged in research limits the productivity growth in and the growth perspectives of many developing countries.

Much of the innovation benefitting developing countries has been generated by the **Consultative Group on International Agricultural Research (CGIAR)**, a partnership of research centres that develop technologies to address problems of poverty and hunger in developing countries. These centres aim to become clusters of innovation and to provide new varieties and other technologies to be further developed and diffused in different countries. CGIAR was crucial in introducing the Green Revolution in the 1950s and 1960s and continues to introduce innovations today. However, climate change, which is likely to affect developing countries close to the equator more severely, has increased the need for research to develop new technologies that allow both mitigation and adaptation. **Climate-smart agriculture** is an approach that aims to meet these objectives. Adaptation to climate change will entail significant investment in infrastructure to control rising sea levels and more frequent flooding, development of new varieties to adapt to changing climate conditions, and new institutional arrangements that address the challenges of immigration and relocation. Climate change will provide opportunities for benefiting from efforts to sequester carbon as part of future carbon trading schemes (Lipper et al. 2017). The research infrastructure in developing countries needs to be expanded and redesigned to develop and implement climate-smart agricultural strategies. This requires expanding the range of research topics covered by the public sector in developing countries, and intensive collaboration between public and private research efforts. The challenge of climate change also requires well-trained professionals who can pursue research and assess and implement new strategies.

7.3. Assessment of research efforts and new technologies

Research efforts and the introduction of new technologies require investment that will bear fruit over time. A key element of the economics of technological change is the assessment of investments in technologies and the determination of where and how to implement them. There are several measures of the impact of research, including the net present value of investment in research, internal rate of return of these investments, and the impact of research on productivity. The literature on investment in agricultural research and technology has several important strands. It is useful to distinguish between **ex-post** studies that assess the performance of past investments and **ex-ante** analyses used to assess the potential impact of new projects (Alston et al. 2009c, 1995). Of course, the lessons from ex-post studies affect the future direction of investment in research. Moreover, it is valuable to assess the accuracy of ex-ante studies by means of ex-post studies, in order to improve the prediction and assessment of future investments. Unfortunately, this type of ex-post validation is not done enough.

Maredia et al. (2000) provide a very good overview of different approaches for ex-post studies that are also applicable for ex-ante studies. They distinguish between assessments at different levels of aggregation, e.g. national investment in research, allocation of research to a certain area, and assessment of individual products. Econometric techniques are used to assess national or other large programmes and frequently aim to evaluate the impact of research investment on productivity. One approach to assess productivity of agricultural research is the **internal rate of return (IRR)**. The IRRs of agricultural research tend to be very high (sometimes above 90%). Hurley et al. (2014) suggest using a modified internal rate of return (MIRR) that accounts for borrowing and reinvestment rates. But even after adjustment, the MIRR based on multiple studies of agricultural research projects is about ten percent, which still implies that there is underinvestment in agricultural research.

Fuglie et al. (2012) assemble global results on productivity growth in agriculture, including the contribution of research, by estimating production functions, assessing the contribution of inputs such as capital, labour and soil, and then assessing the contribution of research. Two masterful overviews of the US research system, introducing and applying assessment methodologies, appear in Huffman and Evenson (2008) and Alston et al. (2009a). These studies provide alternative approaches to estimate the effects of investment in research over time on total factor productivity at different levels of aggregation. Econometric estimation of aggregate production functions is very useful for providing a bird's-eye view of the productivity of investment in research and innovation. With more advanced data, we are able to utilise more granular approaches.

One approach uses a **computable general equilibrium (CGE)** model to assess the impact of research projects or different technologies. CGE models aim to assess the interaction of multiple markets within the economy, and integrate the behaviour of consumers, firms, and governments. CGE models can be both static or dynamic and they can interact with models that may focus on specific sectors. Mahaffey et al. (2016) use a general equilibrium framework to assess the benefits of **genetically modified organisms (GMO).** They find the social cost of a complete ban of GMO is about 10 billion dollars annually.

Different types of programming models are used to assess the impact of technologies or policies ex-post but mostly ex-ante. Howitt (1995) developed a detailed positive mathematical programming framework to assess the economic effects of policies, as well as technologies, over multiple related markets and locations. It has been incorporated with entropy models to obtain econometric estimates of impacts (Heckelei and Wolff 2003). McCarl and Schneider (2001) developed a mathematical programming model to assess the potential of soil carbon and tree carbon in mitigating climate change. Their analysis emphasises that the effects of new innovations depend both on their features as well as the policies that are used to enhance commercialisation. Khanna and Zilberman (2017) review some of the methodologies that are used for assessing technologies and associated policies, mostly in the context of biofuels and their impact. Their analysis emphasises that assessment technologies evolve and since they vary in their degree of aggregation, multiple approaches are integrated within a single framework.

Much of the analysis of the impact of new technologies is done with partial equilibrium models. This line of research originated with the seminal work of Griliches (1958), which was expanded to assess both technologies and regulations at different degrees of aggregation. For a given project, let investment in period t be denoted by I_t. The benefits resulting from the technology consist of changes to consumers' surplus, ΔCS_t, as well as to producers' surplus, ΔPS_t, and to environmental surplus, ΔES_t. The discount rate is denoted by r. When the planning horizon is of T years, the social **net present value (NPV)** is

$$NPV = \int_0^T e^{-rt}\{\Delta CS_t + \Delta PS_t + \Delta ES_t - I_t\} \quad (2)$$

An alternative measure of the performance of a technology is its internal rate of return (IRR), defined as the discount rate in equation 2 at which the technology's net present value (NPV) is 0. That is, a research project yields positive net present value if and only if its IRR is greater than the discount rate.

The criteria for the NPV vary based on the decision maker. For example, a private company will not consider consumers' surplus and externalities, which leads to a possible deviation of private investments from socially optimal choices. Environmental policies and other regulations can modify technology choices by the private sector in order to better align them with social criteria. The NPV and IRR are used for both ex-ante and ex-post analysis. The literature suggests that the social rates of return for public research in agriculture are much higher than the commercial interest rate (sometimes more than ten times as high), as the meta-analysis of Hurely et al. (2016) documents. This implies that there is underinvestment in public research in agriculture. However, the private rates of return may be smaller, which may motivate the agricultural sector to use its political clout and oppose the expansion of research, especially when innovation might expand supply and reduce the well-being of producers (de Gorter and Zilberman 1990).

Equation (2) suggests that when assessing the effects of a technology, one needs to obtain multiple relationships to compute consumer, producers, and environmental surplus. The analysis leading to the assessment, especially ex-ante, may require estimation of a production function and the relationship between output and inputs (including capital), and determination of decisions of investment and other inputs used in various periods. It also requires the analyst to assess the impact of technologies on externalities and risk, and the ability to predict the behaviour of input and output markets, as well as regulation. Obtaining data to assess innovations or technologies is very challenging. It is often easier in the case of ex-post analysis, where data are more likely to exist, but the analysis may nevertheless require statistical estimation of the impact of the technology on multiple variables.

Limited micro-level studies can assess the impact of a technology under a specific set of circumstances. Emerick et al. (2016) use a randomised controlled trial to quantify the risk reduction effect of a flood-tolerant rice variety. **Meta-analysis** is used to provide a broader picture of technological impacts. For example, Klümper and Qaim (2014) estimate the impact of GMO crop varieties based on hundreds of studies. They find that the adoption of GMO technology on average increased crop yields by 22% and reduced pesticide use by 37%. Farmers' profits increase especially in developing countries.

To assess the effects of a new technology on consumer and producer surplus, one needs to assess the extent to which the technology has been adopted. Barrows et al. (2014) use country-level data on production and land-use under alternative technologies to estimate the impact of GMO crops on yields per unit of land, and this information, combined with land-use, is then used to assess the impacts on output supply. They show that the GMO crops reduce the price of soybeans by 20% on average, and the corn price by around 10%. Both meta-analyses and aggregate analyses are far from perfect, but together they provide a base for reasonable assessments. With larger datasets on both yields, input-use, and technologies, one can estimate outcomes at the micro-level and then aggregate them to obtain macro-level predictions. However, since the adoption of innovations is generally country-specific, aggregation over a set of countries may limit the accuracy of the predictions.

Gollin et al. (2021) use country-level data to assess the effects of the Green Revolution. This Revolution, by introducing high-yielding crop varieties, deeply transformed agricultural production in developing countries in the last century. It is estimated to have led to a 44% increase in yields between 1965 and 2010. Taking its impact on structural transformation into account, the Green Revolution is estimated to account for about half of the growth in GDP per capita in the sample period (Gollin et al. 2021). This highlights that agricultural innovations have tremendous implications within and beyond the agricultural sector.

When it comes to ex-ante studies that assess investment in new innovations, the analyst may rely on predictions or expert opinion on the impact of the technology on supply or demand of the affected products, and use these to conduct economic welfare analysis. Alston et al. (1995) suggest that the impact of a new technology can be approximated by either **additive or multiplicative shifts in supply** and that the challenge for the researcher is to estimate the most likely shift or the plausible distribution of the shift's value. To assess the welfare effect of a technology that shifts supply, one needs to assess equilibria given demand and then derive output and prices. For example, when the initial supply is $Q = S(P)$, where P denotes price and Q denotes quantity, a multiplicative shift of supply results in $Q =$

$S(P)(1+a)$, where a is a percentage increase in output. If demand is denoted by $Q = D(P)$, the new equilibrium price is where $Q = S(P)(1+a) = D(P)$. Higher shifts result in stronger price reductions and larger increases in output, both in a closed economy or worldwide. The outcomes for additive shifts are determined similarly.

Since agricultural markets are not necessarily competitive, Sexton and Zhang (2001) develop a formula to compute consumer and producer prices when an intermediary has significant market power in the farm commodity and the retail market.[4] Let P^C denote price paid by consumers, and P^f denote price paid by farmers. The relationship between the prices is

$$P^C\left[1-\frac{\alpha}{\eta}\right] = P^f\left[1+\frac{\beta}{\zeta}\right] + C_r \tag{3}$$

where α (which is between 0 and 1) is the market power of the intermediary in the final product market and η is the elasticity of consumer demand. Similarly, β is the intermediary power in the input market, and ζ is the price elasticity of supply. Finally, C_r is the cost of retail marketing per unit of output. In the case of multiplicative shifts, where cost of production declines by a fraction of γ, equation (3) is modified so that

$$P^C\left[1-\frac{\alpha}{\eta}\right] = P^f\left[1+\frac{\beta}{\zeta}\right](1-\gamma) + C_r \tag{4}$$

Trilnick and Zilberman (2021) use such a model to assess the effects of micro-climate engineering (mechanisms for reducing the impacts of temperature spikes on blooming) in pistachios in California, using both multiplicative and linear impact estimates based on biological studies. They account for the market concentration in the pistachio supply chain and demonstrate that the estimated effects of the technology are sensitive to the market concentration parameter.

Ex-ante assessment of innovation is not limited to evaluating returns in order to guide choices regarding investments in research and development (R&D), but also regarding the timing of these investments. Research agencies may engage in many projects, and the prospects of these projects depend on the economic situation, as well as progress of other projects. An emerging body of literature assesses the timing of investment in research. Childs and Triantis (1999) develop a model of managing a portfolio of innovation with active learning, where funding allocation changes over time

[4] Similar formulae are developed and discussed in detail in chapters 8 and 10.

based on learning by doing, changes in market conditions, and the state of competing innovations. The analysis accounts for random shocks to the system and develops the critical values that will trigger changes in strategies. Deeney et al. (2021) develop a real option model to manage R&D investment, taking into account technological and market uncertainties, and identifying the accomplishments that would lead to extra investment in research. The model is applied to assess investment in carbon recycling strategies, and simulations suggest that the expected progress of R&D is an S-shaped function of time, i.e. it is slow in the beginning, has a period of fast progress, and then progress slows as the technology refines.

While active dynamic modelling is likely to become more widely used in technology assessment and management, the expected IRR and NPV will continue to be the workhorses of technology assessment, especially when innovative efforts are launched and decision makers have limited flexibility about timing. However, the future of an innovation is determined by the way it is implemented and adopted. Frequently, implementation of new innovations requires establishing supply chains, the design of which depends on the assessment of the potential for adoption at different locations and time.

7.4. Designing the supply chain to implement innovation

Recall that Schultz (1975) emphasises that modern economies are in disequilibrium and subject to continuous change. Aghion et al. (2021) develop a model of "**creative destruction**" based on Schumpeter (2017). They argue that in a modern economy, research discovery and institutions such as intellectual property and competition lead to continuous introduction of innovations that lead to the commercialisation of new technologies. Furthermore, they state that innovations cannot flourish on their own without a supporting policy environment, which consists of promoting competition and improving financial institutions. This includes banks and private investors that enable the implementation of new innovations and lead to elimination of unprofitable technologies.

Most innovations modify existing supply chains, but major innovations lead to the introduction of entirely new supply chains and markets. Entrepreneurs who implement innovations in agriculture – for example a new agricultural product such as flowers in Kenya, or a new input such as drip irrigation – recognise that the use of innovation requires a multi-stage supply chain. Zilberman et al. (2019) developed a conceptual framework to analyse a two-stage supply chain for implementing a new product. The first stage is the production of an agricultural input (maybe flowers, corn or sugarcane as feedstock for biofuel, etc.). The second stage is the processing and distribution of the final product. The entrepreneur tends to manage the second stage and has to determine the scale of the operation, the amount of agricultural input produced in-house, and the amount purchased through the market or contracting. The pursuit of profits will lead to decision rules whereby the expected marginal gain from all activities will be equal to the expected costs, subject to credit constraints, resource availability, and risk. The investment decisions are dynamic and should consider expectations regarding learning and the expansion of supply. When the innovator controls vast resources and has relative advantage in all elements of the supply chain, the new product may be produced by a vertically integrated entity (as is frequently the case in the production of palm oil in plantations). In other cases, credit constraints, desire for fast expansion, and lack of access to resources may lead the entrepreneur to specialise in processing and rely on contractors for the provision of inputs (as is frequently the case in meat production). Often mixed arrangements emerge where the processor produces some of the inputs and purchases or contracts for others. For example, a winery may grow some of the grapes that it processes but contract with other farmers to procure the rest. This arrangement helps the winery overcome credit and other resource constraints.

Frequently, a new product innovation leads to the establishment of new markets, and the initial entrepreneur who controls the innovation will affect the structure of these markets. Profit-pursuing innovators will aim to establish a monopolistic output market and monopsonistic input markets. Entry to the industry by competitors may lead to an oligopolistic market structure, as modelled by Sexton and Zhang (2001).

The two-stage supply chain is a simplification. Agricultural supply chains can extend over multiple states, encompassing the production of agricultural inputs, agricultural production, processing, wholesaling, and retailing. The structure of a supply chain is affected by policy as well as technological and institutional innovation. For example, legislation that allows breweries to sell beer on their premises led to the emergence of micro-breweries in the US and thus contributed to changes in the structure of the US beer industry (Garavaglia and Swinnen 2017).

It has become common to analyse a three-stage supply chain that includes upstream farming, midstream processing and wholesaling, and downstream retailing. Barrett et al. (forthcoming) surveyed the literature on the transformation of agri-food systems in low- and middle-income countries. Much of this transformation was associated with revolution in the midstream and downstream stages, in particular the adoption of refrigeration and weather control systems, improved processing of food products, and the spread of supermarkets.

In the early stages, innovations tend to be implemented in the location where they are most profitable, but over time they expand. For example, supermarkets originated in the US and Europe, but migrated first to Asia, then Latin America, and then Africa. The transfer of technology was associated with globalisation, foreign direct investment, and the development of human capital and local capacity to introduce new technologies. Once technologies move over space, they are adapted to local conditions. An entrepreneur introducing a technology to a new location may initially import inputs from the technology's origin before establishing suppliers in the new location. Thus, the introduction of supermarkets in developing countries led them to establish suppliers of both raw and processed food products that could meet the standard of the supermarket chain. Ogutu et al. (2020) show that supermarket contracts may reduce poverty in the rural sector and have diverse distributional effects.

Innovations evolve. For example, a process innovation such as **drip irrigation** has improved over time in terms of accuracy, ability to maintain pressure, and lower costs. It also requires further innovation to be introduced to new crops. Drip irrigation initially was utilised for tree crops and fresh vegetables. While the private sector improved the hardware, extension services in California developed new varieties and agronomical practices that allowed it to be adopted on processing tomatoes and lower-value crops. **Private-public collaboration** across the supply chain contributed to the spread of the technology in California and developed countries. The spread of the technology in some developing countries was less successful because of limited capacity for local adaptation and maintenance (Taylor and Zilberman 2017).

7.5. Adoption of technologies

One key measure of the success of an innovation is the extent to which it is adopted. The predicted expected rate of adoption is also a very important determinant of investment in a new innovation, and therefore it has been a major topic of research.

It is useful to distinguish between **a technology's diffusion and its adoption**. Diffusion is an aggregate measure of the fraction of the potential adopters or resources (land) that adopt a technology, while adoption reflects decisions by individual producers. Because aggregate data on diffusion of technologies over time at different locations have been easier to obtain, early empirical work studied diffusion under the assumption that adoption is the process of imitation. Griliches (1957) established an econometric procedure that allowed to estimate diffusion as an S-shaped function of time, where the rate of diffusion in period *t* (S_t) is,

$$S_t = L/\left(1 + e^{-(\rho_0 + \rho_1 t)}\right) \quad (5)$$

where L is the long-run rate of diffusion which obtains as t gets very large, ρ_0 is the initial rate of diffusion, and ρ_1 is the rate of diffusion over time. Higher values of S_t are an indication of faster rates of diffusion. The availability of microlevel data on adoption rates as well as panel data led to the estimation of adoption by individuals, using econometric techniques that accommodate discrete choices including logit, probit, and Tobit models (Greene 2009).

Feder et al. (1985) argue that imitation is one of the contributors to adoption, but adoption remains an explicit economic decision-making process, with multiple components affected by risk, credit, institutions, and the heterogeneity of biophysical and socio-economic conditions. The modified threshold model (Zilberman et al. 2012) views adoption as a **multi-stage decision-making** process in which decision makers first become aware of a technology through media or interactions with other agents, then evaluate it, and subsequently make a decision that may be reversed. The assessment may use profit maximising or other criteria, and heterogeneity among individuals may lead to different choices. However, processes of learning by doing, learning by using, and network externalities result in increased benefits of the technology over time, thus enhancing diffusion. On the other hand, the obsolescence of existing technologies and the arrival of new innovations may lead to replacement of technologies and **dis-adoption**.

A special issue of the journal *Applied Economic Perspectives and Policy* addresses some of the recent findings from the literature on adoption in agriculture (Pannell and Zilberman 2020). The literature emphasises that adoption decision making is a process and that there is heterogeneity in the key considerations that affect adoption in different contexts. Learning and social networks are important for awareness and the decision-making process. Potential adopters learn from extension agents, input-providers, and peers, and digital sources of information continue to increase in importance. Education and human capital are key contributors to adoption of more advanced technologies, and when technologies have strong economies of scale, adoption may lead to concentration and other structural changes in the industry.

Much of the econometric analysis on adoption aims to understand past adoption behaviour, but one of the biggest challenges is to develop a better ability to predict adoption. This is especially important when it comes to policies that hope to enhance adoption to combat climate change, enhance food security, or foster rural development. New, multidisciplinary software that allows the prediction of adoption behaviour is being developed, borrowing methods from traditional econometrics and machine learning. Prediction of adoption may become more accurate if there is more understanding about the importance of the rate of adoption over time and the determinants of the gap between known technologies and their use.

One of the major challenges facing the research on adoption is explaining why technologies that appear to be worth adopting are not adopted. There are several explanations for this phenomenon. Adoption of technology can be viewed as an investment, and a simple criterion for investment in a new technology is that its expected NPV exceed that of continuing with the traditional technology. However, recent literature based on the option value approach considers that decision makers not only choose whether to adopt a technology, but also when to adopt it (Dixit and Pindyck 1994). In doing so, they take random events (e.g. changes in prices, weather shocks, etc.) into account. For example, when deciding when to adopt modern irrigation technologies that save water compared with traditional technology, the farmers may have a critical price of water that would trigger adoption. As long as the price is below this critical value, it is not worthwhile to adopt the technology. Taylor and Zilberman (2017) confirm that droughts were a big trigger to the adoption of drip irrigation in California and elsewhere.

Another explanation emphasised by Suri (2011) is the heterogeneity of potential adopters. Ex-ante assessment of the profitability of a technology is based on average conditions, but farms and farmers vary in their capacity to adopt and the potential of the technology to provide the expected benefits. According to the modified threshold model (Zilberman et al., 2012), the heterogeneity among potential adopters is the main contributor to gradual S-shaped diffusion curves of technology over time, which may result in a significant number of non-adopters. There are many sources of heterogeneity among potential adopters, such as size, access to credit, human capital, land quality. Sunding and Zilberman (2001) provide evidence on how these sources of heterogeneity have slowed and limited diffusion processes. Wuepper and Lybbert (2017) provide evidence that differences in self-efficacy (perceived self-esteem) are a major factor that influence whether individuals adopt a new technology. Hence, education and training that enhances self-confidence and familiarity with the technology can enhance adoption.

Two other sources of heterogeneity are **reliability risk** and **fit risk**. Reliability risk is a concern that the technology may break or not perform as expected. One reason modern irrigation technologies have not been adopted in developing countries is a lack of support and maintenance. Potential adopters of farm machinery (e.g. a harvester) expect to be able to get back-up equipment if the machine fails to work. Without a network of reliable support dealers, adoption of such equipment will be limited to (typically larger) producers who can better cope with mishaps.

Fit risk reflects the concerns of individuals that the technology does not fit their own personal situations and needs. Concerns about fit have been shown to prevent adoption and marketers have developed multiple strategies including demonstrations, money-back guarantees, and sampling to enhance adoption. Marketing activities are generally important to enhancing adoption because they provide information to enhance awareness (Heiman et al. 2020). Failure to select the appropriate marketing or extension strategy by the promoter of a technology may retard its adoption.

Decision makers are not necessarily economic maximisers and their choices are affected by **cognitive limitations** that are addressed by behavioural economic models (Thaler 2015). Behavioural economic analysis identifies several reasons why adoption patterns might deviate from what is expected based on traditional economic considerations. Streletskaya et al. (2020) find that technology may not be adopted because economic agents tend to over-weight low probability events. If a new technology has a low probability of failure, potential adopters may over-weight this probability in their technology assessment. Another behavioural pattern that may delay or prevent adoption is a tendency to procrastinate. Decision-makers may over-weight the immediate cost required to adopt the technology compared to its benefit.

Finally, adoption of new technologies depends on supportive policy environments. Since human capital is a main contributor to the adoption of modern technologies, government investment in education and extension services as well as in information infrastructure is important to enhance adoption. Lack of credit is a main obstacle for adoption, and government policy can reduce credit constraints and encourage institutions such as cooperatives that can share the financial risk to adoption. Finally, Rogers (1983) emphasises the role of location in enhancing adoption. Locations that are closer to urban centres where technologies are introduced are more likely to adopt than locations that are far away. Investment in infrastructure, including roads and internet, thus tend to increase adoption.

7.6. Political economy aspects

Research on innovation has found that the social rate of return on public agricultural research tends to be much higher than the market rate of return (Alston et al. 2009c). Decisions regarding public research, both in terms of levels and source of financing, are political and may reflect the distribution of political power (Rausser et al. 2011). When producers have strong influence over research, they may lobby for policies that under-finance it, especially research that may lead to higher production and lower prices. Similarly, there may be over-investment in public research if it serves the interest of private groups with significant political power. There is evidence that private sector support for research in universities may bias public research towards private ends (Ulrich et al. 1986). Alston et al. (2009c) note the decline in public support for agricultural research while private support is increasing in developed countries. They find this trend alarming because public research and private research are complementary; breakthroughs from private research will likely slow without sufficient public funding for basic research. Developing mechanisms to improve the effectiveness of public research is another challenge, since the allocation of research funds among scientists is conducted under uncertainty, and thus the provision of information and accountability require significant transaction costs. Huffman and Just (2000) suggest rules that combine competitive grants with formula funding (where certain funds are allocated among research stations based on capacity to maintain ongoing research) to support the allocation of resources among research projects, to reduce the time required to prepare proposals, and to award researchers for output rather than input.

Political economic considerations affect innovation through many channels. Support for research and education are obvious channels, but policies that affect the relative prices of market and environmental goods are another channel. Carbon pricing and penalties for pollution are likely to reduce greenhouse gases and improve environmental quality. Chen et al. (2012)

suggest that incentives for the introduction of biofuels led to significant investment in research and development that reduced the cost of producing both traditional and advanced ethanol by 50% or more. Regulation can play a critical role in affecting innovation. The *de facto* ban on GMO in Europe has slowed agricultural productivity growth in Europe and in Africa. Herring and Paarlberg (2016) suggest that Europe has more political sway in Africa, while the US has stronger impact in the Western Hemisphere, and thus the regulatory regimes of many countries in Africa and Latin America reflect this situation. Political economic considerations, including the influence of environmental groups, concerns about the wellbeing of incumbent industries, and concerns about unexpected consequences, have led to inefficient regulations of biotechnology. For example, they have largely limited the utilisation of GMO to producing fibres and animal feed, rather than food crops. This has resulted in immense loss in the capacity to address both climate change and food security problems, and thus limited our capacity to transition to a renewable economy.

7.7. Conclusion

Innovations were crucial to enabling global agriculture to feed a growing population and to supporting a transition to a highly productive, knowledge-intensive farming system that enhanced human wellbeing and enabled billions of people to leave the farm and adopt other livelihoods. But many challenges remain. Populations continue to grow, and, with increased income, food production must increase. Most of the world's farmers are still poor, and it is imperative that we face the challenge of improving their quality of life and opportunities. Agriculture is a major source of greenhouse gas emissions and contributes to deforestation and environmental degradation. To address climate change, agriculture must play a crucial role in carbon sequestration and the transition to a renewable economy, increasing input-use efficiency, reducing negative externalities, and producing new environmental amenities. New innovations are crucial for meeting the new challenges facing agriculture. They require continued investment in research and the development of human capital across the world, as well as policies and regulations that allow for the implementation of new technologies to meet efficiency, distributional, and environmental objectives. Economic research on innovation, combining economic principles with multidisciplinary knowledge, can play a crucial role in developing policies that allow agriculture and humanity to meet the challenges of the future.

7.8. Keywords

- Additive and multiplicative supply shifts
- Applied research
- Basic research
- Categorising innovations based on outcome
- Categorising innovations based on implementation
- CGIAR (Consultative Group on International Agricultural Research)
- CGE (computable general equilibrium)
- Climate smart agriculture
- Cognitive limitations
- Creative destruction
- Diffusion and adoption of technologies
- Dis-adoption
- Drip irrigation
- Endogenous growth
- Ex-post and ex-ante analysis
- Fit risk
- GMO (genetically modified organisms)
- Human capital
- Innovation clusters
- Intellectual property protection
- IRR (internal rate of return)
- Meta-analysis
- Multi-stage decision making
- NPV (net present value)
- Private-public collaboration
- Reliability risk

References

Aghion P, Antonin C and Bunel S (2021) The Power of Creative Destruction. Harvard University Press.

Alston JM, Andersen MA, James JS and Pardey PG (2009a) Persistence pays: US agricultural productivity growth and the benefits from public R&D spending. Natural Resource Management and Policy Vol. 34. Springer Science & Business Media.

Alston JM., Beddow JM and Pardey PG (2009b) Agricultural research, productivity, and food prices in the long run Science 325(5945): 1209-1210.

Alston JM, Pardey PG, James JS and Andersen MA (2009c) The economics of agricultural R&D. Annual Review of Resource Economics 1(1): 537-566.

Alston JM, Norton GW and Pardey PG (1995) Science under scarcity: principles and practice for agricultural research evaluation and priority setting. Cornell University Press, 1995.

Alston JM and Pardey PG (forthcoming). The Economics of Agricultural Innovation. Handbook of Agricultural Economics.

Barrett CB, Reardon T, Swinnen J and Zilberman D (forthcoming) Agri-food value chain revolutions in low-and middle-income countries. Journal of Economic Literature.

Barrows, G, Sexton S and Zilberman D (2014) The impact of agricultural biotechnology on supply and land-use. Environment and Development Economics 19(6): 676-703.

Binswanger HP (1974) A microeconomic approach to induced innovation. The Economic Journal 84(336): 940-958.

Chen X, Khanna M and Yeh S (2012) Stimulating learning-by-doing in advanced biofuels: effectiveness of alternative policies. Environmental Research Letters 7(4): DOI:10.1088/1748-9326/7/4/045907

Childs PD and Triantis AJ (1999) Dynamic R&D investment policies. Management Science 45(10): 1359-1377.

De Gorter H and Zilberman D (1990) On the political economy of public good inputs in agriculture. American Journal of Agricultural Economics 72(1): 131-137.

Deeney P, Cummins M, Heintz K and Pryce MT (2021) A real options based decision support tool for R&D investment: Application to CO2 recycling technology. European Journal of Operational Research 289(2): 696-711.

Dixit RK and Pindyck RS (2012) Investment under uncertainty. Princeton University Press.

Emerick K, De Janvry A, Sadoulet E and Dar MH (2016) Technological innovations, downside risk, and the modernization of agriculture. American Economic Review 106(6): 1537-61.

Evenson RE and Kislev Y (1976) A stochastic model of applied research. Journal of Political Economy 84(2): 265-281.

Feder G, Just RE and Zilberman D (1985) Adoption of agricultural innovations in developing countries: A survey. Economic development and cultural change 33(2): 255-298.

Federico G (2004) The growth of world agricultural production, 2004, 1800–1938. In: Research in economic history. Emerald Group Publishing Limited.

Fuglie KO, Wang SL and Ball VE (eds.) (2012) Productivity growth in agriculture: an international perspective. CABI, Wallingford, UK.

Garavaglia C and Swinnen J (2017) The Craft Beer Revolution: An International Perspective. Choices 32(3).

Gollin D, Hansen CW and Wingender AM (2021) Two blades of grass: The impact of the green revolution. Journal of Political Economy 129(8): 2344-2384.

Graff GD (2007) Echoes of Bayh-Dole? A survey of IP and technology transfer policies in emerging and developing economies. Intellectual property management in health and agricultural innovation: a handbook of best practices, Volumes 1 and 2: 169-195.

Graff G, Heiman A and Zilberman D (2002) University research and offices of technology transfer. California Management Review 45(1): 88-115.

Greene W (2009) Discrete choice modeling. In Palgrave handbook of econometrics: 473-556. Palgrave Macmillan, London.

Griliches Z (1957) Hybrid corn: An exploration in the economics of technological change. Econometrica 25(4): 501-522.

Griliches Z (1958) Research costs and social returns: Hybrid corn and related innovations. Journal of political economy 66(5): 419-431.

Heckelei T and Wolff H (2003) Estimation of constrained optimisation models for agricultural supply analysis based on generalised maximum entropy. European review of agricultural economics 30(1): 27-50.

Heiman A, Ferguson J and Zilberman D (2020) Marketing and technology adoption and diffusion Applied Economic Perspectives and Policy 42(1): 21-30.

Herring R and Paarlberg R (2016) The political economy of biotechnology. Annual Review of Resource Economics 8: 397-416.

Howitt RE (1995) Positive mathematical programming American Journal of Agricultural Economics 77(2): 329-342.

Huffman WE and Evenson RE (2008) Science for agriculture: A long-term perspective. John Wiley & Sons.

Huffman, WE and Just RE (2000) Setting efficient incentives for agricultural research: Lessons from principal-agent theory. American Journal of Agricultural Economics 82(4): 828-841.

Hurley TM, Rao X and Pardey PG (2014) Re-examining the reported rates of return to food and agricultural research and development. American Journal of Agricultural Economics 96(5): 1492-1504.

Khanna M and Zilberman D (2017) Handbook of Bioenergy Economics and Policy: Volume II. Springer.

Klümper W and Qaim M (2014) A meta-analysis of the impacts of genetically modified crops. PloS one 9(11),

https://doi.org/10.1371/journal.pone.0111629.
Lipper L, McCarthy N, Zilberman D, Asfaw S and Branca G (2017) Climate smart agriculture: building resilience to climate change. Springer Nature.
Mahaffey H, Taheripour F and Tyner WE (2016) Evaluating the economic and environmental impacts of a global GMO ban. Journal of Environmental Protection 7: 1522-1546.
Maredia MK, Byerlee D and Anderson JR (2000) Ex post evaluation of economic impacts of agricultural research programs: a tour of good practice. https://cgspace.cgiar.org/bitstream/handle/10947/503/expostevaluation_2001_anderson.pdf?sequence=1. Accessed February 18, 2022.
McCarl, BA and Schneider UA (2001) Greenhouse gas mitigation in US agriculture and forestry. Science 294: 2481-2482.
Ogutu S, Ochieng DO and Qaim M (2020) Supermarket contracts and smallholder farmers: Implications for income and multidimensional poverty. Food Policy https://doi.org/10.1016/j.foodpol.2020.101940.
Pannell D and Zilberman D (2020) Understanding adoption of innovations and behavior change to improve agricultural policy Applied Economic Perspectives and Policy 42(1): 3-7.
Rausser GC, Ameden H and Stevens R (eds.) (2016) Structuring Public–Private Research Partnerships for Success: Empowering University Partners. Edward Elgar Publishing.
Rausser GC, Swinnen J and Zusman P (2011) Political power and economic policy: Theory, analysis, and empirical applications. Cambridge University Press.
Rogers E (1983) Diffusion of Innovations (3rd edition). New York: Free Press of Glencoe.
Romer PM (1990) Endogenous Technological Change, Journal of Political Economy 98(5): 71-102.
Romer PM (1994) The origins of endogenous growth. Journal of Economic Perspectives 8(1): 3-22.
Schultz TW (1964) Transforming traditional agriculture. Yale University Press.
Schultz TW (1975) The value of the ability to deal with disequilibria. Journal of Economic Literature 13(3): 827-846.
Schumpeter JA (2017). The Theory of Economic Development: An Inquiry into Profits, Capita I, Credit, Interest, and the Business Cycle. Routledge.
Sexton RJ and Zhang M (2001) An assessment of the impact of food industry market power on US consumers. Agribusiness 17(1): 59-79.

Streletskaya NA, Bell SD, Kecinski M, Li T, Banerjee S, Palm-Forster LH and Pannell D (2020) Agricultural adoption and behavioral economics: Bridging the gap. Applied Economic Perspectives and Policy 42(1): 54-66.

Sunding D and Zilberman D (2001) The agricultural innovation process: research and technology adoption in a changing agricultural sector. Handbook of Agricultural Economics Vol. 1: 207-261.

Suri T (2011) Selection and comparative advantage in technology adoption. Econometrica 79(1): 159-209.

Taylor R and Zilberman D (2017) Diffusion of drip irrigation: the case of California. Applied Economic Perspectives and Policy 39(1): 16-40.

Thaler RH (2015) Misbehaving: The Making of Behavioral Economics. WW Norton & Company.

Trilnick I and Zilberman D (2021) Microclimate Engineering for Climate Change Adaptation in Agriculture: The Case of California Pistachios. American Journal of Agricultural Economics 103(4): 1342-1358.

Ulrich A, Furtan H and Schmitz A (1986) Public and private returns from joint venture research: An example from agriculture. The Quarterly Journal of Economics 101(1): 103-129.

Wuepper D and Lybbert TJ (2017) Perceived self-efficacy, poverty, and economic development. Annual Review of Resource Economics 9: 383-404.

Zilberman D, Lu L and Reardon T (2019) Innovation-induced food supply chain design. Food Policy 83: 289-297.

Zilberman D, Zhao J and Heiman A (2012) Adoption versus adaptation, with emphasis on climate change. Annual Review of Resource Economics 4(1): 27-53.

Exercises

1. Explain why agricultural innovations will likely be introduced less rapidly in a country with comparatively small farms.

2. Discus the importance of national trade and international trade for the adoption of innovations.

3. What can a government do to speed up the introduction of innovations?

4. Discuss hypotheses that explain the difference in the changes in agricultural production and labour input that occurred in Ukraine and in the former German Democratic Republic in the first years of their

transformations from planned to market economies (see Figures 3 and 4 in chapter 1).

5. Intellectual property protection in the form of plant breeders' rights is a controversial topic. Discuss arguments in favour of and against allowing plant breeders to patent varieties of plants used in agriculture, or specific gene sequences in crops.

CHAPTER EIGHT

PRICING UNDER IMPERFECT COMPETITION

CHRISTOPH WEISS

8.1. Introduction and learning objectives

Under perfect competition the actions of an individual agent are irrelevant to all other economic agents in the same market. No single agent has direct influence on the overall result (e.g. prices) on the market; the term 'atomistic market' is sometimes used to describe this situation. Perfect competition is intended less as a description of actual markets, and more as a thought experiment that describes an extreme situation. In the vast majority of agri-food markets, competition is imperfect and the actions of individual firms typically play an essential role in determining the market outcome.

Numerous examples from all stages of the agri-food value chain illustrate this. Global production of mineral fertilisers, for instance, is dominated by about ten internationally active companies. High development costs for new seeds are a major reason for increasing market concentration in the field of plant breeding; here, too, only a few firms are active worldwide. The process of concentration is particularly pronounced in food retailing. Retail chains may be able to use their bargaining power in negotiations with food processors. In addition, the high concentration in food retail in many countries raises the question whether consumers pay too much for food.

In this chapter we discuss:

- how prices are determined in different types of markets and the consequences of imperfect competition (market power) for the prices of goods,

- how different business strategies affect market equilibrium (in the short and long term),

- what factors influence the intensity of competition in a market, and under what conditions collusion between companies is likely to take place,
- why the diversity of products in the agri-food industry has increased so much,
- what factors influence product diversity in a market and how food diversity is related to imperfect competition,
- how the market power of companies can be measured, and what practical problems arise when measuring market power,
- if and how businesses can be prevented from exercising market power, and
- how competition policy works in Europe and what problems it entails.

As mentioned above, under perfect competition the prices of goods are exogenous from the point of view of the individual suppliers; firms will therefore aim to produce goods at minimum cost. In markets with imperfect competition, the decision-making of firms is more complex, because a single firm can influence the market price through its behaviour. In deciding on the optimal price and whether or not to change its price, two issues are particularly relevant for a firm: (a) how will consumers react to a price (change), and (b) how will competitors react. Before we explore strategic interaction between firms in more detail, we will first briefly discuss consumer behaviour.

8.2. Consumer behaviour

> "Essentially, all models are wrong, but some are useful".
> Box und Draper (1987, p. 424).

Knowledge of consumer behaviour is essential for corporate decision-making, and also for the economic analysis of businesses' pricing decisions under imperfect competition. Due to its importance, a vast economic literature has accumulated on consumer behaviour. We cannot provide a comprehensive treatment here; instead, to provide a basis for the subsequent analysis of corporate strategies, we will only present a simple model of the demand for differentiated products.[1]

We begin by assuming that a representative consumer's preferences for the n goods of interest are characterised by a quadratic utility function (Häckner 2000):

$$U(q, q_0) = \sum_{i=1}^{n} s_i q_i - \frac{1}{2}\left(\sum_{i=1}^{n} q_i^2 - 2d \sum_{j=1}^{n} q_i q_j\right) + q_0 \quad \text{for } i \neq j \qquad (1)$$

where q_i is the quantity of the i-th good consumed, and n is the number of different goods. This utility function also includes the utility of other products consumed, labelled q_0, a composite commodity that is assumed to be independent of the n goods (i.e. it is neither a complement nor a substitute to these n goods). q_0 is assumed to be the numeraire (i.e. its price is set equal to one: $p_0 = 1$). The parameter $d \in [-1,1]$ measures the degree of horizontal differentiation between products i and j. For our purposes it does not matter whether i and j are objectively different (i.e. have different physical characteristics) or are only subjectively judged to be different by the representative consumer.[2] If $d = 0$, the products are independent, and each firm enjoys monopoly power for its product. $d = -1$ describes the case of perfect substitutes (the products are not differentiated at all), while $d > 0$ describes a complementary relationship between the products. Finally, the parameter s_i as a measure of product quality, also known as vertical differentiation. *Ceteris paribus*, an increase in s_i leads to an increase in the marginal utility of consuming one unit of product i.

Linear demand functions for each of the n goods are obtained by maximising the utility in equation (1) subject to the budget constraint $y = \sum_{i=1}^{n} p_i q_i + q_0$ (where y is income – see Appendix 8.1 for details):

---

[1] A comprehensive account of the theory and empirical analysis of demand behaviour can be found in Deaton (1986). Angus Deaton received the 2015 Alfred Nobel Memorial Prize in Economics "*for his analysis of consumption, poverty and welfare*" (Nobelprize.org 2020).

[2] Note that the model assumes that the degree of substitutability d is identical between all products. In other words, if the products are different, they are all equally different from one another. This is a major limitation of this simple model.

$$p_i = s_i - q_i + d\sum_{j=1}^{n} q_j \tag{2}$$

or

$$q_i = \sigma_i - \beta p_i + \delta\sum_{j=1}^{n} p_j \qquad \text{for } j \neq i \tag{3}$$

We obtain the demand function in equation (3) by rearranging the inverse demand function in equation (2) and defining the following parameters:

$$\sigma_i = \frac{[1 - d(n-2)]s_i + d\sum_{j=1}^{n} s_j}{(1+d)[1 - d(n-1)]}, \qquad \beta = \frac{1 - d(n-2)}{(1+d)[1 - d(n-1)]}$$

and

$$\delta = \frac{-d}{(1+d)[1 - d(n-1)]} \tag{4}$$

If the goods are independent ($d = 0$), the quantity of good i demanded only depends on its own price p_i and not on the prices of other goods p_j (because $\sigma_i = s_i$, $\beta = 1$ and $\delta = 0$). If the goods are perfect substitutes ($d \to -1$), then $\beta \to \infty$ and $\delta \to \infty$ in equation (3), which indicates that consumers react with infinite price-sensitivity to changes in the prices of both goods. In the more common case of imperfect substitutes ($-1 < d < 0$), which we will consider in greater detail below, we obtain $\beta > \delta > 0$ (for $n \geq 2$).

The influence of quality differences between goods is represented by the parameter σ_i. If the n substitutes are of the same quality (i.e. the goods are differentiated horizontally but not vertically), then $s_i = s_j$ and $\sigma = \frac{s}{1-d(n-1)} > 0$. If the goods differ in quality, σ_i increases with the quality of good i (s_i), and decreases with the quality of competing goods (s_j). If company i succeeds in increasing the perceived (subjective) quality of its own good (s_i) through advertising, σ_i and the demand for its own good q_i in equation (3) increase, while σ_j and demand for the competing product q_j decrease. This case is referred to as **predatory advertising**. By contrast,

cooperative advertising describes a positive relationship between the advertising expenditure for good i and the demand for other goods j.[3]

The demand model described above is limited, e.g., by the assumption of a quadratic utility function, and by the assumption of identical substitutability d between all goods. Nevertheless, the model is comparatively simple and provides a sufficient basis for the following analysis of strategic interaction between suppliers of differentiated goods.

8.3. Short-term strategic interaction in a duopoly

Markets with imperfect competition are characterised by the fact that economic agents interact strategically: the behaviour of one actor influences the behaviour of another, and *vice versa*. Even very large suppliers with large market shares pay close attention to what their competitors are doing and adjust their own behaviour accordingly. In this regard, markets with imperfect competition differ from monopolies and competitive markets.[4]

In general, we distinguish between two types of competition (i.e. types of strategic interdependence): Competition with **strategic substitutes** and competition with **strategic complements.**[5] If x_i is an action by an economic agent i (e.g. to produce a certain quantity, to set a particular price, or to spend a certain amount of money on advertising), either $\frac{\partial x_j}{\partial x_i} < 0$ (strategic substitutes, the actions offset) or $\frac{\partial x_j}{\partial x_i} > 0$ (strategic complements, the actions reinforce one another) will apply. As we demonstrate in the next section, when firms compete with one another by adjusting the quantities of goods that they sell, their actions can be characterised as strategic substitutes. When firms compete with one another on the basis of price their

---

[3] Whether advertising actually is predatory or cooperative is case-specific. Gasmi et al. (1992) study the market for Pepsi Cola and Coca-Cola in the US and find that advertising expenditures in this market have predatory effects. According to Rojas (2008) advertising expenditures in the American beer market have predominantly cooperative effects.

[4] We assume that the reader is familiar with the economic analysis and consequences of monopoly behaviour. Appendix 8.2 contains a brief refresher on monopoly behaviour in a model with two goods.

[5] The terms 'strategic substitutes' and 'strategic complements' refer to relationships between the actions of companies and should not be confused with the terms 'substitute' and 'complement' as they refer to relationships between goods from the perspective of customers.

actions are typically strategic complements. Which type of competition prevails has important implications for the choice of optimal long-run strategic decisions.

8.3.1. Competition with strategic complements (price competition)

In the short term, pricing is one of the most important business decisions. To determine the profit-maximizing price for a particular product, firms must consider three factors: the consumers' willingness to pay, production costs, and competitors' reactions. To illustrate this with a simple model, we begin by considering a duopoly ($n = 2$). Each firm produces one of two differentiated products, which they produce at constant marginal costs ($c_i' \equiv \frac{\partial c_i(q_i)}{\partial q_i}$) and fixed costs ($f_i$). What price should a firm ($i = 1,2$) choose if it aims to maximise its profit and must decide simultaneously (i.e. it cannot observe its competitor's price before deciding)? The solution to this question is closely linked to the name of the French mathematician Joseph **Bertrand**, who was the first to analyse price competition in a duopoly.

Given the demand equation (3), the profit maximisation problem of the first firm ($i = 1$) is:

$$\max_{p_1} \pi_1 = (p_1 - c_1')q_1 - f_1 = (p_1 - c_1')(\sigma_1 - \beta p_1 + \delta p_2) - f_1.$$

The first-order condition for a profit maximum is:

$$\frac{\partial \pi_1}{\partial p_1} = \sigma_1 - 2\beta p_1 + \delta p_2 + \beta c_1' = 0.$$

Hence, the first firm's profit-maximising price must satisfy the following first-order condition:

$$p_1 = \frac{\sigma_1 + \delta p_2 + \beta c_1'}{2\beta} \equiv R_1 \qquad (5)$$

Equation (5) shows that the first firm's optimal (profit-maximising) price depends on the parameters of the demand function (σ_1, δ and β), on the firm's own marginal costs c_1', and on the competitor's behaviour (expressed by the price p_2). Since p_2 is not observable when the two firms decide simultaneously, firm 1 must react to the expected price p_2. A firm's optimal pricing rule as a function of its competitor's behaviour is referred to as its

reaction function or best response function (R_1). The reaction function in equation (5) shows that the first firm's profit-maximising reaction to a price increase by its competitor is to increase its own price: $\frac{\partial p_1}{\partial p_2} = \frac{\delta}{2\beta}$, where $0 < \frac{\delta}{2\beta} < 1$ (since $\beta, \delta > 0$ and $0 < \delta < \beta$ for $n \geq 2$ follow from equation 4). If the price of product 2 increases, then firm 1 will expect an increase in demand for its own product 1, and will therefore increase the price of this product. Since action (p_2) and reaction (p_1) reinforce one another, prices are strategic complements if the goods being considered are substitutes (i.e. $d < 0$ and therefore $\delta > 0$).

We can describe the second supplier's situation in the same way. Firm 2's optimal pricing decision will also depend on demand parameters, production costs, and the competitor's expected behaviour. Maximising profits for firm 2 leads to:

$$p_2 = \frac{\sigma_2 + \delta p_1 + \beta c_2'}{2\beta} \equiv R_2 \qquad (6)$$

Given the behaviour that is described by the reaction functions in equations (5) and (6), does an equilibrium exist in this market and, if so, what prices are chosen for the two goods? To answer this question and analyse the resulting behaviour, a graphical representation is useful.

Figure 8.1 shows the reaction functions for the two firms. As mentioned above, firm i reacts to a price increase by its competitor j by also increasing the price of their own product, with $0 < \frac{\partial p_i}{\partial p_j} < 1$. For example, suppose the first firm considers setting a price of p_1^0 for its product. Whether this price is the best possible choice for firm 1 will depend, among other things, on how firm 2 responds to that price. Figure 8.1 shows that the best response by firm 2 is to choose a price of p_2^0 on its response function R_2. If firm 1 correctly anticipates this reaction, it will conclude that p_1^0 is not the best possible decision. If the second firm were indeed to respond by choosing p_2^0, then according to the response function R_1 the first firm's best choice would be p_1^1, not p_1^0.

Figure 8.1: Reaction functions in a duopoly with price competition

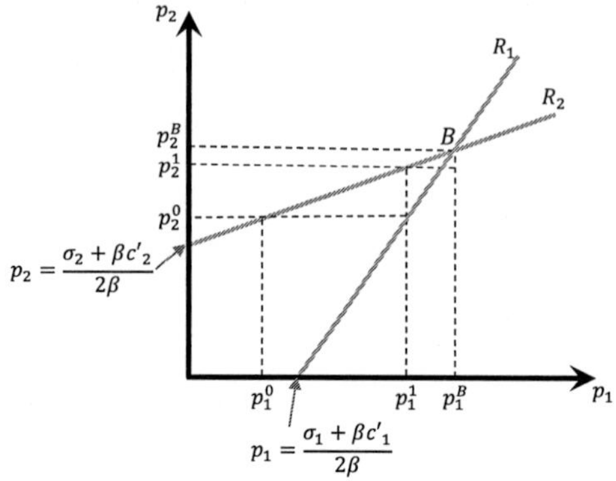

Source: Own depiction

The first firm will evaluate all possible price choices based on similar considerations. For each price that it could choose, it will try to anticipate its competitor's reaction and then, in light of this reaction, evaluate whether its original choice was optimal. These considerations will lead the first firm to the conclusion that there is only one price that maximises its own profits given a profit-maximising response by the second firm. This price is p_1^B. Firm 2 will respond to this price with p_2^B. If the first firm correctly anticipates this, it will conclude that selecting price p_1^B was the best possible decision and that there is no way to further increase profits, given the second firm's behaviour (i.e. p_2^B).

The second firm will conduct analogous thought experiments. In this way, it will also reach the conclusion that the price p_2^B maximises its own profits given its competitor's optimal reaction. The price combination (p_1^B, p_2^B) is the only combination for which neither competitor wishes to revise its pricing decision, given the other competitor's anticipated behaviour; at these prices there is no ex post regret. The first firm's decision to choose p_1^B is optimal given that the competitor chooses p_2^B, and vice versa. This form of equilibrium is called a **Nash-Bertrand equilibrium.**[6]

[6] John Forbes Nash (1928 - 2015) was an American mathematician who, together with Reinhard Selten and John Harsanyi, received the Alfred Nobel Memorial Prize in Economics in 1994. His story became known to a wider audience in 2001 through the film "A Beautiful Mind".

In our example, the equilibrium can be calculated by solving equations (5) and (6) ($R_1$and R_2):

$$p_i^B = \frac{2\beta(\sigma_i + \beta c_i') + \delta(\sigma_j + \beta c_j')}{4\beta^2 - \delta^2} \quad \text{for } i,j = 1,2 \text{ and } i \neq j \tag{7}$$

In the simple case of symmetric demand ($\sigma_1 = \sigma_2 = \sigma$) and identical marginal costs ($c_1' = c_2' = c'$) the two firms will choose the (same) price $p^B = \frac{\sigma+\beta c'}{2\beta-\delta}$. The equilibrium price of a product will increase as consumers' willingness to pay or product quality (σ) increase, as consumer sensitivity (β) decreases, and as the marginal cost of production (c') increases. Furthermore, the degree of product differentiation plays an important role: the more differentiated the products, the higher the equilibrium price. In the extreme case of completely independent products ($d = 0$), the price corresponds to $p^B = \frac{\sigma+c'}{2}$ (since $\delta \rightarrow 0$ and $\beta = 1$ if $d \rightarrow 0$). Appendix 8.2 proves that this corresponds to the price p^M that a monopolist would charge. This makes sense, because if the two products are completely independent, then each of the duopolists is the monopoly supplier of a product that has no substitutes. If, instead, the two goods are perfect substitutes ($d = -1$), then it follows from equation (4) that $\delta = \beta$ and $\beta \rightarrow \infty$, and thus $p^B = \frac{\sigma}{\beta} + c' = c'$. In this extreme case, the duopoly price equals the marginal production costs and the duopolists do not earn any excess profits.

In the case of differentiated products and different production technologies, the firms' profits in equilibrium are:

$$\pi_i^B = \frac{\beta[2\beta\sigma_i - (2\beta^2 - \delta^2)c_i' + \delta(\sigma_2 + \beta c_j')]^2}{[4\beta^2 - \delta^2]^2} - f_i \tag{8}$$

with $2\beta^2 - \delta^2 > 0$ since $\beta > \delta$. A firm's profits increase as its own marginal costs (c_i) and fixed costs (f_i) decrease. Therefore, spending on research and development (R&D) to reduce production costs (so-called process innovation) is a key business strategy in markets characterised by price competition. Furthermore, the profitability of enterprises is also determined by the degree of product differentiation. While prices for homogeneous products (perfect substitutes) decline to marginal costs and firm profits thus fall to zero, profits under maximum product differentiation

$(\delta = 0 \Rightarrow \beta = 1)$ are $\pi_i = \frac{(\sigma_i - c_i')^2}{4} - f_i$ and thus identical to monopoly profits (see also Appendix 8.2).

In competition policy, the so-called **Lerner index** (Lerner, 1934) is often used as a measure of the market power of firms. This index measures by how much prices exceed marginal costs. In the case of symmetric demand $(\sigma_1 = \sigma_2 = \sigma)$ and identical marginal costs $(c_1' = c_2' = c')$ we obtain:

$$L^B = \frac{p^B - c'}{p^B} = \frac{\sigma + (\delta - \beta)c'}{\sigma + \beta c} \qquad (9)$$

If the products are perfect substitutes $(d = -1, \delta = \beta$ and $\beta \to \infty)$, the Lerner index is zero. Otherwise, the Lerner index increases with the degree of product differentiation.

Case study 1: Pricing and product differentiation for yoghurt

In an empirical analysis, Loy and Weiss (2019) examined the influence of product differentiation on price formation on the German yoghurt market. The authors observed prices of 30 different yoghurt products in 432 stores over a period of 312 weeks and created a measure of product differentiation using various product characteristics (fat and calorie content, taste, brand name, etc.). Using these data, they estimated the effect on yoghurt prices of changes in raw milk prices (an essential component of the marginal cost of yoghurt production) and product differentiation. The authors show (a) that ceteris paribus the price of a product increases the more it differs from competing products, and (b) that yoghurt prices increase significantly over time with the price of raw milk. These results confirm two important predictions of the duopoly model: both marginal costs and the degree of product differentiation have a positive effect on price levels.

8.3.2. Competition with strategic substitutes (quantity competition)

While the price of a product was a firm's the decision variable (x_i) in the previous section, we now look at a situation in which the two competitors simultaneously choose the quantity produced. This situation is referred to as **Cournot competition.**[7] Using the demand function (equation 2), the first firm's profit maximisation problem is:

$$\max_{q_1} \pi_1 = (p_1 - c_1')q_1 - f_1 = (s_1 - q_1 + dq_2 - c_1')q_1 - f_1.$$

The first-order condition is:

$$\frac{\partial \pi_1}{\partial q_1} = s_1 - 2q_1 + dq_2 - c_1' = 0.$$

Solving for q_1 gives the following best response function for the first firm:

$$q_1 = \frac{s_1 + dq_2 - c_1'}{2} \equiv R_1. \qquad (10)$$

If the products under consideration are substitutes ($d < 0$), then the reaction function in equation (10) shows that the best (i.e. profit-maximising) response by firm 1 to an increase in q_2 is a reduction in quantity q_1: $\frac{\partial q_1}{\partial q_2} = \frac{d}{2} < 0$. An increase in q_2 will lower the market price, which is why firm 1 will reduce the quantity supplied. The fact that action and reaction offset shows that quantities are strategic substitutes (provided that the goods being considered are substitutes: $d < 0$).

Similarly, a response function for the second firm can be calculated as follows: $q_2 = \frac{s_2 + dq_1 - c_2'}{2} \equiv R_2$. A **Cournot-Nash equilibrium** is realised at the intersection of the two reaction curves: $q_i^C = \frac{2(s_i - c_i') + d(s_j - c_j')}{4 - d^2}$. In the simple case of symmetric demand ($s_1 = s_2 = s$) and identical marginal costs ($c_1' = c_2' = c'$), the two suppliers will supply the same quantity $q_1^C = q_2^C = q^C = \frac{s - c'}{2 - d} > 0$ for $s > c'$. This results in an equilibrium price of $p^C = \frac{s + (1-d)c'}{2-d}$, a profit of $\pi_i^C = \frac{(s-c')^2}{(2-d)^2}$ and a Lerner index of $L^C = \frac{s - c'}{s + (1-d)c'}$. The equilibrium in a symmetric Cournot duopoly is shown in Figure 8.2.

[7] Antoine-Augustin Cournot (1801-1877) was a French mathematician and economist who first, within the framework of a formal model, described the strategic interaction of two competitors and the resulting equilibrium on the product market.

Figure 8.2: Reaction functions in a Cournot duopoly

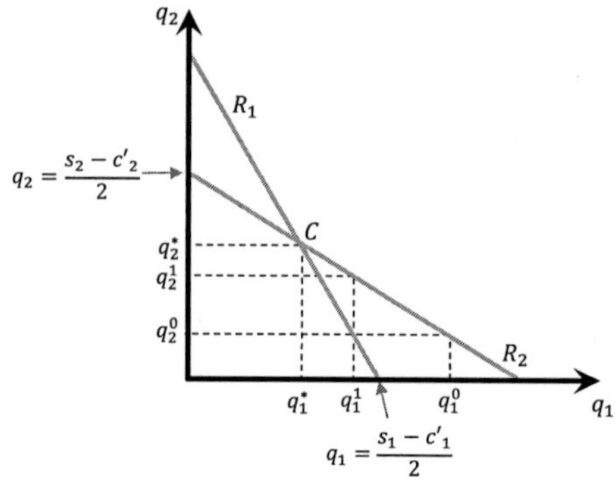

Source: Own depiction.

We see from the expression for the equilibrium price that this price will increase if the willingness of consumers to pay or the quality of the product (s) increases, if the marginal costs of production (c') increase, and if the products become more differentiated and therefore less substitutable, i.e., if d increases ($\frac{\partial p^C}{\partial d} > 0$). If products are independent ($d = 0 \Rightarrow s = \sigma$), the price $p^C = \frac{s+c'}{2} = \frac{\sigma+c'}{2}$ corresponds to the monopoly price p^M, while the price is $p^C = \frac{s+2c'}{3}$ in the case of perfect substitutes ($d = -1$).

Comparing the results obtained for Bertrand and Cournot competition shows that the firms' prices and profits are lower under price competition: one might say that Bertrand competition is more aggressive than Cournot competition. This is particularly evident for homogeneous products. In this case (i.e. when the products are perfect substitutes), $d \to 1$. The Lerner index is then $L^B = 0$ for price competition, $L^C = \frac{s-c'}{s+2c'} > 0$ for quantity competition, and $L^M = \frac{s-c'}{s+c'}$ in a monopoly, with $L^B < L^C < L^M$.

8.4. Short-term strategic interaction in an oligopoly

The discussion of strategic interaction in a duopoly in the previous section is based on a number of simplifying assumptions (such as the quadratic utility function in equation (1) and the resulting linear demand functions in equations (2) and (3)). In this section we examine an oligopoly, i.e., a market with $n > 1$ identical firms, using a more general model. We assume that the willingness of consumers to pay is given by the inverse demand function $p(Q)$, and that the i-th firm's variable and fixed costs of production are $c_i(q_i)$ and f_i, respectively. The profit maximisation problem for firm i is $\max_{q_i} \pi_i = p(Q)q_i - c_i(q_i) - f_i$, from which we obtain the following first-order condition: $\frac{\partial \pi_i}{\partial q_i} = \frac{\partial p(Q)}{\partial Q}\frac{\partial Q}{\partial q_i} q_i + p(Q) - c_i'(q_i) = 0$, where $c_i'(q_i) \equiv \frac{\partial c_i(q_i)}{\partial q_i}$ are the firm's marginal production costs. The term $\frac{\partial Q}{\partial q_i}$ captures the change in the total quantity supplied by all firms (Q) as a result of the change in the quantity supplied by firm i. If firm i supplies an additional unit of the good and all other firms respond by changing their combined supply by the amount θ, we can write $\frac{\partial Q}{\partial q_i} = 1 + \theta$. Parameter θ is called the conjectural variation. This parameter measures the aggregate response of all other firms to a change in quantity q_i: $\theta \equiv \frac{\partial Q_{-i}}{\partial q_i}$ (with $Q_{-i} = \sum_{j=1}^{n} q_j$ for $i \neq j$). As above, since all decisions are taken simultaneously, firm i does not know how its competitors will react if it changes q_i; θ measures how firm i anticipates (i.e. conjectures) that its competitors will react. It follows from the first-order condition that:

$$p(Q) = -\frac{\partial p(Q)}{\partial Q}(1+\theta)q_i + c_i'(q_i) \tag{11}$$

Expanding and rearranging terms for the case of n identical firms (i.e. for $c_i'(q_i) = c'(q)$ and $q_i = q = \frac{Q}{n}$) gives:

$$\begin{aligned} p(Q) &= -\frac{\partial p(Q)}{\partial Q}\frac{p(Q)}{p(Q)}\frac{Q}{Q}(1+\theta)q + c'(q) \\ &= \frac{1}{\varepsilon}(1+\theta)\frac{q}{Q}p(Q) + c'(q), \end{aligned} \tag{12}$$

where $\varepsilon = \left|\frac{\partial Q}{\partial p(Q)}\frac{p(Q)}{Q}\right|$ is the absolute value of the own-price elasticity of demand, which in turn depends on the extent of the products' substitutability. The resulting equilibrium price is:

$$p(Q) = \frac{c'(q)}{1-(1+\theta)/\varepsilon n} = \mu c'(q) \tag{13}$$

The equilibrium price in an oligopoly is determined by marginal production costs ($c'(q)$), and the size of the **mark-up** $\mu = \frac{1}{1-(1+\theta)/\varepsilon n}$. The level of this mark-up, in turn, depends on three factors:

The own-price elasticity of demand (ε): The lower the absolute price elasticity of demand (i.e. the more urgently consumers want to buy the product), the higher the equilibrium price $p(Q)$. The price elasticity of demand also highlights the importance of product differentiation: the more readily consumers substitute the products for one another, the more price-elastic demand will be (from $d \rightarrow -1$ it follows from equation (4) that $\beta \rightarrow \infty$ and thus $\varepsilon \rightarrow \infty$), and the lower the equilibrium price.

The number of suppliers (n): The higher the number of competitors, the lower the equilibrium price.

The behaviour of the suppliers (θ): The concept of conjectural variation is the main innovation of this oligopoly model compared with the duopoly model described above. For this reason, we study its implications in greater detail in the following.

Very aggressive market conduct is reflected in a conjectural variation of $\theta = -1$. For example, if firm i reduces output in an attempt to raise the market price, $\theta = -1$ implies that competitors will completely counteract this measure by increasing their output by the same amount. As can be seen in equation (13), if $\theta = -1$ the mark-up μ equals one and the price equals marginal cost. Note that marginal cost prices arise whenever $\theta = -1$, regardless of the number of competitors (as long as $n > 1$) and the price elasticity of demand. This illustrates an important insight: the number of firms is not, *per se*, a reliable indicator of the intensity of competition in a market. As we saw above, two competitors can be enough to guarantee perfect competition and thus efficient market outcomes. Hence, focusing exclusively on indicators of market structure (i.e. the number of firms and their relative sizes) can be misleading; competition policy must focus on firms' actual conduct.

Perfect competition ($p = c'(q)$) will also be the result of an atomistic market, i.e. if $n \rightarrow \infty$. Furthermore, the oligopoly price equation (13) above can also depict monopoly outcomes as a special case. A conjectural variation of $\theta = n - 1$ means that the firms' conduct is perfectly synchronised; an increase (a reduction) in q_i by one unit is copied by all other firms; each increases (decreases) quantity q_j by one unit and, therefore, quantity Q_{-i} increases (decreases) by another $n-1$ units. This synchronised behaviour leads to the same market outcome as if the n firms had reached an explicit collusive agreement, and the market price is exactly the same as in a monopoly: $p = \frac{c'(q)}{1+1/\varepsilon} = p^M$.

Finally, a conjectural variation of $\theta = 0$ is referred to as Cournot-Nash behaviour. In this case, firm i assumes that its competitors will not react at all if it changes its output.

The concept of conjectural variation is particularly useful for illustrating the different paradigms of competition policy. The Lerner index of firm i's market power can be calculated from equation (6) as follows: $L_i^{CV} = \frac{p(Q)-c'(q_i)}{p(Q)} = \frac{1}{\varepsilon}(1+\theta)\frac{q_i}{Q} = \frac{1}{\varepsilon}(1+\theta)r_i$, where $0 < r_i = q_i/Q \leq 1$ is the market share of supplier i. The aggregate Lerner index for the entire market, can be calculated from the individual firms' Lerner indices, each weighted by the respective firm's market share:

$$L^{CV} = \sum\nolimits_{i=1}^{n} r_i L_i^{CV} = \sum\nolimits_{i=1}^{n} \frac{1}{\varepsilon}(1+\theta) r_i^2 = \frac{1+\theta}{\varepsilon}\sum_{i=1}^{n} r_i^2 = \frac{1+\theta}{\varepsilon} HHI \qquad (14)$$

where $HHI = \sum_{i=1}^{n} r_i^2$ is the Herfindahl-Hirschman index of supplier concentration. This index ranges from $1/n$ (when all firms have an equal market share of $r_i = r = 1/n$) to 1 (in the case of a monopoly, when $r_i = 1$ and $n = 1$).

Equation (14) can be interpreted in a number of ways. First, for a given consumer behaviour (represented by the price elasticity of demand ε), the mark-up on marginal costs increases with market concentration (measured by the Herfindahl-Hirschman index HHI). Thus, competition policy should aim at preventing (excessive) increases in market concentration, by regulating mergers or by breaking firms that have market power. The so-called Harvard School of competition policy supports this view. According to the Chicago School, however, a high Lerner-index is not (necessarily) caused by firms exploiting their market power in concentrated markets. Instead, the superior efficiency (i.e. low marginal costs) of individual firms leads to both a high Herfindahl-Hirschman index and a high Lerner-index. In this case, consumers benefit when inefficient firms are taken over by efficient competitors, and restrictive competition policies that prohibit such takeover will result in welfare losses. Divergent perspectives and sometimes diametrically opposed competition policy recommendations by economists are often a consequence of different interpretations of equation (14).

The key advantage of the conjectural variation model is that the entire range of competitive conduct (from perfect competition to monopoly) is represented by a single parameter (θ). This makes it easy to analyse the consequences of entrepreneurial behaviour for market outcomes such as prices, quantities, and profits in equilibrium. However, and this is the main drawback of the model, entrepreneurial behaviour is only represented by θ and not explained; θ is exogenous. Why and under what conditions businesses act aggressively or collude remains unanswered.

In addition, as mentioned above, this static model does not capture reactions in the usual sense of the word. Firms do not react to previous actions by other firms in the model, instead they anticipate the reactions of other firms when they make simultaneous decisions. Hence, long-term (strategic) business decisions are, by definition, not considered.

Case study 2: (Common) ownership matters

The basic oligopoly models discussed above ignore important issues, such as the internal organization of firms and their ownership. Ownership and market power, however, are interrelated. The rapid growth in investment funds has had a significant impact on the ownership structure of large firms. Institutional investors today hold substantial shares in multiple firms in the same industry (common ownership). Common ownership of same-industry firms incentivizes both investors and managers to maximize portfolio rather than firm profits, which could lead to anti-competitive outcomes.

Torshizi and Clapp (2021) study the impact of common ownership in the US seed sector. In this sector, the 'Big 6' (Monsanto, Bayer, Dow, DuPont, Syngenta, and BASF) control the majority of seed and chemical sales. The authors document that the largest asset management companies (BlackRock, Vanguard, State Street, Capital Group, and Fidelity) collectively hold substantial shares in the 'Big 6' (see Figure 8.3) and argue that this network of common owners and the ownership linkages among rival firms could further reduce the intensity of competition in this sector.

Figure 8.3: Total percentage ownership shares of institutional investors in Bayer, Monsanto, DuPont, Syngenta, and Dow, 2000–2016.

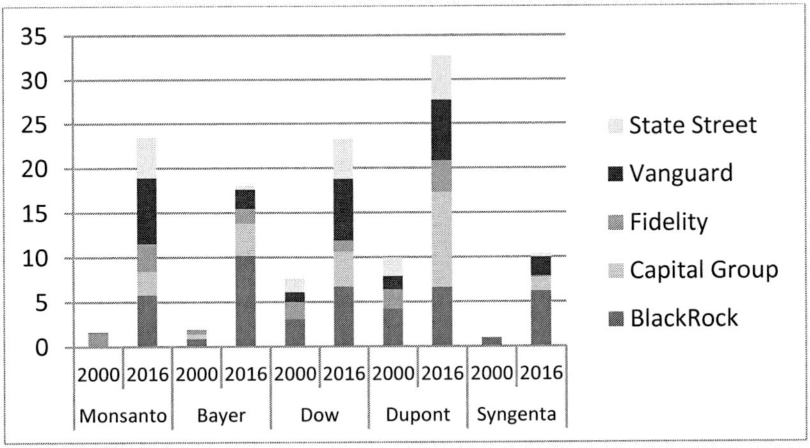

Source: Torshizi and Clapp (2021, p. 42).

Following previous research in the area of finance and industrial organization, Torshizi and Clapp (2021) show how common ownership moves the market from the more competitive standard Cournot-Nash oligopoly equilibrium toward a less competitive outcome (which implies an inward shift of firms' reaction functions – more details are provided in an online appendix of their paper). This implies an increase in "effective concentration", which can be represented by a modified Herfindahl-Hirschmann Index $MHHI = HHI + \Delta$ (where Δ measures the effects of common ownership). The authors' empirical calculations for the US seed market show that the mean of Δ across corn, soybeans and cotton is almost as high as the HHI market concentration index. In an econometric analysis, they investigate the impact of common ownership on seed prices for soybean, corn, and cotton seed prices over the 1997–2017 period. Their analysis suggests that, on average, 14.6% of the increase in corn, cotton, and soybean seed prices can be attributed to the increase in common ownership. Common ownership matters in the US seed market.

8.5. The behaviour of businesses in the long run

If a model only depicts a single point in time, it cannot distinguish between tactical (short-term) and strategic (long-term) decisions. Such a model cannot provide answers to many important questions. For example: What strategies can firms use to force existing competitors out of the market (or prevent new competitors from entering)? Under what conditions are mergers between firms profitable? How much should an entrant differentiate its product from that of an incumbent, and should the entrant supply higher or lower quality? How much should a firm invest in advertising or in R&D to improve production technology? These and many other strategic decisions change the environment (market structure) within which firms make the short-term (tactical) decisions discussed in previous sections (i.e. decisions on optimal prices or quantities).

Strategic questions are analysed in modern industrial economics using two- or multi-stage games. These games show that the decision for or against a particular strategic measure is influenced by the nature of competition (strategic complements or substitutes). In the following we will illustrate this using a simple example of a market with two firms (duopoly) and two time-periods.

Consider the first firm's strategic decision to invest in improving its production technology. From the firm's point of view, expenditures on research and development (R&D) in the first period (t_1) constitute fixed costs. If the R&D efforts are successful, firm 1 will be able to compete with firm 2 in the following period (t_2) with a more efficient production technology (i.e. the first firm's marginal costs will decrease). This competitive advantage will influence the firm's tactical price or quantity decisions in the second period. When making a strategic decision, firm 1 must consider how firm 2 will respond to this decision. The two diagrams in Figure 8.4 show that the second firm's reaction in period t_2 will depend on the nature of the competition, and that this plays an essential role in assessing the profitability of the original strategic R&D decision in t_1.

Figure 8.4: Direct and indirect effects of R&D expenditure

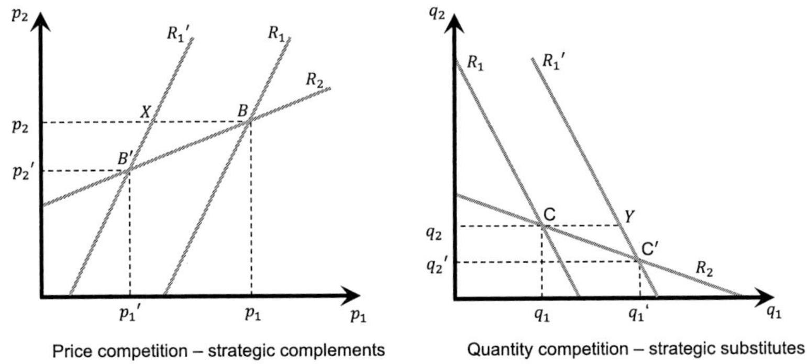

Source: Own depiction.

Figure 8.4 shows the tactical decisions of the two firms in t_2. Due to the first firm's investments in R&D in t_1, its marginal costs decline. This reduction in marginal costs changes the first firm's choice of an optimal price or quantity in t_2. In the case of Bertrand competition (price competition), reduced marginal costs will lead firm 1 to lower the price of its own product. This tactical decision is apparent from equation (5), in which $\frac{\partial p_1}{\partial c_1'} = \frac{1}{2} > 0$: for a given competitor's price (p_2), if c_1' decreases then so does the optimal price p_1. This corresponds to a shift of the first firm's reaction function from R_1 to R_1' in the left panel of Figure 8.4. Firm 2 will respond to a decline in p_1 with a price reduction for its own product. The adjustments in both prices in period t_2 as a consequence of the first firm's R&D expenditures in t_1 (and the associated reduction in marginal costs) are represented by a movement from point B to a new equilibrium point B' in Figure 8.4.

For the overall assessment of the first firm's strategic decision, two countervailing effects are important. First, the first firm's profit increases due to the reduction in its production costs and the associated optimal adjustment of price p_1. This direct effect corresponds to the movement from point B to point X (with unchanged p_2) in the left panel of Figure 8.4. Second, however, the competitor's response (the indirect or strategic effect) acts in the opposite direction; firm 2 reduces its price to p_2', which reduces the demand for firm 1 and thus reduces its profits. This strategic effect of the competitor's reaction corresponds to the movement from point X to point B' in Figure 8.4.

Hence, under Bertrand competition (strategic complements) the direct and indirect effects of the first firm's strategic decision to invest in R&D work in opposite directions. In contrast, the same strategic decision under conditions of Cournot competition (strategic substitutes) will trigger mutually reinforcing direct and indirect effects. The right panel of Figure 8.4 shows that in the case of Cournot competition the reduction in marginal costs will lead to an increase in the first firm's output; the reaction function shifts to the right from R_1 to $R_1{}'$. This shift is due to the fact that $\frac{\partial q_1}{\partial c_1'} = -\frac{1}{2} < 0$ in equation (10). The direct effect therefore leads to a move from point C to point Y. The second firm's response benefits firm 1 in this case; firm 2 will, in its own interest, reduce its output from q_2 to q_2', to which firm 1 will respond by further increasing its output to q_1'. The indirect (strategic) effect therefore leads to a movement from point Y to point C'. Both the direct and indirect effects increase profits for firm 1.

This example illustrates that the profitability of a firm's long-term (strategic) decisions is determined by the nature of market competition (strategic complements or strategic substitutes).[8] The form of competition in a market thus not only influences the level of prices or quantities in the short term but is also decisive for assessing the profitability of long-term business strategies. The effects described in the example above are relevant not only for the specific case of R&D expenditures, but also for other strategic decisions such as advertising, the outsourcing of production processes, the bundling and coupling of products, and strategic trade policy.

8.6. Extensions and modifications

8.6.1. The choice between price and quantity competition

Which strategy (price- or quantity-setting behaviour) should a firm choose? Under what conditions would it be profitable for a firm to fix a particular price and let consumers decide how much they want to consume (Bertrand competition)? When would the alternative strategy of setting the optimal quantity (Cournot competition) be more profitable? What happens when firms choose different strategies? While we have so far assumed that the

[8] Fudenberg and Tirole (1984) also distinguish between "soft" and "tough" strategies. In the situation just described, reductions in marginal costs caused by expenditures on R&D will induce firm 1 to lower its price and increase output. This will reduce the competitor's profits. Such strategies are called "tough". A "soft" strategy increases the competitor's profits.

form of competition (price or quantity competition) is exogenous, we now want to examine the choice between these two strategies as a managerial decision.

When firms are not perfectly informed about consumer demand, the choice between price and quantity competition depends crucially on the characteristics of the production technology. If production technology is characterised by sharply increasing marginal costs (i.e. an increase in output is associated with high additional costs in the short term), quantity setting is more profitable. If firms were to fix prices instead of quantities in this situation, any fluctuation in demand would have to be met by adjusting quantities, which would entail high additional costs. However, if marginal costs are constant (or only rise moderately), price-setting behaviour becomes more attractive. Sharply increasing marginal costs are to be expected *ceteris paribus* where firms face short-term capacity constraints. In contrast, constant or moderately increasing marginal costs are more plausible where firms have excess capacity or are taking a long-term perspective.

What happens if individual businesses choose different strategies? Assume for example, that one firm opts for the Bertrand strategy, while the competitor chooses a Cournot strategy. In this case, which is an example of a so-called **mixed oligopoly**, it can be shown that Cournot behaviour will prevail over Bertrand behaviour as a dominant strategy. Overall, the assumption of quantity-setting behaviour has established itself as the starting point for numerous applied analyses, especially in studies of relatively homogeneous products. As Shapiro (1989, p. 346) concludes in an excellent survey: "For homogenous goods, Cournot's model remains the workhorse oligopoly theory".

8.6.2. Competition with endogenous market structure

So far, we have analysed imperfect competition under the assumption that the market structure (i.e. the number of competitors, production technology and consumer preferences) is exogenous. In this framework, the given, exogenous market structure determines firm conduct (the aggressiveness of competition as expressed in the choice of prices and quantities, advertising expenditure, investments in R&D, etc.) which again affects market performance in equilibrium (prices, quantities, profits and consumer welfare). However, this framework, which is referred to as the classic structure-conduct-performance (SCP) approach in industrial economics, ignores the fact that some firms might exit the market if they perform poorly, or that new firms might be attracted by high profits and enter the market. Market structure (the number of firms, for example) therefore depends on firms' conduct and performance, and is thus endogenous. Similarly, attempts by firms to improve their production technology (through R&D) or to influence consumer preferences (e.g. through advertising) might change production technology and consumer demand; effects which are also not considered in the SCP approach.

Modern theories therefore use two- or multi-stage models to account for the endogeneity of market structure. In a first stage, the long-term (strategic) decisions (the number of competitors or products supplied in the market, the amount of expenditure on advertising or R&D, etc.) are modelled. On this basis, the short-term (tactical) decisions (choice of prices or quantities) are investigated in a second stage. We use backward induction to identify the sequence of actions in the Nash equilibrium. This means that we first determine the optimal second-stage (short-term, tactical) decision for each possible outcome of the first-state (long-term, strategic) decision. Given the optimal decisions from the second stage, we then calculate optimal strategic decisions in the first stage. The following case study illustrates this approach by investigating market structure (the number of restaurants and cuisines) in the food sector.

Case study 3: Competition between restaurants

Over the past decades, out-of-home consumption has become a major economic factor in developed economy food sectors. In a two-stage, spatial model, Schiff (2015) describes the behaviour of firms in this business and their customers. Firms have to make two decisions: the first-stage, long-term (strategic) decision is whether to open a new restaurant in a city and, if so, what type (cuisine) of restaurant. Given the long-term decisions of all competitors, and the potential customers' behaviour, short-term price decisions are made in the second stage. Under the assumption that restaurants enter a market only if expected profits are positive (or that they leave a market if profits are negative), Schiff calculates so-called "entry thresholds". These indicate the number of consumers in a given region required for profitable market entry. The larger the number of potential customers in a region (or the higher their purchasing power), the greater the number of restaurants in that region. The entry thresholds depend, among other things, on the preferences of consumers for particular cuisines. While a restaurant that serves a standard cuisine for a broad public can operate profitably in a comparatively small town, a restaurant that serves a specialty cuisine for select customers can only survive in a comparatively large city.

Replicating Schiff's (2015) analysis, Pennerstorfer et al. (2020) apply this model to observations of 101 cuisines in 24.454 restaurants in 1.883 Austrian municipalities. In Figure 8.5, each point represents a city/cuisine combination. On the horizontal axis the cities are sorted according to their rank in the number of different cuisines offered ("city rank"). The city with the smallest number of different cuisines is ranked first (to the left of Figure 8.5). On the vertical axis ("cuisine rank") the 90 cuisines are sorted according to their prevalence in the 1.883 municipalities. The cuisine which is offered in the fewest municipalities is ranked first (to the bottom of Figure 8.5). We see that cities with many restaurants (to the far right of the figure) also have a larger variety of different cuisines, including cuisines that are offered only rarely (to the bottom of the figure). Cities with few restaurants (on the left), however, only offer common or widespread cuisines (at the top of the figure) that are offered in most municipalities.

Figure 8.5: Relationship between 'city rank' and 'cuisine rank' (explanation in text)

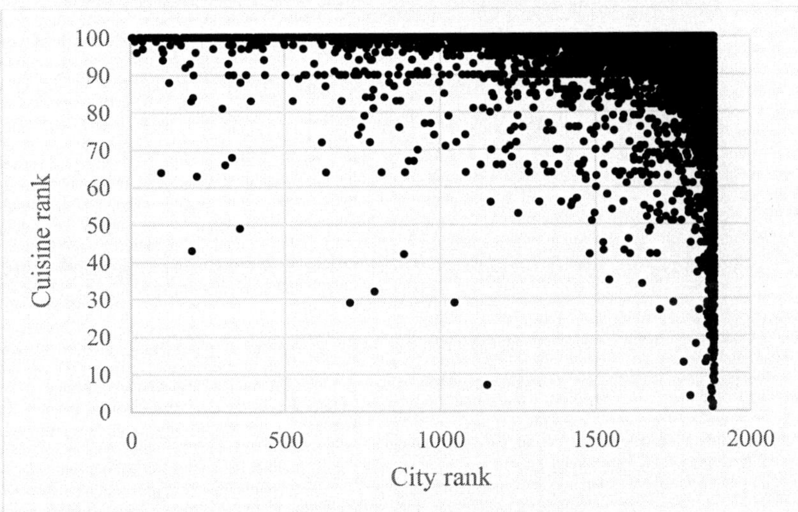

Source: Pennerstorfer et al. (2020, p. 48).

8.6.3. Competition over time

A limitation of static models of imperfect competition is that they neglect time. All decisions are taken simultaneously; there is neither a future (for which one might be willing to make investments today) nor a past (from which economic agents could learn for today's and tomorrow's decisions). Game-theoretical models show that the behaviour of economic agents depends heavily on whether they interact only once or whether they meet and interact repeatedly. In the latter case, in **repeated games**, it is important to distinguish between finite games in which players are aware that the game will be played a known, finite number of rounds, and games in which the players do not know how many rounds will be played (so-called **super games**). Super games deliver important new insights, particularly regarding the likelihood of collusion between firms. While static models and finite games cannot adequately explain collusion between firms, super games generate a number of empirically supported hypotheses about the occurrence and durability of collusive behaviour and cartels. Without going into detail, the following ten stylised facts summarise the main results in the literature (see Feuerstein 2005):

i. A small number of suppliers and high barriers to entry facilitate collusive behaviour.

ii. Large differences in market shares between individual firms make collusive agreements more difficult.

iii. Frequent interactions among firms and a high frequency of price adjustment facilitate collusive behaviour.

iv. High transparency in markets facilitates the maintenance of collusive agreements.

v. For a given number of firms, collusive agreements are more likely to be maintained in growing markets.

vi. Fluctuations in demand (e.g. pronounced seasonal fluctuations) reduce the likelihood of collusion.

vii. Innovations (product and process innovations) make it difficult to maintain agreements.

viii. Large differences in cost structures or capacity limits between firms make collusive behaviour more difficult.

ix. Multi-market contacts (i.e. situations in which firms with broad product palettes compete with one another on different markets) facilitate collusive behaviour.

x. A high price elasticity of demand reduces the likelihood of collusion and cartels between firms.

An extensive empirical literature analyses food industry cartels such as the Lysine Cartel and the Citric Acid Cartel (see Case Study 4). Levenstein and Suslow (2006) provide a detailed overview of the factors that influence the success and longevity of cartels.

Case study 4: The Lysine Cartel and other examples from the food industry

In the mid-1990s, five global suppliers of lysine, an amino acid used in animal production, started price-fixing. The companies involved were American (ADM), Japanese (Ajinomoto and Kyowa Hakko Kogyo), and Korean (Sewon America Inc. and Cheil Jedang Ltd.). A senior ADM official, Mark Whitacre, made tape recordings of conversations between the cartel members for the FBI. The US Bureau of Competition imposed heavy fines on ADM, and responsible company managers received prison sentences. The story of the lysine cartel was made into a film "The Informant" starring Matt Damon. A number of economic studies (including Bolotova et al. 2008) have analysed the lysine cartel in great detail.

The food sector provides numerous further examples of collusion and cartels. These include the following cases in Germany alone: the coffee market (Bundeskartellamt 2009); the market for milk and dairy products (Bundeswettbewerbsbehörde 2013b); the beer market (Bundeskartellamt 2014a); sausage production (Bundeskartellamt 2014b); sugar production (Bundeskartellamt 2014c); and food retailing (including the Bundeswettbewerbsbehörde 2013a; Bundeskartellamt 2016).

8.6.4. Competition in space

Consumers are diverse; they have different preferences and face different budgetary constraints. We have ignored this consumer heterogeneity in the model above by assuming a representative consumer (sections 8.2 and 8.4). This model does account for product variety, and a preference for variety is built into the representative consumer's utility function.[9] However, since this preference for variety is represented by a single parameter, the model

---

[9] In the utility function in equation (1), the marginal utility of good i decreases with the quantity consumed of that good (q_i), and increases with the quantity consumed of the substitute (q_j). Hence, a balanced consumption bundle (in which the available budget is divided equally among all n goods) generates a higher utility than a specialised bundle (in which the entire budget is spent on only one product only).

assumes that all products are equally substitutable: the products are different but they are all equally different from one another (see footnote 2), and each product therefore competes with equal intensity with each other product (global competition). In reality, of course, some products are close substitutes in the eyes of consumers and therefore in close competition with one another, while others are so different that they hardly compete.

Products can be differentiated geographically as well as in terms of characteristics such as ingredients, taste, quality, or packaging. Geographical differentiation occurs when transport costs are so high that firms in a geographic region compete with one another, but not with firms in other regions. The following case study illustrates differentiation based on product characteristics for the cereals market.

Case study 5: Product differentiation in the breakfast cereal market

In the business literature, so-called perceptual maps are often used to position individual products or services in characteristic space (Kotler and Keller, 2012). The example in Figure 8.6 depicts competition between individual brands in the US breakfast cereal market.

In Figure 8.6, various cereal brands are positioned in a two-dimensional space based on the characteristics Healthfulness and Sweetness. The perceptual map suggests, for example, that Special K is a close substitute for Total Corn Flakes, so that these products compete intensively for customers who value Healthfulness and prefer cereals that rank low in Sweetness. In contrast, the large distance between Special K and Cocoa Crispies suggests that competition between these products for consumers is weak.

Models of product differentiation account for the fact that consumers differ because they are located in different places and have different preferences for product characteristics. Products and consumers can be positioned in space based on these differences, where 'space' can refer to location but also characteristic space, as for example in the perceptual map above. Competition on goods markets takes place only between firms that are located close to one another in 'space'. If this is the case, the demand for one product is strongly influenced by the prices of similar (or nearby) products, but only reacts weakly to the prices of other products.

Figure 8.6: Perceptual map of the US breakfast cereal market

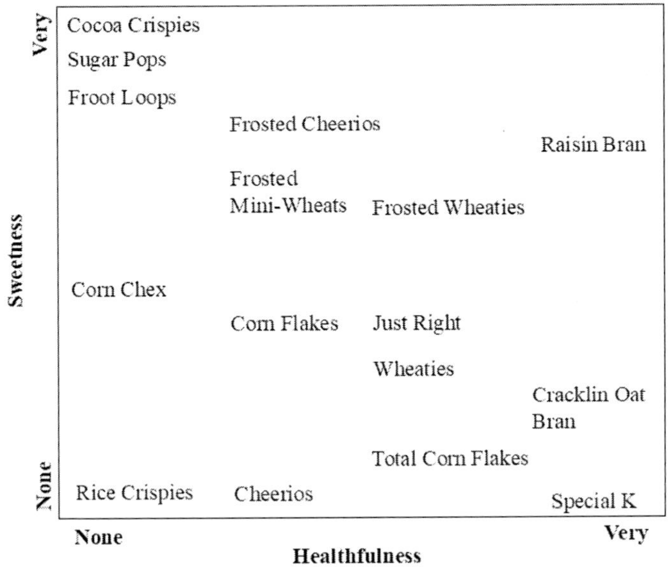

Source: Pindyck (2011).

8.7. Empirical analyses of market power

"Market power is like the wind. You can feel it but you cannot see it". Kohls and Uhl (2002, p. 270).

8.7.1. Structure-conduct-performance approach

(How) can we prove the existence of market power empirically? The industrial organisation literature has applied various methods. As described above, the traditional SCP approach assumes that market structure (e.g. the number of competitors) is exogenous. Market structure determines firm conduct, which in turn determines market outcomes (e.g. equilibrium prices and profits). For example, equation (13) shows that equilibrium prices are determined both by market structure (the number of suppliers n, the marginal production costs c', and the preferences of consumers expressed by the price elasticity of demand ε) as well as by firm conduct (the intensity of competition represented by the conjectural variation θ). Empirical studies based on the SCP approach typically examine the relationship between indicators of market structure and market performance in order to draw conclusions about the (unobservable) conduct of competitors in between. The following case study illustrates this procedure.

Case study 6: Market power in the US food industry

Empirical SCP analyses attempt to establish a direct relationship between market structure (measured for example by supplier concentration) and market performance (e.g. the level of profits). Zellner (1989) is a typical example of SCP analysis. Based on cross-sectional data for 75 branches of the US food industry, Zellner analyses how structural characteristics of these industries influence firm behaviour (such as expenditure on advertising) and performance (profitability). The following equation shows one of the many empirical results provided in this study (Zellner 1989, p. 113, t-statistics of the estimated coefficients in brackets):

$$\text{Lerner index} = \underset{(0.31)}{-1.76} + \underset{(2.82)}{14.82}Growth + \underset{(3.96)}{0.40}CR4 + \underset{(1.72)}{1.22}ASR + \underset{(2.49)}{0.13}Brands$$

$$\underset{(1.85)}{-1.58}Innov + \underset{(1.91)}{0.16}COR - \underset{(2.67)}{0.99}Disp$$

Zellner calculates the Lerner index (equation 9) using average production costs. He observes a significant positive effect of industry growth rates ($Growth$), the concentration ratio ($CR4$, the share of the four largest firms in total industry turnover), the capital-output ratio (COR), the advertising-to-sales ratio (ASR), and product differentiation measured by the number of different products ($Brands$). He also notes a significant negative effect of innovation ($Innov$ measures the number of new products in an industry) and an indicator of geographical dispersion ($Disp$) on the Lerner index.

The analysis presented in case study 6 is based on a cross-sectional regression over a large number of different branches of the food industry. One weakness of such analyses is that they assume that market structure has the same effect on performance in all branches of an industry. In addition, while these analyses might find that concentration and profitability are correlated, the reasons underlying such correlations remain unclear. A positive correlation might, for example, be the consequence of firms exercising market power in highly concentrated branches or industries (Harvard school). However, it might also be due to the higher efficiency of larger companies, which translates into both higher profits and higher concentration ratios (Chicago school). These weaknesses of the traditional

SCP approach can be mitigated by analysing prices (rather than profits) with firm-level data from a specific industry or branch, as illustrated in the following example.

Case study 7: Market power in food retailing in Vermont

Based on price observations for 121 representative products in August 1981, Cotterill (1986) calculated a price index for individual supermarkets in 18 different regions of Vermont in the US. He then looks for evidence that differences in price levels between supermarkets are caused by regional differences in supermarket concentration, while controlling for other characteristics of the individual supermarkets. The following equation shows the results of one of his estimated models (Cotterill 1986, p. 383, t-statistics in brackets).

$$PI = 99.837 + \underset{(5.49)}{8.912HHI} + \underset{(2.72)}{2.241Indep} + \underset{(0.82)}{0.007Size} + \underset{(2.10)}{4.665Sales/Size} + \underset{(0.33)}{0.002Dist}$$

$$-\underset{(0.36)}{0.017Popgr} + \underset{(0.17)}{0.044Income}$$

The food price index (PI) increases significantly with the Herfindahl-Hirschman-Index of regional supermarket concentration (HHI). In addition, PI is significantly higher for independent supermarkets ($Indep = 1$) and supermarkets with high sales per unit area ($Sales/Size$). Supermarket size ($Size$, measured by their sales area), the regional population growth rate ($Popgr$), and average per capita income in the region ($Income$) have no significant influence on PI. The author concludes: "The estimated structure-price relationships suggest that firms with strong market positions enjoy high profits because they raise prices rather than lower unit costs" (p. 385). Based on a much larger number of observations, Asplund and Friberg (2002) as well as Barros et al. (2006) obtain similar results for supermarkets in Sweden and Portugal respectively.

Caves (2007) outlines the merits of the traditional SCP approach compared with more recent empirical approaches. An important advantage of the traditional SCP approach is that it can be used to analyse the intensity of competition and its effects across industries, while more recent studies often focus on firms in a single industry. However, this advantage is also a weakness, because industries differ in many respects besides the intensity of competition, and it is difficult to adequately control for all of these other possibly confounding factors. Furthermore, as mentioned above, the SCP approach assumes that market structures are exogenous and therefore ignores the fact that firms that perform poorly will exit the market, and other firms might enter the market if industry profits are high. It also fails to account for attempts by firms to improve their production technologies (process innovation) and to influence consumer preferences (e.g. through advertising and/or product innovation). Finally, the SCP approach does not analyse the actual behaviour or conduct of firms. It focusses on the relationship between market structure and market performance, while conduct remains unobserved and implicit between them. Hence, compared with more recent approaches, some of which will be discussed below, the SCP only estimates a reduced form of a more extensive structural model.[10]

8.7.2. Direct measurement of the Lerner index

Measuring market power would be straightforward if, in addition to product prices, firms' marginal production costs were also observable. In this case, it would be straightforward to calculate the Lerner index ($L_i = \frac{p_i - c_i'}{p_i}$), which provides explicit information on a firm's mark-up. However, reliable information on a firm's marginal costs is rarely available. Empirical studies often solve this problem pragmatically by using average costs to approximate marginal costs (see for example case study 6). This, however, can lead to systematic bias, because marginal and average costs are only identical if marginal costs are constant and fixed costs equal zero. In addition, and perhaps more important, firms with market power have strong incentives to misreport their marginal costs. Figure 8.7 illustrates this problem for the simple case of constant marginal costs.

[10] Reiss and Wolak (2007) discuss in detail the distinction between estimating a model in 'structural form' and in 'reduced form', and the advantages and disadvantages of the two approaches.

Figure 8.7: Identifying market power: the case of demand shocks

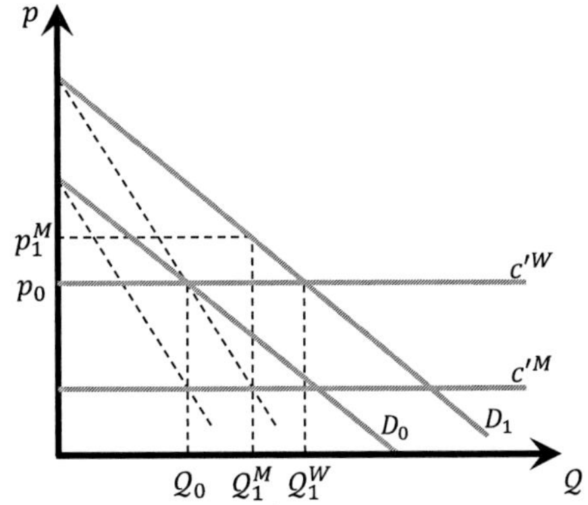

Source: Own depiction.

Consider a market with demand curve D_0 on which we observe the price p_0 and aggregate quantity Q_0. This price-quantity combination could be the outcome of a monopoly market with marginal cost curve c'^M. However, the identical price-quantity combination could also result from perfect competition if the marginal cost curve is c'^W. A monopolist will have a strong incentive to inflate its actual marginal costs in an attempt to hide the fact that it is exercising market power from the competition authorities. Phlips (1996) calls this the **indistinguishability theorem** and formulates "10 commandments" for firms with market power in their dealings with competition authorities. The fifth commandment is "Thou shalt exaggerate the level of costs" (p. 509). In addition to eight further recommendations for misleading competition authorities, the tenth commandment is: "Thou shalt otherwise tell the truth" (p. 510).

Despite this problem, it is sometimes possible to identify market power even when marginal costs are unknown by observing how firms react to exogenous shocks. Consider, for example, a firm's optimal response to an exogenous demand shock. If the demand curve shifts outwards to D_1 in Figure 8.7, prices will not react in a competitive market (with constant marginal costs of c'^W); we will only observe an increase in the equilibrium quantity from Q_0 to Q_1^W. In contrast, a monopolist with constant marginal costs of c'^M would increase prices to p_1^M in response to the same shock. The situation described in Figure 8.7 can be extended to the case of rising rather than constant marginal costs (Breshnahan 1982) and to differentiated products (Nevo 1998). In this way it is possible to use market reactions to demand fluctuations to draw conclusions about market structure.

8.7.3. Analyses of price transmission

Even if marginal costs are unobservable, it is frequently possible to observe individual components of these costs. The prices of dairy products, for example, will depend critically on the producer price of milk (see case study 1). The producer price of milk is not the only component of a dairy's marginal costs of yoghurt, of course, but it is a large and essential component. Under very specific assumptions about the form of demand and cost functions, the transmission of exogenous cost shocks also would allow identification of market power. In Chapter 9 we analyse vertical price transmission in the food chain, in other words the question how prices and margins in the food chain react to changes in the prices of agricultural raw products such as milk, wheat and slaughter pigs. Among other things, we demonstrate in Chapter 9 that market power can be identified using empirical price transmission analysis, but only under exacting conditions that are often not met.

8.7.4. Production-theoretic approaches

Following Hall's (1988) seminal study, production-theoretic approaches attempt to measure marginal costs (c') and the mark-ups ($\mu = \frac{p}{c'}$) by econometric estimation of production or cost functions. If we consider the simplest case, producing the amount q requires only two inputs, labour l (which is variable) and capital k (which is fixed). Production $q = q(l, k)$ is associated with the cost function $c = wl + rk$ where w and r are the prices of l and k, respectively. For a given output $\bar{q}$, a firm's cost minimisation problem can be stated in the following Lagrange function: $\min L = wl + rk + \lambda[\bar{q} - q(l, k)]$. The Lagrange multiplier $\lambda = \frac{\partial L}{\partial \bar{q}}$ shows how production costs change with the output quantity $\bar{q}$, and thus is a measure of marginal costs ($\lambda = c'$). The first-order condition for the variable factor (l) is: $\frac{\partial L}{\partial l} = w - \lambda \frac{\partial q(l,k)}{\partial l} = 0$. After expanding by $\frac{l}{q(l,k)}$ and transforming the equation, we obtain: $\frac{w}{\lambda} \frac{l}{q(l,k)} = \frac{\partial q(l,k)}{\partial l} \frac{l}{q(l,k)}$. Combining this expression with the definition of the mark-up $\mu = \frac{p}{c'} = \frac{p}{\lambda}$ leads to $\mu = \left(\frac{\partial q(l,k)}{\partial l} \frac{l}{q(l,k)}\right) / \left(\frac{w}{p} \frac{l}{q(l,k)}\right) = \frac{\xi}{\frac{wl}{pq(l,k)}}$, where $\xi \equiv \left(\frac{\partial q(l,k)}{\partial l} \frac{l}{q(l,k)}\right)$ is the production elasticity of the variable factor l, and $\frac{wl}{pq(l,k)}$ is the cost share of input l in the value of production. The production elasticity ξ can be determined by estimating a production function or a cost function.[11] The ratio between the estimated production elasticity and the cost share of l is an estimate of the mark-up ($\mu = \frac{p}{c'}$), and also provides us with an estimate of the Lerner index (since $L = \frac{\mu-1}{\mu}$, see equation 9).

Production theoretic approaches are particularly well-suited for the analysis of markets when the production technology can be represented econometrically (i.e. if suitable data and good knowledge of production technology are available). As the following case study shows, this approach can take specific production conditions, such as economies of scale, into account. Economies of scale will lead to systematic differences in mark-ups between large and small firms.

Case study 8: Market power on the German beer market

The German beer brewing companies have repeatedly been the subject of antitrust proceedings by the German competition authorities (Bundeskartellamt 2014a and 2016). Based on data from 197 breweries over 13 years, Karagiannis et al. (2018) estimate a flexible form of production function (a so-called translog production function) and calculate production elasticities for three inputs (labour, intermediate inputs, and capital). The authors calculate an average mark-up of 1.65 from the ratio of the production elasticity of intermediate inputs to their cost share; this corresponds to a Lerner index of $L = 0.4$. The results of the econometric estimation also point to the existence of economies of scale in the brewing industry. Economies of scale mean that large firms can charge higher mark-ups than small firms. The authors' calculations suggest a Lerner index of $L = 0.47$ for large breweries (with an annual production of more than 100,000 hl) compared with $L = 0.28$ for small breweries (with an annual production of less than 25,000 hl).

---

[11] For example, given the Cobb-Douglas production function $q = \tau l^{\xi} k^{\gamma}$, the production elasticity ξ can be estimated by taking logarithms, which gives $\ln(q) = \ln(\tau) + \xi \ln(l) + \gamma \ln(k)$ (see Appendix 2.3 in chapter 2). Many empirical studies estimate cost functions (the dual representation) rather than production functions to obtain production elasticities.

8.7.5. Market power and consumer demand for differentiated products

As shown in section 8.4., the Lerner index is calculated from a conjectural variation model as follows (see equation 14): $L = \frac{p-c'}{p} = \frac{1+\theta}{\varepsilon} HHI$. Direct measurement of L requires information on prices (p) and marginal costs (c'), but this equation suggests an alternative based on θ, ε, and HHI. Since information on the market shares of individual firms is generally readily available, calculation of the Herfindahl-Hirschman index (HHI) is straightforward. This can be combined with an econometric estimate of the price elasticity of demand (ε), and an assumption about the degree of competition in a market (i.e. the conjectural variation θ), to calculated the Lerner index.

Econometric estimation of price elasticities is comparatively simple for homogeneous goods. In the case of differentiated products, it is more difficult due to the large number of substitute goods. If several competing firms each supply a number of substitutes, the number of cross-price elasticities that must be accounted for in the estimation can easily exceed the number of available observations. The market for breakfast cereals, for example, includes more than 50 different brands. Since the uncompensated cross-price elasticities between two brands do not have to be symmetric, it would be necessary to estimate 2,500 own- and cross-price elasticities for this market. This is referred to as the **curse of dimensionality**. The challenge for empirical researches is to formulate flexible demand systems that require the estimation of fewer parameters (such models are sometimes referred to as parsimonious).

Multi-stage models (hierarchical decision models) are one way to reduce the complexity of an empirical model. These models assume that households make sequential consumption decisions. At the top stage, for example, a household decides which share of its budget to allocate to breakfast cereals (relative to other foods). At the next stage, this budget share is sub-divided into different categories of cereals (for children, adults, organic products, etc.). The final stage then models the decisions to purchase individual brands within each category. In this way, the number of substitution parameters to be estimated is reduced significantly. At the same time, it is still possible to represent all substitution possibilities between brands within individual categories. Case study 9 describes an empirical application of this approach for the US beer market.

Case study 9: Market power on the US beer market (1)

Hausman et al. (1994) estimate price elasticities on the US beer market in a three-stage approach. In the first stage, the authors use a double-logarithmic demand function to estimate the price elasticity of demand for beer altogether. They estimate a value of -1.37. In the second stage, the authors distinguish between three segments of the beer market ('premium', 'popular' and 'light'). For each segment, they calculate own- and cross-price elasticities again using a double-logarithmic demand function and assuming that total demand for beer is constant. The point estimates for the own-price elasticities are -2.7 for 'premium' and 'popular beer' and -2.4 for 'light beer'. In the third stage, they estimate the demand for various brands (and thus the substitution relationships within each of the three segments) using an Almost Ideal Demand System. The estimated own-price elasticities differ between the various brands of beer and range from -3.5 to -5.0. The results of this study show that estimated own-price elasticities of demand depend on the level of aggregation that is studied. The higher the level of aggregation (e.g. beer as a whole compared with individual brands of beer), the fewer the consumers' substitution possibilities and, thus, the lower the estimated elasticities.

An alternative response to the curse of dimensionality in demand analysis is to assume that substitution relationships between products depend on the similarity of their characteristics. Rojas' (2008) study of the American beer market in case study 10 provides an example of this approach.

Case study 10: Market power on the US beer market (2)

Rojas (2008) uses a natural experiment to gain insights about the intensity of competition on the US beer market. In 1991, the sales tax on domestic and imported beer in the United States was doubled. The author analyses consumer demand for beer using 20 observations of quarterly price and quantity data for 64 different brands of beer in 58 US cities between 1988 and 1992. Rojas applies a so-called distance metric approach to reduce the number of substitution possibilities in this market. He uses information such as alcohol content, geographical distribution, product segment (light beer, lager, etc.) and packaging size to characterise each brand, and calculates the distances between brands in characteristics space. The distance between two brands i and j in n-dimensional characteristic space is $D_{ij} = [\sum_{n=1}^{N}(i_n - j_n)^2]^{\frac{1}{2}}$, where i_n (j_n) represents the nth characteristic of product i (j). Rojas assumes that the cross-price elasticity of demand between products i and j

is a linear function of the distance between these products in characteristics space (D_{ij}). Using the resulting estimates of own- and cross-price elasticities, Rojas calculates Lerner indices in a conjectural variation framework. Regarding the practicability of this empirical approach, Rojas (2008 p. 26) concludes: "As in previous work, the inference conducted in this paper depends crucially on the precision of demand estimates. The distance metric method employed here is effective in reducing the number of … cross-price effects, but it relies heavily in the researcher's ability to have data on all product characteristics that effectively determine substitution effects. Results may change if there are important unobserved product characteristics".

8.7.6. Market analyses in structural form

The analysis of structural, simultaneous models of supply (cost) and demand is the best option for identifying market power, provided that the necessary data are available. The so-called **New Empirical Industrial Organisation** (NEIO) literature frequently applies structural models to measure firms' market power, but recent empirical studies in business economics also rely on this approach to analyse the effects of different firm-level marketing activities.

Case study 11: NEIO on the banana market

Deodhar and Sheldon (1995) is one of the first applications of structural market analysis in the NEIO literature. They analyse the period between 1970 and 1992, when a few companies dominated the world market for bananas. United Brands, Standard Fruit and Noboa, for example, controlled more than 70% of the market in Germany. Deodhar and Sheldon use a simple NEIO model to measure these firms' market power on the German banana market.

The starting point is equation (11). In the case of n identical firms with constant marginal costs (c'), this equation becomes $p(Q) = -\frac{\partial p(Q)}{\partial Q}(1+\theta)\frac{Q}{n} + c'$. The authors assume a linear market demand function: $Q = \alpha_0 + \alpha_1 p + \boldsymbol{Z\beta}$, where Z is a vector of exogenous factors. The authors further argue that the supply of bananas on the German market is characterised by constant marginal costs: $c' = \gamma_0 + \boldsymbol{X\delta}$, where $\boldsymbol{X}$ is a vector of exogenous supply-shifting factors. Inserting marginal costs into the price equation, we get: $p(Q) = -\frac{\partial p(Q)}{\partial Q}(1+\theta)\frac{Q}{n} + \gamma_0 + \boldsymbol{X\delta} = \gamma_1 Q + \gamma_0 + \boldsymbol{X\delta}$, with $\gamma_1 =$

$-\frac{\partial p(Q)}{\partial Q}\frac{(1+\theta)}{n} = -\frac{1}{\alpha_1}\frac{(1+\theta)}{n}$ (using $\alpha_1 = \frac{\partial Q}{\partial p}$ from the demand function). The authors estimate demand and supply functions based on annual observations for the period 1970 to 1992 to obtain point estimates for $\alpha_0, \alpha_1, \gamma_0, \gamma_1$, and the vectors $\boldsymbol{\beta}$ and $\boldsymbol{\delta}$. Specifically, the authors report the following estimates: $\alpha_1 = -0.32$ and $\gamma_1 = 0.91$. From this they calculate an indicator of the intensity of competition on the German banana market: $\lambda = \frac{1+\theta}{n} = -a_1\gamma_1 = 0.29$. Assuming that there are three (dominant) firms in the market ($n = 3$), this leads to an estimate of the conjectural variation θ of -0.13. Hence, the firms' behaviour on this market differs significantly from perfect competition ($\theta = -1$) and from collusive behaviour (for $n = 3$, collusive behaviour would imply $\theta = n - 1 = 2$). However, it is not significantly different from Cournot-Nash behaviour ($\theta = 0$). Deodhar and Sheldon (1995 p. 345) conclude: "… the hypothesis of perfect competition and collusive behaviour could be rejected, but the hypothesis of Cournot-Nash behaviour could not be rejected ".

Digal and Ahmadi-Esfahani (2002), Sheldon and Sperling (2003) and Perekhozhuk et al. (2017) provide surveys of numerous empirical applications of the NEIO approach for a wide range of agri-food markets. Kim and Cotterill (2008), which focuses on the cheese market, is an especially interesting application because it compares the results obtained from a structural model with those of a reduced form model, and thus highlights the additional insights into the exercise of market power that structural models are capable of generating.

In this section we have provided only a brief overview of the comprehensive literature on different approaches to measuring market power. Research on these issues is still very active, not least because robust empirical results on the existence and scope of market power are of great importance for competition policy. In the final section of this chapter, we will discuss some important aspects of competition policy and the institutions that implement it.

8.8. Competition policy and institutions

8.8.1. The importance of competition policy and the institutional framework

In a modern market economy, **competition policy** is one of the cornerstones of economic policy. [12] From medieval guild rules, to laws against cartels and monopolies, competition policy can be traced back to the Codex Hammurabi. [13]

Compared with other areas of economic policy, competition policy is very integrated in the EU. This is largely due to the fact that much economic activity in the EU takes place at a supranational level, i.e. many firms do business across borders within the EU. As a result, many questions and conflicts that arise in the area of competition policy also extend beyond national borders in the EU.

A special feature of competition policy in the EU is that not only the legislative body but also the executive authority is located at European level. The EU Commission proposes legislation and, together with the competition authorities of the member states, also enforces EU competition rules. The Commission's Directorate-General for Competition is the authority that is primarily responsible for these executive tasks. The Commission is also the investigative authority, prosecutor and decision-making authority in the first instance. The Directorate-General for Competition exercises broad powers in the assessment of subsidies by member states, in merger proceedings, and in antitrust investigations. These powers also affect multinational companies with head offices outside the EU that do business in the EU. The Commission's decisions can be challenged in the European courts.

Because they are so important for the design and functioning of the EU common market, the basic provisions of European competition law are stated in the Treaty on the Functioning of the European Union (Art. 101 et seq. TFEU). Article 101 TFEU prohibits horizontal and vertical "agreements between undertakings, decisions by associations of undertakings and concerted practices which may affect trade between

---

[12] Motta (2004) and Bishop and Walker (2009) provide detailed discussions of key topics in modern competition policy.

[13] The Codex Hammurabi is the oldest completely preserved collection of legal acts and was enacted in Babylon in the 18th century BC.

Member States, and which have as their object or effect the prevention, restriction or distortion of competition within the internal market". This includes, for example, price-fixing agreements between firms, and arrangements whereby firms agree to sell their products or purchase inputs only within demarcated territories.

Article 102 TFEU stipulates that any "abuse by one or more undertakings of a dominant position within the internal market or in a substantial part of it shall be prohibited as incompatible with the internal market in so far as it may affect trade between Member States". A violation of Article 102 would be, for example, if a dominant firm were to sell its products below costs with the objective of driving competitors out of the market. Merger controls also fall under Article 102 TFEU.

In the EU, competition policy is implemented both by the EU and by national competition authorities. The EU is responsible for cases with supranational implications while national authorities are responsible for cases that do not affect trade between the member states. Since it is not always possible to sharply divide jurisdictions, EU and national authorities sometimes work on a case simultaneously. However, merger controls are always pursued exclusively at one level or the other, as we discuss in the next section.

8.8.2. Subfields of competition policy

Competition policy in the EU (and in most developed economies) rests on three pillars: **abuse supervision, antitrust supervision**, and **merger control**. The first two pillars (abuse and antitrust supervision) are predominantly *ex post*-oriented. In both of these areas, the competition authority only becomes active when economic damage has occurred (or is suspected). Merger control is *ex ante*-oriented and seeks to prevent firms from acquiring dominant positions on markets.

a) Ex post approaches: abuse and antitrust supervision

A proceeding against a horizontal or vertical restriction of competition is initiated by an application from an eligible party. Such an application must include a specific demand, for example that firms stop fixing prices. In practice, the competition authorities themselves conduct investigations and collect evidence on the possible abuse of market power or antitrust behaviour by firms. Firms are legally required to cooperate with such investigations, and they can be fined for failure to do so.

Abuse supervision is often considered a comparatively weak instrument of competition policy. Illegal cartels and price-fixing take place in secret, often on the basis of verbal agreements and without documentation. Hence, they are difficult to detect and prove. Insider knowledge is often the key to detecting illegal cartels. Hence, competition laws often contain provisions that allow the competition authority to waive or reduce penalties for whistle-blowers who provide evidence that leads to the detection of a cartel in which they have participated. In Germany, for example, about half of all antitrust proceedings investigated by the Bundeskartellamt (Federal Cartel Office) are triggered by whistle-blowers. In addition, whistle-blower provisions create uncertainty among the members of a cartel; they undermine trust and thus the stability of a cartel. In an empirical analysis of the effects of the whistle-blower provisions introduced in EU competition law in 1996, Brenner (2009) evaluates 61 antitrust decisions reached by the European Commission between 1990 and 2003, and finds that the whistle-blower provisions led to significantly increased penalties and shorter proceedings. Miller (2009) provides a similar empirical analysis for the US.

b) Ex ante approach: Merger control

Of the three pillars of competition policy, merger control is perhaps the most important; it aims to prevent firms from acquiring market power through mergers. Planned mergers must be notified to the competition authority if the annual turnover of the participating firms exceeds a given threshold, and a planned merger cannot be completed as long as the authority is carrying out its investigations. The turnover thresholds also determine whether a merger control is carried out by the EU competition authority or at the national level. The competition authority for its part must reach a decision to permit or forbid a planned merger within a maximum length of time (which is uncommon in other areas of legal practices).

In national merger control cases in Germany, the competition authority has one month to decide in Phase I (pre-investigation) whether a planned merger should be permitted or is subject to further investigation. If there is reason to believe that the planned merger could have negative implications for competition, the competition authorities open Phase II (main investigation). Phase II is an in-depth analysis of the merger's effects on competition. The competition authority must within 4-5 months either forbid the merger or approve it, sometimes subject to conditions. Completing a merger without permission can lead to financial penalties for the participating firms, and invalidation of the merger.

Because the time available is limited, especially in Phase I, the competition authority is not in a position to carry out detailed empirical analyses. For a first rough assessment of the price effects of a merger, the conjectural variation model (Section 8.4) is useful. According to equation (14), the aggregate Lerner index for a market in equilibrium is $L = \frac{1+\theta}{\varepsilon} HHI$. If a merger does not affect firm conduct (represented by parameter θ), and if the price elasticity of demand (ε) remains unchanged, then a merger will affect the price mark-up (the Lerner index L) by changing the market shares of the firms in the industry and, thus, the Herfindahl-Hirschman index (HHI). The difference between the pre- and post-merger HHI in an industry is sometimes referred to as the 'delta'.

In its *Guidelines on the assessment of horizontal mergers*, the European Commission (2004, p. 7) provides some guidance for assessing horizontal mergers with the HHI. "The Commission is unlikely to identify horizontal competition concerns in a market with a post-merger HHI below 1 000. Such markets normally do not require extensive analysis. The Commission is also unlikely to identify horizontal competition concerns in a merger with a post-merger HHI between 1 000 and 2 000 and a delta below 250, or a merger with a post-merger HHI above 2 000 and a delta below 150, except where special circumstances … are present", which are further explained in the Guidelines.

However, a fundamental condition for the calculation of the HHI (and for making informed decisions on competition issues in general) is accurate information on the market shares of the firms in an industry. This requires an accurate definition of the relevant market, which plays a central role in many cases that are considered by competition authorities.

8.8.3. Criteria for defining the relevant market

Determining whether a firm is abusing market power, or whether a merger will give a firm a dominant position on a market, critically depends on how narrowly (or broadly) the relevant market is defined. Firms that want to merge understandably have an interest in defining their market as broadly as possible[14], while others who want to prevent the merger will benefit from a narrow market definition.

Competition policy defines the relevant market in two dimensions; geographic space and product space. "The objective of defining a market in both its product and geographic dimension is to identify those actual competitors of the undertakings involved that are capable of constraining those undertakings' behaviour and of preventing them from behaving independently of effective competitive pressure" (European Commission 1997, paragraph 2). The relevant behaviour in this context is price setting, and the crucial question is the extent to which a firm's ability to raise prices is constrained by competing firms. Hence, the definition of the relevant market and market power are closely intertwined.

As an example of geographic market definition consider a situation in which there are two firms, *A* and *B*, which both supply an identical product but are located at different places. Assume further that there are costs associated with transporting the product to customers. If the geographic distance between *A* and *B* is so large that *B*'s activities (such as choosing the product price) do not affect the competitive situation for *A*, then we can conclude that the markets are (geographically) separate, and *A* can behave as a monopolist on its market. However, if *B*'s activities influence the competitive situation for *A* (for example, because transport costs fall so that *A*'s and *B*'s markets begin to overlap), *A* can no longer behave as a monopolist. *B*'s activities now have a disciplining effect on firm *A*, which can no longer raise its prices without fear of losing customers to *B*. In this case, the two firms operate in the same (geographic) market.

A similar definition underlies the definition of the relevant market in product space: "A relevant product market comprises all those products and/or services which are regarded as interchangeable or substitutable by the consumer, by reason of the products' characteristics, their prices and their intended use" (European Commission 1997, paragraph 7).

The relevant market is based on a combination of the geographic and the product dimensions, and the following three criteria:

---

[14] An example of a very broad definition of the relevant market is the definition suggested by the Coca-Cola company: "*The company's (Coke) executives are fond of saying that every human needs to consume an average of 64 ounces of fluid each day ... to survive. Of that total, Coke calculates it now accounts for less than two ounces.*" (Wall Street Journal, May 8, 1997).

a) Product characteristics

The Commission is very cautious about this criterion for market definition. "An analysis of the product characteristics and its intended use allows the Commission, as a first step, to limit the field of investigation of possible substitutes. However, product characteristics and intended use are insufficient to show whether two products are demand substitutes. Functional interchangeability or similarity in characteristics may not, in themselves, provide sufficient criteria, because the responsiveness of customers to relative price changes may be determined by other considerations as well." (European Commission 1997, paragraph 36). Regarding the "responsiveness of customers to relative price changes", a distinction is made between substitutability on the supply and on the demand side.

b) Demand-side substitutability

The EU competition authority correctly attaches the greatest importance to demand-side substitutability. Substitution by customers is the most immediate and effective disciplining factor for a firm. Competition authorities analyse which alternatives (substitutes) exist for a product, and to what extent customers would switch to these substitutes if the product's price were to rise. It is not necessary that all customers switch to an alternative product for it to be considered a substitute; what matters is whether a sufficient number of consumers switch. Those consumers who are most likely to switch are referred to as marginal consumers. If a sufficient number of consumers is likely to switch to a substitute, then it will not make sense for a firm to increase its price.

c) Supply-side substitutability

A firm's price-setting behaviour will also be constrained if there is sufficient supply-side substitutability. Supply-side substitutability is given when competitors are able to react to a price increase for a product by increasing the supply of that product quickly and without incurring significant additional costs or risks. The terms "quickly" and "significant additional costs or risks" are admittedly vague and require case-by-case elaboration. Supply-side substitutability plays an important role in practice, especially when suppliers offer a wide range of differentiated products. [15] The quantitative importance of supply-side substitutability is reflected in statistics on product innovation. For example, a large share of the product innovations in the German food industry can be considered so-called me-too innovations, i.e., the attempt by firms to enter their rivals' profitable market segments.

8.8.4. Instruments and methods for defining the relevant market

Numerous instruments and methods for defining the relevant market have been proposed in the economic literature. The European Commission states that it "does not follow a rigid hierarchy of different sources of information or types of evidence" but rather "follows an open approach to empirical evidence, aimed at making an effective use of all available information which may be relevant in individual cases" (European Commission 1997, paragraph 25). In many cases important data are missing and the competition authorities have to work with approximations and indirect estimates.

The methods for defining relevant markets that we will discuss below are often also used by competition authorities when they investigate possible abuse of market power. In the following we mainly focus on application to defining the relevant market; applications to the measurement of market power and the abuse of market power are addressed separately.

---

[15] For example, shoes of different sizes clearly belong to the same market. From an individual customer's point of view, switching from size 8 to size 6 would entail significant costs (physical pain); demand-side substitution is therefore limited. However, shoe producers can adjust the production of shoes of different sizes in a short time period without incurring significant additional costs or risks. Hence, supply-side substitutability is given.

a) Price-based procedures for defining the relevant market

Many economists refer to the **law of one price** (LOP) when determining the extent of a market.[16] The test on uniform price development proposed by Horowitz (1981) builds on this idea. The LOP is relaxed somewhat to account for transfer costs between locations and possible random disturbances, but even after allowing for these effects, prices at different locations will tend to move in parallel with a fixed margin between them if the locations are part of the same market. To quote Horowitz (1981, p. 8): "if two geographic areas ... encompass a single market for a particular product, then over time the price at which the product exchanges in one area cannot remain continually out of line with the price at which it exchanges in the other".

In empirical applications, partial correlations between prices of different products are often calculated in order to determine whether these products belong to the same market. If two products A and B are close substitutes, then their prices should exhibit a strong and positive correlation. For example, if, in Figure 8.8, an increase in the marginal cost of product A leads to a shift in the supply curve from S_0^A to S_1^A, the price increase for product A will lead to increased demand for product B; the demand curve for product B will shift from D_0^B to D_1^B. Given the supply curve S_B (for product B), a price increase will also be observed for product B (from p_0^B to p_1^B). The positive correlation between the prices of A and B will increase with the degree of substitutability between the two products.

---

[16] The LOP states that under perfect competition and in the absence of any barriers to trade, identical goods in different locations will be sold for identical prices. If the prices for identical goods in different locations are not identical, then the two locations are not part of the same market. „*It is well known that by market economists mean, not a certain place where purchases and sales are carried on, but an entire territory of which the parts are so united by the relations of unrestricted commerce that prices there take the same level throughout, with ease and rapidity*" (Cournot 1897, S. 51-52).

Figure 8.8: Price-based definition of the relevant market

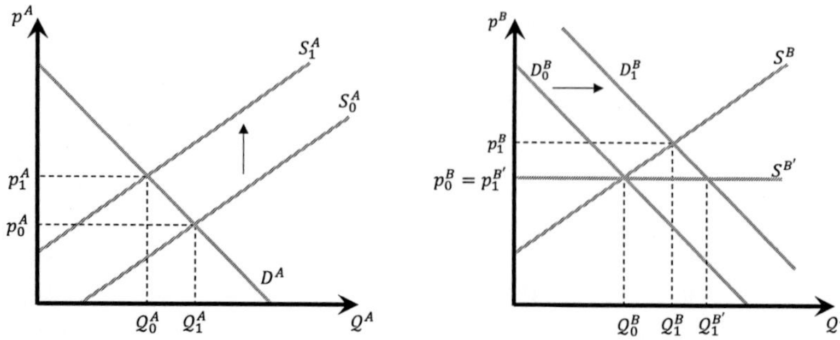

Source: Own depiction.

In more recent applications, advanced time series methods (Granger causality tests and cointegration methods) rather than simple correlation coefficients are used to measure the extent of a market. These methods are better able to determine the direction of causality between prices, to capture the dynamic relationships between prices, and to distinguish between short- and long-term price adjustments. [17] Such price-based approaches have several advantages. They are comparatively simple to implement and to interpret (which can be especially important in court proceedings). In addition, they require only price data, which are often readily available.

However, price-based approaches also have important disadvantages. In many markets, list prices differ from actual transaction prices. Furthermore, correlation analysis can produce different results for the same market depending on the frequency of the price data that are used. In addition, distinguishing between true and spurious correlation is sometimes difficult: prices for two products can be (spuriously) correlated even if there are no supply-side or demand-side substitution relations between them, for example if both are subject to the same inflation or business cycle fluctuations. Moreover, there are no objective benchmark values that can be used to determine what constitutes a 'large' or 'small' correlation between two prices.

[17] These time series methods are also used to analyse relationships between prices at different levels of the food chain. These price relationships are often referred to as **vertical**, while price relationships between locations are referred to as **spatial** or **horizontal**. We discuss vertical price relationships and also provide a brief introduction to the relevant time series methods in Chapter 10.

Finally, the results of price-based analyses are sometimes difficult to interpret, as illustrated in Figure 8.8. An increase in the price of product *A* (from $p_0^A$to p_1^A), and the resulting increase in demand for product *B* (from D_0^B to D_1^B, due to demand-side substitutability), will only trigger an increase in the price of product *B* if the supply of *B* is not perfectly elastic. This will be the case if the supply-side substitutability between *A* and *B* is relatively weak. However, if suppliers can shift their production from *A* to *B* quickly and without incurring significant additional costs or risks (i.e. if there is strong supply-side substitutability between *A* and *B*), then the supply of *B* will be elastic and the correlation between the prices for *A* and *B* will be low. In the extreme case in which the supply of *B* is perfectly elastic (supply curve $S^{B'}$ in Figure 8.8), p^B will remain constant ($p_0^B = p_1^{B'}$). Hence, an empirical analysis would find a weak (or no) correlation between the prices of the two products and thus conclude that *A* and *B* are weak substitutes, although they are actually characterised by high supply-side substitutability.

The main problem with purely price-based attempts to define the relevant market is that price levels and price relationships between markets depend on supply and demand conditions (the shapes of the supply and demand curves) on those markets. However, information on consumer behaviour (reflected in the price elasticity of demand) and on production technologies and costs (reflected in the price elasticity of supply) are not included in purely price-based analyses.

b) The SSNIP Test (HM Test)

The SSNIP (small but significant non-transitory increase in price) or HM (hypothetical monopoly) test was incorporated into the merger guidelines of the US Department of Justice in 1984. It also plays a central role in the European Commission (1997) Guidelines for defining and delineating relevant markets. This test has become one of the most important instruments for defining the extent of markets in merger cases.

The following example illustrates the procedure. In order to determine whether two products *A* and *B* belong to the same market, we assume that product *A* is supplied by a (hypothetical) monopolist. The SSNIP test examines whether it would be profitable for this monopolist to increase the price of *A* from its current level by 5 to 10%. If such a price increase is profitable because the quantity of *A* demanded does not fall substantially, then *A* and *B* can be considered separate markets. If, however, the price increase is not profitable, because many consumers do switch to product *B* (or simply stop purchasing product *A* altogether), then *A* and *B* are considered to belong to the same market.

If more than two products must be considered, the test proceeds iteratively. The test starts from the smallest relevant market (candidate market) and adds further products (the next best substitutes) to the candidate market step-by-step. The relevant market is defined as the narrowest set of products for which it would be profitable for a hypothetical monopolist to impose a small but significant and permanent price increase.

Whether a price increase is actually 'small but significant' is subject to interpretation and depends on a number of factors such as the magnitude of typical price fluctuations on the markets in question, and the rate of inflation. The US Department of Justice uses a 5% price increase, while the European Commission investigates the effects of 5 to 10% price increases, depending on the product. It is also not entirely clear what period of time should be used when testing for an increase in profits with the SSNIP test. In the very short run, consumers will not be able to search for possible substitute products, and other enterprises will not be able to enter the market with their competing products. In the very long run, consumers and competitors will be able to react and it will be difficult for any hypothetical monopolist to generate excess profits via inflated prices. In practice, competition authorities work with a period of one year, however there is no compelling economic rationale for this choice.

A key element of the SSNIP test is determining when it would not be profitable for a firm to increase prices. Following a price increase, some customers will stop consuming the firm's product altogether, while others will switch to rival products (demand-side substitution). At the same time, competing firms will increase their production or launch entirely new substitute products (supply-side substitution). If demand- and supply-side substitution effects are strong, demand will be price-elastic and the price increase will lead to a large reduction in the firm's sales. As the firm sells less, it will reduce production and its costs will fall as well.

The competition authorities therefore focus on measuring the demand and cost changes that result from a price increase. How high can the price elasticity of demand be so that a price increase is just barely (un)profitable? The answer to this question is sometimes referred to as the critical demand elasticity (Werden 1998), as illustrated in case study 12.

Case study 12: The SNIPP test on the beer market

In March 2016, competition authorities of various countries were notified about the proposed acquisition of the world's second largest brewery (SABMiller) by the world's largest brewery (Anheuser-Busch InBev). Competition authorities examined and finally approved this acquisition (see, among others, the European Commission, 2016). The first step involved a detailed analysis of the relevant market (in terms of geographical and product space). Gürkaynak and Kalkan's (2017) conducted a SSNIP test to determine the relevant market in Turkey. Based on monthly sales data for 145 products over the period from March 2013 to March 2016, they estimated own- and cross-price elasticities of demand. For the premium segment of the market, they found an own-price elasticity of retail demand of -7.99 (this figure is much higher than Hausmann et al.'s (1994) estimate for the US beer market - see case study 9). They found that the average own-price elasticity of demand for an individual brand is -12.83. At the wholesale level, the authors find a lower price elasticity of -3.47. This result suggests that the demand for beer is price elastic even at the wholesale level, and that the scope for brewers to raise prices is therefore limited. The authors then compare the actual elasticity with a critical demand elasticity (ε^{krit}), defined as the elasticity value at which the consumer response would be just elastic enough to render a price increase of α% unprofitable for the seller (in this case brewer). The authors use a formula proposed by Werden (1998) to calculate the critical elasticity: $\varepsilon^{krit} = \frac{100}{L+\alpha}$. In their application, the Lerner index for 2015 is $L = 46.6$. For $\alpha = 5$ or $\alpha = 10$, they find that ε^{krit} is smaller than the estimated elasticity at the wholesale level (in absolute values): $\varepsilon^{krit}_{\alpha=5} = \frac{100}{(46.6+5)} = 1.94 < \varepsilon = 3.47$ or $\varepsilon^{krit}_{\alpha=10} = \frac{100}{(46.6+10)} = 1.77 < \varepsilon = 3.47$ "It has been shown that actual elasticity of demand for the premium segment is higher than the critical elasticity … These findings lead to the conclusion that the relevant product market regarding beer brands in Turkey must be wider than the premium segment" (p. 345).

The application of the SSNIP test is comparatively complex and data-intensive. Beginning with the smallest relevant market, products are added one-by-one and the SSNIP test repeated for each iteration. At each step, own and cross-price elasticities of demand and the Lerner index must be estimated in order to determine whether a price increase would be profitable. Carrying out this procedure often requires more time than is available. In addition, the marginal costs of the relevant firms are generally unknown, and price elasticities of demand are often difficult to estimate reliably.

In view of these difficulties and since competition authorities must often reach decisions within short periods of time, practical applications of the SNNIP test often depart from the procedure described above. For example, the selection of the products that are added to the candidate market is often made on an *ad hoc* basis and the SSNIP test is only carried out for those products that are considered particularly interesting based on *a-priori* considerations. Rather than estimating demand elasticities econometrically, they are roughly assessed based on readily available information. In addition, the application of the test can be further simplified by making assumptions about the conduct of firms on the market under consideration. As shown in Section 8.4, in a Cournot model ($\theta = 0$) with identical suppliers the Lerner index simplifies to $L = \frac{p-c}{p} = \frac{1}{\varepsilon}r$, where r represents firms' market shares. If one believes that this model is a reasonable approximation of reality, then the Lerner index can be calculated without information on marginal costs by using the price elasticity of demand and the firms' market shares.

The SSNIP test is well established as tool for defining the extent of the relevant market. However, it has an important weakness as an instrument for identifying the abuse of market power. The problem is known as the **cellophane fallacy**, a term that refers to a 1956 US Supreme Court decision on whether the company *du Pont* held a dominant market position and was abusing the associated market power. According to a narrow definition of the relevant market that considers only the product cellophane, *du Pont* had a market share of about 70%. According to a broader definition argued by *du Pont*, other packaging materials (such as aluminium foil, wax paper and polyethylene) are close substitutes for cellophane, and du Pont's market share was only roughly 17%, in which case it did not have a dominant market position. The Supreme Court based its decision to define the market broadly on estimates of cross-price elasticities; high cross-price elasticities indicated that consumers consider alternative packaging materials as sufficiently close substitutes for cellophane.

This case highlights an important weakness of the SSNIP test as an instrument for identifying market power abuse. In the case of a merger, the possible creation of market power is examined *ex ante*. However, the possible abuse of market power is assessed *ex post*. If a firm is abusing market power, then the price it charges will lie above its marginal cost, and it will already have implemented any profitable price increases.

As a result, the estimation and interpretation of the price elasticity of demand in the application of the SNNIP test can be misleading. Unless the demand function is iso-elastic, the price elasticity of demand will vary with price p. This is particularly evident in the case of a linear demand function, where ε is directly proportional to p/q. While the market price and the price elasticity of demand will be low in a competitive market, the price elasticity of demand will typically be high in a monopoly. In this case, therefore, a high price elasticity of demand will be the result of the monopolist's abuse of market power and cannot be interpreted as indicating the absence of market power, as a mechanical application of the SSNIP test would suggest.

Hence, in a highly concentrated market, the prevailing price elasticity of demand cannot be used to define the extent of the relevant market. The European Commission acknowledges this issue as follows: "Generally, and in particular for the analysis of merger cases, the price to take into account will be the prevailing market price. This may not be the case where the prevailing price has been determined in the absence of sufficient competition. In particular for the investigation of abuses of dominant positions, the fact that the prevailing price might already have been substantially increased will be taken into account." (European Commission 1997, paragraph 19). However, the extent to which a market is classified as concentrated itself depends on how the extent of the market is defined in geographic and product space.

This brief overview of competition policy illustrates the close links between economic theory and policy: the empirical analysis that is used in applied competition policy is based on solid microeconomic models. However, we have also seen that for some problems (such as defining the extent of the relevant market) methods that are both theoretically well founded and meet the practical requirements of applied competition policy are still lacking. As ongoing globalisation leads to increasing horizontal and vertical integration of production processes, defining the extend of the relevant market will continue to pose a major challenge.

8.9. Keywords

- Abuse and antitrust supervision
- Cellophane fallacy
- Competition policy
- Conjectural variation
- Cournot-Nash equilibrium
- Curse of dimensionality
- Indistinguishability theorem
- Law of one price
- Lerner index
- Mark-up
- Merger control
- Mixed oligopoly
- Nash-Bertrand equilibrium
- New Empirical Industrial Organisation
- Perceptual maps
- Predatory and cooperative advertising
- Strategic complements and strategic substitutes
- Repeated games
- Spatial and vertical price relationships
- Structure-conduct-performance
- Super games

References

Asplund M and Friberg R (2002) Food Prices and Market Structure in Sweden. The Scandinavian Journal of Economics 104(4): 547-566.

Barros PP, Brito D and de Lucena D (2006) Mergers in the food retailing sector: An empirical investigation. European Economic Review 50: 447-468.

Bishop S and Walker M (2009) The Economics of EC Competition Law: Concepts, Application and Measurement. 3rd Ed., Sweet & Maxwell, London.

Bolotova Y, Connor JM and Miller DJ (2008) The Impact of Collusion on Price Behavior: Empirical Results from Two Recent Cases. International Journal of Industrial Organization 26(6): 1290-1307.

Box GEP and Draper NR (1987) Empirical Model-Building and Response Surfaces, John Wiley & Sons, New York, NY.

Brenner S (2009) An Empirical Study of the European Corporate Leniency Program. International Journal of Industrial Organization 27(6): 639-645.

Breshnahan TF (1982) The Oligopoly Solution Concept is Identified. Economics Letters 10(1-2): 87-92.

Bundeskartellamt, (2016) Vertikale Preisbindung im Lebensmitteleinzelhandel – Nun auch Bußgeldverfahren in der Warengruppe Bier weitgehend abgeschlossen. Pressemitteilung vom 09.05.2016. https://www.bundeskartellamt.de/SharedDocs/Meldung/DE/Pressemitteilungen/2016/09_05_2016_Bier.html. Accessed on January 16, 2021.

Bundeskartellamt (2014a) Erste Bußgelder im Kartellverfahren gegen Bierbrauer verhängt. Press release 13.01.2014. https://www.bundeskartellamt.de/SharedDocs/Meldung/DE/Pressemitteilungen/2014/13_01_2014_Fernsehbiere.html?nn=3591568. Accessed on January 16, 2021.

Bundeskartellamt (2014b) Bundeskartellamt verhängt Bußgelder gegen Wursthersteller. Press release 15.07.2014. Retrieved from: https://www.bundeskartellamt.de/SharedDocs/Meldung/DE/Pressemitteilungen/2014/15_07_2014_Wurst.html. Accessed on January 16, 2021.

Bundeskartellamt (2014c) Bußgelder gegen Zuckerhersteller. Press release 18.02.2014. Retrieved from: https://www.bundeskartellamt.de/SharedDocs/Meldung/DE/Meldungen%20News%20Karussell/18_02_2014_Zucker.html. Accessed on January 16, 2021.

Bundeskartellamt (2009) Bußgeldverfahren gegen Kaffeeröster wegen Preisabsprachen. Case study 14.01.2010. Retrieved from: https://www.bundeskartellamt.de/SharedDocs/Entscheidung/DE/Fallberichte/Kartellverbot/2009/B11-18-08.pdf?__blob=publicationFile&v=6. Accessed on January 16, 2021.

Bundeswettbewerbsbehörde (2013a) BWB/K-313 Kartellgericht verhängt Geldbuße im Lebensmittelhandel. Press release 3.10.2013. Retrieved from: https://www.bwb.gv.at/kartelle_marktmachtmissbrauch/entscheidungen/detail/bwbk-313-kartellgericht-verhaengt-geldbusse-im-lebensmittelhandel. Accessed on January 16, 2021.

Bundeswettbewerbsbehörde (2013b) BWB/K-311 Milch- und Molkereiprodukte. Press release 06.02.2013. Retrieved from: https://www.bwb.gv.at/kartelle_marktmachtmissbrauch/entscheidungen/detail/bwbk-311-milch-und-molkereiprodukte. Accessed on January 16, 2021.

Caves RE (2007) In Praise of Old I.O. International Journal of Industrial Organization 25(1): 1-12.

Cotterill RW (1986) Market Power in the Retail Food Industry: Evidence from Vermont. The Review of Economics and Statistics 68(3): 379-386.

Cournot AA (1897) Researches into the Mathematical Principles of the Theory of Wealth. Translated by Nathaniel T. Bacon. The MacMillan Company, London.

Deaton A (1986) Demand Analysis. In: Griliches Z. und Intriligator, M.D. (Eds.). Handbook of Econometrics, Volume III, Chapter 30. Elsevier Science Publishers BV, Chapter 30: 1767-1839.

Deodhar SY and Sheldon IM (1995) Is Foreign Trade (Im)Perfectly Competitive? An Analysis of the German Market for Banana Imports. Journal of Agricultural Economics 46(3): 336-348.

Digal LN and Ahmadi-Esfahani FZ (2002). Market Power Analysis in the Retail Food Industry: A Survey of Methods. The Australian Journal of Agricultural and Resource Economics 46(4): 559-584.

European Commission (2016) Case M.7881 - AB INBEV / SABMILLER. Press release 24.5.2016. Retrieved from: http://ec.europa.eu/competition/mergers/cases/decisions/m7881_3286_3.pdf. Accessed on January 16, 2021.

European Commission (2004) Guidelines on the assessment of horizontal mergers under the Council Regulation on the control of concentrations between undertakings. Official Journal of the European Union, February 5, 2004 (2004/C 31/03). Retrieved from: https://eur-lex.europa.eu/legal-content/EN/TXT/PDF/?uri=CELEX:52004XC0205(02)&from=DE. Accessed on January 16, 2021.

European Commission (1997) Commission notice on the definition of relevant market for the purposes of Community competition law. Official Journal of the European Union December 9, 1997(C 372 / 03) Retrieved from: https://eur-lex.europa.eu/legal-content/EN/TXT/PDF/?uri=CELEX:31997Y1209(01)&from=DE. Accessed on January 16, 2021.

Feuerstein S (2005) Collusion in Industrial Economics—A Survey. Journal of Industry, Competition and Trade 5(3/4): 163-198.

Fudenberg D and Tirole J (1984) The Fat-Cat Effect, The Puppy-Dog Ploy, and The Lean and Hungry Look. The American Economic Review 74(2): 361-366.

Gasmi F, Laffont JJ and Vuong Q (1992) Econometric Analysis of Collusive Behaviour in a Soft-Drink Market. Journal of Economics & Management Strategy 1(2): 277-311.

Genesove D and Mullin WP (1998) Testing Static Oligopoly Models: Conduct and Cost in the Sugar Industry, 1890 – 1914. The Rand Journal of Economics 29(2): 355-377.

Gürkaynak G and Kalkan E (2017) Testing Justification for Segment Based Relevant Product Market Definition in Merger Control: Evidence from Turkey. Journal of Competition Law & Economics 13(2): 328-345.

Häckner J (2000) A Note on Price and Quantity Competition in Differentiated Oligopolies. Journal of Economic Theory 93(2): 233-239.

Hall R (1988) The Relation between Price and Marginal Cost in U.S. Industry. Journal of Political Economy 96: 921-947.

Hausman J, Leonard G and Zona JD (1994) Competitive Analysis with Differentiated Products. Annales d'Économie et de Statistique 34: 159-180.

Horowitz I (1981) Market Definition in Antitrust Analysis: A Regression-Based Approach. Southern Economic Journal 48(1): 1-16.

Karagiannis G, Kellermann M, Pröll S and Salhofer K (2018) Mark-ups and product differentiation in the German brewing sector. Agribusiness 34(1): 61-76.

Kim D and Cotterill RW (2008) Cost Pass-Through in Differentiated Product Markets: The Case of U.S. Processed Cheese. The Journal of Industrial Economics 56(1): 32-48.

Kohls RL and Uhl JN (2002) Marketing of Agricultural Products. 9th Ed., Prentice Hall, Upper Saddle River.

Kotler P and Keller KL (2012) Marketing Management, 14th Ed., Prentice Hall, Boston, MA.

Lerner AP (1934) The Concept of Monopoly and the Measurement of Monopoly Power. The Review of Economic Studies 1(3): 157-175.

Levenstein MC and Suslow VY (2006) What Determines Cartel Success? Journal of Economic Literature 44(1): 43-95.

Loy J-P and Weiss CR (2019) Product Differentiation and Cost Pass-Through. Journal of Agricultural Economics. 70(3): 840-858.

Miller NH (2009) Strategic Leniency and Cartel Enforcement. American Economic Review 99(3): 750-68.

Motta M (2004) Competition Policy: Theory and Practice. Cambridge University Press, Cambridge, UK.

Nevo A (1998) Identification of the Oligopoly Solution Concept in a Differentiated-Products Industry. Economics Letters 59(3): 391-395.

Nobelprize.org (2020) Angus Deaton: Facts. https://www.nobelprize.org/prizes/economic-sciences/2015/deaton/facts/. Accessed on January 16, 2021.

Pennerstorfer D, Schindler N, Weiss C and Yontcheva B (2020) Income Inequality and Product Variety: Empirical Evidence. Working Paper No. 2017, University of Linz, Austria.
Perekhozhuk O, Glauben T, Grings M and Teuber R (2017) Approaches and Methods for the Econometric Analysis of Market Power: A Survey and Empirical Comparison. Journal of Economic Surveys 31(1): 303-325.
Phlips L (1996) On the Detection of Collusion and Predation. European Economic Review 40(3-5): 495-510.
Pindyck RS (2011) Lecture Notes on Bundling and Brand Proliferation. MIT. Retrieved from: http://www.mit.edu/~rpindyck/Courses/BBP_11.pdf. Accessed on January 16, 2021.
Reiss PC and Wolak FA (2007) Structural Econometric Modeling: Rationales and Examples from Industrial Organization. In: Heckman JJ and Leamer EE (Eds.), Handbook of Econometrics, Volume 6, Part A, Chapter 64, Elsevier: 4277-4415.
Rojas C (2008) Price Competition in U.S. Brewing. The Journal of Industrial Economics 56(1): 1-31.
Schiff N (2015) Cities and Product Variety: Evidence from Restaurants. Journal of Economic Geography 15(6): 1085-1123.
Shapiro C (1989) Theories of Oligopoly Behavior. In: Schmalensee R and Willig RD (Eds.) Handbook of Industrial Organization, Volume 1, North-Holland, Chapter 6: 329 -414.
Sheldon IM and Sperling R (2003) Estimating the Extent of Imperfect Competition in the Food Industry: What Have We Learned? Journal of Agricultural Economics 54(1): 89-109.
Torshizi M and Clapp J (2021) Price Effects of Common Ownership in the Seed Sector. The Antitrust Bulletin 66(1): 39-67.
Werden GJ (1998) Demand Elasticities in Antitrust Analysis. Antitrust Law Journal 66(2): 363-414.
Zellner JA (1989 A Simultaneous Analysis of Food Industry Conduct. American Journal of Agricultural Economics 71(1): 105-115.

Appendix 8.1 Derivation of (inverse) demand functions for n goods

To maximize the quadratic utility function

$$U(q,q_0) = \sum_{i=1}^{n} s_i q_i - \frac{1}{2}\left(\sum_{i=1}^{n} q_i^2 - 2d\sum_{j=1}^{n} q_i q_j\right) + q_0$$

for $i \neq j$ with respect to the budget constraint

$$y = \sum_{i=1}^{n} p_i q_i + q_0$$

we formulate the Lagrangian equation:

$$L = \sum_{i=1}^{n} s_i q_i - \frac{1}{2}\left(\sum_{i=1}^{n} q_i^2 - 2d \sum_{j=1}^{n} q_i q_j\right) + q_0 + \lambda(y - \sum_{i=1}^{n} p_i q_i - q_0)$$

The first derivatives with respect to q_i, q_0 and λ are:

$$\frac{\partial L}{\partial q_i} = s_i - q_i + d \sum_{j=1}^{n} q_j - \lambda p_i = 0 \tag{15}$$

$$\frac{\partial L}{\partial q_0} = 1 - \lambda = 0 \tag{16}$$

$$\frac{\partial L}{\partial \lambda} = y - \sum_{i=1}^{n} p_i q_i - q_0 = 0 \tag{17}$$

Note that the Lagrange multiplier (λ), which measures the shadow price of income, is constant ($\lambda = 1$ in equation 16). This allows us to conduct a partial equilibrium analysis of the n goods, since there are no interaction (income) effects with other goods (represented by the composite commodity q_0). For $\lambda = 1$, the inverse demand equation for the n goods from equation (15) is: $p_i = s_i - q_i + d \sum_{j=1}^{n} q_j$. This corresponds to equation (2) above. The demand for the composite commodity q_0 is given by equation (17): $q_0 = y - \sum_{i=1}^{n} p_i q_i$.

To derive equation (3) from the inverse demand equation (2), we aggregate equation (2) over all n goods:

$$\sum_{i=1}^{n} p_i = \sum_{i=1}^{n} s_i - \sum_{i=1}^{n} q_i - d \sum_{i=1}^{n} \sum_{j=1}^{n} q_j,$$

which is equivalent to

$$\sum_{i=1}^{n} p_i = \sum_{i=1}^{n} s_i - \sum_{i=1}^{n} q_i - d(n-1) \sum_{i=1}^{n} q_i$$

because $\sum_{i=1}^{n}\sum_{j=1}^{n} q_j = (n-1)\sum_{i=1}^{n} q_i$, for $i \neq j$.[18]

This gives $\sum_{i=1}^{n} q_i = \frac{\sum_{i=1}^{n} s_i - \sum_{i=1}^{n} p_i}{1-d(n-1)}$. Inserting this into equation (2) we obtain

$$q_i = s_i - p_i + d(\sum_{i=1}^{n} q_i - q_i)$$

which can be transformed into

$$q_i(1+d) = s_i - p_i + d\frac{\sum_{i=1}^{n} s_i - \sum_{i=1}^{n} p_i}{1-d(n-1)}$$

or

$$q_i(1+d) = s_i - p_i + d\frac{\sum_{j=1}^{n} s_j - \sum_{j=1}^{n} p_j}{1-d(n-1)} + d\frac{s_i - p_i}{1-d(n-1)}.$$

After further transpositions we obtain:

$$q_i(1+d) = \frac{[1-d(n-1)]s_i + ds_i + d\sum_{j=1}^{n} s_j}{1-d(n-1)} - \frac{[1-d(n-1)]p_i + dp_i}{1-d(n-1)} - \frac{d\sum_{j=1}^{n} p_j}{1-d(n-1)}.$$

Dividing by $(1+d)$ and rearranging terms leads to equation (3):

$$q_i = \frac{[1-d(n-2)]s_i + d\sum_{j=1}^{n} s_j}{(1+d)[1-d(n-1)]} - \frac{[1-d(n-2)]p_i}{(1+d)[1-d(n-1)]} - \frac{d\sum_{j=1}^{n} p_j}{(1+d)[1-d(n-1)]}$$

$$= \sigma_i - \beta p_i + \delta\sum_{j=1}^{n} p_j$$

Appendix 8.2 Pricing in a two-product monopoly

In the following, we examine the profit maximisation problem of a monopolist who sells two differentiated products to customers. Consumer demand is given by equation (8.3). The monopolist maximises the total profit for all n markets: $\Pi^M = \sum_{i=1}^{n} \pi_i^M = \sum_{i=1}^{n}\left[\left(\sigma_i - \beta p_i + \sum_{j=1}^{n} \delta\, p_j\right)(p_i - c_i') - f_i\right]$ for $i \neq j$. Here, the monopolist's marginal and fixed costs are represented by c_i' and f_i. For $n = 2$, the first-order

[18] This can be illustrated for the case of $n = 3$. For $i \neq j$, $\sum_{i=1}^{3}\sum_{j=1}^{3} q_j = (q_2 + q_3) + (q_1 + q_3) + (q_1 + q_2) = (n-1)\sum_{i=1}^{3} q_i$.

conditions are: $\frac{\partial \Pi^M}{\partial p_i} = \sigma_i - 2\beta p_i + \delta p_j + \beta c_i' + \delta(p_j - c_j') = 0$ for $i,j = 1,2$. From this, we obtain the following profit-maximising prices and quantities: $p_i^M = \frac{(\beta^2-\delta^2)c_i'+\beta\sigma_i+\delta\sigma_j}{2(\beta^2-\delta^2)}$ and $q_i^M = \frac{\sigma_i-\beta c_i'+\delta c_j'}{2}$. Profits are $\Pi^M = \pi_i^M + \pi_j^M = \frac{(\sigma_i-\beta c_i'+\delta c_j')[\beta\sigma_i-\delta\sigma_j-(\beta^2-\delta^2)c_i']}{4(\beta^2-\delta^2)} - f_i + \frac{(\sigma_j-\beta c_j'+\delta c_i')[\beta\sigma_j-\delta\sigma_i-(\beta^2-\delta^2)c_j']}{4(\beta^2-\delta^2)} - f_j$. For $c_i' = c_j' = c'$, $\sigma_i = \sigma_j = \sigma$ and $f_i = f_j = f$, this equation simplifies to $\Pi^M = \pi_i^M + \pi_j^M = 2\frac{[\sigma-(\beta-\delta)c']^2}{4(\beta-\delta)} - 2f$. In the case of independent products ($\delta \to 0 \Rightarrow \beta = 1$), we get $p_i^M = \frac{\sigma+c'}{2}$, $q_i^M = \frac{\sigma-c'}{2}$ and $\pi_i^M = \frac{(\sigma-c')^2}{4} - f$ as well as $\Pi^M = 2\pi_i^M = \frac{(\sigma-c')^2}{2\beta} - 2f$. This corresponds to the standard one-product monopoly market with linear demand and cost functions, which can be found in every introductory textbook of microeconomics.

Exercises

1. The big agricultural machinery manufacturers spend considerable sums on advertisement and promotion, for example in agricultural magazines and trade fairs. Do they engage primarily in cooperative or predatory advertising?

2. Your consulting company estimates that the own-price elasticity of demand for a client's product is -0.6. The client is the only firm that is entitled to sell this product in a particular region. In order to raise profits from selling this product, you recommend that the client:
   a) increase production,
   b) lower the price,
   c) reduce production,
   d) choose output such that price equals marginal cost,
   e) choose output such that price equals average costs.

   Hint: Only one answer is correct.

3. In a detailed econometric analysis, Gasmi et al. (1992) estimate demand and cost functions for two competing firms (*Coca-Cola Comp.* and *Pepsico Inc.*) in the US soft-drink market for the period 1968 to 1986. On the basis of Table 11 (page 294) of their study, we obtain (after rounding the parameter estimates) the following demand functions:

$q_{CO} = 60 - 4p_{CO} + 2p_{PE}$ and $q_{PE} = 50 - 5p_{PE} + p_{CO}$, where the subscript CO denotes *Coca-Cola Comp.* and PE denotes *Pepsico Inc.*. Following Gasmi et al. (1992, Table 11) we also assume (constant) marginal production costs of $c_{CO} = 8$ and $c_{PE} = 7$.

a) If *Pepsico Inc.* were to sell its product at a price of $p_{PE} = 8$, what profit-maximizing price p_{CO} should *Coca-Cola Comp.* (p_{CO}) choose under price (Bertrand) competition?
b) Compute the prices (p_{CO} and p_{PE}) and quantities sold (q_{CO} and q_{PE}) for both companies in Bertrand equilibrium.
c) Compute the Lerner-Index for both companies (L_{CO} and L_{PE}) as well as the Herfindahl-Hirschmann-Index (HHI) for this market in Bertrand equilibrium.

4. In an oft-cited study, Genesove and Mullin (1998) analyse the US sugar industry at the end of the 19th century. The technology for producing refined sugar was simple back then, which enables the authors to calculate the producers' marginal costs. Specifically, they find $c^L = 3.78$ and $c^H = 3.87$ (in cents per 100 pounds of sugar), where H denotes the high and L the low season. Based on the study (see Genesove and Mullin, 1998, Table 3 on p. 366) assume that the demand for sugar (which is a comparatively homogeneous produce) is given by the following linear functions $Q^L = 13.37 - 2.30p^L$ and $Q^H = 10.74 - 1.36p^H$, where prices (p^L and p^H) are in cents per 100 pound, and quantities (Q^L and Q^H) are in 100 pound.
   a) In 1892 the *American Sugar Refining Company* (ASRC) had a market share of 95%. On the assumption that this company was effectively the monopoly supplier of sugar in the US, what profit-maximizing prices should it have charged in the high and in the low season? What would have been the corresponding mark-ups (μ) and Lerner indices (L)?
   b) The actual average price of sugar was $p^N = 3.99$ in the high and $p^H = 4.14$ in the low season. Calculate the actual mark-ups (μ) and Lerner indices (L) corresponding to these prices. What might explain the fact that the actual prices were considerably lower than the profit-maximising monopoly prices, even though the market was highly concentrated?
   c) In the ensuing years up to 1914, other producers entered the US sugar market and ASRC's market share steadily fell. Assume that two firms entered the market, so that $n = 3$. In addition, assume for simplicity that all firms were identical. Using the information provided above on the demand function and the marginal costs in the

high season, calculate the equilibrium prices for a conjectural variation model with (i) $\theta = 0$ and (ii) $\theta = -0.5$.

d) Assume that the number of (identical) competitors was $n = 3$ and the actual price of sugar in the high season was $p^H = 4.14$. How high must the parameter of conjectural variation θ have been to generate this equilibrium outcome?

5. The so-called ABCD companies (*ADM*, *Bunge*, *Cargill* and *Louis Dreyfus*) control a large share of the international grain trade. What factors suggest that these firms will (will not) behave collusively? Consider Feuerstein's (2005) ten stylized facts when formulating your answer to this question. How might the growing importance of the Chinese state trading enterprise *Cofco* affect the conduct of the ABCD companies?

CHAPTER NINE

PRICE RELATIONSHIPS AND PRICE CHANGES IN SELECTED AGRICULTURAL MARKETS

SEBASTIAN HESS AND ULRICH KOESTER

9.1. Introduction and learning objectives

This chapter examines selected relationships between individual agricultural prices. Terms that are sometimes used more or less synonymously in this context are the **agricultural price structure, price relations** or **price ratios.**

In Chapter 2 we derived various optimal equilibrium price relationships between outputs and inputs under neoclassical conditions. We seldom observe these price relationships in reality, however, because the assumptions of neoclassical economics are often violated. In addition, agricultural markets are seldom in equilibrium. Instead, markets are typically adjusting to shocks, for example because market participants have received new information, due to changes in behaviour, preferences and technology, and in response to changes in institutions such as government regulations. As a result of such shocks, equilibria are disturbed, which triggers market processes that change prices and quantities in the direction of new equilibria. Since markets are interrelated, adjustments on one market will inevitably lead to adjustments on others.

In this chapter we will analyse the reactions of farmers and processors of agricultural products to selected changes in agricultural prices. As we will see, changes in price relations on agricultural markets are often delayed compared with other sectors. Adjustments are delayed by specific conditions in agriculture, such as biological production processes that take time to unfold (think of tree crops, or the time it takes to expand a dairy herd), the limited availability of land, and the fact that agriculture often produces joint products (such as protein and fat in milk, or oil and meal in oilseeds). But institutions such as laws and the culturally determined behaviour of farmers can also slow down market adjustments in agriculture. It is not the aim of this chapter to derive exactly which price relations will arise in reality as a result of certain shocks. Instead, the primary aim is to analyse and explain how price relationships can be expected to change in response to selected shocks.

Changes in agricultural price relations are not only caused by changes in economic incentive structures but also by institutions. Agriculture produces both private and public goods, and both types of goods are important for the achievement of agricultural policy goals. It is therefore understandable that governments often intervene directly or indirectly on agricultural markets through a large variety of measures (laws and regulations, i.e. institutions) that influence price relations. Laws and regulations that affect agricultural price relationships are not only implemented by national governments, but also at the supra-national level, for example by the EU or the World Trade Organisation (WTO).

In addition, agricultural markets are integrated in increasingly complex value-added chains. Value is added to an agricultural raw product at each link in the chain, for example as milk is processed into milk powder, then baby formula, etc. Hence, price relationships in agriculture are not only horizontal (for example between wheat and barley, or milk and beef), but also vertical (for example between milk and butter, or wheat and bread).

In this chapter we will:

- analyse horizontal price relationships between agricultural products using selected examples,
- discuss price relationships between agricultural raw products and the joint products that they are processed into (for example between milk, milk fat and protein),
- provide an overview of how institutions can affect agricultural price relations using several important examples from the history of agricultural policy in the EU.

9.2. Price relationships between agricultural goods at the same processing stage

Neoclassical models of agricultural pricing usually assume that goods are homogeneous, i.e. different qualities of a good such as wheat are treated as separate goods. In this section, therefore, we will first discuss price determination for homogeneous agricultural goods at the same processing stage, before considering heterogeneous goods. After that we will present examples that illustrate how the effectiveness of policy measures on a particular market are affected by interactions with other markets.

9.2.1. Equilibrium price relationships for related agricultural goods

Price changes between two related agricultural markets can first be examined using a simple, comparative-static partial equilibrium model.[1] Consider two interrelated markets in a closed economy, i.e. one that does not trade with other countries. Without loss of generality we refer to the two markets as 'poultry meat' (M) and 'grain' (G). The supply and demand curves for these markets are:

poultry meat supply: $q_M^S = A\, p_M^a\, p_G^{-b}$ (1)

poultry meat demand: $q_M^D = B\, p_M^{-d}$ (2)

grain supply: $q_G^S = C\, p_G^e$ (3)

grain demand: $q_G^D = E\, p_G^{-g}\, p_M^h$ (4)

where the constants A, B, C and E are all greater than zero, as are a, b, d, e, g and h.

In equation (1) the market supply for poultry meat is an increasing function of the meat price, and a decreasing function of the grain price, the latter because grains are an important feed input in poultry meat production. Rising grain prices thus increase the marginal costs of meat production; *ceteris paribus* this leads to a reduction in the supply of meat. The supply of grain in equation (3) is an (increasing) function of the grain price alone, and the demand for meat in equation (2) is a (decreasing) function of the meat price alone. However, the demand for grain in equation (4) depends on both the grain price and the meat price. An increase in the meat price increases the demand for grain by way of an expansion in meat production.

---

[1] See Roningen (1997, pp. 231-257) and Francois and Hall (1997, pp. 122-155).

We solve for equilibrium prices by equating supply and demand:

Equilibrium condition:

$$\mathrm{A}\, p_M^a\, p_G^{-b} = \mathrm{B}\, p_M^{-d} \text{ and } C p_G^e = E p_G^{-g}\, p_M^h \tag{5}$$

Equilibrium prices:

$$p_M^* = \left(\frac{B}{A}\right)^{\left(\frac{1}{a+d}\right)} p_G^{\left(\frac{b}{a+d}\right)} \text{ and } p_G^* = \left(\frac{E}{C}\right)^{\left(\frac{1}{e+g}\right)} p_M^{\left(\frac{h}{e+g}\right)} \tag{6}$$

We see that the equilibrium price of poultry meat is a function of the grain price, and *vice versa*. The interactions between these prices are determined by the relative magnitudes of the various supply and demand elasticities.

The price of grain has always played a particularly important role in the history of agricultural price and market policy. This price is sometimes referred to as **pivotal agricultural price** because of grain's importance for human nutrition, as a feedstuff in livestock production, and also as feedstock in energy production (e.g. when maize is processed into ethanol). Hence, the grain price has a similar effect on the overall agricultural price structure as the basic wage rate has on the wage structure in an economy.[2]

The model in equations (1) through (6) shows how a change in the grain price affects other agricultural prices and thus the overall agricultural price structure. In reality, of course, more than two markets and prices will interact. The resulting price effects will, as a rule, be non-linear and depend on the relative magnitudes of the supply and demand elasticities involved. As a result, a shock on one market can trigger disproportionately smaller or larger price reactions on other markets.

9.2.2. The supply of and demand for inputs

The supply and demand functions in equations (1) through (4) above depict the aggregated behaviour of many individual market participants (producers and consumers). On the supply side, for example, each individual poultry producer contributes to aggregate supply based on the size of his/her operation and the specific production technology used. This technology

---

[2] In some countries where wages are set by collective bargaining agreements between groups of employers and large unions, the agreement reached in a particular sector will define a basic wage rate that serves as a benchmark for negotiations in other sectors.

describes how inputs such as feed are combined and transformed into an output (poultry meat). To illustrate this let us assume that poultry meat production follows the following Cobb-Douglas production technology: $q_M = {q_G}^{0,5}{q_S}^{0,5}$.

According to this technology, poultry meat (q_M) is produced using the inputs grain (q_G) and soymeal (q_S). The exponents on the input quantities are **production elasticities** that indicate by how many percentage points the output of poultry meat will increase if the respective input amount is increased by 1%. Since the assumed production technology is characterised by constant returns to scale (the sum of the production elasticities equals 1) the exponents can also be interpreted as cost shares. Hence, grain and soymeal each account for 50% of the costs of production.

The indirect (or **dual**)[3] Cobb-Douglas **cost function** corresponding to this production technology is:

$$cost^{min} = 2q_M(p_G)^{0,5}(p_S)^{0,5} \tag{7}$$

The derivation of this function assumes that the producer always aims to produce a given quantity of poultry meat (q_M) at minimum cost ($cost^{min}$) given the prices of grain (p_G) and soymeal (p_S).

Making use of **Shephard's Lemma**, differentiating equation (7) with respect to the two input prices leads to the (Hicksian or compensated) input demand functions. These functions describe poultry meat producers' behaviour on the markets for grain and for soymeal. The resulting input demand for grain is:

$$\frac{\partial c^{min}}{\partial p_G} = q_M(p_G)^{-0.5}(p_S)^{0.5} = q_G \tag{8}$$

and the corresponding input demand for soymeal is:

$$\frac{\partial c^{min}}{\partial p_S} = q_M(p_G)^{0.5}(p_S)^{-0.5} = q_S \tag{9}$$

The demand functions in equations (8) and (9) can be linearized by taking logarithms. This makes it possible to estimate the production elasticities directly using regression techniques and subsequently to test hypotheses about the magnitudes of these elasticities. For the example of the input

[3] Snyder et al. (2015) explain microeconomic duality theory.

demand for grain in equation (8), equation (10) shows the log-linear regression model that can be estimated using a sample of observations on $i = 1, 2, \dots N$ poultry meat producers:

$$ln(q_G)_i = \hat{\beta}_0 + \hat{\beta}_G ln(p_G)_i + \hat{\beta}_S ln(p_S)_i + \hat{u}_i \quad (10)$$

Estimation of equation (10) can be used to test hypotheses such as $\beta_G = -0.5$ and $\beta_S = 0.5$ about the individual production elasticities, or $|\beta_G| + \beta_S = 1$ (i.e. whether the production technology is characterised by constant returns to scale). In equation (10) the coefficients β_G and β_S can also be interpreted as price elasticities of factor demand.

Table 9.1 presents estimated price elasticities of demand for different feedstuffs that have been econometrically estimated for the EU. We see that the demand for the cereal substitute tapioca is especially price elastic, as a 1% increase in the price of tapioca in the EU (for example as a result of an increase in the world market price) leads to a 2.1% reduction in demand.

Table 9.1: Price elasticities of demand for different feedstuffs in the EU (1979-1998).

	A 1% increase in the price of…			
…leads to an X% change in the demand for	Wheat	Other cereals	Protein	Tapioca
Wheat	-1.212	1.412	-0.160	-0.040
Other cereals	0.541	-0.704	0.137	0.026
Protein	-0.105	0.233	-0.323	0.194
Tapioca	-0.264	0.440	1.956	-2.132

Source: Rude and Meilke (2000).

The cost function in equation (7) can also be used to derive the marginal costs of poultry meat production and thus the market supply. For this purpose (7) is differentiated with respect to q_M which results in:

$$\frac{\partial c^{min}}{\partial q_M} = 2(p_G)^{0.5}(p_S)^{0.5} \quad (11)$$

9.2.3. Agricultural goods with heterogeneous qualities: Hedonic prices

In the previous sections we analysed price relationships between products such as poultry meat and grain that we assumed to be homogeneous. However, it is also possible to analyse price relationships between different qualities or types of the same product, for example between different vintages and varieties of wine.[4] In this case, the product in question is heterogeneous. Often, the market prices for agricultural products that are published, for example by government statistical offices, are averages of prices from a large number of individual transactions over a specific period of time. Of course, not every piglet or ton of barley that was traded in a given week, for example, changed hands at the exact price shown in the respective weekly price quotation. If the underlying distribution of individual transaction prices is skewed, then the average transaction price will not equal the most frequent (modal) transaction price. If the underlying price distribution is multi-modal, then the average price might not provide any meaningful information at all. For this reason, it can be instructive to take a closer look at the distribution of prices for heterogeneous good, as we illustrate in the following for the example of horses.[5]

At the end of an auction it is possible to calculate the average price paid over all of the horses sold. However, the price of a particular horse sold at an auction will not depend only, and perhaps not at all, on the total number of horses sold and the total number of buyers present. Instead, the price of a particular horse $k \in \{1, 2, \ldots, K\}$ will depend on a vector of its performance characteristics and other factors. If there are n such characteristics, then horse k can be described by the vector $Z_k = z_{1k}, z_{2k}, \ldots, z_{nk}$, and the price of that horse is given by:

$$p_k(Z_k) = p(z_{1k}, z_{2k}, \ldots, z_{nk}) \quad (12)$$

A seller will not only offer horse k but will also sell it if the auction price $p_k(Z_k)$ equals the marginal costs $MC(Z_k)$ of raising a horse with the characteristics Z_k. Hence, the number of horses sold at an auction, Q^* depends on the prices $p_k(Z_k)$ which in turn depend on the characteristics of the individual horses:

---

[4] See for example Schäufele et al. (2016).

[5] See for example Stowe (2013) or Hess et al. (2014). The implications of product differentiation for (imperfect) competition are analysed in detail in Chapter 8.

$$Q^{k*} = Q^{k*}(P, Z_1, Z_2, \ldots, Z_k) \tag{13}$$

On the demand side, we assume that the different performance characteristics in the vector Z generate benefits for the buyer according to a utility function: $U = U\ (z_1, z_2, \ldots,\ z_n, x)$, where x is a vector that includes all other relevant factors that are not specific to a particular horse (such as the distance of the auction from the buyer's home, and any fees that must be paid to participate in the auction). Horse buyers maximise their utility by demanding horses with certain characteristics, subject to their budget constraints:

$$I = p_x x + p(z_1, z_2, \ldots, z_n) \tag{14}$$

A buyer's expenditure for a certain desired characteristic thus depends on the horse's other characteristics and their prices, as well as the cost of any other expenses as captured by x.

On a market with many suppliers of horses and many buyers, there will be a supply $S_z(z_n)$ and a demand $D_z(z_n)$ for each individual characteristic z_n, and together these will determine the equilibrium amount of this characteristic $S_z^*(z_n) = D_z^*(z_n)$ and its equilibrium price $p_z^*(z_n)$. These prices for individual characteristics are rarely observed, but they are aggregated over all characteristics for each individual horse leading to its specific price $p_k(Z_k)$. For example, in an auction of race horses one does not explicitly observe how much the price of a horse increases for each additional 1000 Euro of prize money it has won to date. However, given sufficient information on the characteristics and sales prices of a sufficiently large number of horses, it is possible to calculate the implicit value of an additional 1000 Euro of prize winnings, using what is referred to as the **hedonic price model**. The hedonic price model explains the variation in prices among a set of heterogeneous goods within a product category (such as horses) as a function of the goods' characteristics and the equilibrium prices of these characteristics:

$$P_k^*(Z_k) = f(z_{1k}^*, z_{2k}^*, \ldots, z_{nk}^*) \tag{15}$$

Hedonic price models are of great practical importance in empirical market analysis. For estimation purposes, a stochastic error term is added to the equation (15), which is then estimated using regression techniques:

$$P_k^*(Z_k) = \beta_0 + \beta_1 z_{1k}^* + \beta_2 z_{2k}^* + \cdots + \beta_n z_{nk}^* + u_k \tag{16}$$

For the example of a horse auction, the $p_k^*(Z_k)$ are the observed auction prices for a sample of horses. On the right side of the equation, the explanatory variables z_{1k}^* to z_{nk}^* are the relevant characteristics of each horse, such as its height, gender, colour, and jumping ability, etc. The regression coefficients β measure the marginal increase in the auction price for an average horse if the corresponding characteristic increased by one unit. Hedonic price models are thus used to estimate the market mark-ups (or mark-downs) that correspond to specific product characteristics. Hedonic analysis has been used in the economic literature for a wide variety of heterogenous products such as wine, real estate, and agricultural land, and it often underlies online market portals that provide value estimates for products such as used vehicles and homes.

9.2.4. The practical importance of substitutability on agricultural markets

Price relationships also arise between goods at the same processing stage when they are substitutes for one another. In the following we discuss this using the example of grain and grain substitutes in animal feed that was touched upon above (see Table 9.1). The competitiveness of a particular feedstuff depends on its nutrient content and its price relative to those of other feedstuffs.

In practice, linear programming (LP) models are often used to optimise feed rations. In addition, a method proposed by Löhr for evaluating the value of a feedstuff can be used. This method considers two nutrients, for example protein and energy. For dairy cattle, the energy content of feed is often measured in MJ NEL (megajoule net energy content for lactation), which indicates the energy content in joules that can be metabolised for milk production per kg of the feed. Protein is measured according to the raw protein content. **Löhr's method** can be used, for example, to calculate how much wheat and soybean meal are required to replace one kg of another feed. Alternatively, the method can be used to calculate up to what price a substitute feed can compete with other feeds such as wheat and soybean meal.

To illustrate Löhr's method we use information about the raw protein and energy content as well as the prices of wheat, soybean meal, and the potential substitute feed. This is demonstrated in the following example in which we calculate the prices at which rapeseed meal and other feedstuffs can compete with a mixture of soybean meal and wheat in dairy rations.

First, the necessary information on protein and energy contents and prices for wheat and soybean meal are presented in Table 9.2.

Table 9.2: Comparative feed levels in a dairy cattle ration.

Alternative feed	Raw protein in g / kg	MJ NEL / kg dry matter	Market prices in € / dt
Soybean meal	425	7,59	28.00
Wheat	121	7,49	14.00

Source: Own depiction based on Groß (2010).

Based on this information, Löhr's method begins by solving the following system of equations to calculated the implicit prices of raw protein (x) and energy (y) in wheat and soybean meal:

Soybean meal: $425x + 7.59y = 28$ (17)

Wheat: $121x + 7.49y = 14$ (18)

The resulting values are

$y = 1.1312$ (the implicit price of energy), and

$x = 0.0456$ (the implicit price of raw protein).

With the help of these implicit prices, we next calculate maximum price at which an alternative feedstuff can compete with a mixture of wheat and soybean meal. One kg of rapeseed meal, for example, contains 330 g of raw protein and 6.51 MJ NEL (see Table 9.3). A reference price (p^{ref}) for rapeseed meal is calculated by multiplying these amounts with their respective implicit prices:

$$p^{ref} = 330 \cdot 0{,}0456 + 6{,}51 \cdot 1{,}1312 = 22{,}44 \quad (19)$$

Hence, as long as its price is lower than the reference price of 22.44 €/dt, rapeseed meal is less expensive than any mixture of wheat and soybean meal that provides equal amounts of protein and energy. However, if the price of rapeseed meal is higher than the reference price, it is less expensive to obtain energy and protein from wheat and soybean meal. Table 9.3 presents analogous calculations for a number of substitute feedstuffs.

Table 9.3: Reference prices for selected feedstuffs for dairy cattle compared with wheat and soybean meal

Feedstuff	Raw protein in g / kg	MJ NEL / kg dry matter	Reference price in € / dt
Rapeseed meal	330	6.51	22.44
Molasses pulp	115	6.93	13.09
Grain corn	93	7.38	12.60
Peas	221	7.51	18.59
Barley	109	7.11	13.02

Source: Own depiction based on Groß (2010).

Of course, whether rapeseed meal or a mixture of wheat and soybean meal is fed depends not only on protein and energy, but also on the composition (amino acid profile) of the protein, on other nutrients, and on palatability. In practice, therefore, and depending on the animal species in question, substitution between feedstuffs is only possible within a limited range.

9.2.5. The effect of policy measures at the same processing level

The previous section dealt with the practical importance of technical substitutability for price relationships between feedstuffs. In this section we present two well-known examples from the history of the EU's **Common Agricultural Policy (CAP)** that show how protection for specific domestically produced products was undermined by duty-free imports of substitutes, leading to large economic distortions. The first case (the so-called Open Flank of the CAP) involves cereals and cereal substitutes, the second case involves sugar and alternative sweeteners such as isoglucose.

9.2.5.1. The Open Flank of the CAP

In the CAP, cereals prices are political prices that are influenced by a common market organisation. Under this common market organisation, administrative support prices (so-called threshold and intervention prices) are set by policy makers. In the past, market prices for cereals (and other agricultural products) in the EU were strongly influenced by these administrative prices and the support measures designed to implement them (such as intervention purchases and export subsidies).

In the course of a series of reforms beginning in the early 1990s, the EU's administrative prices were progressively reduced. As a result, producer prices fell, as did the EU's spending on price support measures. Both of these effects can be seen for the case of wheat in Figure 9.1. In addition, and as also apparent in Figure 9.1, starting in 2007/08 world market prices for wheat increased strongly, further reducing the need for price support in the EU.

Figure 9.1: EU producer and world market prices for wheat, and EU expenditure on wheat price support measures

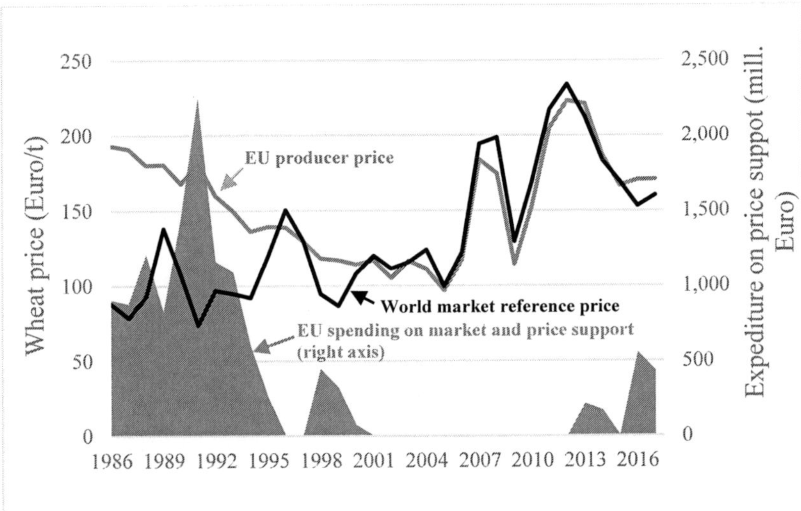

Source: OECD (2022).

The so-called **Open Flank of the CAP** dates back to the beginnings of the CAP, when the EU was designing and first implementing its common market organisations. At this time, the EU (which was then called the European Economic Community – EEC) established a customs union, which means that its members replaced their national tariffs with common EU-wide tariffs. In the early 1960s, before it was clear how high the EU would set its common tariffs, many of the EU's trading partners were worried that it would set high, protectionist and trade-diverting tariffs.[6] As

[6] Josling et al. (1996) describe the negotiations that took place at the time. See Koester (1988) for a detailed discussion of the Open Flank.

a result, in the so-called Dillon Round of GATT[7] negotiations, which lasted from 1960 to 1962, these trading partners – especially the US – demanded compensation from the EU. The EU rejected these demands but did agree to make what appeared, at the time, to be a small concession: it committed itself to import a wide range of oilseeds, protein feeds and cereal substitutes (often collectively referred to as **cereal substitutes**) duty free in perpetuity. Josling et al. (1996, p. 46) consider it "… doubtful if the chief American and EEC agricultural negotiators … realised the significance of their decision at the time it was made". Back then, the EU only imported very small amounts of cereal substitutes. Hence, agreeing to zero or very low levels of import duties for these products appeared, for the European negotiators, to be a harmless concession.

However, in the course of the 1970s this concession developed into a major burden for the CAP because it distorted price relationships between domestic cereals, which were heavily protected, and cereal substitutes, which could enter the EU duty free. Livestock producers in the EU responded to price incentives and increasingly began to feed imported feedstuffs to their animals rather than domestically produced cereals. For example, the right mixture of imported tapioca and soybean meal can largely replace domestically produced wheat or barley. As a result of the Open Flank, total EU imports of cereal substitutes increased from under 2 million tons in the early 1960s to over 18 million tons in 1987 (Josling et al. 1996, p. 46). The cereals that were no longer being fed to animals boosted the EU's cereal surplus and, therefore, its spending on measures such as intervention storage and export subsidies. Imported oilseeds also contributed to growing surpluses and public spending on EU dairy markets. First, margarine produced with oil from duty-free imports of oilseeds reduced the demand for butter in the EU. Second, imported protein feeds replaced skim milk powder in EU feed rations.

Duty-free imports of cereal substitutes, coupled with price support for domestic cereal and livestock production fuelled a strong expansion of intensive livestock production (beef, pork, poultry and dairy products) in the EU, especially in coastal regions with good access via ports to the world markets for cereal substitutes. The current regional pattern of livestock production in the EU, for example the concentration of German livestock

---

[7] **GATT** is an abbreviation for *General Agreement on Trade and Tariffs*, the predecessor of the **WTO** (*World Trade Organisation*) in the early 1990s.

production in the north-western Weser-Ems region, is legacy of the Open Flank.

The Open Flank was ultimately closed by the series of reforms referred to above, which progressively reduced the EU's price support for cereals and thus brought EU cereal prices in line with those on world markets (see Figure 9.1). Figure 9.2 shows how the closing of the Open Flank changed the composition of animal feeds in the EU. In 1990, prior to the reforms, tapioca accounted for 5-6% of compound feed in the EU. As cereal prices in the EU fell, tapioca lost its artificial cost advantage. Its share dropped to around 0.5% in 2005, and by 2018 the use of tapioca in animal feed had become negligible. Additional cereal substitutes in the category 'other' experienced similar declines over this period, while the share of cereals grew from one third to one half.

Figure 9.2: The ingredients in compound feed in the EU (1990, 2005 and 2018)

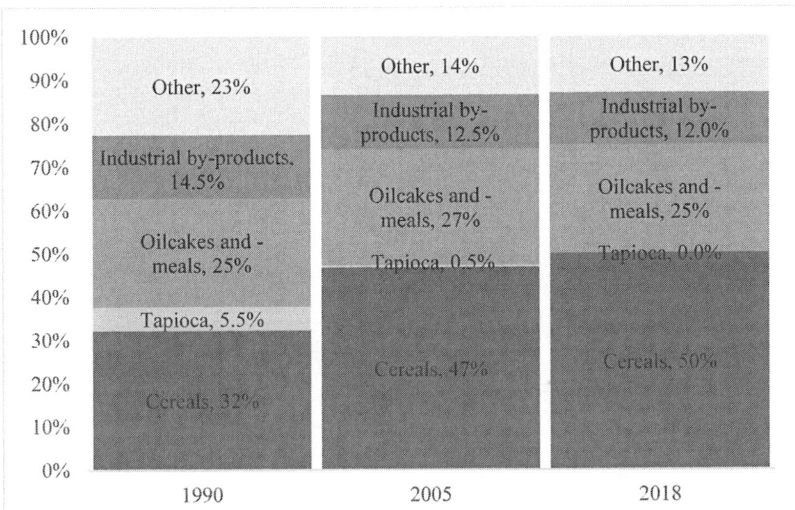

Source: Own depiction with data from FEFAC (2018).

Cereal substitutes are still used in the EU today. Their use depends on their prices relative to cereals, without the cost advantage that existed previously due to the Open Flank. The prices of substitutes relative to cereals, and thus the use of cereals in animal feed, are lower in coastal regions of the EU, and higher in land-locked regions. Nutritional and physiological considerations also influence the composition of animal feed. Soybean meal is a source of high-quality protein (digestibility, amino acid profile). Figure 9.2 shows that the share of oilseed cakes and meals in animal feed in the EU has remained roughly constant (25-27%) over time; imported soybeans (both genetically modified and non-genetically modified) account for the largest share in this category.

9.2.5.2. Sugar, isoglucose and biofuels

Sugar not only plays an important role in human nutrition, it is also an important input in the production of biofuels and in the chemical industry. The term 'sugar' usually refers to sucrose, which is mainly derived from sugar beet and sugar cane. Fructose and lactose are other important types of sugar that are also found in agricultural products, but sucrose is the main output of the sugar industry.

In the EU, there are sugar factories that process sugar beets, as well as refineries that process raw cane sugar. The latter comes from several former French colonies in the Caribbean that remain part of the French state (the so-called Départements d'Outre-Mer), as well as from a number of **African, Caribbean and Pacific** (ACP) countries that have been granted preferential access to the EU sugar market (see below).

The original aim of the EU sugar market organisation was to support the sugar price by restricting sugar beet production. To this end, a fixed production quota was established. This quota was distributed among the sugar processing firms, which further allocated it to individual sugar beet producing farms in the EU. By artificially reducing supply, the quota increased sugar prices in the EU. To keep out imports of cane sugar that would otherwise have been attracted by high prices and thus undermined the quota, the EU also introduced high import duties for sugar. However, it granted some low-income ACP countries duty-free access to the EU market under schemes such the EPA (**Economic Partnership Agreements**) and the EBA (**Everything but Arms**) initiative. Despite the quota, the EU remained over 100% self-sufficient in sugar, and the preferential imports added to its export surplus. In 2005, a WTO panel found that the EU was exporting more sugar than permitted with the help of export subsidies.[8] As a result of this finding, the EU was obliged to reduce its sugar exports.

---

[8] The EU argued that it was not subsidising its sugar exports at all. However, the panel found that sugar companies were using their inflated earnings on the domestic EU market to indirectly subsidise exports. See Burrell et al. (2014) for details.

Figure 9.3 summarises the complex constellation of interacting markets, stakeholder interests and international commitments that EU policy makers had to navigate in their efforts to support prices for domestic sugar beet producers. The oval background area represents the EU internal market that was protected by external tariffs on sugar imports, but to which some countries had preferential access (dotted brackets at the top). Rectangular brackets symbolise quantity restrictions. Food industry use and industrial sugar use formed two separate market segments until the sugar quote was abolished on October 1, 2017.

Figure 9.3: Schematic depiction of substitution relationships and interactions on the EU sugar market from 2006 to the end of the quota system in 2017

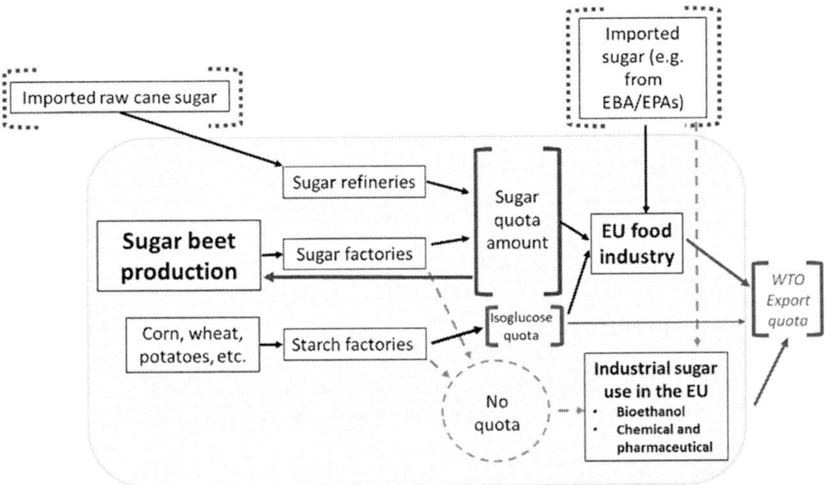

Source: Own depiction based on Agrosynergie (2011).

Sugar can be largely and sometimes completely replaced by glucose-fructose syrup – which is often referred to as isoglucose – in a number of food industry uses, for example to sweeten soft-drinks. Isoglucose is not produced from sugar beets or sugar cane, but rather from the starch in products such as corn, wheat, and potatoes. If the EU sugar market organisation had only imposed a production quota on sugar from beets and cane, making it more expensive, then the food industry would have replaced as much sugar as possible with isoglucose, triggering an expansion in isoglucose production. This would have undermined the sugar quota and depressed sugar prices. To avoid this, EU agricultural policy makers had to impose a quota on isoglucose production as well.

Figure 9.3 also shows that sugar and starch for industrial use were not subject to any quantitative restrictions. For example, there was no limit on the production of biofuels from sugar. Hence, if fossil fuel prices were high enough, ethanol production based on unrestricted 'industrial' sugar beets became attractive.

Since the sugar quota was abolished on October 1, 2017, prices for domestic beet sugar, imported cane sugar, and isoglucose are freely determined. Nevertheless, the linkages between the beet sugar, cane sugar, starch and isoglucose markets depicted in Figure 9.3 remain. These linkages connect food markets to industrial and fuel markets, resulting in a complex, dynamic price structure.

9.3. Price relationships between joint agricultural products

In the previous section we considered price relationships between agricultural products at the same processing stage, for example different feedstuffs that compete for inclusion in feed rations. In this section we turn our attention to the fact that many agricultural products contain several components that can be processed into different intermediate or final food products. For example, oilseeds such as soybeans and rapeseed can be processed into oil and protein (meal) components by crushing. The resulting **joint products** are sold for further processing and/or final consumption on different markets, where they do not compete with one another.[9] Similarly, higher- and lower-quality cuts of meat from, for example, a chicken, can be viewed as joint products, although in this case they do compete because consumers might switch from higher- to lower-quality cuts if prices increase, and vice versa. A further example of joint production is milk, which has the two main components fat and protein. Dairy products contain different combinations of these two components: for example, butter is mainly composed of the fat component, while skim milk powder is mainly composed of the protein component. Note that not all joint products are separated from one another at the processing stage, like cuts of meat in a slaughterhouse or fat and protein in a dairy processing plant. For example, milk and meat emerge separately as joint outputs of dairy farming.

---

[9] The relationship between prices for agricultural products at different processing stages, for example the relationship between the prices of soybeans and soybean oil and meal, are referred to as vertical price relationships, and are discussed in detail in Chapter 10.

9.3.1. The supply of joint products[10]

In section 9.2.1 we discussed the connection between two markets that arises when one (e.g. grain) is an input in the production of another (e.g. poultry meat). The opposite is the case if two outputs are generated by a production process, and (some of) the inputs into this process cannot be unambiguously assigned to one or the other output. Most agricultural production processes produce multiple outputs using multiple inputs, and often it is not possible to clearly allocate all of the input use to specific outputs, i.e. to measure what amount of an input Z is responsible for output Q_1, and what amount is responsible for another output Q_2.

The implicit production function in equation (20) describes a production system that produces two joint outputs, Q_1 and Q_2, using two inputs, Q^x and Z.

$$F(\mathrm{Q}_1, \mathrm{Q}_2, Q^x, \mathrm{Z}) = 0 \tag{20}$$

The input Q^x can be allocated, i.e. we know how much of it led to the production of Q_1 (Q_2). The other input Z cannot be allocated. We can re-write the production function as follows, where $Q^x = Q_1^x + Q_1^x$:

$$Q_1 = f^1(Q_1^x, Z) \tag{21}$$

$$Q_2 = f^2(Q_2^x, Z) \tag{22}$$

A typical example of a production process according to equation (20) is the production of milk Q_1 and beef Q_2 using feed Q^x and a cow Z. The feed use can be allocated to the individual outputs using information on the underlying physiological relationships, but the cow, which produces milk and calves jointly, cannot be allocated.

From the perspective of profit maximisation, the production function in equation (20) leads to the following optimisation problem:

$$\pi = P_1 Q_1 + P_2 Q_2 - P^x Q_1^x - P^x Q_2^x - P^z Z \tag{23}$$

or

$$\pi = P_1 f^1(Q_1^x, Z) + P_2 f^2(Q_2^x, Z) - P^x Q_1^x - P^x Q_2^x - P^z Z \tag{24}$$

[10] This section is based on Chapter 5.5 in Beattie et al. (2009).

The first-order conditions for a profit maximum are determined by differentiating equation (24) with respect to the input quantities and setting the derivative equal to zero:

$$\frac{\partial \pi}{\partial Q_1^x} = P_1 \frac{\partial Q_1}{\partial Q_1^x} - P^x = 0 \tag{25}$$

$$\frac{\partial \pi}{\partial Q_2^x} = P_2 \frac{\partial Q_2}{\partial Q_2^x} - P^x = 0 \tag{26}$$

$$\frac{\partial \pi}{\partial Z} = P_1 \frac{\partial Q_1}{\partial Z} + P_2 \frac{\partial Q_2}{\partial Z} - P^z = 0 \tag{27}$$

Equations (25) and (26) tell us that profit is maximised when the price of the input that can be allocated (e.g. feed) is equal to its marginal value product in the production of Q_1 (e.g. milk) and to its marginal value product in the production of Q_2 (e.g. beef). Hence, these two marginal value products must be equal. Rearranging equation (27) to isolate P^z on the right-hand side reveals a further condition for profit maximisation: that the price of the input that cannot be allocated (e.g. the cow) equals the sum of its marginal value products for Q_1 and Q_2 (e.g. milk and beef).

By simultaneously solving equations (25), (26) and (27) for the input quantities Q_1^x, Q_2^x and Z, we obtain the (uncompensated) input demand functions.[11] These demand functions are referred to as 'uncompensated' because they capture both substitution effects and effects due to changes in the output quantities that result from price changes.[12] These functions show that the demand for an individual input is not only a function of its own price, but also of the two output prices and the price of the other input. Furthermore, inserting the input demand functions into the production functions in equations (21) and (22), we obtain the output supply functions which show that the supply of each output is also a function of all input and output prices. This means, for example, that the output of beef depends not only on the beef price and the feed price, but also on the milk price, since beef and milk are joint products that are linked by the input that cannot be allocated (in this example, the cow).

---

[11] For the derivation of these input demand functions and the output supply functions referred to below see Beattie et al. (2009).

[12] Compensated or Hicksian input demand functions compensate or correct for output changes to isolate substitution effects. For details see Beattie et al. (2009) and Snyder et al. (2012).

Whether or not an input can be allocated to different outputs is somewhat arbitrary and depends on the costs of a detailed, definitive analysis. It might be possible, based on detailed analysis of physiological and metabolic processes, to trace and separate a cow's contributions to milk and meat production. However, this would not change the fact that in reality the living cow is a single input with a single market price.

9.3.2. Price relationships between joint products – the example of milk

In this section we take a closer look at price relationships between joint products by analysing the case of raw milk that is processed into butter and skim milk powder (SMP). This analysis can be applied to other markets, for example oilseeds that are processed into oil and meal. Figure 9.4 presents several important technical relationships that apply in the case of milk.

Figure 9.4: Technical relationships between milk products at different processing levels*

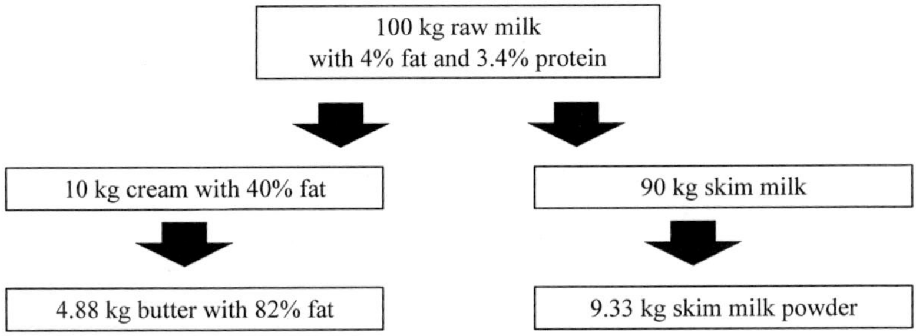

Source: Own depiction based on DairyCo (2014).
** Simplified, and without considering processing losses.*

Figure 9.4 shows that the main marketable components of raw milk are the fat component and the protein component. The market demand for raw milk is therefore ultimately derived from the final consumer demand for products that contain milk fat on the one hand, and for products that contain milk protein on the other. In the following we simplify by assuming that the fat component can only be processed into butter, and the protein component only into SMP.

If only the fat component of milk had a market value, we could derive the price of raw milk from the price of butter. We would start with the butter price, subtract processing and marketing costs, and divide by an appropriate **technical transformation coefficient** (see Figure 9.4) that indicates how many kg of milk are required to produce 1 kg of butter. However, dairies can also process and sell the protein component of milk. Hence, the price that they can pay farmers for raw milk will also reflect the value of the protein component, as reflected in the following equation:

$$MV^{raw\,milk} = bP^{butter} - bc^{butter} + dP^{SMP} - dc^{SMP} \tag{28}$$

In equation (28), the marginal value of one kg of raw milk ($MV^{Raw\,milk}$) equals the revenue from the sale of its fat and protein components (bP^{butter} and dP^{SMP}, respectively), minus the costs of processing each of these components (bc^{butter} and dc^{SMP}, respectively). Table 9.4 presents information on these costs, and based this information Table 9.5 calculates the marginal value of one kg of raw milk using market prices for butter and SMP in the EU in June 2018.

Table 9.4: Assumed costs of processing 100kg of raw milk into butter and skim milk powder (SMP)

Symbol in equation (28)	Description	Source / Assumption
MV	Derived marginal value of raw milk	Calculated using equation (28)
P	Market prices	Current market prices
b	Technical transformation coefficient for butter	100 kg raw milk → 4.88 kg butter, or 20.49 kg raw milk → 1 kg butter (see Figure 9.4)
c	Processing and marketing costs*	€ 32.03 / 100 kg butter € 43.47 / 100 kg SMP
d	Technical transformation coefficient for SMP	100 kg raw milk → 9.33 kg SMP, or 10.72 kg raw milk → 1 kg SMP (see Figure 9.4)

Source: Own depiction based on DairyCo (2014)
* *Processing costs do not include the cost of the raw milk itself.*

Table 9.5: The marginal value of raw milk in the EU in June 2018 based on average butter and skim milk powder (SMP) prices

Butter price (€/kg)	5.82
Costs of processing for butter (€/kg)	0.32
SMP price (€/kg)	1.52
Costs of processing for SMP (€/kg)	0.43
Derived marginal value of raw milk (€/kg)	**0.37**

Source: Own illustration based on equation (28) and Table 9.4.

The marginal value of raw milk derived according to equation (28), and illustrated in Table 9.5, is based on a number of assumptions. Do dairy processors pay corresponding prices to farmers for the raw milk that they deliver? Figure 9.5 shows that the average monthly farm-gate price for raw milk in the EU is correlated with the derived marginal value, but not perfectly. Since 2007 in particular we can see that movements in the farm-gate price have tended to lag behind movements in the derived marginal value by several months. We can also see that the farm-gate price fluctuates less (lower peaks and higher troughs) than the derived marginal value.

Figure 9.5: Derived marginal values of raw milk and average farm-gate prices of milk in the EU (monthly averages, 2001-2018)

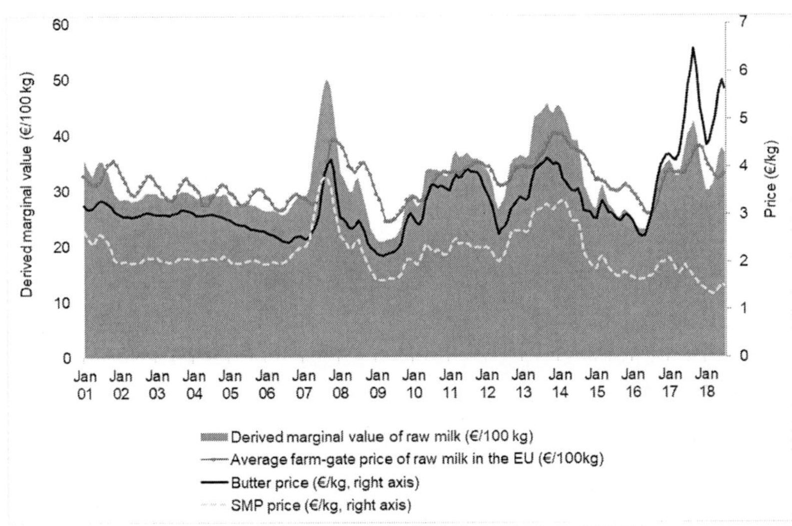

Source: Own depiction with data from the EU Commission (2020b).

Possible explanations for these observations include the following:

- Dairy processors try to smooth the prices that they pay to farmers for raw milk over time.
- The actual marginal value of a kg of raw milk does not depend exclusively on butter and SMP prices. Diary companies process milk into a much wider range of products, including for example cheese. Cheese contains both fat and protein, and some varieties of cheese command premium prices on consumer markets. The mix of consumer products that a dairy company produces has a strong influence on the prices that it can pay farmers for raw milk; companies that produce more high-value products such as cheese can pay farmers higher prices for raw milk.

9.3.3. The effects of policy measures on prices for joint products

In this section we discuss several examples of how political market interventions influence and are influenced by price interactions between joint products.

9.3.3.1. The EU's intervention price system for milk

The EU's CAP attempts to support the farm-gate price of raw milk by setting support prices for butter (the fat component of milk) and SMP (the protein component) (see the previous section). This makes sense, because raw milk is perishable and expensive to store even in the short run. Butter also requires refrigeration, but it is less perishable and has lower storage costs relative to its value. Hence, so-called intervention purchases of butter and SMP are used to indirectly support the price of raw milk in the EU. Support policy could focus instead on other processed dairy products such as cheese, but butter and SMP have the advantage of being comparatively homogeneous.

As a result of reductions in support prices and increases in world market prices for cereals, the EU has not intervened significantly on cereals markets since roughly the turn of the century (see Figure 9.1). Cereal support prices still exist, but market prices have been consistently and often considerably higher. The situation on EU milk markets is different, as support prices and the so-called intervention system have continued to play an important role through a series of milk price crises.

The farm-gate price of milk is not directly supported by the intervention system; instead this system supports the prices of butter and SMP for dairy companies and thus puts them in a position to pay higher prices to the farmers who deliver milk. For example, Table 9.6 presents calculations – similar to those in Table 9.5 above, but more detailed – that show that in 2015, EU intervention prices for butter and SMP supported a derived farm-gate price for raw milk of 19.7 Cent/kg.

Table 9.6: Derivation of the farm-gate value of raw milk from intervention prices for butter and skim milk powder (SMP)

	Item	Value	Unit
	Reference price butter	246.4	€/100 kg
I	Intervention price butter (90% of reference)	221.8	€/100 kg
II	Reference price SMP	169.8	€/100 kg
	Transport costs butter/SMP		
	Dairy to intervention warehouse	350.0	km
IIIa	- Transport costs butter	29.8	€/t
IIIb	- Transport costs SMP	23.5	€/t
	Financial costs		
IVa	- Financial costs butter	23.7	€/t
IVb	- Financial costs SMP	18.1	€/t
	Marketing and processing costs		
V	- Marketing costs	10.0	€/t
VI	- Processing costs butter/SMP	320.0	€/t

Value of raw milk to dairy processor derived from intervention prices:

$$\underbrace{(\text{I} - (\text{IIIa}+\text{IVa}+\text{V}+\text{VI})/20.49)}_{\text{Fat component (butter)}} + \underbrace{(\text{II} - (\text{IIIb}+\text{IVb}+\text{V}+\text{VI})/10.72)}_{\text{Protein component (SMP)}}$$

= Value of raw milk at processing plant	21.1	Cent/kg
- Collection costs from farm to plant	1.44	Cent/kg
Farm-gate value of raw milk	19.7	Cent/kg

Source: Thiele et al. (2015). Calculations assume milk with 4% fat and 3.4% protein. Financial costs are caused by delays in receiving payment for butter and SMP delivered to intervention. See Thiele et al. (2015) for details.

Whether dairy companies in the EU pass on supported prices for butter and SMP to milk-producing farmers depends on several factors. As mentioned above, dairy companies do not only produce butter and SMP. Some produce higher-value products that can be sold at premium prices on consumer markets, and are thus able to pay farmers more for raw milk. In addition, since the dairy industry is highly concentrated in Germany[13] and many other EU countries[14], dairy companies may be able to exercise market power to depress the prices that they pay farmers for raw milk. In 2016, for example, during a period of relatively high milk production (due in part to abolishment of the milk quota in 2015), spot market prices for raw milk fell significantly below the values derived from intervention prices for butter and SMP.

Figure 9.6 shows how the value of raw milk can be derived from the prices of its fat and protein components. The **iso-price line** for milk in Figure 9.6 is the set of all combinations of the prices for the fat component and the protein component that lead to the same value of raw milk. It follows that the relationship between the price of raw milk and the price of the processed product butter is not constant, but rather depends on the price that is obtained for the protein component. A given value of raw milk can be attained with high fat and low protein prices, but also with low fat and high protein prices. The slope of the iso-price line is determined by the relative amounts of fat and protein in a kg of raw milk. Which point on the iso-price line is realised depends on demand conditions for different milk products and the resulting relative prices of fat and protein.

---

[13] Bundeskartellamt (2012).
[14] EU Commission (2016).

Figure 9.6: Iso-price line for raw milk

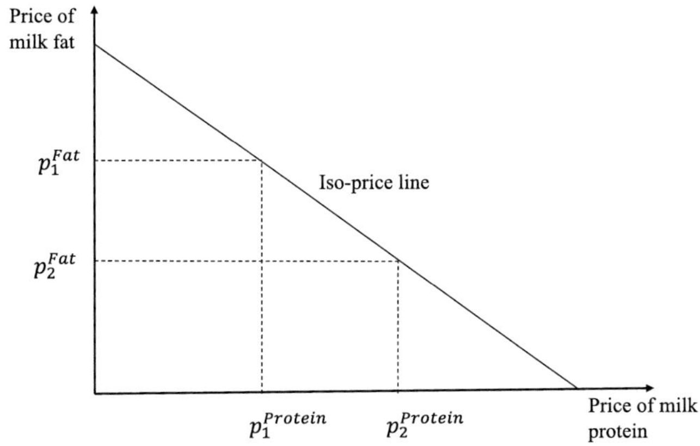

Source: Own depiction.

In the following it will be shown how the price relation of protein to fat changes as a result of shock to the equilibrium in one of the markets:

The intervention prices of butter and SMP will, by influencing the prices of milk fat and milk protein, also influence the prices of other milk products that are not subject to intervention. For example, as a result of an increase in the intervention price for butter, less milk fat will be available for the production of other dairy products that require milk fat, such as some types of cheese. The increase in the intervention price for butter increases the opportunity costs of using milk fat in other dairy products. This shifts the supply curve of these products upward, and increases their prices. These price increases will be smaller than the original increase in the price of butter, unless the demand for these other products is perfectly inelastic, or their supply is perfectly elastic. Hence, while the market prices of butter and SMP will follow the corresponding intervention prices closely, the prices of other dairy products that contain milk fat will be affected less strongly, depending on product-specific market conditions.

Imagine a situation in which the demand for milk protein increases, i.e. the demand curve shifts to the right (from D_0 to D_1 in the left panel of Figure 9.7). This might occur as a result of an increase in consumer demand for 'high protein' foods that are produced using milk protein. The price of milk protein will increase and with it the price of milk. This will trigger an increase in milk production, leading to an increase in the quantity of milk protein supplied (from $q_0^{Protein}$ to $q_1^{Protein}$).

Figure 9.7: The effect of an increase in the demand for milk protein on the markets for milk protein and milk fat

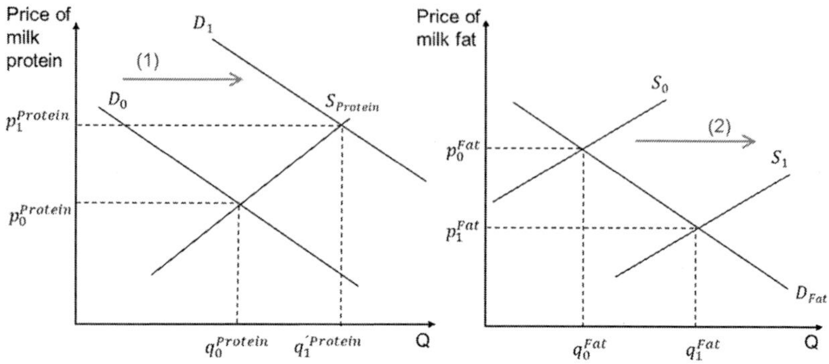

Source: Own depiction.

However, since milk protein and milk fat are joint products that are produced in fixed proportion[15], the increase in protein production will be accompanied by an increase in fat production as the supply curve of milk fat shifts to the right (from S_0 to S_1 in the right panel of Figure 9.7). The original increase in demand for milk protein therefore leads to two opposite price movements: an increase in the price of milk protein, and a reduction in the price of milk fat. The result is a shift in the price relationships among raw milk and its fat and protein components.

9.3.4. Energy prices and agriculture

The interaction between agricultural prices and energy prices has become increasingly important in recent years. In this section we will discuss three aspects of these interactions. These three aspects do not cover all dimensions of the interactions between agriculture and energy markets, but they illustrate how agricultural price relationships can be influenced by policies and market interventions in other, non-agricultural sectors of the economy.

[15] This proportion is fixed in the short run. However, farmers can influence the composition of milk by changing the cows' feed, and in the longer run by switching to other breeds of dairy cow.

9.3.4.1. Food or fuel: agricultural prices and the energy market

The finite nature of fossil fuel supplies and the problematic accumulation of CO_2 from non-renewable sources in the atmosphere has prompted many governments worldwide to subsidise the production of energy using agricultural raw materials, such as ethanol based on sugar, and biogas (methane) based on corn silage. The aim of these subsidy programs is usually to improve the competitiveness of energy (such as electricity or fuels) from renewable sources vis-à-vis traditional, non-renewable fossil energies.

These policies have given farmers in many countries new options for generating income with their land, labour, and capital. At the same time, however, these policies have highlighted the fact that bioenergy production competes with food production for limited agricultural land – the so-called **food or fuel conflict**. Awareness of this conflict was heightened when world market prices for agricultural raw materials increased sharply in 2006/07.[16]

For example, since 2009 the EU's Renewable Energy Directive (RED) requires that 10% of the fuel used in European road transport must come from renewable sources. The new edition of this directive (RED II) requires that in all EU member states 14% of the energy used in road and rail traffic must come from renewable sources by 2030 (EU Commission 2019). This has led to significant production of biodiesel using rapeseed in the EU; ethanol production based on sugar beet, wheat or corn plays a smaller role. US biofuel policy has promoted ethanol production from corn and thus influenced world market prices for these products (Koirala et al., 2015), while in Brazil the government's *Proálcool* program has supported the production of ethanol from sugar cane since 1975 (Andrietta et al. 2007).

The EU's promotion of biodiesel production is a controversial issue because it affects oilseed prices, but also because it has led to increased imports of palm oil for biodiesel production. New technologies that make palm oil more attractive relative to rapeseed have contributed to this trend (Bureau and Swinnen, 2018). This in turn has contributed to the expansion of palm oil plantations in Asia but increasingly also in South America and Africa, which can have negative effects on biodiversity and the maintenance of rainforests.

---

[16] See Mitchel (2008).

At the same time, EU and US biofuels policies have also created employment and income opportunities in agriculture in many low-income countries. These can contribute to economic development and improvements in food security. Households that are net producers of agricultural products will generally benefit from higher demand and prices for agricultural products as a result of policies that encourage the production of biofuels. However, low-income households that spend a significant proportion of their income on food will be negatively affected by global food price increases (Swinnen 2011).

9.3.4.2. Competition for land

Renewable energy production can compete with food production even if the relevant production factors, land and capital, are not exclusively owned by farmers. Food and energy production compete with one another for the use of land. The resulting changes in agricultural factor prices will have an indirect effect on the prices of agricultural products.

As an example of this consider the influence of wind turbines on agricultural land prices in Germany. In an attempt to increase the share of renewable energy in national energy use, many European countries, including Germany, have subsidised wind turbines that generate electricity. In Germany this is accomplished by means of the EEG (Renewable Energy Law) which obliges utility companies to purchase electricity from wind turbines at guaranteed prices, and to pass on the resulting additional costs to final consumers of electricity.

Locations that have frequent and sustained winds are especially attractive for the construction of wind turbines. Most wind turbines are constructed on agricultural land, but even the largest models do not require much area. Compared with other renewable energies such as biodiesel or biogas, therefore, electricity generation with wind turbines does not interact directly with agricultural production.

However, since the EEG makes it profitable to operate a wind turbine, and since these turbines cannot be built too close to one another, operators compete for spaces and pay correspondingly high rental or purchase prices to landowners at favoured locations. Ritter et al. (2015) present evidence that agricultural land prices have increased strongly at such locations.

The increasing generation of renewable energy can thus increase competition for land and, by increasing land prices, also affect the competitiveness of agricultural production in some locations. Similar to the case of wind turbines in Germany, extensive solar parks in other parts of the world can also compete with agricultural production for land.

9.3.4.3. Energy prices and the marginal cost of agricultural production

Energy is generally not considered to be one of the primary factors of production in agriculture (land, labour and capital). Nevertheless, many agricultural production processes use energy – from renewable or non-renewable sources – for heating, drying or to power machinery. Furthermore, as outlined above, energy prices can indirectly affect land prices. Energy costs therefore account for an important share of production costs for many types of agricultural production.

Energy prices also affect agriculture via fertiliser costs. Figure 9.8 shows that the global production of mineral fertilisers continues to increase steadily. The production of nitrogen fertilisers using the **Haber-Bosch process** is particularly energy-intensive. Altogether, fertiliser production accounted for roughly 2% of global energy use in the 1990s, and the Haber-Bosch process accounted for 5% of global natural gas use (IFA 1998, p. 33-34). Hence, the influence of fertiliser production on energy prices is likely limited. Nevertheless, the production and prices especially of nitrogen fertiliser depend heavily on energy prices.

Figure 9.8: Global fertiliser production

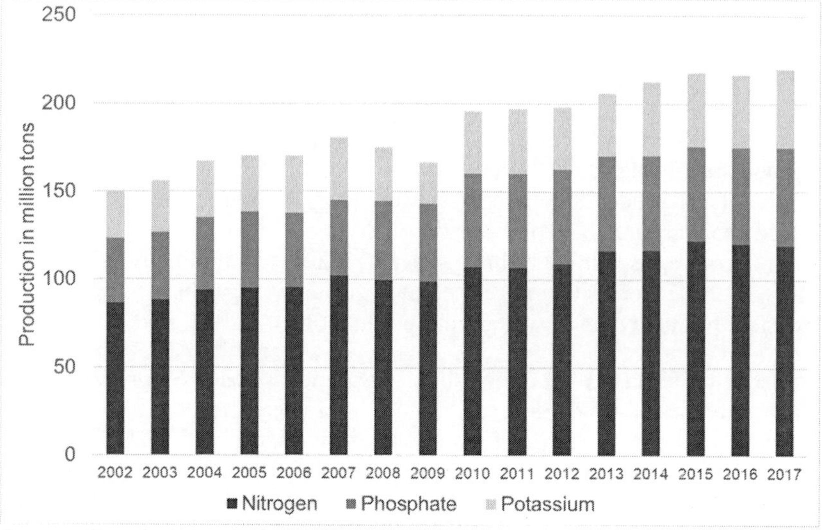

Source: Own depiction with data from FAO (2020).

Because it is difficult to allocate spending on energy to different types of production on a farm, it is often considered among overhead costs. Figure 9.9 presents information on the composition of overhead costs in German agriculture from 2004 to 2013. We can see that over time the energy costs developed approximately in proportion to the other overhead costs and accounted for between 25% and 30% of the total. Figure 9.9 is based on data from the FADN (Farm Accountancy Data Network), which the EU operates in all member states (EU Commission 2020a). It depicts average values across all farm types and size classes in all German regions. Clearly, such averages hide considerable variation, and the share of energy costs can vary considerably from farm to farm and over time.

Figure 9.9: The share of energy costs in total overhead costs of agricultural holdings in Germany

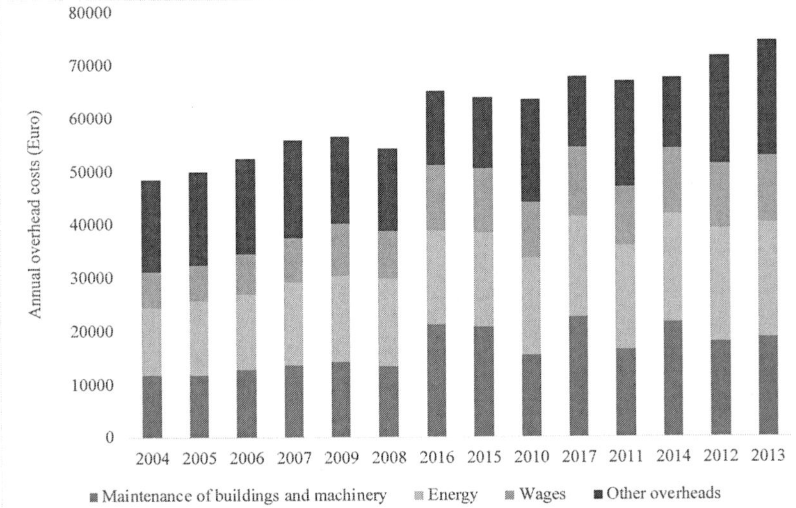

Source: Own depiction with FADN data (EU Commission 2020a).

The share of energy in the costs of transporting and processing food vary considerably. In some energy-intensive cases, for example when products must be refrigerated or frozen, or when SMP is produced by drying, energy costs can play a very important role.

These considerations show that changes in energy prices on world markets, but also changes due to government interventions on domestic energy markets, can influence the competitiveness of individual agricultural products, and the competitiveness of agriculture relative to other sectors of the economy. In the future, trading CO_2 emission certificates could create a new source of income for agriculture. In comparison with other energy-intensive sectors, some types of farming activity can create CO_2 sinks, for example by increasing the humus content of soils or by means of bioenergy generation with carbon capture and storage (BECCS). Not all farms will be able to take advantage of trade in emission certificates to the same extent, and the benefits will depend on whether certificate prises increase in line with energy prices in the future (see Sands et al. 2011).

9.4. Keywords

- ACP (African, Caribbean and Pacific)
- Agricultural price structure, price relationships, price ratios
- Common Agricultura Policy (CAP)
- Cereal substitutes
- Dual cost function
- EBA (Everything But Arms)
- EPA (Economic Partnership Agreements)
- Food or fuel conflict
- GATT (General Agreement on Trade and Tariffs)
- Haber-Bosch process
- Hedonic pricing model
- Iso-price line
- Joint products
- Löhr's method
- The Open Flank of the CAP
- Pivotal agricultural price
- Production elasticity
- Shephard's lemma
- Technical transformation coefficient
- WTO (World Trade Organisation)

References

Agrosynergie (2011) Evaluation of CAP Measures Applied to the Sugar Sector. Report prepared for the European Commission. https://ec.europa.eu/info/sites/info/files/food-farming-fisheries/key_policies/documents/ext-eval-sugar-synth-sum_2011_en.pdf. Accessed February 7, 2022.

Andrietta MGS, Andrietta SR, Steckelberg C and Stupiello E (2007) Bioethanol - Brazil, 30 years of Proálcool. International Sugar Journal 109: 195-200

Beattie B, Taylor R and Watts MJ (2009) The Economics of Production. Second Edition, Krieger Publishing Company, Florida. ISBN 978-1-57524-295-8.

Bundeskartellamt (2012) Sektoruntersuchung Milch. Abschlussbericht gemäß § 32e GWB – Januar 2012.

http://www.bundeskartellamt.de/SharedDocs/Publikation/DE/Sektoruntersuchungen/Sektoruntersuchung%20Milch%20-

%20Abschlussbericht.pdf?__blob=publicationFile&v=4. Accessed February 7, 2022.

Bureau JC and Swinnen J (2018) EU policies and global food security. Global Food Security 16: 106-115.

Burrell A, Himics M, Van Doorslaer B, Ciaian P and Shrestha, S (2014) EU sugar policy: A sweet transition after 2015? EU Joint Research Centre Scientific and Policy Report EUR 26530 EN. https://publications.jrc.ec.europa.eu/repository/bitstream/JRC76619/jrc%20tr%20sugar_study_pubsy_v6.pdf. Accessed February 7, 2022.

DairyCo (2014) Review of Dairy Market Indicators. Report produced by Ken Burgess Associates on behalf of AHDB/DairyCo. https://projectblue.blob.core.windows.net/media/Default/Market%20Intelligence/dairy/Files/Prices/Wholesale%20prices/Dairy%20market%20indicators%20review%20full%20report-2014.pdf. Accessed February 7, 2022.

EU Commission (2016) Report from the Commission to the European Parliament and the Council: Development of the dairy market situation and the operation of the "Milk Package" provisions. https://eur-lex.europa.eu/resource.html?uri=cellar:8ae294cd-b2f7-11e6-9e3c-01aa75ed71a1.0010.02/DOC_1&format=PDF. Accessed February 7, 2022.

EU Commission (2019) Renewable Energy – Recast to 2030 (RED II). https://ec.europa.eu/jrc/en/jec/renewable-energy-recast-2030-red-ii. Accessed February 7, 2022.

EU Commission (2020a) FADN - Farm Accountancy Data Network https://ec.europa.eu/info/food-farming-fisheries/farming/facts-and-figures/farms-farming-and-innovation/structures-and-economics/economics/fadn_en. Accessed February 7, 2022.

EU Commission (2020b) Milk Market Observatory: EU historical prices per EU country. https://ec.europa.eu/agriculture/market-observatory/milk_en. Accessed February 7, 2022.

FEFAC (European Feed Manufacturers Federation) (2018) Feed & Food Statistical Year-book 2018. https://fefac.eu/wp-content/uploads/2020/07/feedfood2018.pdf. Accessed February 7, 2022.

FAO (Food and Agriculture Organization of the United Nations) (2020) FAOSTAT – Food and Agriculture Data. http://www.fao.org/faostat/en/#home. Accessed February 7, 2022.

Francois J and Hall H (1997) Partial Equilibrium Modeling. In: Francois J, Reinert K. (eds.) Applied Methods for Trade Policy Analysis: A Handbook. Cambridge University Press, Cambridge

Groß D (2010) Preiswürdigkeit von Futtermitteln (Rinder) mit Berechnungsprogramm. http://www.dlr.rlp.de/internet/global/themen.nsf/ALL/1E4E76E878B0F3F9C12576EF004472E8?OpenDocument. Accessed February 7, 2022.

Hess S, Surry Y, Kron R, Liljenstolpe C, Lindberg G and Andersson H (2014) A hedonic analysis of the price for horse riding lessons in Sweden. Journal of Outdoor Recreation and Tourism 7: 65-74.

IFA (International Fertilizer Industry Association) (1998) The Fertilizer Industry, World Food Supplies and the Environment. IFA, Paris. http://large.stanford.edu/courses/2014/ph240/yuan2/docs/1998_IFA_UNEP_worldfoodsupplies.pdf. Accessed February 7, 2022.

Josling TE, Tangermann S and Warley TK (1996) Agriculture in the GATT. MacMillan, London.

Koester U (1988) An Inventory of Disharmonies in EC Agricultural Policy Measures. Diskussionsbeiträge Nr. 62, Institut für Agrarpolitik und Marktlehre der Christian-Albrechts-Universität zu Kiel.

Koirala KH, Mishra AK, D'Antoni JM and Mehlhorn JE (2015) Energy prices and agricultural commodity prices: Testing correlation using copulas method. Energy 81: 430-436.

Mitchel, D (2008) A note on rising food prices. The World Bank. Policy Working Research Paper 4682. The World Bank, Washington DC.

OECD (2022) PSE database, European Union. https://www.oecd.org/eu/producerandconsumersupportestimatesdatabase.htm. Accessed February 7, 2022.

Ritter M, Hüttel S, Walter M and Odening M (2015) Der Einfluss von Windkraftanlagen auf landwirtschaftliche Bodenpreise. Berichte über Landwirtschaft – Zeitschrift für Agrarpolitik und Landwirtschaft 93(3): 1-16.

Roningen V (1997) Multi-Market, Multi-Region Partial Equilibrium Modeling. In: Francois J and Reinert K. (eds.) Applied Methods for Trade Policy Analysis: A Handbook. Cambridge University Press, Cambridge

Rude J and Meilke K (2000) Implications of CAP Reform for the European Union's Feed Sector. Canadian Journal of Agricultural Economics 48(4): 411-420.

Sands R, Westcott P, Price JM, Beckman J, Leibtag E, Lucier G, McBride WD, McGranahan D, Morehart M, Roeger E and Schaible G (2011)

Impacts of Higher Energy Prices on Agriculture and Rural Economies. Economic Research Report 262236, United States Department of Agriculture, ERS, Washington DC

Schäufele, I, Herrmann, R and Szolnoki, G (2016) Do High-quality Wines Capture Higher Prices? A Hedonic Analysis on DLG Quality Tests. German Journal of Agricultural Economics 65(2): 132-150

Snyder C, Nicholson W and Stewart R (2015) Microeconomic theory: Basic principles and extensions. Centage Learning EMEA, Andover, UK

Stowe CJ (2013) Breeding to sell: a hedonic price analysis of leading Thoroughbred sire stud fees. Applied Economics 45: 877-885

Swinnen J (2011) The right price of food. Development Policy Review 29(6): 667-688.

Thiele H, Richards E and Burchadi H (2015) Expertise Kriseninstrumente im Milchmarkt. Study commissioned by the Ministry for Rural Areas and Consumer Protection of Baden-Württemberg. Institut für Ernährungswirtschaft, Kiel. https://www.ife-ev.de/attachments/article/71/Endbericht%20Kriseninstrumente%20Mai%202015.pdf. Accessed February 7, 2022.

USDA-ERS (United States Department of Agriculture, Economic Research Service) (2019) Commodity and Food Elasticities. USDA, Washington DC. https://www.ers.usda.gov/data-products/commodity-and-food-elasticities.aspx. Accessed February 7, 2022.

Exercises

1. In 2017, butter prices in the EU reached a very high level. Nevertheless, butter production initially increased very little. Could this be explained by the fact that cheese prices were also relatively high at the same time?

2. In the EU, many supermarket chains and some dairies required that farmers only feed non-GM soy to their cows. Discuss what effect this will have on the supply and demand of domestic protein crops.

3. The pork producers in a closed economy produce according to the following function $Output_{Pork} = q_{Labour}^{0.2} q_{Feed}^{0.8}$. If the market price for pork is $Price_{Pork}$ = 20 €/dt, how high are the wages and feed prices per unit of labour and feed, respectively?

4. Assume that after abolishing the milk quota, the EU would like to slow down the increase in milk production by raising beef prices. Discuss the short-run and the long-run effects of this measure.

5. In the function $c^{min} = 2Qw_G^{0.5}w_E^{0.5}$, production costs are a function of the output quantity Q and the input prices w_G and w_E, but input quantities are not mentioned. Explain why this is the case.

6. Assume that the wheat price in the EU is 15 €/dt, and that the price for non-genetically modified soybean meal increases to 40 €/dt. Using Löhr's method and the information in Table 9.3, calculate the maximum market prices up to which European peas and grain corn can compete in feed rations.

7. By lowering its domestic grain prices, the EU has reduced domestic demand for imported cereal substitutes such as oilseeds. Discuss the effects of this policy change on world market prices for vegetable oils.

8. Data Exercise: Search the internet for estimates of price elasticities of demand for different oilseed products in the EU and China. A possible source is USDA-ERS (2019). Both the EU and China are important importers of oilseeds on the world market. How do you interpret their respective elasticities?

9. Data exercise: Download recent price data from the *Milk Market Observatory* (EU Commission 2020b) and use equation (28) as well as the information in Table 9.4 to calculate the marginal value of raw milk. Compare this with the average EU farm-gate price for raw milk.

CHAPTER TEN

VERTICAL PRICE RELATIONS IN AGRICULTURE

STEPHAN VON CRAMON-TAUBADEL

10.1. Introduction and learning objectives

With few exceptions, consumers in industrialised countries buy little food directly from the farm. Instead, most agricultural products are consumed at the end of a long and multi-linked chain from farm to fork. Along this chain, agricultural products are sorted, inspected, transported, stored, packaged and placed on retail shelves. In most cases they are also physically transformed and combined with other products. For example, apples become juice, cattle become cuts of meat, sausage and leather, and tomatoes, onions and broccoli are combined with other ingredients to make vegetarian pizza.

Hence, the money that consumers spend on food does not only pay for the agricultural raw products contained in this food, but also for the many goods and services that are added to these raw products between the farm and the fork. In 2018, farmers in Germany for example received on average 20.8 cents of every euro consumers spent on food (see Figure 10.1). However, this share varies considerably across products and time. First, while grain farmers received only 4.1% of consumer expenditure for bread in 2018, egg producers received 48.5% of consumer expenditure on eggs in shell. Second, the farm share of consumer expenditure on food has fallen over time. In the early 1970s, farmers in Germany received 47.5 cents of every euro (or DM) that consumers spent on food, more than twice as much as 20.8 cents in 2018. However, Figure 10.1 also shows that the farm share of consumer expenditure on food has stabilised over the last roughly 10 years and may even be rising again for eggs.[1]

Figure 10.1: The farmers' share of consumer expenditure on food in Germany (%)

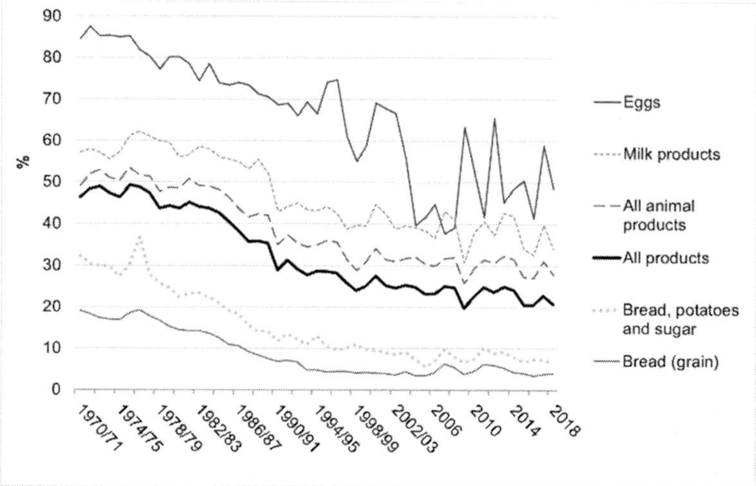

Source: Thünen Institute (2020), own depiction. Data for West Germany up to and including 1990/91. After the 2004/05 marketing year, reporting changed to calendar years.

The farm share of the consumer food bill is a controversial topic. It is often argued that farmers are subject to unfair competition and do not receive a fair share of consumer expenditure on food because of the structure of competition in the food chain (with often only few processors and retailers dominating the chain between farmers and consumers). A typical accusation is that food processors pass increases in the prices of raw agricultural products on to consumers faster and more completely than reductions in raw material prices. Sometimes consumers are accused of inappropriate behaviour as well. It is argued that bargain-hunting consumers do not show sufficient appreciation for the true value of food, and that the resulting pressure on prices is passed back along the food chain to farmers. This has led to calls for policy makers to enforce minimum retail prices to ensure that food is not sold below its cost of production. In Germany in recent years,

---

[1] Producing data on the farmers' share of consumer expenditure on food is a complex undertaking. Sinabell (2005) discusses the statistical challenges involved. Schnepf (2015) presents facts and figures on the development of the farmers' share of consumer expenditure on food in the USA.

this discourse has triggered several so-called food summits and other initiatives involving high-ranking politicians and representatives of agriculture, the processing industry, retailers and consumers.[2]

Against the background of these sometimes very heated discussions, what can economic analysis tell us about so-called **vertical price relationships**[3] in the food chain? Some of the issues raised above, such as the definition of the intrinsic value of food, are beyond the scope of economic analysis. However, economics can formulate models that provide insights into how prices in vertically integrated markets react to one another under certain conditions, what factors influence these price reactions, and what consequences they have for the actors in the food chain. The transmission of price signals along food and other chains is crucial for the efficient functioning of a market economy. Therefore, in this chapter we provide an introduction into the economic analysis of the relationships between the prices of agricultural raw products at the farm gate and the prices of corresponding food products along the food chain, e.g. at the wholesale and retail levels.

In this chapter we:

- discuss which factors influence vertical price relations and, consequently, the farm share of consumer expenditure on food;
- describe how these factors have changed over time and why farmers in Germany received 47.5 cents of every euro spent by consumers on food in the early 1970s, but only 20.8 cents in 2018;
- outline the models and empirical methods that economists use to analyse vertical price relations in agricultural and food markets;
- analyse the factors that determine the speed with which price changes at one stage in the food chain are passed on to other stages;

---

[2] For example, one such summit took place on 3 February 2020 in the Federal Chancellery in Berlin: see https://www.agrarheute.com/politik/live-merkel-kloeckner-altmaier-treffen-lebensmittelwirtschaft-564454.

[3] Price relationships along the chain from farm to fork are often referred to as vertical price relationships to distinguish them from spatial price relationships, which are sometimes referred to as spatial.

- discuss whether and how concentration in many branches of food processing affects vertical price formation (i.e. whether processing or retail companies use their market power to distort vertical price relations to the disadvantage of farmers and/or consumers); and

- explain what is meant by the term asymmetric price transmission, and what can cause asymmetric price transmission in the food chain.

10.2. The determinants of the long-term evolution of the farm-retail price spread in agriculture

We begin by considering why the farm share of consumer expenditure on food has tended to fall over time, as shown for the example of Germany in Figure 10.1. Consumer expenditure on a food product is the sum of payments to farmers for the agricultural raw products that they produce, and payments to the suppliers of the **complementary goods and services** (CGS) that are added to these raw products along the chain. The following formula illustrates this relationship.

$$P_{Cons} = P_{raw}\alpha_{raw} + \sum_{i=1}^{k} P_i\alpha_i \quad (1)$$

where P_{cons} denotes the per unit consumer price of the final food product, and P_{raw} the per unit price of the agricultural raw product. α_{raw} is a **transformation coefficient** that indicates how many units of the raw product are needed to produce one unit of the consumption product. The farm share of consumer expenditure on the food product is thus the ratio $\frac{P_{raw}\alpha_{raw}}{P_{cons}}$. The **unit margin** $\sum_{i=1}^{k} P_i\alpha_i$ is the total value of the $i = 1,2, \dots k$ CGS that are added to the agricultural raw product; P_i is the per unit price of the i-th CGS, and α_i as the corresponding transformation coefficient. Figure 10.2 illustrates these relationships for the example of fluid milk in Germany in October 2018. The consumer price of milk was 69 cents/litre, of which the farm-gate price of raw milk accounted for 30 cents/litre, and the various CGS added between the farm and retail for the remaining 39 cents/ litre.

Figure 2: The composition of the price fluid milk in Germany (October 2018, in cents/litre)

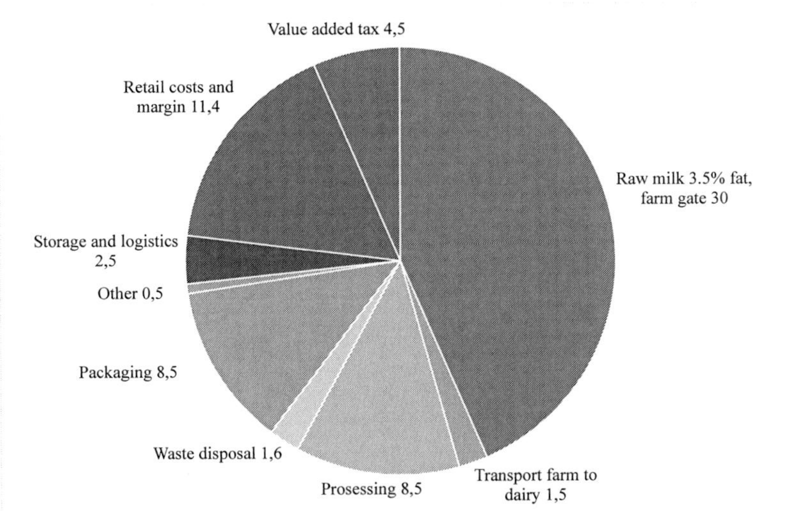

Source: Own depiction with data from Institut für Ernährungswirtschaft (2018).

If P_{cons} in equation (1) is multiplied by the total quantity demanded of the final food product Q_{cons}, we obtain

$$P_{cons}Q_{cons} = P_{raw}\alpha_{raw}Q_{cons} + \sum_{i=1}^{k} P_i\alpha_i\, Q_{cons} \quad (2)$$

or

$$consumer\ expenditure = P_{raw}Q_{raw} + \sum_{i=1}^{k} P_iQ_i \quad (3)$$

since $\alpha_{raw}Q_{cons}$ equals the quantity of the raw agricultural product (Q_{raw}) that is required to produce Q_{cons}, and α_iQ_{Cons}, by analogy, equals the required quantity of the i-th CGS (Q_i).

The sum $\sum_{i=1}^{k} P_iQ_i$ in equation (3) is called the **market margin**. We see that the market margin is the product of a **price vector** $\{P_1, P_2, \ldots, P_k\}$ and a **quantity vector** $\{Q_1, Q_2, \ldots, Q_k\}$. The determinants of the market margin can thus be divided into those that influence the quantity vector, and those that influence the price vector (Koester 2016, p. 142 ff.).

10.2.1. Factors that influence the quantity vector

a) **Rising incomes**. The demand for most food is known to be income inelastic in industrialised countries such as Germany. The demand for CGS is usually more income elastic. The demand for CGS therefore expands more as a result of an income increase than the demand for raw agricultural products. For example, we do not necessarily demand more potatoes as our incomes rise, but we purchase more processed potato products and eat in restaurants more often, where we pay to have potatoes prepared into different dishes. Hence, as incomes rise, the quantities of CGS (Q_i) in equation (3) increase and/or the dimension of the quantity vector (k) increases as new CGS are added to a food product. Both of these changes (more CGS and new CGS) increase the market margin.

b) **Household structures and preferences.** Economic development and rising incomes have been accompanied by far-reaching changes in the structure and preferences of households, not only in industrialised countries. Women, who in many societies traditionally prepared meals and thus added many CGS to food (usually without pay), are increasingly employed outside the home and spend less time preparing meals. As women's opportunity costs have increased, so has the willingness of households to pay for so-called **convenience foods** that are more processed and easier to prepare. This leads to an increase in the dimension k in equation (3): CGS that used to be added in households (free of charge) are increasingly added by firms in the food chain (and paid for).

c) **The outsourcing of CGS formerly added on farms**. Not only consumer households but also farms have outsourced food processing functions over time. Many farms used to, for example, process milk into butter and cheese, or slaughter animals and produce sausages and other meat products for sale. As farms have become more specialised, firms in the food chain have taken over these processing steps. In terms of equation (3), this means that in the past the raw product sold by the farmer was often partially processed and thus less 'raw' than it is today. Hence, over time some CGS have shifted from farm income to the market margin.

The first two factors listed above, rising incomes and the outsourcing of processing steps from consumer households, both increase the market margin but, *ceteris paribus*, leave farm revenues largely unchanged.[4] Therefore, the farm share of consumer expenditures for food falls, but farm incomes are not negatively affected. However, if farms outsource functions and sell products that are less processed over time (the third factor listed above), then farm-gate prices and farm revenues fall. This does not necessarily imply that farm household welfare will fall. On-farm processing steps requires labour and other resources that are saved when these functions are outsourced. Farm household members are freed to pursue other, more rewarding work, or to enjoy more leisure time. Furthermore, specialisation in pure agricultural production can lead to efficiency gains and better utilisation of economies of scale, thus increasing the overall profitability of the farm.

10.2.2. Factors that influence the price vector

Changes in the price vector can also affect the market margin. Declining **agricultural terms of trade** compared with other sectors over many decades means that the prices of agricultural products have tended to fall relative to the prices of many industrial products and services. If P_{raw} falls relative to an index of the CGS prices $\{P_1, P_2, \dots, P_k\}$ in equation (3), the market margin will increase. State intervention can also play a role, for example when the prices of agricultural commodities are supported, as was (and is) the case in many industrialised countries. For example, the steady reduction of price support for agricultural products in the EU that began with the so-called MacSharry-reform of 1993, had tended to reduce P_{raw} and, thus, increase the market margin.[5]

Taxes and duties can also contribute to a widening of the market margin. In the example of fluid milk presented in Figure 10.2, value added tax accounts for 4.5 cents/litre or roughly 11.5% of the market margin. A further 1.6 cents/litre (4.1% of the market margin) is attributable to waste disposal costs under the so-called Grüner Punkt system in Germany.[6] For some consumer products of agricultural origin (e.g. cigarettes), taxes account for over half of the consumer price. Government regulations also influence the market margin, for example best-before dates, nutrition labelling, minimum wages for workers in the food processing industry, and the increased

[4] Rising incomes will lead to some increase in the demand for food, and thus boost farm revenues, depending on income elasticities for different types of food.

[5] EU price support via the intervention system and its reduction over time is discussed in Chapter 9.

[6] See https://www.gruener-punkt.de/en/company/about-us.

documentation and labelling that is required to ensure the traceability of food. These regulations both add CGS to the quantity vector of the market margin and increase the prices of individual CGS in the market margin.

The factors discussed above have contributed to a widening of the market margin over time. As shown Figure 10.1, the farm share of consumer expenditure on food in Germany has tended to fall and, conversely, the market margin has grown. The situation in many other countries is similar. However, we should be cautious about extrapolating these trends into the future. As noted above, there are signs in Figure 10.1 that the farm share of consumer expenditure on food has stabilised over the last decade in Germany. This has been helped by the fact that the trend of falling real agricultural prices has slowed down and, at least in phases (notably during the so-called agricultural price crisis of 2007/08), has been reversed. The boom in cooking at home and the popularity of cooking shows and celebrity chefs has led to many households buying less processed food and preparing it more elaborately themselves; the number of farms selling agricultural products directly to consumers (farm shops, weekly markets, delivery services) has increased.

Whether these trends will continue remains to be seen. The Covid-19 pandemic will likely lead to at least a temporary decline in the market margin because of the associated reductions in household incomes, but also because eating away from home (e.g. in restaurants and canteens) has fallen sharply due to infection control restrictions. The pandemic has led to a scarcity of seasonal workers in many countries and, thus, to reductions in supply and increases in the farm-gate prices of fruit and vegetables. This will likely reduce market margins for these products, but other pandemic-related factors such as transportation and logistic bottlenecks will work in the opposite direction. In the longer term, changes in the structure and functions of trade (e.g. new platforms such as online trade or online retail shopping) will also affect the level and evolution of the market margin.

10.3. Gardner's model

The previous section discussed factors that influence the market margin between farm-gate and consumer prices for food in the long run. These factors include rising incomes and changes in both farm and consumer preferences. In the long run, these factors have led to the addition of more and more CGS in the food chain. In the following section, we assume that incomes and preferences are given and examine the short-run relationships between farm-gate and consumer prices - the so-called vertical price relationships. The aim is to better understand the factors that influence whether and how fully consumer prices and producer prices react to one another.

10.3.1. Basics

The starting point for much of the literature on vertical price relationships in recent decades is a model that was originally proposed by Gardner (1975). The title of Gardner's seminal paper refers to the *farm-retail price spread*, a term that is often used to describe the margin between farm-gate and consumer prices. In Gardner's model, under conditions of perfect competition, food-processing firms (the processors) produce a final consumer product x using two inputs; a raw agricultural product a and a non-agricultural input (or bundle of CGS) b. The first equation in the model is a linear homogeneous production function[7] that describes how a and b are transformed into the consumer product x:

$$x = f(a, b) \text{ (supply of the consumer product } x\text{)} \quad (4)$$

The production function in equation (4) is not necessarily limitational, i.e. a and b do not have to be combined in fixed proportions. In equations (1) to (3) above we implicitly assumed limitational production technology defined by the fixed transformation coefficients α_{raw} and α_i. Instead, the production function in equation (4) allows for substitution between inputs depending on the **elasticity of factor substitution** σ. σ can be interpreted as a measure of the curvature of the isoquants of a production function and is defined as:

$$\sigma = \frac{\partial(a/b) / (a/b)}{\partial(P_b/P_a) / (P_b/P_a)} \quad (5)$$

Equation (5) shows that the elasticity of substitution indicates which proportional adjustment of the factor input ratio $(a\ /\ b)$ is triggered by a 1% change in the factor price ratio (P_b/P_a). If the production technology is limitational, even large changes in the factor price ratio do not lead to an adjustment in the factor input ratio. This is because input use is governed by fixed transformation coefficients and more of both inputs, in fixed proportion, is needed to increase production. In this case the elasticity of

[7] See Appendix 2.3 in Chapter 2.

factor substitution equals 0 and the isoquants are shaped as right angles (Figure 10.3, left panel). At the other extreme, if the isoquants are straight lines, a very small change in the factor price ratio leads to a jump from one corner solution with $(a / b) = 0$ to the other corner solution with $(a / b) = \infty$ (or vice versa). In this case the elasticity of factor substitution equals ∞ (Figure 10.3, right panel). If $0 < \sigma < \infty$, then the isoquants are the familiar convex (from the origin) curves (Figure 10.3, middle panel) that are typically shown in textbooks. In this case some, but not unlimited input substitution is possible.

Figure 10.3: Different isoquants and elasticities of factor substitution

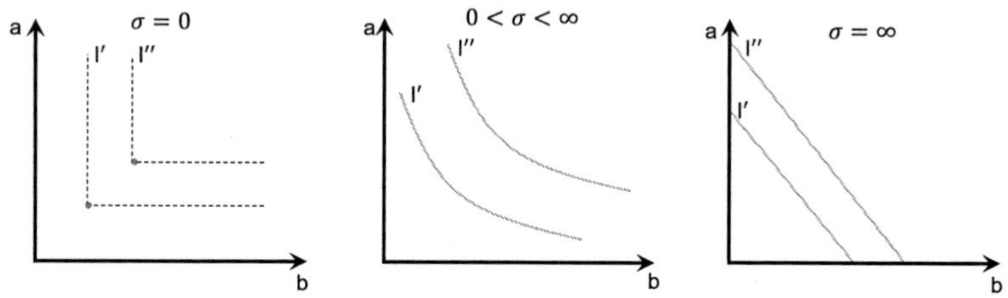

Source: Own representation.

The elasticity of factor substitution σ depends on the production technology and is often relatively low in food processing technologies. For example, the production of potato chips (x) requires a certain quantity of potatoes (a); these cannot be substituted in the short term, or only to a very limited extent, by using more CGS such as labour, energy and capital in the input bundle (b). However, technical progress can increase σ in the medium and long term. For example, breeders might develop new potato varieties whose shapes allow a higher yield of potato chips.

In addition, the elasticity of factor substitution can also be influenced by institutions. One example is the German *Reinheitsgebot* (purity law) for beer, which prohibits input substitutions that are technically possible and permitted in other countries (e.g. brewing beer with maize or rice rather than barley).[8] Another example are standards for the use of natural and other flavours (case study 1).

---

[8] The *Reinheitsgebot* stipulates that, with a few exceptions, beer can only be brewed with four ingredients: hops, barley, yeast and water. The example of the *Reinheitsgebot* shows that laws that restrict substitution possibilities in the

Case study 1: Standards and substitution possibilities in the production of raspberry yoghurt in Germany

Producers can add raspberry flavour to 100 kg of yoghurt in a variety of ways (Ahlers 2019). First, fresh raspberries can be used, which costs about 31.50 euros. Natural raspberry flavouring extracted from raspberries costs about 12.50 euros. Raspberry flavouring, which can be obtained from fungal cultures and sawdust, for example, costs about 3.75 euros. Finally, there are raspberry flavouring preparations that can be produced from artificial raw materials and that cost only about 0.06 euros. These various technical possibilities give producers considerable scope (and considerable financial incentives) to substitute the agricultural raw product raspberry with other, non-agricultural inputs. However, labelling regulations limit these substitution possibilities. If the words "natural raspberry flavouring" appears on the label, then no less than 95% of the flavouring must have been obtained from either fresh raspberries or natural raspberry flavouring (Verbraucherzentrale 2016). If raspberry flavouring (for example from fungal cultures) was used, then the words "natural flavouring" (but not "natural raspberry flavouring") may appear on the label. Consumer advocate groups in Germany complain that this is misleading and lobby for stricter labelling requirements that would increase transparency for consumers but also further limit substitution possibilities in food processing.

The production function in equation (4) describes the supply of the consumption product x as a function of the input quantities a and b. Gardner's model is completed by five further equations that describe the demand for x as well as supply and demand for a and b.

$$x = g(P_x) \qquad \text{(Demand for the consumer product x)} \qquad (6)$$

$$a = h(P_a) \qquad \text{(Supply of the raw agricultural product } a\text{)} \qquad (7)$$

---

production of food are sometimes introduced or maintained for protectionist reasons. For a long time, beer that had been brewed abroad but not in accordance with the *Reinheitsgebot* could not be sold as beer in Germany. The enforcement of the *Reinheitsgebot* thus restricted foreign competition on the German beer market. In 1987, the European Court of Auditors ruled that this violated the free movement of goods in the EU internal market. Since then, foreign beers that are not brewed according to the *Reinheitsgebot* can be offered for sale in Germany as beer (see, for example, Dornbusch 2013).

$$\frac{\partial(f(a,b))}{\partial a}P_x = P_a \qquad \text{(Demand for the agricultural raw product } a\text{)} \qquad (8)$$

$$b = k(P_b) \qquad \text{(Supply of the non-agricultural input } b\text{)} \qquad (9)$$

$$\frac{\partial(f(a,b))}{\partial b}P_x = P_b \qquad \text{(Demand for the non-agricultural input } b\text{)} \qquad (10)$$

Here, g, h and k denote functions that satisfy plausible, general conditions. For example, the function g should be such that the demand for x falls as P_x rises, i.e. ${\partial(g(P_x))}/{\partial P_x} < 0$. Equations (8) and (10) describe the derived demand for factors of production a and b under conditions of perfect competition.[9] The model thus comprises a total of six equations (4, 6, 7, 8, 9 and 10) and six unknowns (the quantities x, a and b, and the corresponding prices P_x, P_a, and P_b).

Comparative-static analyses are performed on the model by first totally differentiating and linearising all equations. These steps are detailed in Appendix 1.[10] Equation (7), for example, gives rise to:

$$\dot{a} = \varepsilon_{a,P_a}\dot{P}_a \qquad (7')$$

with $\dot{a} = {da}/{a}$, $\dot{P}_a = {dP_a}/{P_a}$ and ε_{a,P_a} the own-price elasticity of supply of a.

This is often called the **equilibrium displacement form of an equation** because it can be used to study transitions between equilibrium states that are triggered by shocks. It must be emphasised that equations like (7′) are only local approximations. They provide good approximations of the behaviour of the variables in question in response to small changes (say 5% or 10%). Hence, equation (7′) tells us that in response to a small percentage change in P_a (measured by $\dot{P}_a$), a will change by approximately $\varepsilon_{a,P_a}\dot{P}_a$ percent. However, since we do not know the exact mathematical form of the underlying function (in this case the supply function $a = h(P_a)$), the

---

9 In equations (8) and (10), the marginal value product (marginal product*output price) is on the left-hand side, and the factor price is on the right-hand side. See the explanation of marginal productivity theory in Chapter 2.

10 These are the same steps used in section 3.4.2 of Chapter 3 (to model the impact of a product price increase on land prices), and in section 4.7 of Chapter 4 (to model the impact of income and technical progress on agricultural prices).

approximation in equation (7′) can become increasingly inaccurate for larger changes. Equilibrium displacement models are very useful tools for studying the behaviour of interdependent variables in economics; however, one should be wary of applications in which they are used to simulate the consequences of large changes such as doubling or halving of prices or quantities.

10.3.2. The elasticity of vertical price transmission - the response to producer price changes

The *equilibrium displacement* form of Gardner's model, shown in Appendix 1, can be used to examine the effects of various exogenous shocks. For example, to determine the impact of a change in the price of the raw agricultural product a on the price of the consumer product x, the supply equation for a (equation (7)) is replaced by $\dot{P}_a = \dot{\bar{P}}_a$, where $\dot{\bar{P}}_a$ represents an exogenously given proportional change in the price of a. Such an exogenous change could be triggered, for example, by the state adjusting the support price for a, which is what the EU used to do each year when it fixed the intervention prices for agricultural products. The system is then solved for the so-called **elasticity of vertical price transmission**: $\dot{P}_x / \dot{P}_a$ (henceforth E_{P_x,P_a}). The result is:[11]

$$E_{P_x,P_a} = \frac{S_a(\sigma+\varepsilon_{b,P_b})}{\varepsilon_{b,P_b}+S_a\sigma-S_b\eta_{x,P_x}} \qquad (11)$$

where $S_i = \frac{iP_i}{xP_x}$ is the cost share of production factor i, σ is the elasticity of substitution between factors a and b, ε_{i,P_i} is the own-price elasticity of supply of factor i, and η_{x,P_x} is the own-price elasticity of demand for the consumer product x.

All terms in equation (11) are positive except for the own-price elasticity of demand for x (which, however, is in a term with a minus sign). Hence, we can conclude that $E_{P_x,P_a} > 0$. Moreover, it can be proved as follows that $E_{P_x,P_a} < 1$:

$$E_{P_x,P_a} < 1 \text{ if } S_a\left(\sigma + \varepsilon_{b,P_b}\right) < \varepsilon_{b,P_b} + S_a\sigma - S_b\eta_{x,P_x}$$

[11] Equation (19) in Gardner (1975).

$$S_a\sigma + S_a\varepsilon_{b,P_b} < \varepsilon_{b,P_b} + S_a\sigma - S_b\eta_{x,P_x}$$

$$S_a\varepsilon_{b,P_b} - \varepsilon_{b,P_b} < -S_b\eta_{x,P_x}$$

$$(S_a - 1)\varepsilon_{b,P_b} < -S_b\eta_{x,P_x}$$

$$(1 - S_a)\varepsilon_{b,P_b} > S_b\eta_{x,P_x}$$

$$\varepsilon_{b,P_b} > \eta_{x,P_x}$$

since under full competition $P_a a + P_b b = P_x x$ and thus $S_a + S_b = 1$ or $S_b = 1 - S_a$.[12]

$\varepsilon_{b,P_b} > \eta_{x,P_x}$ will always be true under normal conditions ($\varepsilon_{b,P_b} > 0$ and $\eta_{x,P_x} < 0$). Thus, $0 < E_{P_x,P_a} < 1$. In other words, a 1% increase in the price of the agricultural commodity a leads to a positive but less than 1% increase in the price of the processed consumer product x.

This result sounds plausible at first. If car tyres increase in price by X%, the price of a new car will increase by less than X%; if tomato prices increase by Y%, the price of a pizza will increase by less than Y%.[13] The proof presented above can be slightly modified to show that $E_{P_x,P_a} = 1$ will only hold if $\varepsilon_{b,P_b} = \eta_{x,P_x}$, which will never be the case as long as the demand for x falls as the price P_x rises, and the quantity of b supplied increases as the price P_b rises.

Equation (11) can be simplified under certain conditions. If the elasticity of factor substitution is very low ($\sigma \to 0$), we obtain:

$$E_{P_x,P_a} = \frac{S_a(\sigma+\varepsilon_{b,P_b})}{\varepsilon_{b,P_b}+S_a\sigma-S_b\eta_{x,P_x}} = \frac{S_a(0+\varepsilon_{b,P_b})}{\varepsilon_{b,P_b}+S_a 0-S_b\eta_{x,P_x}} = \frac{S_a\varepsilon_{b,P_b}}{\varepsilon_{b,P_b}-S_b\eta_{x,P_x}} \tag{12}$$

[12] See equation (81) in Appendix 2.3 in Chapter 2. In a linear homogeneous production function, if all factors are remunerated according to their marginal value products, there is no residual income.

[13] However, as Kinnucan and Zhang (2015) show, even respected agricultural economists have argued that the elasticity of vertical price transmission should ideally be one (*perfect vertical price transmission*). And it is not uncommon for farmers or consumers to claim instinctively that if slaughter pigs become 5% cheaper, the retail prices of pork chops and bacon should also fall by 5%.

If in addition S_a (the cost share of the raw agricultural product in the consumer product) is relatively large, then since $S_a + S_b = 1$, S_b must be relatively small. Finally, if the demand for the consumer product is inelastic, then the product $S_b\eta_{x,P_x}$ in the denominator of equation (12) will be very small, and we can conclude:

$$E_{P_x,P_a} \approx \frac{S_a\varepsilon_{b,P_b}}{\varepsilon_{b,P_b}} = S_a \tag{13}$$

Flour milling is an example of food processing in which these conditions apply. It is possible to produce roughly 0.75 tons of flour from one ton of wheat. There is very little scope for substituting wheat with labour, capital or other inputs in the milling process, at least in the short run.[14] Furthermore, the cost share of wheat in the value of flour is relatively high, and the price elasticity of demand for flour, which is a staple food flour, is low. Case study 2 presents the empirical example of wheat-flour price transmission in Ukraine.

Case study 2: The elasticity of vertical price transmission between wheat and flour in Ukraine

Brümmer et al. (2009) study weekly Ukrainian wheat and flour prices from July 2000 to November 2004. In Figure 10.4 we can see that these prices appear to move together. The large price swings in Figure 10.4 are mainly due to the fact that Ukraine imported wheat following very poor harvests in 2000 and 2003. As a result, import parity prices rather than export parity prices for wheat prevailed in those years.

[14] In the long run, milling machines that yield more flour per ton of wheat could perhaps be developed, but milling technology is mature.

Figure 10.4: Weekly milling wheat and flour prices in Ukraine (July 2000 to November 2004, in Ukrainian Hryvnia (UAH) per ton)

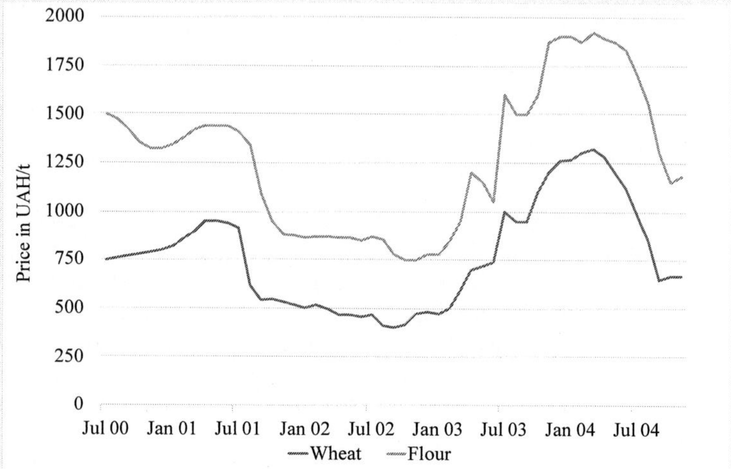

Source: Bruemmer et al. (2009).

The average wheat price over the observation period was 766 Ukrainian Hryvnia (UAH)/t; the average flour price was 1275 UAH/t. Since about 0.75 tons of flour can be obtained from one ton of wheat, 1.33 tons of wheat are needed to produce one ton of flour. These 1.33 tons of wheat cost an average of 1021 UAH (= 1.33 t * 766 UAH/t) during the observation period; the cost share of wheat in flour production was therefore 0.80 (= 1021 UAH/1275 UAH). Thus, in this case all of the conditions for the simplified result $E_{P_x,P_a} \approx S_a$ in equation (13) apply: a low elasticity of substitution σ, a relatively high cost share S_a of the raw agricultural product a, as well as a price-inelastic demand for the consumer product x. Consequently, according to Gardner's model, the elasticity of vertical price transmission between wheat and flour should be roughly equal to $S_a = 0.80$. And indeed, a simple regression between the log wheat and flour prices in Figure 10.4 yields the following results:

$$lnP_t^{wheat} = 1.790 + (0.808 * lnP_t^{wheat})$$

The estimated elasticity of vertical price transmission between wheat and flour is thus 0.808 (with a standard error 0.015), which is very close to the expected value of 0.80.

10.3.3. The elasticity of vertical price transmission - the response to consumer price changes

In the previous section, the elasticity of vertical price transmission was derived using Gardner's model and the assumption that the price of the agricultural raw product a is exogenous. This elasticity can be referred to as the farm price elasticity of the consumer price and will be labelled $E_{P_x,\underline{P_a}}$ in the following to illustrate that the farm-gate price P_a has triggered the price adjustments. This elasticity was important in the past when agricultural policy makers in the EU set new intervention prices for agricultural products each year, and economists wanted to forecast the effects of increases or decreases in intervention prices on consumer prices.

However, it is possible to derive another elasticity of vertical price transmission using Gardner's model, specifically $E_{\underline{P_x},P_a}$. This can be called the consumer price elasticity of the farm price, and it measures the effect on the farm-gate price of an exogenous change in the consumer price.[15]

$$E_{\underline{P_x},P_a} = \frac{\sigma + S_a \varepsilon_{b,P_b} + S_b \varepsilon_{a,P_a}}{\sigma + \varepsilon_{b,P_b}} \tag{14}$$

Since all parameters in equation (14) are greater than zero under normal conditions, $E_{\underline{P_x},P_a}$ will always be greater than zero. It can also be shown that $E_{\underline{P_x},P_a} < 1$ holds if $\varepsilon_{b,P_b} > \varepsilon_{a,P_a}$. This condition is likely to hold in the vast majority of agricultural applications, especially in an industrial country where food processing is a relatively small sector and acts as a price taker on markets for the CGS in b (e.g. capital, labour and energy).[16] Thus, just as $0 < E_{P_x,\underline{P_a}} < 1$ is true under normal conditions, so too is $0 < E_{\underline{P_x},P_a} < 1$. Yet $E_{\underline{P_x},P_a} \neq E_{P_x,\underline{P_a}}$: the elasticity of vertical price transmission differs

[15] Equation (14) is the inverse of equation (18) in Gardner (1975).

[16] If $\varepsilon_{b,P_b} = \infty$, i.e. the supply of all CGS is infinitely price elastic, then $E_{\underline{P_x},P_a} = E_{P_x,\underline{P_a}} = S_a$, regardless of the values of the other parameters in equations (11) and (14). In the short run, however, it cannot be assumed that the supply of all CGS will be infinitely elastic. Some CGS may be provided by specialised skilled workers or require specialised processing facilities for which the supply curves are upward sloping in the short run.

depending on whether the price adjustments are triggered by a change in the farm-gate price P_a, or a change in the consumer price P_x.

Assume, for example, the following values for the model parameters: $\sigma = 0.5$; $\varepsilon_{a,P_a} = 1$; $\varepsilon_{b,P_b} = 2$; $\eta_{x,P_x} = -0.5$; $S_a = 0.5$. Then $E_{P_x,\underline{P_a}} = 0.5$, but $E_{\underline{P_x},P_a} = 0.8$. In other words, a 1% increase in the producer price leads to a 0.5% increase in the consumer price, but a 0.5% increase in the consumer price leads to an increase in the producer price of only 0.625%. Kinnucan and Zhang (2015, p. 733, Table 1) compare $E_{P_x,\underline{P_a}}$ and $E_{\underline{P_x},P_a}$ for various plausible parameter constellations, and it is always the case that $0 < E_{P_x,\underline{P_a}} < E_{\underline{P_x},P_a} < 1$.

Which elasticity of vertical price transmission should be applied in which situations: $E_{P_x,\underline{P_a}}$ or $E_{\underline{P_x},P_a}$? The answer depends on the source of the exogenous shock, in other words which price has triggered the price adjustments. Case study 2 above presents the example of wheat and flour in Ukraine. Since wheat is tradable and Ukraine actively participates in international wheat trade, it is plausible to assume that the price of wheat in Ukraine is largely determined on world markets, i.e. it is exogenous from Ukraine's perspective. Flour, on the other hand, is internationally traded much less than wheat due to its higher perishability and transport costs. Consequently, the flour price in Ukraine is largely determined on a closed domestic market. Therefore, most of the shocks that affect the vertical price relationship between wheat and flour in Ukraine can be expected to arise on the world market for wheat; any shocks that might occur on the Ukrainian flour market will have only negligible effects on international wheat markets. In such a setting, the elasticity $E_{P_x,\underline{P_a}}$ is appropriate. In contrast, consider price transmission between farm and consumer prices for pork in Germany. Germany exports pork, and some important recent shocks (e.g. the outbreak and spread of African swine fever in China) have presumably affected this export market. These shocks did not arise at the level of the raw product a, but rather at the level of the processed product x. The consequences of such shocks can be better studied with the elasticity $E_{\underline{P_x},P_a}$.

10.4. Vertical price adjustments under imperfect competition

An important assumption of Gardner's model is that of perfect competition. Since we observe high concentration in many branches of the food processing industry as well as in food retailing in many countries, this assumption can be questioned. Of course, concentration is not a sufficient condition for the exercise of market power. Whether concentration leads to price fixing or other collusive behaviour depends on how firms behave. But as explained in case study 3 in Chapter 8, the German Federal Cartel Office has imposed fines for various forms of collusion in several branches of the food industry over the last 20 years, including milk and dairy products, the coffee market, sausage production, sugar production and food retailing. There are similar concerns about imperfect competition in the food chain in other countries.[17]

Various authors have therefore extended Gardner's model to account for market power. These contributions draw on the concept of conjectural variations introduced in Chapter 8. In the case of an oligopoly, the conjectural variation parameter (θ) measures how all other firms together react to a change in quantity by firm i:

$$\theta = \frac{\partial X_{-i}}{\partial x_i} \text{ where } X_{-i} = \sum_{j=1}^{n} x_j \text{ for } i \neq j \tag{15}$$

θ thus measures how the other firms adjust their supply of the consumer product x when firm i, out of a group of $i = \{1,2, \dots, n\}$ firms, supplies an additional unit of x. $\theta = -1$ represents aggressive behaviour by competitors; if i lowers its supply by one unit in an attempt to raise the price, this move is fully compensated by the other firms. In this case, the market outcome is identical to the outcome under perfect competition. At the other extreme, $\theta = n - 1$ means that all firms increase or decrease their supply by the same amount, which corresponds to coordinated or collusive behaviour. In this case, the n firms behave together like a monopolist.

In his extension of Gardner's model, Weldegebriel (2004) assumes that processors can exercise oligopoly power over the consumers of x. He therefore adds the parameter θ to the model as a measure of the implementation of oligopoly power on the part of processors. However, Weldegebriel also assumes that processors can exercise oligopsony power vis-à-vis producers of the raw product a. For this purpose, he again resorts to the concept of conjectural variations and defines:

$$\phi = \frac{\partial A_{-i}}{\partial a_i} \text{ with } A_{-i} = \sum_{j=1}^{n} a_j \text{ for } i \neq j \tag{16}$$

[17] Sexton and Xia (2018), for example, discuss the available evidence for the US.

ϕ measures how the other firms adjust their demand for the raw product a when firm i demands an additional unit of a. Analogous to θ, ϕ lies between -1 and $n-1$. $\phi = -1$ implies that if firm i demands less of a in an attempt to push the price of a down, the other firms counteract by increasing their demand by an identical amount. $\phi = n-1$ means that the firms collude and behave together as if they were a monopsonist.

These extensions have consequences for some of the equations in Gardner's model. For example, equation (8), which describes the demand for the raw agricultural product a, becomes:

$$\frac{\partial(f(a,b))}{\partial a} P_x \left(1 + \frac{(1+\theta)}{\eta_{x,P_x}} \frac{x_i}{x}\right) = P_a \left(1 + \frac{(1+\phi)}{\varepsilon_{a,P_a}} \frac{a_i}{a}\right) \tag{17}$$

If $\theta = \phi = -1$, then the processing firms behave aggressively towards each other, i.e. the attempts of firm i to exercise market power are always counteracted by the other firms. In this case, equation (17) reduces to equation (8), which holds under perfect competition. If, on the other hand, the n processing firms manage to collude perfectly, then $\theta = \phi = n-1$. Assuming n identical firms, $\frac{x_i}{x} = \frac{a_i}{a} = \frac{1}{n}$ and equation (17) can be simplified to:

$$\frac{\partial(f(a,b))}{\partial a} P_x \left(1 + \frac{1}{\eta_{x,P_x}}\right) = P_a \left(1 + \frac{1}{\varepsilon_{a,P_a}}\right) \tag{18}$$

Equation (18) describes the factor demand of a firm that is simultaneously a monopolist in the sale of x and a monopsonist in the purchase of a.[18]

After the equations in Gardner's model have been modified to account for imperfect competition, the resulting system of equations is solved once more. One important result that we can compare with the case of perfect competition is the farm price elasticity of the consumer price, which now takes the following form:[19]

$$E_{P_x,\underline{P_a}} = \frac{(1+\delta)S_a(\sigma+\varepsilon_{b,P_b})}{(1-\mu)(\varepsilon_{b,P_b}+S_a\sigma)-S_b\eta_{x,P_x}} \tag{19}$$

---

[18] The parameters θ and ϕ are simple mathematical expressions for a variety of possible entrepreneurial strategies, on which there is a very extensive literature. See, for example, Belleflamme and Peitz (2015, chapter 17).

[19] Equation (19) in Weldegebriel (2004).

The parameters δ and μ in equation (19) are functions of the parameters of conjectural variations θ and ϕ. Under conditions of perfect competition, $\delta = \mu = 0$ and equation (19) reduces to equation (11). However, δ and μ also depend on the exact functional forms of the demand for x and the supply of a: the definition of δ contains a term $\frac{\partial \varepsilon_{a,P_a}}{\partial P_a}$ and the definition of μ contains a term $\frac{\partial \eta_{x,P_x}}{\partial P_x}$.[20] These terms indicate how the own-price elasticities of the supply of a and the demand for x, respectively, change when the corresponding prices (P_a and P_x, respectively) change. For iso-elastic functions, these terms are zero by definition. For linear and other functional forms, however, this is not the case; the price elasticities vary along the corresponding curves.

Due to this dependence on the exact functional form of the supply and demand curves, no generally valid statements can be made about the effects of market power on vertical price adjustments. Weldegebriel (2004) shows that the farm price elasticity of the consumer price $E_{P_x,\underline{P_a}}$ can be higher but also lower under imperfect competition than under perfect competition. Whether imperfect competition reduces or increases the elasticity depends on the behaviour of the processing firms, and on the functional form of the demand for x and the supply of a. For example, if the functional forms are linear, the supply of a is relatively price elastic ($\varepsilon_{a,P_a} > 1$), and the demand for x is relatively price inelastic ($-1 < \eta_{x,P_x} < 0$), then the exercise of oligopoly power increases the elasticity $E_{P_x,\underline{P_a}}$ compared with perfect competition. However, when oligopsony power is exercised, $E_{P_x,\underline{P_a}}$ will be lower. A clear statement on which effect dominates requires a detailed analysis of consumer behaviour (the demand curve $x = g(P_x)$), farmer behaviour (the supply curve $a = h(P_a)$), as well as processor behaviour (the conjectural variations θ and ϕ).

Case study 3: Market power in the Ukrainian milling industry?

Case study 2 presented the following least squares estimation results for the vertical price transmission between wheat and flour prices in Ukraine:

$$lnP_t^{flour} = 1{,}790 + (0{,}808 * lnP_t^{wheat})$$

We noted that the estimated elasticity of vertical price transmission between

[20] See equations (13) and (14) in Weldegebriel (2004).

wheat and flour of 0.808 is very close to the value of S_a= 0.80 that would be expected under conditions of perfect competition according to Gardner's model. Can we conclude from this coincidence that there is perfect competition in the Ukrainian milling industry? Unfortunately, the simple answer to this question is 'no'.

First, note that the milling industry in Ukraine is concentrated: in 2019, according to Latifundist.com (2020), 10 milling firms produced about 47% of flour in Ukraine (0.7674 of 1.630 million tons). Some milling firms are controlled by economically and politically influential so-called oligarchs. Collusive behaviour, e.g. price fixing but also territorial agreements, where competing firms divide the market among themselves into geographical areas, is therefore a distinct possibility. We cannot rule out the possibility that some milling firms simultaneously exercise oligopsony power when they purchase wheat from local farmers and oligopoly power when they sell flour. If this is true, the corresponding effects on vertical price transmission could roughly offset one another, in which case the estimated elasticity would only coincidentally resemble the elasticity expected under perfect competition. As Weldegebriel (2004, p. 113) summarises: "without knowledge of the functional forms of retail demand and farm input supply, little can be inferred from the numerical value of a price transmission coefficient. In particular, it is not generally possible to attribute low (or high) values of the price transmission coefficient to market power".

10.5. Empirical methods for measuring vertical price adjustment processes

The following section provides a brief overview of the empirical methods used in most studies on vertical (and spatial) price adjustment processes. The workhorse model in these studies is the so-called **error correction model** (ECM), which will be briefly explained below[21].

The ECM has dominated the empirical literature on price adjustment processes since the mid-1990s.[22] Before that, relationships between prices at different stages of the food chain were often analysed with simple correlation coefficients or least-squares regressions. However, these

---

[21] The ECM is a key element of cointegration analysis, which is a branch of (time series) econometrics. A comprehensive introduction to cointegration analysis would go beyond the scope of this chapter. Hendry and Juselius (2000, 2001) provide a detailed but accessible introduction for agricultural economists.

[22] The first application in a leading agricultural economics journal is Ardeni (1989).

methods were criticised because they were prone to misinterpretation. Prices at different stages of the chain might be correlated because farmers, processors and consumers interact on markets under conditions of more or less perfect competition as described in Gardner's model. In this case, prices at different stages of the chain will be interrelated because the markets in which they are formed are integrated.

But prices can also be correlated because inflation is strong in a country and all nominal prices therefore follow similar rising trends, even when the markets in question are not integrated. Furthermore, prices can be correlated because the state intervenes in price formation by prescribing fixed margins or price formulas (e.g. that the price of flour must be exactly 120% of the price of milling wheat).

Finally, there is also the danger of so-called **spurious correlation**, which can occur when time series variables (such as prices) are not stationary. A stationary time series has a constant mean as well as a constant variance and constant covariances, regardless of which segment of the series is viewed. A stationary time series can temporarily deviate upwards or downwards from its long-term mean, but will always tend back to this mean. Many economic variables such as prices, however, are characterised by non-stationary behaviour; they rise or fall over longer periods and show no inherent tendency to return to a constant mean. In a seminal study, Granger and Newbold (1974) showed that when X_t and Y_t are two independent non-stationary time series (with $t = 1,2,\ldots T$ observations) and the regression $Y_t = \beta_0 + \beta_1 X_t$ is estimated, the null hypothesis $H_0\colon \beta_1 = 0$ (which is actually true) is rejected far too often.[23] This means that regressions between non-stationary variables often produce what appear to be statistically significant relationships that are actually just statistical artefacts. Since many prices have non-stationary properties, regressions such as $P_t^A = \beta_0 + \beta_1 P_t^B$ are also susceptible to the phenomenon of spurious correlation.

In summary, a high correlation or significant regression between two prices does <u>not</u> necessarily mean that these prices are actually linked in an

[23] In Granger and Newbold's (1974) experiment with non-stationary variables (so-called random walks), the true null hypothesis $H_0\colon \beta_1 = 0$ was rejected in about 75% of all cases at the 5% level of significance. In 2003, Clive W.J. Granger, together with Robert F. Engle, received the Nobel Memorial Prize in Economic Sciences in recognition of his many contributions to the analysis of economic time series, including the estimation and interpretation of ECMs.

equilibrium relationship determined by market processes and the behaviour of economic agents. Simple correlation coefficients and least squares estimates are not able to distinguish between price correlations that arise on integrated markets and those that are due to other causes such as inflation or spurious correlation.

As these insights were increasingly recognised, econometricians responded by estimating dynamic regression models with lagged so-called lag terms (e.g. $P_t^A = \beta_0 + \beta_1 P_t^B + \beta_2 P_{t-1}^B + \beta_3 P_{t-1}^A$) or models in differences (e.g. $\Delta P_t^A = \beta_0 + \beta_1 \Delta P_t^B$, where $\Delta X_t = X_t - X_{t-1}$). Then, Engle and Granger (1987) showed how the ECM could be used to estimate relationships between non-stationary time series. A simple ECM for two price series P^R and P^C (R denotes the raw agricultural product and C the consumer product) takes the following form:

$$\Delta P_t^C = \alpha_C (P_{t-1}^C - \beta_0 - \beta_1 P_{t-1}^R) + \delta_{C1} \Delta P_{t-1}^C + \delta_{R1} \Delta P_{t-1}^R \quad (20)$$

The dependent variable on the LHS of equation (20) (ΔP_t^K) measures the change in P^C between the previous and current periods. The term in parentheses on the RHS of equation (20) captures deviations from the long-run equilibrium relationship $P_t^C = \beta_0 + \beta_1 P_t^R$ between P^C and P^R. The non-stationary price series P^C and P^R are connected by a stable long-run equilibrium relationship only if the deviations from this long-run relationship ($P_{t-1}^K - \beta_0 - \beta_1 P_{t-1}^R$, the so-called error correction term) are stationary and thus always tend to return to their mean value of zero. $\beta_1 = {\partial P^C}/{\partial P^R}$ is the long-run price adjustment coefficient; if the prices P^R and P^C are in logarithms, β_1 represents the elasticity of vertical price transmission.

If prices are in equilibrium, then $P_t^C = \beta_0 + \beta_1 P_t^R$ and hence the error correction term ($P_t^C - \beta_0 - \beta_1 P_t^R$) equals 0. If the long-run equilibrium is temporarily disturbed, for example by an unexpected shock, then $P_t^C - \beta_0 - \beta_1 P_t^R \neq 0$. The parameter α_C (often called the adjustment parameter) measures how P^C reacts in the next period to correct part of the deviation from equilibrium. For example, if P^C is too large relative to P^R, then a positive deviation or error from the long-run equilibrium exists because $P_t^C - \beta_0 - \beta_1 P_t^R > 0$. If, for example, $\alpha_C = -0{,}5$ (-0.20), then P^K will fall to correct 50% (20%) of this error in the next period. α_C must be less than zero so that a too high (low) P^C is corrected downwards (upwards) in the next period, thus correcting the error and restoring the long-run equilibrium between P^R and P^C.

The two lagged price change terms on the right-hand side of equation (20), $\delta_{C1}\Delta P_{t-1}^{C}$ and $\delta_{R1}\Delta P_{t-1}^{R}$, measure short-term dynamic interactions between prices. Equation (20) contains only one lag each of the price changes (ΔP_{t-1}^{C} and ΔP_{t-1}^{R}), but further lags can be added in empirical applications.

A similar ECM can be specified for changes in the raw product price P^R:

$$\Delta P_t^R = \alpha_R(P_{t-1}^C - \beta_0 - \beta_1 P_{t-1}^R) + \gamma_{C1}\Delta P_{t-1}^C + \gamma_{R1}\Delta P_{t-1}^R \quad (21)$$

If P^C is too large relative to P^R ($P_t^C - \beta_0 - \beta_1 P_t^R > 0$), P^R must increase in the next period to contribute to correcting the deviation from long-run equilibrium. Therefore, $\alpha_R > 0$ must hold in equation (21). The sum $|\alpha_C| + \alpha_R$ thus measures how fast the prices P^C and P^R react together to correct temporary deviations from equilibrium. Equations (20) and (21) together form a so-called vector ECM (abbreviated in the literature as VECM for **vector error correction model**). The equations in a VECM are usually estimated simultaneously using a method developed by Johansen (1991).

Case study 4: A VECM for wheat and flour prices in Ukraine

In case study 2, the elasticity of vertical price transmission between wheat and flour prices in Ukraine was estimated using the following least squares regression: $lnP_t^{flour} = 1.790 + (0.808 * lnP_t^{wheat})$. However, the prices used in this regression might be non-stationary (see Figure 10.4), and if that were true these regression results might reflect spurious correlation. To rule out this possibility, a typical price transmission analysis follows the following steps. First, the individual price series are tested for non-stationarity. So-called unit root tests are used for this purpose. If both series are non-stationary, there is a risk of spurious correlation. Therefore, the second step is to test whether deviations from the estimated long-term relationship between the prices are stationary. So-called **cointegration tests** are used for this purpose. If the deviations are stationary, spurious correlation can be excluded; there is a valid, interpretable long-term relationship between the prices. In this case, third, a VECM can be estimated for these prices.

The technical details of these various test and estimation procedures cannot be explained here. As mentioned above, Hendry and Juselius (2000, 2001) are useful sources. For Ukrainian wheat and flour prices, first, the results of unit root tests show that both prices are non-stationary. Second, cointegration tests show that there is a valid long-run relationship between these prices - the regression results presented above are therefore not due to spurious correlation. Third and finally, the following VECM can be estimated for the prices (standard errors in brackets):

$$\Delta lnP_t^{flour} = -0.124\left(lnP_{t-1}^{flour} - 1.607 - 0.835 lnP_{t-1}^{flour}\right) + 0.367\Delta lnP_{t-1}^{flour} + 0.024\Delta lnP_{t-1}^{wheat}$$

(0.023) (0.246) (0.037) (0.061) (0.049)

$$\Delta lnP_t^{wheat} = 0.002\left(lnP_{t-1}^{flour} - 1.607 - 0.835 lnP_{t-1}^{wheat}\right) + 0.208\Delta lnP_{t-1}^{flour} + 0.203\Delta lnP_{t-1}^{wheat}$$

(0.036) (0.246) (0.037) (0.094) (0.074)

The estimated long-run relationship in the VECM $lnP_t^{flour} = 1.607 + (0.835 * lnP_t^{wheat})$ is slightly different from the long-run relationship presented above in case study 2. The differences arise because the VECM is estimated using the maximum likelihood method rather than least squares. However, the differences are minor and do not change the key results, especially the estimated elasticity of vertical price transmission, which remains slightly above 0.8.

The estimated adjustment parameters $\alpha_{flour} = -0.124$ and $\alpha_{wheat} = 0.002$ indicate that the flour price responds when there are deviations from the long-run equilibrium between wheat and flour prices, by about 12.4% of the deviation per week. The wheat price, on the other hand, does not react (the estimated value of 0.2% per week is very small and statistically insignificant). This result is expected because, as explained above, the wheat price in Ukraine depends on the world market, while the flour price is formed on the domestic market. If an imbalance arises between wheat and flour prices in Ukraine, the much larger world market for wheat cannot be expected to react significantly; instead, the comparatively small Ukrainian flour market will adjust to restore equilibrium (the dog wags the tail, not the other way around). Correcting roughly 12.4% of a disequilibrium each week is not very fast; at that rate it will take several months to restore equilibrium. One possible explanation for this result could be that mills do not purchase the wheat they need in small batches on a weekly basis. Instead, they usually purchase larger batches at longer intervals. Hence, the flour a mill sells today was probably milled from wheat purchased several weeks or even months ago. Therefore, it can take time for price signals to be transmitted from wheat to flour markets.

The use of VECMs to estimate price transmission processes has several advantages. First, equilibrium relationships can be distinguished from spurious correlations. Second, not only the long-run equilibrium relationship between two prices is estimated, but also the short-run reactions of prices to shocks that disturb this equilibrium. In this way we can gain insights into the pattern and speed of a price adjustment process.

10.6. Asymmetric vertical price transmission

A price adjustment is **asymmetric** if the magnitude and/or speed of the response of one price to a change in another price depends on the direction of the original price change. Figure 10.5 is a schematic depiction of both types of asymmetry: the response of P_x to an increase in P_a is complete after two periods and equals $\beta^{\uparrow}$, but the response of P_x to a decrease in P_a is only complete after four periods and is smaller ($\beta^{\downarrow} < \beta^{\uparrow}$). This type of asymmetry is often called **rockets and feathers**, suggesting that prices rise quickly (like rockets) but fall slowly (like feathers).

Rockets and feathers behaviour is often suspected: car owners and households that heat with oil claim that the prices of gasoline or heating oil rise quickly when the price of crude oil rises, and fall slowly when the price of crude oil falls. Pig farmers sometimes claim that slaughter companies and retailers use their market power to pass price increases for slaughter pigs on to consumers very quickly, because these price increases would otherwise squeeze their margins. However, farmers claim that the same slaughter companies and retailers will pass price reductions for slaughter pigs on to consumers more slowly, because these price reductions stretch their margins, and they are in no hurry to pass on this benefit. Case study 5 shows that empirical evidence of asymmetric vertical price transmission of the rockets-and-feathers type can be found in the German market for slaughter pigs.

Figure 10.5: Schematic depiction of asymmetric vertical price adjustments

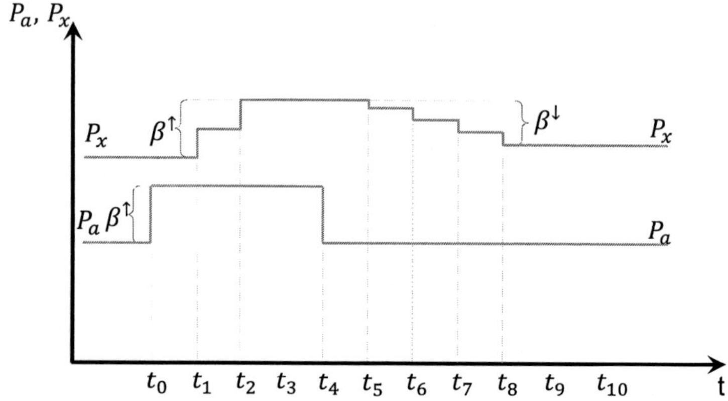

Source: Own depiction.

Case study 5: Asymmetric price adjustments in the market for slaughter pigs in Germany

Von Cramon-Taubadel (1998) analyses vertical price transmission between producer prices for slaughter pigs and wholesale prices for pork cuts in northern Germany using weekly data from January 1990 to February 1993. He uses the following asymmetric specification of the ECM:

$$\Delta P_t^{whole} = \alpha_{wholw}^{+}(u_{t-1}^{+}) + \alpha_{whole}^{-}(u_{t-1}^{-}) + \delta_1 \Delta P_{t-1}^{whole} + \gamma_1 \Delta P_{t-1}^{prod} + \gamma_2 \Delta P_{t-2}^{prod} + \gamma_4 \Delta P_{t-4}^{prod} \quad (22)$$

with $u_t = P_t^{whole} - \beta_0 - \beta_1 P_t^{prod}$, the deviation from the long-run equilibrium relationship between the wholesale price of cuts (P^{whole}) and the producer price of slaughter pigs (P^{prod}). Possible asymmetry is captured by decomposing the deviation from equilibrium (u_t) into two components. The component u_t^{+} equals the positive values of u_t, and is otherwise zero; the component u_t^{-} conversely equals the negative values of u_t, and is otherwise zero:

$$u_t^{+} = \begin{cases} u_t \; \forall \, u_t > 0 \\ 0 \; \forall \, u_t \leq 0 \end{cases} \text{ and } u_t^{-} = \begin{cases} u_t \; \forall \, u_t < 0 \\ 0 \; \forall \, u_t \geq 0 \end{cases}$$

The corresponding symmetric ECM

$$\Delta P_t^{whole} = \alpha_{whole}(u_t) + \delta_1 \Delta P_{t-1}^{whole} + \gamma_1 \Delta P_{t-1}^{prod} + \gamma_2 \Delta P_{t-2}^{prod} + \gamma_4 \Delta P_{t-4}^{prod} \quad (23)$$

is a restricted form of the asymmetric ECM in equation (22), in which the restriction $\alpha^{+}_{whole} = \alpha^{-}_{whole}$ is imposed (since $u^{+}_{t} + u^{-}_{t} = u_t$). The corresponding null hypothesis H_0: $\alpha^{+}_{whole} = \alpha^{-}_{whole}$ can therefore be tested by means of an F-test. For the German pork price data this H_0 can be rejected (p-value equals roughly 0.02). The following (simplified) estimation results for the asymmetric ECM are presented (see von Cramon-Taubadel 1998, Table 2; standard errors in brackets):

$$\Delta P^{whole}_{t} = -0.057(u^{+}_{t-1}) - 0.270(u^{-}_{t-1}) + 0.164\Delta P^{whole}_{t-1} + 0.114\Delta P^{prod}_{t-1} - 0.093\Delta P^{prod}_{t-2} - 0.107\Delta P^{prod}_{t-4}$$

$$(0.041) \quad (0.083) \quad (0.062) \quad (0.054) \quad (0.045) \quad (0.035)$$

These results indicate a rockets and feathers asymmetry. $u_t > 0$ implies that the wholesale price P^{whole} is too high relative to the producer price P^{prod}, i.e. the slaughter companies are enjoying an above-average margin. If this is the case, only a relatively small and statistically insignificant correction ($\alpha^{+}_{whole} = -0.057$) takes place. $u_t < 0$ implies that the wholesale price P^{whole} is too low relative to the producer price P^{prod} , i.e. that the slaughter margin is below-average. In this case, the correction is about five times larger ($\alpha^{-}_{whole} = -0.270$). Deviations from the long-term equilibrium that stretch the margin are thus corrected significantly more slowly than those that squeeze the margin. Simulations for Germany as a whole, calculated under the assumption of symmetric price adjustment with an adjustment parameter of $\alpha^{+}_{whole} = \alpha^{-}_{whole} = 0.270$, show that asymmetry increased the slaughter margin by about 28 million euros per year.

However, results such as those presented in case study 5 do not conclusively prove that the companies in the German slaughter industry have used market power to expand their margins and thus their profits during the observation period. In terms of the classical **structure-conduct-performance** approach (SCP, see section 7 in Chapter 8), we observe a certain market *structure* (many pig farmers, but few large slaughter companies) and a certain market *outcome* (asymmetric vertical price adjustments). But since we do not directly observe the *behaviour* (conduct) of the slaughter companies, we cannot be sure that the market structure is causing the outcome. The fact that asymmetric price transmission is observed does not prove that the companies colluded or otherwise coordinated their behaviour to generate it. It would therefore be premature to attribute the observed asymmetry to market power. This caution is called for because, first, **asymmetric price adjustment** can be caused by factors other than the exercise of market power and, second, because market power does not necessarily lead to rockets and feathers asymmetry.

10.6.1. Alternative causes of asymmetric price adjustment

Asymmetric price adjustments can occur in the absence of market power. Several alternative causes of asymmetry have been proposed in the literature. [24] According to Kinnucan and Forker (1987), one possible explanation for asymmetric price adjustments could be agricultural policy. If farmers in a country traditionally benefit from price support, processors will expect the government to step in and support farmers' prices whenever they fall. Processors will therefore expect farm-gate price reductions to be short-lived. Accordingly, they will not reduce the sales prices of their consumer products when farm-gate prices fall. In comparison, processors will expect increases in farm-gate price to be longer-lived, and they will therefore be more likely to pass on the resulting cost increases to their customers. The result will be rockets-and-feathers price adjustment that is not caused by market power.

Another alternative explanation for asymmetric price adjustments is proposed by Ball and Mankiw (1994). In their model, inflation in conjunction with so-called **menu costs** causes asymmetric price adjustment. Menu costs are the costs incurred by a firm when it changes its prices. In the original sense of the words, menu costs refer to the costs that a restaurant incurs when it adjusts its prices and therefore has to redesign and reprint its menu. More generally, the term refers to all costs associated with changing price lists, catalogues, websites, etc. As a result of menu costs, a firm will not adjust its sales prices in response to every small change in its input costs. Instead, it will only adjust its sales prices if the profit loss due to the input cost change exceeds the menu costs caused by the sales price change. Some firms will only adjust their sales prices at regular, often seasonal intervals (e.g. the summer catalogue, the autumn collection, the Christmas menu, etc.), and use these scheduled opportunities to respond to any input price changes that have occurred in the interim.[25]

[24] Surveys of the literature on asymmetric price adjustment processes are provided by Frey and Manera (2007) and Meyer and von Cramon-Taubadel (2004). Loy et al. (2016) provide a comprehensive recent overview of the various causes of asymmetric vertical price adjustment that have been proposed in the literature.

[25] Firms might also worry that too frequent adjustments of their sales prices will confuse or annoy customers. Rotemberg (2010) argues that this danger is particularly present in the case of storable products: if prices increase for a storable product, consumers will regret that they did not buy it earlier; if prices fall, consumers will regret that they did not wait longer. This worry on the part of firms will, like menu costs, make them less likely to change their sales prices.

In Ball and Mankiw's model, firms must take both menu costs and inflation into account when setting prices. All other things being equal, over time inflation causes a firm's margin to decline in real terms. After a certain period of time, its margin will have fallen so much that a firm will respond by increasing its sales price, despite menu costs. If, however, input prices have fallen in the meantime, this counteracts inflation; it increases the firm's margin and enables the firm to postpone or cancel the sales price increase (and save the menu costs that it would otherwise have incurred). If, instead, input prices have increased in the meantime, the firm's margin is doubly squeezed (by both inflation and the input price increase). In this case the firm will be obliged to increase its sales price sooner. Viewed from outside, it will appear that input price reductions do not or less often lead to adjustments in sales prices, compared with input price increases. The result, again, is asymmetric price adjustment that is not caused by the exercise of market power.

Yet another explanation for asymmetric price adjustment proposed in the literature relates to so-called **stock-out costs**. A stock-out occurs when a product that is normally part of a retailer's assortment is sold out and therefore temporarily unavailable to customers. If a stock-out occurs, the retailer incurs costs in the form of reduced sales. However, there is also the danger that customers will look for and find the missing product at a competing retailer and, in the worst case, switch to the competing retailer altogether. As Gaur and Park (2007, p. 227) state: "in practice, customers do react substantially and negatively to poor service (e.g., stock-outs), which may lead them to switch retailers on subsequent trips". This risk is particularly high for perishable staples such as fresh milk, which households cannot store in large quantities; if such a product is stocked-out in one store, customers are very likely to look for it elsewhere.

To reduce the risk of stock-outs, retailers might therefore tend to reduce their sales prices only slowly when their input prices fall, especially for perishable products, so as not to stimulate demand too much. If, on the other hand, purchase prices rise, retailers will pass this cost increase on to their customers more quickly. This asymmetry will not occur or will be less pronounced for products that are easier and less expensive to stock.[26]

---

[26] Slonim and Gabarino (2009) develop a formal model in which the strength of the resulting asymmetry in vertical price adjustment depends, among other things, on the storability/perishability of the product.

Finally, an explanation for asymmetric price adjustments can also be derived from the results of Gardner's model, which was presented above. In section 10.3.3 we saw that the elasticity of vertical price transmission is higher when price adjustments are triggered by a change in the price of the consumer product x, rather than by a change in the price of the raw farm product a ($E_{P_x,\underline{P_a}} < E_{\underline{P_x},P_a}$). If, over time, price reductions are more often triggered by shocks on the market for a, while price increases predominantly arise as a result of shocks on the market for x, rockets and feathers asymmetry can occur even under conditions of full competition.

10.6.2. Does market power necessarily lead to rockets and feathers asymmetry?

It certainly is conceivable that firms that have oligopoly power might collude to coordinate rockets and feathers asymmetry. Over time, this would increase average margins for these firms. Of course, the firms could simply agree to permanently raise their sales prices in order to permanently increase their margins. However, if they worry that permanent increases might quickly come to the attention of competition authorities, they might consider rockets and feathers behaviour as a subtler and less conspicuous way of turning market power into profits.

However, collusive price manipulation is not the only behaviour that can arise in concentrated markets. Imagine, for example, an oligopoly consisting of a financially strong firm that has substantial financial reserves, and several other firms that are in financially weaker positions and, in some cases, highly indebted. In such a situation, the strong firm might be willing to forego profits in the short run in order to drive some competitors out of the market and thus expand its market share in the medium or long run. If the firm pursues such a strategy, it is unlikely to participate in collusion that leads to rockets and feathers asymmetry. After all, rockets and feathers asymmetry would increase average margins over time, and thus reduce the pressure on financially weaker firms. Instead, the strong company might try to implement the opposite asymmetry. If input prices were to fall, the strong firm would immediately reduce its sales prices to maintain economic pressure on its competitors. If input prices were to rise, the strong firm could leave its sales prices unchanged and temporarily absorb below-average margins in the hope that these might force some weaker competitors to exit the market. The result would be the exact opposite of rockets and feathers.

In conclusion, asymmetric price adjustments do not necessarily result from the exercise of market power, and the exercise of market power does not necessarily lead to rockets and feathers asymmetry. The following case study presents evidence for the dairy market in Germany.

Case study 6: Price transmission and market power in the German dairy market

Loy et al. (2016) analyse an extensive dataset of weekly price data for 90 different brands of fluid milk (3.5% fat content in one litre containers) in 327 retail stores from 2005 to 2008. The retail price of milk is strongly influenced by the wholesale prices that dairies charge. The authors analyse which factors, such as market power, influence the transmission of prices between the wholesale and the retail level in the 327 shops.

In a first stage, the authors estimate an ECM for each brand of milk in each shop (referred to as "product" in the following). Both symmetric (α) and asymmetric adjustment parameters (α^+ and α^-) are estimated (see case study 5). These indicate how quickly prices for a particular product react to deviations from the long-run equilibrium and whether these price reactions are symmetric. In a second step, the authors use the adjustment parameters estimated in the first stage as endogenous variables in cross-section regressions. The aim of these cross-section regressions is to test whether there is a systematic relationship between the speed of vertical price adjustment or the extent of estimated asymmetry on the one hand, and metrics of market power and other characteristics of dairy markets on the other.

The results reveal a negative correlation between a retailer's market power (measured using the price-cost margin, see chapter 8) and the speed of price adjustment. In other words, retailers with more market power appear to adjust their retail prices more slowly in response to wholesale prices changes. The authors also find clear evidence of rockets and feathers asymmetry. However, they find that the extent of this asymmetry <u>de</u>creases with increasing market power. This result contradicts the common expectation that rockets and feathers asymmetry is a consequence of market power. Finally, the authors find that price adjustment asymmetry is significantly stronger for fresh milk than for ultra-heat treatment (UHT) milk that can be stored for longer periods of time. They interpret this result as a possible indication that asymmetric price adjustment is being caused by retailers' reactions to stock-out costs.

10.7. Implications for agricultural and food policy

As noted in the introduction to this chapter, vertical pricing is a controversial topic. Farmers and other stakeholders often call for political interventions such as minimum farm-gate prices, bans on the sale of food below production costs, and restrictions on market power in food processing and retailing. What conclusions for agricultural and food policy can we draw based on the economic concepts and models presented in this chapter?

Competition policy

First, we have seen that the effects of market power on vertical price transmission are complex. The exercise of market power can increase but also reduce elasticities of vertical price transmission. It can lead to asymmetric price adjustment, but asymmetry can also have other causes. The empirical analysis of prices at different levels of the food chain, e.g. by means of ECMs, can provide important insights into price adjustment processes, but can only generate limited evidence on the existence and exercise of market power. Therefore, and as explained in detail in chapter 8, competition policy must also rely on other analytical methods and instruments. In this chapter we have focussed on vertical price relationships in the food chain. However, market participants negotiate not only prices, but also other contractual conditions such as supply guarantees, exclusivity, payment conditions, and premiums and penalties for quality, punctuality, and other contract fulfilment criteria. Thus, analysis of price data alone can only be one ingredient in a comprehensive competition policy.

Food processing and food retailing in Germany are characterised by high concentration. Concentration does not automatically imply the exercise of market power. However, in recent decades the Germany Federal Cartel Office has investigated many branches of the food processing industry as well as food retailing, and these investigations have often led to the imposition of fines. The situation is similar in many other industrialised counties. Accordingly, there are indications that competition is less than perfect in the food chain in many countries. This underlines the crucial need for competition authorities that are equipped with sufficient resources and regulatory power.

Minimum prices and other interventions in price formation

As explained in section 10.2, the widening of the market margin for food over time is due to many factors including technical change, rising incomes, and changes in farm and consumer households' preferences and behaviour. The widening of the market margin therefore does not in itself provide a justification for government intervention.

In public debates it is often argued that food prices in Germany are too low and that policy makers should intervene to correct or improve price formation in the food chain. Statements such as the following quote by the President of the German Farmers' Union Joachim Rukwied meet with approval among the population: "Food should not be dumped at bargain-basement prices" (DBV 2020). In a survey conducted in early 2020 (Heinrich 2020), 73% of respondents were in favour of a ban on the sale of food at prices below production costs.

The implementation of such a ban, however, would be associated with considerable difficulties and side effects. First, references to "the" production costs fail to recognise that agriculture is heterogeneous. The production costs of a litre of milk or a ton of wheat can vary, both regionally and from farm to farm. If average production costs were used as the minimum price in food retailing, food would continue to be sold at prices below the production costs of farms that have above-average costs. If, instead, the production costs of the marginal supplier were used to determine the minimum price, very high margins would arise in the food chain.

Second, the enforcement of a minimum retail price would increase consumer spending on food and retailers' revenues, but it would not necessarily lead to higher prices for farmers or a larger farm share in consumer expenditure on food. For the latter to happen, the state would have to regulate not only retail prices but also pricing along the entire food chain. In any event, it cannot be assumed that the percentage increase in farm-gate prices would equal the percentage increase in consumer prices. This is because, as shown above, the elasticity of vertical price transmission is only equal to one under very restrictive conditions.

Third, while it is conceivable that minimum prices could be set for comparatively simple food products such as milk, eggs and flour, this would be much more complicated for highly processed food products that are composed of several raw products such as frozen pizzas and muesli mixes.

In order to ensure that the cost of production (however defined) of each individual ingredient is not undercut, policy makers would require extensive and constantly updated information on prices, recipes and the costs of complementary goods and services. It is unlikely that the state would be able to obtain this information and use it effectively. In the planned economies of Eastern Europe before 1989, policy makers attempted to control prices and margins along the entire food chain; the results were chronic shortages, often very limited product variety, and considerable inefficiencies in the system.

Finally, calls for minimum prices and bans on dumping in the food chain often implicitly assume that Germany (or whatever other country is under consideration) is a closed economy, i.e. they fail to account for international trade. In the single European market, not everything that is sold below production costs in a particular country is automatically a case of dumping. For example, it is not dumping if a processor combines expensive ingredients from Germany with less expensive ingredients from other EU countries, and sells the end product at a price that reflects the average ingredient costs. Similarly, it is not dumping if a processing firm sells a product in Germany that was produced exclusively on the basis of raw materials from other EU countries where production costs are lower than in Germany.[27]

If there is imperfect competition in the food chain, it should be addressed using the instruments of competition policy (see chapter 8); minimum prices and other market interventions will generally be less effective and less efficient. In some cases, legislation and government programmes can help farmers coordinate and bundle their market power and, thus, better assert their interests vis-à-vis other stakeholders in the food chain. From the 1960s until the 1990s the EU provided farmers with high levels of price support. Nevertheless, the farm share in consumer expenditure on food fell and structural change in agriculture continued. There is no reason to expect that these trends could be arrested by re-implementing price support today.

---

[27] Provided, of course, that the imported raw materials were produced in compliance with the quality standards (health, animal welfare, environment, etc.) that apply in the EU, and that were adopted by the EU with Germany's participation.

10.8. Keywords

- Agricultural terms of trade
- Asymmetric price adjustment
- Complementary goods and services
- Convenience foods
- Cointegration test
- Elasticity of factor substitution
- Elasticity of vertical price transmission
- Equilibrium displacement form of an equation
- Error correction model (ECM)
- Market margin
- Menu costs
- Price vector
- Quantity vector
- Rockets and feathers
- Spurious correlation
- Stock-out costs
- Structure, conduct, performance (SCP)
- Unit margin
- Transformation coefficient
- Vector error correction model (VECM)
- Vertical price relationships

References

Ahlers F (2019) Verantwortung bei FRoSTA. Presentation held at the *ttz Zukunftsforum* „Wie und was essen wir morgen?" ttz Bremerhaven, June 12-13, 2019.

Allen RGD (1938,) Mathematical Analysis for Economists. Macmillan & Co., London.

Ardeni P (1989) Does the Law of One Price hold for Commodity Prices? American Journal of Agricultural Economics 71: 661-669.

Ball L and Mankiw NG (1994) Asymmetric Price Adjustment and economic Fluctuations. The Economic Journal 104: 247-261.

Belleflamme P and Peitz M (2015) Industrial Organization: Markets and Strategies. Cambridge University Press, Cambridge.

Brümmer B, Cramon-Taubadel S and Zorya S (2009) The impact of market and policy instability on price transmission between wheat and flour in Ukraine. European Review of Agricultural Economics 36: 203-230.

DBV (Deutscher Bauernverband) (2020) Bauernverband zum Lebensmittelgipfel. Press release on February 3, 2022. https://www.bauernverband.de/fileadmin/user_upload/dbv/pressemitteilungen/2020/KW_06/2020-027_LEH.pdf. Accessed on February 18, 2022.

Dornbusch H (ed.) (2013) Reinheitsgebot. In: The Oxford Companion to Beer. Oxford University Press, doi: 10.1093/acref/9780195367133.001.0001.

Engle RF and Granger CWJ (1987) Co-integration and error-correction: Representation, estimation and testing. Econometrica 55: 251-276.

Frey G and Manera M (2007) Models of Asymmetric Price Transmission. Journal Economic Surveys 21: 349-415.

Gardner BL (1975) The Farm-Retail Price Spread in a Competitive Food Industry. American Journal of Agricultural Economics 57: 399-409.

Gaur V and Park Y-H (2007) Asymmetric consumer learning and inventory competition. Management Science 53: 227-240.

Granger CWJ and Newbold P (1974) Spurious Regressions in Econometrics. Journal of Econometrics 2: 111-120.

Heinrich R (2020) Eine Studie zur politischen Stimmung im Auftrag der ARD-Tagesthemen und der Tageszeitung DIE WELT. https://www.infratest-dimap.de/fileadmin/user_upload/DT2002_Bericht.pdf. Accessed on February 18, 2022.

Hendry DF and Juselius K (2000) Explaining Cointegration Analysis: Part I. The Energy Journal 21: 1-42.

Hendry DF and Juselius K (2001) Explaining Cointegration Analysis: Part II. The Energy Journal 22: 75-120.

Institut für Ernährungswirtschaft (2018) Wert und Kosten der Trinkmilch (October 2018). Institut für Ernährungswirtschaft Kiel e.V.
https://www.ife-ev.de/index.php/ife-publikationen/branchenuebersicht-milch. Accessed on February 18, 2022.

Johansen S (1991) Estimation and Hypothesis Testing of Cointegration Vectors in Gaussian Vector Autoregressive Models. Econometrica 59: 1551-1580.

Kinnucan HW and Forker OD (1987) Asymmetry in Farm-Retail Price Transmission for major Dairy Products, American Journal of Agricultural Economics 69: 285-292.

Kinnucan HW and Zhang D (2015) Notes on farm-retail price transmission and marketing margin behavior. Agricultural Economics 46: 729-737.

Koester U (2016) Grundzüge der landwirtschaftlichen Marktlehre. 5. Auflage, Verlag Franz Vahlen, München.

Latifundist.com (2020) Flour production 2019: Ukraine's market leaders. https://latifundist.com/en/novosti/48774-nazvany-top-10-proizvoditelej-muki-v-ukraine-v-2019-g. Accessed on February 18, 2022.

Loy J-P, Glauben T and Weiss CR (2016) Asymmetric Cost Pass-Through? Empirical Evidence on the Role of Market Power, Search and Menu Costs. Journal of Economic Behavior and Organization 123: 184-192.

Meyer J and von Cramon-Taubadel S (2004) Asymmetric Price Transmission. Journal of Agricultural Economics 55: 581-611.

Nivievskyi O and von Cramon-Taubadel S (2011) Dairy Supply Chain in Belarus – Bottlenecks and scope for improvements. Studie für BE Berlin Economics GmbH im Auftrag des Bundesministeriums für Ernährung, Landwirtschaft und Verbraucherschutz.

Rotemberg J (2010) Altruistic dynamic pricing with customer regret. Scandinavian Journal of Economics 112: 646-672.

Schnepf R (2015) Farm-to-Food Price Dynamics. Congressional Research Service (CRS) Report R40621. Washington DC. https://digital.library.unt.edu/ark:/67531/metadc818396/. Accessed on February 18, 2022.

Sexton RJ and Xia T (2018) Increasing competition in the agricultural supply chain: Implications for market power and sector performance. Annual Review of Resource Economics 10: 229-251.

Sinabell F (2005) Marktspannen und Erzeugeranteil an den Ausgaben für Nahrungsmittel. Studie des Österreichischen Instituts für Wirtschaftsforschung im Auftrag des Bundesministeriums für Land- und Forstwirtschaft, Umwelt und Wasserwirtschaft. https://www.wifo.ac.at/jart/prj3/wifo/resources/person_dokument/person_dokument.jart?publikationsid=25398&mime_type=application/pdf. Accessed on February 18, 2022.

Slonim R and Garbarino E (2009) Similarities and differences between stockpiling and reference effects. Managerial and Decision Economics 30: 351-371.

Thünen Institut (2020) Anteil der Verkaufserlöse der Landwirtschaft an den Verbraucherausgaben für Nahrungsmittel inländischer Herkunft in Deutschland. https://www.thuenen.de/media/institute/ma/Downloads/Tabelle1_Anteilsberechnung_2018.pdf. Accessed on February 18, 2022.

Verbraucherzentrale (2016) Lebensmittelklarheit. Aromastoffe: viele Geschmack, weniger natürliche Zutaten. https://www.lebensmittelklarheit.de/informationen/aromastoffe. Accessed on February 18, 2022.

von Cramon-Taubadel S (1998) Estimating asymmetric price transmission with the error correction representation: An application to the German pork market. European Review of Agricultural Economics 25: 1-18.
Weldegebriel HT (2004) Imperfect Price Transmission: Is Market Power Really to Blame? Journal of Agricultural Economics 55: 101-114.

Appendix 10.1: The solution of Gardner's model

The six initial equations of Gardner's (1975) model are:

$x = f(a, b)$	(supply of the consumption product x, a production function)	(4)
$x = g(P_x)$	(demand for the consumption product x)	(6)
$a = h(P_a)$	(supply of the raw agricultural product a)	(7)
$\frac{\partial(f(a,b))}{\partial a}P_x = P_a$	(demand for the raw agricultural product a)	(8)
$b = k(P_b)$	(supply of the non-agricultural input b)	(9)
$\frac{\partial(f(a,b))}{\partial b}P_x = P_b$	(demand for the non-agricultural input b)	(10)

These equations are put into *equilibrium displacement* form by totally differentiating them and converting all unknowns into proportional changes. For equation (4), this leads to the following steps, where a variable with a dot (e.g. $\dot{x}$) represents the proportional change of this variable ($\dot{x} = {dx}/{x}$):

$dx = \frac{\partial(f(a,b))}{\partial a}da + \frac{\partial(f(a,b))}{\partial b}db$	(totally differentiate equation 4)
$\frac{dx}{x} = \frac{\partial(f(a,b))}{\partial a}\frac{a}{x}\frac{da}{a} + \frac{\partial(f(a,b))}{\partial b}\frac{b}{x}\frac{db}{b}$	(divide by x, multiply RHS terms by $\frac{a}{a}$ and $\frac{b}{b}$, respectively)
$\frac{dx}{x} = \frac{P_a}{P_x}\frac{a}{x}\frac{da}{a} + \frac{P_b}{P_x}\frac{b}{x}\frac{db}{b}$	(replace $\frac{\partial(f(a,b))}{\partial i}$ using equations 8 and 10)
$\frac{dx}{x} = S_a\frac{da}{a} + S_b\frac{db}{b}$	($S_i = \frac{iP_i}{xP_x}$, the cost share of production factor i)

$\dot{x} = S_a\dot{a} + S_b\dot{b}$ $\quad\quad$ $\frac{dx}{x} = \dot{x};\ \frac{da}{xa} = \dot{a};\ \frac{db}{b} = \dot{b}$ (4′)

Equations (6), (7) and (9) all have the same form and are linearised as follows:

$m = l(P_m)$ $\quad\quad$ where $m = \{x, a, b\}$ and $l = \{g, h, k\}$, respectively.

$dm = \frac{\partial(l(P_m))}{\partial P_m} dP_m$ $\quad\quad$ (totally differentiate)

$\frac{dm}{m} = \frac{\partial(l(P_m))}{\partial P_m}\frac{P_m}{m}\frac{dP_m}{P_m}$ $\quad\quad$ (divide by m, multiply RHS by $\frac{P_m}{P_m}$)

$\dot{m} = \epsilon_{m,P_m}\dot{P_m}$ $\quad\quad$ ($\epsilon_{m,P_m} = \frac{\partial(l(P_m))}{\partial P_m}\frac{P_m}{m}$, the own-price elasticity of demand for $m = x$, or supply for $m = a$ or b).

These derivations therefore lead to:

$\dot{x} = \eta_{x,P_x}\dot{P_x}$ $\quad\quad$ (η_{x,P_x} is the own-price elasticity of demand for x) (6′)

$\dot{a} = \varepsilon_{a,P_a}\dot{P_a}$ $\quad\quad$ (ε_{a,P_a} is the own-price elasticity of supply of a) (7′)

$\dot{b} = \varepsilon_{b,P_b}\dot{P_b}$ $\quad\quad$ (ε_{b,P_b} is the own-price elasticity of the supply of b) (9′)

The linearisation of equations (8) and (10) is somewhat more complicated, as it requires derivatives of the marginal products $\frac{\partial(f(a,b))}{\partial a}$ and $\frac{\partial(f(a,b))}{\partial b}$ (i.e. second derivatives of the production function $x = f(a, b)$). The following notation simplifies the presentation: $\frac{\partial(f(a,b))}{\partial a} = f_a$, and $\frac{\partial(f(a,b))}{\partial b} = f_b$. Equation (8) is transformed as follows:

$P_a = f_a P_x$

$dP_a = \frac{\partial P_a}{\partial P_x} dP_x + \frac{\partial P_a}{\partial f_a} df_a$ $\quad\quad$ (totally differentiate)

$dP_a = f_a dP_x + P_x df_a$ $\quad (\frac{\partial P_a}{\partial P_x} = f_a$, and $\frac{\partial P_a}{\partial f_a} = P_x)$

$dP_a = f_a dP_x + P_x(\frac{\partial f_a}{\partial a} da + \frac{\partial f_a}{\partial b} db)$ $\quad$ (expand df_a)

$\frac{dP_a}{P_a} = f_a \frac{dP_x}{P_a} + \frac{P_x}{P_a}(f_{aa} da + f_{ab} db)$ $\quad$ (divide by P_a , $\frac{\partial f_a}{\partial a} = f_{aa}$, $\frac{\partial f_a}{\partial b} = f_{ab}$)

$\frac{dP_a}{P_a} = \frac{P_a}{P_x}\frac{dP_x}{P_a} + \frac{P_x}{P_a}(f_{aa} da + f_{ab} db)$ $\quad$ ($f_a = \frac{P_a}{P_x}$ from equation 8)

We now use the following definitions of the elasticity of factor substitution according to Allen (1938, p. 343): $\sigma = -\frac{b}{a}\frac{f_a f_b}{x f_{aa}}$ and $\sigma = \frac{f_a f_b}{x f_{ab}}$, or equivalently $f_{aa} = -\frac{b}{a}\frac{f_a f_b}{\sigma x}$ and $f_{ab} = \frac{f_a f_b}{\sigma x}$.

$$\dot{P}_a = \frac{P_a}{P_a}\frac{dP_x}{P_x} + \frac{P_x}{P_a}(-\frac{b}{a}\frac{f_a f_b}{\sigma x} da + \frac{f_a f_b}{\sigma x} db)$$

$\dot{P}_a = \dot{P}_x - \frac{P_x}{P_a}\frac{b}{a}\frac{P_a P_b}{P_x P_x}\frac{1}{\sigma x} da + \frac{P_x}{P_a}\frac{P_a P_b}{P_x P_x}\frac{1}{\sigma x} db$ $\quad$ ($f_a = \frac{P_a}{P_x}$ and $f_b = \frac{P_b}{P_x}$ from equations 8 and 10)

$\dot{P}_a = \dot{P}_x - \frac{P_x}{P_a}\frac{b}{a}\frac{P_a P_b}{P_x P_x}\frac{1}{\sigma x} da + \frac{P_x}{P_a}\frac{P_a P_b}{P_x P_x}\frac{1}{\sigma x}\frac{b}{b} db$ $\quad$ (multiply the last term on the RHS by $\frac{b}{b}$)

$\dot{P}_a = \dot{P}_x - \frac{bP_b}{xP_x}\frac{1}{\sigma}\frac{da}{a} + \frac{bP_b}{xP_x}\frac{1}{\sigma}\frac{db}{b}$ $\quad$ (simplify)

$\dot{P}_a = \dot{P}_x - \frac{S_b}{\sigma}\dot{a} + \frac{S_b}{\sigma}\dot{b}$ $\quad (\frac{bP_b}{xP_x} = S_b)$ $\quad$ (8′)

Analogously, equation (10) can be transformed into

$\dot{P}_b = \dot{P}_x + \frac{S_a}{\sigma}\dot{a} - \frac{S_a}{\sigma}\dot{b}$ $\quad$ (10′)

The model's six equations in *equilibrium displacement* form are thus summarised:

$$\dot{x} = S_a\dot{a} + S_b\dot{b} \tag{4'}$$

$$\dot{x} = \eta_{x,P_x}\dot{P}_x \tag{6'}$$

$$\dot{a} = \varepsilon_{a,P_a}\dot{P}_a \tag{7'}$$

$$\dot{P}_a = \dot{P}_x - \frac{S_b}{\sigma}\dot{a} + \frac{S_b}{\sigma}\dot{b} \tag{8'}$$

$$\dot{b} = \varepsilon_{b,P_b}\dot{P}_b \tag{9'}$$

$$\dot{P}_b = \dot{P}_x + \frac{S_a}{\sigma}\dot{a} - \frac{S_a}{\sigma}\dot{b} \tag{10'}$$

In matrix form this system of six equations and six unknowns is:

$$\begin{bmatrix} 1 & 0 & -S_a & 0 & -S_b & 0 \\ 1 & -\eta_{x,P_x} & 0 & 0 & 0 & 0 \\ 0 & 0 & 1 & -\varepsilon_{a,P_a} & 0 & 0 \\ 0 & -1 & S_b/\sigma & 1 & -S_b/\sigma & 0 \\ 0 & 0 & 0 & 0 & 1 & -\varepsilon_{b,P_b} \\ 0 & -1 & -S_a/\sigma & 0 & S_a/\sigma & 1 \end{bmatrix} * \begin{bmatrix} \dot{x} \\ \dot{P}_x \\ \dot{a} \\ \dot{P}_a \\ \dot{b} \\ \dot{P}_b \end{bmatrix} = \begin{bmatrix} 0 \\ 0 \\ 0 \\ 0 \\ 0 \\ 0 \end{bmatrix}$$

Exercises

1. Determinants of the marketing margin.
   a) Discuss the impact of future technological developments (e.g. digitalisation) and new regulations (e.g. labelling requirements for food) on the farm share in consumer expenditure on food.
   b) The published data on the farm share in consumer expenditure on food in Germany do not distinguish between raw products from conventional and organic agriculture. For which type of agriculture do you expect that the farm share of consumer expenditure will be higher? Justify your answer.

2. The following error correction model was estimated using weekly producer prices for slaughter pigs (P^{prod}) and wholesale prices for pork cuts in northern Germany (P^{whole}) in the period January 1990 and February 1993 (standard errors in parentheses):

$$\underset{}{\Delta lnP_t^{whole}} = \underset{(0.045)}{-0.100}\left(lnP_{t-1}^{whole} - \underset{(0.047)}{0.746} - \underset{(0.043)}{0.676}lnP_{t-1}^{prod}\right) + \underset{(0.093)}{0.006}\Delta lnP_{t-1}^{whole} + \underset{(0.058)}{0.249}\Delta lnP_{t-1}^{prod}$$

$$\Delta lnP_t^{prod} = \underset{(0.086)}{0.016}\left(lnP_{t-1}^{whole} - \underset{(0.047)}{0.746} - \underset{(0.043)}{0.676}lnP_{t-1}^{prod}\right) - \underset{(0.172)}{0.166}\Delta lnP_{t-1}^{whole} + \underset{(0.110)}{0.327}\Delta lnP_{t-1}^{prod}$$

a) What is the estimated elasticity of transmission between producer and wholesale prices?
b) According to the estimates, which of the two prices responds significantly to deviations from the long-run equilibrium between producer and wholesale prices?
c) Assume that the prices are initially in equilibrium and that the producer price is 2.00 euro/kg. An outbreak of African swine fever in Poland leads to a 0.25 euro/kg increase in producer prices in Germany. Describe the adjustment paths of the two prices. Roughly how many weeks will it take for the two prices to return to equilibrium?

3. Political intervention.
   a) On 4 June 2009, the Parliament of Ukraine passed Law No. 1447-VI "On amendments to certain laws of Ukraine respecting the improvement of state regulation of the agricultural market". One clause of the law stipulates that the market margin in the food chain shall not exceed 20%. Do you think that this clause can be implemented, and what effects might it have on the agri-food sector in Ukraine?
   b) Nivievskyi and von Cramon-Taubadel (2011) report that local administrations in Belarus force farms that produce milk in their respective regions to deliver all their milk to specific local dairies, even if other dairies in neighbouring regions offer higher prices for the milk. What effects would you expect from this regulation, for the milk farms but also for the development of the dairy sector as a whole?

CHAPTER ELEVEN

PRICE FORMATION IN FOOD RETAILING

JENS-PETER LOY

11.1. Introduction and learning objectives

Most agricultural commodity markets exhibit an atomistic structure and are characterised by perfect competition. Most commodities are highly homogeneous and traded all over the world. Trading is often standardised, for example on futures markets. However, food retailing, which we all experience almost daily, is very different. The food retail market is highly concentrated in many countries. The top five food retailers account for roughly 75% of the food spending by the 40 million households in Germany. In addition, food prices often display levels of dispersion over time, between products, and between stores, that exceed the costs of physical arbitrage. Finally, food products are highly differentiated. Consumers in Germany can, for example, choose between more than 2000 different yoghurt products. While many models of agricultural markets focus on single products, the food retail market clearly is a multiproduct business with manifold substitutional and complementary relationships between products. This all leads to a highly complex system of food retail pricing, many aspects of which are not fully understood. The emergence of online food retailing is adding another dimension to the system, as retailers increasingly use big data and artificial intelligence algorithms to better adjust products and prices to consumers' behaviour.

Against this background, we present some of the basic theories that have been developed to explain important characteristics of food retail pricing. In this chapter we will:

- present an overview of the structures and organisation of food retailing,

- explain the price phenomena and strategies prevalent in food retailing,
- outline the main economic models of food retail pricing, and
- summarise the main findings of several empirical case studies of food retail pricing.

In the following section (11.2), we define specific terms that are used throughout the chapter. Section 11.3 provides an overview of the food retail sector in Germany, and in section 11.4 we present various economic models and concepts that are applied to study food retail pricing. We summarise and discuss various empirical case studies in section 11.5 and close the chapter with an outlook for future research on food retail pricing in section 11.6.

11.2. Definition of terms[1]

In this section, we briefly define and discuss several terms that are used in this chapter. Some of these terms will be familiar to many readers, while others might not be fully comprehensible without additional context. Hence, the reader might skip this section for the time being and return to it later for reference, if and as required.

Brand: a brand is a name, term, design, symbol or any other feature that identifies one seller's good or service as distinct from those of other sellers.

Brand loyalty: brand loyalty is "a deeply held commitment to rebuy or re-patronise a preferred product/service consistently in the future, thereby causing repetitive same-brand or same brand-set purchasing, despite situational influences and marketing efforts having the potential to cause switching behaviour" (Oliver 1999, p. 34). As there is no consensus on the definition of brand loyalty, we present two additional definitions in section 11.4.

Bundling: bundling is when companies package several of their products or services together as a single combined unit, often for a lower total price than they would charge customers to buy each item separately. The products and services are usually related, but they can also consist of dissimilar items which appeal to one group of customers. ***Pure bundling*** occurs if only the

[1] Some of these definitions are based on https://dictionary.cambridge.org/.

packaged good is available; if both the packaged good and the individual goods are on sale, we refer to ***mixed bundling***.

Buying-in price: the price at which a firm can buy a good or input (purchasing or cost price).

Cartel: a cartel is a group of similar independent companies who join together to control prices, production, or other marketing activities in order to limit competition, to the advantage of the group.

Cherry picking: cherry picking refers to a consumer purchasing only products with the best price at a store, for example, only those products that are on sale at a reduced price. An extreme cherry picker is a customer who generates negative gross profits for a store on a sustained basis.

Concentration ratio (CR): the sum of the market share percentages held by the largest firms (a specified number, taken together) in an industry. The CR5, for example, measures the cumulative market share of the five largest firms in a market.

Fast-moving consumer goods (FMCG): FMCG, also known as consumer-packaged goods, are products that are sold and consumed quickly at relatively low cost with a high inventory turnover. Examples include packaged foods, beverages, toiletries, candy, cosmetics, etc.

Lerner Index: a measure of market power, the Lerner Index is the difference between the (monopoly) price and the marginal cost, divided by the (monopoly) price.

Market power: market power is the ability of a firm to profitably raise the market price of a good or service over its marginal cost. In retailing, the definition is more general: market power is the ability of a firm to influence the terms of a contract with a buyer or seller in its favour.

Mark-up: an increase in price, usually to provide a profit to the person selling. The mark-up is often measured as a percentage.

Menu costs: the costs to firms of changing prices. These costs include retraining sales staff, reprinting price lists, relabelling products and informing customers. Menu costs also include the costs of making price decisions, developing algorithms etc. High menu costs discourage firms from changing prices frequently.

Mixed strategy: in a mixed pricing strategy, a firm (randomly) sets different prices, often based on a probability distribution, in order to avoid being predictable.

Monopoly rent: the difference between the monopoly price and the marginal costs.

National brand (manufacturer brand): a brand owned and controlled by a manufacturer.

Price discrimination: price discrimination takes place when the mark-up that is charged by a firm for a product differs for different buyers, for different volumes or qualities, for different groups of buyers, or for different bundles of products, etc.

Price dispersion: variation among sellers in the price of a homogeneous good or service. Price dispersion can be interpreted as a measure of trading frictions or viewed as violation of the law of one price.

Private label (retailer brand): a brand owned and controlled by a retailer.

Promotion: activities to advertise something. Sales promotion is a set of marketing technologies aimed to stimulate the demand for a particular product and increase brand awareness.

Price promotion (sale's price): "A sale is a temporary (significant) reduction in the price of an item that is unrelated to cost changes" (Hosken and Reiffen 2001).

Reaction function: a reaction function, also called best-reply function, is the locus of optimal, i.e. profit-maximising actions that a firm may undertake in response to any given action by a rival firm. The reaction function of firm 1, for example, describes the relationship between the quantity (price) of firm 1 and the (given) quantity (price) of firm 2.

Residual demand (curve): the demand curve facing a particular firm is called the residual demand curve. The residual demand is the market demand that is not met by other firms in the industry at a given price. Hence, it is the market demand minus the supply of other firms.

Store format: retail stores can be categorised into different retail formats with respect to size, layout, product assortment, and pricing policy. The categories commonly considered in Germany are listed in Table 11.1.

Table 11.1: Food retail store formats in Germany

Store format	Size in square meters	Number of stock keeping units (SKU)	Pricing strategy*	Share of private labels
Hard discounter	<1000	1500-4000	EDLP	high
Soft discounter	<1000	2000-5000	EDLP/HiLo	medium
Small supermarket	100-399	1000-7000	HiLo	low
Large supermarket	400-999	7000-12000	HiLo	low
Small consumer market	1000-2499	12000-25000	EDLP/HiLo	medium
Large consumer market	>2500	25000-200000	EDLP/HiLo	medium

* *EDLP = everyday low price, HiLo = High-Low pricing. Source: Based on Nielsen categories (Nielsen 2018a).*

Stock keeping unit (SKU): a stock keeping unit is a distinct item for sale such as a product or service and all of the attributes associated with this item that distinguish it from other items, such as package size and packaging.

11.3. Food retailing in Germany

11.3.1. History

Self-service in grocery shopping was first introduced early in the 20th century and marked a fundamental change in food retailing. In Germany, the first self-service grocery store started in 1938 in Osnabrück, and the first supermarkets opened in the 1950s. Before, the very first supermarkets had been introduced in the 1930s in the USA. They became popular around the world and are still seen as the gold standard today. Desai et al. (2013:3) call this initial period "retail 1.0". About fifty years later, Carrefour and Walmart developed the concept of food stores which offer everything in one place and promoted the idea of one-stop-shopping, referred to as "retail 2.0". At roughly the same time, discounters began to operate in Europe. Discount outlets typically have simple interior designs and product placement. They are further defined by narrow product assortments and **everyday low-price (ELDP) strategies**. Retailers also began to introduce **private labels** to strengthen their bargaining power vis-à-vis manufacturers, as well as to advertise their respective retail chains. At first, these brands were low-price and low-quality, as befits the discount idea. Later, private labels began to imitate higher quality manufacturer brands and cover a larger assortment of products. What we see today is the fourth generation of private labels in food retailing.[2] Aided by the adoption of these innovations, retail chains quickly grew in size, which improved their bargaining power vis-à-vis food processors.

In 1990, Jeff Bezos founded Amazon and started a new era of online retailing, thus initiating the rise of e-commerce or "retail 3.0" (Desai et al. 2013:5). From an online bookstore, Amazon quickly expanded to offer music, electronic equipment and most other fast-moving consumer goods. In 2017, Amazon offered 230 million items, a number that had doubled in only three years since 2014 and that far exceeds the number of **stock keeping units (SKU)** of even the largest consumer markets (see Table 11.1).

Today we are on the brink of "retail 4.0" which is characterised by multichannel food retailing. Online retailers such as Amazon are establishing brick-and-mortar outlets, and many traditional brick-and-mortar retailers are operating online food retailing formats. Stores routinely experiment with alternative modes of distribution, such as delivery stations and home delivery. The future of retail 4.0 is expected to bring even more virtual stores, mobile payment, self-checkout, social media marketing, and dynamic pricing strategies (Desai et al. 2013).

The World Wide Web has changed consumers' communication and information search behaviour. Over 90% of the German population has access to and uses the internet. The share of users only drops sharply (to 50%) for individuals aged 70 and above. The internet is mainly used for information searches and private e-mails (60-70%). 30% of the population uses online shopping and watches movies via streaming services (AGOF 2020). The role of information has fundamentally changed: while information was once scarce and costly to obtain, today it is abundantly available in real time, and the emphasis has shifted from finding information

[2] The first generation of private labels are low-price, no-name brands, as found with many discounters. Second generation private labels are quasi-brands for large packs of single products. In the third generation, private labels are used as corporate brands for groups of products, also with a view to promoting the specific retail chain. The fourth generation of private labels mimics manufacturer brands in order to compete directly with them and further improve the quality image of the retail chain. Private labels account for about 40% of the total turnover in fast moving consumer goods in Germany.

to selecting and processing relevant information (Verbeke 2005, p. 347ff). As Shapiro and Varian (1998, p. 6) put it, "nowadays the problem is not information access but information overload".

Furthermore, information is no longer exclusively in the hands of traditional providers such as manufacturers, news agencies, and service providers. Information is a new currency that is produced, consumed, and traded at high speed (Shapiro and Varian 1998, p. 5). Consumers can also become part of the information chain by posting personal ratings on electronic marketplaces and rating platforms. As so-called influencers, some consumers participate actively in the creation and dissemination of information, using social media platforms to rate and promote goods, services and ideas (Labrecque et al. 2013).

11.3.2. Market structure and firm organisation

Food products are sold in a variety of store formats. According to Nielsen, we can distinguish between supermarkets, consumer markets, and discounters (Table 11.1). In terms of sales area, supermarkets range from 100 to 999 m^2 and mainly sell food products. Discounters have a narrow product assortment and mostly follow an EDLP strategy. Consumer markets are larger than supermarkets, with sales areas ranging from 1000 to more than 5000 m^2, and selling a broad range of food and non-food products.

Food products are also sold in drugstores, gas stations, off-licence stores, kiosks, cash-and-carry markets, specialised food stores (bakeries, butchers, fish shops, etc.) and weekly markets. In the following discussion we focus on supermarkets, consumer markets, and discounters, although drugstores are included in some statistics. In Germany, the number of stores with a sales area greater than 100 m^2 declined from 37,109 in 2014 to 34,947 in 2018. Their turnover increased from € 167 billion in 2013 to € 188 billion in 2017 (Nielsen 2018b). Table 11.2 shows turnover and market share figures for the different store formats in 2017. Consumer markets and discounters account for 84% of the total turnover of food stores larger than 100 m^2.

Table 11.2: Turnover in German food retailing in 2017

Store format	Turnover in million Euro	Share of total turnover in %
Large consumer market	45213	24.1
Small consumer market	40665	21.7
Discounter	70080	37.4
Large supermarket	13622	7.3
Small supermarket	1815	1.0
Drugstore	16108	8.6
Total	187503	100

Source: Nielsen 2018a, p. 111.

As mentioned above, the five biggest food retail chains in Germany dominate the market with a combined market share of about 74% for food products. Table 11.3 shows that if non-food sale by the food retailers is also considered, the picture does not change substantially. Edeka is the leading food retail chain in Germany with a market share of 25.7% and 376,000 employees. Netto, another chain of discounters and supermarkets, belongs to Edeka. The first Edeka cooperative was founded in 1898 in Berlin. Edeka still is a cooperative of about 4000 mostly independent merchants who run the individual stores. These stores are supplied by seven regional trading companies that trade food products and produce some of their own. The regional trading companies also consult the Edeka food stores and organise marketing, advertising, and provide financial services through a bank.

The Rewe Group started in 1927 as a cooperative and transformed into a non-listed stock company in 1972. About 10,000 food stores and 330,000 employees are part of the Rewe Group in Germany today. Another 5000 food stores in other countries (such as the Billa chain in Austria) belong to the Rewe Group, as well as the German discounter Penny, two DIY (do it yourself) superstore chains, and several travel agencies.

Aldi and the Schwarz group are the two top-ranked private companies in Germany. Aldi actually consists of two separate regional companies, namely Aldi North and Aldi South, that are commonly taken together as Aldi and count a total of 62,000 employees. The Schwarz group has 320,000 employees.

Finally, the Metro group is a joint-stock company with two major private shareholders accounting for roughly 64 % of the shares. The Real consumer markets and the Metro cash-and-carry markets belong to the Metro group.

Table 11.3: Turnover in German food retailing by retail chain in 2017

Retail chain	Total turnover in million Euro	Share of total turnover in %	Food turnover in million Euro	Share of food turnover in %
Edeka	56497	23.3	51650	25.7
Rewe Group	42599	17.6	31837	15.9
Schwarz Group	38610	15.9	31359	15.6
Aldi	29665	12.3	24325	12.1
Metro	13623	5.6	9882	4.9
Total	242129	74.8	200612	74.3

Source: Nielsen 2018b.

11.3.3. Food retail prices

Compared with farm, wholesale, or futures prices, food retail prices exhibit some unique characteristics. Food retail prices in Germany are roughly 6% above the EU average, but relative to above-average incomes in Germany food prices are low. One of the reasons for low relative food prices is that German consumers are particularly price sensitive. For 75% of German consumers the price-quality relationship is the most important measure of a food retailer's performance, followed by quality, product range and convenient location. Price promotions are very important to consumers in choosing products, brands, and stores. The corresponding price strategy based on price promotions or sales is called a **High-Low or HiLo strategy**.

Figure 11.1 shows typical price charts for different items of the same good in different stores over time. It reveals strong price dispersion over time, across stores and brands. We see frequent temporary price reductions (sales) in some cases, and long periods of rigid prices in others. On average, private labels exhibit lower prices and fewer price promotions. Berck et al. (2008) show that it is not profit-maximising for private labels priced close to their marginal costs to offer promotional sales. National brands exhibit strong variation in average prices; some are even priced as low as comparable private labels. Unlike national brands, private labels show significant co-movement (synchronisation) of prices. Private labels often represent the lowest price possible, which is almost the same across stores. Some retailers even explicitly advertise their private label as offering the lowest price on the market.

Figure 11.1: Four examples of weekly retail prices for butter in Germany

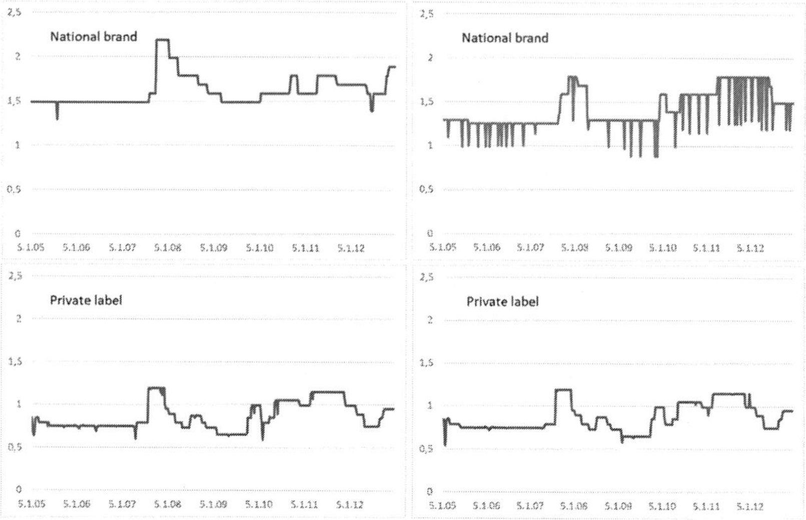

Note: Prices in € per 250g.
Source: Own based on IRI Symphony (2014).

Price promotions

Price promotions are used for various reasons. They might introduce a new product or advertise a product to the consumer. They can be used to clear stocks or to lure customers into a store. In addition, promotions can motivate consumers to switch brands and products. Figure 11.2 summarises the potential effects of promotions.

Promotional sales are a major feature in the marketing mix of many food retailers (Simon 1992, p. 51), accounting for between 20% and 50% of the variation in food retail prices (Hosken and Reiffen 2004, p. 137; Berck et al. 2008, p. 1261). Many models have been proposed to explain sales in an equilibrium price-setting framework, based on different assumptions about retailer motives and consumer behaviour. The **loss-leader** model proposed by Lal and Matutes (1994) assumes advertisement and menu costs. According to this model, retailers only advertise a selection of products. Because consumers have travel costs, they prefer one-stop shopping. Consumers choose a particular store based on the advertised price promotions. Since consumers rationally expect high prices for non-advertised products, stores set some promotional prices even below cost prices (loss leaders) to attract consumers who then also buy the higher-priced products. An alternative model is Blattberg et al.'s (1981) model of consumer storage. A price promotion gives consumers the incentive to stock up on a storable product, and thus allows the retailer to save on storage costs. In another model, Blattberg and Neslin (1990) show that promotional sales can be the outcome of a prisoner's dilemma. We return to this issue and explain three other models of promotional pricing in more detail in section 11.4.

Figure 11.2: The possible effects of price promotions

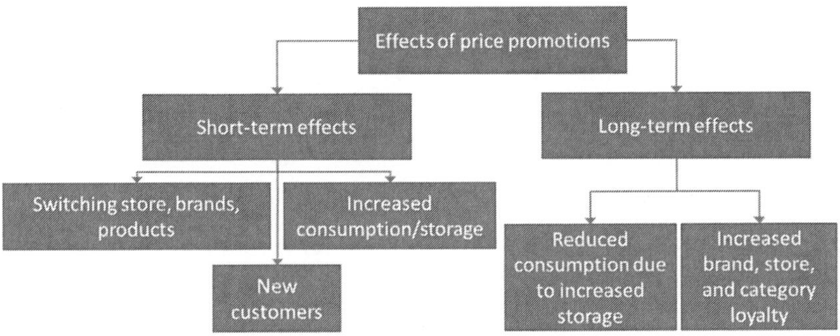

Source: Own depiction based on Gedenk (2002, p. 104).

Rigid prices

Menu costs are often used to explain why firms sometimes maintain retail prices at constant nominal levels over several and sometimes lengthy periods of time (see Figure 11.1). Menu costs include all costs related to the adjustment of prices. Food retailers, for instance, often announce their prices by printing price lists, through advertisements, and through in-store labels. Adjusting prices therefore requires printing new lists, placing new advertisements, and changing in-store labels, all of which incurs menu costs. A retailer will only adjust prices if the change in economic conditions, and hence the potential losses from not adjusting prices, exceed these menu costs.[3] Dutta et al. (1999) provide evidence that menu costs can be high enough to impede price changes in supermarket and drugstore chains. They estimate that the ratio of menu costs to revenues is 0.70% for supermarket chains, and 0.74% for drugstore chains. Under these conditions, marginal

[3] Menus costs are also discussed with respect to asymmetric price transmission in Chapter 10.

changes in the economic environment do not automatically lead to product price changes.

Odd prices and 9-endings

Odd pricing is a strategy whereby a retail price is set just below a round number, for example 9.99 or 8.95. Especially 9-endings are common in food retailing, accounting for 70% to 80% of all prices (Levy et al. 2011; Loy and Weiss 2002). **9-endings** are so-called psychological pricing points that affect consumers' price perceptions. Snir et al. (2017) discuss two underlying mechanisms, the level effect and the image effect. The former occurs when consumers, due to bounded rationality, round prices down or process prices from left to right and ignore the rightmost digit (Stiving and Winer 1997; Thomas and Morwitz 2005). The image effect draws consumers' attention and signals low prices even when alternative products are priced lower (Anderson and Simester 2003). Because of these psychological effects, prices with 9-endings are more rigid (Anderson et al. 2015; McShane et al. 2015).

Price staggering and synchronisation

Rigid prices for a particular firm and product, whatever their underlying cause, do not necessarily imply price rigidity at the aggregate (industry or sectoral) level. At the aggregate level, price rigidity depends on the relative timing of price changes by individual firms. Whether all firms review prices simultaneously (synchronisation) or different firms adjust their prices at different times (staggering) has important macroeconomic consequences. If all firms change their prices simultaneously with a lag of one period following an exogenous shock, the aggregate price level will have adjusted fully to the new equilibrium level by the end of this period and the shock will have no persistent real consequences. If, however, price-setting is staggered, the effect of a nominal shock will be prolonged. In two seminal papers, Taylor (1979, 1980) shows that price staggering can lead to macroeconomic price rigidity. Loy and Weiss (2004) find that price setting is characterised by almost perfect staggering across and within stores in German food retailing.

11.3.4. Regulations

Free competition is a key element of functioning market economies. It stimulates economic performance and offers consumers a broad choice of high-quality products and services at competitive prices. European Union

(EU) competition policy ensures that competition is not distorted in the internal market by ensuring that similar rules apply to all companies operating in the EU. Title VII, chapter 1 of the Treaty on the Functioning of the European Union establishes the legal basis for Community rules on competition. In Germany, the Antitrust Commission is tasked with enforcing the EU competition law.[4]

The laws against unfair competition and against restraints of competition constitute the basis for prosecuting certain business practices. Many forms of aggressive business practices, such as direct threats against competitors or business associates, are forbidden. Comparative advertising is not allowed. Some forms of (price) discrimination, in particular discrimination with respect to religion, ethnicity, or gender, are prohibited. In addition, dominant firms are not allowed to ask for material benefits from their business associates without an objective reason. Permanently setting prices below cost prices is also forbidden. Before 1974, many manufacturers in Germany set fixed resale prices to control the retail prices of their brands. Since 1974 this practice is prohibited, and manufacturers may only make non-binding price recommendations.

11.3.5. Different types of consumers

Consumer expenditures for food, beverages, and **food away from home (FAFH)** in Germany amounted to € 274 billion in 2018, of which € 81 billion was spent on FAFH in restaurants, fast-food restaurant, and canteens etc. The food processing industry has a turnover of € 180 billion and the farm production value is at € 59 billion. Food expenditures altogether account for 11% of total consumer expenditures in Germany.[5] In Europe, this share ranges from 8% in the UK to 29% in Romania.

Consumers are not homogeneous. Retailers try to take advantage of this variety by offering different products, brands, promotions, and package sizes etc. Marketing activities aimed at individuals have become increasingly prevalent with the advent of internet shopping. Digital marketplaces allow firms to collect and process information about individuals and to process it in real time. This enables them to generate

---

[4] Section 8 of Chapter 8 ("Pricing under imperfect competition") discusses EU competition policy in detail.

[5] At the beginning of the 20th century, the share of food expenditures (including tobacco and alcohol) was about 60%. By 1950 it had dropped to 44% and in 1975 it was 23% (Federal Statistical Office 2020).

individual advertisements, offers, and deals, and thus exploit differences between consumers systematically.

Traditional strategies in food marketing are based on a more general segmentation of consumers. Nielsen, for example, classifies consumers into the following groups: young singles, mid-age singles, old singles, young couples without children, mid-age couples without children, full nest 1, 2 and 3 (households with children at different ages; for example, full nest 1 has one child under 6 years of age), and empty nest with no children. Single households buy less often and spend less money on fast-moving consumer goods. Young singles spend less than elderly singles. The most frequent buyers are mid-age couples whose children no longer live in the household, and old singles (Nielsen 2018b). "By understanding how consumers view themselves, as well as what they prioritise as important, companies can create more tailored strategies, from product development and innovation through to sales and marketing" (Euromonitor International 2020). According to Euromonitor International, German consumers can be classified into five main categories (Figure 11.3): (1) undaunted strivers (10%), (2) empowered activists (21%), (3) cautious planners (26%), (4) secure traditionalists (18%), and (5) inspired adventurers (25%).

Figure 11.3: Future consumer types in Germany

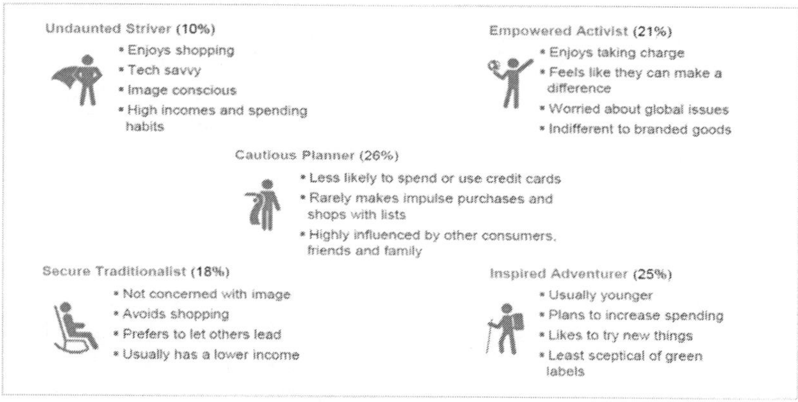

Source: Euromonitor International 2020.

11.3.6. Data sources

Various organisations collect information on consumer behaviour and food retailing. In the following we present four sources of such information in

Germany. These are: consumer panel data provided by the Gesellschaft für Konsumforschung (GfK); retail scanner data from the Information Resources Incorporation Symphony Group (IRI); consumer expenditure data from the Einkommens- und Verbrauchsstichprobe (EVS, translation: Income and Consumption Panel) survey; and price data gathered by scraping websites.

Consumer panel data

The GfK runs household and individual consumer panels to collect reports on food and fast-moving consumer good purchases. These self-reports include prices, volumes, promotion indicators, points of purchase, and dates of purchase, as well as information on the reporting person or household. Depending on the product, panellists report their own purchases or the purchases of the household, generally aggregated on a weekly basis. The GfK is a German marketing research and consulting company, founded in 1934 as a non-profit organisation. It now operates worldwide and is ranked sixth among the top market research companies with an annual revenue of $US 1,626 million in 2018.[6]

The GfK launched its first household panel in 1957. Today the household panel includes over 30,000 of the 39 million households in Germany. Since about 20% of the panellists leave every year, the GfK has to promote panel participation continuously to find replacements. The panel is organised to be representative of the population in dimensions such as regional origin, age, income, employment and household size. Participation is voluntary and panellists receive no financial benefits. Panellists scan their grocery shopping at home, using a scanner device provided by the GfK. Panellists enter the price of every item, point of purchase and whether a product was on (price) promotion. Data are transferred online to the GfK, where they are validated before they are added to the database. For scanning the GfK uses the **EAN (European Article Number)** code. EAN codes need to be updated for new or modified products, which can make it difficult to analyse longer time periods. While the GfK data cover household fast-moving consumer goods purchases, they do not capture purchases by big consumers, the catering trade, tourists, or households' external food purchases. As consumers do not purchase every product in every week at every store, no

---

[6] Another important supplier of consumer panel data in Germany is The Nielsen Company, which also operates worldwide with a head office in the USA (https://www.nielsen.com/de/). The Nielsen Group is ranked first with a revenue of over $US 6,500 million (ESOMAR Global Market Research Report 2019).

continuous time series of prices at retail stores can be constructed from this GfK data set.

Retail panel data

Another source of information is retail scan data. All retailers use electronic check-outs to record the volume and price data of every purchase. Some retailers sell these data to market research companies or make them available to researchers. One of the market research companies working in this field is IRI, located in Düsseldorf. IRI operates worldwide and is the seventh-ranked market research company. It purchases retail scan data, analyses it for customers such as brand manufacturers, and resells it. Retail scan data consists of weekly sale volumes and prices for every retail outlet and every product sold by retailers in the sample. Price promotions are not reported by the retailer. IRI adds a promotion indicator variable for each product item by applying a simple algorithm. If a price is reduced by more than 5% against the regular price and if the reduced price is effective for no more than 4 weeks, then it is considered a promotional price. Hence, any price that is maintained for more than 4 consecutive weeks is considered a regular price.

A major disadvantage of retail scan data is self-selection by retailers; for example, the chains Aldi and Lidl do not sell their scanned data. In addition, specialised food stores such as bakeries or butchers and online food stores are not covered by the sample. However, an advantage of retail scan data is that, for individual products, complete time series of prices can be retrieved for each retail outlet in the sample that carries the product.

Income and Consumption Panel

The German EVS (income and consumption panel) provides official statistics on the living conditions of private households. Among other variables, the consumption expenditures of a representative set of private households are recorded. The data are used to determine consumer price indices, to calculate the income distribution in Germany, to define poverty lines, and to feed into the national accounts. The survey is voluntary and is conducted every five years. The sample is selected according to population parameters and consists of about 60,000 households. All participants report their income and expenditures for three consecutive months. To capture seasonal fluctuations, the total sample is divided into four equal parts that report in consecutive quarters. A detailed monthly record is compiled for foods; however, no brands or other product-specific information is gathered, and product groups are highly aggregated. The data are available to researchers for a small fee, but the low frequency of data collection and lack of brand information are major disadvantages.

Web scraping

Web scraping is also called web harvesting or web data extraction. Web scraping software can be employed to access the World Wide Web using the Hypertext Transfer Protocol, or through a web browser. Web scraping can be done manually or by automated processes using a bot or web crawler. Specific data are gathered and copied from web sites, usually into a local database or spreadsheet. The programming languages Python and R are typically used to write web scraping code. Regular prices, price promotions, product information, product numbers etc. can be extracted *ad infinitum*. The advantages of these data are their high frequency and the fact that information on promotions is provided by the retailer and does not have to be constructed by the market research company or the researcher (see below). A disadvantage is that no information on regular or promotional sales' volumes is available.

Unless it is clearly forbidden by the online retailers or they take countermeasures, web scraping is possible for every public web site. However, some legal aspects of web scraping are unclear. As long as only publicly available information is scraped and no general terms and conditions of business are signed, web scraping appears to be legal. Generally, web scraping should not extract massive data (considered to be more than 20% of all data available). Data extraction that disturbs the operation of the target website is likely to be illegal. Data gathered for scientific research purposes is probably uncritical.

Data quality and discussion

Data quality has two dimensions: data needs to be representative with respect to the research question at hand (validity) and with respect to the underlying population (reliability). We cannot discuss the validity of the four data sources presented above without first defining a specific research question. The research question also determines the relevant underlying population and therefore the reliability of the data. Assume, for example, that the relevant population is all food consumers in Germany. In this context we have already discussed some shortcomings of the consumer scan and retail scanner data: participation in the GfK panel is voluntary and not all retailers share their retail scan data. Further data shortcomings can arise from measurement and processing errors.

Figure 11.4 shows two time series with potentially inconsistent data. Retail price 1 includes an observation of € 0.08 per 250 g of butter. This price is far below the wholesale price of butter, which is above € 0.5. Perhaps this observation is the result of an entry or processing error. Retail price 2 is below the wholesale price over the entire sample period. Perhaps this retail price is actually for a different package size.

Figure 11.4: Examples of potentially inconsistent retail scan prices of butter

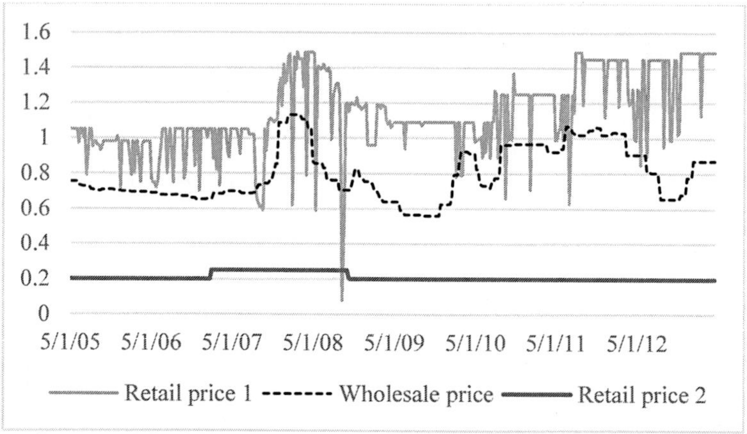

Note: Prices in € per 250g.
Source: Own based on IRI Symphony (2014).

Another issue is the identification of promotional price sales, which are not indicated by the retailers in scanner data. The algorithm that IRI applies was described above. This algorithm has several obvious problems in identifying price promotions. Holzer and Bittmann (2019), based on Eichenbaum et al. (2011) and Kehoe and Midrigan (2015), developed an algorithm that uses rolling-window modal prices to identify first regular prices and then promotional prices. Figure 11.5 presents two retail price series for butter before (above, original price series) and after (below, sales price removed) the application of this algorithm. In Figure 11.5, each promotional sales price identified by the algorithm in the original series is replaced by the last regular price. For the price on the left, the algorithm works as expected and all obvious temporary price reductions are removed. For the price on the right, some observations that cannot be attributed to either promotional or regular prices remain after application of the algorithm.

A variety of other methods for identifying promotions in retail price series have been proposed – see Tifaoui and von Cramon-Taubadel (2016) for an overview.

Figure 11.5: Identification of promotional sales prices in a retail scan price of butter

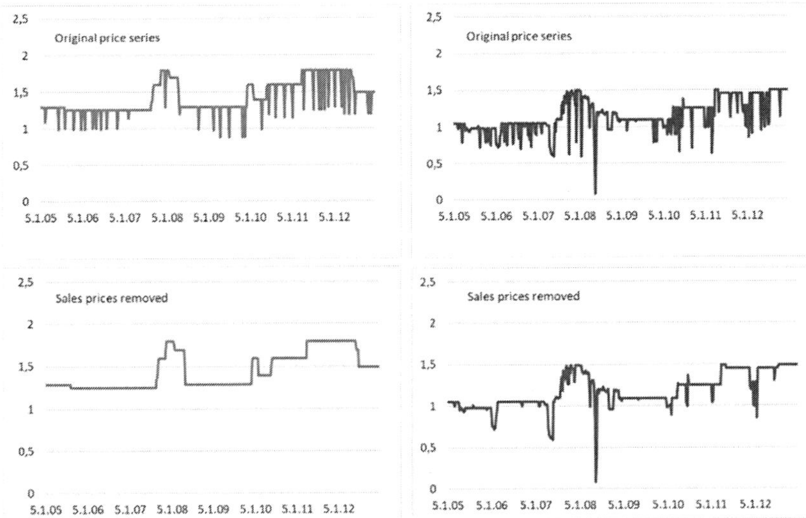

Source: Own based on IRI Symphony (2014).

While retail scanner data may contain fewer processing errors, consumer scan data rely heavily on entries made by consumers. Prices and promotion indicators have to be manually entered by the panellist. This is a major source of errors, as panel members enter their data at home after returning from shopping. Thus, they need to precisely recall prices and promotions for all items bought. Errors in recollection will lead to noise in the price and promotion information in the data.

11.4. Models and price systems in food retail pricing

As described above, food retailing in Germany is dominated by a few large retail chains. The same is true in many other countries. Only a few large food manufacturers are in a position to deal on equal terms with these retail chains. Thus, retailers can exert market power vis-à-vis food manufacturers.

It is obvious that they can also exert market power vis-à-vis the many consumers.

The traditional starting point for the analysis of market power vis-à-vis consumers is the monopoly model, which we present next in section 11.4.1. Monopolistic competition (section 11.4.2) builds on the monopoly model and introduces the idea of differentiated products. Food retailing is a multiproduct business with several thousand products that are linked by relationships ranging from substitution to complementarity. Retail pricing needs to account for these relationships, which we discuss in section 11.4.3. In section 11.4.4 we look at the retailers' purchases of inputs. The traditional starting point is here the monopsony model. However, the underlying idea that a monopsonist will push down cost prices by cutting demand appears implausible in the case of food retail. We therefore present a model in which the monopsony retailer negotiates both cost prices and volumes.

The oligopoly model best reflects actual retail market structures in many countries. In section 11.4.5 we therefore briefly present basic oligopoly models and an extension of these models under product differentiation, as well as its implications for cost pass-through, which is a key term in the evaluation of vertical markets. In sections 11.4.6 to 11.4.8 we address specific problems and phenomena in retail pricing, such as price discrimination, promotional sales, and brand loyalty.

11.4.1. Monopoly

A monopoly sells to many buyers who have no alternatives to satisfy their demand. The monopoly firm does not take the market price as given, instead it recognises its influence on the market price and will choose the price that maximises its profit. Consumers are confronted with prices when they purchase food, so it is intuitive to think of the monopolist setting the price (p). However, the monopolist can equally maximise profit by choosing the appropriate quantity. In fact, casting the model in terms of profit maximisation with respect to quantity (q) (as we do in the following) is also analytically more convenient.[7]

$$\max_q [p\{q\}q - C\{q\}] \tag{1}$$

[7] Maximisation with respect to price results an equivalent condition (see Varian 2014, p. 457 and Tirole 1988, p. 66).

$$\frac{\partial p}{\partial q}q + p\{q\} - C'\{q\} = 0 \tag{2}$$

$$\frac{\partial p}{\partial q}\frac{q}{p}p + p = C'\{q\} \tag{3}$$

$$MR \equiv p\left(1 + \frac{1}{\varepsilon^D}\right) = C'\{q\} \equiv MC \tag{4}$$

In food retailing, many costs such as labour, store and equipment are *quasi* fixed. Menu costs are variable to some extent. The most significant variable cost is the purchase (or cost) price of products such as transportation and logistics services. To simplify the model, we assume that the marginal cost (MC) equals the purchase price of these services. To maximise profits, the monopolist must equate marginal revenues (MR) to MC. MR depends on the price and the price elasticity of demand for the food product.

The degree of market power can be measured by **the Lerner Index**, which is defined in equation (5). The extent of market power depends directly on the elasticity of demand. If the consumer's reaction is inelastic, the Lerner Index tends towards 1.[8] If consumers react perfectly elastically, then the Lerner Index, even for a monopolist, is zero.

$$\text{Lerner-Index} \equiv \frac{p-MC}{p} = \frac{1}{|\varepsilon^D|} \tag{5}$$

For linear demand, marginal revenue is also linear. The marginal revenue function intersects the price axis (*q=0*) at the same point as the demand function. The slope of the marginal revenue function is negative and twice that of the demand function. The following derivation proves this.[9]

$$p = a - bq \text{ with } a > b > 0 \tag{6}$$

$$R \equiv pq = aq - bq^2 \tag{7}$$

$$MR \equiv \frac{\partial R}{\partial q} = a - 2bq \tag{8}$$

[8] The Lerner Index will exceed 1 if the elasticity of demand is less than one, but a profit maximising monopolist would, in the short term, never operate on the price inelastic range of a demand curve.

[9] The sufficient condition for profit maximisation is that the second derivative of the profit function is negative. This is fulfilled for a linear demand function (Tirole 1988, p. 69).

Since the optimal quantity for a monopolist (q^M) obtains where *MR* equals *MC*:

$$q^M = \frac{a-MC}{2b} \tag{9}$$

$$p^M = a - b\left(\frac{a-MC}{2b}\right) \tag{10}$$

$$p^M = \frac{a+MC}{2} \tag{11}$$

Hence, for a linear demand function the monopoly price (p^M) is equal to half of the sum of a plus MC. Furthermore, assuming constant *MC*, the quantity offered by the monopolist (q^M) is half of the volume that would be offered on a perfectly competitive market. Otherwise, the slope of the *MC*-curve also determines the equilibrium quantity. The steeper the *MC*-curve, the smaller the difference between q^M and the perfect competition equilibrium quantity.

In the following section, we briefly analyse cost pass-through (CPT), which is defined as the change in price caused by a change in *MC*. “Cost pass-through is relevant to an extensive range of competition issues” (Walters et al. 2014, p. 9). We obtain the CPT by deriving the equilibrium price in equation (11) with respect to *MC*:

$$\frac{\partial p^M}{\partial MC} = \frac{\partial p^M}{\partial a} = \frac{1}{2} \tag{12}$$

Hence, under monopoly conditions, only 50% of a variation in MC is passed on to consumers. Under perfect competition, the equilibrium condition is $p = MC$, so CPT is one-to-one.

Linear demand functions cause moderate CPT because the demand elasticity increases with price. When the monopolist raises the price, consumer reactions become more elastic and therefore a lower mark-up maximises profits. For isoelastic demand functions, the optimal mark-up for profit maximisation is the same regardless of the cost. For a MC-curve with a positive slope, the partial derivatives do not change; however, for discrete changes the CPT depends on the slopes of the supply and the demand curves, even under perfect competition. In this case, the CPT reference is not one-to-one: the pass-through rate for a monopoly is still lower than under perfect competition, but the difference can be small. For non-linear demand functions, no general statement can be made, and the CPT rate might even be higher for a monopoly than under perfect competition. For an isoelastic demand and constant marginal costs, for example, a cost change implies a one-to-one pass-through rate for perfect competition, while a monopolist will keep the same relative mark-up, implying that the price in absolute terms increase more than the cost.

Figure 11.6 shows that a monopolist would offer at most half of the saturation quantity (market demand at a price of zero). Therefore, under conditions of linear demand a monopolist will never enter the region of inelastic demand (see also footnote 9). Inelastic demand implies negative marginal revenues, hence any quantities supplied in this region reduce revenues while increasing costs, which is not compatible with profit maximisation. However, this might be short-sighted if consumers react more elastically in the long-term. When the government enforces a minimum supply or when potential rivals enter the market at higher prices, a monopolist might also supply an inelastic (low price) demand.

Figure 11.6: The monopoly market

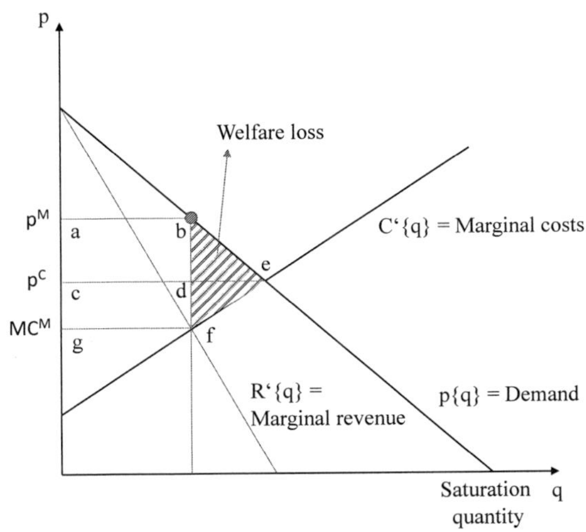

Compared with the outcome under perfect competition, the monopoly outcome leads to welfare losses equivalent to the area ***bef*** in Figure 11.6. Consumers lose ***abce*** of their net surplus, while the monopolist loses producer surplus ***def*** but gains ***abcd*** due to the price increase. As the monopolist maximises profits, the net effect must be positive; thus ***abcd*** > ***def***. The net welfare loss for society is ***bef*** due to reduced production compared with perfect competition. The net welfare effect may be less negative or even positive if the monopolist has a cost advantage, e. g. due to economies of scale. The difference between the monopoly price and the marginal cost, the area ***abfg*** in Figure 11.6, is called the monopoly rent.

Monopolistic profits create incentives to develop new products, and patent protection ensures that firms can realise monopoly rents for their inventions. However, inventions in the food industry most often take the form of new recipes, which become known when inventors register patents. Thus, most food processors choose to keep their recipes secret.

11.4.2. Monopolistic competition

The food retail market in Germany is not a monopoly; it is dominated by more than one large retail chain. However, some products or brands might be unique from a consumer perspective, and this might allow the corresponding manufacturers and retailers to exercise monopoly power. It is possible to estimate the extent of this market power by comparing prices between manufacturer (national) and basic retailer (private label) brands. To this end, Connor and Peterson (1992) and Barsky et al. (2003) use retailer brand prices as an indicator of marginal costs to calculate mark-ups on national brands. Low price private labels best represent purchasing prices or production costs. Thus, all mark-ups on national brands compared with low-price private labels can be interpreted as short-run excess profits and an indication of the degree of market power exercised by manufacturers and/or retailers. The extra profit may be divided between manufacturer and retailer, depending on their respective negotiation positions, consumer loyalty towards the brand, and long-term costs.

We illustrate this using fluid milk from the Rewe group's online grocery store as an example. In total, the Rewe online store offers more than 50 different fluid milk items. In Table 11.4 we present data on 30 of these items to illustrate the main factors that influence in-store product price dispersion. Drinking milk is differentiated with respect to the brand (private label, national brands, brand characteristics), the fat content (1.5 to 3.9%), the production process (pasture-fed, organic, etc.), with or without lactose, perishability (pasteurised, extended shelf life, ultra-high temperature), and package size (tetra pack or glass bottle). The lowest-priced private label is "ja!" milk, which sells for 0.79 €/l (3.5% fat). "Weihenstephan" brand milk with 3.5% fat is priced at 1.29 €/l. The price difference between the two brands is 0.50 €/l., which suggests a Lerner Index of roughly 39%.

The most expensive milk is from Demeter, an organic milk with 3.7% fat in a glass bottle at a price of 1.89 Euro/l. Rewe offers the low-price private label "ja!", as well as several higher-quality labels such as "Rewe Beste Wahl" and "Rewe Bio", which are priced close to the lowest-price manufacturer brand, which is "Berchtesgadener Land" at a price of 1.15 €/l for 3.5% fat milk.

As long as the entry to the market is free, all manufacturers' profits should be zero in the long-term. If mark-ups vary as much as the example in Table 11.4 suggests, and if indeed all profits are zero, then additional fixed and variable costs must explain the different mark-ups. The idea of monopolistic competition is that the average cost curve touches the demand curve at the monopoly price to ensure an equilibrium (Figure 11.7). In reality this equilibrium might never be attained. However, it is reasonable to assume that strong brands have higher marketing and advertising costs that account for most or at least some of their mark-ups. In addition, there are significant costs associated with the research, development, and introduction of new brands, many of which fail. These costs have to be borne by those brands that are successful, which can also explain higher mark-ups.

Figure 11.7: Monopolistic competition

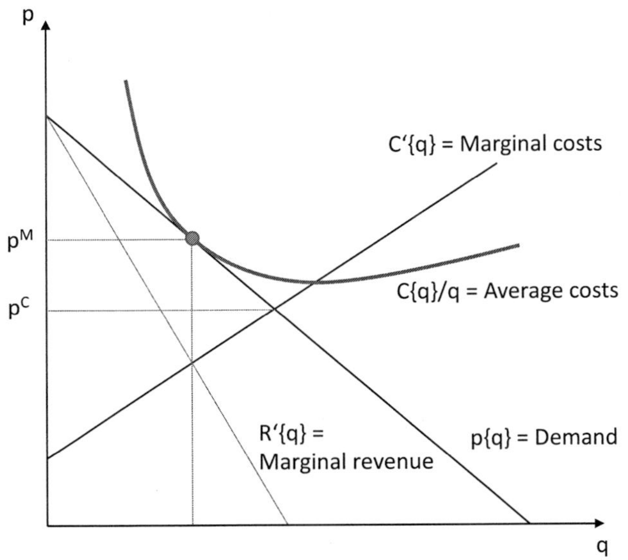

Table 11.4: Drinking milk prices at the Rewe online store on March 3, 2021

Brand	Type	Description	Size	Package	Fat (%)	Lactose	Perishability	Price (€/l)	Nutri-score
ja!	PL	Skim	1L	TP	1.5	yes	P	0,71	A
ja!	PL	Skim long-life	1L	TP	1.5	yes	UHT	0,71	A
ja!	PL	Whole	1L	TP	3.5	yes	P	0,79	B
ja!	PL	Long-life	1L	TP	3.5	yes	UHT	0,79	B
Hansano	NB	Skim long-life pasture-fed	1.5L	TP	1.5	yes	UHT	0,90	A
Rewe Bio	PL	Organic skim long-life	1L	TP	1.5	yes	UHT	0,99	A
Rewe Beste Wahl	PL	Pasture-fed	1L	TP	3.5	yes	P	1,09	B
Berchtesgadener Land	NB	Fresh, skim alpine farmers	1L	TP	1.5	yes	ESL	1,09	A
Rewe	PL	Long-life, lactose-free	1L	TP	3.5	no	UHT	1,09	B
Rewe Bio	PL	Organic long-life	1L	TP	3.8	yes	UHT	1,09	B
Berchtesgadener Land	NB	Fresh, alpine farmers	1L	TP	3.5	yes	ESL	1,15	B
Bärenmarke	NB	Fresh, alpine farmers	1L	TP	1.8	yes	ESL	1,19	A
Weihenstephan	NB	Fresh, skim alpine farmers	1L	TP	1.5	yes	ESL	1,19	A
Weihenstephan	NB	Fresh, alpine farmers	1L	TP	3.5	yes	ESL	1,29	B
Hansano	NB	Fresh, pasture fed	1L	TP	1.8	yes	ESL	1,29	A
Weihenstephan	NB	Long-life	1L	TP	3.5	yes	UHT	1,29	B
Landliebe	NB	Fresh, country	1.5L	TP	3.8	yes	ESL	1,33	B
Hansano	NB	Fresh, pasture-fed	1L	TP	3.9	yes	ESL	1,35	B
Hamfelder Hof	NB	Organc long-life	1L	TP	3.8	yes	ESL	1,35	B
Hamfelder Hof	NB	Organic skim	1L	TP	1.5	yes	ESL	1,35	A
Hofmolkerei Dehlwes	NB	Organic	1L	TP	3.5	yes	P	1,39	B
Andechser	NB	Organic skim	1L	TP	1.5	yes	ESL	1,39	A
Andechser	NB	Organic	1L	TP	3.8	yes	ESL	1,49	B
Arla	NB	Fresh, skim organic pasture-fed	1L	TP	1.5	yes	ESL	1,49	A
Arla	NB	Fresh, organic pasture-fed	1L	TP	3.8	yes	ESL	1,59	B
Landliebe	NB	Fresh, country	1L	B	3.8	yes	ESL	1,59	B
Landliebe	NB	Lactose-free	1L	TP	3.8	no	P	1,65	B
Hansano	NB	Fresh, pasture-fed	0,5L	TP	3.9	yes	ESL	1,7	B
Hansano	NB	Fresh, skim lactose-free	1L	TP	1.5	no	P	1,75	A
Demeter	NB	Organic	1L	B	3.7	yes	P	1,89	B

Notes: PL = private label; NB = national brand; TP = tetrapack; B = bottle; P = pasteurised; ESL = extended shelf life; UHT = ultra-high temperature. Source: Own depiction based on https://shop.rewe.de/, accessed on March 3, 2021.

How many and how differentiated should products be produced under monopolistic competition? Carlton and Perloff (2015, p. 244) describe the optimal solution graphically as depicted in Figure 11.8. First, the production possibility frontier indicates that there is a trade-off between producing variety and quantity; firms can produce greater variety but at the expense of quantity. Second, the convex social indifference curves indicate that the marginal benefits of increasing variety and increasing quantity, respectively, are decreasing. The social optimum is reached at point O, where a societal indifference curve is tangent to the production possibility frontier, n^* different products are produced and the output quantity is q^*.[10]

Monopolistic competition equilibrium can lead to equilibria with either too much variety (such a A) or too little (such as B) relative to the social optimum (Carlton and Perloff 2015, p. 243). While fixed costs and economies of scale lead firms to produce too few brands, substitution between products increases a firm's profits by reducing the demand for the products of competing firms. This results in firms offering too many brands.

So far, we have implicitly assumed a representative consumer, for whom all brands are equally good substitutes. In reality, however, it is rarely the case that consumers view different brands as equally good substitutes. Furthermore, individual consumers differ in their perceptions of brands and brand substitutions. To overcome this limitation, Hotelling (1929) introduced a location model of product differentiation. Salop (1979) extended the linear model to a circular model. The difference between products is represented by the geographical distance between firms' or products' locations. The closer products are in geographical or characteristic space, the better substitutes they are. Depending on their preferences, consumers also have locations in geographic or product space.

[10] Carlton and Perloff (2015, p. 259 ff.) argue that if products are homogeneous, only one firm should produce at the level where marginal cost equals price. To prevent shutdown, the firm's losses should be levelled by a subsidy.

Figure 11.8: Optimal allocation of quantity and variety of products

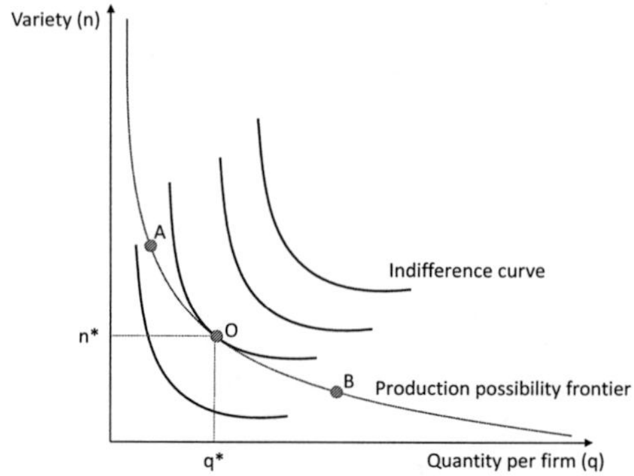

Source: Own based on Carlton and Perloff (2015, p. 244).

11.4.3. Multiproduct monopoly

Food retailing is a multiproduct business. Models of product differentiation, such as the monopolistic competition model, are a first step when considering multiple products and the relationships between them. We now introduce multiple products to a monopoly model to extend the analysis.

If a firm produces *n* products, it has to consider the relationships between them in consumption and production. If the products were independent in production and consumption, each could be analysed using a standard single-product model. Accounting for interdependence requires more complex models. In this section, we focus on relationships between products in consumption and assume that the products are independent in production. Niehans (1956) investigated this setting and presented a solution, sometimes referred to as the 'Niehans-Rule'. A very similar result was published by Ramsey (1927) in his theory of optimal taxation. Thus, the resulting prices are also called Ramsey prices.

Products can be either substitutes or complements in consumption, depending on consumer preferences. Products can be chemically or physically different, but nevertheless viewed as substitutes by consumers. Conversely, products can be identical but nevertheless be viewed as different by consumers. Some consumers may perceive cola and lemonade as substitutes, others might prefer "mezzo mix" and thus perceive cola and lemonade as complements. "The consumer is always right" (Carlton and Perloff 2015, p. 227).

To keep the algebra simple, we assume two products and the following profit function:

$$\max_{p_1}\left[p_1 q_1\{p_1,p_2\} + p_2 q_2\{p_1,p_2\} - C\{q_1\{p_1,p_2\}, q_2\{p_1,p_2\}\}\right] \tag{13}$$

We differentiate equation (13) with respect to the price of product 1 (p_1), and set the derivative equal to zero. After a few modifications, we obtain the optimal $p_1(q_1^*)$:

$$q_1\{p_1,p_2\} + p_1\frac{\partial q_1}{\partial p_1} + p_2\frac{\partial q_2}{\partial p_1} - \frac{\partial C}{\partial q_1}\frac{\partial q_1}{\partial p_1} - \frac{\partial C}{\partial q_2}\frac{\partial q_2}{\partial p_1} = 0 \tag{14}$$

$$q_1\{p_1,p_2\} + \frac{\partial q_1}{\partial p_1}\left(p_1 - \frac{\partial C}{\partial q_1}\right) + \frac{\partial q_2}{\partial p_1}\left(p_2 - \frac{\partial C}{\partial q_2}\right) = 0 \tag{15}$$

$$p_1 + \frac{\partial q_1}{\partial p_1}\frac{p_1}{q_1}\left(p_1 - \frac{\partial C}{\partial q_1}\right) + \frac{\partial q_2}{\partial p_1}\frac{p_1}{q_2}\frac{q_2}{q_1}\left(p_2 - \frac{\partial C}{\partial q_2}\right) = 0 \tag{16}$$

$$p_1 + \varepsilon_{11}\left(p_1 - \frac{\partial C}{\partial q_1}\right) + \varepsilon_{21}\frac{q_2}{q_1}\left(p_2 - \frac{\partial C}{\partial q_2}\right) = 0 \tag{17}$$

$$p_1^* = \frac{\varepsilon_{11}}{1+\varepsilon_{11}}\frac{\partial C}{\partial q_1} - \frac{\varepsilon_{21}}{1+\varepsilon_{11}}\frac{q_2}{q_1}\left(p_2 - \frac{\partial C}{\partial q_2}\right) \tag{18}$$

In these equations, ε_{11} and ε_{12} are the elasticities of demand for product 1 with respect to the prices of product 1 and product 2, respectively. The first term of the right-hand side of equation (18) is the standard profit maximising price for a single-product monopoly. The sign of the second term depends on the cross-price elasticity ε_{12}. For substitutes, $\varepsilon_{12} > 0$, and for complements $\varepsilon_{12} < 0$. Note that $1 + \varepsilon_{11} < 0$, as monopolists only supply in the price-elastic range of the demand curve. Moreover, the quantities q_1 and q_2 and the mark-up $\left(p_2 - \frac{\partial C}{\partial q_2}\right)$ must be greater than zero. Thus, the second term is positive for substitutes $\left(-\frac{\varepsilon_{21}}{1+\varepsilon_{11}}\frac{q_2}{q_1}\left(p_2 - \frac{\partial C}{\partial q_2}\right) > 0\right)$. This implies that the profit maximising p_1 will be higher than the standard single-product monopoly price if the monopolist is also selling a substitute product 2. The additional price mark-up increases with the substitutability of the products, the magnitudes of ε_{11} and ε_{12}, the ratio of quantities $\frac{q_2}{q_1}$, and the mark-up for product 2.

This result makes intuitive sense. For independent products, profits are maximised when marginal revenue equals marginal cost. For substitutional products, the monopolist has to consider the additional demand for product 2 that is caused by an increase in p_1. This additional demand increases the marginal revenue by increasing p_1. For complements, the sign of the second term on the right-hand side of equation (18) is negative, implying that the profit maximising p_1 will be lower than in the independent-product monopoly case.

A similar interpretation follows from the profit maximising Lerner Index in equation (19). For the general case with *n* products, we can similarly derive the profit maximising price and the Lerner Index (equations 11.20 and 11.21). The price effect depends on the number and nature (substitutes, complements) of the product relationships in the monopolist's assortment.

$$\frac{p_1^* - \frac{\partial C}{\partial q_1}}{p_1^*} = -\frac{1}{\varepsilon_{11}} - \frac{\varepsilon_{21}}{\varepsilon_{11}} \frac{q_2}{p_1 q_1} \left(p_2 - \frac{\partial C}{\partial q_2}\right) \tag{19}$$

$$p_i^* = \frac{\varepsilon_{ii}}{1+\varepsilon_{ii}} \frac{\partial C}{\partial q_i} - \sum_{j \neq i} \frac{\varepsilon_{ji}}{1+\varepsilon_{ii}} \frac{q_j}{q_i} \left(p_j - \frac{\partial C}{\partial q_j}\right) \tag{20}$$

$$\frac{p_i^* - \frac{\partial C}{\partial q_i}}{p_i^*} = -\frac{1}{\varepsilon_{ii}} - \sum_{j \neq i} \frac{\varepsilon_{ji}}{\varepsilon_{ii}} \frac{q_j}{p_i q_i} \left(p_j - \frac{\partial C}{\partial q_j}\right) \tag{21}$$

Applications of the Niehans-Rule are rare - even in scientific journals - for the following reasons. First, it requires estimates of own-price and cross-price demand elasticities for all products. Even in a small supermarket, the number of products can easily exceed 5000. Although it can safely be assumed that $\varepsilon_{ij} = 0$ for many product pairs, many thousand elasticities remain to be estimated. Estimation is further complicated by the fact that many prices are highly collinear over time, which inflates standard errors, and by price promotions, as it is almost impossible to disentangle their various effects such as increased storage, brand switching, etc.

11.4.4. Monopsony

Average retail chain profits are lower in Germany than in other European countries. Relative to income levels, retail prices in Germany are also comparatively low. This suggests that German retailers are exercising little or no market power as sellers to consumers. Nonetheless, the market concentration ratio is very high. Therefore, the German Antitrust Commission has investigated in the market power of food retailers vis-à-vis the manufacturing or food-processing industry.

Analogous to section 4.1 above, where we considered retailers' market power as sellers to consumers, we now begin the discussion of retailers' market power as buyers, with the monopsony model for one product and one input. The main input factor for food retailers, however, is the same as their output good; retailers do not produce goods but rather provide retail services to re-sell food products that they have previously purchased. In this process, product loss (quality and/or quantity) can take place. In addition, retailing involves short-term fixed costs (*C*), predominantly for labour and capital. Assume a single retailer with given (competitive) output prices, many input (product) suppliers, and the following profit function:

$$\max_{x}[pq\{x\} - r\{x\}x - C] \tag{22}$$

where r is the purchase price of the input x. We differentiate equation (22) with respect to the input x and set the first derivative equal to zero. After a few modifications, we obtain the profit maximisation condition that the gross value added (*GVA*) – here, the retail sale price – is equal to the marginal expenditure (*ME*) of the monopsonist for the input x:

$$p\frac{\partial q}{\partial x} - \frac{\partial r}{\partial x}x - r\{x\} = 0 \tag{23}$$

$$p\frac{\partial q}{\partial x} = \frac{\partial r}{\partial x}\frac{x}{r}r + r\{x\} \tag{24}$$

Assuming that $\frac{\partial q}{\partial x} = 1$ (one unit of input x is resold as one unit of output q), and rearranging:

$$GVA \equiv p = r\left(1 + \frac{1}{\varepsilon^S}\right) \equiv ME \tag{25}$$

$$\text{Lerner-Index}^* \equiv \frac{GVA - r^M}{r^M} = \frac{1}{\varepsilon^S} \tag{26}$$

where ε^S is the price elasticity of supply of the input x. If the input supply is linear, the marginal expenditure function is also linear and intersects the price axis (r given $x = 0$) at the same point as the input supply function. The slope of the marginal expenditure function is twice the slope of the input supply function.

$$r = h + kx \tag{27}$$

$$rx = hx + kx^2 \tag{28}$$

$$ME \equiv \frac{\partial rx}{\partial x} = h + 2kx \tag{29}$$

Since the monopsonist's optimal purchase quantity x^M obtains where $ME = GVA$:

$$GVA = h + 2kx \tag{30}$$

$$x^M = \frac{GVA-h}{2k} \tag{31}$$

$$r^M = h + k\left(\frac{GVA-h}{2k}\right) \tag{32}$$

$$r^M = \frac{h+GVA}{2} \tag{33}$$

Hence, the monopsonist will purchase half as much x as would be purchased under perfect competition, if consumer demand for the output q is perfectly price elastic so that $P = GVA$ is fixed. Otherwise, the slope of the consumer demand function determines the market volume (Figure 11.9).

Figure 11.9: Monopsony market

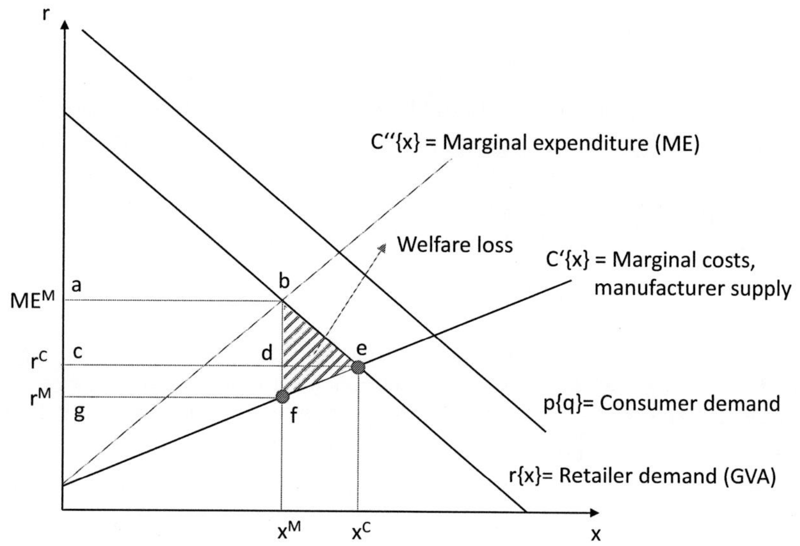

As in the monopoly case, the steeper the demand, the closer the equilibrium quantity x^M is to the volume under perfect competition x^c. Differentiation of equation (33) with respect to *GVA* and with respect to c provides information similar to CPT rates:

$$\frac{\partial r^M}{\partial h} = \frac{\partial r^M}{\partial GVA} = \frac{1}{2} \qquad (34)$$

Both derivatives equal ½. *GVA* changes when either retail prices or variable retailing costs change. Thus, if these increase by one unit, the purchase price of the input x increases by ½. The same applies for factors that shift manufacturers' costs (for example when the prices of agricultural raw products change). As before, these results assume a perfectly elastic *GVA* (demand) function. For falling *GVA*, the effects of manufacturer cost changes on r can exceed ½, and the effects of changes in *GVA* on r can be smaller than ½.

Haucap et al. (2015) state that this standard monopsonistic model is not capable of illustrating the exploitation of market power by food retailers. Instead of reducing demand in order to push down purchase prices, food retailers negotiate delivery conditions. If we assume that retailers can negotiate prices and delivery volumes, the equilibrium changes. If the retailer has perfect market power, the food manufacturers will have to forego all profit and transfer it to the retailer. The retailer will negotiate the same quantity as under perfect competition at a price that extracts the entire gross margin from the manufacturer(s). This outcome is depicted in Figure 11.10, where the retailer chooses the perfect competition volume x^c but uses market power to push the purchase price down to r^{M*}. As a result, the manufacturers' profits on the first x' units (abc) exactly compensate their losses on the units between x' and x^c (bde).

Even though this is an extreme outcome that might not occur in practice, the idea remains that retailers can use market power to push purchase prices down without reducing the quantity demanded. If retailers pass on reduced purchase prices to consumers, they will need to negotiate even higher volumes to satisfy the increase in consumer demand.

Figure 11.10: Market outcome under buyer market power, negotiating price and volume

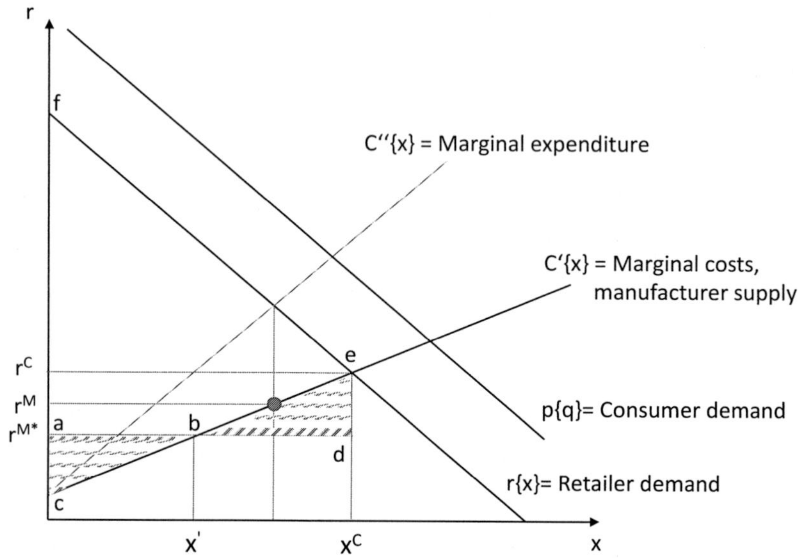

In a sector study, the German Antitrust Commission (2014) clearly states that the four leading retail chains in Germany (Edeka, Rewe, Schwarz Group, and Aldi) dominate the competition in the market, in terms of supply and input demand. These four retail chains use negotiations with food processors to their advantage, which causes further concentration in food retailing and the food processing industry. However, concentration in food processing does not necessarily improve the processors' negotiating position, as large food processors have no or fewer fall-back options besides the four leading retail chains. Thus, large food processors may have less power in negotiations with the retail chains than smaller processors. Only a few large food processors that produce 'must have' brands negotiate on an equal footing with the big food retail chains (German Antitrust Commission 2014).

High market shares of private labels support the superior position of food retail chains in negotiations with food processors. However, a food processor that produces a national brand as well as a private label will be better off than a pure national brand manufacturer, if the retailer and processor can agree on a consistent price differentiation strategy for these brands.

Smaller retail chains in Germany organise purchasing cooperatives, which enable them to generate market power comparable to that of the leading retail chains. Some of these purchasing cooperatives are led by one of the 'big four'. The additional profit generated by these cooperatives might be small for the big retail chain, but it allows the chain to offer private labels in the cooperatives' stores, which might ease future mergers, and increase the popularity of the chain.

11.4.5. Oligopoly

An oligopoly is a market with few suppliers or producers and a large number of consumers. This market structure almost perfectly describes the retail food markets in industrialised countries such as Germany.

Oligopoly models can be classified into cooperative and non-cooperative models. Cooperative models refer to cartels, the members of which coordinate some or all of their relevant production and marketing decisions. Ideally a cooperative oligopoly behaves as one firm, i.e. a monopoly. The coordination of the cartel group's actions is easier, when (a) the product is homogeneous, (b) there are few group members, (c) group members have the same production costs, (d) group members are of the same size, and (e) antitrust laws are weak. Under German antitrust laws, cartels are illegal and the German Antitrust Commission actively investigates suspected cases. Examples are reported on the website of the German Antitrust Commission at https://www.bundeskartellamt.de.

In non-cooperative oligopolies, the competitors' reactions to each other's actions are essential. In the following section, we briefly describe the three traditional approaches to modelling competition among oligopolists. A more comprehensive presentation can be found in Chapter 8 ("Pricing under imperfect competition"). After presenting these models, we discuss an oligopolistic model to investigate the impact of product differentiation on CPT. This provides the theoretical background to an empirical case study presented in section 5.4.

Augustin Cournot developed an oligopoly model in 1838. In the simplest variant he assumed two firms, a duopoly, which produce a homogeneous product. Both firms have the same production function and the same constant marginal costs of production. The strategic variable is the quantity produced. Cournot assumes that once a firm (firm 2) has decided the quantity of its production (q^{F2}), it does not react to the competitor's (firm 1) response. Thus, firm 1 takes the firm 2's production as given. In this case the firms 1's residual demand equals the total demand minus firm 2's production, as depicted in Figure 11.11. Firm 1 applies monopolistic behaviour to its residual demand function and thus chooses to produce q^{F1}. For any q^{F2} chosen by firm 2, firm 1 can calculate its optimal q^{F1}, and vice versa. Based on these considerations, each firm can calculate its own and its competitor's **reaction function**. These reaction functions are depicted in Figure 11.12.

Figure 11.11: Residual demand in the Cournot duopoly

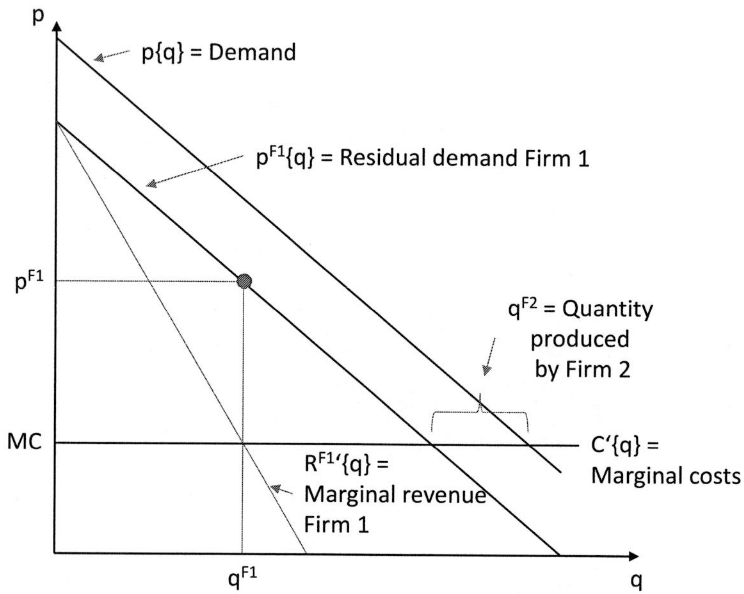

The intersection of the reaction functions marks the **Cournot-Nash-Equilibrium**. Following Carlton and Perloff (2015, p. 185) "a set of strategies is called a Nash-Equilibrium if, holding the strategies of all other firms constant, no firm can obtain a higher payoff (profit) by choosing a different strategy". The duopoly model can be extended to *n* firms, and the market equilibrium demonstrably converges to the competitive equilibrium as *n* approaches infinity. For $n = 1$, the monopoly price equilibrium results. Thus, competition increases monotonically with *n*.

Figure 11.12: Reaction functions in the Cournot duopoly

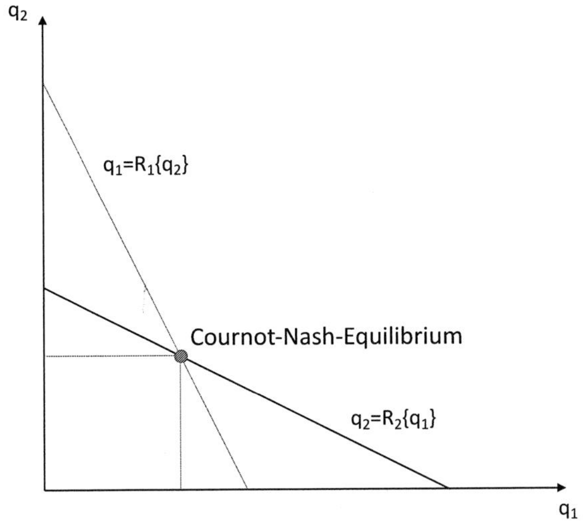

In the Cournot model, the quantity is the strategic variable and actions take place simultaneously. Stackelberg (1934) also developed a duopoly model in which quantity is the strategic variable, but actions take place sequentially, starting with the market leader (*L*). The follower (*F*) observes the leader's choice and reacts to it. The leader assumes that the follower will react as a competitor in the Cournot model would, and anticipates this reaction when deriving his/her own residual demand function. For the linear case the leader's residual demand starts at the monopoly price and ends at the equilibrium under perfect competition (Figure 11.13). When the leader supplies nothing, the follower realises the monopoly price equilibrium (p^M). When the leader supplies as under perfect competition, then no demand is left for the follower. The equilibrium price in the Stackelberg duopoly is lower than the Cournot equilibrium price, but the market leader realises a higher profit than the firms in the Cournot duopoly.

In both the Cournot and Stackelberg models, the oligopolists choose quantities. It might be more realistic to assume that the price is the strategic variable on food markets. Therefore, in 1883 Bertrand developed a model of two firms that simultaneously set prices rather than quantities. What does the residual demand function of firm 1 look like, when firm 2 sets a price in the range between the consumers' maximum willingness to pay and the competitive price?

Figure 11.13: The Stackelberg leader (*L*) follower (*F*) model

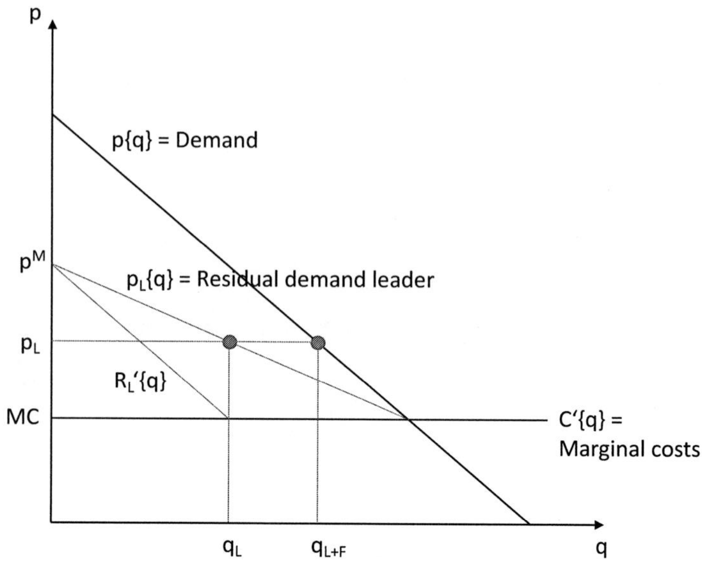

The answer to this question is depicted in Figure 11.14. When firm 2 sets price p_2, firm 1 can underbid this price and receive the total demand. Thus, as long as p_2 is above the competitive price, which equals the constant marginal cost of production *MC*, firm 1 will underbid it to capture the entire market demand. Hence, as shown in Figure 11.15, the price reaction functions lie closely above and below the 45-degree straight line, starting at *MC*, where both functions intersect. Thus, the Bertrand-equilibrium is the same as the competitive equilibrium. This is an astonishing result: for a monopoly or monopsony the choice of the strategic variable is irrelevant to the outcome, but for a duopoly it makes a substantial difference.

Figure 11.14: Residual demand in the Bertrand model

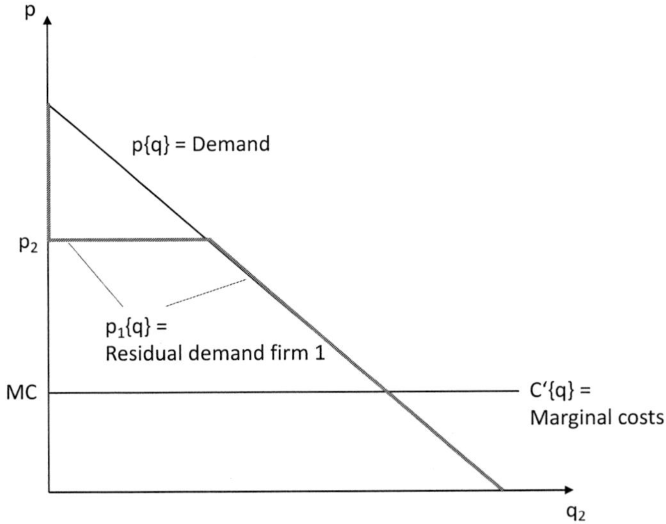

In section 4.2 on monopolistic competition, we introduced the term **product differentiation** without providing a clear definition. Product differentiation in a loose sense may be defined as "any set of commodities closely related in consumption and/or production" (Eaton and Lipsey 1989). Product differentiation has a horizontal and a vertical dimension. If consumers rank products at the same price differently, product differentiation is said to be horizontal. If consumers similarly rank products at the same price, product differentiation is called vertical (Beath and Katsoulacos 1991). Product differentiation is an important feature, not only in food markets. In many industries we find a large number of similar but differentiated products. "There must hardly be a reader who is not aware of the daunting array of breakfast cereals, detergents, toiletries on the average supermarket shelf" (Beath and Katsoulacos 1991 p. 7). Almost no processor produces identical products, and every processor produces a range of differentiated products. Individual consumers, however, only consume a small subset of all available products (Eaton and Lipsey 1989).

Figure 11.15: Price reaction functions for the Bertrand model

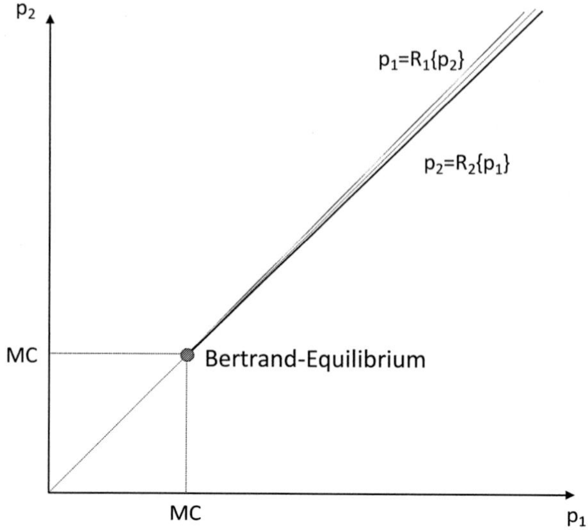

In the following we present a Cournot and a Bertrand oligopoly with product differentiation, employing the representative consumer approach. We follow Shubik and Levitan (1980), Zimmermann and Carlson (2010), and Wang and Zhao (2007), and start with a market of i symmetric non-cooperative competitors offering n differentiated products, where $\phi \in [-1,0]$ reflects the degree of product differentiation. Zero indicates the maximum level of product differentiation, at which products are completely independent. When all products are perfect substitutes, $\phi = -1$.[11] Hence, an increase in ϕ represents an increase in average product differentiation or a corresponding reduction in substitutability. q_i is firm i's output. Equation (35) shows an inverse firm-specific linear demand function (Zimmerman and Carlson 2010).[12]

[11] The definition of product differentiation in Zimmerman and Carlson's (2010) model is reversed ($-\phi \in [0,1]$, where 1 indicates perfect substitution). For ease of comparison, we use $\phi \in [-1,0]$ throughout.

[12] The assumption of linear demand is important in this setting. As Weyl and Fabinger (2013) show, for non-linear demand functions and market power, CPT rates may be higher than under perfect competition.

$$p_i = \alpha - q_i + \phi \sum_{j \neq i} q_j \tag{35}$$

We derive the profit maximising quantity of firm i under a symmetric Cournot-Nash Equilibrium (sCN), where q_j is a vector of outputs excluding firm i, by solving the reaction function for marginal costs c, assuming symmetric firms. This leads to the following optimal output and equilibrium price-cost relationships:

$$q_i^{sCN} = \frac{\alpha - c}{2 - \phi(n-1)} \tag{36}$$

$$p_i^{sCN} = \frac{\alpha + (1 - \phi(n-1))c}{2 - \phi(n-1)} \tag{37}$$

The resulting CPT under Cournot-Nash price-cost equilibrium is positive, yet smaller than one:

$$\frac{\partial p_i^{sCN}}{\partial c} = \frac{1 - \phi(n-1)}{2 - \phi(n-1)} > 0 \tag{38}$$

For a given number of firms, perfectly differentiated products ($\phi = 0$) produce a pass-through rate of 50% and each individual firm engages in monopolistic pricing for its product. This result is similar to the monopoly case. When all competitors offer homogeneous products ($\phi = -1$), the right-hand side of equation (38) reduces to (n / n +1), CPT depends on the number of firms, and approaches 1 as $n \rightarrow \infty$.

To investigate the impact of product differentiation on firms' equilibrium prices, we differentiate equation (37) with respect to the product differentiation parameter ϕ:

$$\frac{\partial p_i^{sCN}}{\partial \phi} = \frac{(n-1)(\alpha - c)}{\left(2 - \phi(n-1)\right)^2} > 0 \tag{39}$$

In equation (39), prices increase with product differentiation. To determine the effect of product differentiation on the degree of CPT, we partially differentiate equation (38) with respect to ϕ:

$$\frac{\partial^2 p_i^{sCN}}{\partial c \partial \phi} = -\frac{(n-1)}{\left(2 - \phi(n-1)\right)^2} < 0 \tag{40}$$

Product differentiation reduces the CPT, or in other words, closer substitutive relationships between products suggest a higher CPT.

Zimmermann and Carlson's (2010) analysis focuses on the role of competition, namely the number of firms in the market. CPT increases with the number of firms and converges to complete (one to one) CPT under perfect competition ($n \to \infty$). Therefore, product differentiation and a declining number of firms both reduce CPT by increasing the sellers' market power.

So far, we have assumed symmetric firms, but in a differentiated product market this appears to be rather restrictive. Firms have different product portfolios and different firm-specific marginal costs. Retail purchase prices can therefore differ not only due to product differentiation but also due to the cost structures of the food processors and the volumes that they produce.

Wang and Zhao (2007) extend Shubik and Levitan's (1980) model to introduce firm asymmetry. Equation (41) shows the non-symmetric Cournot-Nash (*nsCN*) price-cost equilibrium relationship that they derive (Wang and Zhao 2007, p. 178). Again, for ease of interpretation we transform the product differentiation measure, which ranges from minus infinity to zero ($\phi \in [-\infty, 0]$) (see footnote 11). However, the interpretation of ϕ remains unchanged as higher parameter values indicate more differentiated products.

$$p_i^{nsCN} = \frac{(n-\phi)\alpha}{2n-(n+1)\phi} - \frac{n\phi\bar{c}(n-\phi)}{(2n-\phi)(2n-(n+1)\phi)} + \frac{nc_i}{2n-\phi} \tag{41}$$

where $c_i, \bar{c} \equiv \sum \frac{c_i}{n}$ are firm-specific and average marginal costs, respectively. To determine the effect of changes in firm-specific marginal costs on CPT, we differentiate equation (41) with respect to c_i.

$$\frac{\partial p_i^{nsCN}}{\partial c_i} = \frac{2n^2-n(n+2)\phi+\phi^2}{(2n-\phi)(2n-(n+1)\phi)} > 0 \tag{42}$$

As for the case of symmetric firms, when $n = 1$ (monopoly) and products are independent ($\phi = 0$), the rate of CPT is ½. As the number of firms increases, CPT remains at ½, regardless of the level of product differentiation. Zimmermann and Carlson (2010, p. 11) simulate the CPT for different numbers of asymmetric firms. For a single firm (monopoly), the CPT rate is ½ and declines with an increasing number of firms. After reaching a minimum, the rate increases and converges back to the monopoly CPT of ½. Firms have little incentive to adjust prices to changes in firm-specific costs because if they do, consumers will quickly switch to other firms that have not experienced cost changes. Hence, firm-specific costs are passed on at lower rates than for the monopoly case. This effect becomes stronger with an increasing number of firms and with a lower degree of product differentiation. The number of firms, however, also flattens the reaction function in the Cournot model. This leads to a more uniform firm behaviour and to an increasing CPT rate as the number of firms increases until the monopolistic CPT rate is reached (Zimmerman and Carlson 2010).

To derive the impact of product differentiation on firms' equilibrium prices, we differentiate equation (41) with respect to product differentiation ϕ. The result shows that firms increase prices of more differentiated products:

$$\frac{\partial p_i^{nsCN}}{\partial \phi} = \frac{(n-1)n\left(4n^2\alpha+n\left(c(\phi-4)\right)\phi+(2c+\alpha)\phi^2-4\alpha\right)}{(\phi-2n)^2(n(\phi-2)+\phi)^2} > 0, \text{ for } n > 1 \quad (43)$$

In equation (44) we differentiate the CPT from equation (42) with respect to the measure of product differentiation (ϕ). Contrary to the finding for the symmetric case, firms offering more differentiated products increase their CPT. The upper limit for the firm-specific CPT is the monopoly rate of ½; the lower limit is zero.

$$\frac{\partial^2 p_i^{nsCN}}{\partial c_i \partial \phi} = \frac{(n-1)n\phi(n(\phi-4)+2\phi)}{(\phi-2n)^2(n(\phi-2)+\phi)^2} > 0, \text{for } n > 1 \quad (44)$$

To assess the robustness of the Cournot-Nash model under asymmetric cost structures, Zimmermann and Carlson (2010) also derive the Bertrand price-cost equilibrium relationship. They confirm the Cournot-Nash results. The individual CPT rates have the same upper limit. Under competition, CPT rates are always higher, and the rates monotonically decrease with the number of firms. The result with respect to product differentiation is the same: CPT of firm-specific costs increases for more differentiated products. Contrary to the Cournot-Nash model outcome, the presence of product differentiation reinforces the effect of intensified competition; an increase in ϕ positively affects a firm's response to rivals' output decisions. Consequently, CPT rates strictly decline with the number of competing firms (Zimmerman and Carlson 2010).

In conclusion, *ceteris paribus* we expect the prices of more differentiated products to be higher, and CPT of industry-wide cost shocks to be lower: CPT decreases with product differentiation. For homogeneous products and a large (infinite) number of firms, the CPT rate is 1. As in the monopolistic case, the minimum CPT rate of industry-wide cost shocks is ½, implying that 50% of a cost shock is passed on to the retail price. For individual cost shocks, CPT rates increase with product differentiation, starting at a rate of zero for homogeneous products. Independent (perfectly differentiated) products show a CPT rate of ½ for firm-specific cost shocks. For homogeneous products, individual costs cannot be passed on to consumers as demand reacts perfectly elastically. For differentiated products, firms can pass on costs. For independent products, CPT rates converge to the monopolistic rate of ½.

The theoretical models discussed here do not make any predictions about the dynamics of the CPT process. Borenstein and Shepard (2002) argue that market power slows down CPT. Baker and Bresnahan (2008) point out that product differentiation is a means of generating market power. Thus, CPT will become more sluggish as product differentiation increases. Many empirical studies test for asymmetric dynamic responses, namely the "rocket and feathers" phenomenon (Tappata 2009). Retailers may exert market power by differentiating their product portfolio to raise prices more rapidly when costs increase than they reduce prices when costs decrease. Borenstein et al. (1997, p. 324) argue that "prices are sticky downward because when input prices fall the old output price offers a natural focal point for oligopolistic sellers". Thus, for more differentiated products, we expect retailers to adjust prices more asymmetrically.[13]

11.4.6. Price discriminations and bundling

Product differentiation and price discrimination are related, as the former is often a means to achieving the latter. Price discrimination, however, can also work without product differentiation. Price discrimination is sometimes defined as setting different prices for the same product. "However, this definition fails on two accounts: different prices charged to different consumers could simply reflect transportation costs, or similar costs of selling the good; and price discrimination could be present even when all consumers are charged the same price" (Varian 1989, p. 598). We therefore use Stigler's (1987) definition: "a firm price discriminates when the ratio of prices is different from the ratio of marginal costs for two goods offered by a firm."

$$\frac{P_1}{P_2} \neq \frac{\frac{\partial C}{\partial q_1}}{\frac{\partial C}{\partial q_2}} \tag{45}$$

[13] Chapter 10 includes a detailed discussion of the causes and empirical measurement of asymmetric CPT.

Clerides (2002, 2004) points out that absolute deviations between prices and marginal costs also qualify as price discrimination, and that price discrimination can occur in the short and/or long term depending on whether one considers marginal or total costs.

$$P_1 - \frac{\partial C}{\partial q_1} \neq P_2 - \frac{\partial C}{\partial q_2} \qquad \text{short term} \qquad (46)$$

$$P_1 - \frac{C}{q_1} \neq P_2 - \frac{C}{q_2} \qquad \text{long term} \qquad (47)$$

Under perfect competition, prices should equal marginal costs in the short term and average costs in the long term. Thus, under perfect competition we do not expect price discrimination. Three conditions are necessary to successfully discriminate in terms of price. Firms need to have market power; they require knowledge of differences in consumer demand and the ability to sort customers; and they must be able to prevent resales.[14]

Price discrimination is defined by differences in the mark-ups of similar products. Market power is defined by the ability to enforce mark-ups. We assume that profit maximisation is the main incentive for price discrimination, but it can result from the pursuit of other objectives, such as redistribution of income or state regulation. Low-price meals for students or uniform postage charges for standard letters are examples of price discrimination that is not driven by the profit motive. University cafeterias in Germany charge students less than they charge staff and guests for the same meals, not to maximise profit but rather to indirectly support student incomes. In Germany, the cost of sending a standard letter by mail is fixed by law, regardless of the distance between sender and destination.

Figure 11.16 shows the magnitude of price discrimination in a university cafeteria in Germany. Even though the marginal cost of preparing a meal is the same regardless of who eats it, guests pay the highest prices, followed by university staff and then by students, who pay only 40% to 60% of what guests are charged. The ratio is higher for more expensive meals.

Students also get discounts at theatres, movie theatres, museums, and for public transportation. Movie theatres differentiate not only between consumer groups (student, but also children under a certain age) but also for the day of the week. The cost of admission for a regular movie in many

[14] Due to self-selection, resales do not need to be prevented under second-degree price discrimination and mixed price bundling.

German movie theatres will typically be lower early in the week (Monday through Wednesday) than later (Thursday through Sunday).

Figure 11.16: Prices of meals in a German student canteen 2020.

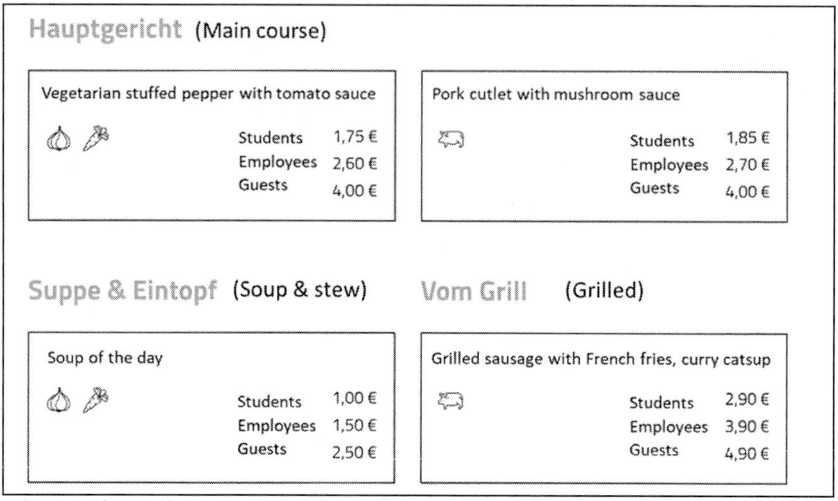

Source: https://www.studierendenwerk-bonn.de/.

Another example of price discrimination is provided by the book market. In March 2021, Varian's "Microeconomic Analysis" was listed on Amazon (www.amazon.de) for €55.99 in hardcover, and for 53% less at €29.95 in paperback. Although the marginal cost of producing hardcover is higher than that of paperback, this is very likely a case of price discrimination.[15]

Price discrimination can affect different dimensions, e. g. in respect of customer groups, volumes purchased, qualitatively differentiated products, over time, over space, etc. We distinguish four different types of price discrimination: first, second, and third degree, and bundling (over different products).

[15] According to Gorham Printing (https://gorhamprinting.com/prices-book-printing/price-charts.html) the cost of printing a softcover book with 300 pages including interior colour pages and a print run of 500 is $16.20; the same book in hardcover costs $26.08. Hence, both the absolute and the relative prices cited here for Varian's textbook cannot be explained by marginal production costs.

First-degree price discrimination

For first-degree price discrimination, firms need to know the demand of all individual buyers and need to make sure that no reselling takes place. For each and every unit of sale, firms set a price based on the consumer's willingness to pay. By this strategy, firms skim the entire willingness to pay for each and every unit. Alternatively, firms set a take-it-or-leave-it price for a fixed quantity that equals the consumer's entire willingness to pay.[16] Another strategy is a two-tier pricing scheme by which customers pay a price equal to the marginal costs plus a fixed amount (entry fee), which must be paid before purchase. First-degree price discrimination is an ideal; the required information on each individual consumer's willingness to pay and/or the ability to prevent resales are often missing. Theoretically, first-degree price discrimination by a monopolist leads to the same allocation as perfect competition; thus, there is no net welfare loss, but the monopolist receives the entire sum of producer and consumer surplus.

Second-degree price discrimination

"Second-degree price discrimination encompasses a variety of pricing schemes through which the firm is able to induce consumers with high valuations to pay higher prices than consumers with low valuations" (Carroll and Coates 1999, p. 469). Consumers self-select into groups based on their willingness to pay. Firms have no information on individual consumers' willingness to pay. However, they know that the willingness varies among consumers, and they have some idea of the (approximate) size of groups of consumers with different preferences, for example with respect to the quantity or the quality of the product. Examples are volume discounts or different mark-ups for different qualities, e. g. paperback and hardcover books.

Consider the following simple example of second-degree price discrimination. Assume that we run a pizza delivery service. Half of our potential customers prefer smaller pizzas and the other half larger pizzas. Demand (marginal willingness to pay) functions for these two groups are depicted in Figure 11.17. These demand functions have been corrected for the respective variable costs of production, which might vary somewhat with pizza size. Thus, the areas beneath these demand functions show the maximum profit that could be generated through sales to individual

[16] Such a take-it-or-leave-it offer would already be an example for bundling over the same good or second-degree price discrimination.

customers. Under first-degree price discrimination, the areas under these demand functions plus the variable costs of production are the take-it-or-leave-it prices for the two groups of individuals. The small pizza has the optimal size q_S and the large pizza has the optimal size q_L. Selling small pizzas earns $A+B$, and selling large pizzas earns $A+B+C+D+E$, plus the sum of variable costs. The total profit is $2(A+B)+C+D+E$. These prices and sizes are optimal if we can distinguish between the customers and present them with corresponding take-it-or-leave-it offers, and provided they are not able to resell.[17] However, under self-selection the large pizza lovers will not choose large pizzas because choosing small pizzas provides them with a consumer surplus of $D+E$ (compared with zero if they choose large pizzas). To prevent this, we can reduce the price of large pizzas by $D+E$. Thus, the total profit increases from $2(A+B)$, when both groups order small pizzas, to $2(A+B)+C$.

Figure 11.17: Second degree (quantitative) price discrimination

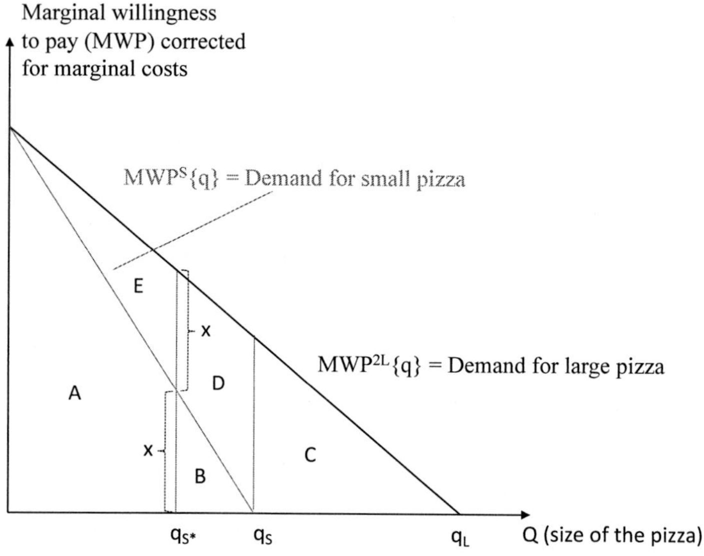

Instead of only decreasing the price for large pizzas, the firm can additionally change the size of the pizzas to maximise profits. Increasing the sizes beyond q_S and q_L makes no sense as the respective willingness to

[17] Under second degree price discrimination, buyers self-select into the pricing arrangement that is best for them and for the seller (Carroll and Coates 1999).

pay does not increase beyond q_S and q_L. Making large pizzas smaller than q_L has no positive effect either, because it would only reduce the area *C*. The only relevant option is making small pizzas smaller than q_S. As a consequence, we need to reduce the price of small pizzas, for example to *A*. Thus, we lose profit equivalent to area *B* from the small pizza lovers. However, we can now increase the price of the large pizza by *B+D*. Our net gain is (*D-B*), which is positive. The profit *2A+B+D+C* is maximised by reducing the size of the small pizzas until resulting marginal reduction in B equals the marginal gain in D, which is the case for q_{S*} in Figure 11.17 (where both marginal changes equal *x*). This result holds as long as the shares of small and large pizza lovers are the same. If, for example, the restaurant has twice as many small pizza lovers than large pizza lovers, then the marginal loss in B needs to be half of the marginal gain in D.

Third degree price discrimination

Third-degree price discrimination is based on differences between groups of consumers in their price sensitivity. Intuitively, less sensitive consumer groups pay higher prices. Groups need to be identified and separated, and reselling needs to be restricted. Groups such as students, children, retired or handicapped individuals can easily be identified by identification cards. In some cases, identification is not necessary if groups are naturally separated by region or time (for example, customer groups who want to see a movie on different nights of the week). Assuming the supplier has information on the total demand of each group, and constant marginal costs, the problem simplifies to the monopoly equilibrium in each individual market. If marginal costs are increasing, the solution is more complicated. The necessary condition remains: marginal cost equals marginal revenue in both markets. Figure 11.18 shows an example with two groups of customers. The profit maximising quantity sold ($q^M = q^{D1+D2}$) is reached where aggregate marginal revenue ($R'\{q\}$) equals marginal cost ($C'\{q\}$). This quantity is then divided between groups 1 (q^{D1}) and 2 (q^{D2}), such that the marginal revenue of the last item sold is the same in both groups.

Bundling

Bundling is the practice of selling two or more goods in a package. Pure bundling is when products are only available in a package; mixed bundling is when the bundle and the individual goods are both available to the consumer. Examples are menu offers in a restaurant or in fast food chains, hardware purchases combined with service contracts, season tickets, etc. Second-degree price discrimination can be viewed as a special kind of bundling over the same product. Bundles can be fixed or flexible. For example, some printer brands insist that consumers use same-brand toner refills. Like other forms of price discrimination, bundling is often used to maximise profits. Further arguments for bundling are efficiency in production or assembling, quality assurance, avoiding price regulations, promotion of (new) products, and price-fixing agreements.

Sometimes it is more efficient to sell bundles. There are strong economies of scale associated with the production of many manufactured goods such as automobiles, kitchen appliances and cameras; few, if any, consumers would consider assembling these products themselves, even though the component parts could, at least in principle, be purchased separately. Many such products can thus be viewed as bundles. Some firms sell complements in bundles or require the follow-up purchase of another product to activate a quality agreement or service guarantee. Examples are car brands that require certain operating supplies or analogue cameras which required film rolls and processing services. Kodak, for example, gave away free tickets for processing with each film roll sold to ensure a certain quality standard. Another reason for bundling is to avoid price regulations. If a firm is limited by a minimum price regulation or cartel agreement, selling product bundles enables it to mask individual prices and thereby avoid the price regulation and possible associated penalties.

Figure 11.18: Third degree price discrimination, monopoly, and perfect competition.

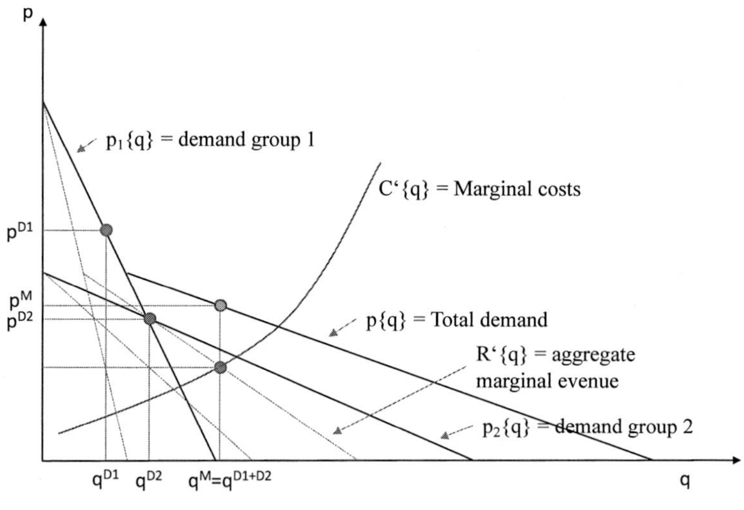

If the supplier is a profit maximiser, bundling works well if the consumers' willingness to pay is negatively related. If one consumer is willing to pay more for one and less for the other product than another consumer, then bundling is the best way to extract the consumers' willingness to pay. Assume, for example, that consumer 1 is willing to pay €12 for good 1 and €8 for good 2, and consumer 2 is willing to pay €15 for good 1 and €5 for good 2. A monopolist selling these products separately would charge €12 for good 1 and €5 for good 2. If the two consumers are prepared to buy at most one unit of each product and assuming zero production cost, the profit is €34. However, if the monopolist bundles and sells the goods together for €20, both consumers will buy the pure bundle and the total profit is €40.

Mixed bundling is more complicated due to the additional alternative of buying the single products. Figure 11.19 is a schematic depiction of the situation. The monopoly firm chooses the individual prices (P_1 and P_2 for goods 1 and 2, respectively) and the bundle price (P_{Bundle}) in order to maximise profits. The consumers choose depending on their willingness to pay (WTP). Area *A* in Figure 11.19 contains the WTP combinations for which consumers would only buy product *1*. Area *C* is the corresponding area for good *2*. Area *D* contains the WTP combinations for which consumers do not buy at all, and area *B* those for which consumers choose to buy the bundle. The monopoly firm can change the relative sizes of these areas by adjusting the prices for the single products, and by moving P_{Bundle} closer to or farther away from the origin.

Figure 11.19: Mixed bundling

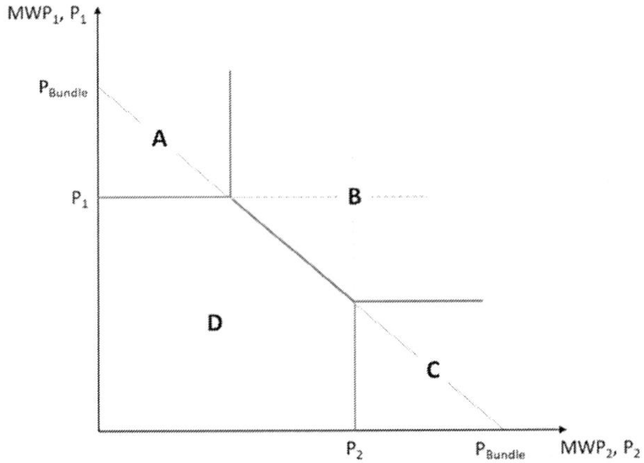

Source: Own based on Carlton and Perloff (2015:350).

The following example illustrates an optimisation problem with two goods and three consumers. The monopoly supplier has constant marginal costs of production of €6 per unit of good *1* and €10 per unit of good *2*. The willingness to pay for the two goods (good *1*/good *2*) is €20/€4 for consumer *1*, €16/€8 for consumer *2*, and €8/€16 for consumer *3*. If we apply fixed bundling, the best bundle price is €24. All three consumers would buy the bundle and the profit is: (3*€24) – (3*€10) – (3*€6) = €24. If the monopolist sells the products separately, the optimal prices are €16/€8 resulting in a profit of: 2*(€16 + €8) – (2*€10) – (2*€6) = €16. The optimal mixed bundling strategy would be to sell consumer *1* only good *1*, to sell consumer *2* the bundle, and to sell consumer *3* only good *2*, with the bundle price set at €24, the price of good *1* at €19.99, and the price for good *2* at €15.99. The profit under mixed bundling is then: €19.99 + €24 + €15.99 – (2*€10) – (2*€6) = €27.98.

11.4.7. Information and models of sales

We live in an information society. It has never been easier to obtain information about all manner of things. Often not a lack of information but rather information overload causes difficulties in decision making, for example in consumer choice. Everybody individually relates to the term information, but what exactly is it? According to Shapiro und Varian (1998, p. 3) information is "anything that can be digitised - encoded by a stream of bits". Thus, many things may be viewed as information. Information often has a positive connotation, as something that is objective, correct, or useful. However, this is not necessarily the case. Key properties of information include: (1) not all information is correct, (2) not all information is processed, (3) information gathering and processing is costly, (4) not all information is readily available at all times, (5) information can change over time, (6) not everybody can correctly process each piece of information, (7) information is subjective, and (8) information may not be structured and may even be without value (Case 2012, p. 45 ff.).

Information on prices, product quality, quantities, etc. is relevant for market participants. In his paper "The Market for Lemons", for example, Akerlof (1970) analyses the implications of imperfect (asymmetric) information about product quality. He shows that there will be no market for high quality goods unless, for example, sellers offer product guarantees or warranties. In the following, we focus on the role of price information. To simplify the issue, we first assume that information is just about the product price, it is always correct, and all agents can correctly process it. Time is not an issue.

However, information gathering is costly and/or consumers have different levels of price information (knowledge). The motivation of the following models is to demonstrate the possible existence of multi-price equilibria under this setting. Salop and Stiglitz (1977) first present a model of the role of information, which results in a two-price equilibrium with high- and low-price stores. Varian's (1980) model of sales produces mixed pricing strategies, with a continuum of prices in the range between low promotional sales' prices and high reservation prices. We begin with Salop and Stiglitz's (1977) model of bargains and rip-offs.

11.4.7.1. Bargains and rip-offs (Salop and Stiglitz 1977):

Salop and Stiglitz (1977) analyse the effect of information costs in the context of (food) retailing. They assume two types of consumers. One type has low marginal costs of gathering and processing price information (c_1), and the other has high costs ($c_2 > c_1$). The model assumes one identical product. Each consumer demands a maximum of one unit of this product, and each is willing to pay at most P^u for this unit. There are n firms, manufacturers or retailers who have free entry into the market. Thus, profits are zero. The average production and/or retailing cost curve (AC) is U-shaped and identical for all firms (Figure 11.20).

Figure 11.20: The Salop and Stiglitz (1977) model of bargains and rip-offs

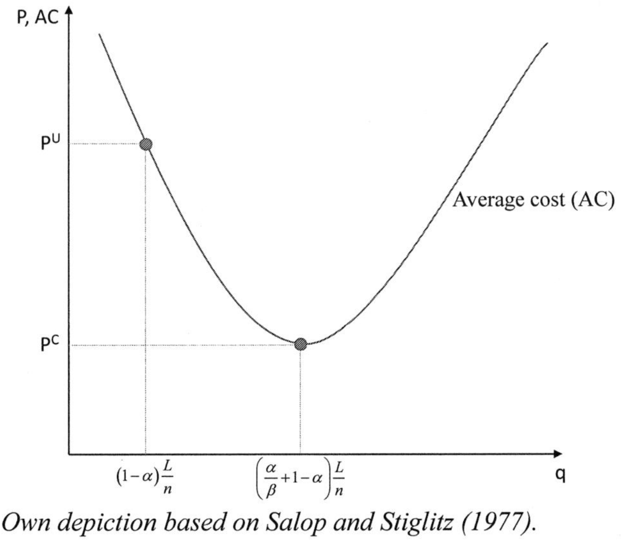

Source: Own depiction based on Salop and Stiglitz (1977).

The minimum of the average cost curve is at P^C. If consumers invest the costs of gathering and processing information, they become informed about all prices in the market. If not, they do not know any prices charged by firms in the market. Though the location of the firms is not relevant, each consumer can only buy from one firm. Informed consumers buy from the firm with the lowest price. Consumers with no price information randomly choose a firm. The share of informed consumers is α and the share of uninformed consumers is therefore $1\text{-}\alpha$. The number of consumers in the market is L.

Based on the model assumptions, three different price equilibria can result. First, when all consumers are informed, the price P^C results. To prove this, we start at a price above P^C. If all firms set a price above P^C, each firm has an incentive to marginally lower the price to attract all informed consumers. Because the price decrease is only marginal and average costs fall, demand and profits increase significantly. Thus, firms will underbid each other down to P^C. No firm will bid below P^C, which represents the minimum average cost.

The second price equilibrium is P^U, the maximum WTP common to all consumers. A price above P^U would lead to zero demand, zero sales, and zero profit. If all consumers are uninformed due to high costs of information, consumers randomly choose firms. In this situation, a price decrease would not generate an increase in demand for a firm because there are no informed consumers. Therefore, the profit-maximising price is at P^U.

Third, a two-price equilibrium can occur if some consumers are informed and others are not. This equilibrium occurs if the following condition is met:

$$c_1 < (1-\beta)(P^U - P^C) < c_2 \tag{48}$$

Consumers search because the reward of the search exceeds its costs. In this case, the reward takes the form of finding the low-price firm. A potential equilibrium with two prices in the market is represented by a low price at P^C and a high price at P^U. Prices above P^U and below P^C are not set by firms because there is no demand above P^U and costs exceed prices below P^C. Prices between P^U and P^C are suboptimal because firms that set such prices would not attract informed consumers, and therefore, they would be better off charging P^U. Only firms that charge P^C share the informed consumers. Thus, if a two-price equilibrium exists, then because some firms set P^U and others P^C. Due to free entry, profits are zero for all firms. Average costs at the demand of high-price firms need to equal P^U and average costs at the demand of low-price firms need to equal P^C. The demand (the number of consumers expected) at the high-price firms is equal to the share of uniformed consumers times the total number of consumers divided by the number of firms:

$$d_{pU} = (1 - \alpha)\frac{L}{n} \tag{49}$$

The demand at the low-price firms is the demand at the high-price firm plus an even share of the informed consumers at low-price firms, where β is the share of low-price firms.

$$d_{pC} = (1 - \alpha)\frac{L}{n} + \alpha\frac{L}{n\beta} = \frac{((1-\alpha)\beta+\alpha)L}{n\beta} \tag{50}$$

By substituting the demand at high-priced firms in equation (49) into equation (50), we can determine the share of low-price firms β:

$$\beta = \frac{\alpha d_{pU}}{(1-\alpha)\left(d_{pC}-d_{pU}\right)} \tag{51}$$

The share of low-price firms increases with the share of informed consumers and with the individual demand at high-price firms; in addition, the share of low-price firms decreases with the share of informed consumers and the demand at low-price firms.

Salop and Stiglitz show that it is possible to have a two-price equilibrium for a homogeneous good market. The retail food market, where we observe significant product price differences between low-priced discounters and high-priced supermarkets, is a good example. However, the model cannot explain price differences between products within a retail store, nor can it explain price changes over time, e. g. promotional prices. In addition, the model does not explain which store sets what price and why, because the decision-making process at the store level is not modelled. Finally, the model is dynamically inconsistent. Uninformed consumers randomly visit stores. Thus, some of them will find a low-price store by chance. After finding such a store, consumers will return to it in the future. Thus, in the long run, all consumers will become informed either systematically or randomly, and the two-price equilibrium will dynamically converge to a one-price equilibrium at P^C with only informed consumers. Varian (1980) takes up this critique in the model that we consider next.

11.4.7.2.A model of sales (Varian 1980):

In the late 1970s Hal Varian shopped for a new TV and noticed that there were substantial price differences and special offers. Inspired by these observations, Varian developed a model of (promotional price) sales. Varian (1980, p. 651) states “Economists have belatedly come to recognise that the "law of one price" is no law at all. Most retail markets are instead characterised by a rather large degree of price dispersion”.

Varian (1980) and Salop and Stiglitz (1977) make very similar assumptions. The main difference is the assumption of a monotonically decreasing average cost curve. Salop and Stiglitz (1977) assume a U-shaped average cost curve with a low-cost minimum. Varian argues that retailing costs are, for the most part, fixed and that as a result, average retailing costs monotonically decline with sales volume. Instead of introducing search costs, Varian assumes a fixed share of informed and uniformed consumers.

Following Varian’s (1980) notation there are n firms or retail stores, and market entry is free. There are I informed and M uniformed consumers. Each consumer demands at most one unit of the homogeneous good. Uniformed consumers randomly choose a store; thus, every store gets the same share ($U = M/n$) of uninformed consumers. The maximum WTP, or reservation price for the good (r), is the same for each consumer. All informed consumers choose the lowest-price store. The number of consumers at the store with the lowest price is $U + I$.

For these assumptions, Varian (1980) shows that there exists no symmetric price equilibrium (not all stores set the same price). Instead, an equilibrium can only exist for a mixed pricing strategy based on a continuous price distribution (probability density function, $f(P)$). Figure 11.21 shows the setting for the Varian (1980) model. First, we define the maximum price range. The maximum price is equal to the reservation price (r). The minimum price equals the average costs for a sales volume of $I + U$ units and is marked P^* in Figure 11.21. Neither r nor $P*$ represent symmetric price equilibria. If all stores offer at price r, then every store has an incentive to underbid competitors in order to attract the informed shoppers. If all firms set $P*$, then all stores make losses as they will each attract an equal share of the informed consumers ($U + I/n$). Varian (1980) argues that there can be no mass (price) points in the interval between r and $P*$. If a mass point in the distribution of prices did exist, stores would have an incentive to underbid this price in order to attract all informed consumers. Therefore, the price distribution must be continuous.

To derive the probability density function of P ($f(p)$), we follow Varian's (1980) initial idea and derive the expected profit ($\pi(P)$) of a store that sets price P:

$$E[\pi(P)] = \pi_S(1 - F(P))^{n-1} + \pi_f\left(1 - (1 - F(P))^{n-1}\right) \tag{52}$$

$F(P)$ is the cumulative probability density function or the integral of $f(P)$. Figure 11.21 illustrates the expected profit if the firm sets price P. In that case, we have two potential outcomes. First, if the store setting price P is the lowest price store, it gets $I + U$ consumers and the profit amounts to the area π_s $(= (P - P^*)(U + I) > 0)$. If the store's price P is not the lowest price in the market, then the store only sells U units at the average cost of r and makes the profit $\pi_f(= (P - r)U < 0)$; thus, the retailer makes a loss equivalent to area π_f. The expected profit is the sum of the π_s times the probability that P is the lowest price in the market $((1-F(P))^{n-1})$ and π_f times the residual probability $(1 - (1 - F(P))^{n-1})$. The probabilities depend on P. If the firm sets a higher price, the probability that it will be the low-price supplier decreases. To calculate the probability of being the lowest price store, we start with the probability that a competitor sets a price above P. The probability that one other store sets a price above P is 1 minus $F(P)$. The probability that all other stores set prices above P is $(1 - F(P))^{n-1}$, which is the probability that the store setting price P is the lowest price store. The probability that the store is not the lowest price store is $(1 - (1 - F(P))^{n-1})$. Because of free entry, the expected profits of all firms at all prices in the range between r and P^* are zero.

If we set the expected profit to zero, we can rearrange equation (52) which results in:

$$F(P) = 1 - \left(\frac{\pi_f}{\pi_f - \pi_S}\right)^{\frac{1}{n-1}} \tag{53}$$

The store's profit at price P is negative when P is not the lowest price in the market. The store's profit at price P is positive, when P is the lowest price. Thus, the term in brackets in equation (53) is positive and smaller than 1. The likelihood that P is the lowest price depends on the ratio of the firm's profits at P, when P is the lowest and when P is not the lowest price in the market. For higher prices, π_f is decreasing and π_s is increasing; thus, the ratio tends to zero. For lower prices, π_f increases and π_s decreases and the ratio approaches 1. From equation (53) we can derive the equilibrium price probability density function.

Figure 11.21: The Varian (1980) model of sales

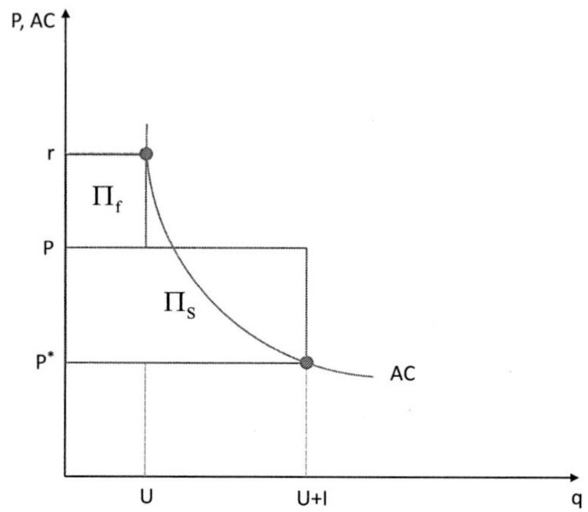

Source: Own depiction based on Varian (1980, p.655).

For $P = r$ we can conclude that the price cannot be the lowest in the market and thus the profit is equal to $r \cdot M/n - k$, where k are the fixed costs. Due to free entry, the profit even in this extreme case is zero and therefore $U = k/r$. The other extreme is P=P*, which is the lowest price in the market. In this case the profit is $P^*(I + k/r) - k = 0$; thus $P^* = k/(I + k/r)$. We introduce the general profit equations $((PU - k), P(U + I) - k)$ to equation (53) and simplify:

$$F(P) = 1 - \left(\frac{PU-k}{PU-k-P(U+I)+k}\right)^{\frac{1}{n-1}} \tag{54}$$

$$F(P) = 1 - \left(\frac{PU-k}{-PI}\right)^{\frac{1}{n-1}} \tag{55}$$

$$F(P) = 1 - \left(\frac{k-\frac{k}{r}P}{PI}\right)^{\frac{1}{n-1}} \tag{56}$$

$$F(P) = 1 - \left(\frac{k}{I}\left(\frac{1}{P} - \frac{1}{r}\right)\right)^{\frac{1}{n-1}} \tag{57}$$

Next, we differentiate equation (57) with respect to P. After some rearrangements, and assuming that n goes to infinity, Varian (1980) shows that the price density is proportional to the expression on the right-hand side of the following equation:[18]

$$\underset{n\to\infty}{F'(P)} \equiv \underset{n\to\infty}{f(P)} \propto \frac{1}{P\left(1-\frac{P}{r}\right)} \tag{58}$$

The density in equation (58) is U-shaped as shown in Figure 11.22, indicating high probabilities for low as well as for high prices.

Figure 11.22: Equilibrium price density for the Varian model

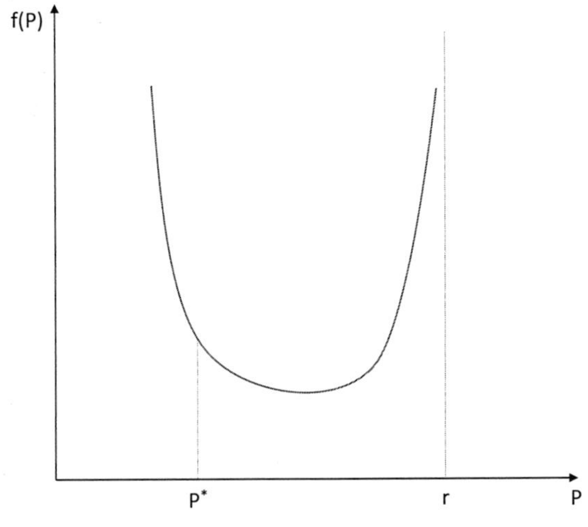

Source: Own depiction based on Varian (1980, p. 656).

The Varian (1980) model can explain price differentiation at the same store in time. The model produces high and low prices as an outcome of a mixed strategy equilibrium. However, it is unrealistic that retail managers would set prices by randomly drawing from a distribution every day or week. Further, the focus on one product oversimplifies the market situation in retailing, where there are thousands of products per store, as well as the interactions between them in demand and supply. Richards (2006) develops a multiproduct model of sales based on Varian (1980) to prove the existence

---

[18] A detailed derivation of Varian's (1980) results is presented in the Appendix to this chapter.

of a complementary relationship between breadth and depth of sales. Loy and Weiss (2009), however, show that the model results in a substitutional relationship; thus, the number of sales and the average level of discounts are substitutes.

In the following, we add a second product to study multiple products and the role of brands and brand loyalty in price setting and promotion.

11.4.8. The effects of brand loyalty (Raju et al. 1990):

At the beginning of this chapter we saw that brands play a major role in food retailing. By establishing brands, manufacturers and retailers try to differentiate the food retail market horizontally and/or vertically. "A brand is a name, term, design, symbol or any other feature that identifies one seller's good or service as distinct from those of other sellers" (Muñiz 2015). A brand "is an intangible asset" that is intended to create "distinctive images and associations in the minds of stakeholders, thereby generating economic benefit (value)". In practice, strong brands attract customers, and add revenue through increased price or volume premiums and repeat purchase loyalty. Brands can create economic benefit, if a brand producer can raise prices above competitors' level without losing too much sales volume. Brand loyalty is the key term behind the strength of brands. According to Jacoby and Kyner (1973, p. 2) "brand loyalty is a biased (non-random) behavioural response expressed over time by some decision-making unit with respect to one or more alternative brands out of a set of such brands and is a function of psychological (decision making, evaluative) processes." Brands add extra value to the product, for which the consumer is willing to accept a higher price. Agrawal (1996, p. 87) defines the "strength of brand loyalty … as the price differential needed before the consumer will switch away to the less favoured brand". Hence, a consumer is loyal with an intensity l_1 to brand *1* if he/she does not switch until:

$$P_{i\neq 1} < P_1 - l_1 \text{ with } l_1 > 0 \tag{59}$$

Raju et al. (1990) built on this definition and developed a model of brand loyalty with two competing products. They assume two producers, one of which markets a strong *(s)* brand, while the other markets a weak *(w)* brand, with $l_s > l_w$. There are two groups of customers, one of which is loyal to the weak brand while the other is loyal to the strong brand. The reservation price is *r* for all consumers, and every consumer demands at most one unit of each good. Raju et al. (1990) abstract from production and transaction costs. The demand functions for the weak and for the strong brands are shown in equations (60) and (61), respectively.

$$q_s(p_s, p_w) = \begin{cases} 0 & if \quad p_w < p_s - l_s \\ 1 & if \quad p_w - l_w \leq p_s \leq p_w + l_s \\ 2 & if \quad p_s < p_w - l_w \end{cases} \tag{60}$$

$$q_w(p_s, p_w) = \begin{cases} 2 & if \quad p_w < p_s - l_s \\ 1 & if \quad p_w - l_w \leq p_s \leq p_w + l_s \\ 0 & if \quad p_s < p_w - l_w \end{cases} \tag{61}$$

Figure 11.23 illustrates the demand for the strong brand. Like Varian (1980), Raju et al. (1990) find a mixed pricing strategy for both firms. The main result is that the strong brand promotes less often and at higher discounts than the weak brand. Promotion of the strong brand is used to attract consumers loyal to the weak brand (aggressive promotion), while promotion of the weak brand is used to discourage its loyal customers from switching to the strong brand (defensive promotion). Figure 11.24 shows the equilibrium probability density functions for both brands.

Figure 11.23: Demand for the strong brand in the Raju et al. (1990) model

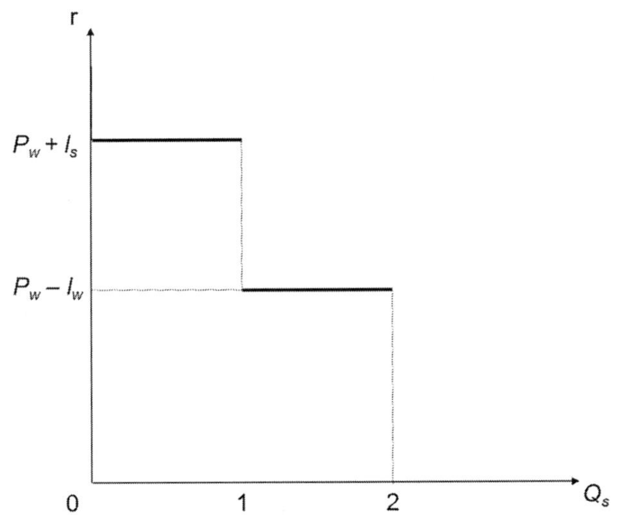

Source: Own depiction based on Raju et al. (1990).

Agrawal (1996) extends this model by introducing a retailer as an intermediary between the producers and the consumers. Agrawal's (1996) model generates significantly different outcomes, for the following reason. In the Raju et al.*'s* (1990) model there is no coordination of promotion between manufacturers. In Agrawal (1996), however, the monopolistic retailer has full control over promotional sales. For the retailer it is not profitable to defend customers loyal to the weak brand against promotions of the strong brand. The retailer only sets price promotions in order to encourage consumers to switch to the promoted brand. The retailer sets price promotions for both brands, but not at the same time; the discount for the strong brand is lower than the discount for the weak brand, according to the intensity of consumer loyalty. Compared with the weak brand, the strong brand needs less (price) incentive to attract the consumer of the competing (weak) brand. The producer of the strong brand will offer a better deal for discounts than the producer of the weak brand. Thus, the retailer will promote the strong brand more often than the weak brand, but at lower discounts. This result is exactly opposite to that of Raju et al. (1990). The five series of orange juice prices in the same retail store presented in Figure 11.25 appear to confirm one of Agrawal's (1996) results, as they show no evidence of synchronised brand promotions.

Figure 11.24: Probability density functions for the Raju et al. (1990) model

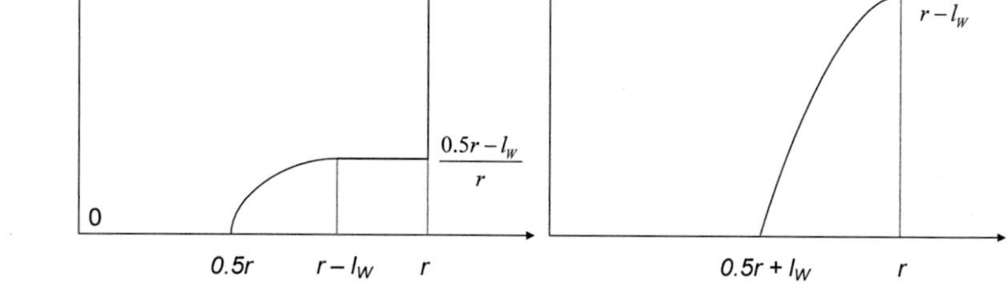

Source: Own depiction based on Raju et al. *(1990, p. 287).*

In this section we have introduced some models that aim to explain why price promotions are used in food retailing. We have seen that these models shed some first light on the complex problem of explaining the phenomena in retail price setting. In the next section we present a number of specific case studies of price behaviour in food retailing to further explore empirical evidence in this field.

11.5. Case studies

11.5.1. Why don't prices rise during periods of peak demand (Chevalier et al. 2003)?

Chevalier et al. (2003) examine retail and wholesale prices for a large US supermarket chain over a period of more than seven years. They find that prices on average fall during seasonal demand peaks for a product, such as holidays, largely due to changes in retail margins. Retail margins for specific goods fall during peak demand periods, even if these periods do not coincide with aggregate demand peaks for the retailer.

Chevalier et al. (2003) present different theories to explain this countercyclical pricing: a model of countercyclical collusion, a model of cyclical elasticity of demand, and a model of loss leader. All of these models are potentially consistent with seasonally falling food retail prices for particular products at demand peaks.

Economies of scale in search

Warner and Barsky (1995) model economies of scale in consumer search. The costs of search and travel between retail stores are fixed for consumers. Thus, when demand is high, fixed costs are spread over a higher purchase volume and consumers search more. This makes consumers more price sensitive, leading to lower retail margins and prices. Therefore, prices tend to fall for example at Christmas or Easter, when overall demand is at a peak.

Countercyclical collusion model

Another explanation is based on dynamic interactions between firms. If retailers compete repeatedly, tacit collusion can emerge. Rotemberg and Saloner (1986) consider tacit collusion under variable demand. In periods of high demand, the temptation to defect and increase market shares by lowering prices is highest. Moreover, the possible resulting punishment for defecting is lowest, because it will occur in later periods of low demand. Bernheim and Whinston (1990) extend this analysis to the multiproduct environment and prove that prices of various products fall during periods of peak demand.

Loss-Leader model

The Lal and Matutes (1994) loss-leader model (see section 3.3) provides another explanation of falling prices in periods of peak demand. The model assumes costs of shopping and costs of advertising. Furthermore, it assumes that consumers do not have any information on retail store prices, unless they are advertised. To attract consumers, retailers advertise low prices for some products and maintain regular high prices for the others. Consumers choose a store based on advertised prices. Because of advertisement costs, retailers do not advertise all prices, but rather only those with a high demand. Thus, in periods of high demand more products are chosen for advertisements than in periods of normal demand.

Chevalier et al.'s (2003) empirical results show that prices, and retail margins, fall in periods of peak demand, but only for seasonal products. Estimated price elasticities for these products also display significant seasonal variation. Furthermore, the authors find that advertising activity and seasonal demand are positively correlated, i. e. seasonal products are more advertised in peak demand periods. These empirical results are consistent with Lal and Matutes' (1994) loss-leader theory of retailer competition. Models that stress cyclical demand elasticities or cyclical firm conduct are less consistent with the empirical findings. Hence, it appears that manufacturer behaviour plays a limited role in the countercyclicality of prices.

11.5.2. Sales: Tests of theories on causality and timing (Berck et al., 2008)

Modern theories of promotional sales make controversial predictions about the temporal pattern of sales. Berck et al. (2008) analyse grocery scanner data for orange juice in the USA to test these theories. Using correlations, runs tests, probit regressions, and vector-autoregressive analyses, they investigate the following hypotheses: (1) private label products are less often on sale than national brands; (2) manufacturers determine sales rather than retailers; (3) price distributions over longer time periods are (a) continuous (U-shaped, bell-shaped), (b) have a mass point at the highest price, or (c) have two mass points for each major brand and a single mass point for the private label; (4) price distributions vary with the perishability of the product; (5) regarding the timing of sales across firms: (a) sales patterns are random across firms, (b) firms lower prices simultaneously, (c) national-brand firms alternate sales, but private labels do not have sales, (d) the probability of a sale rises with the time since the last sale of the relevant brands, (e) the largest brand is a pricing leader, (f) prices fall slowly and then jump to a high level." (Berck et al. 2008, p. 1260).

The authors use retail prices of major brands and private labels of orange juice in 22 stores in 13 US cities collected by IRI Symphony for 1998 and 1999. The authors include a wholesale price for orange juice and a consumer price index in their analysis. The results show that retail prices vary strongly across stores and over time. The variation in both dimensions is largely due to temporary price promotions for individual brands. The authors define promotional sales in a store as price reductions of at least 25%, 35% or 50% against the mode price of the product in the store calculated for the two-year period.

Berck et al. (2008) find that private label orange juice is put on sale at least as frequently as the manufacturer brands. Thus, they reject the first hypothesis. However, Loy and Schaper (2014) find the opposite result for a range of products in German grocery stores: retailer brands are put on sale significantly less frequently than national brands. Figure 11.25 shows an example for 5 different orange juice brands in a German retail store in 2000. While we observe promotional price sales for three of four manufacturer brands, we observe none for the private label TIP.

Figure 11.25: Weekly retail prices of orange juice in a German food store

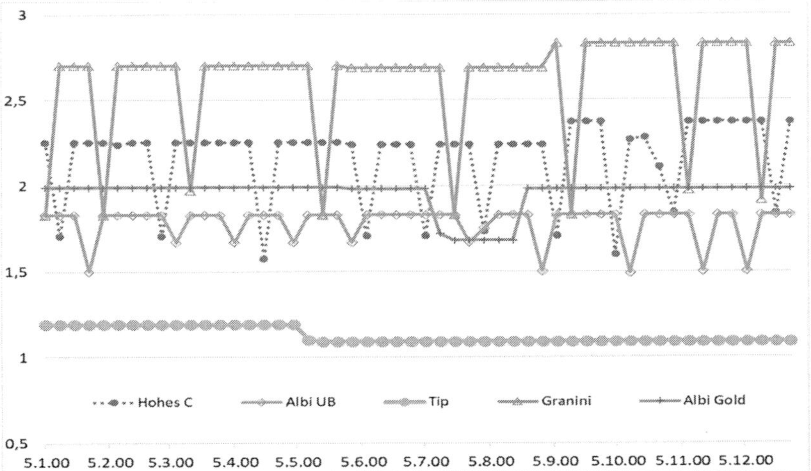

Source: Own depiction with price data from MaDaKom 2002.

Berck et al. (2008) also investigate the correlations of promotions for the same brands in different stores at the national, market and chain levels. They find relatively low level of correlations. For refrigerated juice, the level of correlations increases from national to chain level, but for frozen juice this is not the case. Berck et al. (2008) therefore conclude that manufacturers do not determine the timing of sales for refrigerated or frozen orange juice.

For the distribution of prices Berck et al. (2008) reject hypotheses (a) and (b). They also find little evidence for hypothesis (c) that the distribution is bimodal with one mass point at the sale's price and another mass point at the regular price. Berck et al. (2008, p. 1265) conclude that "price distributions differ in no obvious pattern by brand and by store. Little support was found for any one of the three clearly predicted price distributions." In the case presented in Figure 11.25, three of four manufacturer brands show a clear bimodal distribution with the sales' price and the regular price as mass points. The private label shows a unimodal distribution at the regular price.

For hypothesis 5 (f) Berck et al. (2008) show that prices do not fall slowly before they rise to the highest price. For the prices in Figure 11.25 it is clear that prices rise and fall equally fast. Similar to Villas-Boas (1995), Slade (1994), and Pesendorfer (2002), Berck et al. reject the null hypothesis 5 (a) that promotional price sales are random. They find some evidence that sales are intentionally dispersed between brands. Figure 11.25 supports this finding, as we cannot observe many overlaps between brands' sales. In most cases, there is only one brand on sale at any given time and all sales last only one week. Similarly, Berck et al. (2008) fail to confirm hypothesis 5 (d) that the probability of a sale increases with the time elapsed since the last sale. In addition, the price leader hypothesis 5 (e) cannot be confirmed.

11.5.3. Brand loyalty (Empen et al., 2015)

Following Narasimhan's (1988) seminal work, many research papers have modelled the pricing strategies used by retailers to exploit brand loyal consumers. Empen et al. (2015) merge consumer and retail scanner data sets to provide a comprehensive basis for investigating the relationship between measures of brand loyalty and retailers' price promotion strategies. The study contributes to previous work by analysing two different dimensions of brand loyalty (size and strength) for the ready-to-eat cereal market.

Theoretical as well as empirical models employ a reduced brand architecture (product line management) that is focused on one brand for each manufacturer (corporate brand). The models arrive at different conclusions depending on the various assumptions. For example, Koças and Bohlmann (2008) find that the stronger brands are promoted more aggressively, while, as discussed in section 11.4.8, Agrawal (1996) predicts that they will be promoted less deeply but more often. In the real world, manufacturers often establish a corporate brand with several sub-brands, something that is not addressed in the existing models. In the sample analysed by Empen et al. (2015), each corporate brand sells several sub-brands. For example, Kellogg's sells Frosties and Special K; Nestlé sells Trio and Fruit Loops. This type of product line management can be found in other product markets such as soft drinks (consider for example the range of Coke products), yoghurts or automobiles. Empen et al. (2015) distinguish between corporate and sub-brands by introducing corporate brand dummies. They find that Kellogg's sub-brands on average capture a larger loyal consumer segment and a higher strength of loyalty than Nestle's sub-brands. According to the theory of Koças and Bohlmann (2008), Nestlé follows an aggressive promotional strategy by offering more sales at a higher discount because Nestlé sells to more customers who switch (higher switching to loyal ratio). Hence, Nestlé relies on being the cheapest alternative and may therefore offer more aggressive trade deals to retailers.

Empen et al. (2015) capture corporate brand effects with dummy variables; the remaining variation in promotional strategies indicates the variations between the different sub-brands. While some sub-brands, e. g. Kellogg's Frosties, have a large loyal consumer segment, the strength of the loyalty is comparatively low. Other sub-brands, e. g. Kellogg's Toppas Classic, have a smaller but strongly loyal consumer segment. These differences between sub-brands determine the relationship between brand loyalty and price promotions. Empen et al. (2015) find strong evidence that the loyal segment size has a positive impact on promotional measures, whereas the strength of consumer loyalty negatively impacts the depth and the frequency of sales. As can be seen in Table 11.5, the segment size positively affects the depth of discounts (0.062) and the frequency of discounts (0.263). The loyalty strength has a negative impact on both measures, -0,075 and -0.283 respectively.

To date, there is no consistent theory in the literature that explains this result. Empen et al. (2015) hypothesise that it is caused by the retailers' strategy to choose sub-brands for promotional sales. If retailers use brand promotions mainly to lure customers into their stores, then they will choose sub-brands that have large loyal segments; this ensures that the promotion will attract a large number of customers. However, retailers will not choose sub-brands with strong brand loyalty, because they would rather exploit strongly loyal customers through high prices. Promotions for such sub-brands are costly, as prices have to be reduced heavily to reach new customers. Thus, there are many promotions with higher discounts for sub-brands with large loyal segments and only few promotions with low discounts for sub-brands with strong loyal segments. Price promotions for these sub-brands are not motivated by loss leadership but are rather attempts to increase the sub-brands' loyal segments to prevent customers from switching to competitors' brands.

The results suggest that weaker corporate brands, such as Nestlé, are promoted more aggressively, which supports the model hypotheses by Koças and Bohlmann (2008) (see the estimates for corporate brand dummies in Table 11.5). Within the manufacturer's product line, sub-brands with larger loyal consumer segments and moderate consumer loyalty are more often used for effective price promotions, which reflects the idea of loss leading.

Table 11.5: Results for the frequency and depth of price promotion models

Independent variables	Dependent variable	
	Depth of discount sales (Tobit model)	Frequency of discounts (OLS estimation)
Constant	0.116 (7.89)	-2.924 (-20.39
Brand loyalty		
Loyalty strength	-0.075 (-3.71)	-0.283 (-1.74)
Segment size / 1000	0.062 (7.98)	0.263 (3.48)
Retailer dummies		
Markant	-0.022 (-2.28)	-0.156 (-1.93)
Metro	0.001 (0.15)	0.161 (2.38)
Rewe	-0.173 (-13.03)	-0.139 (-1.09)
Tengelmann	-0.039 (-2.67)	-0.792 (-8.57)
Discounter	-0.173 (-8.07)	-0.902 (-6.23)
Others	-0.016 (-0.98)	-0.869 (-7.98)
Corporate brand dummies		
Kelloggs	-0.025 (-2.75)	-0.212 (-1.77)
Koelln	-0.091 (-4.46)	-0.913 (-6.34)
Nestlé	0.039 (4.17)	0.503 (4.37)
Number of observations	1729	1012
R^2		0.23

Note: t-values in brackets.
Source: Empen et al. (2015, p. 747).

11.5.4. Product differentiation and cost pass-through (Bittmann et al. 2020)

Many studies that estimate CPT rates or vertical price transmission for agricultural and food product markets focus on short-run dynamics, and in particular on asymmetric 'rocket and feathers' adjustments of prices to shocks. [19] Loy and Weiss (2019) introduce a measure of product differentiation into a reduced form model of retail CPT. The analysis in the paper by Bittmann et al. (2020) builds on Loy and Weiss (2019), and uses an oligopoly model approach to derive and empirically estimate the effects of product differentiation on CPT for industry-wide and firm-specific cost shocks. Theory points to the importance of distinguishing between industry-wide and firm-specific cost shocks and their interactions with product differentiation in the context of retailers' price-setting behaviour (see section 4.5 in this chapter).

Bittmann et al. (2020) analyse CPT in differentiated oligopolies using data on ready-to-eat soup products in the Canadian retail market that includes detailed information on product-specific purchase prices. This allows them to differentiate between and estimate industry-wide and firm-specific costs. The availability of detailed UPC-level product and brand information allows them to construct and estimate several distance measures of product differentiation, and to merge these variables with a large panel of purchase and retail prices. Using these data, they test the following hypotheses: (1) more differentiated products show higher retail prices, (2) more differentiated products have a lower CPT elasticity of industry-wide cost shocks, (3) more differentiated products have a higher CPT elasticity of firm-specific cost shocks, (4) more differentiated products return more slowly to the long-run price-cost equilibrium, and (5) product differentiation reinforces the asymmetric CPT and slows down the price adjustment process.

The results in Table 11.6 provide support for hypotheses 1 to 5. Product differentiation is associated with higher margins; CPT rates for industry-wide cost shocks are lower for more differentiated products; CPT rates for firm-specific cost shocks are higher for more differentiated products; retail prices adjust less rapidly to cost shocks for more differentiated products; and for more differentiated products the 'rocket and feathers' phenomenon becomes more pronounced. These results confirm that product

[19] A detailed discussion of asymmetric vertical price adjustment is provided in Section 6 of Chapter 10.

differentiation serves as a tool of market segmentation to reduce price competition, and that it is a source of retail market power which directly effects product-specific mark-ups and CPT rates.

11.6. Outlook

This chapter presents an overview of theories and facts about food retail pricing. Some aspects have been covered briefly, and others in more detail. However, many aspects have been left out due to space limitations. In this final overview, some relevant missing aspects are mentioned.

First, promotional sales are key measures of food retail marketing. Many scientific papers analyse the effects of promotional prices on sale volumes, consumer loyalty, stockholding, brand switching etc. Gedenk (2002) and Blattberg and Neslin (1990) provide excellent introductions to the literature in this field.

Second, the literature is dominated by studies that use data from US food retail markets. More studies need to be carried out on markets in other countries, and the results need to be compared to deepen our understanding of food retail pricing. Among the few such comparative studies, Lamey et al. (2007) compare private labels in the US and Europe.

Table 11.6: Fixed and random effects panel model of long- and short-run CPT

Long-run CPT Dependent variable: retail prices Independent variables	Random Effects Model	**Short-run asym. CPT** Dependent variable: First differences of retail prices Independent variables	Random Effects Model
Measure of Product differentiation (PD)	0.04 (0.01)	Error Correction Term$^+$	-0.60 (0.05)
Industry-wide costs	0.97 (0.05)	Error Correction Term$^-$	-0.88 (0.05)
Industry-wide costs x PD	-0.09 (0.03)	Error Correction T.$^+$ x PD	0.27 (0.03)
Firm-specific costs	0.84 (0.02)	Error Correction T.$^-$ x PD	0.02 (0.01)
Firm-specific costs x PD	0.09 (0.02)		
Constant	0.31 (0.01)		
R^2 within	0.84	R^2	0.41
R^2 between	0.90		
R^2 overall	0.84		
Observations	101,104	Observations	98,264

Note: Robust standard errors in parentheses.
Source: Based on Bittmann et al. (2020).

Third, increasing market shares of private labels and the development of alternative private label brand formats demand further theoretical and empirical research on the effects of private labels for retail competition and the performance of retail markets. Steiner (2004) discusses the issue in his paper on the nature and benefits of national brand and private label competition.

Fourth, not all products are regularly promoted. Food stores use a selection of goods that is repeatedly promoted. So-called signpost items are products of high consumer price sensitivity. Lal and Matutes (1994) discuss this without describing the selection of products. Hosken and Reiffen (2004) present a model to derive some properties of promoted products and SAP and GfK (2010) publish lists of signpost items and their price sensitivities.

Fifth, the Covid-19 pandemic has shifted food demand towards online retailing. This will alter food marketing to use more individual data, individually tailored promotions, and social media-based advertising. Developing and investigating optimisation methods based on artificial intelligence is an area of emerging research. Chintagunta et al. (2016) look at the potential of big data in marketing science. Culotta and Cutler (2016) propose a novel and fully-automated method for inferring attribute-specific brand perception ratings based on mining a brand's social connections on Twitter.

11.7. Keywords and Terms

- Brand
- Brand loyalty
- Bertrand
- Buying-in price
- Cartel
- Cherry picking
- Concentration ratio (CR)
- Cournot-Nash equilibrium
- European article number (EAN)
- Everyday low-price (EDLP)
- Fast-moving consumer goods (FMCG)
- Food away from home (FAFH)
- High-Low or HiLo strategy
- Lerner index
- Loss-leader

- Market power
- Mark-up
- Menu costs
- Mixed bundling
- Mixed strategy
- Monopolistic competition
- Monopoly rent
- National brand (manufacturer brand)
- Odd pricing
- Price discrimination
- Price dispersion
- Price rigidity
- Product differentiation
- Promotional pricing (sales)
- Private label (retailer brand)
- Pure bundling
- Reaction function
- Residual demand (curve)
- Stackelberg
- Store format
- Store keeping unit (SKU)
- 9-endings

11.8. References

AGOF (2020) Digital report. Frankfurt. www.agof.de. 20.03.2021.

Agrawal D (1996) Effect of brand loyalty on advertising and trade promotions: a game theoretic analysis with empirical evidence. Marketing Science 15 (1): 86-108.

Akerlof GA (1970) The Market for "Lemons": Quality Uncertainty and the Market Mechanism. The Quarterly Journal of Economics 84(3): 488-500.

Anderson E, Jaimovich N and Simester D (2015) Price stickiness: empirical evidence of the menu cost channel. The Review of Economics and Statistics 97 (4): 813–826.

Anderson E and Simester D (2003) Effects of $9 Price Endings on Retail Sales: Evidence from Field Experiments. Quantitative Marketing and Economics 1: 93-110.

Baker J and Bresnahan TF (2008) Economic evidence in antitrust: defining markets and measuring market power. P. Buccirossi (ed) Handbook of Antitrust Economics: 1-42.

Barsky RB, Bergen M, Dutta S and Levy D (2003) What can the price gap between branded and private-label products tell us about markups? Feenstra RC and Shapiro MD (eds) Scanner Data and Price Indexes. University of Chicago Press: 165-228.

Beath J and Katsoulacos Y (1991) The economic theory of product differentiation. Cambridge University Press. Cambridge.

Berck P, Perloff JM, Brown J and Villas-Boas SB (2008) Sales: tests of theories on causality and timing. International Journal of Industrial Organization 26: 1257-1273.

Bernheim BD and Whinston MD (1990) Multimarket contact and collusive behavior. RAND Journal of Economics, 21(1): 1-26.

Bittmann T, Loy J-P and Anders S (2020) Product differentiation and cost pass-through: industry-wide versus firm-specific cost shocks. Australian Journal of Agricultural and Resource Economics 59: 1-26.

Blattberg RC, Eppen GD and Lieberman J (1981) A theoretical and empirical evaluation of price deals for consumer nondurables. Journal of Marketing 45(1): 116-29.

Blattberg RC and Neslin SA (1990) Sales promotion. Concepts, methods, and strategies. Prentice Hall. Englewood Cliffs, New Jersey.

Borenstein S and Shepard A (2002) Sticky prices, inventories, and market power in wholesale gasoline markets. RAND Journal of Economics 33 (1): 116-39.

Borenstein S, Cameron AC and Gilbert R (1997) Do gasoline prices respond asymmetrically to crude oil price changes? The Quarterly Journal of Economics 112(1): 305-339.

Carlton DW and Perloff JM (2015) Modern industrial organization. 4th Ed. Addison Wesley.

Carroll K and Coates D (1999) Teaching Price Discrimination: Some Clarification. Southern Economic Journal 66(2): 466-480.

Case DO (2012) Looking for information. Third Edition. Emerald. Bingley, UK.

Chevalier JA, Kashyap AK and Rossi PE (2003) Why don't prices rise during periods of peak demand? Evidence from scanner data. American Economic Review 93 (1): 15–37.

Chintagunta P, Hanssens DM and Hauser JR (2016) Editorial - marketing science and big data. Marketing Science 35(3): 341-42.

Clerides SK (2002) Book value: intertemporal pricing and quality discrimination in the US market for books. International Journal of Industrial Organization 20: 1385-1408.
Clerides SK (2004) Price discrimination with differentiated products: definition and identification. Economic Inquiry 42: 402-12.
Connor JM and Peterson EB (1992) Market-structure determinants of national brand-private label price differences of manufactured food products. The Journal of Industrial Economics 40(2): 157–171.
Culotta A and Cutler J (2016) Mining brand perceptions from twitter social networks. Marketing Science 35(3): 343-62.
Desai P, Potia A and Salsberg B (2013) Retail 4.0: The future of retail grocery in a digital world. https://www.supplychain247.com/papers/the_future_of_retail_grocery_in_a_digital_world/mckinsey.
Dutta S, Bergen M, Levy D and Venable R (1999) Menu costs, posted prices, and multiproduct retailers. Journal of Money, Credit and Banking 31(4): 683-703.
Eaton BC and Lipsey RG (1989) Product differentiation. Handbook of Industrial Organization 1: 723-68.
Eichenbaum M, Jaimovich N and Rebelo S (2011) Reference Prices, Costs, and Nominal Rigidities. American Economic Review 101 (1): 234 – 62. https://doi.org/10.1257/aer.101.1.234.
Empen J, Loy JP and Weiss C (2015) Price promotion and brand loyalty: empirical evidence for the German ready-to-eat cereal market. European Journal of Marketing 49(5/6): 736-59.
ESOMAR (2019) Global Market Research Report. Cited on https://www.researchworld.com/. Accessed 08. April 2023.
Euromonitor International (2020) Consumer types in Germany. https://www.euromonitor. com/. Accessed 08. April 2023.
EVS (Einkommens- und Verbrauchsstichprobe: Income und Consumption Panel): https://www.destatis.de. Accessed 08. April 2023.
Federal Statistical Office (2020) https://www.destatis.de.
Gedenk K (2002) Verkaufsförderung. Verlag Vahlen. München.
German Antitrust Commission (Bundeskartellamt) (2014) Sektoruntersuchung Lebensmitteleinzelhandel. Bonn. www.bundeskartellamt.de. Accessed 08. April 2023.
GfK Gesellschaft für Konsumforschung, 2004, Consumer scan data. Nürnberg.
Haucap J, Heimeshoff U, Thorwarth S and Wey C (2015) Die Sektoruntersuchung des Bundeskartellamts zur Nachfragemacht im

Lebensmitteleinzelhandel. Ein Kommentar aus ökonomischer Perspektive. DICE Consult GmbH, Düsseldorf.

Holzer PS and Bittmann T. (2019) Regular Price Stickiness in German Food Retailing. Journal of Agricultural & Food Industrial Organization, DOI: https://doi.org/10.1515/jafio-2019-0027

Hosken D and Reiffen D (2001) Multiproduct retailers and the sale phenomenon. Agribusiness: An Interantional Journal 17(1): 115-37.

Hosken D and Reiffen D (2004) Patterns of retail price variation. RAND Journal of Economics 35(1): 128-46.

Hotelling H (1929) Stability in competition. Economic Journal 39: 41-57.

IRI Symphony Group (2014) Retail scanner data Düsseldorf. SymphonyIRI Group GmbH.

Jacoby J and Kyner DB (1973) Brand loyalty vs. repeat purchasing behavior. Journal of Marketing Research 1: 1-9.

Kehoe PJ and Midrigan V (2015) Prices Are Sticky After All. Journal of Monetary Economics 75: 35 – 53. https://doi.org/10.1016/j.jmoneco.2014.12.004.

Koças C and Bohlmann JD (2008) Segmented switchers and retailer pricing strategies. Journal of Marketing 72(3): 124-42.

Labrecque LI, vor dem Esche J, Mathwick C, Novak TP and Hofacker CRF (2013) Consumer power: evolution in the digital age. Journal of Interactive Marketing 27 (4): 257-69.

Lal R and Matutes C (1994) Retail pricing and advertising strategies. The Journal of Business 67(3): 345-370.

Lamey L, Deleersnyder B, Dekimpe MG and Steenkamp JEBM (2007) How business cycles contribute to private-label success: Evidence from the U.S. and Europe. Journal of Marketing 71(1): 1-15.

Levy D, Lee D, Chen H, Kauffman R and Bergen M (2011) Price points and price rigidity. The Review of Economics and Statistics 93(4): 1417-31.

Loy J-P and Schaper F (2014) Preisrigidität bei Lebensmitteln. In: Schmollers Jahrbuch 134: 25 – 60.

Loy J-P and Weiss C (2002) Staggering and synchronisation of pricing behaviour: new evidence from German food retailers. Agribusiness 18(4): 437-457.

Loy J-P and Weiss C (2004) Synchronization due to common shock? Evidence from German grocery prices. Economics Letters 81(1): 123-7.

Loy J-P and Weiss C (2009) Sales by multi-product retailers: a comment. Managerial and Decision Economics 30: 513-5.

Loy J-P and Weiss C (2019) Product differentiation and cost pass-through. Journal of Agricultural Economics 70(3): 840-58.

MaDaKom (2002) Markt Daten Kommunikation GmbH. Retail scan data. Düsseldorf.

McShane B, Chen C, Anderson E and Simester D (2015) Decision stages and asymmetries in regular retail price pass-through. Marketing Sciene 35 (4): 619-29.

Muñiz AM (2015) Brands and Branding. In: The Blackwell Encyclopedia of Sociology, Ritzer G (ed.).

Narasimhan C (1988) Competitive promotional strategies. Journal of Business 61(4): 427-49.

Niehans J (1956) Preistheoretischer Leitfaden für Verkehrswissenschaftler, Schweizerisches Archiv für Verkehrswissenschaft und Verkehrspolitik 11: 293-320.

Nielsen (2018a) Nielsen Consumers, Deutschland – Verbraucher – Handel – Werbung. Frankfurt. www.nielsen.com/.

Nielsen (2018b) Nielsen trade dimensions. Frankfurt. https://nielseniq.com/global/de/insights/analysis/2018/tradedimensions-topfirmen-2017/. Accessed 08. April 2023.

Oliver RL (1999) Whence consumer loyalty? Journal of Marketing 63: 33-44.

Pesendorfer M (2002) Retail sales: a study of pricing behavior in supermarkets. Journal of Business 75: 33–66.

Raju JS, Srinavasan V and Lal R (1990) The effects of brand loyalty on competitive price promotional strategies. Management Science 36(3): 276-304.

Ramsey FP (1927) A contribution to the theory of taxation. Economic Journal 37: 47-61.

Richards TJ (2006) Sales by multi-product retailers. Managerial and Decision Economics 27: 261-77.

Rotemberg JJ and Saloner G (1986) A supergame-theoretic model of price wars during booms. American Economic Review 76(3): 390-407.

Salop S (1979) Monopolistic competition with outside goods. The Bell Journal of Economics 10(1): 141-56.

Salop S and Stigliz JE (1977) Bargains and ripoffs: a model of monopolistically competitive price dispersion. The Review of Economic Studies 44 (3): 493-510.

SAP and GfK (ed.) (2010) Preisoptimierung im deutschen Lebensmitteleinzelhandel.Von einer Wettbewerbs- zur Kundenorientierten Preisfindung. Retrieved February 26, 2021 from http://www.gruenderlexikon.de/magazin/preisoptimierung_im_deutschen_lebensmittelhandel.pdf. Accessed 08. April 2023.

Shapiro C and Varian HR (1998) Information rules: a strategic guide to the network economy. Harvard Business School Press. Boston, USA.

Shubik M and Levitan R (1980) Market structure and behavior. Harvard University Press.

Simon H (1992) Preismanagement Analyse - Strategie – Umsetzung. Springer Gabler.

Slade M (1994) Optimal Pricing with Costly Adjustment and Persistent Effects: Empirical Evidence. mimeo, University of British Columbia.

Snir A, Levy D and Chen HA (2017) End of 9-endings, price recall, and price perceptions. Economics Letters 155: 157-63.

Stackelberg, H. von (1934) Marktform und Gleichgewicht. Julius Springer. Wien.

Steiner RL (2004) The nature and benefits of national brand/private label competition. Review of Industrial Organization 24: 105-27.

Stigler G (1987) The theory of price. McMillan. New York.

Stiving M and Winer R (1997) An empirical analysis of price-endings with scanner data. Journal of Consumer Research 24 (1): 57–67.

Studierendenwerk Bonn https://www.studierendenwerk-bonn.de.

Tappata M (2009) Rockets and feathers: understanding asymmetric pricing. RAND Journal of Economics 40: 673-87.

Taylor JB (1979) Staggered price setting in a macro model. American Economic Review 60: 108-13.

Taylor JB (1980) Aggregate dynamics and staggered contracts. Journal of Political Economy 88: 1-24.

Thomas M and Morwitz V (2005) Penny wise and pound foolish: the left-digit effect in price cognition. Journal of Consumer Research 32(1): 54–64.

Tifaoui S and von Cramon-Taubadel S (2016) Temporary Sales Prices and Asymmetric Price Transmission. Agribusiness 33: 85-97.

Tirole J (1988) The Theory of Industrial Organization. Cambridge, MA: MIT Press.

Varian HR (1980) A model of sales. American Economic Review 70(4): 651-59.

Varian HR (1989) Price discrimination. Handbook of Industrial Organization Vol. 1 ed. By Schmalensee R., Willig R. D. Elsevier Science Publisher.

Varian HR (2014) Intermediate microeconomics: a modern approach. 9th ed. W.W. Norton and Company. London.

Verbeke W (2005) Agriculture and the Food Industry in the Information Age. European Review of Agricultural Economics 32(3): 347-68.

Villas-Boas JM (1995) Models of competitive price promotions: some empirical evidence from the coffee and saltine crackers markets. Journal of Economics and Management Strategy 4: 85–107.

Walters C, Williams I, Durand B, Majumdar A, Alvim N, Armstrong R, Manganelli A, Reuter T, Sodano V, Stoddart P and Whelan C (2014) Cost pass-through: theory, measurement, and potential policy implications. Report prepared for the Office of Fair Trading, London. RBB Economics. London 2014.

Wang XH and Zhao J (2007) Welfare reductions from small cost reductions in differentiated oligopoly. International Journal of Industrial Organization 25(1): 173-185.

Warner E and Barsky RB (1995) The timing and magnitude and retail store markdowns: evidence from weekends and holidays. Quarterly Journal of Economics 110(2): 321-52.

Weyl EG and Fabinger M (2013) Pass-through as an economic tool: Principles of incidence under imperfect competition. Journal of Political Economy 121(3): 528-583.

Zimmerman PR and Carlson JA (2010) Competition and cost pass-through in differentiated oligopolies. MPRA Paper No. 25931, online at http://mpra.ub.uni-muenchen.de/25931/. Accessed 08. April 2023.

11.9. Appendix: Derivation of Varian's (1980) model result.

$$F(P) = 1 - \left(\frac{k}{I}\left(\frac{1}{P} - \frac{1}{r}\right)\right)^{\frac{1}{n-1}} \tag{1}$$

$$\frac{\partial F(P)}{\partial P} = -\frac{1}{n-1}\left(\frac{k}{I}\left(\frac{1}{P} - \frac{1}{r}\right)\right)^{\frac{1}{n-1}-1}\left(-\frac{k}{IP^2}\right) \tag{2}$$

$$\frac{\partial F(P)}{\partial P} = \frac{1}{n-1}\left(\frac{k}{I}\right)^{\frac{1}{n-1}}\left(\frac{1}{P} - \frac{1}{r}\right)^{\frac{1}{n-1}-1}\frac{1}{P^2} \tag{3}$$

Let $m = 1 - 1/(n-1)$. It holds that $n = rM/k$. Thus $m = (rM - 2k)/(rM - k)$

$$\frac{\partial F(P)}{\partial P} = \frac{k}{rM-k}\left(\frac{k}{I}\right)^{m-1}\left(\frac{1}{P} - \frac{1}{r}\right)^{-m}\frac{1}{P^2} \tag{4}$$

With $n -> \infty$, $m -> 1$ and $k/(rM-k)$ is a constant factor it follows:

$$\frac{\partial F(P)}{\partial P} \overset{n\to\infty}{\approx} \left(\frac{1}{P} - \frac{1}{r}\right)^{-m}\frac{1}{P^2} \tag{5}$$

$$\frac{\partial F(P)}{\partial P} \overset{n\to\infty}{\approx} \frac{1}{\left(\frac{r-P}{rP}\right)^m P^2} \tag{6}$$

$$\frac{\partial F(P)}{\partial P} \overset{n\to\infty}{\approx} \frac{1}{\left(\frac{r-P}{r}\right)^m P^{2-m}} \tag{7}$$

$$\frac{\partial F(P)}{\partial P} \overset{n\to\infty}{\approx} \frac{1}{\left(1-\frac{P}{r}\right)^m P^{2-m}} \tag{8}$$

$$\frac{\partial F(P)}{\partial P} \overset{n\to\infty}{\approx} \frac{1}{P\left(1-\frac{P}{r}\right)} \tag{9}$$

11.10. Exercises

1. Bartels and Langness (BeLa) is a regionally operating food retailer in Northern Germany. Write up a small portrait of the company (https://www.bela.de/en/).

2. How have consumer trends and attitudes changed during the Covid-19 pandemic? Which of these changes are likely short-term, and which are likely long-term?

3. List some examples of monopolistic price setting in (German) food retailing and discuss graphically the welfare effects of a monopoly that is more cost efficient than the supply under perfect competition.

4. What concepts are used to measure the degree of market power in food retailing?

5. List some examples of monopolistic competitive price setting in food retailing.

6. What approaches are used to estimate the marginal costs of retailing?

7. Discuss the welfare effects of monopolistic competitive price setting in food retailing.

8. Summarise the main challenges of multiproduct pricing.

9. Visit the webpage of the German Antitrust Commission and summarise one of the cases on illegal cartel actions in the field of food retailing or food processing (https://www.bundeskartellamt.de/EN/).

10. Find examples for food retail product price discrimination and estimate relative mark-up differences.

11. Draw a graph of an individual demand function and explain the implementation of a take-it-or-leave-it price or a two-tier pricing scheme, and the effects on welfare of first-degree price discrimination.

12. Describe several real-world examples of two-tier pricing schemes.

13. For the pizza example under 'second-degree price discrimination' in Section 4.6: Maximise the profit and calculate the optimal size for the small pizza, when MWP_1=100-2q und MWP_2=100-q. Discuss how the results change if the shares of pizza lovers change from 1:1 to 2:1 or to 1:2.

14. Explain why the aggregated marginal revenue of two or more markets is not necessarily similar to the marginal revenue of the aggregated demand over the same markets.

15. Discus potential differences in the market outcomes between uniform monopoly pricing and third-degree price discrimination.

16. Discuss examples of bundling in food retailing, classify the type of bundling in each case, and explain the motivation for the bundling.

17. Test your knowledge of food retail prices. Write down 10 items (e. g. 1kg bananas, 1L milk, etc.) and their prices. Check your data against prices at an online retailer such as Rewe.

18. Read the paper by Varian (1980) and summarise his model assumptions. Which assumptions differ from Salop and Stiglitz (1977)? What are the main findings and shortcomings of Varian's (1980) model?

19. Set the expected profit in equation (52) equal to zero and derive F(P) in equation (53).

20. In Varian's (1980) model, stores discriminate between informed and uninformed consumers. Explain this statement and describe the type of discrimination.

21. Read the paper by Chevalier et al. (1994) and describe the variables used in their empirical analysis. What are the main results of their analysis, and how do they support the overall conclusion of the paper?

22. Compare the results presented in Figure 11.25 and your personal observations with the results found by Berck et al. (2008).

CHAPTER TWELVE

PRICE VOLATILITY IN AGRICULTURE

BERNHARD BRÜMMER

In memory of Dr. Stefan Busse (†2020)

12.1. Introduction and learning objectives

For many years, the volatility of prices on agricultural markets received little attention in the EU. This began to change around the turn of the century. In many other especially low-income countries, price volatility has always been an important issue. In recent memory, a first episode of high food price volatility occurred in the early 1970s, partly related to the first oil price crisis in the fall of 1973, but also triggered by global supply and demand conditions and short-sighted and ill-advised policy responses by the US and other governments.[1]

Attention returned to agricultural price volatility in the EU during a more recent episode of volatility, the so-called 'agricultural price crisis' of 2007/08, when prices for the most important cereals (wheat, maize and rice) initially rose sharply, only to fall again within a relatively short period of time. In the aftermath of these price developments, food price volatility even became an issue for the G20 group of major economies (G20, 2014). Most recently, Russia's military aggression in Ukraine in late February 2022 shocked global grain markets that were already characterised by under-supply, sending price levels and volatility to new highs (von Cramon-Taubadel 2022).

The fact that the price peaks in 2007/08 and early 2022 led to a resurgence of interest in price volatility among policymakers and academics, suggests

[1] This episode is sometimes referred to as the 'Great Grain Robbery'. See Schnittker (1973) for a description and an assessment.

that price levels and price volatility are related and sometimes conflated in people's minds. Also, some measures that are ostensibly used to combat price volatility are in fact aimed more at influencing price levels. This is the case, for example, when prices are low and there are calls for price support to 'stabilise' prices.

For decision-makers in agricultural value chains, such as farmers, traders and processors, understanding and measuring volatility is an important prerequisite for formulating effective risk management strategies. For policy makers, understanding volatility is crucial for developing and implementing appropriate policy responses.

In this chapter we will therefore:

- show how agricultural price volatility can be defined and interpreted;
- explain which theoretical determinants of price volatility are of particular importance for agricultural markets;
- outline the models and empirical methods that economists use to analyse price volatility in agricultural and food markets; and
- discuss what need for action arises from agricultural price volatility for producers, for other actors in the food chain, and for agricultural policy.

12.2. Conceptual considerations

The concept of price volatility was developed in the literature on financial markets in the middle of the 20th century. However, fluctuating prices were discussed extensively in the early economic literature. For example, as early as 1789, Adam Smith addressed the role of trade for the stability of grain prices and concluded that free trade in grain provided a more stable supply with less fluctuation in prices (Smith 1793).

However, in the more recent literature on price fluctuations a key conceptual distinction was introduced, between those fluctuations that are **expected** by market participants, and those that are unexpected. Today, only **unexpected fluctuations** are considered to be price volatility. Consequently, we will use the following typical definition of **volatility**:

Price volatility is a measure of unforeseen deviations in a market price from its expected level. Volatility therefore refers to the unexpected part of total price fluctuations.

Based on this definition, price data can be used to develop various empirical measures of agricultural price volatility. Since volatility is defined as unexpected fluctuations from an expected price level, irrespective of the direction of these fluctuations, it makes sense to measure volatility using the second moment of the price distribution (i.e. the variance). In general, for a price series $p_t = \{p_1, p_2, \ldots, p_n\}$ the standard deviation of the first differences of the logarithmic price series is used to measure volatility.

$$\text{Volatility} = \sqrt{\frac{\sum_{t=1}^{n}(\Delta lnp_t - \overline{\Delta lnp_t})^2}{n-1}} \qquad (1)$$

$\Delta \text{ln}p_t$ can be interpreted as the relative change p_t from period $t-1$ to t (the so-called 'return'). Hence, equation (1) measures volatility in percentage units. Equation (1) is based on a simple decomposition of the price changes into an expected component (the mean value of the returns, $\overline{\Delta lnp_t}$) and an unexpected component (deviations from this mean value).

Consider an example in which the mean return is 1% and volatility measured using equation (1) equals 2%. How do we interpret this result? As Goldstein and Taleb (2007) show, this question poses challenges not only to students but also to experienced bankers. Most importantly, the interpretation depends on the probability distribution that is assumed for the returns. If the returns are normally distributed, then just over 68% of all returns will lie within an interval of plus/minus one standard deviation from the mean, i.e. between -1% and +3% in our example. If the returns follow a Student's t-distribution with three degrees of freedom, only about 60% of all returns will lie within this interval. In any event, it is not correct to interpret volatility measured using equation (1) as an average absolute change, even if this is intuitively appealing to many market participants (Goldstein and Taleb 2007).

The above definition of price volatility implies that price level and price volatility should be treated as separate concepts. However, certain characteristics of agricultural markets, particularly the role of storage, often lead to a positive correlation between price levels and price volatility. This contrasts with many financial markets, where low prices are often associated with high volatility. This correlation will be examined in more detail below.

12.3. Theoretical foundations

Why are unexpected price fluctuations on markets for storable agricultural products more likely to occur when prices are at above-average levels? A simple explanation is based on the role of the **demand for stocks** and the fact that stocks can never be negative (in other words, that it is not possible to store quantities that have not yet been produced). The illustration of the model in Figure 11.1 follows Wright (2011), who decomposes the total demand for a storable product (e.g. wheat) into two components.[2] The market demand curve, which reflects the current consumption of the commodity, is relatively inelastic. The demand for stocks, however, typically has a different shape, which results from the speculative motives of the stockholders. Stockholders will demand products for storage when they think that prices are relatively low; they expect that by some future date prices will have increased sufficiently to allow them to sell their stocks for a profit, net of the storage costs that have accumulated in the interim. If stockholders think that prices are high, they will be less likely to expect prices to increase sufficiently to make storage profitable. Hence, when prices are high they will only demand relatively small quantities for speculative stockholding. However, even when prices are very high, there will be a demand for a basic level of so-called working stocks that are necessary to maintain operations. Together, the demand for speculative and working stocks will generate an aggregated demand curve that is increasingly elastic at lower prices, as depicted in Figure 11.1.

The left panel of Figure 11.1 shows a situation with low prices (P_0) and large stocks. Total demand is split roughly equally between demand for stocks and market demand. Supply is seen as fixed in the short run, and expected production is indicated by Q_0. In the right-hand panel, the initial price P_0 is higher and the expected supply Q_0 is lower. In this situation demand for stocks accounts for a smaller share of total demand and is composed largely of demand for working rather than speculative stocks.

[2] Deaton and Laroque (1992) is a seminal paper on commodity price behaviour, which cites "pioneering" work by Gustafson (1958) on the demand for and fundamental asymmetry of commodity storage.

Figure 11.1 The demand for stocks, market demand, price levels and volatility

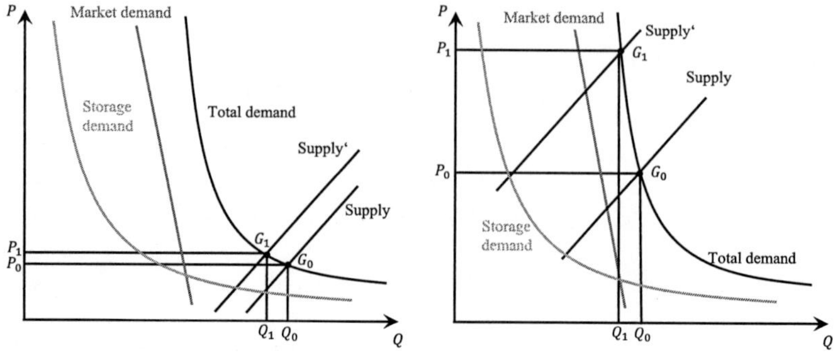

Source: Own illustration based on Wright (2011).

Now consider the effects of an unexpected shock, for example a lower than expected harvest, on prices in these two scenarios. In the left panel of Figure 11.1, prices react very little because the shortfall in supply is almost completely compensated by a reduction in speculative storage, which is price elastic in equilibrium. Price volatility is correspondingly low. In the right panel, the price reaction is much stronger. Since storage has already fallen to the level of working stocks, speculative storage cannot adjust to help buffer the supply shock. Total demand is price inelastic in this situation, and the supply shock leads to a larger price increase. Price volatility is correspondingly high. Altogether, this results in the pattern of price volatility on markets for storable products that we described above: when prices are high (a situation which typically coincides with low stock levels), price volatility tends to be high, while when prices are low and stock levels are high, price volatility tends to be low.

It is clear from Figure 11.1 that the size of the shock, in this case the poor harvest, affects the magnitude of the price fluctuations. However, the size of the market also plays an important role. Assume two identical countries, both of which are initially in autarky. A poor harvest will trigger the same price increase in either country, because the countries have identical demand curves by assumption. Now assume that the countries begin to trade freely with one another, creating a larger common market. Unless harvest quantities in the two countries are positively correlated (which is unlikely), then average year to year harvest fluctuations in the two countries together will be smaller relative to the size of the common market than fluctuations in any one country individually were relative to the size of its national market. As a result, harvest fluctuations will trigger smaller average price changes on the common market. This explains why prices are more stable in regionally integrated markets than in individual autarchic markets.[3]

How do phases of increased price volatility affect the players on agricultural and food markets? For farmers, price volatility is first and foremost a problem of individual farm **risk management**. Volatile agricultural prices are a source of substantial uncertainty for farm revenues. As a rule, highly **specialised** farms that depend on sales of one agricultural product, are more susceptible than more **diversified** farms.

But even if agricultural product prices are stable, unexpected price changes for agricultural inputs will lead to changes in production costs and perhaps even operational losses. From the farmers' point of view, increased price volatility can thus jeopardise **profitability**. **Stability** and **liquidity** are also obviously negatively affected by price volatility. When input and/or output prices fluctuate strongly, profits vary more, and a larger liquidity cushion is required to ensure solvency than when prices are stable. Companies and industries upstream and downstream from agriculture face fundamentally similar challenges. Especially less diversified companies that are strongly dependent on agriculture (e.g. dairy processors) can be susceptible to price fluctuations.

Comparative-static analysis shows that price volatility can also have negative effects on general economic welfare. Sandmo (1971) shows that as prices become more volatile, risk-averse producers will supply less. Furthermore, volatility dampens the propensity to invest because it makes future cash flows less certain. This reduces supply further in the long run. In extreme cases, investment might cease altogether.

There are also negative effects on the consumer side. Simple comparison of consumer surplus in a two-period model shows that consumers are worse off in a scenario with constant prices than in a scenario with symmetrically fluctuating prices (Waugh 1944).[4] However, Samuelson (1972) shows that fluctuating prices are detrimental to consumers if they result from the distribution of a constant crop quantity over time.

---

[3] This important benefit of regional integration is elaborated by Koester (1986).

[4] Consumer surplus is a quadratic function of the price level. Therefore, consumers gain more when prices fall by a certain amount than they lose when prices rise by the same amount.

Consequently, excessive price volatility can be considered as an example of relative market failure, which, at least in theory, could justify state intervention to improve economic welfare. However, state intervention will not necessarily lead to welfare improvements; it can also result in policy failure and welfare losses. We discuss this in greater detail in section 5 below. In the following section 4, however, we first review the empirical methods that are used to measure price volatility.

12.4. Estimating volatility in agricultural markets

12.4.1. Methods

Conceptual considerations

Different methods are used to estimate price volatility. However, all approaches share some basic conceptual considerations. Recall that volatility was defined above as the standard deviation of the unexpected price return. Andersen et al. (2010, p. 69) emphasise that the measurement of volatility defined in this way requires a distinction between "the component of a given price increment that represents a return innovation as opposed to an expected price movement". This requires splitting observed price fluctuations into expected and unexpected components. Hence, not every observed price fluctuation represents volatility. The need to distinguish between unexpected and expected price movements means that we cannot measure price volatility directly. Instead, we must first estimate a model of expected price changes based on market data, and then estimate volatility based on the unexplained residuals from this model.

Volatility measures can be **backward-looking** based on historical price data, or **forward-looking** based on a forecasting model. The underlying model of expected price changes can be either non-parametric or parametric. For the latter, time series models are usually employed. Alternatively, implicit volatility can be derived from the current valuation of financial derivatives such as options, which is suitable for both backward-looking and forward-looking volatility estimation. Table 11.1 provides an overview of these measures.

Table 11.1: Overview of different approaches to the measurement of volatility in agricultural markets

	Parametric	Non-parametric	Assessment-based
Backward-looking	GARCH Stochastic volatility	Realised volatility	Implicit volatility from historical prices
Forward-looking	Predictions from GARCH/SV		Implicit volatility from current prices

Source: Own illustration.

The estimation of expected price movements: To distinguish between unexpected and expected price movements, a model of the latter is required. For several reasons this is especially important for agricultural markets compared with financial markets. First, for many agricultural products only low-frequency price data (i.e. weekly or monthly) are available. Furthermore, these products are often storable and display seasonal price patterns due to factors on the supply side (e.g. production cycles, annual harvests) and/or the demand side (e.g. the BBQ-season). Second, and related, while it is often assumed that the expected returns for financial products are zero, this is a questionable assumption for agricultural products. Third, observed market prices for agricultural products are often a mixture of current spot prices and longer-term, contract-based prices. When this is the case, for example for sugar and milk, observed prices do not necessarily reflect all of the information available to market participants at a given point in time, so that consideration must be given to additional fundamental factors when modelling expected price movement.

Forward or backward-looking (historical) approach: The forward-looking approach forecasts future volatility using an estimated model of expected price changes that is based on data available up to the present time. The backward-looking perspective uses all the information available for the entire period under consideration to estimate the expected price changes and the historical price volatility within that period. Figure 11.2 schematically illustrates the two approaches. Forward-looking analysis is shown above the central timeline, and backward-looking analysis below.

Figure 11.1: Schematic representation of forward-looking and backward-looking volatility measurement

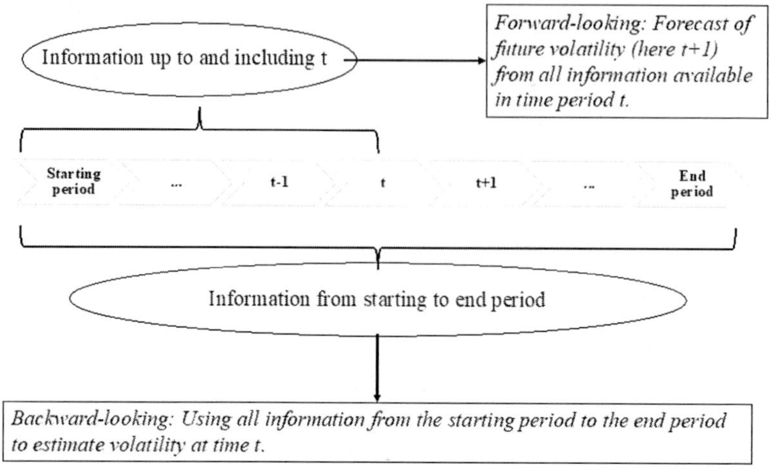

Source: Own illustration.

The choice of a forward- or a backward-looking approach depends on the objective of the volatility measurement. The forward approach is useful for volatility analysis with a view to future market developments. Examples of the forward-looking approach are the Chicago Board Options Exchange's volatility index (VIX) for the American stock market, and the Deutsche Börse's VDAX-NEW volatility index for the shares listed in the DAX. In both cases, price movements for the next 30 days are estimated using an implied volatility measure based on option prices. Historical analysis is useful when the focus is on the development of agricultural price volatility and its drivers over a specific period of time, for example if one wishes to analyse whether and how a certain factor has influenced price volatility in the past. The above-mentioned 'agricultural price crisis' of 2007/08 gave rise to many studies that employed a backward-looking approach. Those analyse what caused price levels and volatility to increase so strongly, and whether factors such as biofuel subsidies, speculation on futures markets or trade policy interventions played a role (for an overview, see Brümmer et al. 2016c).

Time scale: The temporal frequency of the available price data has important implications for the estimation approach. As a rule, the price process is modelled for the frequency at which the necessary data are available. If, for example, daily data are available, analysis is based on a model of daily returns.[5] However, it is often the case that some data on market fundamentals (for example, stock levels) are only available at lower frequencies than the price data. Finally, volatility is always measured for a certain time horizon; the volatility measure in equation (1), for example, will differ depending on whether it is based on daily, weekly or monthly returns. This time horizon can differ from the frequency of the available data. In general, conversion between time horizons is carried out by multiplying a higher-frequency measure of volatility by the square root of the number of high-frequency observations within the lower-frequency period. For example, annualised volatility is often used in the literature; if the original volatility measure is based on stock market trading days, of which there are 256 per year, then multiplication by the factor $16 = \sqrt{256}$ is necessary to convert daily into annualised volatility.

Estimation methods

Various methods can be used to estimate volatility. A first distinction is between those based on direct price quotations for the agricultural commodity in question, and those based on financial derivatives for this product, e.g. options, which are traded on sufficiently liquid markets. In the latter case, the option prices indirectly express the market participants' expectations of the current volatility, and the observed prices for the financial derivatives can thus be used to estimate the so-called implicit volatility. To do this, a model for the valuation of volatility by market participants must be assumed. Probably the best-known approach is based on the Black-Scholes equation[6] for valuing options (Black and Scholes 1973). The original Black-Scholes model describes how a fair valuation for an option can be determined given its maturity and strike price, a known risk-free interest rate, a valuation of the underlying asset, and a given level of volatility. The concept of implicit volatility turns this around; the observed market valuation of an option is taken as given, and the implicit

---

[5] There are approaches that deviate from this rule, such as mixed data sampling (MIDAS, see Engle et al. 2013). For an agricultural application, see Brümmer et al. (2016a).

[6] This equation was developed jointly by Fischer Black, Robert C. Merton and Myron S. Scholes and should also bear Merton's name. However, this is not common practice in the literature, as Merton did not publish an independent paper on the equation. When the Nobel Prize was awarded for this work in 1997, it went to both Merton and Scholes; Black passed away in 1995 and was therefore not eligible to receive the Nobel Prize.

volatility for which this valuation can be considered fair is calculated. This approach is not used very often for agricultural commodities, because liquid commodity futures markets and the associated options are often unavailable for these products, especially in Europe.

Implicit volatility estimation is not possible if only market prices for the product in question are available. Volatility must then be estimated directly from these prices. This can be done using either parametric or non-parametric approaches. The basic premise of **non-parametric models** is simple. In efficient markets, current prices reflect all publicly available information. The expected price changes over a given period of time can therefore be assumed to be constant, and volatility will be reflected in the variation of price changes around this constant value. Under these assumptions, so-called **realised volatility** can be estimated as the empirically observed standard deviation of prices over the given period (Andersen and Bollerslev 1998). If, for example, we are interested in daily price volatility and have access to intra-day price quotations, then the standard deviation of the returns within a day will provide an unbiased estimator of the desired daily volatility. In principle, this procedure can also be applied to lower-frequency price series, e.g. we can estimate a monthly volatility as the standard deviation of the daily returns within that month. However, in statistical terms the realised volatility approach is based on the integrated volatility of a continuous time process (Andersen and Teräsvirta 2009). Hence, in practice this approach requires high-frequency prices. This limits its applicability for agricultural products, for which spot market prices are often only available at daily or even lower (i.e. weekly or monthly) frequencies. However, if high-frequency futures price data are available, measuring price volatility using the realised volatility approach is often a reasonable choice.

The specification of a **parametric model** requires a trade-off between data availability and the desired frequency of the volatility measure. In empirical applications, time-series models are most common. On most markets, price volatility is not constant over time, but varies. Therefore, in empirical volatility analysis using parametric models, a price process with a variable conditional standard deviation is postulated. The simplest specification is the so-called **ARCH** model (Engle 1982).[7] As explained above, the key to measuring volatility is the distinction between expected and unexpected price fluctuations. From an econometric point of view, this requires that the

---

[7] Robert Engle was awarded the Nobel Prize in Economics in 2003 for the development of the ARCH model.

mean value process of the returns (i.e. the expected fluctuations) be modelled in such a way that the residuals (the unexpected fluctuations) are free of autocorrelation and stationary. An ARCH(q) model for these residuals can be described by the following multiplicative structure:

$$u_t = \varepsilon_t \sigma_t \quad (2)$$

$$\varepsilon_t \sim i.i.d.\, N(0,1) \quad (3)$$

$$\sigma_t^2 = \omega + \sum_{i=1}^{q} \alpha_i u_{t-i}^2 \quad (4)$$

In these equations, ε_t is an independently and identically distributed (i.i.d.) normal random variable, ω and $\alpha_i, i = 1 \dots q$, are parameters to be estimated, and σ_t^2 is the conditional variance, the root of which is the volatility measure. The assumption of an i.i.d. normal random variable makes estimation with maximum likelihood methods possible. However, other distributions for ε_t can be and often are specified. For example, the t-distribution (which includes the normal distribution as a special case) can be used to account for the common observation that large returns are more frequent than predicted by the normal distribution, i.e. that the residual distribution has so-called 'fat tails'.

As can be seen in equation (2) through (4), in an ARCH(q) model the conditional variance σ_t^2 is represented as a function of the lagged squared residuals weighted by α_i, the parameters to be estimated. This results in a variance that can assume a different value at each time t, conditional on the information available at time t. The unconditional variance is given by

$$\sigma^2 = \frac{\omega}{1 - \sum_{i=1}^{q} \alpha_i} \quad (5)$$

and requires as stationarity conditions that $\omega > 0$ und $\sum_{i=1}^{q} \alpha_i < 1$. The parameters α_i measure the influence that new information arising in one period has on volatility in subsequent periods. In this model, the conditional variance will tend to display so-called **volatility clusters**, i.e. high values of σ_t^2 will tend to be followed by high values of σ_{t+1}^2, σ_{t+2}^2 etc. This is consistent with the empirical observation that volatility does not remain uniform over time; when increased volatility occurs, it often does so in clusters over longer periods of time.

Few time series models have been extended as often as the ARCH model. In the following we review some extensions of the ARCH model that have proven important for the analysis of agricultural price volatility.

GARCH: Probably the most important extension, certainly when measured in terms of citations, is the extension of the ARCH model to including lagged conditional variances in the equation for the conditional variance itself:

$$\sigma_t^2 = \omega + \sum_{i=1}^{q} \alpha_i u_{t-i}^2 + \sum_{j=1}^{p} \beta_j \sigma_{t-j}^2 \qquad (6)$$

In this Generalised ARCH (GARCH) model, first proposed by Bollerslev (1986), the parameters α_i again indicate the effect of new information on the conditional variance, and the parameters β_j measure the persistence of volatility. In practice, the simplest GARCH model with $p = q = 1$ is often sufficiently flexible to capture the dynamics of price volatility in agricultural markets.

Asymmetry: In Section 3 of this chapter we explained that due to the behaviour of speculative stockholders, unexpected price fluctuations on markets for storable agricultural products are more likely to occur when prices are high. When prices are high, stocks will tend to be low and new information will trigger large unexpected price swings. This suggests that when prices are already high, new information that points further price increases will increase volatility, while new information that points to price reductions will be less likely to increase volatility.[8] In this setting it makes sense to extend the GARCH model in such a way that upward price changes, (i.e. positive residuals of the returns), exert a greater influence on the conditional variance than downward price changes (negative residuals of the returns). A large number of models allow for such asymmetries. The most important are the exponential GARCH model (EGARCH, Nelson 1991), the GJR model (Glosten et al. 1993) and the TGARCH model (Zakoian 1994). In the EGARCH model, the natural logarithm of the conditional variance $ln(\sigma_t^2)$ replaces σ_t^2 in equation (6). Furthermore, the effect of the squared residuals u_{t-i}^2 is split into a magnitude and a direction effect. In the GJR model, the desired asymmetry is achieved by introducing an additional binary variable D_t^- which takes the value one for negative values of u, and zero otherwise. The extended form on the right-hand-side

---

[8] A similar but opposite effect is found on markets for financial securities, where unexpected price reductions lead to increased volatility.

of equation (6) becomes $\sum_{i=1}^{q}(\alpha_i u_{t-i}^2 + \gamma_i D_t^- u_{t-i}^2)$, and the statistical significance of the parameters γ_i provide a test for asymmetry. In TGARCH a similar approach is taken, but the conditional standard deviation replaces the conditional variance, and absolute values of the residuals $|u_{t-i}|$ replace their squared values u_{t-i}^2.

Finally, we briefly mention the so-called stochastic volatility models. They differ from the GARCH models primarily in that an additional error term is introduced into equation (4) for the conditional variance. This makes it possible to account for 'fat tails' and asymmetry, but it also makes estimation considerably more complicated. Therefore, despite their theoretical advantages, these models have rarely been applied to agricultural markets and will not be discussed further here. Shephard and Andersen (2009) provide an introduction.

12.4.2 Selected results

The extent of price volatility in key agricultural markets

A very extensive literature on price volatility in agriculture has accumulated over the decades, covering a wide variety of products, markets and methods. Any overview is therefore inevitably subjective. In the following we first focus on grain and specifically wheat markets, because wheat is a key staple for human consumption but also an important feed input in livestock production. International trade in wheat has been established for centuries and is now organised in well-integrated global supply chains. The wheat market is therefore often viewed as a cornerstone for global agricultural price formation, which justifies a closer examination.

In Figure 11.3 we present weekly spot market prices for US soft wheat (SRW No2, fob Gulf of Mexico – left axis, in US$/t) and the annualised volatility of these prices (right axis, in percent – estimated with a GJR-GARCH model). No single price can reflect price dynamics for all major wheat export regions (besides the US, Argentina, Australia, Canada, the EU, Russia and Ukraine are major exporters), but this US fob Gulf price is often used as a barometer of conditions on global markets.

Figure 11.3: Weekly prices and volatility for US wheat, Gulf of Mexico, 2005-2020

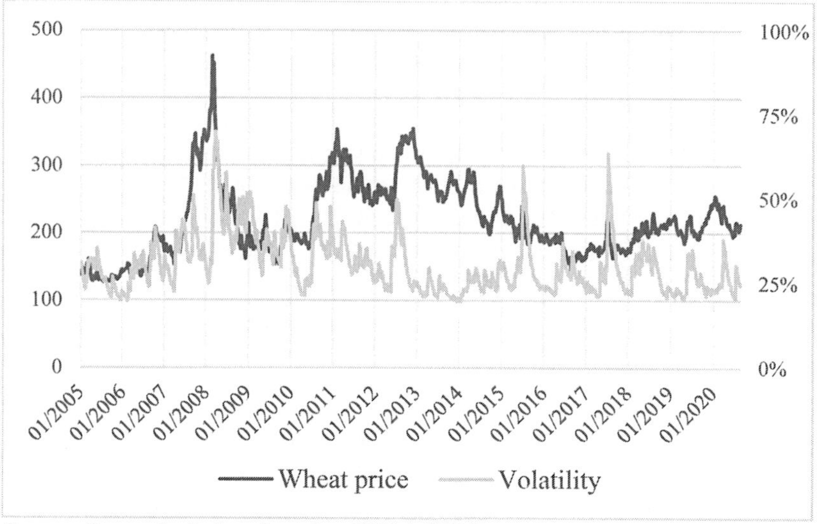

Source: Own calculations based on USDA (2021).

In Figure 11.3 we see that the volatility of the US price varies greatly over time. Three phases in which the volatility exceeds 50% stand out. The first of these phases begins in March 2008. It persists into May, and high levels of volatility continue to be observed sporadically throughout the rest of 2008. This phase coincides with the end of the agricultural price crisis of 2007/08 and begins just as the prices begin to fall from their highest levels. Two further peaks in volatility are found in July 2015 and 2017; again, the pattern of rapidly rising prices followed by a rapid price decline is repeated.

Figure 11.3 also reveals evidence that wheat price volatility is seasonal. The highest volatilities are often observed around June, i.e. immediately before the wheat harvest in the northern hemisphere, where roughly 80% of global export supplies are produced (Canada, EU, Russia, Ukraine and US). During this period, markets are particularly sensitive to new information about weather conditions and crop conditions, until reliable information on the size and quality of the harvest becomes available.

For many years, wheat prices in the EU were insulated from these price fluctuations by the intervention price system of the Common Agricultural Policy (CAP), which used variable import levies and export refunds to support and stabilise domestic prices.[9] When a large country such as the EU stabilises its domestic prices, it effectively exports price instability to global markets. This, in addition to the direct effects of the price support (increased production and subsidised exports by the EU), led to conflicts with trading partners, especially other large exporters. The so-called MacSharry Reforms in 1992 marked the beginning of a shift to a less protectionist CAP and of a gradual integration of the EU into global agricultural markets. Today, farmers in the EU face international price levels and fluctuations for most important agricultural products.

Case study 1: Variable import levies in the EU and international price volatility

In an empirical analysis of the maize market, Berger et al. (2021) examine the relationship between the EU's variable import levies and an international maize price. The variable import levy was an integral part of the CAP's intervention price system that protected high support prices for grains in the EU in an import situation. The variable import levy adjusted to bridge the gap between a fixed EU domestic price and the variable world market price at any point in time. This ensured that imports would not enter the EU as long as domestic prices were below a politically desired target level. In this way, the EU, a major importer of maize in the sense of trade theory, decoupled itself from international market events. As a result, international price changes did not trigger domestic supply or demand reactions in the EU, and the EU made no contribution to buffering international maize price shocks.

Berger et al. (2021) estimate an EGARCH model in which variable import levies (expressed in percentage ad valorem terms) are included as an exogenous variable in the volatility equation. For the 2002-2017 period, they analyze the relationship between EU and Argentine maize prices and how import levies affect the volatility of both prices. They find that the import levy has proportionally equal but opposite effects on both markets, i.e. as the import levy reduces volatility in the EU, it increases volatility in the Argentine market.

[9] This system also applied to other grains as well as milk, sugar and beef. See, for example, Koester (2020) for details.

12.5. Determinants of agricultural price volatility

Why do agricultural prices exhibit pronounced volatility, as illustrated for the wheat market in Figure 11.3, and why is this volatility not constant over time? The determinants of volatility can be rooted in the specific market under consideration, but can also lie beyond this market. The term **volatility spill-over** is often used to describe the latter case. Among the market-specific determinants, we have already discussed the role of stockholding and often inelastic supply and demand in section 11.3. In the following we will focus on the determinants that cause volatility spill-overs.

Spill-overs from other agricultural and input markets: The prices of different agricultural products are often linked by demand-side and/or supply-side effects. On the demand side, agricultural products are often substitutes for one another. For example, different feed grains (wheat, barley, maize) are largely interchangeable, as are vegetable oils (rapeseed, soya, palm, sunflower oil, etc.) or meats (beef, pork, poultry), always subject to technical limitations and/or consumer preferences. Substitutability implies that the prices of these products are linked and, thus, that price shocks on one market are transmitted to other markets. The strength of the resulting volatility spill-overs will depend not only on the substitution possibilities but also on how price discovery takes place on the markets in question. If forward contracts and futures markets play a significant role in price discovery, then short-term price volatility will generally tend to be limited to the market in question and spill over less to other markets.

On the supply side, competition for common production factors (e.g. for arable land) typically does not play an important role in the transmission of volatility between markets, because the allocation of these inputs to different uses (e.g. wheat vs. barley production) is largely fixed in the short run. However, volatility does spill over vertically along supply chains due to vertical price relationships. [10] Unexpected fluctuations in feed grain prices, for example, can trigger meat price volatility via adjustments in supply behaviour. Price volatility for intermediate inputs such as fertilisers or fuel can also contribute to the volatility of agricultural product prices.

Relations with energy markets: Energy markets, especially those for fossil fuels, deserve closer examination. The expansion of biofuel policies in recent decades has added a new dimension to price formation in agricultural

[10] Vertical price relationships are discussed in detail in Chapter 10.

markets, reinforcing the already strong supply-side influence of energy as an important input in agricultural production. The subsidised production of bioethanol, especially from maize in the USA and sugar in Brazil, as well as the production of biodiesel from vegetable oils (such as rapeseed, soya and palm oil), creates an additional demand-side link between the prices of fossil fuels and the prices of corresponding agricultural raw materials. The crude oil market – which is the most important energy market – is characterised by relatively high price volatility and trading volumes that are orders of magnitude larger than on agricultural markets. Hence, the empirical literature usually concludes that volatility spills over unidirectionally from energy to agricultural markets. This pattern is found for biodiesel and the associated feedstocks (Busse et al. 2012; Brümmer et al., 2016b) as well as for the bioethanol complex (Serra et al. 2011).

Agricultural and trade policy interventions: Bioenergy policy is not the only area in which government interventions have consequences for agricultural price volatility. Market interventions that target completely different policy objectives can have unintended side effects on price volatility. The example of the intervention price system, which stabilised prices in the EU but increased volatility elsewhere, has already been mentioned. Today, such trade-distorting domestic policies are subject to commitments that countries make under the WTO Agreement on Agriculture. This agreement also restricts the use of import tariffs and export subsidies. However, analogous restrictions in the area of export restrictions are largely missing. If a large exporter introduces an export restriction such as an export tax or quota, as for example Russia and Ukraine have done several times since 2006 for wheat, this will increase both the level and the volatility of international prices. This effect is amplified by the fact that countries applying export restrictions often do so in an intransparent and discretionary manner.

The institutional framework and market transparency: In addition to specific policy interventions, the broader institutions that govern agricultural markets, especially the embedded or first-order institutions (Williamson 2000, as presented in Chapter 2), also influence agricultural price volatility. For example, in Germany, agricultural futures markets were forbidden for many decades. Even though they are permitted today, they are heavily criticised by many individuals and NGOs who consider futures trade in agricultural commodities to be a morally questionable 'speculation with food' that increases price levels and volatility. If explicit restrictions or moral censure limits the use of futures markets as a risk management tool, price volatility can be expected to increase, and market participants such as farmers and traders will suffer more from its consequences.

Market transparency is also an important institutional factor. We have stressed the influence of stockholding on price formation for storable agricultural commodities. Hence, market participants rely heavily on accurate information on stock levels. However, the availability of such information is limited on many agricultural markets. Estimates of stock levels are often residual estimates, i.e. the change in a country's stocks over a certain period is calculated as the difference between total supply and total demand in that period. It is seldom possible to confirm the accuracy of these residual estimates because even if private actors such as trading companies and farmers are required to report on their stockholding activities (which is the case in some countries but not, for example, the EU), public stocks of staple food products are considered to be strategic secrets in many countries. For example, while China is estimated to hold as much as 60% of all global grain stocks (UDSA 2022), it is not possible to directly confirm the accuracy of these estimates. There is also little clarity about the level of stocks bound in maritime shipping at any given time. Due to the considerable transit times involved in intercontinental maritime trade, these stocks can make up a considerable part of total stocks. Information on these stocks is available to the private trading shipping companies involved, but not publicly available. As a result, unexpected price fluctuations will be more likely to occur and price volatility will be higher.

Financialization of agricultural markets: The agricultural price crisis of 2007/08 triggered an intensive discussion on the role of the so-called **financialization of agricultural markets**. Financialization in this context generally refers to the increasing importance of financial markets for agricultural commodities. Phenomena that are typically considered to be symptoms of financialization include: the inflow of liquidity to commodity futures markets for agricultural products; the increasing role of institutional investors – especially index and hedge funds – on these markets; and the growing involvement of actors who have no direct relationship to value chains for the products in question, i.e. no interest as producers, processors or consumers in the underlying physical products. [11] Even though the

---

[11] In 2008, fund manager Michael Masters testified to the US Senate "that institutional investors are one of, if not the primary, factors affecting commodities prices today" (Masters 2008, p. 1). This so-called Masters hypothesis attracted considerable media attention. In Chapter 13 we discuss the role of speculation in price formation on futures markets.

discussion initially focused on the effect of financialization on price levels, it has subsequently shifted to price volatility. As mentioned above, many individuals and NGOs are convinced that financialization increases price levels and volatility. However, convincing empirical support for this assertion is lacking in the literature (see for example Will et al. 2015).

Macroeconomic factors: Finally, the macroeconomic environment can also influence price volatility. Unexpected changes in prices for agricultural products can be caused by general price instability, for example in economies suffering from high inflation rates. In this case, there is often also a close connection with the exchange rate, since changes in exchange rates are the consequences of different inflation trends between currency areas. The exchange rate vis-à-vis the US dollar is of particular importance here, as a large share of international agricultural trade is transacted in this global reserve currency. In countries that are heavily dependent on export earnings from primary goods such as agricultural commodities and fossil fuels, commodity price volatility can play an important role in the so-called Dutch disease phenomenon. Commodity price volatility can trigger exchange rate volatility that leads to fluctuating terms of trade for the economy as a whole, which is detrimental to overall economic development (Cavalcanti et al. 2015).

12.6. Coping with agricultural price volatility – responses by farmers, policy makers and other stakeholders

12.6.1. The farmer's perspective

From the farmer's perspective, agricultural price volatility means that risk management strategies have to cope not only with the production risks inherent to agriculture, but also with fluctuations in input and output prices.

Agricultural price volatility generally gives rise to risk as defined by Knight (1921).[12] This means that as a rule, a probability distribution for price fluctuations can be used for risk management purposes. Information on the probability distribution can be derived from the analysis of price data, for

[12] Frank Knight (1921) distinguished between risk and uncertainty. Both are characterised by the fact that outcomes are unknown, but in the case of risk, the probability distribution of the outcomes is known. Whether a fair coin will show heads or tails is a matter of risk; whether an animal disease outbreak will occur in a particular region is a matter of uncertainty. Knight's students included Nobel Prize winners Milton Friedman, George Stigler and James Buchanan.

example from private and public **market information systems**, from trade publications or from scientific studies. Individual farm-level and market-based strategies can be used to manage risk. Individual farm-level approaches include the use of planning methods that consider liquidity and stability in addition to profitability. This usually results in the need to review and, if necessary, reorganise the farm's financial relationship with its bank(s). Farm-level risk management strategies also include diversifying production to reduce exposure to fluctuations in individual prices, and expanding on-farm storage capacities so that the farmer has more control over when to sell. However, both diversification and storage strategies are associated with sometimes considerable opportunity costs.

Market-based approaches include forward sales of agricultural products and forward purchases of agricultural inputs such as fertiliser or feed. In agriculture, such forward contracts are relatively widespread. Price hedging via commodity futures markets is also possible but used less frequently by farmers directly.[13]

12.6.2. The value chain perspective

We discussed volatility spill-overs along the value chain in the previous section. Options for mitigating price volatility are especially available in sub-sectors in which farmers sell their output to only one or a few processers. Examples of such sub-sectors are milk, sugar and, to some extent, meat (in Germany mainly poultry, internationally also pork). Vertical integration in the corresponding chains can range from purchase contracts at pre-determined prices between farmers and processors, to various forms of contract production in which processors provide inputs and exercise varying degrees of control over on-farm production processes, to complete vertical integration in which farm production and processing take place within a single commercial entity. Each of these gradations offers opportunities for allocating risk between farms and processors. Since input and output prices are often positively correlated, for a vertically integrated company price volatilities can offset; unexpectedly low sales prices can be at least partially offset by lower input prices. However, these benefits have to be weighed against the opportunity costs of vertical integration.

There is usually little transmission of price volatility along vertically differentiated value chains. Since market power often grows with increasing processing depth, such chains need to be carefully monitored by

[13] Forward contracts and commodity futures are explained in Chapter 13.

competition authorities.[14] However, greater price rigidity in such chains can also be related to other causes such as psychological price thresholds, and adjustment or menu costs. Regardless of the degree of market power, different types of contractual arrangements can have very different consequences for the vertical transmission of price volatility. In the sugar chain in Germany, for example, contracts between farmers and processors generally fix a minimum basis price. In the German milk chain, however, the price that a farmer receives for milk delivered in the previous month is typically corrected *ex post* to account for the processor's revenue in the current month. In this way, current volatility is effectively transmitted into the past, an effect that is especially strong if a large part of the processor's output is not sold through stable contractual relationships with food retailers. In this case, alternative contractual arrangements could mitigate the consequences of price volatility.

12.6.3. The policy maker's perspective

The increased challenges posed by agricultural price volatility (at least in the EU) have triggered debates on the need for agricultural policy responses. In the following we briefly list and critically assess some of the most important policy responses that have been proposed at the international level. Since most agricultural markets in the EU have been largely integrated into global agricultural trade since the mid-2000s, international policy responses seem most appropriate, especially because – as we have seen – national measures that reduce domestic price volatility typically do this at the expense of increased volatility elsewhere in the world.

Improving market transparency: Market information can help market participants to formulate more realistic expectations and thus reduce the magnitude of unexpected price fluctuations. Since market information, when made publicly available, has the characteristics of a public good, government intervention to establish **market information systems** can generate important benefits. The more information public and private actors contribute, the more effective such systems will be. In the aftermath of the agricultural price crisis of 2007/08, the Agricultural Market Information System (AMIS) was launched at the G20 level.[15] AMIS collects up-to-date information on supply, demand, stocks, price levels and volatility, and publishes it together with assessments of the overall market situation. AMIS is certainly a step in the right direction, but it remains incomplete, both in

---

[14] Chapter 8 takes a detailed look at pricing under imperfect competition.

[15] See http://www.amis-outlook.org/.

terms of the number of agricultural markets covered and the level of detail of the market information collected.

Regional and national market information systems also exist, but they usually have correspondingly regional or national foci. An important exception are the USDA's World Agricultural Supply and Demand Estimates (WASDE, see USDA 2022). These monthly reports cover key global agricultural markets and are a valuable source of information to market participants all over the world.

Multilateral measures for the coordination of trade policies: The lack of binding WTO rules on the use of export restrictions has repeatedly proven to be a driver of agricultural price volatility during episodes of high and increasing prices. In the absence of such binding rules, an effective voluntary commitment by countries to refrain from export restrictions would certainly be welcome. However, a complete renunciation of export restrictions on foodstuffs will probably be difficult to achieve; when food prices rise, national governments come under strong pressure to put domestic interests first. It would help if at least some disciplines on the implementation of export restrictions could be adopted, to increase transparency, reliability and ensure that export restrictions are not used to discriminate against specific (often foreign) traders. The WTO would be the appropriate forum for negotiating such disciplines, but as we write (2022) the most recent Doha Round of WTO negotiations has been ongoing and making little headway for over twenty years.

Physical storage for price stabilisation: The use of state-controlled stocks, often referred to as **buffer stocks,** to stabilise prices is almost as old as trade in agricultural goods. The basic idea is simple: the state keeps stocks on hand; if prices rise too much, stocks are released; when prices fall again, stocks are replenished. This basic principle was also the basis of many of the so-called commodity agreements that were concluded in the 20th century for some agricultural goods (especially tropical export goods such as coffee, cocoa or rubber). However, the widespread failure of these agreements to achieve the goal of price stabilisation shows that the implementation of a coordinated storage strategy is extremely difficult in practice. First, storage is expensive. Second, stockholding by the state can crowd out private stockholding. Third, it is not objectively possible to define the 'right' price levels at which the replenishment and release of stocks should take place. Finally, if prices enter a prolonged slump, the state's capacity to accumulate stocks will at some point be exhausted; similarly, if prices peak for a protracted period, stocks can only be released until they are empty. If international coordination is also required, there is the problem of free riding. Each individual country has an incentive to defect, as long as all other participants play by the rules. Given these challenges, the effectiveness of government stockholding to reduce price volatility is limited. Similar reservations apply to the idea of using financial derivatives instead of physical stocks to stabilise markets. Such virtual warehousing avoids physical storage costs, but all of the other challenges outlined above remain.

12.7. Keywords and terms

- ARCH and GARCH models
- Backward- and forward-looking volatility estimation
- Buffer stocks
- Demand for stocks, stockholding
- Diversification, specialisation
- Expected and unexpected fluctuations
- Financialization of agricultural markets
- Market information systems
- Parametric and non-parametric estimation
- Profitability, stability, liquidity
- Realised volatility
- Risk management
- Volatility
- Volatility clusters
- Volatility spill-overs

References and further readings

Andersen TG and Bollerslev T (1998) Answering the Skeptics: Yes, Standard Volatility Models do Provide Accurate Forecasts. International Economic Review 39: 885–905.

Andersen TG, Bollerslev T and Diebold FX (2010) Parametric and Nonparametric Volatility Measurement. In: Aït-Sahalia Y and Hansen LP (Eds): Handbook of Financial Econometrics. North-Holland, pp. 67–137.

Andersen TG and Teräsvirta T (2009) Realized Volatility. In: Mikosch T et al. (Eds): Handbook of Financial Time Series. Springer Berlin Heidelberg, Berlin, Heidelberg, pp. 555–575.

Berger J, Dalheimer B and Brümmer B (2021) Effects of variable EU import levies on corn price volatility. Food Policy, https://doi.org/10.1016/j.foodpol.2021.102063
Black F and Scholes M (1973) The Pricing of Options and Corporate Liabilities. Journal of Political Economy 81: 637–654.
Bollerslev T, 1986, Generalized Autoregressive Conditional Heteroskedasticity. Journal of Econometrics 31: 307–327.
Brümmer B, Dönmez A, Jamali Jaghdani T, Korn O, Magrini E and Schlüßler K (2016a) Has agricultural price volatility increased since 2007. In: Garrido A et al. (Eds): Agricultural markets instability. Revisiting the recent food crises. Earthscan food and agriculture. Routledge, London, New York, pp. 29-58.
Brümmer B, Korn O, Schlüßler K and Jamali Jaghdani T (2016b) Volatility in Oilseeds and Vegetable Oils Markets: Drivers and Spillovers. Journal of Agricultural Economics 67: 685–705.
Brümmer B, Korn O, Schlüßler K, Jamali Jaghdani T and Saucedo A (2016c) Volatility in the after-crisis period: A literature review of recent empirical research. In: Garrido A et al. (Eds): Agricultural markets instability. Revisiting the recent food crises. Earthscan food and agriculture. Routledge, London, New York, pp. 15-28.
Busse S, Brümmer B and Ihle R (2011) Emerging linkages between price volatilities in energy and agricultural markets. In: Prakash A. (Ed): Safeguarding food security in volatile global markets. Food and Agriculture Organization, Rome, pp. 107-126.
Busse S, Brümmer B and Ihle R (2012) Price formation in the German biodiesel supply chain: a Markov-switching vector error-correction modeling approach. In: Agricultural Economics 43: 545–560.
Cavalcanti TV de V, Mohaddes K and Raissi M (2015) Commodity Price Volatility and the Sources of Growth. Journal of Applied Econometrics 30: 857-873.
Deaton A and Laroque G (1992) On the behaviour of commodity prices. Review of Economic Studies 59: 1-23.
Engle RF (1982) Autoregressive Conditional Hetero-scedasticity with Estimates of the Variance of United Kingdom Inflation. Econometrica 50: 987.
Engle RF, Ghysels E and Sohn B (2013) Stock Market Volatility and Macroeconomic Fundamentals. Review of Economics and Statistics 95: 776–797.
FAO (Food and Agricuture Organisation), 2021, Food Price Monitoring and Analysis. http://www.fao.org/giews/food-prices/en/.
G20, 2014, G20 Food Security and Nutrition Framework.

http://www.g20.utoronto.ca/2014/g20_food_security_nutrition_framework.pdf. Accessed 27. August 2022.
Glosten LR, Jagannathan R and Runkle DE (1993) On the Relation between the Expected Value and the Volatility of the Nominal Excess Return on Stocks. The Journal of Finance 48: 1779–1801.
Goldstein DG and Taleb NN (2007) We Don't Quite Know What We Are Talking About. Journal of Portfolio Management 33: 84–86.
Gustafson RL (1958) Carryover Levels for Grains, US Department of Agriculture, Technical Bulletin 1178, Washington DC.
Knight FH (1921) Risk, Uncertainty and Profit. Houghton Mifflin, Boston, New York.
Koester U (1986) Regional cooperation to improve food security in Southern and Eastern African countries. Research Report No. 53. International Food Policy Research Institute, Washington, DC.
Koester U (2020) Foundations of Agricultural Market Analysis and Agricultural Policy, Vahlen.
Masters MW (2008) Testimony of Michael W. Masters before the Committee on Homeland Security and Governmental Affairs of the United States Senate, https://www.hsgac.senate.gov/imo/media/doc/052008Masters.pdf. Accessed 27. August 2022.
Nelson DB (1991) Conditional Heteroskedasticity in Asset Returns: A New Approach. Econometrica 59: 347.
Samuelson PA (1972) The Consumer Does Benefit From Feasible Price Stability. The Quarterly Journal of Economics 86: 476.
Sandmo A (1971) On the Theory of the Competitive Firm Under Price Uncertainty. The American Economic Review 61: 65–73.
Schnittker JA (1973) The 1972-73 Food Price Spiral. Brookings Papers on Economic Activity, No. 2. https://www.brookings.edu/wp-content/uploads/1973/06/1973b_bpea_schnittker.pdf. Accessed 27. August 2022.
Serra T, Zilberman D and Gil J (2011) Price volatility in ethanol markets. European Review of Agricultural Economics 38: 259–280.
Shephard NG and Andersen TG (2009) Stochastic volatility: origins and overview. Handbook of financial time series. Springer, Berlin, pp. 233–254.
Smith A (1793) An inquiry into the nature and causes of the wealth of nations. London: Printed for A. Strahan and T. Cadell, in the Strand.

USDA (2022) World Agricultural Supply and Demand Estimates (WASDE) Reports. https://www.usda.gov/oce/commodity/wasde. Accessed 27. August 2022.
von Cramon-Taubadel S (2022) Russia's Invasion of Ukraine – Implications for Grain Markets and Food Security. German Journal of Agricultural Economics, doi: 10.30430/71.2022.5.Apol.
Waugh FV (1944) Does the Consumer Benefit from Price Instability? The Quarterly Journal of Economics 58: 602.
Will MG, Prehn S, Pies I and Glauben T (2015) Is Financial Speculation with Agricultural Commodities Harmful or Helpful? The Journal of Alternative Investments 18: 84–102.
Williamson OE (2000) The New Institutional Economics: Taking Stock, Looking Ahead. Journal of Economic Literature Vol. 38: 595–613.
Wright BD (2011) The Economics of Grain Price Volatility. Applied Economic Perspectives and Policy 33: 32–58.
Zakoian J-M (1994) Threshold heteroskedastic models. Journal of Economic Dynamics and Control 18: 931–955.

Exercises

1. Theoretical determinants of price volatility in agricultural markets:
   a. Discuss the main determinants of price volatility in agricultural markets.
   b. Using a suitable diagram, show the way in which volatility is influenced by stock levels.
   c. Discuss to what extent regional integration can influence the volatility of agricultural product prices.

2. Empirical estimation of price volatility in agricultural markets: Busse et al. (2011) estimate price volatilities for the most important oilseeds and crude oil for the period from 1999 to 2009 using a GARCH(1,1) model with weekday data from commodity futures markets. The following results for the conditional variance $\sigma_{i,t}^2 = \omega + \alpha u_{i,t-1} + \beta \sigma_{i,t-1}^2$, with i = {rapeseed oil, crude oil} are estimated:

$$\sigma_{rape\ oil,t}^2 = 0.00 + 0.37 u_{rape,t-1} + 0.55 \sigma_{rape,t-1}^2$$
$$\sigma_{crude\ oil,t}^2 = 0.00 + 0.04 u_{crude\ oil,t-1} + 0.94 \sigma_{crude\ oil,t-1}^2$$

   a. Are the conditions for stationarity met in both markets?
   b. What are the reasons for the different estimators for α and β in the two equations? Which of the two markets reacts more strongly to

new information, and why is this the case?

c. The authors further find that the conditional correlation between the returns for rapeseed oil and for crude oil increases dramatically from mid-2006, and this increase continues until 2009. Discuss which factors could be responsible for this increase in dynamic correlation.

3. Policy measures and price volatility:
In April 2018, China imposed an additional 25% tariff on imports of US soybeans. This was in response to US punitive tariffs on imports from China. China was the world's largest importer of soybeans at the time. Before the tariffs, the USA was the main supplier of soybeans to China. What was the expected impact on price volatility? Distinguish between the USA, China and the rest of the world.

CHAPTER THIRTEEN

FORWARD AND FUTURES MARKETS AND THEIR INFLUENCE ON AGRICULTURAL PRICE FORMATION

TERESA VOLLMER, LUDWIG STRIEWE AND STEPHAN VON CRAMON-TAUBADEL

13.1. Introduction and learning objectives

Agricultural production is a decentralised activity. Most agricultural goods must therefore be transported to the places where they are processed and consumed (**spatial transformation**). In addition, many products such as grains, oilseeds, potatoes, sugar beets, fruits, and vegetables are harvested seasonally. Other products, such as milk and meat are produced continuously, but even for these products supply and demand typically display seasonal fluctuations (for example due to the seasonal availability of pasture for animals, or special holiday demand such as Thanksgiving turkey). Hence, storage (**temporal transformation**) is required to match agricultural production and consumption over time.

Production, processing and consumption can all take place within a single vertically integrated company. For example, a farmer might produce grain and feeds it to her own pigs, another might grow grapes and produce wine. However, most of the grain, sugar beets, and oilseeds produced in industrialised countries is processed by third-party companies such as oilseed crushers, sugar factories, compound feed mills and flour mills. The resulting products are then in turn either raw materials for companies in the food industry or are sold directly to retailers for sale to consumers.

The farmers, traders, processors and retailers who are part of this food chain coordinate their activities on markets by means of contracts. Contracts allow the market participants to plan their production, input needs, plant capacity utilisation, storage and transportation needs, quality requirements, cash flows, etc. Contracts are also important for price determination. In particular, they allow market participants to fix the prices at which future transactions will take place. Since future conditions cannot be known with certainty, fixing prices for future transactions via contracts is a means of allocating risk between market participants who have different preferences for risk (**risk transfer**).

In this chapter we discuss two types of contracts, forward contracts and futures contracts, both of which play a key role in the pricing of many agricultural products. In particular, we will explain:

- how forward contracts are defined and how they are used by market participants,
- the advantages and disadvantages of forward contracts for market participants,
- how futures contracts and futures trading work,
- how market participants can hedge risk via futures contracts – so-called hedging,
- how grain traders can implement risk management strategies using futures contracts, and how this can benefit farmers who do not engage in futures trade themselves,
- that speculation plays an essential but also controversial role on futures markets, and
- that futures markets can only function effectively if price determination on futures and spot markets is not distorted by state intervention.

13.2. Forward contracts

When classifying contracts, a basic distinction can be made between those that are fulfilled immediately and those that are fulfilled at a future date. The definition of 'immediate' depends on the market in question. If one purchases a downloadable item such as an e-book online, immediate means within a few seconds or minutes. However, if the Kingdom of Saudi Arabia buys a 60,000 ton shipload of barley in a major German port, transport time dictates that the earliest possible delivery will take 30 days. In international grain trade, 'immediate' by convention refers to the fastest possible delivery of the contracted quantity and quality of grain to the agreed place of delivery by the agreed mode of transport.

In contrast to immediate delivery, **forward contracts** regulate the future delivery or acceptance of goods. Hence, a forward contract can be defined as a contract that is fulfilled later than immediately.

13.2.1. Design of forward contracts

Forward contracts are contracts negotiated individually between contracting parties in which, in addition to the standard contract parameters (such as product, quantity, quality and place of delivery) the date or period of delivery is also specified. The defining characteristic of a forward contract is therefore the future date or period of fulfilment. The price of a forward contract can be determined when the contract is signed, at the time of delivery, or sometime in between. There is also a great deal of flexibility in defining the delivery date or period, depending on the preferences of the contracting parties. To illustrate this, consider the following typical forward contractual arrangements in the grain trade:

1. The simplest form is a contract for fulfilment at a fixed time. *Example: Delivery of 500 tons of feed wheat, 2021 harvest, ciffo/franko*[1] *Hamburg, fulfilment in the 1st half of May 2022.*

2. Forward contracts can also be fulfilled in fixed monthly or semi-monthly instalments over a specified period of time. *Example: 3,000 tons of feed wheat, 2021 harvest, ciffo/franko Hamburg, delivery of 500 tons per month from January to June 2022.*

3. In international grain trade, optional contracts are also common. According to these contracts, the buyer takes delivery of a shipment,

---

[1] The abbreviation cif (*cost, insurance, freight*) means that the buyer pays for the goods in the port of destination including costs for insurance and freight. If the contracting parties also agree that the buyer pays for the goods after they have been unloaded at the port of destination, the contract contains the clause ciffo (cif + fo for *free out*). In German, the abbreviation franko has the same meaning for transport by truck as ciffo has for transport by ship, i.e. that all costs of transport, insurance and unloading are covered.

for example **fob**[2] at a specified seaport, but is free to choose the time of delivery within a defined period. Such optional contracts usually contain clauses that specify how much advance notice the buyer must give the seller prior to fulfilment, and what storage charges the buyer incurs per interval of elapsed time within the defined period. These storage charges are called reports and can be defined on a daily, semi-monthly or monthly basis. *Example: Purchase of 60,000 tons of wheat, fob Rostock, 2021 harvest, minimum 12.5% protein, maximum 14% moisture, buyer's option of delivery between February and May 2022, buyer must give 10 days' notice, price + 0.70 €/ton report per half-month.*

13.2.2. Economic motives for conclusion of forward contracts

In the grain trade, forward contracts are the rule and **spot contracts** tend to be used only when farmers sell directly after the harvest. Forward contracts are the central control instrument for sales, production, storage and logistics between the economic actors on grain markets. In addition, they allow actors to fix or hedge price in advance and thus to control revenues (sellers) and costs (buyers).

Processors of agricultural products such as grain and oilseed often sell more or less continuously – e.g. flour mills to retailers and bakers; oilseed crushers to retailers, compound feed and biodiesel producers. Hence, processors require a sufficient supply of raw materials throughout the year. A processor can ensure this supply by own stockholding or by contract suppliers to make continuous deliveries. Own storage makes a processor independent. However, it is expensive to store the amount of raw material required for an entire year of processing, because of the physical costs of storage, and the financial costs of the money tied up in stocks. Furthermore, many processing sites are centrally located on waterways or in large agglomerations. At harvest time, when logistics are tight, it is scarcely possible to transport large quantities of grain from decentralised production centres over several hundreds of kilometres to these concentrated locations. Consequently, most processors only have storage capacities of a few weeks or months of production, and they use forward contracts with suppliers to ensure supply in instalments over the course of a year.

---

[2] The abbreviation fob (*free on board*) means that the buyer takes delivery of the goods on board a ship in the specified export harbour, and is responsible for all costs such as insurance and freight incurred thereafter.

Forward contracts for delivery in instalments also provide planning security for the grain suppliers, for example large farms or traders with country elevators who purchase from farms. Forward contracts enable these suppliers to calculate how much storage capacity they require. In addition, grain processors usually buy grain delivered to the plant, i.e. the supplier provides the transport carrier. Forward contracts for delivery in instalments therefore allow for a continuous utilisation of the suppliers' transport carriers - truck, rail or ship. Forward contracts are thus a central element of cost management and the efficient utilisation of storage and processing capacities, and transport infrastructure.

Both forward as well as spot contracts specify all of the parameters that are important for the suppliers and processors. Very large processors usually specify their own individual purchasing conditions. In some markets, standardised forward contracts have also emerged that are used by several processors as a point of reference. Dozens of parameters can be specified in forward contracts. In addition to basic parameters such as the product, quantity, and the date and location of fulfilment, contracts often include detailed clauses on:

- transport carriers; the mechanism for triggering instalments,
- tolerances and associated penalties for over- or under-delivery,
- quality parameters and tolerances as well as surcharges and/or discounts for qualities that do not fall within these tolerances,
- the right to refuse a delivery if certain parameters are not met,
- agreements on the quality management system to be used, on controls, and on the way in which sampling is carried out, and
- agreements on the responsible mediator or jurisdiction in the event of a dispute.

13.2.3. Risks and disadvantages of forward contracts

Forward contracts are basically individually negotiated contracts. It is not easy for either the seller or the buyer to withdraw from a forward contract in the event of a change in the conditions for fulfilment. If a seller is unable to supply as foreseen in a forward contract, he can purchase goods at the same conditions (quality, location, etc.) from a third party to fulfil the contract. Nevertheless, the original seller remains the buyer's contract partner. When the forward contract is fulfilled, the buyer pays the original seller, who in turn pays the third party from whom he purchased the goods.

Such chain transactions involving standardised contracts for typical qualities of grain and delivery locations are quite common in grain trading. In Germany, for example, standard contracts for milling wheat and feed barley franko/ciffo Hamburg are sometimes sold and resold as often as five or even ten times. The same holds for standardised contracts for wheat, barley or rye franko Südoldenburg in northwest Germany, where there is a concentration of compound feed producers for the local livestock industry. At each link in such a chain, contract conditions and payments have to be controlled and processed, which can be complicated, time-consuming and error-prone.

Forward contracts, like all physical contracts, are associated with the risks of non-performance and non-payment. The contracting parties therefore pay close attention to whom they do business with, and almost all trading houses assess the so-called **counterparty risk** before concluding a contract, i.e. they check the creditworthiness of the contracting party and how well it has executed contracts in the past.

In summary: forward contracts are appropriate instruments for planning and controlling procurement, storage, production, logistics and sales. They also serve to fix prices between contract partners. However, this form of contract is very individual, and only fungible and liquid to a limited extent. Futures contracts can be seen as a reaction to these disadvantages. As we will show in the following sections, futures and forward contracts together provide market participants with highly customised price-fixing and risk-hedging instruments.

13.3. The futures contract

Futures contracts and their predecessors were already being used in the 17th century, e.g. at the Osaka rice exchange in Japan. In Chicago, the Chicago Board of Trade (CBOT) was founded in 1848 and the first forward contract was traded in 1851 (Chicago Board of Trade, 1997). Starting in 1865, the CBOT took steps to standardise these contracts. Such contracts were called **futures contracts** (futures for short). Futures were also traded in Germany, on the Berlin Commodity Exchange. However, futures trade in Germany was stopped in 1886 because Prussian Junkers (a class of aristocrats with large agricultural estates and considerable political influence) suspected that speculation on the futures market was lowering grain prices. Hence, they lobbied successfully for stricter regulation of exchanges. It would take until 1993 for an amendment to the law to make futures trading possible in Germany again.

13.3.1. The role of futures contracts

Futures contracts can be traded for a variety of different product groups. The *Futures Industry Association* (FIA) collects data from 52 exchanges worldwide and publishes statistics on the trade in futures and options on futures[3] for seven product groups: stock indices, stocks, interest rates, currencies, energy (including electricity), agricultural products, non-precious metals and precious metals. According to FIA (2020), almost 34.5 billion contracts were traded worldwide in 2019, including roughly 19 billion futures and 15 billion options contracts. With 12.5 billion contracts, futures on stock indices accounted for around 36% of global trading volume, followed by stocks with 17.6%, interest rates with just under 14%, and currency futures with just over 11%.

Futures trading in agricultural products has developed rapidly over the past 20 years (Fig. 13.1). According to FIA, only 137 million contracts were traded in 2000, but by 2019 this number had risen to 1.65 billion. North America (especially the US) has accounted for only 20-30% of the number of contracts traded over the last 5 years, compared with 68-80% in Asia (especially China), which has become by far the most important trading centre for futures on agricultural products. In Europe, the number of contracts traded has increased steadily from 4 million in 2000 to 14 million in 2010 and 27 million in 2017. Overall, however, the exchanges in Europe are less important, with a constant share of only about 2% of the global trading volume.

In Europe, futures trading for agricultural products takes place on several commodity futures exchanges. Of particular importance are Euronext (*MATIF - Marché à Terme International de France*, with futures on wheat, rapeseed, rapeseed meal and rapeseed oil, maize and contracts on skimmed milk powder, sweet whey powder, butter and fertilisers), and the Liffe

---

[3] An option is the right to buy or sell something at a later date and at a fixed price. Whereas futures establish obligations, options merely establish rights. Options also play a role in agriculture but are not discussed further here. For more information on options, see e.g. Hull (1998).

(*London International Financial Futures and Options Exchange*), which is part of the NYSE (*New York Stock Exchange*) and on which contracts on sugar and feed wheat are traded.

Figure 13.1 The number of traded futures on agricultural product markets by region of the world

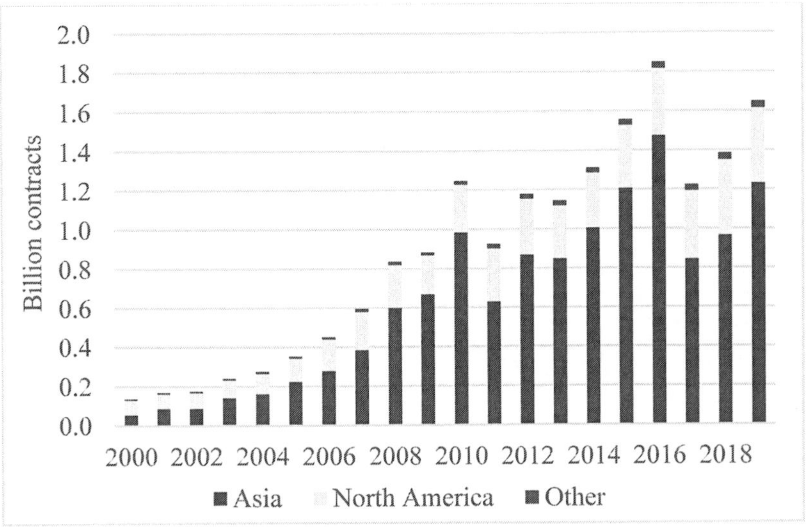

Source: FIA (2020), own illustration.

13.3.2. The nature of futures contracts

Futures contracts are agreements to buy or sell an asset at a specific future settlement date. The detailed contract specifications are standardised and defined by the exchange that provides the contract, e.g. Euronext. The only remaining parameter that the transacting parties must agree on is the price. Due to its great importance for the European grain trade, we present in Table 13.1 the specification of the Euronext MATIF wheat No. 2 futures contract (hereinafter the MATIF wheat contract).

Table 13.1 The specification of the Euronext MATIF wheat No. 2 futures contract

Designation	MATIF-wheat No. 2 futures contract
Contract code	EBM
Trading place	Paris
Clearing	LCH S.A. (a company based in Paris, see below)
Algorithm	The central order book applies a price/time trading algorithm, priority is given to the first order at the best price
Product	Wheat produced in the EU
Moisture	Max. 15%
Broken grains	Max. 4%
Sprouted grains	Max. 2%
Impurities	Max. 2%
Hagberg falling number	Min. 220 seconds
Protein content	Min. 11% in dry matter
Specific weight	Min. 76 kg/hl
Differences between delivered and specified quality	In case of differences, discounts apply in accordance with Incograin No. 23 and Technical Annex 2
Mycotoxins	Applicable EU legislation for unprocessed cereals
Delivery points	In an approved silo in Dunkirk, La Pallice, Montoir, Nantes or Rouen (France).
Delivery months	September, December, March and May
Contract size	50 t
Currency	Euro and Eurocents per t
Tick size	25 Eurocents per t = 12,50 €/contract
Trading times	10:45 – 18:30 (UTC+1)
Last trading day	18:30 (UTC+1) on the tenth calendar day of the delivery month (if no business day, then on the following business day)
Notification day	The first business day following the last trading day
Delivery period	Each business day from the last trading day until the end of the respective delivery month
Delivery limits	Delivery limits are set by LCH S.A. and are published 80 days before the last trading day and are applicable for 12 days before the last trading day of the delivery month

Source: Euronext (2020).

The contract specifications include the trading venue, the responsible clearing institution and a rule for the algorithm of the central order book. We discuss this further below. The contract specifications also include the physical quality parameters described in Table 13.1, such as moisture and protein content, and how differences between these parameters and actual delivered quality will be managed. The specifications also list the possible delivery points, which in the case of the MATIF wheat contract are all accredited silo operations in France. The seller decides at which of the delivery points the delivery will take place. This is called the **seller's option**, and it has important implications for the pricing of a futures contract, as we will explain below in Section 13.3.5.

Based on the specification of the futures contract, the buyer knows exactly which minimum quality he will receive, and the seller knows which minimum quality he must deliver, if the contract is physically delivered. Physical delivery is possible in principle and takes place for all contracts that have not been traded back (**offset** - see below) by the end of their last trading day. The possibility of physically delivering wheat of the quality specified in the futures contract is central to the price formation of the contract. It ensures that on the last trading day of a contract, the price of the contract and the spot market price of wheat (of the quality and at the delivery point specified in the contract) will be equal. On the last trading day, therefore, futures prices and spot prices converge.

All other contract specifications shown in Table 13.1 are of a technical nature. They regulate the contract size (50 t for wheat), the minimum price movement that is traded (0.25 eurocents per t, which corresponds to € 12.50 per 50 t contract), the trading hours, the last trading day and the exact procedures for physical delivery, such as the notification times and the details of where delivery shall take place if the seller exercises the seller's option.

13.3.3. The trading in futures contracts

Since all other parameters of a futures contract are standardised, only the price of the contract remains to be determined. As a rule, futures trading is carried out on behalf of clients by authorised brokerage houses or banks acting as brokers who place buy or sell orders for a specific contract directly in the exchange's trading system. Clients usually place their buy or sell orders with their brokers by telephone or directly via the brokers' electronic trading systems.

The order in which incoming orders are placed on the exchange is regulated by the algorithm described in Table 13.1. In the case of the MATIF wheat contract, for example, this ensures that the sell order for a specific contract and specific price is booked in the same rank order in which it was entered into the exchange's system (first come, first served). If, for example, client X places an order to sell 50 September 2022 wheat contracts, i.e. 2,500 t, at a price of 190 €/t, then this order will enter the queue behind all of the other sell orders for the same contract at the same price. Only when the other contracts ahead in this queue have been purchased will client X's 50 contracts be up for sale. These 50 contracts will then be sold all together or in parts, depending on the number and sizes of the orders in the corresponding queue of buy orders for the same contract at the same price. The exchange's electronic trading system displays the number of sell and buy orders placed for a specific contract. When the electronic trading system has matched client X's sell order with one or more corresponding buy orders, then the seller and the buyer(s) have traded 50 t of wheat as specified in the contract and are informed of this electronically. If this trade is the last one to take place on a given day, the price of 190 €/t will be the official daily closing price for the September 2022 contract on that day. However, exchanges often reserve the right to publish the average price of a number of the last trades as the official closing price.

13.3.4. Market integrity, margin system and the clearing mechanism

Futures trading is anonymous, i.e. the buyers and sellers of a particular contract have no knowledge of each other's identity. Hence, they cannot assess counterparty risk, as described above for forward contracts. Instead, the integrity of the futures contract, i.e. its unconditional fulfilment and the settlement of profits and losses, is guaranteed by a **clearing mechanism**. On the Euronext, this is regulated by the clearing bank LCH S.A. (see Table 13.1).

The clearing mechanism is based on a system of margins. Margins are amounts of money that are deposited in a trustee account with the clearing bank. The clearing bank acts as a third party to the trade between a buyer and a seller and requires that both deposit **margins**, which are either a percentage of the contract value or a fixed amount per contract. When a contract is traded, both the buyer and the seller must first deposit the so-called **initial margin**, which is an amount at least large enough to cover the maximum loss that could be incurred on the next trading day. This maximum loss is determined by the trading limit of the futures contract that is set by the exchange, i.e. maximum amount by which the price of a contract might fluctuate within a certain period of time, beyond which trading for this futures contract will be temporarily suspended.

The buyer of a futures contract suffers a loss if the market price for this contract falls. This is because by purchasing the contract, the buyer has committed to pay a certain price in return for the quantity, quality, time and place of delivery specified in the contract. If the price of the contract falls, then the same quantity and quality at the same time and place could be purchased for less. Consider the example shown in Table 13.2. The futures contract was originally traded for 190 €/t, and in the meantime its market price has fallen to 185 €/t. The initial margin of 5 €/t covers the buyer's loss of 5 €/t exactly. The clearing bank then demands an additional 5 €/t margin from the buyer, the so-called **margin call**. By this mechanism, the buyer of the contract is obliged to always deposit with the clearing bank an amount equal to the maximum loss that he/she might incur in the course of the next day's trading.

Table 13.2 An example of the initial margin and margin calls in €/t for different price developments

Buyer			Euronext	Seller		
Exchange demands	Sum margin	Margin	Price	Margin	Sum margin	Exchange demands
Margin call	€ 35	€ 5	€ 160			
Margin call	€ 30	€ 5	€ 165			
Margin call	€ 25	€ 5	€ 170			
Margin call	€ 20	€ 5	€ 175			
Margin call	€ 15	€ 5	€ 180			
Margin call	€ 10	€ 5	€ 185			
Initial margin	€ 5	€ 5	€ 190	€ 5	€ 5	Initial margin
			€ 195	€ 5	€ 10	Margin call
			€ 200	€ 5	€ 15	Margin call
			€ 205	€ 5	€ 20	Margin call
			€ 210	€ 5	€ 25	Margin call
			€ 215	€ 5	€ 30	Margin call
			€ 220	€ 5	€ 35	Margin call

Price at which the contract was originally traded (→ € 190)

The same logic applies for the seller, who suffers a loss when the price of the contract increases. The seller has committed to deliver the quantity and quality at the time and place of delivery specified in the contract, in return for a certain price. If the price of the contract increases, then the same quantity and quality, at the same time and place, could be sold for more.

Trading in futures contracts can thus bind large amounts of capital in the form of deposited margins. In the event of sharp price hikes, market participants who have sold futures contracts have to inject a lot of capital in the form of margin calls, and may run into liquidity problems as a result. This occurred in 2007/08, for example, or more recently following Russia's attack on Ukraine in February 2022, when prices for many agricultural commodities rose sharply.

13.3.5. Obligations of the market participants

If a contract is traded at time t_0, the seller (A) undertakes to deliver the commodity and quality underlying the future at the specified delivery time and place. The seller's position is called **short**.[4] The buyer of a future (B), on the other hand, undertakes to accept delivery of the commodity in accordance with the contract specifications. The buyer' position is called **long**. Market participant A can cancel his/her delivery obligation (**short position**) in t_1 without affecting B if he/she can find another market participant (C) who is willing to assume this delivery obligation in return for a price. The result would be that C now has a short position and B continues to have a **long position** on the commodity futures market. Participant A would no longer have a position the commodity futures market because his/her initial short position has been **offset**. Of course, B can also offset his/her long position by transferring the associated obligation to accept delivery to another market participant.

On a commodity futures exchange, the margins that the seller and buyer have deposited are matched and balanced by the clearing bank. In the example in Table 13.2, if the price of the contract has fallen to 170 €/t by t_1, the buyer realises a loss of 20 €/t when he/she offsets his/her long position by selling the contract. The clearing bank will therefore retain 20 of the total 25 €/t of margin that the buyer has deposited since t_0, and use this money to cover the profits that the seller has realised since t_0. Thus, commodities do not necessarily have to be physically exchanged as a result of trade in futures contracts. Sellers and buyers can always eliminate their

[4] A helpful mnemonic: 'short' and 'sell' both begin with the letter 's'.

obligations to make/take delivery by offsetting their positions, with the clearing house balancing any accumulated profits and losses. In practice, the share of contracts that are physically delivered is usually less than 1% of the contract volume.

Table 13.3 summarises and contrasts the main characteristics of forward and futures contracts.

Table 13.3 Characteristics of forward and futures contracts

Characteristic	Futures contracts	Forward contracts
Specification	Quantity, quality, and place and time of delivery are standardised	Individually negotiable
Liquidity	Correlated with trading volume on the futures exchange	Must be negotiated individually, not guaranteed. Fungibility is guaranteed only on a few paper markets
Integrity	Guaranteed by the exchange via the clearing bank	Counterparty risk must be managed by the respective contract parties
Payment method	Continuous by means of the margin mechanism	Individual, mostly as a lump sum at or after delivery
Delivery	As a rule, as contracts are offset therefore no delivery	Physical, countertrade or loss compensation
Transaction costs	Broker fees and interest on deposited margin	Negotiation and settlement costs

Source: Nelson (1985, p. 17).

13.3.6. The pricing of futures contracts

In the following section we explain the pricing of futures contracts and how futures prices are linked to spot market prices by the so-called **basis**. The basis is the difference between the current or future spot price at a certain location, and the price of a certain futures contract. A distinction is made between the **forward basis**, which is the difference between the spot price and the forward price ($p_{t_0}^{S} - p_{t_0 \to t_1}^{FUT}$) at a certain point in time t_0, and the **maturity basis**, which is the difference between the spot price and the futures price when the futures contract matures ($p_{t_1}^{S} - p_{t_1 \to t_1}^{FUT}$), i.e. at the time of delivery. In these equations, $p^{FUT}_{t_i \to t_j}$ denotes the price at time t_i of the futures contract with maturity t_j, and $p^S_{t_k}$ denotes the spot price at time t_k.

Arbitrage affects the basis and thus the relationship between futures and spot prices. For example, if the futures price is higher than the spot price for a commodity with identical quality characteristics at time t_1, then arbitrageurs will sell futures contracts at price $p^{FUT}_{t_1 \to t_1}$, purchase equivalent amounts of the commodity in question on the spot market at the lower price $p^S_{t_1}$, and physically deliver the futures contracts. By doing so, the arbitrageurs will tend to drive down the price of the futures contract, and drive up the spot price. As a result, arbitrage will drive the maturity basis to zero. However, the maturity basis will be smaller (larger) than zero if the commodity traded on the spot market is of lower (higher) quality than that specified in the futures contract.

Based on analogous considerations, we expect that in a perfect market futures and forward prices will be almost identical. If, for example, the forward price $p^{FWD}_{t_0 \to t_1}$ exceeds the futures price $p^{FUT}_{t_0 \to t_1}$ at t_0, arbitrageurs will sell commodities forward and buy contracts on the futures market with the intention of insisting on physical delivery of the futures contracts at time t_1 when they mature. With the delivered commodity they can fulfil the forward contract and thus realise the profit $p^{FWD}_{t_0 \to t_1} - p^{FUT}_{t_0 \to t_1}$. Consequently, the prices of forward contracts will generally be derived from futures prices, with adjustments for quality differences. Later in this chapter we show how this relationship affects price determination in the grain trade.

Abstracting from quality differences and different delivery locations, it can be assumed that the forward basis will increase linearly with increasing time horizon in the course of a crop year. Formally, the relationship between a futures price $p^{FUT}_{t_0 \to t_1}$ and the spot price $p^S_{t_0}$ can be represented as follows:

$$p^{FUT}_{t_0 \to t_1} = p^S_{t_0}\left(1 + r_{t_0 \to t_1}\right) + L_{t_0 \to t_1} \quad (1)$$

where

$r_{t_0 \to t_1}$ = the opportunity cost of an amount of capital equal to the spot price over the period from t_0 to t_1,

and

$L_{t_0 \to t_1}$ = the cost of storage per unit of the good from t_0 to t_1.

If equation (1) does not hold exactly, arbitrageurs will be able to realise certain profits. If, for example $p_{t_0 \to t_1}^{FUT} > p_{t_0}^{S}(1 + r_{t_0 \to t_1}) + L_{t_0 \to t_1}$ they will buy the commodity on the spot market for $p_{t_0}^{K}$ and at the same time take a corresponding short position on the futures market (i.e. sell a futures contract for $p_{t_0 \to t_1}^{FUT}$). When the futures contract matures, they can deliver the commodity that they purchased on the spot market, and the difference between $p_{t_0 \to t_1}^{FUT}$ and $p_{t_0}^{K}$ will be more than enough to cover the cost of purchasing the commodity and storing it in the interim.

13.3.7. The seller's option

As we explained above, the seller's option allows the seller to select the delivery point from a specified list. We illustrate this using the example of the MATIF rapeseed contract, which specifies eight delivery points (in France, Belleville, Metz and Frouard on the Moselle River; in Germany, Bülstringen, Vahldorf and Magdeburg on the *Mittellandkanal*, and Würzburg on the Main River; and in Belgium, Ghent).

For the delivery of contracts that have not been offset prior to maturity, sellers will choose a delivery point where they can deliver the rapeseed at the lowest cost. Until 2012, for example, there was a surplus of rapeseed in the new *Länder* of the former German Democratic Republic. This rapeseed had to be transported via the *Mittellandkanal* to oil mills on the Lower Rhine, which cost roughly 12 €/t. The price fob barge *Mittellandkanal* was thus 12 €/t below the price cif on the Lower Rhine. At that time, rapeseed could be transported the Moselle to the Lower Rhine for 6 €/t, so that the price fob Moselle was generally 6 €/t below cif Lower Rhine. Similarly transport costs from the port of Ghent to the Lower Rhine were about 5 €/t, so fob Ghent was correspondingly 5 €/t below cif Lower Rhine. The price at the *Mittellandkanal* was always the lowest price derived from the price cif Lower Rhine and thus represented the most favourable option for sellers who had to deliver. This was anticipated by the market participants. As a result, the maturity basis for the price fob *Mittellandkanal* always amounted to 0 €/t, the MATIF rapeseed contract reflected fob *Mittellandkanal*, and most deliveries took place on the *Mittellandkanal*.

Since then, however, rapeseed processing capacities in the new *Länder* have grown and rapeseed production has declined. As a result, the region has become a net importer of rapeseed. At the same time, the EU as a whole has also developed from a net exporter to a net importer of rapeseed. The lowest price is now usually the cif Ghent price, which in turn represents the cheapest delivery option. The MATIF rapeseed contract therefore now reflects the Ghent location. Oil mills located on the *Mittellandkanal* must now pay a basis (traders refer to it as a 'premium') of up to 14 €/t on top of the MATIF rapeseed price, to cover transport costs from the port of Ghent.

13.4. Risk management with futures markets

13.4.1. Basics of hedging on futures markets

When market participants use futures markets to protect themselves against the risk of price fluctuations for physical goods, they are said to be **hedging**, in the sense of 'fencing in' or 'limiting'. In the following we will explain how a hedge functions, what risks are associated with hedging, and what role speculation plays on futures markets.

In general, a distinction is made between **long** and **short hedges**. A seller who would like to fix the price of a future sale of physical goods on the spot market in order to protect against falling prices, is called a short hedger. A farmer, for example, could try to fix the selling price for his/her next harvest by means of a short hedge. If, on the other hand, a buyer attempts to fix the price of a future purchase of physical goods to protect against rising prices, we refer to a long hedge. Typical long hedgers are processors of agricultural products, such as flour mills, that try to lock in future raw material costs.

As an example of a long (short) hedge, assume that a trader intends to buy (sell) physical goods on the spot market at price $p_{t_1}^S$ at time t_1. To do this, he sells (buys) a forward contract at time t_0 and price $p_{t_0 \to t_1}^{FWD}$. Without hedging, there is a price risk, since $p_{t_1}^S$ is unknown at time t_0. If $p_{t_1}^S$ turns out to be lower than the forward price, the trader has lost, because he/she could have paid less for the goods in question. This risk can be reduced (hedged) by a countertrade on the futures market. For this purpose, the trader buys (sells) futures contracts at price $p_{t_0 \to t_1}^{FUT}$ and time t_0, and thus enters into a long (short) position on the futures market. The purchase of the futures contracts can be viewed as a temporary substitute for the transaction to be carried out later on the spot market. The long (short) futures position is offset by selling (buying) futures contracts at time t_1 and price $p_{t_1 \to t_1}^{FUT}$. The profits or losses from the transactions on the futures market are offset by the clearing house as explained above and either credited or charged to the trader. At the same time, the trader acquires (sells) the physical commodity on the spot market.

Formally, this long hedge can be represented as follows:

$$\begin{aligned} \pi_H &= qp^{FWD}_{t_0 \to t_1} - qp^S_{t_1} - qp^{FUT}_{t_0 \to t_1} + qp^{FUT}_{t_1 \to t_1} \\ &= q(p^{FWD}_{t_0 \to t_1} - p^S_{t_1}) - q(p^{FUT}_{t_0 \to t_1} - p^{FUT}_{t_1 \to t_1}) \end{aligned} \quad (2)$$

where

π_H= the profit after the long hedge,

q = the quantity traded,

$p^{FWD}_{t_0 \to t_1}$= the forward price in t_0 for delivery in t_1,

$p^S_{t_1}$= the spot price in t_1,

$p^{FUT}_{t_0 \to t_1}$= the futures price in t_0 for delivery in t_1, and

$p^{FUT}_{t_1 \to t_1}$= the futures price in t_1 for delivery in t_1.

Thus, the profit of a long hedge π_H equals the change in the value of the quantity traded on the spot market $(p^{FWD}_{t_0 \to t_1} - p^S_{t_1})$ minus the change in the value of the quantity traded on the futures market $(p^{FUT}_{t_0 \to t_1} - p^{FUT}_{t_1 \to t_1})$. If these changes mirror one another, price risk is reduced. This will be the case if both $p^{FUT}_{t_0 \to t_1}$ and $p^{FWD}_{t_0 \to t_1}$, and $p^{FUT}_{t_1 \to t_1}$ and $p^S_{t_1}$ move in parallel. As explained above, arbitrage will ensure that these conditions are met. First, $p^{FWD}_{t_0 \to t_1}$ and $p^{FUT}_{t_0 \to t_1}$ will move in parallel as forward prices are derived from futures prices, with allowance for quality differences between the commodity traded in the forward and futures markets. Second, $p^{FUT}_{t_1 \to t_1}$ and $p^S_{t_1}$ will also move in parallel as the maturity basis tends towards zero, again with allowance for quality differences. Hence, any loss (gain) on the spot market will be compensated by a corresponding gain (loss) on the futures market - i.e. $(p^{FWD}_{t_0 \to t_1} - p^K_{t_1}) \approx (p^{FUT}_{t_0 \to t_1} - p^{FUT}_{t_1 \to t_1})$.

These relationships are illustrated in Table 13.4. A trader buys wheat for 184 €/t on November 28, 2019 (whether on the spot market or on the forward market is irrelevant for the example). At the same time, he sells a March 2020 wheat futures contact (i.e. enters into a short position) on the MATIF at a price of 180 €/t. The basis for this contract is therefore 4 €/t. At this point, the trader has bought (is long on) the physical commodity, and has sold a futures contract (is short on the futures market). This position (physical commodity long, futures short) is called **premium long**. The opposite position, in which a trader has sold the physical commodity and hedged the price by buying a futures contract (physical commodity short, futures long) is called **premium short**.

On February 15, 2020, the trader sells the physical commodity for 180 €/t, which is 4 €/t below the November 2019 purchase price. At the same time, the trader offsets the futures contract, i.e. he takes the opposite position and buys back the futures contract, which has also fallen by 4 €/t. Since the prices on the futures market and the spot market have moved in parallel, as described above (both have fallen by 4 €/t), the basis has not changed. Without a hedge, the trader would have lost 4 €/t on the physical transaction; however, this loss is completely offset by a profit on the futures market. The result is therefore 0 €/t and the hedge is perfect.

Table 13.4 Position premium long: prices fall, basis remains unchanged

	Physical		**MATIF**		**Basis**	**Result**
	Buy	Sell	Buy	Sell		
28 Nov 2019	€ 184			€ 180	€ 4	
15 Feb 2020		€ 180	€ 176		€ 4	
Profit/loss		€ -4		€ 4	€ 0	€ 0

Source: Own illustration.

The same transaction has a different outcome for the trader if the basis increases. This is the case when the physical value falls less (or increases more) than the price on the MATIF. In Table 13.5, the physical price falls by 4 €/t as in the previous example, but the MATIF price falls by 6 €/t. Hence, the basis increases from 4 to 6 €/t. The trader again loses 4 €/t on the physical transaction, but in this case this loss is more than compensated by the gain of 6 €/t from the short hedge on the futures market.

Table 13.5 Position premium long: prices fall, basis increases

	Physical		MATIF		Basis	Result
	Buy	Sell	Buy	Sell		
28 Nov 2019	€ 184			€ 180	€ 4	
15 Feb 2020		€ 180	€ 174		€ 6	
Profit/loss		€ -4		€ 6		€ 2

Source: Own illustration.

Similarly, if the physical price falls more (or increases less) than the price on the MATIF, the trader with the long premium position incurs a loss (Table 13.6). In this case, the loss on the physical transaction is not fully offset by a profit from the short hedge on the futures market. As we will explain in greater detail in the next section, the changes in the basis that we have assumed in the last two examples (Tables 13.5 and 13.6) can be triggered by factors such as volatile transport costs or weather-related changes in the qualities available on the spot market.

Table 13.6 Position premium long: prices fall, basis falls

	Physical		MATIF		Basis	Result
	Buy	Sell	Buy	Sell		
28 Nov 2019	€ 184			€ 180	€ 4	
15 Feb 2020		€ 180	€ 178		€ 2	
Profit/loss		€ -4		€ 2		€ -2

Source: Own illustration.

We present a final example in Table 13.7 to show that a falling basis leads to a profit if the trader is premium short instead of premium long. In this case, the physical commodity is first sold (physical commodity short) and the price is hedged by buying a futures contract (futures long). A falling basis then leads to a profit, since the profit on the physical transaction is greater than the loss from the long hedge on the futures market. Conversely, premium short leads to losses if the basis increases.

Table 13.1 Position premium short: prices fall, basis falls

	Physical		MATIF		Basis	Result
	Buy	Sell	Buy	Sell		
28 Nov 2019		€ 184	€ 180		€ 4	
15 Feb 2020	€ 180			€ 178	€ 2	
Profit/loss		€ 4		€ -2		€ 2

Source: Own illustration.

10.4.1.1. Risks associated with hedging

Hedging is often compared to insurance, but this comparison is flawed. The insurance principle is based on spreading possible losses over many policyholders. In contrast, hedging means offsetting one risk by means of an opposite transaction so that the combined risk of both transactions together is smaller than the risk of one alone. However, as the examples above have illustrated, risk is not completely eliminated. Since the basis can increase or fall, the basis risk always remains.

We introduced the concepts of basis risk and margin risk above. Further risks are the liquidity risk and the standard quantity risk, both of which can also affect the profitability of a hedge. In the following, we review each of these types of risk in turn.

The price risk in spot market transactions can only be reduced by hedging if spot and futures market prices move largely in parallel and the basis is therefore roughly constant over time. In reality, however, this is rarely the case. **Basis risk** arises because the basis in t_1 is unknown and cannot be forecast exactly at time t_0. In fact, a hedge does not completely eliminate price risk on the spot market, it merely exchanges this price risk for basis risk. In the case of a long hedge, a basis that increases over time ($[p^{FUT}_{t_0 \to t_1} - p^{K}_{t_1}] > [p^{FUT}_{t_1 \to t_1} - p^{K}_{t_1}]$) leads to a loss, while a basis that falls over time ($[p^{FUT}_{t_0 \to t_1} - p^{K}_{t_1}] < [p^{FUT}_{t_1 \to t_1} - p^{K}_{t_1}]$) leads to a gain. In the case of a short hedge, the opposite effect occurs in each case.

Changes in basis can be caused by a variety of factors. These include volatile transport costs. If, for example, freight rates increase or important waterways become temporarily impassable due to weather conditions, transport costs will increase. This will affect the costs of physically delivering a futures contract from other locations (in space). As a result, the difference between the futures price and the spot price at another location will increase. Unless transport costs are constant, spot prices are decoupled from the futures prices to a certain extent, resulting in basis fluctuations.

Changes in the relative qualities of the goods on the spot and futures markets can also generate basis fluctuations. While the MATIF wheat contract provides for a minimum protein content of 11% (see Table 13.1), on average over the years, German milling wheat has a roughly 1% higher protein content, which leads to a positive basis. However, if extreme weather in Germany leads to quality losses in a particular year, the basis can weaken.[5]

In most markets, however, the correlation between futures and spot prices is sufficiently high (i.e. basis risk is sufficiently low) to ensure that hedging usually leads to a reduction in the price risk of spot market transactions. Indeed, it is sometimes the case that the correlation between the futures price for one product and the spot price for a different but related product is sufficiently high to allow successful hedging. For example, rapeseed and soybean prices are often so positively correlated that transactions on the spot market for rapeseed can be hedged with soybean futures. In this case, we speak of a **cross hedge**.

Liquidity risk, which has been a problem for example on European commodity futures markets for dairy or meat products, is closely related to basis. A futures market is liquid when a sufficient number of market participants (including speculators[6]) trade on that market and hedgers are therefore able to trade and, in particular, offset any and all open contract volumes at the prevailing market price at any time. In a market with low liquidity, i.e. a low trading volume, it can be difficult to offset an open position because – as explained above – every transaction on a futures market involves matching, i.e. the simultaneous presence of a buyer and a seller who are both willing to trade at a certain price. On a market with low liquidity, hedgers might have to make price concessions to offset large positions, and this can lead to changes in the basis.

Whereas liquidity risk is a characteristic of a particular futures market, **margin risk** can create liquidity problems for individual farmers. As we

---

[5] Prehn et al. (2016) and Vollmer et al. (2020) analyse the determinants of the basis between spot prices for wheat in Germany and the price of the MATIF wheat contract.

[6] The role of speculators on futures markets is discussed in Section 13.4.2.

explained above, a farmer who wants to hedge by selling futures contracts for wheat (short hedge) will have to make margin calls on an ongoing basis if prices rise sharply. Depending on the financial situation of the farm and the size of the short position, this can lead to considerable liquidity problems for a farm (see case study 1 below).

Standard quantity risk is a problem that can arise when a hedger only produces or purchases small quantities. A futures contract specifies a certain quantity of for example 50 tons in the case of the MATIF wheat contract. It is not possible to purchase or sell fraction of a contract. If a farmer who expects to harvest 25 tons of wheat attempts to hedge by selling a futures contract for 50 tons, he/she will be speculating on the futures market with the 25-ton difference. Similarly, a farmer who hedges an expected harvest of 70 tons with a single 50-ton contract will be speculating with 20 tonnes on the spot market.

10.4.1.2. Determining the optimal hedge ratio

A market participant who hedges all of his/her expected spot market transactions on the futures market ton-for-ton is said to have a hedge ratio of 1, or a 'full hedge'. The hedge ratio is defined as the ratio of the quantity that is hedged on the futures market to the quantity that (will be) traded on the spot market.

$$H_R = \frac{q_H}{q_S} \qquad (3)$$

where

H_R = the hedge ratio,

q_H = the quantity hedged on the futures market, and

q_S = the quantity traded on the spot market.

A hedge ratio of 1 means that the hedger does not take on any standard quantity risk. However, a hedge ratio of 1 is not necessarily optimal; depending on the hedger's individual risk affinity/aversion and the level of risk associated with a hedge, the optimal hedge ratio can deviate from 1, sometimes considerably. The term 'under hedge' ($H_R < 1$) is used to describe the situation in which a market participant hedges only a part of the quantity traded on the spot market. Similarly, if a larger quantity is hedged on the futures than on the spot market we refer to an 'over hedge' ($H_R > 1$). A market participant who hedges nothing ($H_R = 0$) is, by definition, a **speculator** who bears the price risk on the entire volume of his/her open spot market position.

What is a market participant's optimal hedge ratio? First of all, it should be clear that even an infinitely risk-averse market participant will not choose a full hedge. This is due to the different types of risk discussed in the previous section, and in particular the basis risk. A risk-averse market participant is interested in minimising overall risk, not only price risk. The overall risk consists of the price risk on the spot market and the basis risk on the futures market. To illustrate this, we begin with equation (2)[7]

$$\pi_H = q(p^{FWD}_{t_0 \to t_1} - p^S_{t_1}) - q(p^{FUT}_{t_0 \to t_1} - qp^{FUT}_{t_1 \to t_1})$$

which can be modified as follows:

$$\pi_H = q_S p^{FWD}_{t_0 \to t_1} - q_S p^S_{t_1} - q_H p^{FUT}_{t_0 \to t_1} + q_H p^{FUT}_{t_1 \to t_1} \qquad (4)$$

where q_S and q_H are the spot and hedged quantities as defined above. The risk-averse hedger is interested in minimising the variance of π_H, defined as:

$$Var(\pi_H) = E\big(\pi_H - E(\pi_H)\big)^2 \qquad (5)$$

where

$Var(\pi_H)$ = the variance of the profit after a hedge (π_H), and

$E(\pi_H)$ = the expected value of π_H.[8]

Substituting equation (4) into equation (5) leads to:

$$Var(\pi_H) = E\Big(\big[q_S\big(p^{FWD}_{t_0 \to t_1} - p^S_{t_1}\big) - q_H\big(p^{FUT}_{t_0 \to t_1} - p^{FUT}_{t_1 \to t_1}\big)\big] - E\big[q_S\big(p^{FWD}_{t_0 \to t_1} - p^S_{t_1}\big) - q_H\big(p^{FUT}_{t_0 \to t_1} - p^{FUT}_{t_1 \to t_1}\big)\big]\Big)^2 \qquad (6)$$

---

[7] See Malliaris (1999, PP. 40-42).

[8] Equation (2) (or 4) applies to the case of a long hedge. In the case of a short hedge, all of the terms in this equation have the opposite sign. However, since these terms are all squared in the derivation of the optimal hedge ratio (below), the derivation applies to both long and short hedges.

Since at time t_0 both the quantity traded on the spot market (q_S) and the two prices $p^{FUT}_{t_0\to t_1}$ and $p^{FWD}_{t_0\to t_1}$ are known, equation (6) can be modified to:

$$Var(\pi_H) = E\Big(\big[q_S(p^{FWD}_{t_0\to t_1} - p^S_{t_1}) - q_H(p^{FUT}_{t_0\to t_1} - p^{FUT}_{t_1\to t_1})\big] - \Big[q_S\left(p^{FWD}_{t_0\to t_1} - E(p^S_{t_1})\right) - q_H\left(p^{FUT}_{t_0\to t_1} - E(p^{FUT}_{t_1\to t_1})\right)\Big]\Big)^2$$

$$= E\left(q_S(E(p^S_{t_1}) - p^S_{t_1}) - q_H(E(p^{FUT}_{t_1\to t_1}) - p^{FUT}_{t_1\to t_1})\right)^2 \qquad (7)$$

We next expand equation (7) to obtain:

$$Var(\pi_H) = E\Big(q_S^2\left(p^S_{t_1} - E(p^S_{t_1})\right)^2 - 2q_Sq_H\left(p^{FUT}_{t_1\to t_1} - E(p^{FUT}_{t_1\to t_1})\right)\left(p^S_{t_1} - E(p^S_{t_1})\right) + q_H^2\left(p^{FUT}_{t_1\to t_1} - E(p^{FUT}_{t_1\to t_1})\right)^2\Big)$$

$$= q_S^2 Var(p^S_{t_1}) - 2q_Sq_H Cov(p^S_{t_1}, p^{FUT}_{t_1\to t_1}) + q_H^2 Var(p^{FUT}_{t_1\to t_1}) \qquad (8)$$

where

$Cov(p^S_{t_1}, p^{FUT}_{t_1\to t_1})$ = the covariance between $p^S_{t_1}$ and $p^{FUT}_{t_1\to t_1}$.

Equation (8) can be further modified as follows:

$$Var(\pi_H) = q_S^2\left(Var(p^S_{t_1}) - 2\frac{q_H}{q_S}Cov(p^S_{t_1}, p^{FUT}_{t_1\to t_1}) + \frac{q_H^2}{q_S^2}Var(p^{FUT}_{t_1\to t_1})\right) \qquad (9)$$

Next, we substitute equation (3) ($H_R = \frac{q_H}{q_S}$) into equation (9):

$$Var(\pi_H) = q_S^2\left(Var(p^S_{t_1}) - 2H_R Cov(p^S_{t_1}, p^{FUT}_{t_1\to t_1}) + H_R^2 Var(p^{FUT}_{t_1\to t_1})\right) \qquad (10)$$

The first-order condition for minimising the variance of π_H by choosing the optimal hedge ratio H_R^* is:

$$\frac{\partial Var(\pi_H)}{\partial H_R} = q_S^2\left(-2Cov(p^S_{t_1}, p^{FUT}_{t_1\to t_1}) + 2H_R Var(p^{FUT}_{t_1\to t_1})\right) = 0 \qquad (11)$$

Solving equation (11) results in:[9]

$$H_R^* = \frac{Cov\left(p_{t_1}^S, p_{t_1 \to t_1}^{FUT}\right)}{Var\left(p_{t_1 \to t_1}^{FUT}\right)} \tag{12}$$

If there is no basis risk, the prices on the spot market and on the futures market are perfectly correlated. The variance of the futures price (in the denominator) and the covariance of the futures and the spot prices (in the numerator) will therefore be identical, and a full hedge will be optimal. As the basis risk increases, the covariance of the futures and spot prices decreases, and with it the optimal hedge ratio. In the extreme case, both the covariance of the futures and spot prices and the optimal hedge ratio equal zero.

An estimate of the optimal hedge ratio can be derived from the linear regression equation of spot prices on futures prices at time t_1.

$$p_{t_1}^S = \beta_0 + \beta_1 p_{t_1 \to t_1}^{FUT} \tag{13}$$

The least squares estimate of the slope coefficient β_1 in equation (13) is:

$$\widehat{\beta_1} = \frac{\Sigma\left(p_{t_1}^S - \overline{p_{t_1}^S}\right)\left(p_{t_1 \to t_1}^{FUT} - \overline{p_{t_1 \to t_1}^{FUT}}\right)}{\Sigma\left(p_{t_1 \to t_1}^{FUT} - \overline{p_{t_1 \to t_1}^{FUT}}\right)^2} \tag{14}$$

Dividing the numerator and the denominator of equation (14) by $(n-1)$ (where n = the number of observations), we obtain:

$$\widehat{\beta_1} = \frac{\Sigma\left(p_{t_1}^S - \overline{p_{t_1}^S}\right)\left(p_{t_1 \to t_1}^{FUT} - \overline{p_{t_1 \to t_1}^{FUT}}\right)/(n-1)}{\Sigma\left(p_{t_1 \to t_1}^{FUT} - \overline{p_{t_1 \to t_1}^{FUT}}\right)^2/(n-1)} = \frac{Cov\left(p_{t_1}^S, p_{t_1 \to t_1}^{FUT}\right)}{Var\left(p_{t_1 \to t_1}^{FUT}\right)} = H_R^* \tag{15}$$

Thus, the optimal hedge ratio H_R^* can be derived as the slope of a linear regression equation of spot prices on futures prices in t_1 ($H_R^* = \widehat{\beta_1}$).

[9] Since the second derivative $\frac{\partial^2 Var(\pi_H)}{\partial {H_R}^2} = 2q_S^2 Var\left(p_{t_1 \to t_1}^{FUT}\right)$ is always positive, equation (12) minimises $Var(\pi_H)$.

Other methods of deriving the optimal hedge ratio besides simple least squares regression have been proposed in the literature. For example, error correction models (introduced in Chapter 10) can also be used. Both least squares and error correction models generate constant values of H_R^* that do not vary over time. Using so-called GARCH models, it is also possible to estimate time-varying hedge ratios that account for the possibility that price variances and covariances might change over time.[10]

Case study 1: Optimal hedge ratios for wheat producers in Germany

Vollmer and von Cramon-Taubadel (2020) empirically analyze the potential of price hedging using the MATIF wheat contract as a risk management tool for farmers in Germany. Among other things, the authors calculate optimal hedge ratios using a simple least squares regression with the spot price of wheat FOB Rostock as the dependent variable (p_t^S) and the price of the MATIF wheat contract as the independent variable (p_t^{FUT}). They use weekly price data from September 2001 to April 2016. They also assume two short hedging strategies: first, that the farmer hedges her crop 12 months in advance directly after sowing, and second, that she waits until the spring and hedges her harvest 6 months in advance. The latter strategy might make more sense, as the farmer can better estimate the harvest volume to be hedged in the spring, after the crops have emerged from the winter months. Vollmer and von Cramon-Taubadel (2020, Table 2) present the following regression results (p-values in brackets):

$p_t^S =< 0.001 + 0.455(p_{t+12Months}^{FUT})$ $\qquad$ $p_t^S =< 0.001 + 0.375(p_{t+6Months}^{FUT})$

(0.001) (0.035) $\qquad$ (0.001) (0.028)

Accordingly, the estimated optimal hedge ratio is 45.5% (37.5%) for the strategy with a time horizon of 12 (6) months. These values are very similar to those estimated using error correction models instead of least squares regression. The authors also estimate time-varying optimal hedge ratios using GARCH models, which will not be discussed further here.

Vollmer and von Cramon-Taubadel (2020, Table 10) also simulate the liquidity risks associated with the hedging strategies mentioned. Their results show that especially in years that were characterised by high swings in wheat prices (e.g. 2006/07 and 2009/10), large margin calls of up to

[10] GARCH models are beyond the scope of this chapter. An overview of different methods for calculating optimal constant or dynamic hedge ratios is provided by Chen et al. (2003).

€ 6,000 per contract could arise. A farmer who sold 10 contracts to hedge 500 t of wheat, for example, would therefore have to have the financial means to make margin calls of up to € 60,000.

13.4.2. Hedging vs. speculation

So far, we have reviewed how reciprocal transactions on spot and futures markets are used by market participants to reduce price risk. However, futures contracts can also be traded by market participants who have no interest in the physical commodity, i.e. who speculate. Speculators are the third (and often the largest) group of participants in futures markets, along with arbitrageurs and hedgers. Speculators trade on futures markets, buying or selling contracts and later offsetting them, without owning or otherwise intending to deal in the corresponding physical commodity.

A distinction can be made between **short speculators** (also called bearish speculators) and **long speculators** (bullish speculators). A short speculator expects prices to fall over time and therefore goes short by selling at t_0 on the futures market for time t_1. He thus enters into a delivery obligation without owning the commodity. At t_1 he offsets his futures position by buying and realises a profit if the price of the contract has fallen since t_0. In contrast, a long speculator bets on rising prices in the future. She goes long in the futures market at t_0 for time t_1 and thus enters into a purchase obligation. At t_1 she offsets her futures position by selling and realises a profit if the price of the contract has increased since t_0. The short speculator's profit expectation is therefore

$$\pi_S = q(p_{t_0 \to t_1}^{FUT} - p_{t_1 \to t_1}^{FUT}) \tag{16}$$

and the long speculator's profit expectation is

$$\pi_L = q(-(p_{t_0 \to t_1}^{FUT}) + p_{t_1 \to t_1}^{FUT}) \tag{17}$$

with

q = the quantity traded on the futures market.

We illustrate these relationships with an example of short speculation in Table 13.8. Assume that a speculator expects wheat prices to fall between November and March. In order to profit from this expected price decline, the speculator goes short on the futures market. She is not using the expected co-movement of futures and cash prices to hedge physical goods; instead she is deliberately speculating that falling prices will lead to a profit on the futures market. This example makes clear that speculation does not minimise but rather entails additional risks.

In scenario 1, prices fall as the trader expected, from 184 €/t in November to 180 €/t in the following March. The trader thus makes a profit of 4 €/t from the futures transaction. In scenario 2, the price rises to 190 €/t and the speculator suffers a loss of 6 €/t.

Table 13.2 An example of short speculation

		Futures price per ton	
		Scenario 1	Scenario 2
November (t_0)	Sale of one March wheat futures contract	184	184
March (t_1)	Purchase of one March wheat futures contract	180	190
Profit on the futures market		4	-6

Source: Own illustration.

A speculator considers whether she believes that the price at t_1 quoted on the futures market at t_0 is correct, or whether she believes that the price will change between t_0 and t_1. For this purpose, she collects and analyses information on the market conditions that will determine the price of the futures contract at t_1. If her analysis leads to a (subjective) price expectation $p_{t_1 \to t_1}^{FUT}$ that differs from the current price $p_{t_0 \to t_1}^{FUT}$, she will take a long or short speculative position depending on the sign of the difference. The speculator's profit, if any is realised, can be interpreted as a reward for the successful collection and analysis of relevant market information. Since false price expectations lead to losses, speculators must take great care when collecting and analysing market information.

The futures price for an agricultural product such as wheat thus reflects all the market information available to all of the market participants at a given time. New information is continuously being generated by factors such as weather developments, exchange rate fluctuations, trade reports, policy changes, epidemics such as African Swine Fever or the coronavirus, and disruptions due to conflict such as Russia's attack on Ukraine. This information is transmitted onto futures markets and thus into futures prices as it arises, often on a minute-by-minute basis.

The speed with which new information is priced into futures markets has increased significantly as electronic trading platforms have replaced the floor trading that was common in the past. At the same time, the importance of so-called algorithmic or automated trading has grown. Algorithmic trading is based on computer programs that are designed to anticipate market developments by evaluating past price movements, the news situation, the weather and developments on other markets worldwide. Estimates suggest that by 2019, algorithmic trading accounted for 50-70% of global agricultural futures trade. At the Chicago Mercantile Exchange, for example, automated computer transactions now account for over 50% of the total trading volume in corn and soybeans futures, and over 60% for wheat and live cattle (Haynes and Roberts 2019, Table 3). Because of their comparatively low transaction costs and high speed of information processing, futures markets often react more rapidly and strongly to new information than spot markets. Futures markets therefore act as a highly efficient and fast form of information exchange.

While speculation is a vital source of information on futures markets, and contributes essentially to their liquidity, it is also controversial. The so-called agricultural price crisis of 2007/08 led to renewed accusations that speculators deliberately manipulate and increase prices for staple foods such as wheat in order to make profits at the expense of the hungry. If these accusations could be substantiated, stronger regulation or even bans on futures trading might be justified. However, there is little sound theoretical or empirical evidence that speculators systematically use futures markets to increase staple food prices.[11]

An important distinction can be made between informed and uninformed speculators. Informed speculators have information about so-called **fundamentals**, i.e. factors that influence demand and supply and thus determine the price level of a good. Informed speculators assume that they have an information advantage, i.e. that they have more, better or earlier information, or that they are able to assess the implications of new information for future pricing earlier or better than other market participants. They use this advantage to form expectations about future prices and take corresponding long or short positions. As explained above,

---

[11] Recall (see section 10.3 above) that futures markets were banned in the 19th century in Germany because producers argued that speculation was <u>lowering</u> grain prices.

their futures trading ensures that futures prices always reflect all available market information.

Uninformed speculators do not base their futures positions on fundamentals. Instead they analyse past price movements for patterns such as trends. If they are convinced, for example, that a sustained rising trend has set in, they take long positions in the expectation of further rising prices. If many speculators follow such a strategy (herd behaviour), their expectations of rising prices can become self-fulfilling and a futures price can move away from its fundamental value, at least temporarily. Algorithmic trading might reinforce such price movements, which are sometimes called price or speculative **bubbles**. A speculative bubble must burst sooner or later: if a futures price has moved away from its fundamental value, informed speculators and other market participants can take counter-positions and make safe profits. To do this, however, they must be able to pick the right time when the herd behaviour will subside and prices will return to fundamental values.[12]

The literature contains some empirical evidence for the existence of price bubbles in staple food futures markets (see case study 2). However, the literature is not unanimous, and there is no convincing evidence to support the claim that the 2007/08 agricultural price crisis was largely or even exclusively triggered by speculation. On the contrary, the 2007/08 price peak can be explained with reference to market fundamentals. The USDA (the US Department of Agriculture) publishes estimates of the global supply situation - i.e. stocks, production, trade and consumption - for all major global agricultural markets in its monthly World Agricultural Supply and Demand Estimates (WASDE) reports (USDA, 2020). These reports represent the most extensive and consistent source of publicly available information on agricultural markets, and they have a correspondingly large influence on markets and prices. However, they are not infallible. The February 2008 WASDE report described an historically tight supply situation on world grain markets, and grain prices peaked after it was released. When the USDA later revised its assessment and released less pessimistic numbers, grain prices quickly fell. Was the price peak thus the result of the USDA's initial misjudgement, or was it caused by speculative market participants who based their trades on the USDA assessments?

[12] As Gilbert (2010, p. 4) aptly writes: "...there is no easier way to lose money than to be right, but to be right too soon".

To prove the existence of a price bubble on a futures market, one must prove that the prices on this market have moved away from their fundamental values. Thus, one must have complete information on all relevant fundamentals and how they influence prices. In practice, however, it is not possible to categorically rule out that an important fundamental factor has been overlooked. When Robles et al. (2009, p. 2), referring to the 2007/08 price crisis, claim that "changes in supply and demand fundamentals cannot fully explain the recent drastic increase in food prices", they are implicitly assuming that they have complete empirical information on all relevant market fundamentals and their effects on price levels – certainly a heroic assumption.

Case study 2: Speculation with agricultural commodities

Adämmer and Bohl (2014) look for evidence of speculative bubbles on American futures markets for maize, soybeans and wheat. To this end, they analyse the relationship between agricultural prices, the price of crude oil and an index of various exchange rates using monthly data from 1993 to 2012. Crude oil prices and exchange rates are considered to be fundamental factors that influence the prices of agricultural commodities. It is expected that rising crude oil prices will lead to increasing agricultural prices, while rising real exchange rates will lead to a decline in demand and thus to falling prices. If rapid increases in agricultural prices are followed by rapid falls, and these peaks are not observed in crude oil prices or exchange rates, this is considered to be evidence of a speculative bubble.

Adämmer and Bohl's (2014) results provide evidence for the existence of speculative bubbles in the wheat futures market. This confirms the findings of earlier studies such as Gilbert (2010) and Gutierrez (2013). For the soybean and maize markets, Adämmer and Bohl (2014) do not find clear evidence that speculation influences price developments.

Another important challenge for studies that analyse the influence of speculation on futures prices lies in the need to categorise market participants into speculators and hedgers. In theory, the speculative motive can be clearly distinguished from the hedging motive, but in practice many participants cannot be unambiguously assigned to one group or the other. A trader can simultaneously hedge and speculate on futures markets, and any hedge that deviates from the optimal hedge ratio contains an element of speculation. An extensive literature has looked specifically at the activity and effect of so-called hedge funds, which clearly act as speculators on agricultural futures markets. But even this literature does not offer firm and robust evidence of a strong influence on futures prices (see e.g. Sanders and Irwin 2010).

Note that farmers often engage in speculative behaviour on agricultural markets. A farmer who does not use forward or futures contracts to hedge his future harvests is automatically in a long position. If a poor harvest leads to expectations of increasing prices, farmers will often speculate by holding back grain for later sale. If many farmers do this, it will reduce supply and drive up prices.

Since there is at least some evidence for the existence of price bubbles on agricultural futures markets, could government regulation of these markets improve their performance and ensure that they do not distort price formation? Yes, perhaps, but not necessarily. Market failure is not a sufficient condition for government intervention, because any such intervention also carries the risk of policy failure. Careful analysis must first consider whether there are feasible government interventions whose costs do not exceed the cost of the market failure that they are supposed to correct. The activity of speculators is essential for the functioning of futures markets as institutions that serve price discovery and that allow for the exchange of risk between market participants with different willingness and ability to bear risk. The call for regulation to curb excessive speculation is understandable, but if such regulation is not able to clearly distinguish and target 'excessive' regulation, it will generate more costs than benefits. Speculation in staple food markets has been debated heatedly for many decades, and it will likely remain a controversial topic in future scientific and political discourse.

13.4.3. Futures markets as reference markets for the pricing of spot and forward contracts

Although farmers in Germany use futures markets as an important source of information, they rarely actively participate in these markets. In a survey conducted by Adämmer et al. (2014), only 10% of farmers reported hedging on commodity futures markets. Even in the US, which is home to many of the largest commodity futures exchanges and where there is a long, unbroken tradition of futures trading, most farmers do not participate - surveys often report shares below 10% (see e.g. Carter 1999, p. 216).

Why is this the case? Possible explanations include small farm structures and the high costs of opening a futures trading account, i.e. high transaction costs per hedged contract.[13] Other explanations are the liquidity risk of possible margin calls (see case study 1 above) as well as the information costs of futures trading for farmers who are already very busy with day-t-day farming operations. Pannell et al. (2008) present simulation results showing that hedging only generates notable benefits for farmers with above-average risk aversion. Farmers in the EU receive secure per hectare direct payments that stabilise their income and thus possibly increase their willingness to take risks when marketing their products, i.e. reduce their demand for risk reduction through hedging.

Another important explanation lies in the fact that many farmers do not need to participate on futures markets directly because they can do so indirectly via forward contracts that are offered to them by traders who do make active use of futures markets. When farms wish to hedge future harvests, they can sign forward contracts with local traders who, in turn, hedge their forward transactions with farmers on futures markets. On Euronext exchange, for example, contracts can be traded up to three years in advance of the delivery date; the May 2025 MATIF wheat contract, for example, has been trading since May 2022. Usually, the volume of trade for a new contract is initially low, but trade picks up over time, and a contract generally becomes sufficiently liquid to permit hedging within 18 to 24 months of its delivery date.

An example of this indirect or derived participation by farmers on futures markets is shown in Table 13.9. In February 2020, a farmer decides to hedge a certain quantity of her upcoming 2020 wheat harvest. Because she has some on-farm storage capacity, she decides to sell forward for October 2020, a few months after the harvest. On February 18, the MATIF wheat contract for December 2020 is quoted at 189.25 €/t. The farmer's local trader expects that it will realise a basis of +3.00 €/t fob Hamburg in December 2020, i.e. a price of (189.25 + 3.00) €/t = 192.25 €/t. The forward price that the traders is prepared to offer the farmer is derived from this price, minus the transport costs from the farm to (the seagoing vessel in) Hamburg. If, for example, handling and loading in Hamburg costs 5.00 €/t and truck transport from the farmer's storage location to Hamburg costs 7.00 €/t, then the trader can offer the farmer a forward contract for October 2020 delivery for a farm gate price of (192.25 - 5.00 - 7.00) €/t = 180.25 €/t.

[13] See e.g. Salhofer and Zoll (2005).

Table 13.3 Derived price hedging through agricultural trade

	Physical		MATIF		Basis	Result
	Buy	Sell	Buy	Sell		
18 Feb 2020	€ 192.25*			€ 189.25	€ 3	
20 Oct 2020		€ 182	€ 181		€ 1	
Profit/loss		€ -10.25		€ -2	€ -2	€ -2

** Farm-gate price 180.25 €/t = (192.25 fob Hamburg less handling 5 and truck transport 7) €/t.*
Source: Own illustration.

The trader thus offers the farmer a price that is the futures price plus or minus the expected basis and corrected for location (i.e. transport and handling charges). To hedge this transaction with the farmer, the trader (who is now in a long position) assumes a short position on the futures market by selling a corresponding number of December 2020 MATIF wheat contracts. The liquidity of the futures market (including the activity of speculators) has put the trader in a position to offer the farmer a forward contract and, by extension, price risk reduction.

To complete the example, assume that prices fall between February and October, so that the trader can only resell the wheat he collects from the farmer for a price of 182 €/t fob Hamburg (rather than the expected 192.25 €/t). The trader therefore suffers a loss of 10.25 €/t on the physical market. When the forward contract with the farmer is delivered (October 2020), the trader offsets his short position on the futures market by buying back the corresponding MATIF wheat contracts. The futures price has fallen in parallel with the price on the physical market, but only by 8.25 €/t. The basis is therefore only 1.00 €/t rather than the expected 3.00 €/t (i.e. the basis has fallen by 2.00 €/t), so the gain of 8.25 €/t on the futures market cannot fully compensate for the loss on the physical market.

Overall, in this example, the trader suffers a loss of 2 €/t because the basis has fallen between February when the forward contract was signed, and October when it was delivered. However, the key point in the example is that hedging on the futures market enables the trader to provide derived price risk reduction in the form of forward contracts to many farmers with smaller volumes of production who might not be willing or able to engage in futures trade themselves.

13.5. Preconditions for the functioning of commodity futures markets

As shown in Section 13.3.1, futures markets exist for a whole range of product groups including cereals, oilseeds, oils, sugar, milk and its processed products, orange juice, tea and piglets. This disproves an assumption often made in the past, according to which futures markets can only be derived for storable and standardisable agricultural products. Milk, for example, is not storable and live animals cannot be standardised. In fact, a futures contract can be designed for any product for which a price can be defined at a precise time and place. Even if no physical delivery is possible - as is the case for futures contracts on shipping routes, for example - the futures can be traded on the basis of so-called cash settlements. In this case, the profit and loss between the future's short and long traders is balanced at the time of settlement on the basis of a transparent and clearly documented price.[14]

The decisive factor for the success of a futures market is whether it is accepted by market participants and, especially in the case of agricultural products, allows participants to hedge prices. There have been many failed attempts to establish futures markets.[15] In Germany, for example, a commodity futures exchange (the WTB) was launched in Hanover in April 1998. Besides potatoes and pork, a wheat futures market was also established on the WTB, but later abandoned. This was probably not due to the design of the WTB wheat contract, but rather to competition from the MATIF in France. For German grain traders, the correlation between futures prices on the MATIF and grain prices in Germany is sufficient for successful hedging. Under these conditions, when a liquid contract already provides sufficient opportunities for hedgers, it is difficult to establish a new contract.

In general, the attractiveness of a futures contract for a commodity will increase with the variability and unpredictability of the commodity's price. The size of the underlying market, and thus the potential volume of futures trade, also influences the success or failure of a contract. The number of possible trading partners for a contract can also play a role. The larger the number of potential participants, the less influence individual traders will

---

[14] For a more detailed analysis of the role of storability in price discovery on futures markets, see Yang et al. (2001).

[15] Till (2015) reviews a large number of examples of futures markets that did or did not succeed.

have on price behaviour and the more attractive the contract. The attractiveness of a future also depends on the alternative price hedging options. For example, there are many different futures contracts for wheat traded on exchanges all over the world, but to the best of our knowledge there is no futures contract for flour. This is probably because flour mills, large bakeries and retailers are generally able to manage price risk using contracts.

Finally, the successful establishment of a futures market also depends on the institutional framework in the country where it is traded. First of all, the integrity of the market must be guaranteed. Trading partners must be absolutely certain that the clearing bank will provide a secure and transparent exchange of profits and losses. In addition, market participants who hedge price risks must be absolutely certain that there will be no government intervention on the market in question. In Ukraine and Russia, for example, there have been several plans and attempts to establish commodity futures markets for wheat and other agricultural commodities. However, since politicians have repeatedly intervened in the markets in a discretionary manner, for example by imposing export quotas or even embargoes, hedging is associated with an enormous basis risk. Consider a trader who holds a physical long position inside Russia, and hedges this with a future based on a fob location, for example at a Black Sea port. If an export restriction is imposed, then the trader's physical long will fall in price, while his futures short will rise. Both ends of the trader's hedge are therefore negatively affected by the government's export restriction. Hedging via futures therefore only works if price formation can take place free of state intervention as a result of the interplay of market supply and demand.

13.6. Keywords

- Basis, maturity basis
- Basis risk
- Bubble
- ciffo
- Clearing mechanism
- Counterparty risk
- Cross hedge
- fob
- Forward contract
- Fundamentals
- Futures contract

- Hedge, long hedge, short hedge, hedge ratio
- Liquidity risk
- Long, long position
- Margin, initial margin, margin call
- Margin risk
- Offset
- Premium long, premium short
- Risk transfer
- Seller's option
- Short, short position
- Spatial transformation, temporal transformaton
- Speculator, long speculator, short speculator
- Standard quantity risk
- Spot contract

References

Adämmer P, Bohl MT (2014) Speculative bubbles in agri-cultural prices. The Quarterly Review of Economics and Finance 55: 67-76.

Adämmer P, Bohl MT and von Ledebur E-O (2014) Die Bedeutung von Agrarterminmärkten als Absicherungsinstrument für die deutsche Landwirtschaft. Thünen Report 14, Johann Heinrich von Thünen-Institut, Braunschweig.

Carter CA (1999) Commodity futures markets: a survey. Australian Journal of Agricultural and Resource Economics 43: 209-247.

Chen S, Lee C and Shrestha K (2003) Futures hedge ratios: a review. The Quarterly Review of Economics and Finance 43: 433-465.

Euronext (2020) Milling Wheat Derivatives. https://www.euronext.com/en/for-investors/commodities/milling-wheat. Accessed 13. June 2022.

FIA (Futures Industry Association) (2020) Exchange Volume Reports. www.fia.org/exchange-volume-reports. Accessed 13. June 2022.

Gilbert CL (2010) Speculative influences on commodity futures prices 2006-2008. United Nations Conference on Trade and Development (UNCTAD) Discussion Paper No. 197, Geneva.

Gutierrez L (2013) Speculative bubbles in agricultural commodity markets. European Review of Agricultural Economics 40: 217-238.

Haynes R and Roberts JS (2019) Automated Trading in Futures Markets – Update #2. Study prepared for die CFTC (Commodity Futures Trading Commission), Washington DC.

https://www.cftc.gov/sites/default/files/2019-04/ATS_2yr_Update_Final_2018_ada.pdf. Accessed 13. June 2022.

Hull JC (1998) Introduction to Futures and Options Markets, 3rd Edition, Pearson, London.

Malliaris AG (1999) Foundations of Futures Markets. Elgar, Cheltenham.

Nelson R, 1985, Forward and Futures Contracts as Pre-harvest Commodity Marketing Instruments. American Journal of Agricultural Economics 67: 15-23.

Pannell DJ, Hailu G, Weersink A and Burt A (2008) More reasons why farmers have so little interest in futures markets. Agricultural Economics 39: 41-50.

Prehn S, Steinhübel L and Glauben (2016) Why temporary silo closures and improper contract specifications endanger the credibility of the No. 2 Milling Wheat futures. Paper presented at the 91st Annual Conference of the Agricultural Economics Society, 24-26 April 2017, Dublin, Ireland.

Robles M, Torero M and von Braun J (2009) When speculation matters. International Food Policy Research Institute (IFPRI) Issue Brief No. 57, Washington.

Salhofer K and Zoll M (2005) Preisabsicherung durch Warenterminhandel: Eine empirische Analyse für den deutschen Schweinemarkt. Jahrbuch der Österreichischen Gesellschaft für Agrarökonomie 14: 235-246.

Sanders DR and Irwin SH (2010) A speculative bubble in commodity futures prices? Cross-sectional evidence. Agricultural Econonomics 41, p: 25-32.

Till H (2015) Case Studies on the success or failure of futures contracts. Journal of Governance and Regulation 4: 30-47.

USDA (United States Department of Agriculture) (2020) World Agricultural Supply and Demand Estimates. https://www.usda.gov/oce/commodity/wasde.

Vollmer T, Herwartz H and von Cramon-Taubadel S (2020) Measuring price discovery in the European wheat market using the partial cointegration approach. European Review of Agricultural Economics 47: 1173-1200.

Vollmer T and von Cramon-Taubadel S (2020) The Optimal Wheat Futures Hedge at the Euronext Paris from a Farmer's Perspective. German Journal of Agricultural Economics 69: 49-63.

Yang J, Bessler DA and Leatham DJ (2001) Asset storability and price discovery in commodity futures markets: A new look. The Journal of Futures Markets 21: 279-300.

Exercises

Consider the following products:

- A: Milling wheat on the spot market
- B: Euronext MATIF Wheat No. 2 Futures Contract (delivery May 2020)
- C: CBOT Wheat Futures Contract (delivery May 2020)

The following series of transactions is carried out by a local trader:

1. January 15, 2020:

   Buy A: 1000 t for 193 €/t

   Sell B: 500 t for 195 €/t

   Sell C: 500 t for 192 €/t

2. February 15, 2020:

   Buy B: 300 t for 194 €/t

   Sell A: 300 t for 190 €/t

3. March 15, 2020

   Buy C: 500 t for 170 €/t

   Sell A: 500 t for 171 €/t

4. April 15, 2020

   Buy B: 200 t for 193 €/t

   Sell A: 200 t for 191 €/t

As of April 15, 2020, all positions have been offset.

a. Calculate the trader's profit or loss from this series of transactions.

b. What would have happened if the land trader had not hedged, but rather simply bought 1,000 t of A on the spot market on January 15 and sold this amount again on April 15?

c. Assess the overall success of the trader's hedge. Was it worthwhile for the trader? What considerations go into your answer?

BIOGRAPHIES

Bernhard Brümmer has been a Professor in the Department of Agricultural Economics and Rural Development at the Georg-August-University of Göttingen since 2005. He studied agricultural economics at the University of Kiel and at Wageningen University, and holds a PhD from Kiel (2001). He has published widely in both disciplinary and general economics journals. He is a member of IAAE and EAAE, where he served on the program committee for several triennial conferences. His current research focuses on efficiency and productivity in agricultural and food value chains, international agricultural trade, and price formation in agricultural output and input markets. He has served as policy consultant for the World Bank in Ukraine and Russia, and for several EU institutions on questions of price formation, in particular price volatility. He is also involved in interdisciplinary research initiatives in Asia, primarily in Bangladesh, China, India, and Indonesia.

Sebastian Hess has held the chair for Agricultural Markets at the University of Hohenheim since 2019 and is Director of the Research Centre for Cooperatives since 2021. From 2014 to 2019 he held the Endowed Chair for Dairy and Food Industry Economics at the University of Kiel. He studied Agricultural Economics in Göttingen and Davis, and completed his PhD at the University of Göttingen and the Docentur in Uppsala. His teaching and research focusses on the quantitative analysis of agri-food markets and value chains, as well as on the role of cooperatives within these markets. He coordinates the Subject Area on Bioeconomy within the Euroleague for Life Sciences.

Ulrich Koester is Professor Emeritus of Agricultural Economics at the University of Kiel and Associated Member of IAMO, Halle. He is the author of an introductory textbook that has been published in German (five editions) as well as in English, Russian and Serbian. His achievements in research and teaching have been recognised by honorary doctorates from the Universities of Gießen, Hohenheim and Ulaanbaatar. His research and several visiting professorships have been supported by institutions including the German Government, the World Bank, the European Union and the FAO.

Jens-Peter Loy has held the Chair for Market Analysis at the University of Kiel since 2003. He studied agricultural economics at University of Kiel and received his PhD there as well in 1995. From 2000 to 2002 he held interim professorships at the Universities of Bonn and Göttingen. He was guest professor for several years at the Vienna University of Economics and Business and spent a postdoc year at the Pennsylvania State University in State College, USA. From 2020 to 2022 he was president of the German Association of Agricultural Economists. His teaching and research focus on the theoretical and empirical study of agricultural and food retail markets, and the functioning of agricultural futures markets.

Ludwig Striewe is member of the Management Board of BAT Agrar, a private agricultural trading company. BAT is run by over 1.500 employees and operates in Germany, Austria, Denmark and Poland. Ludwig Striewe is responsible for the grain division, the inland and port silos, truck logistics and communication. Before joining BAT in 2013, he was responsible in different position in ADM and its daughter company Alfred C. Toepfer International GmbH. Between 1997 and 2020 he served in the German Advisory Group on Economic Reforms in Ukraine as an Agricultural Economist on behalf of the KfW (Kreditanstalt für Wiederaufbau). He holds a Master's Degree in Agricultural Economics from the University of Kiel and an International Master's Degree from Wageningen University.

Teresa Vollmer studied Agricultural Sciences at the University of Göttingen, with a major in agricultural economics. She completed her PhD in Economics in 2019, focusing on time series analysis and the relationship between spot and futures prices for agricultural commodities. Today, she works in the IT services industry.

Stephan von Cramon-Taubadel has held the Chair for Agricultural Policy at the University of Göttingen since 1999. He studied agricultural economics at McGill University and the University of Manitoba in Canada, and completed his PhD at the University of Kiel in Germany. He is a guest professor at Nanjing Agricultural University in China and the Universidad de Talca in Chile, and Secretary-Treasurer of the International Association of Agricultural Economists (IAAE). His teaching and research focus on the analysis the determinants and effects of agricultural policies, the empirical study of market integration and price interactions in space and along the food chain, and the transformation of agriculture in countries of the former Soviet Union, especially Ukraine and Georgia.

Christoph Weiss has been full professor of economics at the Vienna University of Economics and Business since 2002 and prior to that was full professor for food economics and consumption studies at the University Kiel. He has held numerous visiting positions including at Harvard University, the University of California at Berkeley and the University of Technology in Brisbane, and was guest professor at the Universities in Giessen, Munich and Bratislava. He earned his PhD in economics at the University of Linz in Austria. Christoph Weiss has taught courses in industrial organization, microeconomics, and food and agricultural economics. His research investigates the determinants as well as the impact of market structure on firm behavior and performance in different sectors of the economy. He served on various editorial boards and was editor of the European Review of Agricultural Economics between 2009 and 2013.

David Zilberman holds the Robinson Chair in the Agricultural and Resource Economics Department at the University of California at Berkeley. He is the recipient of the 2019 Wolf Prize in Agriculture and was elected a member of the US National Academy of Science 2019. He is Hagler fellow at Texas A&M University. David served as the 2018-19 President of the Agricultural & Applied Economics Association (AAEA). He's a fellow of multiple professional associations and has published in both professional and popular outlets. He has more than 400 referenced articles and has edited 30 books. In addition, he has served as a Consultant to the US Environmental Protection Agency, USDA, the World Bank, FAO, MARS, BP, and others. David's BA is from Tel Aviv University and his Ph.D. from Berkeley. His research analyses water, innovation, supply chain, and the interactions between agriculture, energy, and the environment as well as the political economy of agricultural biotechnology and the potential of the bioeconomy.